T0335122

NEW PHENOMENA
IN LAW AT THE
BEGINNING OF
THE 21ST CENTURY

CZECH LAW
BETWEEN
EUROPEANIZATION
AND GLOBALIZATION

CZECH LAW

BETWEEN

EUROPEANIZATION

AND

GLOBALIZATION

Michal Tomášek
et al.

Charles University in Prague
Karolinum Press 2010

Scientific reviewers:
Professor Emmanuel Decaux (Paris)
Professor Dr. Dr.h.c. Marian Paschke (Hamburg)

This monograph was published within the Research Project MSM 0021620804
entitled "Quantitative and Qualitative Transformation of the Legal Order
at the Beginning of the 3rd Millennium – Roots, Sources and Prospects",
headed by Professor JUDr. PhDr. mult. Michal Tomášek, DrSc.

© Charles University in Prague, 2010
ISBN 978-80-246-1785-5

Authorial team head:
Professor JUDr. PhDr. mult. Michal Tomášek, DSc.

Editor:
PhDr. Marta Chromá, Ph.D.

Authorial team members:
Professor JUDr. PhDr. Karolina Adamová, CSc., DSc.
JUDr. Marek Antoš, Ph.D.
Professor JUDr. Milan Bakeš, DrSc.
JUDr. Vladimír Balaš, CSc.
JUDr. Eduard Barány, DrSc.
Professor JUDr. Miroslav Bělina, CSc.
Associate Professor JUDr. Petr Bělovský, Ph.D.
JUDr. Karel Beran, Ph.D.
JUDr. PhDr. Veronika Bílková, Ph.D., E.MA
JUDr. Radim Boháč, Ph.D.
Professor JUDr. Stanislava Černá, CSc.
Professor JUDr. Dagmar Císařová, DrSc.
JUDr. Zuzana Císařová
Professor JUDr. Milan Damohorský, DrSc.
JUDr. Tomáš Dobřichovský, Ph.D.
Professor JUDr. Jan Dvořák, CSc.
JUDr. Ondřej Frinta, Ph.D.
JUDr. Dita Frintová, Ph.D.
Professor JUDr. Aleš Gerloch, CSc.
JUDr. Bc. Tomáš Gřivna, Ph.D.
Associate Professor JUDr. Mgr. Jiří Herczeg, Ph.D.
JUDr. Irena Holcová
Mgr. Věra Honusková
JUDr. Záboj Horák, Ph.D.
JUDr. Jiří Hřebejk
Associate Professor PhDr. Stanislava Hýbnerová, CSc.
Professor JUDr. Jiří Jelínek, CSc.,
Professor JUDr. Antonín Kerner, DrSc.
Associate Professor JUDr. Vladimír Kindl
JUDr. Veronika Křesťanová, Dr.

Professor JUDr. Jan Kříž, CSc., dr. iur. h. c.
Professor JUDr. Jan Kuklík, DrSc.
Associate Professor JUDr. Jan Kysela, Ph.D.
Professor JUDr. Karel Malý, DrSc., dr. h. c.
Associate Professor JUDr. PhDr. Pavel Maršálek, Ph.D.
JUDr. PhDr. Petr Mlsna, Ph.D.
JUDr. Hana Müllerová
Associate Professor JUDr. Jan Ondřej, CSc., DSc.
Professor JUDr. Monika Pauknerová, CSc., DSc.
JUDr. PhDr. René Petráš, Ph.D.
Associate Professor JUDr. Radim Seltenreich
Professor JUDr. Michal Skřejpek, DrSc.
JUDr. Petra Skřejpková, Ph.D.
JUDr. Michal Sobotka, Ph.D.
Associate Professor JUDr. Ladislav Soukup, CSc.
JUDr. Olga Sovová, Ph.D.
JUDr. Vojtěch Stejskal, Ph.D.
Professor JUDr. Pavel Šturma, DrSc.
JUDr. Radovan Suchánek, Ph.D.
JUDr. Petr Tégl, Ph.D.
Professor JUDr. Luboš Tichý, CSc.
Professor JUDr. PhDr. mult. Michal Tomášek, DrSc.
Professor JUDr. Jiří Rajmund Tretera
JUDr. Jan Tryzna, Ph.D.
Associate Professor PhDr. Ing. Jan Urban, CSc.
JUDr. Alexandra Wünschová Pujmanová
Professor JUDr. František Zoulík, CSc.
JUDr. Karolina Žákovská, Ph.D.
JUDr. Petra Žikovská

Translators:
Mgr. Adéla Bahenská
PhDr. Renata Hrubá
PhDr. Marta Chromá, Ph.D.
PhDr. Martin Starý

Proofreader:
Sean Davidson, J.D.

Technical editing:
JUDr. Jana Ondřejková

TABLE OF CONTENTS

FOREWORD

In 2005 the Ministry of Education, Youth and Sports of the Czech Republic granted to the Charles University Law Faculty funds to carry out a research project entitled "Quantitative and Qualitative Transformation of the Legal Order at the Beginning of the 3rd Millennium – Roots, Sources and Prospects". Academic jurists started their research in all branches of law, and Law Faculty members specialising in areas other than law, such as economy, philosophy or linguistics, also engaged in the project. The objective of the research project was rather challenging since it covered a wide range of special subject-matters. Considering the fact that the outcome of such research is not a mere description of law but rather a scholarly analysis of timeless significance, the first task in the project was to determine the methodology of the scientific work. From the very beginning we attempted to designate the key internal as well as external impulses for the development of Czech law at the beginning of the 21st century and sought to prepare an analysis of their significance. This created a basis for the formulation of the working outcomes with respect to the developmental tendencies in all the branches of law and, at the same time, we tried to establish factors connecting the research between individual branches.

Collecting the sources and classifying the first results showed it was inevitable that a wide exchange of initial opinions and positions among individual research teams would be promoted, and that partial outcomes of individual research stages would be presented to a wider academic community and law practitioners in the Czech Republic and abroad. Such an opportunity was provided in relation to the 660th anniversary of the foundation of Charles University in April 2008. On that occasion there was a common ceremonial session of the Law Faculty Scientific Council and the Academic Senate held on 17th April 2008. Professor Hampl, Rector of Charles University, and Professor Gerloch, Dean of the Law Faculty opened the session. The representatives of all three of the governmental powers took the floor: the President of the Senate, the Speaker of the Chamber of Deputies of the Parliament of the Czech Republic, the members of the Government and the President of the Constitutional Court. Opinions regarding new phenomena in law were presented by the Governor of the Czech National Bank and the President of the Supreme Audit Office, i.e. representatives of institutions often designated as the germ of a newly emerging state power having the potential to complement the existing governmental triad in the future. The international conference entitled "New phenomena in law at the beginning of 21st century" was held on 18th April 2008 in four subject areas: historical impulses for the development of law; theoretical and constitutional impulses for the development of law; Europeanization and internationalization of public law; and Europeanization and internationalization of private law. Heads of individual research teams presented the outcomes of their analysis, and foreign colleagues as well as law professionals expressed their opinions in the subsequent debate. One of the outcomes of the one-day conference was the requirement that a monograph should be published to summarize the results of the whole research project. The conference also served as a meeting of the authorial teams of the respective chapters of the future monograph.

During 2009–2010 four volumes of the monograph entitled "New Phenomena in Law at the Beginning of the 21st Century" were written. The coincidence of the title of the monograph with the name of the international conference is not random: the reaction of Czech and foreign academic and professional legal communities during the conference showed that such a name was well perceived; thus the same title was used for the whole monograph. Titles of individual volumes were also inspired by the subject-areas covered by the international conference in 2008: Volume I was entitled "Historical Impulses for the Development of Law"; Volume II "Theoretical and Constitutional Impulses for the Development of Law"; Volume III "Transformation of Public Law"; and Volume IV "Transformation of Private Law". In discussing the titles of Volumes III and IV we concluded that Czech law, both public and private, is subject to the impact of many more factors than solely external Europeanization and internalization. It was suggested during the preparation of the monograph that, in addition to the four volumes written in Czech, a fifth volume in English should be compiled which would present our opinions regarding the development of Czech law at the threshold of the 21st century to the scientific community abroad.

Each of the four chapters in the present volume of the monograph selects those ideas and thoughts from the respective Czech volume which, in our opinion, should be introduced to the foreign scientific community. Every chapter is appended with a selected bibliography encompassing primarily Czech publications dealing with the respective topic.

Chapter One, an analysis of the historical impulses of the development of law, is based on the presumption that in history some legal issues were resolved in such a way that they may have a direct effect on the law of today or, at least, may be instructive as a valuable source of experience. For example, there is useful experience gained in the field of rent regulation, recovery (restitution) of property seized in the time of non-freedom, the development of the Czech doctrine of federalism, and policies with respect to ethnic (or national) minorities. A Czech comparative view of some constitutional institutions of common law is of a significant value, as is the sensitive analysis of the relationship between church and state.

Chapter Two, which deals with theoretical and constitutional impulses for the development of law, is built upon the defining of the essential elements of a democratic state governed by the rule of law and upon an analysis of the recent model of how the courts are bound by the law. It is emphasized that the scope and content of "the essential elements of a democratic state governed by the rule of law" are not determinate; therefore the concept of the state governed by the rule of law is dynamic and not static. The extent to which the law binds courts in their decision-making is an issue that has become more and more complicated by the plurality of the sources of law – national, European or international. The authors elaborate on the legal reasoning *lege artis* which should replace out-dated and simple application models and, at the same time, restrict the arbitrariness of judicial decision-making.

Chapter Three focuses on the transformation of public law; it emphasizes the fact that Czech public law stems from the continental legal tradition where the state acts to implement common interests as well as the interests of the individual. Unlike the continental tradition, the tradition of common law attaches a narrow role to the state in its actions in furtherance of common social interests. In the common law system, the State is not an automatic protector of common interests since a higher force exists beyond the state, namely "the rule of the law", i.e. a body of clearly defined individual rights and freedoms at the disposal of individuals so that individuals may enforce them against the state. Our theoretical knowledge of public law suggests that today the traditional elements of continental law and common law have been diffused. For example, the system of law in the United Kingdom has been enriched with many continental features due to the transposition of European laws into British legislation. There is other experience illustrating that the strengthening of basic rights and freedoms leads in the continental legal system to the adoption of many Anglo-American legal principles. Criminal proceedings in continental legal systems, for example, have taken a certain shift to the Anglo-American adversarial principle due to an increasing number of procedural rights of parties even in countries that historically have had a rigid inquisitorial system of criminal procedure. This view is supported by the adversarial principle of procedure applied by international criminal tribunals.

Chapter Four reflects on the most important directions of Czech private law. The background of private law has been significantly affected by the phenomenon called publicization of private law, which has brought elements of public law into the domain of originally pure private law. This feature may lead to a certain relativization of the concept of "private law", typically seen in company law; needless to say, procedural law as a whole, i.e. including civil procedure, is public law in its essence. Private law has undergone a certain evolution within European integration. In particular, private law has been circumscribed within the European Union through the harmonization of legislation of individual Member States. European private law and European private international law have become phenomena which may not be disregarded. Also, similar to public law, common law principles and continental law principles are presently commingling in EU private law.

The applicability of the achieved theoretical outcomes in practice has been an important pre-requisite for deeming scientific work as comprehensive and successful. This essential precondition was fully met in the course of work on the research project "Quantitative and Qualitative Transformation of the Legal Order at the Beginning of the 3rd Millennium – Roots, Sources and Prospects". Extensive recodification of the most important branches of Czech law was in progress simultaneously with our research project. A new Criminal Code was passed in Parliament and the work on a new draft of the Civil Code was completed. Whilst the philosophy of the existing Civil Code is based on the codification of property relations, the Draft Civil Code does not consider the regulation of property as its ultimate priority; rather, its priority is the freedom of an individual and the respect thereof. Private law in the Draft Civil Code is not used as a tool for the management of society, but as a guarantee for the free establishment of one's private life in such a way that the greatest space possible is left for the free initiative of an individual. The autonomy of the will of an individual emphasizes the individualist basis of private law in contrast with the social character of public law. The emphasis on basic rights and freedoms was reflected in the new Czech Criminal Code. The Code provides for the full assurance of basic rights and freedoms guaranteed by the Constitution of the Czech Republic and the Charter of Fundamental Rights and Freedoms; the enforcement of important orders to act or to refrain from acting through the instruments of criminal law is the ultimate solution, unavoidable in many respects. The implementation of criminal policy in a democratic society is based upon the principle of humanism; it is directed at the social reintegration of offenders into society, the provision of reasonable satisfaction to the victims of crimes, and at the protection of the society against crime. The emphasis is placed on an individual approach to the solution of criminal matters presuming wide application of alternative punishments (non-incarcerative sentences) in order to positively motivate the offenders. We are proud that our theoretical analyses were incorporated in the above-mentioned principles for the drafting of new codes in the basic branches of law. The most important factors connecting our results and the new Czech codes are included in the respective volumes of the monograph published in Czech, as well as in the relevant chapters of this volume published in English. Considerations of *de lege ferenda* are also included where the newly adopted codes have shown drawbacks, for example, in labour law and in business law.

The monograph is not, and cannot be, the description and explanation of Czech law as a whole. It serves as an analysis of the main factors having an impact on Czech law as internal and external impulses, and presents essential theoretical outcomes. The four volumes written in Czech, as well as this volume published in English, should be read as a mosaic, the pieces of which create a picture of the route for Czech law to enter the 21st century. The intention of the authorial team was not to tell, in a gradual and systematic way, the story of the Czech law of today. Rather, the emphasis was placed on the internal development of thoughts at all stages, generating outcomes in all legal branches subject to the analysis. One of these outcomes is the fact that the penetration of common law into continental law is a process which cannot be discontinued; thus, it is necessary to obtain sufficient knowledge of this traditionally very remote system of law and to identify its positive features. Another important outcome is that the role of the system of fundamental rights and freedoms is expanding; it not only becomes a tool for the approximation of legal systems among individual EU Member States, but also creates the basis for the recodification of Czech law.

The authorial team, composed of dozens of academics completed this work during the past five years. It was decided that the work should be evaluated by those looking objectively at the whole issue from outside. The choice of reviewers was extremely careful and thorough: each reviewer had an outstanding scientific background, and it was decided that review of the four volumes written in Czech was to be completed by one Czech expert not attached to the Charles University Faculty of Law and one foreign expert who was able to understand the text in Czech. The list of foreign reviewers of the four volumes written in Czech includes experts not only from Slovakia, where it is quite common to understand the Czech language even almost twenty years after the split of Czechoslovakia, but also professors from Germany or Sweden having their roots in the former Czechoslovakia and a law degree from a Czech university. The choice of reviewers for the fifth volume was not restricted with respect to language; nevertheless, it was desirable to choose specialists in continental law with a certain level of experience in Czech law. We are honoured that the difficult task was assumed by Professor Emmanuel Decaux, Director of the Centre for Research on Human Rights and Humanitarian Law at the University Paris II (Panthéon – Assas), an expert in public law, and Professor Dr. Dr.h.c. Marian Paschke, Director of the Institute for Commercial, Maritime and Economic Law at the Faculty of Law of the University of Hamburg, an expert in private law. Both professors are internationally recognized as outstanding academic jurists who have acted as visiting professors at the Charles University Law Faculty for many years. Having a close knowledge of Czech law they provided valuable insight, advice and inspiration to the authorial team. Their reviews are enclosed in the annex to this volume. I would like to sincerely thank them on behalf of all co-authors.

Professor JUDr. PhDr. mult. Michal Tomášek, DrSc.

1. HISTORICAL IMPULSES FOR THE DEVELOPMENT OF LAW

It has become the custom in history that great anniversaries or turns of centuries give rise to many reflections and expectations of the arrival of a new, usually better and happier future, and they become a myth and symbol of a new era. It even seems that modern times just follow the predictions of medieval visionaries and prophets announcing the demise of an evil and corrupt world and the arrival of a new, just social order. The end of the 19th and beginning of the 20th centuries, as well as the 21st century, are no exception. The development of industrial and postmodern society based on the so far unthinkable boom of technical progress and scientific knowledge has only strengthened these tendencies.

However, the reality of social development is usually different and it brings disillusion. That is why the beginning of the new century itself, contained in the title of our project, should not be the only impetus to reflections on what new phenomena have been arising or will arise in law over the centuries. The memory of the vain hopes of our forefathers a hundred years ago, who expected the new century as a period of peaceful bloom of mankind and progress in science and learning, warns us against undue optimism since it was the past 20th century which brought the bloodiest war conflicts in human history as well as unbelievable revivals of the horrors of the middle ages in the area of development and application of law. The real challenge for us should be the dynamic of social and legal development which came after the creation of the European Communities and the necessity of approximation of the existing Czech law to European law. For post-communist countries, including ours, the real and urgent necessity which arose after the collapse of the communist regime has been the transformation of the legal order and laying down the democratic forms of law in the entire complex system of legal order.

However, some questions have arisen: how can legal history prove useful in this process of changing and creating new law, and what knowledge can it bring to current legislation and legal theory, to deliberations on trends of our and European legal orders? When looking for answers to these questions it will not be sufficient to refer to the fact that law as such is a historical category, that variability of law and its creation is conditioned by history, that the principle of continuity is being applied in law, that positive law as a part of legal culture has been influenced not only by domestic tradition but also by that of Europe, stemming from the roots of Roman legal thinking and canon law. Legal history offers something more. A specific feature of legal history is that it offers a map of the historical development of legal order, of that ancient river with all its currents, main streams and cut-off meanders, successful and forever accepted principles as well as impasses where some futile attempts of lawmakers ended. In this way legal history substitutes for social tests, substitutes for futile or risky experiments which, if the society chose to perform them, often led to tragic results as we have witnessed not only in our own but also in European history. Legal historical research as an intrinsic part of legal science represents a link, a bridge to other social sciences, to general history, political science, philosophy and it draws them into the research of categories of law, undoubtedly to the benefit of not just legal science but social sciences in general.

There is no doubt legal history can principally contribute to the development of positive law, and to current legislation. By analysing historical concepts and legal theories as well as by showing concrete examples of old legislation and legal practice, it can bring historically demonstrable evidence of possible and impossible legal regulation of social relations, evidence of operation of law in the past and of the success of past solutions. This applies not only to the recent past, i.e. the period of the communist regime, but also to the democratic legal order. As far as the former is concerned, we have not yet overcome it completely, not only in positive law but also in the perception of law within society, where the residues of the past have been surviving longer than one would expect. Concerning the latter, it is not only because the legal practice, courts and lawyers, inevitably have to return far back in the 20th and sometimes even the 19th century, but current legislation does the same as was undoubtedly shown in discussions on the draft of our new Civil Code. Besides, legislative procedures which were started at the beginning of the 1990s clearly demonstrated how strong the traditions of democratic legal culture are and that the models of the democratic legal order of interwar Czechoslovakia still had an influence.

However, the matter is not as simple as it may seem. Legal historical research is a complex procedure which cannot get along only with analysing legal regulations, the wording of codes or other legislation. Not even comparing the sources of law and legal practice and proving the wording of law in its application before courts or in administrative procedure will be sufficient. The sources of knowledge of law are much more complex and abundant – they include perception of law within society, which is difficult and complex to prove; sources of a narrative nature, which bear witness to the social influence of law and individuals who created it or on whom it impacted; legal theories, which influenced, to a varied degree, the creation of law and logically the political life of the society in which the law was created, by which it was influenced or, on the contrary, on which it exerted influence. Hence legal historical research entails other sciences. Besides auxiliary historic sciences which represent the elementary working tool for legal historians, it includes political science, theories of national economy, statistics and philosophy of law, etc., to mention just a few of those disciplines with which legal historians must work. The reason for mentioning it is that we cannot expect legal history to provide us with simple "instructions for use". The utilization of knowledge of legal history by other branches of legal science is a reciprocating process requiring active as well as critical approach.

1.1 SOCIAL LEGISLATION AND CHANGES IN PROPRIETARY RIGHTS

1.1.1 Protection of tenants and housing in the Czechoslovak Republic – aspects of social state (normative image) between 1918 and 1948

The scope of social legislation in the Czechoslovak Republic (CSR) covered financial and material social security of inhabitants. Besides health and social insurance, housing care was also required in order to provide for the existence of inhabitants – citizens of the state both in productive and post-productive age. Housing care was a specific set of regulations by which the Czechoslovak state partially interfered with the private relations of citizens, mainly the freedom of contract, and limited free disposal of flats. It controlled and regulated the financial burden of tenants from low income groups. At the same time it took into consideration legitimate needs and requirements of owners – landlords, who provided the operation, maintenance and construction of flats and residential houses. The beginnings of housing care of this type can be found as early as in the war legislation of Austro-Hungary. Growing interest in flats resulted in a dramatic increase in rent prices and housing shortage which the monarchy tried to alleviate. The first decree for the protection of tenants in the Hungarian Kingdom was issued in November 1916.[1] The government of Austria issued a similar decree in January 1917.[2]

Regarding rents for flats and residential premises, after the creation of the Czechoslovak Republic the protection of tenants was governed by a ministry decree of December 1918.[3] Increases in rent and other charges were thus permissible only in specifically listed cases. The limit of permitted increase was determined for flats where a yearly rent had so far been from one to two thousand crowns. It also applied to subleases. Social aspects were considered in the case of persons who received benefits for the indigent.

The protection of tenants also dealt with the termination of lease contracts by notice, which was possible only because of specifically listed relevant reasons. First of all it was the default in payment of rent on the part of the tenant, then the tenant's refusal to accept a rent increase approved by the relevant authority and notice to persons violating the housing code.

The permissibility of increase in rent was considered upon an application of the landlord or tenant to the relevant rent authority or district court. Rent authorities had been established already in the monarchy in towns and communities having more than twenty thousand inhabitants. They were headed by a chairman and his deputy, other members were appointed in the office of honour by the mayor for a term of one year. The communication between rent authorities and citizens was primarily oral. Their decisions supported by reasoning were declared orally and only then they were executed in writing.

---

[1] Decree No. 3787 M.E. of 12th November 1916.
[2] Decree No. 34/1917 ř. z. (Reich Laws) of 27th January 1917.
[3] Decree of the Minister for Social Care and Minister of Justice, in accord with other participating ministers, No. 83/1918 Sb. z. a n. (Collection of Laws and Regulations) of 17th December 1918, on the protection of tenants. It referred to the Austrian Act No. 307/1917 ř. z. of 24th July 1917 and adopted in full detail the Austrian decree No. 381/1918 ř. z. of 26th October 1918.

Commissions for considering the possibility of increasing the interest rate on mortgages were also created. According to the joint decree of Ministers of Justice and Social Care[4] of February 1919 the possibility to terminate the lease was usually dependent upon the district court approval granted in non-contentious proceedings.

The first complex piece of legislation governing the protection of tenants was the Act of 8th April 1920.[5] It regulated the termination of lease by notice, the rent and modes of its increase, the establishment and operation of rent authorities, the possibilities of flat advertising and the Act incorporated earlier relevant criminal provisions.

A notice of termination of lease was valid only upon approval of the competent district court due to the failure to pay rent or due to causing gross and repeated disorder in the house. A newly introduced reason for notice was the approval of reconstruction of the house granted to the landlord by administrative authorities.

The Act of 1920 newly and clearly defined the modes and limits of the rent increase as a percentage rate of permissible increase relating to the basic rent paid on 1st August 1914. An increase of more than twenty percent on the basic rent of 1914 was only permissible upon the approval of the rent authority or district court. The Act permitted a widespread increase in rents within the community on condition that municipal authorities, having received an official approval, declared the rent increase rate permissible in their community. The effect of the Act was limited by the end of 1921.

Another complex law on the protection of tenants was passed in 1922.[6] It started to remove the protection of tenants but no new flats were being built.[7] The new law was to a high degree concordant with its predecessor. A new reason for notice was added, namely a conviction of a violent crime committed against the landlord. Instead of an adequate substitute flat, the tenant could be assigned just a "sufficient" one. A new ground for giving notice was the property of the tenant, who stated in his assets declaration filed according to the Capital Levy Act that he owned property worth at least two million crowns and did not own any house in the community. Another new provision regulated the situation when the tenant deserted the common household and flat which he had used together with his family. His rights and duties devolved to members of the family remaining in the flat. The new Act did not contain provisions concerning rent authorities which had been abolished.

As of 1st May 1922 the permissible rent increase was at least 20 % on the basic rent depending on the flat category. Three months later another increase of 10 % on the basic rent came, which made a total of 30 %. In case of larger flats the basic rent was increased by 20 %, which made a sum not exceeding 40 % of the original rent. Since 1st November 1922, a new increase of 10 % on the basic rent was permissible in smaller flats and 20 % in larger flats. Thus it was permissible to increase rent in some flats by 60 % in total. Larger flats,

[4] Decree of the Ministry of Justice and the Ministry for Social Care No. 62/1919 Sb. z. a n. of 9th February 1919, on the protection of tenants; it was adopted also in accordance with the Austrian parent act of 1917, see above.
[5] Act No. 275/1920 Sb. z. a n. of 8th April 1920, on the protection of tenants, government bill on the protection of tenants, print No. 2666 of 26th March 1920.
[6] Act No. 130/1922 Sb. z. a n. of 27th April 1922, on the protection of tenants.
[7] Print No. 1322 of the Senate of the National Assembly of the Czechoslovak Republic, 1922, Report of the social-political and budget committee on the resolution of the Chamber of Deputies concerning the government bill on the protection of tenants (print No. 1305).

consisting of four or more dwelling rooms and a kitchen plus rooms for servants, were not subject to regulation of rent and the rent was set by agreement of the contracting parties at any amount.

The fact that the state endeavoured to gradually solve the housing shortage was demonstrated in the proposal of the Ministry of Social Care to allocate 30 million Czech crowns to the support of smaller flats. However, Journals of the Budget Committee of the Senate stressed that at least a billion crowns was needed.

Another Act on the protection of tenants of April 1923[8] amended and specified the previous regulation. A new ground for the termination of a lease was, for instance, the expulsion of the tenant from the territory of the Republic, or the existence of another, sufficient flat in the community which the tenant owned and did not need for the performance of his occupation. Social and economic aspects were included in some newly introduced grounds for termination: a tenant being a natural person who declared assets worth at least 1,500,000 Czech crowns and a tenant being an artificial legal person declaring 20,000,000 Czech crowns could be evicted from a flat with regulated rent.

The Act, in effect from 1st May 1923, provided for the permissible increase in rent in accordance with the size of the flat and the number of dwelling rooms. In a flat with one dwelling room the increase could not be more than 20 % on the basic rent, in a flat with two rooms and a kitchen the rent could be increased by 40 % and in all larger flats it could be increased by 60 %. Rooms for servants and other appurtenances were not included in the number of rooms. The law provided new and detailed specification of charges for services connected with the occupation of a flat. State controlled rent and its limitation applied only to flats consisting of at least four dwelling rooms and appurtenances.

The Act on suspended execution of eviction from rooms[9] had a strong social impact. In the period of the continuing flat crisis, indigent tenants were often in default of their rent and landlords, upon approval of courts, successfully terminated their leases and filed for compulsory eviction from flats. The new Act enabled certain moderation of the harsh measure of execution of eviction. The debtor, sentenced to eviction from the flat, could apply to the execution court for a suspension of eviction for a period of no more than three months. The reason for suspension was a difficult situation for the debtor. The Act permitted no more than three repeated suspensions of execution in a period of three months. The debtor had to pay the rent for the expected period of use of the flat after its extension within eight days of the legal force of the execution court's resolution to suspend eviction. Should he fail to pay, the suspension of execution was cancelled.

Appropriation of flats and limitation on migration of citizens should be seen in connection with difficult social circumstances after World War I, when the housing shortage persisted. Under the government decree of January 1919 on the appropriation of flats by communities[10], the owners of houses and flats as well as their tenants were deprived of their right to dispose freely of the flats which were subject to a decision on appropriation. Lease contracts were cancelled.

8/ Act No. 85/1923 Sb. z. a n. of 26th April 1923, on the protection of tenants.
9/ Act No. 86/1923 Sb. z. a n., on suspended execution of eviction from rooms.
10/ Decree of the Czechoslovak government No. 38/1919 Sb. z. a n. of 22nd January 1919.

Provincial administrative authorities in regions suffering from a serious housing shortage could empower local authorities to impose the duty to notify of empty flats within a given period of time. A list of unused flats was created on the basis of such notices. The duty to notify was also imposed on owners of two or more flats who could expect that only one flat would be left at their disposal.

The decree aimed at resolving the housing shortage with respect to large-sized flats having four or more dwelling rooms if the number of rooms exceeded by at least two the number of persons (excluding servants) using the flat. It was ordered that the owner might retain one room more than the number of persons living in the flat, but three rooms were the minimum. Procedural rules were simple. The decision on appropriation was to be announced to all parties and the date of taking possession of the flat by the authority was determined. The community paid the owner compensation, usually amounting to the rent which the previous tenant had paid. The possibility of reconstruction of appropriated flats was also anticipated. It was possible to file a protest within three days, which was decided by the competent rent authority and then by the administrative authority. No remedy was permissible against the decision. Disputes were decided by ordinary courts.

The Act "on the restriction of the right to migrate" of 1919[11] strictly limited the freedom of movement of citizens. A citizen wishing to move to a community where this Act was applicable had to notify the local authority of his intention not later than one month in advance, even if he wanted to move to his own house. The authority granted or withheld a written permission to the informant (applicant). If the applicant could not prove requisite reasons, moving was not possible. The Act on the restriction of the right to migrate did not apply to persons having the right of abode in the relevant community and explicitly to civil servants and railroad employees in active service.[12] The restriction of the right to change the place of residence was regulated by another law passed in March 1921.[13] The Act on the restriction of the right to migrate applied to the territory of the whole state, including places with a different structure of administrative authorities in historical countries and in the parts of the Republic which once belonged to the Hungarian Kingdom.

In the middle of 1921 a government regulation to implement the Act was issued.[14] It determined a list of towns and cities where the limiting measures against the relocation of new inhabitants could be applied until the end of 1921. The top of the list was engaged by the Capital City of Prague with all the attached communities and settlements as they were mentioned in s. 1 of Act No. 114/1920 Sb. z. a n. Other towns on the list were České Budějovice, Hradec Králové, Liberec, Litoměřice, Pardubice, Plzeň and Ústí nad Labem in Bohemia, Brno, Moravská Ostrava, Olomouc, Prostějov, Znojmo, Opava and Těšín in Moravia, and Bratislava, Báňská Bystrica, Komárno, Košice, Lučenec, Nitra, Nové Zámky, Prešov, Rimavská Sobota, Turčianský svatý Martin, Ružomberok, Lykavka, Trnava and Žilina in Slovakia.

---

[11]/ Act No. 181/1919 Sb. z. a n. of 1st April 1919, on the restriction of the right to migrate.
[12]/ This was explicitly regulated in s. 8 of the Act.
[13]/ Act No. 118/1921 Sb. z. a n. of 17th March 1921.
[14]/ Decree of the Czechoslovak Government No. 235/1921 Sb. z. a n. of 15th July 1921.

In the end of 1922 the effect of the Act and the government regulation[15] was extended[16] for another year.

Interference with private ownership of residential and other buildings continued in 1919 by the passage of another law. On 11th June 1919 the Act on the appropriation of buildings or their parts for public purposes[17] was adopted. If no suitable rooms were available, the Provincial Authority (political administration of the province) could appropriate buildings having many rooms for its use. The appropriation should have been carried out after preliminary investigation by competent authorities and interested parties. The owners were to receive adequate compensation for possible economic loss. The appropriated buildings were to be restored to their original condition upon return. In the second half of 1921 the problems of appropriation of buildings or their parts for public purposes were regulated again.[18] The wording of the law, with all due implications, took into account the situation in the whole territory of the Republic. It specifically listed the authorities in Slovakia and in Ruthenia (district authorities). It determined immovable property adjoining the appropriated premises, yards, gardens or other types of land. The furnishings of buildings or rooms could also be appropriated. The new law regulated in more detail the relevant administrative procedure. The implementation of the law was assigned to the Minister of Public Works.

In autumn 1919 a new law on the appropriation of flats by communities was adopted.[19] It stemmed from the mentioned decree of the government, but it was more specific and stricter. Unlike under the former regulation, common housing authorities were subjected to state control; only civil servants were to work there without any private representatives of flat owners and tenants. They were appointed to their office by provincial authorities and, in Slovakia, by district authorities. The Act imposed the duty on owners to notify of flats and rooms they intended to lease. It concerned flats which had not been occupied at all, or only scarcely, for at least three months, or flats used as warehouses. The acquisition of new residential premises should have also led to the discovery of flats used by an identical user within one community or within the district of a common housing authority.

The new law introduced a stricter classification of flats for the determination of their adequacy to the needs of individual users. If the household consisted of a single person, he was to give notice of his flat bigger than two dwelling rooms; similarly, two adults had to give notice of a flat having more than three rooms. All flats having more than five dwelling rooms were subject to the notification duty. Persons older than fourteen years of age were considered adult members of the household, two younger children were counted as one adult. Servants and sub-tenants were not considered members of the household. Large flats could be divided. The scope of flats which could not be appropriated and used for solving the housing crisis was determined by the Act similarly as by the previous decree of the government, for instance, the depositories of valuable art or scientific collections.

15/ Decree of the Czechoslovak government No. 32/1922 Sb. z. a n. of 9th February 1922.
16/ Act No. 31/1922 Sb. z. a n. of 25th January 1922.
17/ Act No. 332/1919 Sb. z. a n. of 11th June 1919.
18/ Act No. 304/1921 Sb. z. a n., on the appropriation of buildings or their parts for public purposes of 12th August 1921.
19/ Act No. 592/1919 Sb. z. a n. of 30th October 1919, on the appropriation of flats by communities.

On the date of legal force of the decision to appropriate the flat, the current owner and tenant lost the right to dispose freely of the relevant premises regardless of possibly valid lease contracts. Similarly to the previous regulation, the Act provided for the possibility to simultaneously appropriate common furnishings of the flat. Procedural aspects of the appropriation were not different from the previous regulation. After a hearing, the minutes of which were taken, a decision was made and delivered to all parties in writing.

While the conception of the Act of 1919 aimed at the acquisition of more flats or more residential space for needy applicants and it had the character of a social measure within the area of housing care, it still permitted renting the appropriated flats for other than residential purposes.

In the times of non-freedom, i.e. in the post-Munich Czecho-Slovak Republic and mainly during the so called Protectorate of Bohemia and Moravia and the Slovak clerical-fascist republic, many regulations, government decrees and measures of the Permanent Committee of the National Assembly were issued and implemented in practice. Their legal force was usually rather short and had to be repeatedly extended due to the housing and economic situation. Extraordinary measures were caused by the influx of inhabitants drawn out from the occupied border and other areas inland and later also by the German population coming from the Reich. Decrees issued by the occupying power harshly intervened in the housing regulation, for instance in provisions for letting Jewish flats. Other measures of German and Protectorate bodies completely ruined the residential market, which had been free until then. In 1944 the Office for the Management of Residential Rooms[20] was established. After the separation of Slovakia in 1939, new housing regulation was focused on the protection of tenants in small flats consisting of a room and a kitchen[21] according to contracts made before 1st January 1940. In conformity with the anti-Semitic regime, protective housing regulation did not apply to Jews.

After World War II, Provincial National Committees in Prague and in Brno issued, within their territorial competence, general rulings governing the use of flats and published them in the Official Journal. They regulated the duty of owners, tenants and other flat users to notify as well as the assignation of appropriate flats by local national committees.

Appropriation of buildings or their parts for public purposes, by which the state administration wanted to contribute to the improvement of the critical housing situation, was newly regulated by the Provisional National Assembly of the Czechoslovak Republic on 7th May 1946. The amendment specified the buildings which could not be subject to appropriation, such as "small flat apartment houses".

The full text of the Act of 1921 was published in the Collection of Laws[22] in May 1946; it provides for the consolidated statute and other issues in a more detailed way. For instance, the appropriating authority had the power to designate rooms which were to be left to the current user, whose building was being appropriated, so that he could continue to execute the purpose for which the building had been used.

---

[20] Government decree No. 166/1944 Sb. z. a n.
[21] Act No. 167/1940 of Slovak Code of Laws (Sl. z.) and regulation with the force of law No. 267/1941 Sl. z.
[22] Regulation of the Minister of Transportation No. 113/1946 Collection of Laws (Sb.) of 23rd May 1946, on the consolidated statute regulating the appropriation of buildings or their parts for public purposes.

On 18th July 1946, the Constitutional National Convention of the Czechoslovak Republic adopted new, principal legislation covering the management of flats in the territory of the state. The Act on extraordinary measures in housing care[23] imposed a duty to notify. It cancelled some provisions and institutions regulating the use of flats in the times of non-freedom; the Office for the Management of Residential Rooms established by the Protectorate government in 1944 where only German officials were employed ceased to exist at the moment of demise of occupation power. The Act also cancelled housing laws and their parts adopted in Slovakia during fascist rule. The explanatory note on the government bill mentioned the three largest cities in the Republic as the places with the worst housing shortage, namely Prague, Brno and Bratislava. The government expected that the planned removal of Germans would reduce the housing shortage on the national scale but not solve the scarcity of flats mainly in industrial cities. The owners of houses were obliged to notify of flats which were not rented or whose tenant died. Then they had to lease the flat to persons determined by the local national committee. Tenants had to be persons loyal to the state, who did not have a flat in the given community, or who lived in a flat endangering their health or inadequate to their needs and who performed occupation which was their source of income in the given community. They were supposed to perform obligations resulting from the lease, namely to pay the rent. Under this Act, persons to which s. 1 of the decree of the President of the Republic No. 108/1945 Sb. did not apply were considered to be persons loyal to the state. Among the assigned tenants were also members of official or semi-official foreign missions as well as persons who used to live in the community and who were deprived of their flats by Nazi bodies or authorities during German occupation. The Act regulated flats in houses which were transferred to new owners under presidential decrees No. 12 and 108 of 1945 in the course of confiscation and expeditious division of property of Germans, Hungarians and traitors or enemies of the Czech and Slovak nations.

Among other things, the Act provided for flats inhabited by civil servants. If such a flat was vacated, the local national committee was to assign it again to a civil servant upon proposal of the personnel department of a state institution. Employees of the army, members of the National Security Corpses, employees of public railroads and teachers in public schools had similar entitlement. Adequacy of the area of the flat was assessed only according to the number of rooms regardless of their size. Their number could not exceed the number of members of the tenant's household. Kitchens and rooms which the members of the family needed for the performance of their vocation or profession or in public interest were not included in the total of dwelling rooms. That was how administrative authorities were offered an opportunity to favour certain tenants. Any spare room was to be rented within fifteen days after becoming vacant to at least one person. Regular students of higher education institutions enjoyed priority. To exchange flats or to join them together was possible only upon prior approval of the competent national committee.

The Act on extraordinary measures in housing care of 1946 provided for detailed regulation of powers of supervisory bodies within housing policy. For instance, it was possible

---

[23] Act No. 163/1946 Sb. of 18th July 1946, on extraordinary measures in housing care.

to examine the tenant carefully to make sure he met the requirement of loyalty to the state. The Act also provided for the possibility that the housing audit would discover any criminal influence exerted on officials in charge of assigning tenants to appropriate flats. In border areas the state wished to newly accommodate citizens in places which had been depopulated. Local national committees were to allocate the requisite number of flats for incoming persons. Owners' and tenants' duty to notify did not apply to houses of the state, provinces and districts used for official purposes; also flats in spa regions were exempt.

In April 1948, a new Act on the management of flats[24] cancelled the regulation of 1946. The duty to report vacated or unused flats was laid down in the statutory provision as well as the duty to notify, imposed on users of oversized flats. The scope of communities to which the Act applied was extended. The requirement of loyalty to the state was newly stipulated also for people who wanted to make a sub-lease contract.

According to the 1948 Act, local national committees were obliged to maintain and continually complement a single list of flat applicants for the given community and, besides that, a list of persons – tenants who had already been assigned flats. The lists were to be open to the public in official rooms. The decision on whether the assigned flat is adequate was left at the discretion of the national committee. It is quite likely that various subjective approaches were used.

The division of large flats to smaller, separate residential units could improve the housing situation. The Act of 1948 skipped reference to the constitutional protection of freedom of one's home which used to be remembered as an indispensable feature of the conduct of official persons. The scope of members of the tenant's family was narrowed.

The Act on management of flats of 28th April 1948 laid down its own retrospective effect. *"Housing decisions and measures issued or taken by action of national committees or their bodies in the period from 20th February 1948 (sic) to the promulgation of this Act shall be deemed legal. They may not be contested by petitions or before administrative authorities (bodies) or before bodies of public prosecution or elsewhere. Local national committee may, upon request of a party or by virtue of office, review such decisions or measures while respecting the principles of this Act."*[25]

In spring 1947, in the period of post war economic reconstruction of the Republic, an Act regulating state subsidies to residential houses[26] was adopted. It applied only to residential houses included in the building programme of a two-year plan. The assistance provided to housing consisted of a state guaranty for mortgage loans granted to cover the costs of construction and a state subsidy to cover expenses connected with the house.

1.1.2 Interference with proprietary rights between 1945 and 1948 and their reflection in so-called "indemnity agreements" and in privatization and "restitution" legislation after 1989

In the course of the restoration of independent Czechoslovakia in 1945 it was of primary importance to tackle the consequences of property persecution suffered during World

---

[24]/ Act No. 138/1948 Sb. of 28th April 1948, on the management of flats.
[25]/ S. 35 of the Act.
[26]/ Act No. 41/1947 Sb. of 7th March 1947, on state subsidies to residential houses.

War II.[27] Some property related acts performed in the so-called "period of non-freedom" were declared invalid which resulted in special "restitution" claims, such as recovery of property or payment of compensation. Restitutions carried out after 1945 were categorized according to the reason which had led to property transfer, the type of property concerned as well as which body performed it – administrative or judicial. Another question was who was entitled to "restitution" and to which proprietary rights the restitution should apply. Restitution of the title to property taken away because of national, political or racial reasons resulting from persecution thus concerned both natural and artificial legal persons since 1945, and the manner in which it was performed varied depending on the type of property and kind of "interference" in the rights in question; in the case of nationalization it depended upon the size of the relevant assets. Different categories of property (such as agricultural land, industrial enterprises, banks, gold, objects of art or money and insurance policies) often had a specific destiny.[28]

The Constitutional Decree of the President of the Republic on the restoration of legal order of 3rd August 1944, published in the Czechoslovak Official Journal No. 11/1944, provided in Article 12a for a so-called stipulation of special rules regulating "redress of harm resulting from exceptional circumstances in the period of non-freedom".[29] This regulation was necessary because the General Civil Code (ABGB) still valid in the Czech Lands provided in s. 869 and the following for "challengability", or the possibility to declare certain legal acts invalid, if they occurred as a result of, for example, "coercion", "trick" or "simulation", but it by no means covered all acts which occurred after Munich.

The principle of restitution of the title to property, which devolved to a third person as a result of national, racial or political persecution, was regulated by the Decree of the President of the Republic No. 5/1945 Sb. of 19th May 1945. In its first part it enabled "challengability" of transfers carried out as a result of persecution, within a statutory limitation period. Next were the provisions which explicitly cancelled the validity of some legal rules adopted in the period of non-freedom (i.e. from Munich to May 1945). The Decree also provided for the option to impose so-called national administration. It secured property for the ensuing confiscation, nationalization or restitution. It did not represent expropriation as such, but the owners' rights were strictly limited and what remained to him was "pure ownership title". National administration was imposed on estates significant for economy reasons, or on property of persons "not loyal to the state", a category under which mainly people of German or Hungarian nationality and collaborationists fell.

Decree No. 5/1945 Sb.[30] made it permissible for workers, peasants, sole traders and small- and medium-size traders or clerks, as members of "socially weaker classes", to apply for

---

27/ Kuklík, J.: Dekrety prezidenta republiky – výraz kontinuity československého právního řádu nebo jeho revoluční změny? [Decrees of the President of the Republic – Expression of Continuity of Czechoslovak Legal Order or its Revolutionary Change?]. In: Malý, K. – Soukup, J. (eds.): Vývoj práva v Československu v letech 1945–1989 [The Development of Law in Czechoslovakia 1945–1989]. Praha: Karolinum, 2004, p. 132 and subs.
28/ Nešpor, Z.: Vrácení majetku persekvovaným [Returning Property to the Persecuted]. Praha: Orbis, 1946, p. 5.
29/ For more see Kuklík, J.: Mýty a realita tzv. Benešových dekretů [Myths and Reality of so-called Beneš Decrees]. Praha: Linde, 2002.
30/ Nešpor, Z.: Komentář k dekretu prezidenta republiky ze dne 19. května 1945 [Comments on the Decree of the President of the Republic of 19th May 1945]. Praha: Ministerstvo financí, 1945, p. 6.

exemption of their property from national administration if they had been deprived of it on the grounds of national, political or racial persecution. However, they must have been Czechoslovak state citizens and persons loyal to the state.

Final regulation of post-war restitutions was brought by Act No. 128/1946 Sb. of 16th May 1946, on the invalidity of certain property-related acts performed in the period of "non-freedom" and on claims resulting from such invalidity and from other interference with property.[31] The law envisaged two principal methods of performing restitution: (1) By the authority which established national administration under Decree No. 5/1945 Sb.; (2) By the court in cases where applications for restitution were completely or partially dismissed by the administrative authority, or where applications were not disposed of within three months of their filing. The application had to be filed to the proper court within a period of three years. Restitution could consist of the return of the right (title), another form of restoration to the former condition, or the payment of monetary compensation. There was also the possibility to pay monetary compensation in cases where the reinstatement would cause a breach of an "important public interest".

To sum up, the legal basis for the performance of restitutions after 1945 was in principle sufficient. However, it contained certain elements which, because of the manner of implementation of the relevant rules, made it impossible to perform restitutions in many concrete cases and many proceedings were not completed before February 1948. "Jewish" restitutions represented the greatest problem as their performance was hampered by confiscation regulations, the movement of population and returns of estates of large size, where the restitution principle collided with nationalization.

Another property-related measure was confiscation. The Decree of the President of the Republic No. 12/1945 Sb. of 21st June 1945 immediately and without compensation confiscated for the purposes of a land reform agricultural property which had been owned by a) persons of German and Hungarian ethnic origin regardless of their citizenship, b) traitors and enemies of the Republic, c) hostile artificial legal persons. Exemptions from confiscation (loyalty to the Czechoslovak state was required) were decided by district national committees. Confiscated estates were managed by the National Land Fund. The Decree also dealt with the distribution of confiscated land.

The most important decree of those dealing with confiscation of enemy property was Decree No. 108/1945 Sb. of 25th October 1945, on confiscation of enemy property.[32] It confiscated without compensation for the benefit of the Czechoslovak Republic movable and immovable property as well as proprietary rights which, on the day of the real end of German and Hungarian occupation or on 30th October, was owned by three categories of persons: German Reich and other enemy artificial legal persons, natural persons of German or Hungarian ethnic origin, and collaborationists.

Personal movable property was exempt from confiscation as well as property lost by Czechoslovak citizens after 29th September 1938 as a result of occupation or national, racial

---

[31] Nešpor *supra* at p. 19.
[32] Drdacký, K.: Všeobecná úprava konfiskace nepřátelského majetku [General Regulation of Confiscation of Enemy Property]. In: *Nové zákony a nařízení československé republiky* [New Laws and Regulations of the Czechoslovak Republic], vol. 1946, No. 7–8, p. 639.

or political persecution. So the principle of confiscation was in line with the above mentioned regulation of restitution. Confiscated property was managed by National Renewal Funds. It was assumed that the confiscated property would be distributed.

Nationalization is yet another category of interference with proprietary rights.[33] Its first wave was carried out by the nationalizing decrees of 24th October 1945. Nationalization was perceived as expropriation, principally for compensation, and the final receiver of the property was the state. Decree No. 100/1945 Sb. of 24th October 1945 on the nationalization of mines and certain industrial enterprises provided for nationalization of all mines and key enterprises in energy industry, ironworks, steelworks, smelteries, foundries, rolling mills, metal processing and electro-technical enterprises having more than 500 employees, armaments and chemical industry and enterprises in a wide scale of other branches. It occurred on the date of effect of the Decree, i.e. on 27th October 1945. The exemption of an enterprise from nationalization was decided by the government upon proposal of the Minister of Industry.

Nationalized assets passed in the form of so-called basic capital to new entities – national enterprises, which were separate legal persons. The state acquired the position of their promoter and also exercised other functions – to control and supervise their operation. Essentially, property was nationalized for compensation which was calculated as the common price of the property according to the official prices as of the date of promulgation of the decree, or according to an official assessment. However, for example, the value of not yet extracted mineral resources was not to be included in the compensation. The compensation was to be paid in securities, in cash or in other values. The compensation was decided in administrative proceedings by the Minister of Industry upon agreement with the Minister of Finance. The compensation was not provided to the German Reich, Hungarian Kingdom and enemy artificial legal persons or to natural persons of German and Hungarian ethnic origin who were deprived of Czechoslovak citizenship. Also, collaborationists were not awarded compensation. Conditions for which compensation was withheld were identical to the conditions on the basis of which property was confiscated under Decree No. 108/1945 Sb. on the confiscation of enemy property. Decree No. 101/1945 dealt with the nationalization of food industry enterprises and Decrees No. 102 and 103/1945 nationalized joint-stock banks and private insurance companies.

In the years 1946–1948, expropriation measures were further complemented by the so-called review of land reform of the First Republic. Act No. 142/1947 Sb. was passed on 11th July 1947; it created the basis for reviewing the application of provisions of the first Land Reform between 1919 and 1920 and the property, which had not been appropriated yet, was actually expropriated and distributed to those who applied for land. The act was implemented by government regulation No. 1/1948 Sb. of 7th January 1948, so most of the "revisions" were carried out after February 1948.

Other expropriation measures were taken, and limitations on proprietary and similar rights were imposed, when the Communists took power in February 1948. First of all, the

---

[33]/ Trnec, M.: Znárodnění dolů a některých průmyslových podniků [Nationalization of Mines and Certain Industrial Enterprises]. In: *Nové zákony a nařízení Československé republiky* [New Laws and Regulations of the Czechoslovak Republic], vol. 1946, No. 11–12, pp. 63–65.

new regime launched the second stage of nationalization.[34] It consisted of amending the original nationalization decrees of 1945 as well as passing new laws which extended nationalization to medium- and small-sized businesses. Formally, the threshold for nationalization was set at fifty employees. However, in the areas of "public interest" or in sectors which were of crucial importance for national economy or for the fulfilment of the centrally designed economic plans, all establishments were nationalized, regardless of the number of their employees. Explicitly, nationalization newly applied to wholesale businesses, public transportation, natural medicinal springs, foreign trade and international shipping agencies. The state extended its monopoly and it was not possible to run private enterprises in these areas any more.

Nationalization was put into practice by ministry regulations, which were issued upon agreement with the Minister of Finance. There were practically no private enterprises having more than twenty employees in Czechoslovakia by the end of 1948. Essentially, nationalization should have been performed for compensation, but no reimbursement was provided to Czechoslovak citizens. The communist regime was only prepared to negotiate compensation for foreign investments.

Besides nationalization, sole trades and private owners of houses were gradually liquidated in several phases in the 1960s. Expropriation frequently took the form of forced donation or execution of repairs to a house at the cost of the owner and the subsequent passage of the property to socialist ownership.[35]

Act No. 46/1948 Sb. on new land reform, determined, in April 1949, new limits of private ownership of land to be 50 hectares per person, on condition the person worked on it. Other land was subject to "compulsory purchase". Allocation of the land acquired thereby was presumed and the purchase was to be carried out for compensation, which, however, was never paid. The execution of the reform was a component part of the so-called socialization of villages whose inseparable parts were collectivization and restriction of private property.

The above mentioned interferences with proprietary relations, carried out after 1945, have had strong international legal and political aspects. First of all, mostly so-called enemy German and Hungarian property was involved and consequently, its confiscation did not have just a national dimension. This issue is interconnected with the question of reparations and Czechoslovak war damage.

Besides that, so-called indemnity negotiations for nationalized property, confiscations and national administration should be mentioned.[36] The thing is that the Czechoslovak state frequently expropriated foreign investments or other foreign property, which could be done only for "adequate" compensation under international law. And the determination of the amount of compensation for expropriated or nationalized property was the subject matter of bilateral inter-state negotiations (also called "indemnity" negotiations) which

---

[34]/ Most recently Kuklík, J. et al.: *Vývoj československého práva 1945–1989* [The Development of Czechoslovak Law 1945–1989]. Praha: Linde 2009, p. 129 and subs.

[35]/ *Ibidem.*

[36]/ On this issue generally, see Kuklík, J.: *Do poslední pence! Československo-britská jednání o finančních a majetkoprávních otázkách 1938–1982* [To the Last Penny! Czechoslovak-British Financial and Property Negotiations 1938–1982]. Praha: Karolinum, 2007, p. 13 and subs.

led to making bilateral, so-called "lump sum agreements". It is the provision of adequate compensation which is one of the basic requirements for legality of nationalization measures. These agreements represent a single and final solution of claims of both natural and artificial legal persons, who are nationals of one state, and their claims arose as a result of nationalization in another state. Proper jurisdiction for artificial legal persons is in such cases determined by their registered office or place of operation of the corporation affected by nationalization. The agreements sometimes cover not only private claims by natural and artificial legal persons, but also claims by an injured state. Lump sum agreements, made by the Czechoslovak Socialist Republic (CSR) from 1948 to 1982, confirmed the standard of so-called effective compensation, as the compensation was paid in freely convertible currency, but on the other hand they weakened the principle of full and immediate compensation. Indemnity agreements signed by the CSR meant as a rule partial compensation, which was in most cases effectively paid only after several years, and in a couple of cases even after decades.

Since November 1945, parallel indemnity negotiations were led with the USA, Great Britain, France, Belgium, the Netherlands, Sweden, Italy and Switzerland. Until mid 1946, most foreign governments were being asked to postpone specific negotiations until the overall value of nationalized investments had been determined. By 1948, an agreement was reached only in the less complicated cases of Belgium, Sweden, Italy and the Netherlands.

In the period between 1948 and 1950, the communist regime strongly preferred making indemnity agreements with a lump sum amount of compensation and always connected the payment of compensation with a surplus or at least an increase in exports to the relevant countries. In December 1949 an indemnity agreement with Switzerland was signed, which followed contractual obligations from 1946–1948.[37] It stipulated a lump sum amount of compensation for Swiss claims affected by Czechoslovak expropriating or restricting measures, i.e. nationalization, confiscation legislation, national administration and land reform, amounting to 71 million Swiss francs. This established the "final settlement" of Swiss claims.

Negotiations with Great Britain were complicated because of questions connected with British loans from 1939–1945 and the issue of Czechoslovak monetary gold. Czechoslovak-British "indemnity" and business negotiations were terminated by a series of agreements of 28th September 1949. Besides an indemnity agreement, stipulating the lump sum compensation amounting to 8 million British pounds, and a business agreement, also a special agreement on intergovernmental debts, particularly from government loans, was signed amounting to 19.7 million British pounds.[38]

The indemnity agreement defined the British individuals and entities to whom the compensation should be paid and who, by accepting the compensation, agreed not to raise

[37] Kuklík, J. – Jančík, D. – Kubů, E. – Novotný, J. – Šouša, J.: „Spící konta" ve švýcarských bankách za znárodněný švýcarský majetek v Československu? Československo-švýcarská jednání o tzv. náhradových otázkách 1945–1967 ["Dormant Accounts" in Swiss Banks for Nationalized Swiss Assets in Czechoslovakia? Czechoslovak-Swiss Negotiations on so-called Indemnity Issues 1945–1967]. In: *Studie k Moderním dějinám. Sborník prací k 70. narozeninám Vlastislava Laciny* [Study in Modern History. Collected Works on the Occasion of 70th Birthday of Vlastislav Lacina]. Praha: Historický ústav AV ČR, 2002, pp. 445–462.
[38] Kuklík *supra* at p. 97 and subs.

against the CSR any more claims resulting from the affected proprietary rights. "Czechoslovak measures" were explicitly mentioned, which referred to nationalization, expropriation, dispossession and other restrictions of proprietary rights. They applied to both artificial legal persons and natural persons, defined as citizens of Great Britain and the colonies as of the date of signature of the agreement, or persons enjoying British protection. Simultaneously, the requirement of British citizenship of persons on the date when the relevant proprietary measure had been carried out had to be met. The agreement also dealt with the property confiscated or dispossessed from British individuals and entities by the enemy state from 17th September 1938 to 9th May 1945.

By actual acceptance of the compensation, the British party bound itself as well as the mentioned British persons to consider this step to be a "complete satisfaction and final settlement of all obligations towards British individuals and entities", "which were considered legal or beneficial owners of claims" with respect to the above mentioned proprietary measures of the Czechoslovak state. The British government also agreed not to raise further claims against the Czechoslovak Government in connection with Czechoslovak proprietary measures, regardless of whether they affected British individuals or entities according to the definition in this agreement.

The non-existence of an indemnity agreement with the USA resulted in the blocking of Czechoslovak monetary gold in the so-called Tripartite Commission.[39] After several non-ratified agreements from the 1960s and 70s, it was only Reagan's administration that managed to make the Czechoslovak state pay 100 % of recognized claims based on nationalized property, interest on this sum and reimbursement of the large part of intergovernmental debts. Thus the Czechoslovak government agreed to pay reimbursement amounting to 81.5 million dollars plus some intergovernmental debts which, after deduction of some counterclaims, totalled 90 million USD. Then the US government was prepared to consent to the release of Czechoslovak monetary gold.

The agreement between the governments of the Czechoslovak Socialist Republic (CSSR) and the USA on the settlement of certain unresolved claims and financial issues was signed on 29th January 1982.[40] The agreed lump sum of 81.5 million USD was declared to be a complete settlement and discharge of *"all claims of the government of the USA or their citizens against the Czechoslovak government resulting from nationalization, expropriation and such measures on the basis of which the assets, rights and interests were disposed of, or based on other restrictive measures, including taking ownership or exercising control over their assets, rights and interests ..., which occurred before the date of force of this Agreement"*.

According to Article 2 of the Agreement, its subject matter was the settlement of *"unresolved and unsettled"* claims of citizens of the USA *"regarding assets, rights and interests affected by nationalization, expropriation and such measures on the basis of which the assets, rights and interests were disposed of, or affected by other restrictive measures, including taking ownership or exercising control over it, which*

39/ Michálek, S.: *Nádeje a vytriezvenia, Československo-americké hospodárske vzťahy v rokoch 1945–1951* [Hopes and Disillusions, Czechoslovak-American Economic Relations in the period 1945–1951]. Bratislava: Veda 1995, p. 54 and subs.

40/ Pěchota, V.: The 1981 U.S.-Czechoslovak Claims Settlement Agreement: An Epilogue to Postwar Nationalization and Expropriation Disputes. *American Journal of International Law* 1982, p. 639 and subs.

affect them." The requisite condition, however, was that they were claims *"which, from the date of such nationalization or other taking ownership or exercising control over it to the date of force of the Agreement belonged continuously to persons who were citizens of the United States, or to all corporations or other legal persons, for which the United States can claim international liability according to its legal order."*

Article 3 provided that *"the distribution of compensation obtained by the government of the United States under this Agreement shall fall within the exclusive competence of the United States in accordance with its legal order and no liability may result from it for the Czechoslovak Government."* Under Article 7, on the "date of settlement", i.e. the date of handing over gold and reimbursement of the agreed lump sum compensation, all the indemnified US citizens to which the Agreement applied were deprived of any other possibility to legally claim their property against the CSSR in the future. By the Agreement the Czechoslovak Government *"was relieved of all obligations towards the USA or their citizens connected with measures taken against assets, rights and interests"* mentioned in the Agreement. In addition, the US government could not submit, by means of diplomatic protection, any such claims of their citizens under international law.

Only after making the Agreement with the USA the complex property negotiations with Great Britain were completed.[41] Britain requested not only the reimbursement of intergovernmental debts but also compensation for some other private claims of British citizens, mainly due to incomplete restitutions and national administration. In return, the blocked Czechoslovak assets in Great Britain were released. The Czechoslovak state finally agreed to pay a lump sum amount of compensation of 24 million 266 thousand pounds on the basis of the Agreement of 2nd February 1982.

Other important indemnity agreements were those made between CSSR and Austria, on the settlement of certain financial and proprietary issues of 19th December 1974, or the indemnity agreement with Canada signed in the same year.

Finally, we will have a look at the reflection of post-war property measures in so-called restitution legislation passed after 1989. One of the principal symbols of the new social arrangement was privatization. It represented a change from state ownership back to private ownership.[42] In the sphere of law it was connected with the effort to remove the distortions of property law as soon as possible.

Privatization had to tackle restitution expectations of the original owners and their heirs, though it was not clear what time limit to choose, whether to support natural restitution or financial compensation, or how to address the issue of restitution of different categories of property with respect to both the original objects of ownership and certain special categories of original owners. This was demonstrated in the case of restitutions of religious and Jewish property. Similarly, it was not possible to pass one general restitution law; special legislation was required, for instance, for restitution of agricultural land.

Initial discussions on passing a general restitution law are linked with so-called "small privatization" carried out under Act No. 427/1990 Sb. on the transfer of title to certain things from the state to other legal entities or natural persons, of 25th October 1990. Property used for agricultural production and those things which could possibly be claimed

---

[41]/ Kuklík *supra* at p. 420 and subs.
[42]/ Plíva, S.: *Privatizace majetku státu* [Privatization of the State Property]. Praha: Prospektrum, 1991, p. 13.

for restitution were excluded from small privatization. They were mostly the things which passed from natural persons and corporations composed exclusively of natural persons to state ownership according to regulations adopted after 25th February 1948, or for other reasons after this date, *"unless and until proprietary claims of these persons are regulated by special legislation".*

It was this Act on small privatization which addressed for the first time the restitution limit and determined it to be 25th February 1948, the date when the Communist Party of Czechoslovakia took over the power. Act No. 403/1990 Sb. (as amended by Act No. 458/1990 Sb.) introduced a new concept into the Czechoslovak legal order, namely "moderation of some property injustice". It applied mainly to compulsory transfers of small businesses and apartment buildings as well as to some cases of nationalization carried out after 1948. The law came into effect on 1st November 1990.

Generally, the Act regulated returning property to the original owner, from whom it was taken away, or returning it to a range of other persons, so-called entitled persons; in fact it was a special regulation of "inheriting" a restitution claim. It also made it possible to grant financial compensation or to return the purchase price and to cover the difference between the possible financial compensation and the purchase price. The Act imposed on organizations the duty to return the property which the organization possessed on 1st November 1990 upon written request of the entitled person. If the parties failed to find an agreement, the court decided. Foreign exchange non-residents could apply for the return of property only if their claim had not been settled by earlier inter-state indemnity agreements.

Since Act No. 403/1990 Sb. applied only to a relatively limited scope of property, it was necessary to formulate a more general regulation. Act No. 87/1991 Sb. on non-judicial restitutions was passed, reflecting an extensive debate on the significance of restitutions for the proposed privatization of state property. This law upheld the proposition of mere "moderation of some property injustice", which occurred as a result of civil and administrative acts in the period from 25th February 1948 to 1st January 1990. The specified relevant period of time was connected with the unlawful character of the communist regime and the violations of basic human and civil rights stipulated in international documents of the UNO.

The Act contained the main principle of restitution, that is "to moderate property injustice", which should be performed, if possible, by returning the very property to the original owner or entitled persons. Only if this was not possible, the law provided conditions for granting monetary compensation. The important feature was the determination of cases where the law imposed the duty to return the property (generally, various cases of persecution and expropriating measures taken by the communist regime) and the determination of the range of entitled persons.

At the same time the law defined cases where it was not possible to return the property and the compensation was to be awarded. From the perspective of this paper it should be noted that the restriction on restitution without a right to compensation applied to persons, who were "not loyal to the state", as well as the declaration of the principle that persons who had acquired property as a result of racial persecution, i.e. those who Aryanized Jewish property, may not apply for its return.

Entitled persons according to this Act were only natural persons. They were mainly the original owners who must have satisfied two requirements: to be a state citizen of the Czech and Slovak Federative Republic (CSFR), or later the Czech Republic, and to have permanent residency in the territory of the CSFR. Besides, the Act also used the term "other entitled persons" to whom the restitution claim passed.

Due to the fact that no compensation was paid in the course of reviewing the first land reform and the new land reform, special regulation was required for the restitution of agricultural land. Act No. 229/1991 Sb. was passed to regulate the ownership of land and other agricultural property. The scope of entitled persons was principally the same as that according to Act No. 87/1991 Sb., and the "relevant period" was also determined identically.

The first "wave" of laws which dealt with the consequences of changes in ownership and proprietary relations which had occurred after 1945, was the so-called large privatization. It meant the transfer of public property to natural and artificial legal persons, both Czechoslovak and foreign. So-called large privatization was regulated by the Act of the Federal Assembly No. 92/1991 Sb. of 26th February 1991 regulating the conditions of the transfer of public property to other entities, which was amended by Act No. 171/1991 Sb. on the competence of the Czech Republic bodies in transfers of public property to other entities and on the National Property Fund. Also the Federal Government regulation No. 383/1991 Sb. of 5th September 1991 on the issuance and use of investment vouchers played a significant role. Governments of the Republic in their resolutions presented principles for compiling the lists of state enterprises and interests earmarked for privatizations.

Excluded from large privatization was the type of property which, according to constitutional or special laws, could be owned only by the state, property which was returned to artificial legal persons by special legal regulations (such as property returned to a private legal entity under Act No. 403/1990 Sb.), property which passed to the state after 25th February 1948 from churches, congregations and religious societies, and the property whose return might be claimed by natural persons under special regulations, namely Acts No. 403/1990 Sb. and 229/1991 Sb. The question whether the property intended for inclusion in privatization should not be excluded from it because of, for example, its possible restitution, was considered in so-called privatization projects. Restitution claims of entitled persons were identified in these projects and proposals for their settlement were presented. It was the National Property Fund that had competence over the settlement of claims of entitled persons. Restitution subsisted in either the recovery of property or assignation of a portion of shares in the privatized enterprise or shares in the so-called Restitution Investment Fund.

However, the regulation from the early 1990s proved to be objectionable in many ways and controversial for the practice and participating entities. Particularly, Acts No. 87/1991 Sb. and 229/1991 Sb. were frequently amended and considered by the Constitutional Court. Questions linked to Czechoslovak citizenship, the requirement of permanent residency, or time limits and ways of submitting applications for recovery of property became commonplace. Terms, such as "performance of nationalization in violation of the then valid legislation" or "other manners of passage of property to state" needed interpretation. The above mentioned indemnity agreements were not left aside. The fact that they were not published in official collections of laws was used several times to cast doubt on their national applicability.

The adoption of Act No. 116/1994 Sb. represented a breakthrough in the original restitution legislation. It enabled people to exercise their claim to recover property under Act No. 87/1991 Sb. in cases where the property was taken from the person during World War II as a result of political, national or racial persecution, and such person's claim, duly filed according to the restitution legislation of 1945 and 1946 (i.e. Decree No. 5/1945 Sb. and Act No. 128/1946 Sb.), had not been properly settled by February 1948. This strongly applied to Aryanized property and thus to so-called Jewish restitutions. Then the requirement for permanent residency was removed on the basis of the Constitutional Court judgment No. 164/1994 and the time limits for filing claims to recover property or to be awarded monetary compensation were extended.

Yet the restitution legislation did not sufficiently take into consideration the specific destiny of Jewish property, such as objects of art, real estate owned by Jewish artificial legal persons or insurance policies. This was done as late as by Act No. 212/2000 Sb. of 23rd June 2000 on the moderation of some property injustice caused by the Holocaust. The Act brought about the moderation of some property injustice sustained by Jewish communities, foundations and associations in the period between 29th September 1938 and 8th May 1945, when their property was taken away on the basis of transfer or passage of proprietary rights, which were declared invalid by Decree No. 5/1945 Sb. or by Act No. 128/1946 Sb. Such property was gratuitously transferred from the state to the ownership of the Federation of Jewish Communities or to Jewish communities themselves. Besides that the state gratuitously transferred individual objects of art to the Jewish Museum in Prague. The Act was also a milestone in restitutions of objects of art, which were taken away from natural persons in the period from 29th September 1938 to 4th May 1945 on the basis of transfer or passage of proprietary rights that were declared invalid by Decree No. 5/1945 Sb. or by Act No. 128/1946 Sb., and which were owned by the state on the date of effect of this Act. The objects of art were to be gratuitously transferred to the ownership of the original owners, or to their spouse or descendants in case of their death. The requirement of state citizenship was removed and, for the first time within the Czech restitution legislation, the question of whether the relevant property had been the subject of special indemnity agreements with other states was not examined any more. The second part of the Act dealt with the extension of agricultural land restitution.

Leaving alone the specific issue of "church restitutions" or "restitution" claims raised from time to time by displaced Germans, the final restitution closure, which would move the matter of proprietary measures taken in the period 1945–1948 definitely to legal history, is yet to be attained in the Czech Republic.

1.2 CONSTITUTIONAL IMPULSES FOR THE DEVELOPMENT OF LAW IN THE 20ᵀᴴ CENTURY

1.2.1 Czechoslovak legislation from 17th November 1989 to 31st December 1992 and its retrospective interventions

Federal (having state applicability), Czech (produced by the Czech National Council) and Slovak (produced by the Slovak National Council) laws in the above mentioned period of time represent the most significant part of legal rules, passed and promulgated in the last 38 months of the existence of the Czechoslovak legal order, which, as it is generally known, did not exist in reality and was not really applicable in temporal and territorial continuity and in the same "focal shape" in which it had been created in 1918.[43] Those 38 months represent a scant 5 % of its approximate length of 74 years. Quantitative data regarding not only laws (legislative measures) but also other legislative types from this period have already been described in literature.[44]

Considering its content, legislation originating in the above mentioned period features two basic, partially contradictory, trends. This, of course, does not mean that each of the laws passed at that time can be affiliated to one or the other, either because they may have aspects of both the trends, or they cannot be placed in either category due to their content.

The first trend represents a tool for the establishment and consolidation of consequences of the systemic political change subsisting in the replacement of the existing situation, created in the end of February 1948 and somewhat simply designated as "communist", by political pluralism whose institutions should respect the democratic rule of law and division of powers in the state, recognize and guarantee civil and political rights and the free market environment with all its consequences, and perceive with solidarity difficult social situations and conditions with which an individual or a family must objectively or may subjectively be confronted. This trend was primary from the temporal point of view; it had an impact

---

[43]/ Professor J. Beňa, an expert in Slovak legal historiography, presents an opinion in his book *Vývoj slovenského právneho poriadku* [The Development of Slovak Legal Order], Banská Bystrica: Právnická fakulta UMB, 2001 that exclusively Czechoslovak legal order can be considered only in the period 1918–1938. In the framework of Czechoslovak legal order a Slovak legal sub-order was created and applied in the years 1938–1939 and 1948–1968. An independent Slovak legal order was constituted for a short period of time from 1944 to 1945, only to exist and apply parallel to the Czechoslovak legal order in the periods 1945–1948 and 1969–1992. Not all Slovak authors fully share this opinion. See, for example, Mosný, P.: *Povstalecká Slovenská národná rada a slovenská štátnosť* [Slovak National Council during the Slovak Uprising and Slovak Statehood]. *Právněhistorické studie* 39/2007, p. 281 and subs.

[44]/ See: Cvrček, F.: *Metamorfózy českého právního řádu z hlediska kvantitativního (fakta a spekulace)* [Metamorphoses of Czech Legal Order from the Quantitative Aspect (Facts and Speculations)]; Novák, F.: *Proměny práva na podkladě kvantitativní analýzy vývoje legislativy v ČR* [Changes in Law on the Basis of Quantitative Analysis of the Development of Legislation in the CR]. Both in: Jermanová, H. – Masopust, Z. (eds): *Metamorfózy práva ve střední Evropě: sborník příspěvků z mezinárodní konference "Metamorfózy práva ve střední Evropě" a kolokvia "Metamorfózy veřejné správy", pořádaných Ústavem státu a práva AV ČR a Fakultou právnickou ZČU v Plzni ve dnech 11.–13.června 2008 ve Znojmě* [Proceedings from the international conference "Metamorphoses of Law in Central Europe" and the colloquium "Metamorphoses of Public Administration" organized by the Institute of State and Law of the Academy of Sciences of the CR and the Faculty of Law of West Bohemian University in Pilsen, 11–13 July 2008 in Znojmo]. Plzeň – Praha: Vydavatelství a nakladatelství Aleš Čeněk – Ústav státu a práva AV ČR, 2008, p. 50 and subs and p. 123 and subs.

on all areas of the legal order and was effected mainly by federal legislation. However, its independent existence was short. At the moment when external features, i.e. the name of the state and its army and the state symbols, or terminological and graphical attributes of the existing power, were to be removed, the second trend arose.

The second trend pervading legislation of this period is the reflection of the relationship between Czech and Slovak political representation, which, from 29th March at the latest, showed the initial signs of erosion of the coexistence of both the nations in the common state, more and more clearly headed for the liquidation of any form of a common legal order and for the creation of two formally separate legal orders, with Slovaks being in advance in making concrete steps in this direction. This trend is represented in fifty Acts of the Federal Assembly, the Czech National Council and the Slovak National Council. There is no need to deal with them here as they have been studied in detail by other authors, not only native but also those working abroad for a long time.[45] Let us just note that the final legal situation of the state can be compared to the historical legal situation of the state before 28th or 30th October 1918.

The agreement between V. Klaus and V. Mečiar, chiefs of the political parties which prevailed in the elections in June 1992, on the division of the Czech and Slovak Federal Republic into two unitary republics as of 1st January 1993, changed the balance between the two almost concurrent legislative trends in favour of the second one, on which the Czech as well as liquidating federal legislatures had to consequently concentrate their attention. Many steps were put off, suspended or slowed down, but the Federal Assembly, working in a mechanical way, never set aside the reform and modernization trend until the end of its operation. It is a mere coincidence that both basic trends in legislation had approximately the same duration in the final stage of the Czechoslovak legal order.

Regardless of the law directed procedure of the relatively cultured demise of the Czechoslovak state, the period from the end of 1989 to the end of 1992 is in the current literature almost generally identified as the decisive stage of the so-called Czechoslovak legal order transformation which by its content fulfils the first legislative trend mentioned earlier. Its essence subsisted both in the removal of legal barriers, connected in one way or other with the communist domination, from the legal order, and in the creation of legal institutions and completely new regulations or modifications of some of the current rules so that the results would summarily agree with the democratic political system, economic structure not directed by central planning and unaffected by the dirigisme of daily control, and provide a free citizen, protected by a system of basic rights and liberties, with the largest possible space for self-actualization.

This transformation was carried out by a varied range of legal processes and techniques. Along with essentially new legislation, which had no repealing clauses and obviously was rather rare, transformation also brought various interventions aimed at the legal past.

---

[45]/ See, for example, Pavlíček, V.: *O české státnosti. Úvahy a polemiky 1/Český stát a Němci* [On Czech Statehood. Reflections and Debates 1/ The Czech State and Germans]. Praha: Karolinum, 2002, pp. 302–316. A treatise on the split of the Czechoslovak state was written by presumably the oldest graduate of the Law Faculty of Charles University in Prague, E. Stein, who has worked for a long time in the USA and is an internationally distinguished expert. See Stein, E.: *Česko-Slovensko. Konflikt, roztržka, rozpad* [Czecho-Slovakia. Conflict, Dispute, Split]. Praha: Academia, 2000.

Having analyzed legislation from the relevant period we can identify as the most frequent the following:

I. Common repealing provisions in legislative acts of the given period were not directed only to the immediate, latest regulation; they were frequently aimed at the distant past. The limit was not only primary and secondary legislation adopted after 25th February 1948 when the Communist Party of Czechoslovakia gained decisive political power. Legislation in the form of presidential decrees issued nationally was also affected (1945), laws in the form of decrees issued in London (1944) and the Slovak National Council legislation issued during the Uprising (1944) were impacted rather exceptionally and indirectly, in their conceptual principia. Abrogation of legal regulations originating in the Second Republic (1939), whose partial applicability persisted, also occurred. The question remains whether it was at all practicable after the repeal of the Constitution of 1920, which was approved in 1948. The duty of constitutional bodies to promulgate consolidated wordings of important legislation caused revisions of so far unabrogated legislation of Austrian and Hungarian legal orders, going as far back in history as the first half of the 1870s.

II. An objectionable, although rather rarely used institution was the so-called inapplicability of either individual provisions (sections) or the whole piece of legislation. Thus the legislature does not repeal the validity of the legal regulation but orders the relevant bodies not to consider the regulation to be a part of the legal order after a certain date, although formally it remains there. The oldest but inapplicable piece of legislation is the so-called Acquisition Act of 1919.

    According to the introductory provision of the constitutional Act on the Charter of Fundamental Rights and Freedoms, the legislative provisions which did not conform to it became ineffective as of 31st December 1991. They have remained a part of the Czechoslovak legal order but cannot be invoked. So the result is identical. A comprehensive list of such regulations within the Czechoslovak legal order has never been compiled. Thus the Czechoslovak legal order disintegrated to a part which is valid and effective, and another part which is only valid. The legislature determined the scope of both the parts only roughly and concrete decisions are up to the discretion of bodies applying law to individual cases.

III. Judicial and administrative decisions, the scope of which was defined in different ways, were affected; sometimes they were repealed by virtue of law, in other cases it happened in situations when natural or private artificial persons concerned, or their successors, relied on such possibility within determined time limits. For instance, in criminal law these decisions were based on conduct which had occurred before 25th February 1948, mostly since 5th May 1945 but also in older times (during Nazi occupation or during the existence of the Slovak State), although most decisions on such conduct were legally effective (final) after 25th February 1948 and some of them even before that date.

IV. Some employment and civil acts, or acts by public bodies lacking legal formality, were repealed, or their consequences were repealed. It applied mainly to acts performed in the period from 25th February 1948 to 1st January 1990 which met some other specialized requirements.

V.   Complete legal regulations, exceptionally codes (the Commercial Code) and legal institutions, which had been legally repealed or effectively abandoned in the past, were renewed or adjusted to contemporary conditions. Legal phenomena to be revived had mostly been legally and practically liquidated in the years 1939-1953. The question of how much inspiration the legislature drew from the legislation of 1918-1938 and how much from comparable contemporary legislation of West European continental democracies cannot be answered generally; it requires an analysis of each individual case. Similarly, it is not possible to say that all fundamental legal regulation from 1948-1989 was removed. For example, in spite of fierce and long lasting criticism and contrary to general expectations, the Act regulating financial support for churches and religious associations (No. 218/1949 Sb.) was not replaced by any essentially new law by the end of 1992; in fact, it has survived until now (written in June 2009).

VI. The findings in constitutional case-law, but mainly the judgments of the Constitutional Court of the Czech Republic in the period 1995-1998, constituted other interventions in the past beyond the wording of laws and beyond their interpretation performed by general courts. This applies mainly to cases of restitution of land and other types of property and the limit of 25th February 1945 was transgressed several times.

The so-called transformation content of the first of the two legislative lines in the period between 17th November 1989 and the end of 1992 was achieved thanks to the extensive usage of various interventions of positive law in the past as well as in the practice of legal history. The extent of this phenomenon cannot be compared to any other situation in the history of the Czechoslovak legal order, neither at its origination in 1918, nor in getting over its imperilment in 1938-1945. Hence this knowledge should be considered in the course of future legal and historical research of the successive legal order of the Czech Republic. We cannot rule out the possibility that it represents a significant cause of its creation and consequently, on the contrary, a significant cause of the demise of the Czechoslovak legal order.

Making a broader generalization, we can say that the transformation of the Czechoslovak legal order is a part of more extensive legal and geographical changes pivoting on the re-consolidation of the continental legal order, whose temporary restriction by socialist legal systems was seemingly restored to its original condition thanks to changes in the legal orders of Europe in the period between 1988 and 1992.

1.2.2 "Legality" of authoritarian regimes in the 20th century

If we consider the role of law and its significance in the 21st century, we need to look back, not only to distant times but also to modern history. Comprehensive assessment and recapitulation of the history of the recently passed century is an indispensable requirement, since during that time mankind suffered two world wars and had to endure fascism[46] and communism. In the past the state had a monopoly on the legitimate use of force. Dispropor-

---

[46]/ See, for example O'Sullivan, N.: *Fašismus* [Fascism]. Praha: Centrum pro studium demokracie a kultury, 2002.

tions between the power of the state and the position of the citizen or individual created a specific order which soldered up the society; it represented a basic framework of, and justification for, the existence of the state. The past century brought about strong shifts in this established model and gave rise to states, which enwrapped the use of unusually intensive force against their own citizens within a "legal" framework.

One of the typical features of European totalitarian regimes of the 20th century[47] was their effort to legalize their position as well as the tools they used to control the society. Along with absolutely extralegal means, such as paramilitary organizations, they used purely legislative tools which, however, served to strengthen their power. So, technically speaking, they were states which respected the rule of law and whose bodies applied the currently valid laws, but the tools they used were far from democratic.

Such an instrument, legalizing a completely extraordinary manner of ruling, were so-called enabling laws[48] which made it possible for ruling elites to pass legal regulations not taking into consideration the procedure of passing laws in Parliament while the image of constitutionality was retained. They can be encountered both in fascist Italy and in Nazi Germany. Yet enabling laws were not typical of only openly fascist or Nazi regimes; they were then adopted in other European states – in Poland in 1926, in Austria in 1934 or in France in 1940.[49]

A kind of analogy of this type of rule-making can be seen as early as in the 19th century in Austrian constitutions. The first such provision can be found in the draft of Kroměříž Constitution (s. 146), then in the so-called March Constitution of 1849 (s. 87), in the so-called February Constitution (s. 13) as well as in s. 14 of the December Constitution of 1867. In Germany, the first enabling provisions appeared in the course of World War I. In August 1914, the Federal Council of the German Reich was authorized to take extraordinary measures to remove economic losses. Many similar regulations were passed during the transformation of Germany to a republic. In the years 1919–1923, seven enabling laws were adopted, again because of a complicated economic and political situation. The same tool was used in the Constitution of The Weimar Republic (Art. 48) to consolidate economic and political conditions.

The first typical example of utilizing enabling laws was fascist Italy. The fascist "revolution" was performed in a constitutional way. In the autumn of 1922, the king Victor Emanuel III appointed Benito Mussolini[50] as Prime Minister and the "old" Constitution remained unaffected. The apparent constitutional continuity was violated only by the passage of an enabling act at the end of 1922. Its validity was limited by the end of the year 1923, but it granted powers of dictatorship to Mussolini which helped him stabilize his regime. The Parliament had not been removed, but this legal rule disrupted, if not destroyed, the

---

[47]/ On the roots of totalitarianism see, for example, Talmon, J. L.: O původu totalitní demokracie. Politická teorie za Francouzské revoluce a po ní [The Origins of Totalitarian Democracy. Political Theory During the French Revolution and After It]. Praha: Slon, 1998.

[48]/ An enabling act denotes an Act which authorizes a constitutional body to act in areas in which it has not been competent to act.

[49]/ On various forms of fascism see, for example, Paxton, R. O.: Anatomie fašismu [Anatomy of Fascism]. Praha: Lidové noviny, 2007.

[50]/ See, for example, Bosworth, R. J. B.: Mussolini. London: Hodder, 2002.

division of powers in spite of the fact that the Parliament retained formal supervisory power. Legislative initiative was transmitted from the law-making body to the Executive under the pretext of national emergency.

During the relatively short life of the enabling law Mussolini managed to push through a principal reform of the electoral system. In 1923 a new election law was passed which introduced majority representation and secured majority for the Government and fascist candidates. In the elections which were held according to this law in April 1924, the Fascists secured a majority of votes and seats in the Parliament, yet the opposition won in some areas (northern Italy and large industrial centres) in spite of open intimidation by fascist commandos. The enabling act of 1922 was followed by other regulations; the most important were passed in 1925–1926. It was namely the Act on attributes and prerogatives of the Head of State (No. 2263 of 24th December 1925) and on the power of the executive to pass legal rules having the force of law (No. 100 of 31st January 1926). The first one endowed Prime Minister Mussolini with unrestricted power in the state, the other provided for the passage of Royal Decrees regulating, with some exceptions, the implementation of laws, execution of state power and organization and activities of state administration. These extraordinary powers were formally limited by a previous resolution of the Council of Ministers and a debate in the State Council, but the key provision was contained in Article 3 of this Act. Royal Decrees could be passed under statutory authorization granted by the fascist Parliament; but exceptionally, if required by serious reasons and in so-called absolute necessity, the authorization was not necessary. Assessment of both the conditions, which were not specified, was performed only by the political control of the Parliament.

These legal rules laid down firm foundations of the power of the Fascist Party in Italy and other laws which completed the fascist "revolution"[51] originated there. It was not only another election reform in 1926, but also replacing the Parliament by a Chamber of Unions and Corporations in 1938, that served to exclude all non-fascist parties from the Parliament.

The manner in which Nazis acquired power in Germany[52] showed some similarities to the advancement of fascism in Italy. It is evident that in Germany the process was in fact constitutional, utilizing the existing Constitution of the Weimar Republic.[53] The extraordinary powers on which Adolf Hitler later relied were brought by the enabling act of 24th March 1933 which suspended basic political rights enshrined in the German Weimar Constitution. First of all, it was the decree of the Reich President von Hindenburg of 28th February 1933 "Act to protect the nation and state" (Gesetz zum Schutz von Volk und Staat).[54] This legal rule was followed by the above mentioned enabling act. Its complete name was "the Act to remove the poverty of the nation and Reich" (Gesetz zum Behebung der Not von Volk

---

51/ On the development of fascism in Italy see Breuer, S.: *Nationalismus und Faschismus. Frankreich, Italien und Deutschland im Vergleich*. Darmstadt: WissenschaftlicheBuchgesellschaft, 2005, chapter Elemente und Ursprunge des Faschismus I: Italien, p. 96 and subs.

52/ See Fest, J.: *Hitler. Eine Biographie*. 8th ed.. Frankfurt a./Main: Fischer Verlag, 2006; also *Enzyklopädie des Nationalsozialismus*. Stuttgart: Klett Cotta Verlag, 1997.

53/ On legal issues of Nazi Germany see Wessel, U.: *Recht, Unrecht und Gerechtigkeit von der Weimarer Republik bis heute*. München: C. H. Beck, 2003, chapter II. Der Staat Adolf Hitlers, p. 47 and subs.

54/ Willoweit, D. – Seif, U.: *Europäische Verfassungsgeschichte*. München: C. H. Beck, 2003, p. 787 and subs.

und Reich, so-called Ermächtigungsgesetz).[55] It was a very short regulation (five articles) having, however, far reaching consequences.

Put simply, the practical consequence of this law was the exclusion of Parliament from the legislative process and the transfer of this procedure to the Executive, specifically to the Reich government. Formally, everything was perfectly correct, as the law was promulgated upon approval of the Reich Council and it was fully conforming to the Constitution of the Weimar Republic.[56] Also, the two thirds majority required for its approval was retained – only 94 deputies of the Reichstag voted against the passage of this law. When we study this piece of legislation in more detail, we have to say that it meant almost the complete destruction of the above mentioned Constitution and a defiance of the elementary principle of democratic ruling – it destroyed the principle of the division of powers. The Reich Government, completely in the hands of Nazis, was thus enabled to decide laws by resolution. They could even be contrary to the Constitution (Art. 2 provides that they can deviate from it) unless they regulated Reichstag and Reich Council. This, however, was not necessary, as both the bodies had been firmly in the hands of Nazis. Laws, including constitutional laws, were adopted without debate in, and approval of the Reichstag, but the Reich Government also created state budgets at its discretion and even concluded international treaties. These laws became valid upon the signature of the Chancellor.

This law stipulated lawmaking authorization in all respects and it appears to be unequivocally formulated as well as problem-free from the point of view of its interpretation. The most principal stipulation was contained in its last provision, Article 5. Time limitation of the regulation can be found there – it was meant to be in force only until 1st April 1937, so the shift of legislative powers to the Executive should have been only temporary. However, in the meantime the power was permanently transferred to the bodies of the Nazi Party, so this temporary provision became absolutely irrelevant. Another provision in the same Article is much more interesting. It states that "it shall expire when a new government replaces the current Reich government". It represented a kind of safeguard in case Nazis lose their influence in the body to which these exceptional powers passed, so that they could not be used against them. It is interesting to note that Hitler himself paid heed to the appearance of legality of his dictatorship by renewing the enabling act several times, namely in 1937 and 1941. The last renewal of the law for an unspecified time occurred in 1943 upon the Fuehrer's order.

As we have already said, enabling legislation was not exclusively in the domain of fascist Italy and Nazi Germany. It can be found in France in the interwar years, where the Govern-

---

[55] *Ibidem* at p. 789.
[56] The fact that participants were aware of the unlawfulness or non-liberal character of the passage of such law is clearly shown in the stenographic records of the proceedings of Reich Council (Bundestag). We can, for example, quote from the speech of Social Democratic Party deputy (SPD) Wels: *"After persecutions suffered recently by the Social Democratic Party no one can request or expect it to vote for the submitted enabling statute. The elections of 5th May brought majority to governing parties and consequently the possibility to rule on the basis of, and in conformity with, the Constitution. Where there is such a possibility, there is also such a duty. Criticism is healthy and necessary. Never during the existence of Reichstag have public matters, governed by the elected representatives of the people, been suppressed to such a degree as we can see it now and as it should continue by means of this enabling statute. The more limited the freedom of movement shall be, the more this arbitrariness of the government shall grow."* In: Verhandlungen des Reichstages, Bd. 457, p. 33.

ment was authorized by the Parliament to pass decrees with the power of law (décrets-loi), and their number was increasing in the 1930s. In the vast majority of cases they were decrees whose passage could not have been postponed, or decrees on such matters for which the political parties represented in Parliament did not want to be politically accountable. In Austria one enabling act can be encountered, namely that passed on 30th April 1934 "on extraordinary provisions in the constitutional area"[57] which authorized the Austrian Government to pass laws. It was this statute that enabled the Austrian Federal Government to pass the "Federal Constitutional Act on Reintegration of Austria with the German Reich" on 13th March 1938, after annexation. The legal regulation stemmed from the Constitution of the same year, under which Bundestag gave way in political decision-making to executive bodies, mainly to the Federal Chancellor and the Federal Government. But most importantly, all legislative initiative passed to the Government. The Constitution also provided for extraordinary legislation. It meant mainly Martial law, which could be imposed by the President or Government. The document was not based on sovereignty of the people but in its preamble it referred to all rights coming from God. It featured strongly an authoritarian and antidemocratic character.[58]

Polish enabling legislation has its foundations in the coup d'état of Marshall J. Piłsudski[59] of May 1926. The Constitution of 1921 was not abolished, but President Piłsudski's friend, Professor I. Mościcki, was authorized by the Act of 2nd August of the same year to issue decrees having the power of law. The Polish modification of the constitutional authoritarian order is connected to the so-called sanitation regime.[60] It was the chief of the Polish state, Marshall J. Piłsudski', who announced "moral sanitation" (i.e. recovery) of public life in Poland. Under power of the above mentioned law, the President could issue decrees having the force of law as well as dissolve the Sejm (Parliament). The freedom of assembly was abolished and local self-government restricted.

There were various ways leading to the consolidation of authoritarian regimes. If we wish to assess the given period, we have to research in detail not only historical and political events which formed it but also its reflection in the legal order of the given country. There can be no doubt that the period researched bears witness to depersonalization, degeneration or degradation of law. The principles of the rule of law were frequently violated or abused for antisocial, authoritarian interferences with the legal order and in the society as a whole. Legislative procedures used in order to change individual legal systems are still appealing and have not been completely analysed yet. Here we can quote H. Hattenhauer, distinguished German legal historian: *"Experiences of the past must be utilized so that we can better solve the conflicts of the present and dangers of the future."*[61] The modest aim of this analysis has been to outline at least some of these questions.

[57] For more details see Willoweit, D. – Seif, U. *supra* at p. 791 and subs.

[58] Brauneder, W. – Lachmayer, F.: *Österreichische Verfassungsgeschichte*. Wien: Manz Verlag, 1989, pp. 231–247.

[59] See, for example, Humphrey, G.: *Pilsudski: Builder of Poland*. New York: Scott and More, 1936; Garlicki, A.: *Józef Piłsudski. 1867–1935*. London: Scholar Press, 1995.

[60] From Latin *sanatio* – recovery.

[61] Hattenhauer, H.: *Die geistesgeschichtlichen Grundlagen des deutschen Rechts*. Heidelberg: C. F. Müller, 1983, p. 299.

1.2.3 Referendum in the second half of the 20th and at the beginning of the 21st century: its potential and limits (On referendum as an institution of direct democracy in Czechoslovakia after 1989)

The historical process of the gradual reconstruction of constitutional foundations of plural democracy, the system of basic political rights, including the institution of referendum and civic initiatives, started in Czechoslovakia as late as after November 1989. However, the initial approaches to application of referendum have not fulfilled the original expectations of democratically oriented citizens.

Some space for the application of direct democracy opened in 1990 just at the lowest tiers of territorial self-governing bodies when the amended Constitution of the Czech and Slovak Federal Republic (CSFR) provided in Article 86 (3) that *"matters of local self-government shall be decided by citizens at local assemblies or by referendum or by representative bodies of the community."*[62]

Meaningful discussions on the inclusion of an institution of direct democracy in the Constitution developed more at the beginning of the 1990s when the proposal of a Constitutional Act on national referendum, introduced by the President of the Republic Václav Havel, was being debated.[63] The submitted bill envisaged that citizens would have an opportunity to express in referendum their opinion not only on bills and proposed Constitutional Acts but also on essential questions of domestic and foreign policy of the state.

Under Article 1 of the submitted draft, the decision of citizens should have had the binding power of a Constitutional Act. Referendum was to be called by the President of the Republic upon proposal of the Federal Assembly or of his own initiative (Art. 2(5)). For adoption of the proposal, participation of a majority of electors was required (Art. 7).

A controversial discussion started due to Article 8, which enabled the combination of a submitted proposal with the claim of the Czech and Slovak nations' right to self-determination. Concerns were expressed mainly over the strengthening of the influence of the Executive at the expense of the legislative power of the Parliament as well as the fear of possible abuse of referendum for the enforcement of separatist demands of Nazi oriented groups both in the Czech lands and in Slovakia.

An explanatory report on the draft of the Constitutional Act on national referendum perceived the direct vote of citizens as a tool for overcoming possible disagreements in the Federal Assembly in case the deputies were unable to find a common solution of debatable issues.

At the same time, there were heated discussions on a possible reform of the Federal Assembly. The idea of a bicameral federal lawmaking body, which should be composed of a Chamber of Deputies and a Senate, was more or less respected.

These efforts were enforced by constitutional committees which proposed, among other things, that the Senate be entitled to initiate a referendum.

---

[62] Pavlíček, V. et al: *Ústavní právo a státověda, II. díl* [Constitutional Law and State Science, Vol. II]. Praha: Linde, 2008, p. 365. See constitutional Act No. 294/1990 Sb. to modify and amend constitutional Act No. 100/1960 Sb., and constitutional Act No. 143/1968 Sb. to restrict the term of office of National Councils.
[63] *Parliamentary print No. 372* – retrieved from http://www.psp.cz/eknih/1990/tisky/t037200.htm

On 29th April 1991, the "Coalition for the Republic – Republican Party of Czechoslovakia" submitted its own proposal of a Constitution. It requested that the change of the Constitution should be preceded by an *"obligatory national discussion whose results would be binding on a Federal Parliament"*.[64]

The Constitutional Act on national referendum was finally adopted in August 1991 (Constitutional Act No. 327/1991 Sb.). It was rather different from the presidential draft of 1990. The issues submitted for popular vote could only be essential questions of state organization of the CSFR (Article 1 (1)). The decision that any of the Republics leave the Federation could only be made by referendum under Article 1 (2) of this Act.

In case any of the Republics really expressed the wish to leave the Czechoslovak Federation, under Article 3 (2) the President was to call a referendum on this question in the given Republic upon proposal of the relevant National Council. In other cases the President was to call a referendum upon proposal of the Federal Assembly after the National Councils had expressed their opinions (Article 3 (1)).

If the question was not clear or unequivocal, the President could refuse to call a referendum; however, if the relevant lawmaking body persisted, then he would be obliged to call it under Article 3 (3).

When assessing Constitutional Act No. 327/1991 Sb. from the point of view of its content and political implementation, some of its specific features were (and most probably will be) adverted to, namely the following:

1. Considering European legal culture, the determination of the subject matter of a referendum is specific. While in most foreign legal systems the determination is negative, in our law the subject matter of a referendum is defined positively;
2. the adoption of a special Constitutional Act on referendum instead of the inclusion of referendum directly into the Constitution itself is considered somewhat nonstandard;
3. the Constitutional Act did not provide for the situation when the Federal Assembly would decide not to accept the results of a referendum and consequently take measures to change the Constitution in such a way that the result of the referendum could not be carried out.

In other articles the law provided that
i. referendum could not be held five months before the end of the term of office of the Federal Assembly or National Councils (Article 4);
ii. the proposal submitted for referendum was approved if an absolute majority of qualified electors voted for it (Article 5 (1) and (2));
iii. before the results of referendum were announced, the Czechoslovak Constitutional Court could, upon proposal of the Presidium of any of the lawmaking bodies, check whether the referendum had been held in conformity with the Constitution (Article 5 (4));

---

[64]/ For more details see Kubát, M.: J. Kysela, Senát Parlamentu České republiky v historickém a mezinárodním kontextu. Příspěvek ke studiu dvoukomorových soustav [The Senate of the Parliament of the Czech Republic in Historical and International Context. Contribution to Research of Bicameral Systems]. *Politologický časopis* 4/2002, p. 454 and subs.

iv. the result of referendum had the binding force of a Constitutional Act (Article 6 (1));

v. if the proposal that a Republic would leave the Federation was approved in referendum, the CSFR would terminate its existence within one year of publishing the results of such public vote (Article 6 (2));

vi. a five year time limit was determined for repeated referendum on the same issue (Article 5 (5)).

It is noteworthy from the historical point of view that referendum did not become the constitutional basis for the split of Czechoslovakia on 1st January 1993, although it represented a constitutional option.

Public opinion was influenced more and more by statements of Czech and Slovak politicians claiming that the split of the CSFR was uncontrollable so that the application of referendum was effectively impossible.[65]

This tragic historical event will probably remain a permanent topic for legal, ethical, social and political reflections on the current standard of democratic awareness, political will and capability of action of wide layers of the Czech and Slovak society and mainly on the level of responsibility of political elites to the citizens of both federal republics.[66]

After the tragic failure of active application of the democratic thinking and activities of both nations' population in the process of disintegration of the Czechoslovak Federation, there were many attempts to codify a national referendum in the independent Czech Republic; however, none of them were successful. Individual drafts were remarkably diverse, as they differed in their party and ideological purposes, the subject matter of referendum, its sponsors, the manner of approval and binding effect.

During the rule of the coalition government of the Civic Democratic Party (ODS), Christian Democratic Party (KDS), Christian Democratic Union-Czech People's Party (KDU-ČSL) and Civic Democratic Alliance (ODA), deputy Jan Kryčer from the Movement for Self-Governing Democracy of Moravia and Silesia submitted a draft of a Constitutional Act on referendum.[67]

According to this proposal, referendum should have been applied for deciding any important question of domestic or foreign policy as well as the question of adoption or abolition of a statute (Article 2 (1)). In addition, citizens should have been enabled to propose a referendum by a petition.

The Chamber of Deputies dismissed this proposal in its session on 16th February 1994.

On 30th June 1995, a draft Constitutional Act on referendum was submitted by deputy Stanislav Gross of ČSSD. The referendum was to be called by the Government or upon a decision of at least two fifths of all deputies.

The proposal did not define issues on which referenda could be held, but it required an obligatory referendum in case of the delegation of powers of state authorities to a su-

[65] For more details see Klíma, K.: *Ústavní právo* [Constitutional Law]. Praha: Victoria Publishing, 1995, p. 115 and subs.

[66] Ambivalent, small-minded pragmatism and frequently also irresponsibility of top party and state representatives "towards the people" is briefly but cogently described in Gál, F.: Kalendárium rozpadu. In: *Rozloučení s Československem* [Farewell to Czechoslovakia]. Praha: Český spisovatel, 1993, pp. 151–155.

[67] Parliamentary print No. 494 – retrieved from http://www.psp.cz/agw/historie.sgw?T=4948&0=1.

pranational body, that is if *"the Czech Republic joins an alliance with other states, to which powers of state authorities defined in the Constitution should be entrusted"*.[68] The government did not support this proposal and the Chamber of Deputies dismissed it.

On 19th January 1996 deputies D. Matulka and J. Navrátil of the Communist Party of Bohemia and Moravia (KSČM) submitted a draft Constitutional Act on referendum and an amendment of Constitutional Act of the Czech National Council (ČNR) No. 1/1993 Sb., the Constitution of the Czech Republic. There was a requirement that a referendum could be called upon an initiative of deputies or by qualified electors through a petition. The proposed subject matters of a referendum were issues connected with sovereignty, territorial integrity and organization of the Czech Republic. The Government did not support the draft and it was dismissed by the Chamber of Deputies on 14th March 1996.[69]

During the rule of the coalition government of ODS, KDU-ČSL and ODA (1996–1998), deputy Zdeněk Jičínský of the Czech Social Democratic Party (ČSSD) submitted a draft Constitutional Act amending Constitutional Act of ČNR No. 1/1993 Sb., the Constitution of the Czech Republic.[70] The subject matter of a referendum defined in this proposal could become an ordinary statute, the change in the constitutional order, or attitude of citizens to the issues of internal and foreign policy of the state.

Referendum could be initiated by the Government, the Chamber of Deputies or by citizens through their petition. However, the result of such referendum was not binding – the Parliament had to consider it, but it had the discretion to accept it or refuse it. At the same time it could not make changes in the considered draft. The draft was dismissed by the Chamber of Deputies on 22nd October 1977.

During the minority government of ČSSD (1998–2002), Zdeněk Jičínský submitted another draft of a Constitutional Act on popular vote. In fact, it was identical; the only difference was that the provision regulating popular initiative was omitted. The Government supported the draft with several comments, but the Chamber of Deputies dismissed it on 2nd February 1999.[71]

On the same day, a draft Constitutional Act on popular vote was submitted by deputy Cyril Svoboda of KDU-ČSL. The draft stipulated that referenda could not be held on bills, but only on the initial outline of a constitutional or ordinary law. It could be initiated by qualified electors through their petition. The proposal provided for obligatory referendum on the accession of the Czech Republic to the European Union. The Government did not support the proposal and the Chamber of Deputies dismissed it on 13th July 1999.[72]

Another draft Constitutional Act on referendum and an amendment to the Constitution of the Czech Republic was submitted by Pavel Rychetský of ČSSD on 29th August 2000. Under this draft, referenda should be held on serious questions of internal and foreign policy of the state. Referenda could be initiated by qualified electors through a petition.

---

[68]/ Parliamentary print No. 1874 – retrieved from http://www.psp.cz/sgw/historie/sqw?T=1874&0=1.
[69]/ Parliamentary print No. 2096 – retrieved from http://www.psp.cz/sgw/historie/sqw?T=2096&0=1.
[70]/ Parliamentary print No. 104 – retrieved from http://www.psp.cz/sgw/historie/sqw?0=2&T=104.
[71]/ Stenographic record of the 9th session of the Chamber of Deputies of the Czech Republic of 2nd February 1999, retrieved from http://www.psp.cz/eknih/1998ps/stenprot/009schuz/&009010.htm.
[72]/ Parliamentary print No. 120 – retrieved from http://www.psp.cz/agw/historie.aqw?0-37T-120.

The proposal of Pavel Rychetský was dismissed by the Chamber of Deputies on 25th January 2001.[73]

On 11th September of the same year, Pavel Rychetský submitted another draft Constitutional Act on referendum and amending the Constitution of the Czech Republic. The content was identical with the previous proposal, but the obligatory referendum on accession of the Czech Republic to the European Union was stipulated.

While this proposal was passed by the Chamber of Deputies on 7th February 2002, the Senate dismissed it on 19th September 2002.[74]

Senators without delay submitted their proposal for a single referendum on the accession of the Czech Republic to the EU. It was passed as Constitutional Act No. 515/2002 Sb., on referendum on the accession of the Czech Republic to the European Union.[75]

It is important to note that the referendum was held on 13th and 14th June 2003 and consequently the Czech Republic acceded to the European Union on 1st May 2004.

More proposals for national referenda were submitted later during the following development of the Czech state. During the coalition government of ODS, KDU-ČSL and the Freedom Union-Democratic Union (US-DEU) in 2002–2006, a government bill on national referendum was submitted by an independent deputy P. Zářecký (10th March 2005).

He proposed that referenda should be held on important questions of trends in domestic and foreign policy of the state. The deputies approved this proposal on 29th June 2005; however, it was rejected by Senators on 5th December 2005.[76]

On 4th October 2006 the Government dismissed a draft Constitutional Act on a referendum on placing US anti-missile defence elements in the territory of the Czech Republic and to amend the Constitution of the Czech Republic, submitted by V. Filip, H. Šedivá, Z. Bebarová-Rujbrová, Z. Jičínský and S. Grospič.

The Government's opinion was that *"the decision on the possible placement of elements of US anti-missile defence in our territory is an exceptionally important matter, where it is necessary to consider not only political aspects, but also highly specialized military, security, legal and economic issues. Because of that the Government prefers that the question of possible placement of elements of anti-missile defence in our territory be decided by the body which is authorized to make such decisions, namely the Parliament of the Czech Republic. The Government would like to remark that principal decisions regarding strategic security issues have been made by the Parliament of the Czech Republic throughout the existence of the Czech Republic. That was the reason why the accession to NATO, the most important step in the sphere of national security in the history of the Czech Republic, was approved by the Parliament of the Czech Republic. There is no reason why to choose a different approach for the case at issue."*

A similar situation occurred during the Coalition Government of ODS, KDU-ČSL and the Green Party (SZ) when Z. Bebarová-Rujbrová of KSČM submitted a draft Constitutional Act. It provided for referendum on serious questions of domestic and foreign policy of the state. The initiators could be the Government, deputies, senators or qualified electors

73/ Parliamentary print No. 695 - retrieved from http://www.psp.cz/sqw/historie.sqw?0=3&T=695.
74/ Parliamentary print No. 1039 - retrieved from http://www.psp.cz/sgw/historie.sqw?0=3&T=1039.
75/ Stenographic record of the 21st session of the Senate of the Czech Republic of 19th September 2002; retrieved from http://www.senat.cz/xgw/pssenat/original/11948/11948.
76/ Parliamentary print No. 914 - retrieved from http://www.psp.cz/sgw/historie.sqw?0=4&T=914.

through a petition. The Government did not support the proposal and the Chamber of Deputies dismissed it on 14th March 2007.[77]

It is obvious from this survey that there have been numerous genuine attempts at establishing the institution of national referendum in the constitutional system of the Czech Republic since its foundation in 1993. And only once a referendum was permitted, when according to a special law, passed ad hoc for this purpose, a referendum on accession of the Czech Republic to the European Union was held.[78]

Deeper analyses of social scientists and deliberations on the reasons of perpetual rejections of referenda as a legitimate and legal tool enabling citizens to participate in making decisions on crucial issues of domestic and foreign policy of the state show that the principal objector to passage of any Constitutional Act on national referendum has been the Civic Democratic Party. ODS sticks to the opinion that referenda should be called only ad hoc, on a single important question.

One of the arguments against national referendum ODS has voiced is that referenda are frequently used to strengthen authoritarian regimes or that they can hamper progress. It is also frequently claimed that representative bodies are elected by the people in order to make decisions and that it is counterproductive to transfer this responsibility to citizens.

On the other hand, the leftist parties, ČSSD and KSČM, supported the introduction of national referendum. The attitude of KDU-ČSL has been and will be hardly predictable and the Greens can be expected to take a quite positive approach to referendum.

The attitude of Czech political representation to local referenda has been rather different. In 1990 Act No. 367/1990 Sb., on communities, was passed; it provided for referendum on merger or division of communities or other local issues on condition that at least one third of local council members and one tenth of citizens older than 18 applied for it (s. 26).

A referendum was obligatory in case of an application for division of the community and if its result was positive, the Ministry of the Interior performed the division.[79]

Under Act No. 298/1992 Sb., on elections to community councils and local referenda, a referendum could be initiated by any qualified citizen on condition his or her application was supported by no less than a qualified minimum percentage of the total of other qualified citizens (s. 11).

The subject matter of a referendum was determined negatively, and it was not permissible to decide issues such as local budget, local charges, etc. (s. 10). It is worth noting, however, that until 2000 no local referendum according to this Act was held.[80]

---

[77] Stenographic record of the 13th session of the Chamber of Deputies of the Czech Republic of 14th March 2007; retrieved from http://www.psp.cz/eknih/2006ps/stenprot/113schuz/s013047.htm.

[78] For more details see Smith, L. M.: *Přímá demokracie v praxi: Politika místních referend v České republice* [Direct Democracy in Practice: The Policy of Local Referenda in the Czech Republic]. Praha: Sociologický ústav AV ČR, 2007, p. 41.

[79] According to a 2001 census, the number of communities increased on the basis of local referenda by 490 in the years 1991–2001. For more details see Smith, L. M.: Cesty k efektivní přímé demokracii: Česká místní referenda v regionálním srovnání [Paths to Effective Direct Democracy: Czech Local Referenda in Regional Comparison]. *Politologický časopis* 4/2006, pp. 399–422.

[80] *Ibidem* at p. 409.

Direct democracy is (and will be even more) the reality of the development of modern constitutionalism within parliamentary representative democracy.[81] Debates presenting pros and cons of referenda have been and will be conducted in Parliament and in media and in expert treatises of jurists and political scientists; we can only hope that the Czech Republic will finally also get closer to the birthplace of referenda – Switzerland.

1.2.4 On current interpretation of the US Constitution

One of the reasons why the issues of current interpretation of the US Constitution are so interesting is the fact that they represent an exceptionally good example of blending historical impulses in the development of law with impulses growing from precipitated development of the information society influenced by new technologies.

This fact deserves even more attention if we realize that the gap between "the age of stagecoaches", when in 1787 the American federal Constitution was created (and ratified in the summer of the following year), and the current character of American civilization (not taking into consideration just a few amendments adopted in the 19th and 20th centuries) is getting wider and wider every year. This long-aged constitutional document demonstrates the respect for constant principles and values, tested by time, which is so typical of the American society.

Obviously, it is necessary to ask certain questions and the following study tries to formulate the answers. First of all – who enjoys the right to provide binding interpretation of the constitutional text? And how can it be ensured that its interpreters, while respecting chief principles embodied in the foundations of the Constitution by its creators and adopters, were at the same time able to respond to the topical problems of the American society, which could by no means be envisaged at the time of the origination of the Constitution? When is such interpretation legitimate and when is it not?

We need to make a short historical excursion to recall that the history of interpretation of the US Constitution is long and troublesome. We can start by remembering The Federalist Papers written originally as a defence of the constitutional draft prepared in summer 1787 in Philadelphia (with the intention to support the ratification process in the state of New York). It is right there where the first attempts to interpret the Constitution appeared, and the main focus is on famous Paper 78 by Alexander Hamilton, where he presented the judiciary as the ideal candidate for the body *"whose duty it must be to declare all acts contrary to the manifest tenor of the Constitution void."*[82]

We also need to remember the first large crisis of American constitutionality at the end of the 18th century, when individual states assumed the right to interpret the Constitution – not to the benefit of the central power. It is necessary to underline the importance of *Marbury v. Madison* of 1803 where it was effectively decided that the binding interpreter of the Con-

---

81/ See Klokočka, V.: *Ústavní systémy evropských států* [Constitutional Systems of European Countries]. Praha: Linde, 1996. Fiala, P. – Pitrová, M.: *Evropská referenda* [European Referenda]. Brno: Centrum pro studium demokracie a kulturu, 2005. Hamon, F.: *Le referendum, Documents réunis et commentés*. Paris: La Documentation française, 1997. On referenda see also Wintr, J.: *Principy českého ústavního práva* [Principles of Czech Constitutional Law]. Praha: Eurolex Bohemia 2006, p. 54 and subs.

82/ Hamilton, A. – Madison, J. – Jay, J.: *The Federalist Papers*. Olomouc: Vydavatelství Univerzity Palackého v Olomouci, 1990, p. 415.

stitution should be deemed the Supreme Court of the USA – in the sense of the statement "*the Constitution is what the court says it is.*"[83]

Logically, the largest part of this study is devoted to the methods used by the US Supreme Court when interpreting the Constitution. First, we mention the inherently significant historical method based on the presumption that this document was meant by its creators and adopters as a formulation, binding on future generations, determining a constitutional framework whose individual principles should be decoded as closely as possible with view to the original intent and which, of course, must be followed.

It is necessary to describe problems which are traditionally connected with the over-emphasis laid on this approach to the Constitution. Of course, the principal issue is the question of "original intent". How can we reliably discover in the depths of the past what the adopters of the Constitution had really meant by this or that provision? And how should such a provision be interpreted with respect to a concrete and topical problem?

If we, for example, look at the First Amendment regulating among other things the freedom of expression, we cannot possibly avoid the question how its adopters at the end of the 18th century meant the sentence "Congress … shall make no law …abridging the freedom of speech, or of the press".[84] Would they assent to the decision of the US Supreme Court applying this provision also to actions such as burning American flags? And how would they apply it in the age of the internet?

In the case of the ban on infliction of "cruel and unusual punishment" under the Eighth Amendment, we can pose a similar question. What did the term mean in 1791 (obviously it did not apply to the death penalty, which was commonly imposed at that time) and what does belong in this category today? Quite understandably, there are a number of similar examples where the Constitution uses terms whose real extent would require retracing back in history with uncertain results to be expected, and we would probably find ourselves embarrassingly facing the possibilities of application to the current problems.

Consequently, it is necessary to further explore the issue of rigorous and moderate "intentionalism"; the decisive factor is the effort made by "intentionalists" towards determination of the concrete scope of the adopters of the Constitution and understanding their original intentions. That logically means that in the case of the original constitutional document, we need to concentrate our attention on those who participated in the ratification process in the respective nine states of the Union and who, by their approach, decided that the proposal worked out in the summer of 1787 in Philadelphia would become a binding constitutional text one year later.

The adopters, whose original intent should be appropriately researched, are obviously not all those who participated in voting, but only those who expressed their consent to ratification. We can proceed analogously in the case of constitutional amendments – it is important to scrutinize the intentions of those who approved their adoption in the Congress and within the required three quarters in state legislatures of the Union.

---

[83]/ Rossum, R. A. – Tarr, G. A.: *American Constitutional Law.* Vol. II. New York: St. Martin's Press, 1981, p. 1.
[84]/ Abraham, H. J. – Perry, B. A.: *Freedom and the Court.* Oxford: Oxford University Press, 1998, p. 469.

To discover a specific original intention of the group of people thus categorized (if we manage to successfully identify them) is not an easy task. To start with, the problem is that many persons who finally vote for adoption simply do not have any opinion concerning some provisions – as is the case even in the present practice of passing laws and constitutions all over the world – so we can speak of frequent non-existence of any original intent. And if we manage to decode relatively well the gist of the original intent on the basis of extant documents (such as transcripts of debates on adoption of a concrete constitutional text), the border areas of its intended application remain disputable and blurred.

The intentionalists must logically turn into historians who earnestly endeavour to delve into the world of the constitutional conceptions and values of adopters; a question remains whether they succeed in completely cutting themselves off from their own value considerations and ideas and not transplanting them intrusively in the researched situation of the 18th or 19th centuries.

Such a "historian" also has to be able to distinguish between the original intent of the adopters concerning a specific provision and their intent with respect to its future application. Only by doing this can he achieve the aim of his efforts, which is the "transfer" of intentions of the constitutional text adopters into the current situation and conditions.[85]

On the other hand, consistent pursuit of original intentions gives rise to negative reactions – mainly of those who do not necessarily want to replace the original constitutional text by a new one, but who wish for more freedom in its interpretation. Understandably, the notion of original intent represents quite a principal obstacle for this conception and it is frequently formulated in the following objection: "Why should the dead rule the living?"

Really, why should people from times long gone, whose original intentions concerning individual constitutional provisions can often only be guessed, control by means of their opinions, conditioned by their times, the lives of contemporary and so very different generations? Do we not just put in their mouths what "people of present times" want to hear? Even the language people used more than two centuries ago is not identical with the current one.

That leads us to the problems of analysis of the constitutional text, which is most tightly connected with the "historical approach". The text of the Constitution obviously needs to be explored in the social and linguistic context in which it was created. The school of thought emphasizing the language of the constitutional document as the primary or even exclusive source of its recognition is denominated "textualism" and its rigorous and moderate versions are distinguished.

It may be useful in this context to quote the statement underlining the importance of the text for determining the binding sense of the Constitution: *"It is a cardinal rule in the interpretation of constitutions that the instrument must be so construed as to give effect to the intention of the people who adopted it. This intention is to be sought in the Constitution itself, and the apparent meaning of the word employed is to be taken as expressing it, except in cases where that assumption would lead to absurdity, ambiguity or contradiction".*[86]

---

[85] For more details see Brest, P.: The Misconceived Quest for the Original Understanding. In: Garvey, J. H. – Aleinikoff, T. A.: *Modern Constitutional Theory: A Reader.* St. Paul: West Publishing Company, 1991, pp. 60–72.

[86] Black, H. C.: *Handbook on the Construction and Interpretation of the Laws.* St. Paul: West publishing Co., 1911, p. 20.

Similarly, it is necessary to pay attention to a structural approach which endeavours to perceive individual provisions of the Constitution in the framework of the American government residing on pillars whose supporting power pervades not only through a federal Constitution, but also through Constitutions of individual states.

Finally, it is necessary to mention a key question (which has been reiterated in the recent years) of the legitimacy of the US Supreme Court in assessing the US Constitution. It was by no means unusual that namely in the second half of the 20th century the Supreme Court Justices declared some laws unconstitutional without finding sufficient backing in the constitutional text itself (see, for example, the famous and frequently cited case *Griswold v. Connecticut*).

So we can encounter critical opinions claiming unsanctioned "judicial legislation" (Robert Bork being one of their famous promoters), rejecting the Supreme Court of the USA as a "naked instrument of power" and demanding that it operate as a "court of law" which attempts in its decisions to consider all aspects of the given case with generality and neutrality exceeding any immediately available result. The main aim of this conception is to prevent the American Constitution from changing in the process of interpretation into the expression of certain economic or ethical ideas, and to remain the epitome of basic legal rules governing the life of the country.[87]

1.3 CHANGES IN CZECHOSLOVAK CONSTITUTIONALITY IN THE 1960s

1.3.1 Czech conceptions of federalism in the 1960s – an inspiration for our time[88]

In the 1960s various political and constitutional debates on the democratic values of European federalism emerged, which were influenced by the atmosphere of "Prague Spring". Studies on this topic, focusing on the preparation of a new constitutional arrangement of relations between Czechs and Slovaks were published namely in journals *Právník* (The Lawyer), *Socialistická zákonnost* (The Rule of Socialist Law) and *Život strany* (The Party Life).

Some inspiring information on the state of federalism in the Europe of that time was compiled by Oldřich Průša in his article "Federace a základní principy její výstavby" (Federation and the basic principles of its construction), which was published in *Právník* 7/1968.[89]

In the beginning he remarked that federation became a constitutional solution of relations between nations not only in the democratic states of Western Europe and America, but also in some socialist states, namely in the USSR and Yugoslavia. Socialist federation was perceived as a temporary resolution to national problems, which arose after the declara-

---

[87]/ It is noteworthy that Robert Bork, famous mostly for his support of these ideas, was an unsuccessful candidate of President Reagan for a Supreme Court Justice (he was not approved by the Senate). More about his criticism of "illegitimate decisions" of the US Supreme Court can be found in his book *The Tempting of America*. Praha: Victoria Publishing, 1993.

[88]/ On problems of federalism compare Pavlíček, V. et al.: *Ústavní právo a státověda, II. díl* [Constitutional Law and Political Science, Vol. II]. 2nd ed. Praha: Linde, 2008, p. 224 and subs.

[89]/ In fact, it was working material prepared in the Institute for State Administration for the Presidium of the Government.

tion of rights of nations to self-determination and independence that brought the necessity to secure by power the cohabitation of many nations on principles of egalitarianism and voluntariness within one state in Russia. However, Communist Parties considered the federative solution to national relations to be a necessary compromise on the requirement of creating unitary socialist statehood, just for the period before the envisaged passage to so called communist self-government would be accomplished.

Further Průša stated that in spite of serious differences existing between federations in capitalist and socialist states, there are also some parallels in their organization of federation and its member states, territorial arrangements and state citizenship, the system of supreme legislative, executive and judicial bodies as well as in earmarking funds flowing to the federal budget and to member states' budgets.

Then the author compared accords and differences in constitutions of the Union of Soviet Socialist Republics, the Socialist Federal Republic of Yugoslavia, the Federal Republic of Germany, the German Democratic Republic, Switzerland and others.

The problems of legal regulation of the open system of dualist federation were researched in detail by Professor Jiří Boguszak[90] in the late sixties. He explained that in contrast to the asymmetric form of mere autonomy, one of the characteristic features is the implementation of the principle of parity representation of member states in the supreme body of state power. The degree to which the federal power reflects the demonstrations of the will of member states, or to which the bodies of the federation are independent of member states may vary. It depends mainly on whether the federation lets the member states regulate the delegation of representatives themselves, or whether the federation regulates it by its own constitutional act, whether the representatives are elected directly or indirectly, etc.

According to Boguszak, it is possible to distinguish three principles of the functioning of a federation: the majority principle, the parity principle and the principle of a ban on outvoting a minority by a majority. In a broader explanation he then assessed how differently these principles work in two-member and multi-member federations. In a two-member federation, the principle of a ban on outvoting a minority by a majority makes it impossible to apply the majority principle and real life solutions always depend on agreement.

The peculiarities and difficulties connected with the creation of a two-member federation are, according to Boguszak, the following: a) the effort to consistently apply the principle of parity shall result in weakening, or even exclusion of, the majority principle on all levels of decision-making and consequently endangering the viability of the federal system; b) the effort to consistently apply the majority principle shall necessarily result in weakening the principle of parity, which is distinctive of a federation and it tends more to an asymmetrical system then to the concept of federation.

In Boguszak's opinion the principle of parity in the form of a ban on outvoting a minority by a majority should be applied in a part of federal legislature competence, while some space should be left for the principle of majority. The only way to minimize the risks of possible conflicts is to precisely and rather narrowly define competences of federal bodies.

---

[90]/ See Boguszak, J.: Otevřený systém dualistické federace [Open System of Dualist Federation]. *Právník* 10/1965, pp. 917–926.

Boguszak considered unacceptable the alternative that in case of parity or a ban on outvoting a minority by a majority, federal bodies would constitutionally have competence over the states, where conflicts could frequently occur if there was not a constitutional provision for the transfer of competences to national bodies in a situation of "inactivity" of federal bodies.

Boguszak suggested a construction of a dualist system of federation in Czechoslovakia based on parity of the two nations, which would limit the risk of constitutional crises caused by the underestimated parity principle or by a ban on outvoting a minority by a majority. He presented a list of issues which should be within the exclusive competence of the federation. Parity in the form of a ban on outvoting a minority by a majority should be implemented only in serious matters, such as passage of constitutional laws.

There were three options according to Boguszak as regards all other competences:

1. all legislative competences, which under the Constitution of 1960 belonged to central bodies, should be granted to the federation;
2. all so-called state competences should be granted to member states;
3. a combination of both the options.

Having considered the possible consequences of implementation of the three mentioned options in the conception of the federal arrangement of Czechoslovakia, Boguszak arrived at the conclusion that option two would be the best one.

An inspiring contribution to theoretical debates on the international competence of member states in a federation was presented by Vladimír Outrata in the *Právník* journal.[91] He concentrated on problematic issues of various types of a composed state form which were being considered in debates on the conception of the new Czechoslovak Constitution.

He started by a brief explanation of legal consequences of the institution of a confederation system, although he was aware that its legal establishment in Czechoslovak situation was unlikely. He reasoned that a constitution in a confederation system would necessarily be an instrument of not only constitutional character, but also of international effect. The large majority of international treaties would be concluded separately by individual national states in their name and implemented by their national bodies.

The confederation as a whole would be competent to conclude only those treaties that would regulate powers delegated to federal bodies by the Constitution (mainly in the area of defence, common diplomatic representation, currency, funds necessary to cover costs of common activities).

For a more probable case that the new Constitution should provide for a federal system in the Czechoslovak Republic arrangement, Outrata focused on clarification of two main forms of federation – intrastate and international. He underlined that in a system of intrastate federation both the national states could implement a vast range of their own legislative, executive and judicial powers; however, in international relations it would be the

---

91/ Outrata, V.: K otázkám mezinárodní způsobilosti členských zemí ve federativním uspořádání [On International Competence of Member States in Federal Arrangement]. *Právník* 12/1968, pp. 1019–1026.

central state who would act for them as a representative of the whole. Only the federation as a whole could be an international legal person.

International law does not preclude normative or executive activities, necessary for intrastate implementation of international treaties, from being performed by national bodies, as an alternative or exclusively. But responsibility for failure to respect such treaties would always be on the federation as a whole.

Outrata considered as an advantage of the intrastate type of federation the simplicity of its constitutional regulation and exclusion of all direct international consequences of federalization: ambiguities in the division of competences between the federation and member states would not penetrate directly to international relations of the federal state, but they would be firstly solved within its structural arrangements.

On the other hand, in case of an international type federation, both the central state and each member state would have certain legal competence under international law. International treaties would be concluded by the federation and its member states in their own name.

Outrata mentioned two main reasons for introducing an international type federation: 1. the existence of specific interests of individual member states; 2. the need to express specificity and political independence of individual member states of the federation at the international level.

If the new Constitution provided for a federation of international type, it would be necessary to anticipate three types of international treaties:

1. those concluded on behalf of the federation and implemented only by its bodies;
2. those concluded on behalf of the federation but implemented by national bodies; and
3. those concluded by member states independently and implemented by them.

The above mentioned opinions and mainly Outrata's reflections on an international type federation are stimulating even today and could be an inspiration to finding solutions for the interstate relations within the European Union.

1.3.2 Constitutional development in Czechoslovakia in the 1960s and problems of ethnicity

The 1960s represent a remarkable period of social changes all over the world. Many of them concerned Czechoslovakia, and not only in 1968. These changes had an interesting impact on the development of law. The radical reconstruction of basic codes of law in the first half of the 1960s was an original, very problematic yet remarkable case from the point of view of research, but we are not going to deal with it in this paper. Let us just note that the codes of 1961–1965 have not yet been sufficiently scholarly evaluated[92] although they remain, in spite

---

[92]/ At least, we can mention some papers in the monograph Malý, K. – Soukup, L. (eds.): *Vývoj práva v Československu v letech 1945–1989* [The Development of Law in Czechoslovakia 1945–1989]. Praha: Karolinum, 2004; Jičínský, Z.: *Právní myšlení v 60. letech a za normalizace* [Legal Thinking in the 1960s and during Normalization]. Praha: Prospektrum, 1992. For the survey of current research see Petráš, R.: Výzkum českých a československých právních dějin po roce 1989 [Research on Czech and Czechoslovak Legal History after 1989].

of many principal amendments, a part of valid legal order. Our attention will be focused on a much narrower topic, namely constitutional development and specifically problems of ethnicity – minority questions. It should be noted that the terminology of this field is far from being uniform. In this chapter the term "ethnicity" or "ethnic minority" denotes what formerly was called "national minority" (*národnostní menšina* in the Czech language). After 1948 a special term was introduced to Czech law, namely *národnost* in Czech, which was usually translated into English as "nationality".

It is necessary to suggest what we mean by "ethnicity problems" and to make an essential stipulation that, unlike in most other legal branches, in the case of legal status of minorities the terminology has not been clean cut. In accordance with the common understanding in the Communist era, by "ethnic group" we mean an ethnic minority, or rather only some of those more numerous, such as Hungarians, Poles, Ukrainians (Ruthenians) and since 1968 also Germans. The term minority was frequently deprecated after 1945. Another complex issue connected with this topic is the status of Slovakia within Czechoslovakia, which was in the 1960s an extremely sensitive question intertwined with the problem of minorities in many aspects as 1968 clearly demonstrated. The problem of ethnic minorities as well as the Slovak question are wedded to the attitude of the state towards ethnic divergences. In the 1960s, and mainly in their beginning, the regime tended to underestimate the problem and even considered the concept of amalgamation of nations. Disregard for distinctions between nations was a specific part of official illusions of both Czechoslovakia and the USSR about a simple path to an almost ideal state of prosperity – communism. Efforts to radically transform the society were manifested in legislation and, of course, in Constitutional Acts. The axis of the development was the Constitution of 1960 (which originated in a very specific atmosphere prevailing in the ruling circles) and the pursuit of reform in 1968, from which only the creation of federation (Constitutional Act No. 143/1968 Sb.) and the provision for the rights of ethnic groups in Constitutional Act No. 144/1968 Sb. remained.

While the Constitution of 1948 (the so-called May Constitution) had been prepared before February 1948, after which a modified Communist proposal was hastily adopted, the Constitution of 1960 (the so-called Socialist Constitution) was created in a completely different situation. The Constitution of 1948 considerably formally followed the democratic models of the First Republic and the general conception of constitutionalism; in 1960, Soviet constitutional theory and terminology completely predominated.[93] The Constitution was prepared by the ideological department of the Central Committee of the Communist Party of Czechoslovakia (ÚV KSČ). It was first approved by the plenary session of the ÚV KSČ and only then, on 11th July 1960, Parliament adopted it as Constitutional Act No. 100/1960 Sb., the Constitution of the Czechoslovak Socialist Republic. When interpreting it we need to understand a specific atmosphere in the society, or rather in a part of its ruling circles,

Právněhistorické studie 39/2007, pp. 41–59. Minority issues were dealt with in detail in Petráš, R.: *Menšiny v komunistickém Československu* [Minorities in Communist Czechoslovakia]. Praha: VIP Books: Eurolex Bohemia, 2007; or Petráš, R.: Menšiny v Československu 1945–1989 [Minorities in Czechoslovakia 1945–1989]. In: Malý, K. – Soukup, L. (eds.): *Vývoj práva v Československu v letech 1945–1989* [The Development of Law in Czechoslovakia 1945–1989]. Praha: Karolinum, 2004, pp. 240–280. A much more detailed annotation is also provided there.
[93]/ Pavlíček, V. et al.: *Ústavní právo a státověda II 1* [Constitutional Law and Political Science, Vol. II 1]. Praha: Linde, 2001, p. 82.

which created a number of unrealistic expectations. The initial building enthusiasm, which should have followed Soviet industrialization in spite of completely different economic conditions in Czechoslovakia, had practically vanished in the first half of the 1950s, but the images of possible quick and radical changes survived. In fact, the most important role was played by the development in the USSR, where at the end of the 1950s a kind of "building" period started, probably for the last time. Optimism stemming from the successful economic development, a number of political achievements and prestigious victories in sports and technology led to ideas of easy attainment of the state of well-being.

Such Utopian images referred mainly to the economic system, but the new, Communist world was to be essentially rebuilt in other aspects, too. From the legal point of view, the idea of the dying off of a state was especially important. It is a tragic example of the standard of legislation of that time that we can find such ideas directly in legislation, namely in the so-called Socialist Constitution – mainly in its infamous, absurd preamble (Declaration). In line with the Soviet pattern, Czechoslovakia at the end of the 1950s started heading for communism as was declared at the XI Congress of the Communist Party in 1958. However, the reality of economic development, which brought stagnancy and even a temporary recession, led to quick disillusion.

Generally shared – often droll – ideas of a quick path to communism illustrate the circumstances of resolving the problems of ethnicity, but the ideas of the future development of the state are much more significant. The importance of its role should decline and many powers of the centre – allegedly unavoidable in the initial stage after the institution of the proletariat dictatorship – were to be limited and transferred to social organizations and national committees.[94] The overall constitutional and political development featured a dual character. On the one hand, the legal standard of the Constitution and many other laws was appallingly low. We cannot ignore the fact that the rather non-legal character of the Constitution corresponded with the overall conception of the state where law was just a more or less flimsy legislative veil covering the real operation of the regime. Moreover, the Constitution of 1960, although apparently representing the embodiment and consolidation of the socialist regime, did not mean the beginning of the sharpening of the social situation. On the contrary, it marked the start of a limited liberalization: in 1960 quite a number of political prisoners were released.

Understandably, the specific development of thought in this period was manifested not only in the constitutional development in general, but in the solution of national and ethnic issues – that is, the problem of Slovakia and the situation of ethnic minorities. Ethnic differences were perceived rather as a kind of archaic deadwood which would disappear almost completely with the development of a new man. The sensitive issue of Slovakia was disregarded as were other ethnic problems. The Party and government circles to a certain extent believed that problems of minorities had been solved by the institution of the Communist regime itself and showed no interest in creating special legal regulation

---

[94] See, for instance, Rataj, J.: *KSČ a Československo I. (1945-1960)* [Communist Party of Czechoslovakia and Czechoslovakia I. (1945-1960)]. Praha: Oeconomica, 2003, pp. 177–178. Klíma, K.: Vývoj československé ústavy – osnova studie [Development of Czechoslovak Constitution – synopsis of a paper]. In: Klíma, K. – Jirásek, J. (eds.): *Pocta Jánu Gronskému.* Plzeň: Aleš Čeněk, 2008, pp. 33–34.

of the status of ethnic groups. Only with time (mainly since the mid 1960s) the country leadership arrived at the conclusion that the situation required some solution. However, a deadly stillness reigned over minority matters, so typical of totalitarian regimes where minorities did not dare to claim any rights for themselves and enjoyed only what the state graciously granted them. At the end of the 1950s the situation in Czechoslovakia partially followed Soviet conceptions – that means the official Soviet model, and its real significance cannot be overrated[95].

Since the war, ethnic minorities had been perceived as a potential threat and the readiness of Czechs and Slovaks to grant them some rights was negligible, mainly as concerned Germans. Since 1918, the Slovak question had been a complicated problem in the basic conception of the state, so that a federalization, for instance inspired by the Soviet model, was far from simple. In theory, there were no problems in following Soviet models – for instance in reflections on more intense links among nations – but the convergence of nations and ethnic groups (i.e. Czechs and Slovaks with Poles, Hungarians and Ukrainians) was discussed there, not their amalgamation as in the USSR. Theoretically, this policy was probably most anti-minority in the whole Communist era; however, in practice in the 1960s, it was relatively moderate for a Communist regime, and it manifested rather in the lack of interest in any provisions regarding questions of ethnicity.

Even after 1945, ethnic minorities represented an important part of the population – according to the census of 1st March 1961 there were 534,000 Hungarians, 140,000 Germans, 68,000 Poles, etc., out of the total of 13,746,000 inhabitants.[96] It is quite surprising though, that in spite of relatively extensive legal regulation of minorities' status in the period 1918-1938, this matter was almost non-regulated by law from 1945 to 1960, or rather until the passage of Constitutional Act No. 144/1968 Sb. There was a conception after the war that non-Slavic minorities would be displaced or assimilated (in case of Hungarians "re-Slovakized"). Other groups, such as Poles, were more or less ignored. This situation lasted until the beginning of the Communist era. Then Hungarians, and later also the remaining Germans were provided equal position, but, save for sporadic exceptions, legal rules regulating this area were not created. Thus a legally absurd situation evolved where the rights of minorities, such as the right to use their language in communication with authorities or to have education provided in their native language, relied on internal guidance notes (namely circulars issued by the Ministry of the Interior for Regional National Committees) and even on Communist Party documents which formally did not have any legal force. In addition, these internal guidelines and Party documents were frequently secret, so the members of ethnic minorities (and sometimes even state officials) did not have the slightest idea what their rights were!

The most important steps were taken in the summer of 1952 although many unclear questions remained. On 17th June 1952 the government and on 1st July 1952 the Slovak Assembly

[95]/ See, for example, Vykoukal, J. – Litera, B. – Tejchman, M.: *Východ. Vznik, vývoj a rozpad sovětského bloku 1944-1989* [The East. The Origins, Development and Disintegration of the Soviet Block 1944-1989]. Praha: Libri, 2000, pp. 323-324.
[96]/ *Federální statistický úřad / Historická statistická ročenka ČSSR* [Federal Statistical Office / Historical Statistical Yearbook of the ČSSR]. Praha: SNTL, 1985, p. 62.

of Representatives set out so-called language rights – principles of bilingualism in ethnically mixed areas as well as the principles of representation of minorities in National Committees and other organizations. However, those resolutions were never published or worked out in any legislation. Later, for instance in 1968, it was critically remarked that they had never been fully implemented: *"It is hardly possible to carry out correct ethnic policy without legally guaranteed rules."*[97] The key role in state policy was played by the ÚV KSČ which issued guidelines regulating not only Party bodies but also state institutions – for instance in 1956 about Germans and in 1959 about Poles; the Central Committee of the Communist Party of Slovakia (ÚV KSS) issued guidelines on Ukrainians in 1955 and on Hungarians in 1958 and 1959.[98]

Around 1952 the status of ethnic groups – Hungarians, Poles, and Ukrainians – was created and consolidated. Altogether, these minorities acquired adequate cultural and language rights. In areas with dense population of ethnic minorities, they could use their native language for communication with authorities and in public life generally, although the institution of bilingualism was far from ideal and, for instance, in the region of Těšín with a Polish minority, there was rather a formidable chaos. National schooling where children were taught in the language of the minority was also provided. Minorities had their own ethnic organizations, which was particularly important in the totalitarian regime. Minorities were also adequately represented in offices and elected positions, including the KSČ.

The status of some minorities featured principal deficiencies resulting from a problematic approach the regime had adopted towards them. The position of Ruthenians (Ukrainians) was problematic for a long time since the state suppressed – probably upon request from Moscow – Ruthenian orientation and preferred that of Ukraine. Consequently, many members of this minority preferably claimed Slovak ethnic origin and sent their children to Slovak schools. The Germans remained not recognized as a group and discriminated against, but they finally acquired civil rights. Disdainful treatment of the members of this minority was surviving very long though, which was a manifestation of the ongoing anti-German chauvinism of the Czech population and its impact on local administration. Jews and Romanies (or Gypsies in the terminology of that time) were not considered a specific ethnic group and were to be assimilated.

The year 1960 brought a number of crucial changes which often affected the status of minorities. The new Constitution was adopted and an administrative reform carried out which was unfavourable for the minorities to a certain degree. Reorganization meant a decomposition of their institutional framework created in the 1950s. In new and large districts, the proportion of minority population dropped. The Constitution of 1960[99], or the

97/ Zvara, J. – Šindelka, J.: Národnostní menšiny a jejich práva / Žijeme v jedné zemi [Ethnic Minorities and their Rights / We Live in One Country]. *Rudé právo*, 16th August 1968, p. 5. *"We did not provide for constitutional and statutory guarantees for rights of ethnic groups and a central protection of such rights was virtually non-existent."*

98/ Nosková, H.: Národnostní menšiny a politika komunistické moci v letech 1948–1989 [Ethnic Minorities and the Policy of Communist Power in the years 1948–1989]. In: Nosková, H. et al.: *K problémům menšin v Československu v letech 1945–1989* [On the Problem of Minorities in Czechoslovakia in 1945–1989]. Praha: Ústav pro soudobé dějiny AV ČR, 2005, p. 81.

99/ Rabl, K.: Über die Verfassungsurkunde der ČSSR vom 11. Juli 1960. *Bohemia* 1961, pp. 537–539. Until the 1960 Constitution, there was no constitutional regulation of ethnic minorities in the ČSR. Kresák, P.: Verfassungsentwicklungen der ČSSR in den Jahren 1948–1968. In: Mohnhaupt, H. – Schönfeldt, H.-A. (eds.):

Socialist Constitution, treated minorities very briefly – it guaranteed rights for Hungarians, Ukrainians, Poles, but not for Germans.[100] Although the rights of some minorities were laid down in the Constitution, legal regulation of their status remained far from perfect and largely insufficient and such situation lasted until 1968. Two Articles of the Constitution of 1960 (namely 25 and 74) were the only legal provisions and resulted in inconsistent application in practice and frequently arbitrary behaviour of lower bodies, as was admitted even during the Communist era.[101]

During the Communist era, the "Gypsy/Roma question" was not usually considered a part of ethnicity problems, as this group had not been recognized as a separate nation. Their problem is very different, too, because the main question is not that of language differences as in the case of "classic" ethnic minorities (language for dealing with authorities, schooling provided in languages of minorities), but mainly social and cultural disparity. Yet we have to briefly mention this topic, since it was the Roma ethnic group with which the state had the most problems when it tried to assimilate it to the majority population – for instance, by settling nomadic Roma (in fact the provision affected almost the entire Roma population) under Act No. 74/1958 Sb., which was performed in February 1959. Besides, this regulation is a typical example of the way of thinking of the regime at the turn of the 1950s and 1960s. In February 1959, a new stage of the Communist solution of the Gypsy question, consisting of the liquidation of the nomadic way of life, engagement of Roma in work and general enhancement of this group, should have started. In reality, however, the new, and for local administration rather demanding, policy was principally disturbed as early as in 1960 by administrative reform; it is a remarkable coincidence with the previous conception announced in 1952 which was practically stopped in the following year by the re-organization of National Committees.[102] Commissions for work with the Gypsy population effectively broke up at the beginning of the 1960s and many other initiatives collapsed as well. On the other hand, the regime also achieved some success. The overall material standard of the Roma population increased and even the most problematic areas – Roma villages in Eastern Slovakia – slowly started to get acquainted with modern amenities.[103] There was an intention to amend the essentially unsuccessful Act No. 74/1958 Sb., but it never happened.[104]

Normdurchsetzung in Osteuropäischen Nachkriegsgesellschaften (1944–1989) 4. Frankfurt am Main: Vittorio Klostermann, 1998, p. 525 and subs.

[100]/ Staněk, T.: *Německá menšina v českých zemích 1948–1989* [German Minority in the Czech Lands 1948–1989]. Praha: Institut pro středoevropskou kulturu a politiku: Panevropa, 1993, pp. 152–153.

[101]/ Šindelka, J.: *Národnostní politika v ČSSR* [National Minorities Policy in the ČSSR]. Praha: Orbis, 1975, p. 125.

[102]/ Grulich, T. – Haišman, T.: Institucionální zájem o cikánské obyvatelstvo v Československu v letech 1945–1958 [Institutional Care for the Gypsy Population in Czechoslovakia in the years 1945–1958]. *Český lid* 73/1986, p. 76. For details see Petráš, R.: Cikánská / romská otázka v Československu na počátku komunistického režimu a návaznost na starší vývoj [The Gypsy / Romany Question in Czechoslovakia at the Beginning of the Communist Regime and Connection with Older Development]. *Právněhistorické studie* 38/2007, pp. 225–247.

[103]/ *Romové v České republice (1945–1998)* [Romanies in the Czech Republic (1945–1998)]. Praha: Sociopress, 1999, p. 171. Pavelčíková, N.: *Romové v českých zemích v letech 1945–1989* [Romanies in the Czech Lands in 1945–1989]. Praha: Úřad dokumentace a vyšetřování zločinů komunismu PČR, 2004, p. 86. Petráš, R.: Právo a romské kočování v českých zemích – historický přehled [Law and the Nomadic Life of Roma – Historical Survey]. In: Šrajerová, O. (ed.): *Migrace – tolerance – integrace II.* Opava – Praha: Slezský ústav Slezského zemského muzea – Informační kancelář Rady Evropy, 2005, pp. 210–219.

[104]/ See Petráš, R.: K právům národností – menšin v českých zemích na počátku komunistického režimu [On the Rights of Ethnic Groups – Minorities in the Czech Lands at the Beginning of the Communist Regime]. In:

The year 1968 witnessed enormous vigour in the society, which strongly impacted Slovak and minority issues; in fact, the Slovak nationhood claims initiated the reform movement itself. Ethnic minorities attracted less attention; however, in the context of conflicts between Hungarians and Slovaks in the South of Slovakia, they earned a fair share. Neglect of differences among nations, so typical of the end of the 1950s and the beginning of the 1960s, was over. Extraordinarily quick animation of the society was manifested not only in democratic pressure and federalist endeavour in Slovakia, but also in a general debate on the system of government. Ethnic minorities hastily revived mainly in Slovakia, which was often a response to Slovak nationhood claims.[105] Unfortunately, the activity of minorities later grew into national riots in some places (mainly in southern Slovakia).

Finally, extensive activities of minorities and notably preparedness of the state leaders contributed to the adoption of the Constitutional Act to regulate the status of minorities in 1968. This issue was tackled together with the problem of federation – Constitutional Acts on federalization and on ethnic groups were prepared at the same time. It is worth noting that the general public as well as legal experts were far more interested in solving the relations between Czechs and Slovaks than in minority issues. There was hardly any mention of minorities in specialist legal journals[106] and this situation was an objective reflection of both the situation in the legal science and the approach of experts dealing with constitutional matters in Czechoslovakia.

A key role in the constitutional development in 1968 was played by the Government Expert Commission on the New Constitutional Arrangement whose main task was to prepare the federalization of the state, but which gradually became involved in the formation of the law regulating the status of ethnic groups. The Commission was one of the signs of advancing democratization after the creation of a new government on 8th April 1968, which immediately, on 12th April, decided to launch the preparation of the new constitutional arrangement. The Commission was presided over by Gustáv Husák, so it is sometimes labelled Husák's Commission, or it is remembered by the place of its work, Koloděje Castle near Prague. It attended not only to the question of federalization but to many other matters, such as democratization, the operation of public administration, and the reform of regional administration. The Slovak part of the Republic strongly insisted that federalization be carried out, but it was by no means the only publicly debated topic. Apart from the issue of Slovakia, mainly the problems of economy or rehabilitations were discussed in the media. As regards minorities, they were mostly just a marginal topic, except for Hungarian-Slovak conflicts and frequent invectives against "West German revenge" which continued as a tradition throughout the Communist era.

Jirásková, V. – Suchánek, R. (eds.): *Pocta prof. JUDr. Václavu Pavlíčkovi, CSc. k 70. narozeninám*. Praha: Linde, 2004, pp. 140–151.

[105]/ Rychlík, J.: *Češi a Slováci ve 20.století / Česko-slovenské vztahy 1945–1992* [Czechs and Slovaks in the 20th century / Czech-Slovak Relations 1945–1992]. Bratislava: Academic Electronic Press, 1998, p. 230. Petráš, R.: Ústavní zakotvení práv národností v Československu v roce 1968 a maďarská otázka [Constitutional Rights of Ethnic Minorities in Czechoslovakia in 1968 and the Hungarian Question]. In: Šutajová, J. (ed.): *Maďarská menšina na Slovensku v procese transformácie (Historické, politologické a právne súvislosti)* [Hungarian Minority in Slovakia in the Process of Transformation (Historical, Political and Legal Connotations)]. Prešov: Universum, 2007, pp. 32–39.

[106]/ For instance, in the years 1966 to 1970 there is not a single article on minorities in the journal *Právník*, but much information is provided on the Slovak question.

The activity of the Commission on the New Constitutional Arrangement was successful and the preparation of legal regulation featured a high standard, but the Soviet occupation disrupted the work on Constitutional Acts, notably the key Act on Federalization. At the turn of August and September 1968, the Party and government bodies did not consider this matter as the solution of the current political situation was much more pressing. The Government Expert Commission – specifically the sub-commission on ethnic minorities – managed to prepare a *"Draft of a Constitutional Act to regulate the status of ethnic groups in the Czechoslovak Socialist Republic"* at the end of September. This draft was rather close to the law adopted later. On 1st October the draft was considered in the Government and then on a plenary session of the Government Expert Commission. A more detailed, implementing version of the regulation was to be issued later by the Czech National Council (ČNR) and Slovak National Council (SNR).[107] So the law was prepared and, after consideration in the ČNR and SNR, could be submitted to the Parliament and to the people for a general discussion, which was a dramatically different legislative procedure compared to methods common in other Communist regimes. In October, the Act on ethnic groups (along with federalization) was discussed in the Constitutional Committee and simultaneously a rather broad public discussion continued. The Act to regulate the status of ethnic groups was considered in the National Assembly on 27th October 1968[108] (on the 50th anniversary of the birth of Czechoslovakia) together with the Constitutional Act on Czechoslovak federation. But for minor changes, the Constitutional Act was adopted as introduced, there was no debate and the voting was unanimous. Unlike the rather stormy preparation of the law, which aroused enormous attention from the public, its passage conformed to the traditions of the regime.

For the first time since World War II, ethnic minorities – that is, nationalities – acquired adequate legal regulation in order to protect their status, which subsisted in laying down existing rights in the Constitution as well as providing for some new rules – making Germans equal to Hungarians, Poles and Ukrainians, creating government bodies for work with minorities, etc. Specifically, Constitutional Act No. 144/1968 Sb. of 27th October represents the most significant legislation on minorities not only within the Communist era, but in fact from 1920[109] to 2001 (Act No. 273/2001 Sb.). Act No. 144 was one of the few things which survived the failure of reform efforts of 1968. However, a question remains of how to evaluate this Constitutional Act. Generally speaking it was a good resource for ensuring fair minority rights; however, without implementing legislation, which was not passed during the normalization period, it remained but a torso. On the other hand, the overall benefits of the Constitutional Act are not low and in comparison with legal regulation from other periods in our history or with other states, it will undoubtedly stand up.[110]

107/ Daily *Rudé právo,* 2nd October 1968, p. 1.
108/ National Assembly of the Czechoslovak Republic 1964–1968 / stenographic records – 28th session of 27th October 1968 (Digital Library – Czech Parliament www.psp.cz). See also, for instance, *Rudé právo* 28th October 1968, p. 2.
109/ See, for instance, Petráš, R.: Minderheiten in der Zwischenkriegs-Tschechoslowakei – ihre rechtliche und faktische Stellung. *Historica* 10/2003, p. 197–228.
110/ See, for instance, Petráš, R.: Právo, právní historie a národnostní výzkumy v ČR [Law, Legal History and Researche on Ethnic Groups]. In: Machačová, J. – Šrajerová, O. (eds.): *Interakce národnostních kultur / teoretické*

Complete neglect of the questions of ethnicity, so typical of the end of the 1950s and the first half of the 1960s, was gone and did not reappear even after the establishment of the relatively rigid, so-called normalization regime. What did reappear was the deadly inaction in this matter which survived until the collapse of the regime in 1989.

1.4 STATE AND CHURCH IN LEGAL HISTORY

1.4.1 Czech state ecclesiastical law at the beginning of the 21st century

State ecclesiastical law, as a body of legal rules, comprises legal regulations of individual states and international regulations applied in individual states, which govern the following areas:

1. legal status of religions, or denominations, i.e. churches and religious societies as a whole in the respective state;
2. provisions for the right of individuals to profess a religious faith individually or together with others or not to profess any religious faith.

State ecclesiastical law, as a branch of jurisprudence, had developed in the Czech Lands since the period of Enlightened Absolutism in the 18th century within a broader discipline called church law, where ecclesiastical regulations were explored along with the rules of canon law of the Catholic Church and internal regulations of protestant churches. In the course of the 18th and 19th centuries, teaching state ecclesiastical regulations was from time to time emphasized more than teaching the church rules themselves.[111]

At the Law Faculty of the Czech University in Prague, state ecclesiastical law explicitly appeared in the curricula of the winter term of the academic year 1912 / 1913.[112] In the years 1918–1939 it was taught again within the subject of church law, although Czech legal literature perceived it as an independent branch.[113]

For individual denominations in the sense of religious communities, the expressions *churches* and *religious societies* have been used in central European countries. The term *church*

a metodologické přístupy [Interaction of National Minorities' Cultures/ Theoretical and Methodological Approaches]. Opava: Slezské zemské muzeum, 2008, pp. 55–62.

[111]/ See Kindl, V.: Církevní právo [Church Law]. In: Skřejpková, P. – Soukup, L. (eds.): *Antologie české právní vědy* [Anthology of the Czech Legal Science]. Praha: Karolinum, 1993, pp. 87–90.

[112]/ See Horák, Z.: Právnická fakulta Univerzity Karlovy a výuka církevního práva za první Československé republiky [Law Faculty of Charles University and the Instruction in Church Law during the First Czechoslovak Republic]. Prepared within the grant Československé právo a právní věda v meziválečném období 1918–1938 a jejich místo ve střední Evropě [Czechoslovak Law and Legal Science in the Inter-war Period of 1918–1938 and their Role in Central Europe], GAČR No. 407/06/0039, *forthcoming*. The subject called "Austrian ecclesiastical law" was taught by doc. JUDr. Antonín Hobza at that time.

[113]/ See, for instance, Bušek, V.: Historický úvod do československého práva konfesního [Introduction in the History of Czechoslovak State Ecclesiastical Law]. In: Bušek, V. – Hendrych, J. – Laštovka, K. – Müller, V.: *Československé církevní zákony* [Czechoslovak Ecclesiastical Laws]. Praha: Kompas, 1931, p. 1–58, or Tureček, J.: *Kapitoly z konfesního práva čsl.* [Chapters from Czechoslovak State Ecclesiastical Law]. Praha: author's edition, 1961, p. 161. More recently see Tretera, J. R. – Přibyl, S.: *Konfesní právo a církevní právo* [State Ecclesiastical Law and Church Law]. Praha: J. Krigl, 1997, p. 331, or Přibyl, S.: *Konfesněprávní studie* [Papers on State Ecclesiastical Law]. Brno: L. Marek, 2007, p. 261.

had originally been connected exclusively with the Christian religious community.[114] Similar communities, other than Christian, are called *religious societies* in the legal tradition of Central Europe: *"... which of the two names, both traditional and used in state ecclesiastical laws, a church or religious society chooses to use shall remain its own free decision. ...there is also a third option: none of the mentioned terms need to appear in the name of the church or religious society."*[115] The entire name of the church or religious society recognized, or registered, by the state is protected. *"No church or religious society shall be allowed to use the name which was already awarded to any of them."*[116]

Is it possible to satisfy the request that some newly established religious societies should be denied the right to freely choose to use the term "church"? In the state, where its intervention in internal matters of churches and religious societies is impermissible, it is not possible. Who would set the requirements (which are theological in their substance) and who would decide on them? In our opinion, state bodies may not decide theological disputes. Unlike in the case of the entire name of a church or religious society, the mere term *church* or *religious society* cannot be declared as protected (reserved for some religions only).

Instead of the double term "churches and religious societies", which is traditionally used in Czech laws regulating their status and which refers to one and the same legal entity, the theory of state ecclesiastical law uses unified terms. The terms worth consideration are confession, or religious community, or denomination. In specialized texts, after an initial explanation, the abbreviation "church" can also be used for churches and religious societies. In the following text we will follow the last option.

State ecclesiastical law systems (the types of relationships between the state and church)

Religious confessional state is the state where government authorities prefer only one, or exceptionally two or several religious confessions, and other confessions are either completely excluded, or merely tolerated. Where confessional states tolerate some other confessions, they are so-called tolerationist confessional states.[117] However, even those states usually do not permit broader confessional diversity.

Since the second half of the 20th century, the theory of state ecclesiastical law in some states has included among "confessional" states also those which elevated an ideology to the position held by a religion, religious faith or confession in classical confessional states. Where atheism is a part of such ideology, the state is usually labelled a confessional state *à rebours*.

Those were mainly totalitarian states ruled by a Marxist-Leninist political party which, instead of an official religion, imposed the atheist ideology on the society as a whole.[118] A similar character featured also other totalitarian systems having only one governing

---

[114]/ Ethymologically it was derived both in Czech and in English from the Greek Kyrios (Lord) in the sense of Jesus Christ, as contained in the Biblical (New Testament) phrase ekklesia toy Kyrioy (congregation of the Lord).

[115]/ Tretera, J. R.: *Stát a církve v České republice* [State and Churches in the Czech Republic]. Kostelní Vydří: Karmelitánské nakladatelství, 2002, p. 70.

[116]/ *Ibidem* at p. 71.

[117]/ The degree of tolerance and inequality can differ. Consequently, the classification of confessional states into tolerationist and non-tolerationist reflects the formal legal characteristics of confessional arrangement of the given state, and it is not the expression of tolerance in the sense of approach.

[118]/ Krukowski, J.: Aktuální otázky polského konfesního práva [Topical Questions of Polish State Ecclesiastical Law]. *Revue církevního práva* 11/98, p. 150.

ideology based on a mechanism, which substituted for a religion and contained elements of cultic or quasi-religious symbolism. A most obvious example was the state built on the idea of "the cult of blood and soil", i.e. the dictatorship of the national socialist workers' party in Germany (1933–1945) and in the territories occupied by Germany during World War II.

In modern democratic and liberal states, the idea of religious freedom and the postulate of confessional neutrality of the state prevailed. There has been a shift from the state focusing on the support of a confession, hence identifying itself with that confession, to the confessionally neutral state, non-church or secular, or more precisely: non-confessional. The presupposition for such a state is that it may not identify with any religious faith, or ideology, including atheism.

The theory of state ecclesiastical law distinguishes two models of non-confessional state: separation and cooperation state.

Separation state minimizes the cooperation with religious communities; sometimes it officially declares that it gives up such cooperation completely. *"The model of separation is applied mainly in West European and American regions in relation to Christian churches."*[119] The manner, in which the separation of state and churches is performed, and its content is very different in individual cases. Mere financial independence of churches is not a separation. Some authors, aiming at a more precise classification, distinguish friendly and unfriendly separation.

The first country where the separation of state and church had been introduced was the United States of America. In the First Amendment to the Constitution of 1791, the Congress was banned from passing laws establishing a church (establishment clause) as well as laws prohibiting freedom of worship (free exercise clause). Similarly friendly separation was performed in Brazil in 1890.

The second French separation (1905) is considered a separation unfriendly to churches. This separation liquidated church legal persons and all institutions of orders and thus made it more difficult for churches to act in public. Portugal and Mexico later followed suit.[120] This trend, frequently assessed as a period of expression of anti-church emotions, was much moderated over time (for example, diocesan associations were permitted in France in 1923 and religious schools were recognized there since 1958). Both the systems of non-confessional state, separation and cooperation, can be considered as approaching, converging systems.

Cooperation state is the type prevailing among non-confessional states. It consists in the state's non-identification with churches and cooperation with them, particularly in mattes of common welfare (schooling, health care, social care).

Some state ecclesiastical phenomena cross the mentioned classification. For instance, the civil effect of religious marriages can be laid down even in a separation state (USA), while some cooperation states have legislation providing for an obligatory civil marriage (Germany). International treaties with the Apostolic See are being concluded by either

---

[119]/ Filipi, P. et al.: *Malá encyklopedie evangelických církví* [Concise Encyclopaedia of Protestant Churches]. Praha: Libri, 2008, see entry: "separation of church (churches) from the state" p. 105–107.
[120]/ The Soviet type of separation is not usually included in the mentioned classification since it was an outer proclamation which served as a shield for an ideological state, as we described above.

type of state and chaplaincy in the army has been introduced in almost all of them. It is a part of state ecclesiastical law systems of all NATO member states with the exception of Turkey.

Types of state ecclesiastical legislation
The following three types are applied in non-confessional states:

a) The type with prevailingly individualized legislation focusing on individual religions, taking into account their specific features, without being discriminatory. This type had been used in the Czech Lands until 1948.
b) The type with mixed legislation, such as that used by the totalitarian state in Czecho-slovakia in the years 1948–1989, if we consider it from a formal legislative perspective. It contained two general laws to regulate churches in 1949[121] and five government decrees where the general principles were applied to individual churches or groups of churches (one more government decree was added in 1968).
c) The type with generalized legislation, which provides for all religions at the same time. It has been applied since the renewal of democracy in Czechoslovakia in 1989. Both the Acts on churches promulgated as Act No. 308/1991 Sb. and Act No. 3/2002 Sb. stem from this conception. The advantage of this type of legislation is that it cannot be suspected of discriminating colouring. Its drawback is that it does not consider specific features and divergence of individual churches and their self-reflection; it can easily be tempted to push churches into organizational uniformity.

The stages of state ecclesiastical legislation in the Czech Lands since the Enlightenment
Confessional state favouring the Catholic Church
Jura maiestatica circa sacra and *Staatskirchentum* had been implemented from the Habsburg vic-tory over the Czech Estates Uprising (1620), even after Emperor Joseph II issued the Edict of Tolerance (1781) and until the changes occurring in the years 1860–1867.

Inconsistent form of a non-confessional cooperation state (1867–1918)
In 1861, legislation provided for equality of protestant churches and the Catholic Church, and in December 1867 basic civic rights, including the freedom of worship, were laid down in the Constitution. Since May 1868, matrimonial matters were subjected to secular law, pri-mary schools to the state, and inter-confessional relationships of state citizens were regulated by the principle of equality of state recognized churches. The status *nondenominational* was established and registers for nondenominational persons were created and legal regulation of their register law followed soon after.

In many areas, however, the parity among churches (and nondenominational status) was not enforced consistently (namely in delegated legislation and guidelines for schools and army).

---

[121] The second one, Act No. 218/1949 Sb. (in force up to date), abrogated all previous regulation of churches.

Non-confessional cooperation state in the Czechoslovak Republic (1918–1948), with a more consistent system of parity

After the liberation of Czech and Slovak nations from the rule of the Austrian-Hungarian Empire in 1918, most political parties declared their will to establish the separation of state and church; however, it was not performed.[122] Czechoslovak legislation disengaged public space from the relics of state churchism and the dominion of the Catholic Church. A treaty was made with the Apostolic See called *Modus vivendi* (1928).

Ideological atheist state (1948–1989)

The period 1948–1989 represented a stern discontinuity from the preceding systems. One of the harshest formal legal measures was s. 7 of Act No. 218/1949 Sb., regulating the provision of economic resources to churches by the state. The Act stipulated that clergy could perform their office only with the consent of the state, which could be removed by the state any time without giving any reasons. Even candidates for church offices needed to obtain the consent of the state before their election or appointment. State consent was required also for unpaid, lay preachers. There were no legal grounds set in legislation which would permit the raid on, and deportation of, votaries on 13th and 27th April 1950; such operations were illegal even in that regime. The same applied to the concentration of nuns in the period 1950–1989, the internment of bishops and other church officials (without a judgment), etc.

The new stage of non-confessional cooperation state since the end of 1989

Along with the renewal of democracy at the end of 1989, the system of non-confessional cooperation state was renewed. The sources of recent Czech state ecclesiastical law are as follows:

a) The Charter of Fundamental Rights and Freedoms (1991), which was included in the constitutional order of the Czech Republic by the Constitution of 1992;

b) International treaties, namely the International Covenant on Civil and Political Rights of 1966, the Convention on the Rights of Child of 20th November 1989 and the European Convention for the Protection of Human Rights and Fundamental Freedoms of 1950;

c) Specialized state ecclesiastical legislation (i.e. laws on churches), namely Act No. 308/1991 Sb., which was replaced by Act No. 3/2002 Sb.;

d) Laws and legal rules of lower legal force regulating churches, either fully or partially (that is providing for state ecclesiastical matters only or partially);

e) Agreements of the state or its public bodies with churches; the international treaty with the Apostolic See was signed in 2002, but it was not ratified. Intrastate agreements with the Czech Bishops' Conference and the Ecumenical Council of Churches in the Czech Republic were made for chaplaincy in prisons (1994, 1999, 2008) and in the army (1998) as well as for some other matters.

---

[122]/ Possible reasons were mentioned in the paper "První republika a otázka odluky státu a církví" [The First Republic and the Question of Separation of the State and Church] within the research project "Československé právo a právní věda v meziválečném období 1918–1938 a jejich místo ve střední Evropě", GAČR No. 407/06/0039, *forthcoming*.

Research into the sources of law is closely connected with the response to their application in judgments of the Constitutional Court, administrative courts and general courts.

Act No. 3/2003 Sb., on churches, brought many changes in state ecclesiastical law when compared to the situation based on the earlier Act No. 308/1991 Sb.; however, the development of state ecclesiastical law since 2002 has not been so dramatically different as to call it a new stage.

Czech state ecclesiastical legislation in the years 1989–2002

On 13th December 1989 Parliament decided to abolish religious crimes, i.e. anti-church provisions of Criminal Code No. 140/1961 Sb. (ss. 101, 178, 211).[123] Negotiations between the representatives of the Czechoslovak Federal Government and the Apostolic See were held between 18th and 20th December 1989. The *Modus vivendi* of 1928 was found antiquated.[124]

Section 7 of Act No. 218/1949 Sb. was abolished on 23rd January 1990. Since then the state has not interfered in internal matters of churches nor in the appointment of any church official.

After the visit of Pope John Paul II in April 1990, the operation of diplomatic missions of the Apostolic See and Czechoslovakia, which had been interrupted in March 1950, was resumed. Apostolic nuncio in Prague is the doyen of the diplomatic corps again and the Czech Republic is represented in the Apostolic See by an ambassador.

State subsidies for clergy salaries paid under amended Act No. 218/1949 Sb. are considered to be an interim replacement for proceeds from church property which has not been returned yet. The return of some buildings to religious orders was another step in the process of remedying wrongs committed against the religious freedom of citizens during the totalitarian regime. Under Act No. 298/1990 Sb., religious orders and congregations recovered 72 buildings, and Act No. 338/1991 Sb. enabled the recovery of another 198 buildings.

Section 29 of Act No. 229/1991 Sb. of 21st May, regulating the ownership of land and other agricultural property, stipulated that *"property, whose original owners were churches, religious orders and congregations, cannot be transferred to the ownership of other persons before the laws regulating such property have been passed."* Restitution of the title to church property is still being negotiated.

The Charter of Fundamental Rights and Freedoms was published as an appendix to Constitutional Act No. 23/1991 Sb. of 9th January 1991. The Charter came into effect on 8th February 1991 and has been in force in the territory of the Czech Republic permanently up to date. On the date of the split of the federal state into two independent states, i.e. on 1st January 1993, the Charter was adopted as part of the constitutional order of the Czech Republic. It was published again under No. 2/1993 Sb. Articles 15 and 16 of the Charter represent the cornerstones of modern Czech state ecclesiastical law. Under Article 16 (3) the conditions for teaching religion at state schools are determined by law. The provisions are as follows:

---

[123] The crimes were namely the abuse of religious office, obstructing the supervision over churches and religious societies, breaches of the Act on Family Law.
[124] The principle of international law "clausula rebus sic stantibus" was invoked, which states that the validity of a contract expires in the case of substantially changed circumstances.

"Article 15

1. The freedom of thought, conscience, and religious conviction is guaranteed. Everyone has the right to change his/her religion or faith or to be nondenominational.

Article 16

1. Everyone has the right freely to manifest his/her religion or faith, either alone or in community with others, in private or public, through worship, teaching, practice, and observance.

2. Churches and religious societies govern their own affairs; in particular, they establish their own bodies and appoint their clergy, as well as found religious orders and other church institutions, independent of state authorities…"

The Charter of Fundamental Rights and Freedoms was followed by Act No. 308/1991 Sb. of 4th July 1991 on the freedom of religious faith and the status of churches and religious societies, which came into effect on 1st September 1991. This Act was a special law governing Czech state ecclesiastical law for more than ten years. It contained 25 sections and, in a schedule, it provided the list of 19 churches and religious societies[125] acting in the territory of the Czech Republic on the basis of law or state approval.[126]

Section 13 (1) (g) of the Act provides that the legal personality of individual bodies of the church (or religious society), its scope and the person authorized to act on behalf of these legal persons are determined by the respective church (or religious society). Act No. 308/1991 Sb. provided in s. 6 (1) a demonstrative list of rights of churches consisting of 12 points.

The amended Family Act No. 234/1992 Sb., in effect since 1st July 1992, restored the traditional alternative forms of contracting marriage in the territory of the Czech Republic. Marriages contracted before bodies of registered churches and religious societies have civil effect.[127]

Legislative changes since 2002

The Act on Churches (No. 3/2002 Sb.) is much more extensive than the previous law;[128] it restates the registration of churches, introducing two stages of registration. It determines church autonomy in a narrower way than the earlier law. In its original wording (before modifications performed by the Constitutional Court, see below) it obviously endeavoured to limit the responsibilities of churches exclusively to the ideological area. In particular, it

---

[125]/ The list has a declarative sense. Other churches, registered in the Czech Republic later, were not listed at the time of their registration in any legislation in accordance with a procedure laid down in Act No. 308/1991 Sb.

[126]/ Another part of the list, which referred to the territory of the Slovak Republic, provided fourteen churches and religious societies.

[127]/ Details see Němec, D.: Příspěvek k diskusi o současné a budoucí sekulárněprávní úpravě uzavírání manželství [Contribution to the Discussion on Current and Future Secular Regulation of Contracting Marriage]. *Revue církevního práva* 2/1995, pp. 73–80; Hrdina, A. I.: Kanonické uzavření manželství v českém právním řádu [Contracting Marriage under Canon Law in Czech Legal Order]. *Právník* 5/1996, pp. 417–424; Horák, Z.: Proč alternativní forma uzavření manželství? [Why an Alternative Form of Contracting Marriage]. In: Winterová, A. – Dvořák, J. (eds.): *Pocta Sentě Radvanové k 80. narozeninám* [Homage to Senta Radvanová on the occasion of her 80th birthday]. Praha: ASPI, 2009, pp. 197–208.

[128]/ The length of both the laws can be assessed if we compare the number of characters in each. While the text of Act No. 308/1991 Sb. had 12,576 characters, the text of Act No. 3/2002 Sb., as amended, has 63,995 characters, i.e. approximately five times as many.

meant losing the existing charitable and health care institutions as well as losing the ability to establish them in future. Unlike the earlier law, the new law lacks the list of rights of churches (see above).

A new list of so-called "special rights" was created, the acquisition of which is effectively the second stage of registration. All twenty one registered churches have been awarded these rights, but they can be removed under circumstances envisaged by the law. The rights are as follows: to teach religion at state schools, to authorize persons performing clerical work to act as chaplains in army and prisons, to obtain subsidies for clergy pay from the state budget in accordance with Act No. 218/1949 Sb., to conduct ceremonies for solemnizing religious marriages recognized under civil law, to establish church schools, and to observe the duty not to disclose confessional or other similar secrets.[129]

As regards registration of a new church, the required number of applicants was decreased from ten thousand adult citizens of the Czech Republic to three hundred.[130] To acquire so-called "special rights", it is necessary to apply for them only ten years after the first registration and to submit the signatures of 0.1 % of citizens, i.e. 10,292 persons according to the latest census.

Soon after the publication of the Act on Churches, a group of 21 senators filed an application with the Constitutional Court for a partial or complete repeal of the law. The finding of the Constitutional Court of 27th November 2002 was published under No. 4/2003 Sb. The Constitutional Court refused to repeal Act No. 3/2002 on the grounds that the mere curtailing of the standard of religious freedoms is not contrary to the constitutional order. It repealed only four provisions which, according to its judgment, had infringed the autonomy of churches guaranteed by the Constitution. One of them was the provision which made it impossible to hold and establish charitable and health care institutions.

After the judgment of the Constitutional Court of 27th November 2002 was issued, the Ministry of Culture started work on an amendment of the Act on Churches, which was introduced to the Parliament of the Czech Republic in 2005. The amendment was promulgated as Act No. 495/2005 Sb. It regulated primarily the procedure of recording artificial legal persons derived from registered churches in the relevant register of the Ministry of Culture of the CR.

As early as on 16th January 2006 the Constitutional Court of the CR was delivered an application by a group of senators for the repeal of Act No. 495/2005 Sb., or for the repeal of some provisions. This time, on 30th October 2007, the Court decided at its plenary session by a narrow margin 8–7 to reject the application. In its judgment the Constitutional Court of the CR states: *"There is no reliable reason to assess ss. 15(a) and 16 (a) of Act No. 3/2002, mentioned in the application…as conflicting with Article 16(2) of the Charter of Fundamental Rights and Freedoms, because (certain) restrictions on the autonomy of churches and religious societies are counterbalanced by another, constitutionally relevant interest, represented by the protection of rights of third persons, or the principle of legal certainty (Article 1 (1) of the Constitution, Article 16 (4) of the Charter of Fundamental Rights and Freedoms). It cannot be effectively proved that the statutory process and conditions of the creation of artificial legal persons established*

129/ This special law can only be granted to those churches which can prove that such a duty has been a traditional part of their teaching for at least fifty years.
130/ From 2002 to 2008 nine churches were newly registered.

under the internal circumstances of registered churches and religious societies is not based on a legitimate aim and that it derogates from the requirements for proportionality."

1.4.2 Core institutions of churches and religious societies in the USA and their legal status

The science of state ecclesiastical law has become an international discipline approximately in the last two decades. The relationship between the state and churches as well as state ecclesiastical law in the territory of a state are strongly influenced by its history and the regulations are determined mainly by the domestic legal order. Yet the systems of state ecclesiastical law in individual countries have been compared more and more frequently both in Europe[131] and all over the world.[132] Contacts among state ecclesiastical law specialists from Europe and the USA have been developed at scholarly conferences called European-American Conferences on Religious Freedom.[133]

The aim of this study is to contribute to the mentioned debates. It deals with the legal status of core institutions of churches within secular law of the USA. That means institutions which perform church services and are active within the religious community: they are parishes or congregations at the local level and dioceses and similar entities of equal rank on a higher level. On both levels they can be associations of Christians or followers of other religions (lay and clerical), religious and similar institutes.[134] This study does not focus on institutions of education, charity or health care through which the churches and their members act outwardly.

Legal status of core institutions of churches

The basis for the current American legal system can be found in English law[135] and this applies also in the area of core institutions of churches. In England a corporation could be established only upon approval of the king.[136] A similar principle is applicable in American law: a corporation may exist only with the approval of state power. Most organizational forms of core institutions of churches in the USA had existed already under English law.

Legal regulation of the status of core institutions of churches is provided mainly in legal orders of individual states of the Union. Each of them governs several ways in which

---

[131]/ Activities of the European Consortium for Church and State Research, established in 1989, contribute to this effort in Europe.

[132]/ It has been manifested, for instance, in the establishment of International Consortium for Law and Religion Studies, whose first congress was held on 22nd–24th January 2009 at the University in Milan.

[133]/ The author of this paper participated in the second conference. See Horák, Z.: *Druhá evropsko-americká konference o náboženské svobodě „Autonomie církve a náboženská svoboda"* [The Second European-American Conference on Religious Freedom "Autonomy of Church and Religious Freedom"], Law School of the University of Trier, 27th–30th May 1999. *Revue církevního práva* 13/99, pp. 178–179. The third conference was held at Emory University in Atlanta, Georgia in 2002.

[134]/ For definitions of religious and secular institutes of consecrated life and societies of apostolic life in Catholic Church see provisions of the Code of Canon Law of 1983, can. 573 and subs.

[135]/ See Farnsworth, E. A.: *An Introduction to the Legal System of the United States.* 2nd ed., London – Rome – New York: Oceana Publications, 1983, p. 6 and subs. Also Kuklík, J. – Seltenreich, R.: *Dějiny angloamerického práva* [The History of Anglo-American Law]. Praha: Linde, 2007. Knapp, V.: *Velké právní systémy. Úvod do srovnávací právní vědy* [The Great Legal Systems. Introduction to Comparative Jurisprudence]. Praha: Beck, 1996, p. 163 and subs.

[136]/ The term *corporation* is used for an association of persons which has legal personality.

churches and religious societies can be established as legal persons. However, it is always necessary to consider the provisions of federal law, namely the First Amendment to the US Constitution of 1791 and its Establishment Clause and Free Exercise Clause: *"Congress shall make no law respecting an establishment of religion, or prohibiting the free exercise thereof; …".*[137]

The existence of unincorporated associations is connected to the fact that many churches and religious societies start to perform their activities without taking formal steps towards independent legal existence. Sometimes it is caused by theological reasons, for instance the fear that the creation of a corporation can constitute impermissible interconnection with the state power. Another reason is the fact that some churches and religious societies do not consider a fixed organizational structure compatible with their theological teachings.[138] This form has been employed by some Catholic dioceses and parishes[139] since their establishment.

An unincorporated association is composed of natural persons who have acceded to its internal regulations governing the administration of the association (such as the rights and duties of members, elections, property management).[140] Historically, such associations did not have the right to own property, to make contracts, to sue and be sued or to have limited liability like corporations. In order to surmount these legal obstacles, many states of the Union passed laws granting to these associations a limited form of legal existence.[141] *"If it is permissible under the state law, an unincorporated association can have a bank account, accept limited donations, hire employees, and accept loans. If it is permitted, it can sue and be sued."*[142] Special regulation of unincorporated associations is provided in the legislation of thirty-three states, while in the other states their rights and duties are governed by case law.[143]

In 1992, the National Conference of Commissioners on Uniform State Laws passed a model law called The Uniform Unincorporated Nonprofit Association Act[144] with the aim to unify legal regulation in this area.

Corporation sole evolved historically in England where the issue of possessory title was regulated by special laws. Individual priests of the Church of England represented corporations sole. The corporation consisted of a natural person and its successors in office, and this person became a corporation. Thus it had perpetual duration, which the natural person could not boast. The king, bishops, some deans and canons as well as all parsons and vicars were corporations sole.[145] Legal identity of the corporation remained separate

---

[137]/ The Supreme Court of the USA decisions regarding this amendment see Horák, Z.: *Právní úprava činnosti náboženských a školských institucí církví v USA* [Legal Regulation of Activities of Religious and Educational Institutions of Churches in the USA]. Dissertation. Praha: Law Faculty of Charles University, 2002, p. 20.

[138]/ For unincorporated associations see Ariens, M. S. – Destro, R. A.: *Religious Liberty in a Pluralistic Society*. Durham, North Carolina: Carolina Academic Press, 1996, p. 498; Hammar, R. R.: *Pastor, Church & Law*. 3rd ed., Matthews, N. C.: Christian Ministry Resources, 1999, § 6–01.1.; Bassett, W. W.: *Religious Organizations and the Law*. Vol. 1, St. Paul: West Group, 2001, pp. 3–77 – 3–101.

[139]/ Chopko, M.: Principal Civil Law Structures: A Review. *The Jurist* 2009, p. 242 (*forthcoming*).

[140]/ Bassett, W. W. *supra* at p. 3–95; Hammar, R. R. *supra* at § 6–01.1.

[141]/ Kauper, P. G. – Ellis, S.: Religious Corporations and the Law. *Michigan Law Review* 8/1973, pp. 1541–1543.

[142]/ Chopko, M. *supra* at p. 244.

[143]/ Bassett, W. W. *supra* at pp. 3.80 – 3.81.

[144]/ Ariens, M. S. – Destro, R. A. *supra* at p. 498.

[145]/ Blackstone, W.: *Commentaries on the Laws of England*. A Facsimile of the First Edition of 1765–1769, Vol. I, Of the Rights of Persons (1765). Chicago/London: The University of Chicago Press, 1979, p. 457.

from the legal identity of the natural person performing the office. Corporation sole could accept donations and hold property.[146]

In American law, a corporation sole can be created by law or under common law.[147] It is an organizational form suitable for churches with a hierarchical structure.[148] It is the most common organizational form of Catholic dioceses in the USA today;[149] it is also used by Episcopal Church dioceses and a number of Orthodox eparchies.[150] It is the form which enables centralized management of church institutions. Its main disadvantage is the fact that it is very vulnerable in the area of legal liability.[151]

Religious trust has its roots in English law. It is connected with transfers of property which the settlor of the trust performs for the benefit of the trustee, who is obliged to exercise proprietary rights for the benefit of a third person – beneficiary.[152] Some property is transferred in the form of a trust to a person who holds an office in the church, and at the same time such use of the property is carried out to bring profits to the church. The person holding office in the church is the trustee.

In the USA, the institution of trust operates in the form of a simple trust or as a trustee corporation, i.e. a corporation composed of several natural persons who are members of the congregation. The property of the congregation is transferred to the trustee corporation.[153]

Religious corporation is related to the fact that in many states core institutions of churches have the legal form of a corporation. Some states promulgated laws which regulate the establishment of corporations of certain churches and religious societies;[154] in other states there is legal regulation requiring that an application be filed with the court where the corporation is located. Detailed regulation is provided in the Model Nonprofit Corporation Act of 1952, or in the Revised Model Nonprofit Corporation Act of 1987.[155] The latter Act provides for a special category of *religious corporation*.

Membership corporation is a corporate body composed of the members of the organization. The collective body of members constitutes the corporation. This form is suitable mainly for churches and religious societies having congregational structure and administration (e.g. Baptist Churches). Membership corporation is recognized by law in the majority of states and the District of Columbia. It is the most democratic organizational form used by churches. At the same time it frequently causes lawsuits over legal title to church property or its possession.[156]

---

[146]/ Maida, A. J. – Cafardi, N. P.: *Church Property, Church Finances, and Church Related Corporations*. St. Louis, MO: Catholic Health Association of the United States, 1983, p. 128.
[147]/ Chopko, M. *supra* at pp. 245–247.
[148]/ Ariens, M. S. – Destro, R *supra* at p. 497.
[149]/ Chopko, M.: An Overview on the Parish and the Civil Law. *The Jurist* 1/2007, p. 200.
[150]/ Bassett, W. W. *supra* at pp. 3–170.
[151]/ Manny, J. S.: Governance Issues for Non-profit Religious Organizations. *Catholic Lawyer* 40/2000, pp. 1–23.
[152]/ Farnsworth, E. A.: *An Introduction to the Legal System of the United States*. 2nd ed., London – Rome – New York: Oceana Publications, 1983, p. 83–84.
[153]/ Bassett, W. W. *supra* at pp. 3–103.
[154]/ For instance, the state New York.
[155]/ Hammar, R. R *supra* at § 6–02.1.
[156]/ Bassett, W. W. *supra* at p. 1–60–1–61.

1.5 ROMAN LEGAL CULTURE AND ITS PRESENT EFFECTS

1.5.1 New paths and methods of Roman law studies

Roman law has had a firm position in the legal systems of all countries that have been influenced by, and based on, ideological sources of continental Europe. The institutions of Roman law form the basis of the codes of private law. The tradition of Roman law as a propaedeutic discipline taught at law faculties originated in the 19th century when it was transformed from a discipline of positive law. And then the modern Roman law science was created. These traditions – but not stereotypes – have their roots in ancient Rome and at the same time they strongly influence the present era. As long as the basic principles and constructions of law are preserved, Roman law, which features a specific type of legal thinking, will remain indispensable to understanding the operation of law.

As well as other disciplines, Roman law, both as a pedagogic and scientific subject, has undergone many changes and witnessed surges of interest in certain topics. It may be sufficient to remember the famous "hunt of interpolations" at the beginning of the 20th century, which resulted not only in countless partial studies, but finally in a list of all identified modifications in the text of Digests, to which Czech Roman law expert Otakar Sommer significantly contributed.[157]

In the existence of every discipline there comes a moment when it is necessary to rest for some period of time, recapitulate what has been achieved and try to suggest the paths of further development. In this text we are going to outline some options available in the research of Roman law. Before doing that, however, it is absolutely crucial to try to characterize Roman law studies. It may seem quite needless to someone, as an oft-repeated matter. What we have in mind is not Roman law as such, but how the science of the legal order in Ancient Rome appears or may appear to extraneous persons.

When we say Roman law, most people will recollect its two principal faces. It is commonly identified with a pedagogical discipline, which is traditionally being taught at law faculties, usually at the very beginning of the course of studies. At the same time it is understood as the research discipline focused on Roman law, or Roman law studies.

Each of these basic forms has not only a slightly different profile, but it is also perceived differently. Obviously, a layman will perceive the character, position and role of Roman law differently than a practicing lawyer, yet another perspective must be expected from historians of antiquity or teachers at law schools. Actually, it is an evergreen and rewarding topic, which even experts in Roman law studies frequently repeat.[158]

Let us start by a quick look at the place of Roman law as the subject of instruction, as this is significantly reflected in the position it takes in the framework of jurisprudence. It is connected with a principal and fundamental problem. Most lawyers, dealing with positive law, understand Roman law as an inherently historical discipline. But is it really the case?

[157]/ *Index interpolationum quae in Iustiniani Digestis inesse dicuntur.* I. Weimar: Böhlaus Nachfolger, 1929. O. Sommer worked on books 1, 2, 5, 8 and 9.

[158]/ Just a few titles from a voluminous bibliography: Bretone, M.: *Diritto e pensiero giuridico romano.* Firenze: Sansoni, 1976; Kupiszewski, H.: *Prawo rzymskie a współczesność.* Warszawa: Panstwowe Wydawnictwo Naukowe, 1988; Kuryłowicz, M.: *Prawo rzymskie. Historia, tradycja, współczesność.* Lublin: Wydaw. Uniwersytetu Marii Curie-Skłodowskiej, 2003.

Is Roman law only concerned with the explanation of the legal status of slaves, so-called noxal liability, the role of a balance-holder in mancipation and other curiosities? Of course, its role could also be interpreted this way, but it would be very far from reality. The purpose and essence of teaching Roman law consists in something completely different. There is no doubt that students reading Roman law will encounter information on legal institutions which had long ago, and deservedly so, fallen into oblivion, but it is important not only to state certain facts but also to ask why it is so and mainly what purpose such lectures serve.

There will always be different approaches to the purpose of teaching Roman law. Sometimes, its role is restricted only to that of a traditional branch of law, the knowledge of which is an inherent part of the general education of a law graduate from any university. Others add that it is a propaedeutic discipline which introduces to students basic terminology of private law and the construction of its institutions, and that it teaches them legal reasoning as well as the specific legal logic at the very beginning of their study. But what is probably most valuable about Roman law is the information which students encounter during lectures, while reading textbooks and on other occasions almost subliminally.

The point is that Roman law, due to its quite incredible and uninterrupted existence, represents almost the ideal tool for showing the regularities of development of, and changes in, particular institutions as well as for searching for ways of creating a truly effective legal order. Last but not least, the fate of Roman law can serve as a demonstration of the tools for creating specific legal sources as well as law itself and mechanisms of its operation. Frequently they are identical with the current ones, sometimes they differ. Can we always say that the present standards are really the best and ideal? The fact that we are accustomed to something and take it for granted does not justify such a conclusion. Moreover, an unbiased retrospect can prove to be a useful inspiration.

If we consider Roman law as a field of research it is necessary to underline the fact that similarly to the previous case, it is not and cannot be a discipline with clear cut borderlines. The research of the legal order of antique Rome would be inconceivable without utilizing knowledge of a number of other scientific branches.

A proposition of the following thoughts, or rather an antithesis, is that Roman law is considered to be in its own way static. It is a completely incompetent idea which, however, is based on two facts that cannot be challenged.

In the first place, it is the content of textbooks which has been standardized for more than a hundred years, from the publishing of the first Czech textbook by Leopold Heyrovský called "Instituce práva římského" [Institutions of Roman Law][159] to the most recent one in 1995.[160] Realizing that this legal order has not faced any amendments for rather a long time, this fact is to be expected. Individual textbooks thus differ only as regards their literary form, arrangement of topics or innovative approach to organization of the text, as was the case of O. Sommer's manuals.[161]

---

[159]/ Praha: J. Otto, 1886.
[160]/ Kincl, J. – Skřejpek, M. – Urfus, V.: *Římské právo* [Roman Law]. Praha: Beck, 1995.
[161]/ Sommer, O.: *Učebnice soukromého práva římského. Obecné nauky* [Textbook of Roman Private Law. General Teachings]. Praha: nákladem vlastním, 1933; Sommer, O.: *Učebnice soukromého práva římského. Právo majetkové* [Textbook of Roman Private Law. Property Law]. Praha: nákladem vlastním, 1935.

The second reason subsists in the relatively stable and at the same time closed range of sources that can be used not only for scientific research but also in teaching. In reality, however, those who specialize in Roman law studies will forever face new challenges and at the same time new methods of research and elaboration on its results emerge.

There is a general misconception that the research of Roman law, both private and public, is severely restricted by the not only limited, but even finite, range of available sources which originated in the ancient world. In fact, with almost no exception they were all "rediscovered" in the early Middle Ages. The most important event was undoubtedly the discovery of the manuscript of Digests in Pisa. As regards Justinian's Institutions, none of the known manuscripts is older than from the 9th century, and the oldest usable manuscript of the Codex called *Summa Perusina*[162] comes from the following century.

Not all sources of information about Roman law are of this nature, indeed. It is obviously true, and to deny such fact would be ridiculous, keeping in mind the character of the discipline and the notion that no discoveries of principal sources can be expected any more. It is definitely unlikely that discoveries will be made like the ones that occurred in the first decades of the 19th century when in 1816 an almost complete manuscript of Gaius' Institutions was discovered on the palimpsest of St. Hieronymus' letters in the Chapter Library at Verona, or when five years later the Cardinal Angelo Mai discovered extensive fragments of a legal manual originating in the 4th or 5th century AD, which is nowadays called Fragmenta Vaticana because that is where it was discovered.

And yet, there still exists some hope even in this respect. Let us just remember important discoveries, such as that of the fragments of the fourth book of Gaius' Institutions which supplemented the text known at that time. Other discoveries include the fragment treating of adjectician actions preserved on one of Oxyrhynchus papyri found in 1927, or the one which was found on another Egyptian papyrus, published by Vincenzo Arangio-Ruiz in 1933 and provided information on the course of process *lege agere*.

Besides the findings of legal texts, archaeological discoveries also represent a significant source of new information. Not only older findings, such as was the brass table called *Tabula Bantina* in 1790 providing information on constitutional life of ancient Rome, but obviously also much more recent ones are significant. Probably the most important was the discovery of stele called *cippus antiquissimus* in 1899 containing the very oldest Roman legal relic.[163] In 1947 a brass table from the beginning of the 1st century AD was discovered. Besides other things, this so-called *Tabula Hebana* contains provisions on the creation of five new electoral centuries, which slightly modifies our perception of the decline of popular assemblies at the beginning of the Principate.[164]

New sources have been discovered quite recently and principal findings, in a way exceptional, can be encountered all the time. Every year a large number of papyri have been

---

[162]/ The oldest text, only fragmentary, comes from the 6th or 7th centuries; it is a palimpsest found in the chapter library at Verona.
[163]/ It is a text in archaic Latin treating of the legal regulation of a sacred place. It was discovered in the center of Rome at the Forum Romanum.
[164]/ This text from the period of rule of the Emperor Tiberius was found in Tuscany, at the site of the ancient colony Heba and it contains *lex de honoribus Germanico decernendis*.

discovered as well as epigraphic relics.[165] The ongoing editions of these discovered sources are indispensable tools for utilizing these artefacts. In the area of epigraphic relics, it is mainly the yearbook "L'Année épigraphique" which René Cagnat started to produce in 1888 and which has been issued without any interruption ever since.[166] This edition supplements the voluminous *Corpus Inscriptionum Latinarum*, as well as the *Inscriptiones Latinae Selectae*, which were derived from it, compiled by H. Dessau.[167] Equally important for papyri discoveries is the edition "The Oxyrhynchus Papyri"[168] published by the Oxford University since 1898, as well as the Gradenwitz' Collection or the collection deposited in Florence. While epigraphic findings contain more official information prevailingly from the area of public law, papyrus scrolls provide the opportunity to have a glance at the everydayness of Roman law.

Regarding new discoveries, we have in mind namely the so-called *Archivium Sulpiciorum*.[169] Thanks to an incidental finding on the construction site of a road from Pompeii and Salerno in April 1959, we hold the archives of the Sulpicii family, engaged in money lending. Due to favourable circumstances the wax tablets containing accounting records were preserved and thus we can have a detailed insight into the operation of an ancient Rome "banking house" in the first half of the 1st century AD.

A question remains of what treasuries lie hiding in the manuscript departments of large libraries, or in private collections, or will yet come to light thanks to archaeological excavations.

Moreover, new possible interpretations of the existing sources have been emerging; their knowledgeable and detailed analysis can bring rather surprising results. A typical example is the breakthrough study by Cosimo Cascione, Roman law expert from Naples, who by rigorous work on the text of "The Old History of Rome" by Dionysos of Halikarnas managed to amend the existing and almost canonized reconstruction of the Law of the Twelve Tables by a fragment concerning the constitutional rule regulating the one-year duration of Roman magistratures.[170]

Recently, attention has been focused more closely on the sources which were not the primary subject of research yet, such as epigraphs, coins, papyri and also non-legal texts. This does not apply only and exclusively to sources of ancient provenance, but also to relics of newer origin. For instance, this applies to medieval illuminated codices which can clearly demonstrate the changes in approach to the nature of Roman law institutions and their later life.[171]

---

[165]/ A good introduction to epigraphy was produced by Vidman, L.: *Psáno do kamene* [Written into Stone]. Praha: Academia, 1975.

[166]/ It is printed by the publishing house Les Presses Universitaires de France.

[167]/ This anthology of Latin epigraphs, arranged according to the subject matter, was most recently published in 1995.

[168]/ New as well as older discoveries are available in electronic form on the website "POxy: Oxyrhynchus Online" (http://www.papyrology.ox.ac.uk/POxy/).

[169]/ Critical edition of these findings was produced by Giuseppe Camodeca, who published this corpus as *Tabulae Pompeianae Sulpiciorum* in 1999. *Edizione critica dell'archivio puteolano dei Sulpici*. Roma: Quasar, 1999. His first book dedicated to this discovery *L'archivio puteolano dei Sulpici* was published in Naples in 1992.

[170]/ *Una norma dimenticata delle XII tavole?* Dion. Hal. 10.60.6. Index, 28, 2000, pp. 187–201.

[171]/ Ebel, F. – Fijal, A. – Koche, G.: *Römisches Rechtsleben im Mittelalter*. Heidelberg: Müller, 1988.

New possibilities of researching into Roman law are not offered only through discoveries of new sources, which are quite limited, but rather through the use of new methods. They subsist in modern technologies brought by the latest development. Due to the fact that virtually all relevant sources, not only written but also a substantial part of papyrological and epigraphic sources have been transformed to electronic form, it is now possible to apply statistical methods to these relics. Research in the sphere of family relations and that branch of law which is currently called constitutional law present themselves in this context.

Another option is the use of classical legal sources in electronic form for finding connotations among different texts. For example, studying the incidence of legal terms in various contexts can bring various surprising results and new perspectives on a matter which may have seemed rather exhausted from the point of view of research.

The search for new topics cannot be forgotten, too. While the Roman law science traditionally focuses on analysis of private institutions, which in principle have been elaborated in much detail, it is still possible to find a *novum* there.

Recently, we have witnessed a growing interest in those areas of law which had not been perceived as separate disciplines in ancient Rome in spite of the fact that they had existed in practical life. It is mainly business law and the law of banking. From among the most recent works in this field we can mention "Diritto commerciale romano. Profilo storico" by Pietro Cerami, Andrea di Porto and Aldo Petrucci, whose second edition was published in 2004.[172] The problems of legal regulation of banking in ancient Rome were dealt with in the monograph by Aldo Petrucci "Profili giuridici delle attività e dell'organizzazione delle banche romane" from 2002.[173]

More and more authors concentrate on issues which had not been in the focus of attention when the autonomous scientific discipline of Roman law studies came into existence, namely on the research of Roman law on the level of province law and thus the creation of the first "pan-European" law of its kind.

The question of which topics of Roman law should be the subject matter of research had been asked not only in the past, it has remained vital up to now. It would be rather cheap and not very beneficial for the development of the discipline to search for, and work on, only such topics which reflect the current changes in the legal order. They cannot be ignored, indeed, as showing the connections between contemporary legislation and Roman law had always been a part of the specialized writing of Roman law experts. What is most important is to look for crucial themes, which would not only fulfil those "white" or "gray" spots in our current understanding of the legal order of ancient Rome but also advance our comprehension of Roman law as a whole.

Recently, we have noticed that Roman law specialists are starting to follow new paths on the one hand, and, on the other, they are diverging from purely descriptive studies. After the period of looking for answers to "what?" and "how?", the time has come to try and find explanations of "why?". It is not exclusively the case of principal questions of the interaction

---

[172]/ Torino: Giappichelli, 2004, 2nd ed.; Torino: Giappichelli, 2001.
[173]/ Torino: Giappichelli, 2002.

between the social and economic areas and the changes in legal order, although they bring about many interesting subject matters helping to clarify genuine grounds for changes. Rather, the point is why Roman law had developed into its particular form, including all its various peculiarities, although they often seem strange only to us who look at Roman law through eyes influenced, or even blinded, by our current conception of law, by what we today consider to be the only possible, hence "perfect" solution. However, the questions are not new, they have not emerged recently and Roman law specialists were already dealing with them in the 1960s,[174] but they appear to be much more pressing today.

What we still need are really big syntheses clarifying the key issues of the development of Roman law. It is sufficient to mention just one example of such a challenge. It is the time of the second century BC, up to now a rather disregarded period, which was absolutely crucial for the further development of Roman law. Completely new methods of hearing cases in courts appeared – procedures embodying the modernity of Roman law were then born. And it is probably not by accident that it happened right in that time and that both private and criminal procedure were modified simultaneously. In the second-to-last year of existence of the Roman Republic, Roma became the hegemonic power of the whole Mediterranean region and its face had changed definitely. It was not a city state any more, even if very strong, but it became the centre of a world empire.

One of the great challenges faced by Roman law experts is a detailed review of some legal-philosophical problems connected with the development of Roman law. It is mainly the issue of ethical values, which appeared in this legal order and influenced its development. Among the most prominent is the question of justice linked to the praetors' creation of law through court edicts.

They are the very fundamental questions of operation, and moreover of justification of the existence of law, not only Roman. These questions call for deeper consideration. It is generally accepted that not only the questions of justice (*aequitas, iustitia*), but also of the widest conception of humanity (*humanitas*) penetrated Roman law thanks to close contacts with the ancient Greek world, and that simply put, they are primarily the ideas originating in stoic philosophy.

It may seem redundant to reference the famous Ulpianus quote: *Jurisprudentia est divinarum atque humanarum rerum notitia, iusti atque iniusti scientia*,[175] as well as Iuvientius Celsus' maxim: *Jus est ars boni et aequi*.[176] But it was Domitius Ulpianus who tells us that the questions of justice were inherent in Roman law from time immemorial and that we have to look for them in the images of how to maintain *pax deorum*, i.e. in the sphere of religious rules called *fas*.

That is why it is so important to study archaic legal rules and their reconstructions. The research of the influence of religious conceptions on law, its development and its origin represents the key to its understanding.[177] Information about Roman law is not sufficient, as detailed knowledge of Roman religion, its character and unique features is indispensable,

---

[174]/ For instance, Kaser, M.: *Zur Methode der römischen Rechtsfindung*. Nachrichten d. Akademie d. Wissenschaften in Göttingen, phil. – hist. Klasse 2/1962. Göttingen: Vandenhoeck & Ruprecht, 1962, pp. 49–78.
[175]/ D. 1, 1, 10, 2.
[176]/ Ulp. D. 1, 1, 1pr.
[177]/ For instance, Voci, P.: Diritto sacro romano in età arcaica. *SDHI* 19/1953, pp. 38–103.

too.[178] Moreover, research into the mentioned issues serves as a typical example of co-operation among different disciplines of sciences on antiquity.

More and more attention has been devoted to the study of general principles called *maximae juris, regulae, definitiones* or *constitutiones*, created by Roman jurists and their reflection in later legal regulation.[179] These principles of Roman law are being implemented by current legislators, parties to court proceedings refer to them, and they can be found in the reasoning of judgments. On the other hand, they are also utilized by politicians and journalists for their purposes. For a long time, Roman law specialists took only marginal interest in the phenomenon of Roman law principles, and not only those included in the last title of the Justinian Digest called "On Various Rules of Ancient Law".[180] Only in recent decades has it earned the deserved attention and expert treatises on this extremely interesting topic can be encountered.[181] But not only specialized texts are being published. More or less successful anthologies of various Latin figurative phrases are being compiled, which assemble legal principles[182] or focus directly on Roman law.[183]

The question whether ancient Roman law principles are directly applicable today is worthy of detailed study. Simultaneously, a question arises whether current legal principles "work" in the Roman law environment. It is a very complicated question requiring really deep knowledge of Roman law and its background. A typical problem could be the issue of applicability of retroactivity, or its inadmissibility. In ancient Rome, it had been a common tool utilized for achieving the above mentioned *aeqitas*, both in private and even in public law. However, it cannot lead us to the conclusion that Roman law was imperfect and that Roman jurists had a flawed conception of justice. The impression that only our contemporary perspective is the perfect model and others are erroneous, without taking into consideration that different legal and social environments exist, or rather existed, can only result in incorrect conclusions.

It is the correlation of traditional and commonly disseminated misconceptions concerning Roman law which represents another challenge for Roman law studies.

Roman law served as a source of inspiration for numerous generations of law makers. Some lawyers took over, without substantial changes, the wording of its rules and incorporated them in domestic legal orders. The reason for this mechanical copying could be undue deference to the work of Roman jurists or just the lack of their own invention. Others used it and still have been using it as a source of inspiration and treat it as a heritage which deserves

[178]/ The classical work on this topic is Dumézil, G.: *La religion romaine archaïque*. Paris: Payot, 1974.

[179]/ For example, Wolodkiewicz, W.: *Regulae iuris. Łacińskie inskrypcje na kolumnach Sądu Najwyższego Rzeczypospolitej Polskiej*. Warszawa: C. H. Beck, 2001.

[180]/ D. 50, 17 *De diversis regulis iuris antiqui*.

[181]/ For example, Nörr, D.: *Spruchregel und Generalisierung*. ZSS 89/1972, p. 18; Schmidlin, B.: *Die römischen Rechtsregeln. Versuch einer typologie*. Köln–Wien: Böhlau, 1970; Stein, P.: *Regulae iuris. From Juristic Rules to Legal Maxims*. Edinburgh: Edinburgh University Press, 1966.

[182]/ For example, Kuťáková, E. – Marek, V., – Zachová, J.: *Moudrost věků. Lexikon latinských výroků, přísloví a rčení* [Wisdom of the Ages. Lexicon of Latin Sentences, Proverbs and Sayings]. Praha: Svoboda, 1988; or Stejskal, M.: *Moudrost starých Římanů* [Wisdom of Ancient Romans]. Praha: Odeon, 1990.

[183]/ For example, Burczak, K. – Dębiński, A. – Jońca, M.: *Łacińskie sentencje i powiedzenia prawnicze* Warszawa: C. H. Beck, 2007; Kincl, J.: *Dicta et regulae iuris aneb právnické mudrosloví latinské* [Dicta et regulae juris or Clever Talk of Latin Jurists]. Praha: Univerzita Karlova, 1990; Rebro, K.: *Latinské právnické výrazy a výroky* [Legal Expressions and Sentences in Latin]. Bratislava: Obzor, 1984.

respect. Yet others condemn it, even today. There is one thing, which is indisputable. Roman law absolutely played a decisive role in shaping the current private law environment. We cannot but agree with Rudolf von Jhering[184] that Rome gave law to the world and unified mankind three times already: firstly in the period of the ancient Roman Empire, secondly through religion and finally in the Middle Ages when *jus commune* was born.

Regardless of how we perceive and assess Roman law, we should always do it on the basis of knowledge and not prejudices. It is the task for researchers in this branch – Roman law specialists – to be able to transmit relevant information not only to a narrow circle of experts but also to all those who are attracted to Roman law.

1.5.2 *Bona fides* in acquisition of things by usucapion (prescription)

An example of the Roman law heritage is the concept of good faith (*bona fides*) which was considered to be a key principle of the acquisition of property already in antiquity.

Good faith of the possessor, as the subjective mental condition resulting from relevant circumstances of possessing, belongs to younger conditions of usucapion in Roman law. It is classified as a subjective condition of usucapion. That means that its fulfilment in a specific case does not depend on objective facts, but it is assessed with regard to the will of the possessor, i.e. the person who acquires a thing by usucapion. It is this feature which influences legal application, because subjective will is assessed according to objective criteria of its outward manifestation. Some ideas of ancient perception of good faith, which had become the basis of its existence in legal orders of continental Europe, were provided to us in fragments by Marcus Tullius Cicero, who believed that the basis of justice is fidelity (*fides*), defined as steadfastness and truthfulness in promises and agreements.

As regards qualification of possession, Roman law insists that the possessor always be in good faith at the moment of acquisition of possession (*initium possessionis*), no matter whether by means of derivative or any other way (for instance, by finding a thing). The requirement of further continuance of the possessor's good faith during the time from acquisition of possession to the elapse of the prescriptive period is connected on the one hand to the negative definition of good faith, i.e. it is sufficient for the possessor to believe that he causes no harm to another, and on the other to the development of the relationship between *bona fides* condition and other conditions of usucapion (namely the title), which also reflect the state of will of the possessor.

Due to the fact that the possessor's will was considered among other conditions of usucapion, Roman jurisprudence was rather liberal in its approach to this requirement. The opinion that subsequent loss of good faith on the part of the possessor need not prejudice, under certain circumstances, the running of usucapion, gradually prevailed. It was mainly the context of Roman conception of usucapion, which frequently permitted lucrative usucapion where the possessor had not been *bona fides* even at the moment of acquisition of possession. This approach had strongly impacted the development of bonitary ownership,

---

[184]/ von Jhering, R.: *Geist des römischen Rechts auf den verschiedenen Stufen seiner Entwicklung.* 1. Leipzig, Breitkopf und Hartel, 1877, p. 1.

whose protection was based on the fiction of usucapion in favour of the possessor who also had not been *bona fides*.

From the point of view of further development of usucapion, however, the approach of Roman jurisprudence was rather unique. Austrian, as well as Czechoslovak, law insisted on permanent good faith of the possessor. The existence of usucapion without good faith on the part of the possessor at the moment of termination of the usucapion period thus belongs among specific features of the Roman institution of usucapion. When assessing the fulfilment of the *bona fides* condition, the decisive factor was the will, or belief of the possessor at a certain specified moment during legal conduct, but this moment was not perceived uniformly until Justinian. The subject matter of disputes among Roman jurists was namely the good faith of purchaser who is the potential acquirer by usucapion of the purchased thing. According to some lawyers, the decisive factor for determining the good faith of purchaser was the moment of perfection of the sales contract, while others believed it was the moment of tradition (i.e. the moment of acquisition of possession) by title of the sales contract, as states Ulpianus: *"If a thing of another was sold in good faith, the question is if the usucapion period may run. We require good faith at the moment of making the sales contract, others at the moment of tradition. The opinion of Sabinians and Cassians that the moment of tradition is to be considered prevailed."*

Thus Ulpianus confirms that the opinion of the Sabinian school, which tended to prefer the moment of tradition prevailed in practice over the opinion of the Proculian school, which connected the purchaser's will with the moment of perfection of the sales contract. However, it was not a binding rule, since there was no concurrence of opinions among distinguished lawyers on this issue. The third opinion, asserted by Paulus, cannot be omitted: *"the moment of tradition suffices ... in purchase, the moment of making the contract is also considered; consequently, the person must be in good faith at the moment of purchase and he must also be in good faith at the moment of acquiring possession."*

The regulation under Justinian Roman law thus provided that subjective belief of the acquirer at the moment of acquisition (*initium possessionis*) was legally relevant for usucapion, and subsequent loss of good faith on his part is not prejudicial to the running of usucapion period. The product of this position is the principle *mala fides superveniens non nocet*, subsequent bad faith is not prejudicial. The approach of Roman jurisprudence and the provisions of Justinian codification were not later reflected in ABGB, nor in the following Czechoslovak regulation of usucapion (if there was any legal regulation of the institution of usucapion at all), where the contrary principle of Canon law applied – *mala fides superveniens nocet*. In the post-war legislation it can be explained on the one hand by a certain degree of continuity with the recent civil regulation, on the other by exclusion of the requirement of title from the conditions of usucapion. Simplification (or facilitation) of usucapion on one side had to be balanced by a stricter requirement of good faith on the other.

According to Obecný zákoník občanský (General Civil Code, GCC), fair possession had to last during the entire usucapion period. The principle *mala fides superveniens nocet* was based mainly on s. 1460 GCC, which required that *"the possession is proper, fair and real and lasts throughout the whole time determined by law."* Randa also refers to s. 1463 GCC which provided that *mala fides* of a legal predecessor did not preclude *bona fides* of an assignee and made it possible to include the time of usucapion from the moment of acquiring possession. He also highlights s. 1477 GCC which provided that if unfair possession was proved, usucapion was impermissible; however, it is necessary to argue that the mentioned provision applies to extraordinary usucapion, which is less stringently regulated as regards requirements for the possessor. Krčmář interprets the mentioned provisions so that ss. 1463 and 1477 GCC emphasize the element of possession, in the sense that the possession must be guileless and not the possessor at the moment of commencement of possession.

Unlike Roman law which defined good faith as the belief of the possessor that, by his possession, he does not cause any harm to the property of another, Austrian law and pandect civil law, GCC as well as Czechoslovak civil law determined good faith positively, i.e. as the belief of the possessor that he is the owner of the thing. Such belief was reflected in the quality of possession, defined as fair (guileless) possession by Austrian law in s. 326: *"A person who, on probable grounds, considers the thing he possesses to be his own, is a fair possessor."* Unlike under Roman law, the possessor's belief that he causes no harm to another is not sufficient; on the contrary, the possessor must positively believe that he exercises proprietary rights by his possession. Thus, the qualification is stricter than under Roman law.

The regulation of GCC did not avoid the traditional problem of doctrine, namely the determination of *bona fides* as opposed to *mala fides*; the question arises whether a denial of good faith of a person can lead to the conclusion that he is in bad faith, or we can talk about some kind of "third mental state", an unnamed "faith". The same question can be reversed, that is whether an exclusion of bad faith in a specific case can lead us to the conclusion of good faith of the person. This problem, however, concerns the general conception of good faith, *bona fides*, in the broader sense.

GCC regulates the relationship between good and bad faith explicitly when it qualifies possession for the purposes of usucapion, where it determines good as well as bad faith, or fair and unfair possessor, in one provision: *"An unfair possessor is a person who knows, or must assume because of circumstances, that the thing in his possession belongs to another person."* As a result, the lack of good faith during possession must be qualified as unfair possession. *Bona fides* and *mala fides* with respect to possession are perceived as contrary terms in GCC, consequently some kind of indifferent possession, belonging to subjective belief corresponding with good and bad faith, is excluded. So the evidence of lack of good faith can be considered as evidence of bad faith of the possessor according to GCC. Thus this conception corresponds with the Paulus' above-mentioned assertion. This approach was further strengthened in a regulation which was later taken over by the Czechoslovak regulation providing that in case of doubt, the possessor is deemed to have fair possession.

The mentioned conception can be compared with the general determination of good faith in Roman law, as it is found in Paulus: *bona fides contraria est fraudi et dolo*, good faith is the negative of fraud and malicious intention. However, the phrase *contraria est* cannot be unequivocally interpreted to mean that the lack of good faith shall be outright assessed as *mala fides*. Such a conclusion could possibly apply to usucapion based on a qualified conception of good faith with negative determination described above. In the case of *bona fides* generally, its relation is different, or rather specific.

A fair possessor under GCC shall be a person who does not know that by the exercise of his right he breaches the right of a third person and at the same time he is not aware of any facts from which such knowledge could be inferred. The commentary by Rouček – Sedláček educes that what is relevant for the possessor' belief is not just the fact that he is the person exercising the right (namely the proprietary right), but the belief that he has good title to such exercise is sufficient. For instance, a proprietor of immovable property, who acquired it by tradition without "intabulation" (i.e. no records in an official register, creating the title, were made), was considered a fair possessor in spite of the fact that he could know he was not the proprietor. However, this is only on condition that he believed that the title, on which the tradition of immovable property was based, was good. Where such possessor even doubts the title, he must be considered an unfair possessor. The same conclusion follows from s. 326 GCC, according to which an error in fact as well as in law does not preclude the situation of fair, yet not proper possession (i.e. not based on appropriate possessory title). Austrian jurisprudence was not quite unified in qualifying a possessor's error as justifiable. While Randa maintained a stricter position insisting on justifiable error, Unger or Burckhard, for instance, did not exclude the application of s. 326 in case of unjustifiable error.

In Roman law, the possessor's mistaken belief that he does not cause damage to a third person, must always be justifiable and only error in fact is permissible. Where the possessor's belief is based on incorrect legal qualification of the assignor's title, then his good faith is excluded as a result of *error juris*. Under Roman law, the error in law is not permissible in usucapion. This consequence is based upon the principle formulated by Pomponius, a lawyer: *juris ignorantiam in usucapione negatur prodesse, facti vero ignorantiam prodesse constat*, ignorance of law is not beneficial in usucapion, while ignorance of fact is beneficial. Here Pomponius follows the general principle of Roman law formulated by Paulus: *regula est juris quidem ignorantiam cuique nocere, facti vero ignorantiam non nocere*, as a rule the ignorance of law is prejudicial, while the ignorance of fact is not. The same lawyer applies this general rule directly to usucapion, when he states: *in jure erranti non procedat usucapio*, in case of error in law there will be no usucapion.

As regards the relevant subject-matter of the possessor's belief with respect to usucapion, according to Randa – Kasanda *mala fides* cannot be based on knowledge of claims upon obligation by third persons. In other words, s. 326 GCC stipulating that the possessor should consider a thing as "his own" must be interpreted in the sense of rights in rem and not obligations.

The Czechoslovak legal regulation of usucapion after World War II followed the conception of the *bona fides* requirement according to GCC, i.e. as part of determination of the quality of possession and not an independent criterion of usucapion. Unlike complicated classification of types of possession under GCC, which had considered good faith in various aspects, Občanský zákoník (Civil Code, CC) of 1950 simplified the combination of usucapion requirements of good faith and possession in a single category of so called lawful (or unlawful) possession.

Lawful possession was stipulated as a usucapion requirement in s. 116 (2) CC 1950. Lawful possession as such, or person having lawful possession, is defined in s. 145 CC 1950:

"If a possessor, having regard to all circumstances, is in good faith that a thing or a right belong to him, he is a lawful possessor."

The mentioned perception of lawful possession clearly shows the influence of s. 326 GCC. Good faith in usucapion conforms to Austrian regulation; it perceives good faith differently from Roman law and is determined positively. The possessor must believe that he can lawfully dispose of the object of possession. Similarly to GCC regulation, he need not believe that a thing (or right) belongs to him on the basis of a proprietary right, but simply on the basis of title with translational effects. It results from the existence of explicit mention of proprietary rights neither in s. 326 GCC nor in s. 145 CC 1950, which instead combine the will of the possessor and his belief that "it belongs to him" (CC 1950) or that "he considers it his own" (GCC). So the conclusion that usucapion need necessarily be based on rights in rem does not follow from either wording.

The regulation in CC 1950 is further developed in Zákoník mezinárodního obchodu (Code of International Trade, CIT) No. 101/1963 Sb., which provided for usucapion in the period when this institution, as well as possession, were formally excluded from CC 1964. In s. 98 CIT the basis of lawful possession remained similar to the previous regulation; however, certain differences appeared: *"A person who disposes of a thing as his own and, having regard to all circumstances, is in good faith that the thing belongs to him as the proprietor shall be considered a lawful possessor."* The earlier regulation was extended by theoretical determination of possession, or a mention of *animus possidendi* as the basic element of possession subsisting in the belief of the possessor that he controls the thing as his own. The positive definition of good faith, complying with the earlier regulation, was preserved. However, unlike in CC 1950, the possessor's belief that the thing (or right) belongs to him did not suffice, but the specification of title to which the belief should be connected was provided. While according to CC 1950 any translational title (including putative) suffices, CIT makes lawful possession subject to the condition of possessor's belief that he is the direct proprietor of a thing. On the other hand, when differentiating forms of ownership, the law does not specify what type of proprietary right it should be. We can assume that the belief in any type of proprietary right, depending on current legal regulation suffices, since its nature usually issues from other relevant circumstances. A thing which can be exclusively an object of private ownership will require the belief that it is of private ownership.

Another aspect in which the new regulation differs from the old is the determination of residual cases, or the relationship between good faith and bad faith. According to s. 145 (2) CC 1950, in case of doubts the possession is deemed lawful. On the other hand, s. 98 CIT provides: *"If he is not in such good faith, he is an unlawful possessor."* This provision, however, performs another role which can be compared to the determination of an unfair possessor under s. 326 GCC.

Amended CC 1964, Act No. 131/1982 Sb. brought back the institutions of usucapion and formally also possession in the Civil Code. The regulation as well as the relationship of these two institutions differed from both the previous CC 1950 and CIT. The amendment did not provide for possession in general; rather, the regulation was only restricted to the protection of possession in s. 132a. It is obvious that lawmakers made a concession to

90

the doctrinal censure of absence of possession and usucapion in the Civil Code, but only when absolutely essential, which interfered minimally with the ideological structure of the original CC 1964. This approach resulted in s. 132a (1) which in fact provides for the legal definition of possession without even mentioning the term "possession". The fact that this regulation applies to possession is suggested in the heading of the section which reads "Protection of Possession".

It is obvious that due to the lack of explicit provision for possession in CC 1964, the term lawful possessor was also missing, but it was regulated in CIT. Nevertheless, s. 132a (1) of the amendment No. 131/1982 Sb. provided: *"The person, who disposes of a thing as his own and, having regard to all circumstances, is in good faith that the thing belongs to him, shall enjoy similar rights of protection as the proprietor of a thing, unless otherwise provided."* The connection between actual disposition of a thing and the person's good faith, and the framework definition of identification of his will in the qualification of good faith, sufficiently indicate that it is *de facto* regulation of *bona fides* possessor, hence an indirect determination of a special type of possession. Jurisprudence of that period, when explaining usucapion, speaks of so called qualified possession.

The lack of statutory definition of lawful or other *bona fides* possession was consequently manifested in the specification of conditions of usucapion, which were under s. 135a (1) of Act No. 131/1982 Sb. *res habilis* (understood as the capability of a thing to be a subject matter of private ownership, not just usucapion), *possessio* and *tempus*: *"The proprietor of a thing, which can be a subject matter of private ownership, shall be the citizen who continually possesses a movable thing for a period of three years and an immovable thing for a period of ten years."* Unlike in earlier regulations, the explicit requirement of *bona fides* is missing and the provision only refers to a qualified possession under s. 132a (1) providing for the actual state. Similarly to previous regulations, the requirement of continuous good faith of the possessor was laid down, i.e. lasting from the commencement of acquisition of possession to the last day of usucapion. The assessment of good faith also followed the criteria set in the earlier legislation. *Bona fides* as well as the will to dispose of a thing as one's own were deduced from the circumstances of possession, in objective perspective and not on the basis of the belief of the possessor. The basic distinctive criterion was whether a possessor showing ordinary diligence, which can be required in a specific case, doubted or could have doubted that the thing under his control belonged to him. Unlike in protection of proprietary rights, the existence of good title was immaterial.

All significant circumstances which could cause doubts in the possessor concerning the lawfulness of his disposition of a thing were considered a violation of good faith. Bringing an action against the possessor was interpreted as an impairment of good faith, hence *mala fides*.

In spite of inspiration from older regulations for understanding the impact of good faith on the quality of possession, certain differences between post-war and pre-war legislation cannot be omitted. GCC reflected good faith in two types of possessory differences – fair and unfair possession, real and unreal possession. Fair possession, described above, was primarily based on the element of good faith. Unreal possession did not issue directly from a subjective belief of the possessor; however, his will was considered when assessing possession as qualifying for usucapion. Thus possession acquired by violence, trick or gratuitous loan was deemed unreal according to GCC. The regulation was based on the Roman law principle, which excluded from usucapion a thing acquired by *vi, clam et precario* (violence, trick or gratuitous loan). Austrian and later Czechoslovak legislation understood unreal possession more extensively. So, in practice, unreal possession could result, for instance, from an invalid contract or from disposition of a thing by a defendant who had been ordered to surrender the thing, etc.

Jurisprudence did not perceive the essence of the distinction between real and unreal possession uniformly and authors clearly groped for answers in the dark when searching for the nature and import of this type of possession. What was not evident was mainly the relationship between real possession and other types of possession. While s. 345 GCC provided that improper and unfair possession is necessarily unreal, which also issued from its general definition in the same section, it was not clear whether real possession also covers the term of proper (titular) possession. According to Randa, unreal possession is a special type of improper possession. But the application of such conclusion was not so obvious in practice. A question was raised whether there could be a case of proper possession which would at the same time be unreal. Krčmář deduces a positive conclusion, but at the same time he indirectly points at a number of conception problems linked to the application of this type of possession.

In this light, and having considered the combination of various types of possession introduced in GCC, we should understand the conclusion of the explanatory report on CC 1950, which described the GCC regulation as cumbersome.

Selected bibliography to Chapter 1
ABRAHAM, H. J. – PERRY, B. A.: *Freedom and the Court*. Oxford: Oxford University Press, 1998.
ARIENS, M. S. – DESTRO, R. A.: *Religious Liberty in a Pluralistic Society*. Durham, North Carolina: Carolina Academic Press, 1996.
ARNDTS, L.: *Učební kniha pandekt* [Textbook of Pandects]. Praha: Právnická Jednota, 1886.
BASSETT, W. W.: *Religious Organizations and the Law*. Vol. I. St. Paul: West Group, 2001.
BĚLOVSKÝ, P.: Bona fides v Ciceronově De officiis [Bona fides in De officiis by Cicero]. In: Veselá, R. – Schelle, K. (eds.): *Římské právo a neprávnické prameny* [Roman Law and Non-legal Sources]. Brno: Masarykova univerzita, 2004, pp. 41–49.
BEŇA, J.: *Vývoj slovenského právneho poriadku* [The Development of Slovak Legal Order]. Banská Bystrica: Právnická fakulta Univerzity Mateja Bela, 2001.
BLACK, H. C.: *Handbook on the Construction and Interpretation of the Laws*. St. Paul: West publishing co., 1911.
BLACKSTONE, W.: *Commentaries on the Laws of England*. A Facsimile of the First Edition of 1765–1769, Vol. I, Of the Rights of Persons (1765). Chicago/London: The University of Chicago Press, 1979.
BLAHO, P.: Bona fides v rímskom záväzkovom práve [Bona Fides in Roman Law of Obligations]. In: Skřejpek, M. – Bělovský, P. (eds.): *Bona fides*. Praha: Univerzita Karlova 2000, pp. 12–24.
BOGUSZAK, J.: Otevřený systém dualistické federace [Open System of Dualist Federation]. *Právník* 10/1965, pp. 917–926.
BOGUSZAK, J.: Politické strany – kontinuita a diskontinuita (právní kazuistika). Státnost česká a československá – tradice a kontinuita [Political Parties – Continuity and Discontinuity (Legal Casuistry). Czech and Czechoslovak Statehood – Tradition and Continuity]. *AUC Iuridica* 1–2/1999, pp. 211–217.
BORK, R. H.: *Amerika v pokušení: právo vystavené svodům politiky* [The Tempting of America]. Praha: Victoria Publishing, 1993.
BRETONE, M.: *Diritto e pensiero giuridico romano*. Firenze: Sansoni, 1976.
BRETONE, M.: *Diritto e tempo nella tradizione europea*. Roma–Bari: Laterza, 1994.
BREUER, S.: *Nationalismus und Faschismus. Frankreich, Italien und Deutschland im Vergleich*. Darmstadt: Wissenschaftliche Buchgesellschaft, 2005.

BURCZAK, K. – DĘBIŃSKI, A. – JOŃCA, M.: *Łacińskie sentencje i powiedzenia prawnicze*. Warszawa: C. H. Beck, 2007.

CERAMI, P. – DI PORTO, A. – PETRUCCI, A.: *Diritto commerciale romano. Profilo storico*. Torino: Giappichelli, 2004.

CHOPKO, M.: An Overview on the Parish and Civil Law. *The Jurist* 1/2007, pp. 194–226.

CHOPKO, M.: Principal Civil Law Structures: A Review. *The Jurist* 2009, pp. 237–260 (*forthcoming*).

ČIČ, M.: *Československý socialistický štát a právo. Vznik a rozvoj* [The Czechoslovak Socialist State and Law. Creation and Development]. Bratislava: Veda, 1987.

Cui bono restituce II [Cui Bono Restitutions II]. 2nd complemented and updated ed., Praha: Centrum rozvoje a prosperity, 2007.

Cui bono restituce? [Cui Bono Restitutions?]. Praha: Český svaz bojovníků za svobodu, 2006.

CVRČEK, F.: Metamorfózy českého právního řádu z hlediska kvantitativního (fakta a spekulace) [Metamorphoses of Czech Legal Order from the Quantitative Aspect (Facts and Speculations)]. In: Jermanová, H. – Masopust, Z. (eds.): *Metamorfózy práva ve střední Evropě: sborník příspěvků z mezinárodní konference "Metamorfózy práva ve střední Evropě" a kolokvia "Metamorfózy veřejné správy", pořádaných Ústavem státu a práva AV ČR a Fakultou právnickou ZČU v Plzni ve dnech 11.–13.června 2008 ve Znojmě* [Proceedings from the international conference "Metamorphoses of Law in Central Europe" and the colloquium "Metamorphoses of Public Administration" organized by the Institute of State and Law of the Academy of Sciences of the CR and the Faculty of Law of West Bohemian University in Pilsen, 11th–13th July 2008 in Znojmo]. Plzeň – Praha: Vydavatelství a nakladatelství Aleš Čeněk – Ústav státu a práva AV ČR, 2008, pp. 50–60.

DEYL, L.: *Sociální vývoj Československa 1918–1938* [Social Development of Czechoslovakia 1918–1938]. Praha: Academia, 1985.

DOBIÁŠ, K.: *Sociální politika Československé republiky v prvním desetiletí jejího trvání* [Social Policy of the Czechoslovak Republic in the First Decade of its Existence]. Praha: O. Janáček, 1929.

DUMÉZIL, G.: *La religion romaine archaique*. Paris: Payot, 1974.

EBEL, F. – FIJAL, A. – KOCHE, G.: *Römisches Rechtsleben im Mittelalter*. Heidelberg: Müller, 1988.

ENGLIŠ, K.: *Sociální politika* [Social Policy]. Praha: Topič, 1921.

FARNSWORTH, E. A.: *An Introduction to the Legal System of the United States*. 2nd ed., London – Rome – New York: Oceana Publications, 1983.

FIALA, P. – PITROVÁ, M.: *Evropská referenda* [European Referenda]. Brno: Centrum pro studium demokracie a kulturu, 2005.

FILIPI, P. et al.: *Malá encyklopedie evangelických církví* [Concise Encyclopaedia of Protestant Churches]. Praha: Libri, 2008.

GÁL, F.: Kalendárium rozpadu. In: *Rozloučení s Československem* [Farewell to Czechoslovakia]. Praha: Český spisovatel, 1993.

GARLICKI, A.: *Józef Piłsudski. 1867–1935*. London: Scholar Press, 1995.

GARVEY, J. H. – ALEINIKOFF, T. A.: *Modern Constitutional Theory: A Reader*. St. Paul: West Publishing Company, 1991.

GRONSKÝ, J.: *Komentované dokumenty k ústavním dějinám Československa IV* [Comments on Documents on the Constitutional History of Czechoslovakia IV]. Praha: Karolinum, 2008.

HAMILTON, A. – MADISON, J. – JAY, J.: *Listy federalistů* [The Federalist Papers]. Olomouc: Vydavatelství Univerzity Palackého v Olomouci, 1990.

HAMMAR, R. R.: *Pastor, Church & Law*. 3rd ed., Matthews, N. C.: Christian Ministry Resources, 1999.

HAMON, F.: *Le referendum, Documents réunis et commentés*. Paris: La Documentation française, 1997.

HATTENHAUER, H.: *Die geistesgeschichtlichen Grundlagen des deutschen Rechts*. Heidelberg: C. F. Müller, 1983.

HEYROVSKÝ, L.: *Dějiny a systém soukromého práva římského* [The History and System of Private Roman Law]. 5th ed., Praha: Otto, 1910.

HORÁK, Z.: Druhá evropsko-americká konference o náboženské svobodě „Autonomie církve a náboženská svoboda" [The Second European-American Conference on Religious Freedom "Autonomy of Church and Religious Freedom"]. Law School of the University of Trier, 27–30 May 1999. *Revue církevního práva* 2/1999, pp. 178–179.

HORÁK, Z.: Obnovení církevních škol v českých zemích v letech 1990–1991. [Restoration of Church Schools in the Czech Lands in 1990–1991]. *Revue církevního práva* 2/2008, pp. 94–114.

HORÁK, Z.: *Právní postavení církví a náboženských společností v USA s důrazem na postavení Katolické církve* [The Legal Status of Churches and Religious Societies in the USA, with Special Focus on the Status of the Catholic Church]. Diploma thesis. Praha: Law Faculty of Charles University, 1998.

HORÁK, Z.: *Právní úprava činnosti náboženských a školských institucí církví v USA* [Legal Regulation of Activities of Religious and Educational Institutions of Churches in the USA]. Dissertation. Praha: Law Faculty of Charles University, 2002.

HORÁK, Z.: Proč alternativní forma uzavření manželství? [Why an Alternative Form of Contracting Marriage]. In: Winterová, A. – Dvořák, J. (eds.): *Pocta Sentě Radvanové k 80. narozeninám* [Tribute to Senta Radvanová on the Occasion of Her 80th Birthday]. Praha: ASPI, 2009, pp. 197–208.

HRABÁNEK, J.: *Co má znáti každý nájemník a majitel domu* [What Should Every Tenant and Every House Owner Know]. Praha: Jan Svátek, 1934.

HRDINA, A. I.: *Náboženská svoboda v právu České republiky* [Religious Freedom in the Law of the Czech Republic]. Praha: Eurolex Bohemia, 2004.

HUMPHREY, G.: *Pilsudski: Builder of Poland*. New York: Scott and More, 1936.

JEŽEK, T.: *Zrození ze zkumavky, Svědectví o české privatizaci* [Test Tube Baby, Testimony on Czech Privatization]. Praha: Prostor, 2007.

JIČÍNSKÝ, Z.: *Právní myšlení v 60. letech a za normalizace* [Legal Thinking in the 1960s and during Normalization]. Praha: Prospektrum, 1992.

KASER, M.: *Zur Methode der römischen Rechtsfindung*. Nachrichten d. Akademie d. Wissenschaften in Göttingen, phil. – hist. Klasse 2/1962. Göttingen: Vandenhoeck & Ruprecht, 1962.

KAUPER, P. G. – ELLIS, S.: Religious Corporations and the Law. *Michigan Law Review* 8/1973, pp. 1499–1574.

KINCL, J. – SKŘEJPEK, M. – URFUS, V.: *Římské právo* [Roman Law]. Praha: Beck, 1995.

KINCL, J.: *Dicta et regulae iuris aneb právnické mudrosloví latinské* [Dicta et regulae iuris or Clever Talk of Latin Jurists]. Praha: Univerzita Karlova, 1990.

KINDL, V.: *Rehabilitace na Právnické fakultě UK v letech 1990–2000* [Reinstatements at Law Faculty of Charles University in 1990–2000]. Praha: Všehrd XXXI, special ed., 2000, pp. 43–55.

KINDL, V.: Zákonné uznání a registrace (Malé srovnání historické a současné formy legalizace církve a náboženské společnosti na územní ČR) [Statutory Recognition and Registration (Brief comparison of the historical and current form of the legalization of churches and religious associations in the territory of the CR)]. Praha: *AUC Iuridica* 1–2/1999, pp. 201–210.

KLÍMA, K.: *Ústavní právo* [Constitutional Law]. Praha: Victoria Publishing, 1995.

KLOKOČKA, V.: *Ústavní systémy evropských států* [Constitutional Systems of European Countries]. Praha: Linde, 1996.

KNAPP, V.: *Velké právní systémy. Úvod do srovnávací právní vědy* [The Great Legal Systems. Introduction to Comparative Jurisprudence]. Praha: Beck, 1996.

KRATOŠKA, J.: *Ochrana nájemníků, zabírání bytů, omezení práva stěhovacího* [Protection of Tenants, Appropriation of Flats, Restriction of the Right to Move]. Praha: Ústřední dělnické knihkupectví a nakladatelství, 1920.

KRČMÁŘ, J.: Poznámky k dekretu prezidenta republiky ze dne 19. 5. 1945, č. 5/45 a k zákonu ze dne 16. 5. 1946 [Comments on the Decree of the President of the Republic No. 5/1945 of 19th May 1945 and on the Act of 16th May 1946]. *Právník* 9–10/1946, pp. 257–261.

KRČMÁŘ, J.: *Právo občanské, I. díl* [Civil Law, Part I]. 4th ed., Praha: nákladem Knihovny Sborníku věd právních a státních, 1946.

KRČMÁŘ, J.: *Právo občanské, II. díl* [Civil Law, Part II]. 4th ed., Praha: nákladem Knihovny Sborníku věd právních a státních, 1947.

KRČMÁŘ, J.: *Základy přednášek o právu občanském* [The Basics of Lectures on Civil Law]. Vol. II, Part 2, Praha: Všehrd, 1925.

KUBÁT, M.: J. Kysela, Senát Parlamentu České republiky v historickém a mezinárodním kontextu. Příspěvek ke studiu dvoukomorových soustav [J. Kysela, The Senate of the Parliament of the Czech Republic in Historical and International Context. Contribution to Research of Bicameral Systems]. *Politologický časopis* 4/2002, pp. 454–456.

KUBIŠTA, H.: *Ochrana nájemníků s doplňky a podpora stavebního ruchu podle zákona ze dne 23. února 1934 č. 32 Sb. z. a n.* [Protection of Tenants with Amendments and the Support for Construction Traffic under the Act of 23rd February 1934 No. 32 Sb. z. a. n.]. Praha: nákladem vlastním, 1934.

KUKLÍK, J. – SELTENREICH, R.: *Dějiny angloamerického práva* [The History of Anglo-American Law]. Praha: Linde, 2007.

KUKLÍK, J. et al.: *Vývoj československého práva od roku 1945 do roku 1989* [The Development of Czechoslovak Law from 1945 to 1989]. Praha: Linde, 2009.

KUKLÍK, J.: *Do poslední pence! Československo-britská jednání o finančních a majetkoprávních otázkách 1938–1982* [To the Last Penny! Czechoslovak-British Financial and Property Negotiations 1938–1982]. Praha: Karolinum, 2007.

KUKLÍK, J.: *Mýty a realita tzv. Benešových dekretů* [Myths and Reality of so-called Beneš Decrees]. Praha: Linde, 2002.

KUPISZEWSKI, H.: *Prawo rzymskie a współczesność*. Warszawa: Panstwowe Wydawnictwo Naukowe, 1988.

KURYŁOWICZ, M.: *Prawo rzymskie. Historia, tradycja, współczesność*. Lublin: Wydaw. Uniwersytetu Marii Curie-Skłodowskiej, 2003.

LEDERER, L.: *Konec ochrany nájemníků, praktické pokyny, změny v bytových zákonech* [The End of Tenant Protection, Practical Guidelines, Changes in Housing Law]. Praha: nákladem vlastním, 1936.

LERNER, M.: *The Mind and Faith of Justice Holmes.* Boston: Little, Brown, 1943.

LHOTA, V.: *Znárodnění v Československu 1945–1948* [Nationalization in Czechoslovakia 1945–1948]. Praha: Svoboda, 1987.

MACEK, J.: *Základy sociální politiky* [Principles of Social Policy]. Praha: A. Svěcený, 1925.

MAIDA, A. J. – CAFARDI, N. P.: *Church Property, Church Finances, and Church Related Corporations.* St. Louis, Catholic Health Association of the United States, 1983.

MALAST, J.: Vybrané aspekty vývoje obecní samosprávy první Československé republiky [Selected Aspects of the Development of Self-Government of Communities in the First Czechoslovak Republic]. In: Knoll, V. (ed): *Pocta Stanislavu Balíkovi k 80. narozeninám.* Plzeň: Vydavatelství a nakladatelství Aleš Čeněk, 2008, pp. 216–228.

MALÝ, K. – SOUKUP, L. (eds.): *Vývoj práva v Československu v letech 1945–1989* [The Development of Law in Czechoslovakia 1945–1989]. Praha: Karolinum, 2004.

MANNY, J. S.: Governance Issues for Non-profit Religious Organizations. *Catholic Lawyer* 40/2000, pp. 1–23.

MARŠÁLEK, P.: Od restituce k revoluci: K právní obnově v poválečném Československu [From Restitution to Revolution: On Legal Restoration in Post-War Czechoslovakia, Czechoslovakia on the Border of Two Epochs of Non-freedom]. In: Kokošková, Z. – Kocian, J. – Kokoška, S. (eds.): *Československo na rozhraní dvou epoch nesvobody. Sborník z konference k 60. výročí konce druhé světové války* [Czechoslovakia on the Border of Two Epochs of Non-freedom. Proceedings from the Conference on the 60th anniversary of the end of World War II]. Praha: Národní archiv: Ústav pro soudobé dějiny AV ČR, 2005, pp. 118–124.

MATES, P.: Reforma územní samosprávy po roce 1989 [Reform of Local Self-Government after 1989]. *PHS* 39/2007, pp. 309–326.

MATES, P.: Vývoj volebního práva v letech 1945–1989 [The Development of the Right to Vote in 1945–1989]. In: Malý, K. – Soukup, L. (eds.): *Vývoj práva v Československu v letech 1945–1989* [The Development of Law in Czechoslovakia 1945–1989]. Praha: Karolinum, 2004, pp. 210–239.

MAZANEC, M.: Zánik bývalého Nejvyššího správního soudu ve světle dokumentů Státního ústředního archivu [The End of the Existence of the Former Supreme Administrative Court in the Light of State Central Archival Documents]. In: Novotný, O. (ed.): *Pocta doc. JUDr. Vladimíru Mikule k 65. narozeninám.* Praha: ASPI, 2002, pp. 159–182.

MICHÁLEK, S.: *Nádeje a vytriezvenia, Československo-americké hospodárske vzťahy v rokoch 1945–1951* [Hopes and Disillusions, Czechoslovak-American Economic Relations in the period 1945–1951]. Bratislava: Veda, 1995.

MLČOCH, L.: *Úvahy o české transformaci* [Reflections on Czech Transformation]. Praha: Vyšehrad, 2000.

NEŠPOR, Z.: *Vrácení majetku persekvovaným* [Returning Property to the Persecuted]. Praha: Orbis, 1946.

NOLTE, E.: *Das 20. Jahrhundert. Die Ideologien der Gewalt.* München: Herbig, 2008.

NÖRR, D.: Spruchregel und Generalisierung. *ZSS* 89/1972, 18–93.

NOVÁK, F.: Proměny práva na podkladě kvantitativní analýzy vývoje legislativy v ČR [Changes in Law on the Basis of Quantitative Analysis of the Development of Legislation in the CR]. In: Jermanová, H. – Masopust, Z. (eds.): *Metamorfózy práva ve střední Evropě: sborník příspěvků z mezinárodní konference "Metamorfózy práva ve střední Evropě" a kolokvia "Metamorfózy veřejné správy", pořádaných Ústavem státu a práva AV ČR a Fakultou právnickou ZČU v Plzni ve dnech 11.–13.června 2008 ve Znojmě* [Proceedings from the international conference "Metamorphoses of Law in Central Europe" and the colloquium "Metamorphoses of Public Administration" organized by the Institute of State and Law of the Academy of Sciences of the CR and the Faculty of Law of West Bohemian University in Pilsen, 11th–13th July 2008 in Znojmo]. Plzeň – Praha: Vydavatelství a nakladatelství Aleš Čeněk – Ústav státu a práva AV ČR, 2008, pp. 123–141.

Nové zákony a nařízení Československé republiky [New Laws and Regulations of the Czechoslovak Republic]. 1945, 1946 and 1947.

O'SULLIVAN, N.: *Fašismus* [Fascism]. Praha: Centrum pro studium demokracie a kultury, 2002.

Ochrana nájemníků [Protection of Tenants]. Praha: Kosmos, 1919.

Ochrana nájemníků a stavební ruch [The Protection of Tenants and Construction Traffic]. Praha: Bursík a Kohout, 1925.

OSTERKAMP, J.: Ústavní soudnictví v meziválečném Československu [Constitutional Judiciary in Inter-War Czechoslovakia]. *Právník* 6/2007, pp. 585–618.

OUTRATA, V.: K otázkám mezinárodní způsobilosti členských zemí ve federativním uspořádání [On International Competence of Member States in Federal Arrangement]. *Právník* 12/1968, pp. 1019–1026.

PAVLÍČEK, V. et al.: *Ústavní právo a státověda II 1* [Constitutional Law and Political Science, Vol. II 1]. Praha: Linde, 2001.

PAVLÍČEK, V. et al.: *Ústavní právo a státověda, II. díl. Ústavní právo České republiky. Část 1* [Constitutional Law and Political Science, Vol. II. Constitutional Law of Czechoslovak Republic, Part 1]. 2nd ed., Praha: Linde, 2008.

PAVLÍČEK, V.: *O české státnosti. Úvahy a polemiky 1/Český stát a Němci* [On Czech Statehood. Reflections and Debates 1/ The Czech State and Germans]. Praha: Karolinum, 2002.

PAXTON, R. O.: *Anatomie fašismu* [Anatomy of Fascism]. Praha: Nakl. Lidové noviny, 2007.

PELIKÁNOVÁ, I.: Právní úprava ekonomických vztahů v období 1948–1989, její povaha a důsledky [Legal Regulation of Economic Relations in 1948–1989, its Nature and Consequences]. In: Malý, K. – Soukup, L. (eds.): *Vývoj práva v Československu v letech 1945–1989* [The Development of Law in Czechoslovakia 1945–1989]. Praha: Karolinum, 2004, pp. 428–456.

PETR, B.: *Vydržení v českém právu* [Prescription in Czech Law]. Praha: Beck, 2002.

PETRÁŠ, R. – PETRŮV, H. – SCHEU, H. (eds.): *Menšiny a právo v České republice* [Minorities and Law in the Czech Republic]. Praha: Auditorium, 2009.

PETRÁŠ, R.: *Menšiny v komunistickém Československu* [Minorities in Communist Czechoslovakia]. Praha: VIP Books: Eurolex Bohemia, 2007.

PETRÁŠ, R.: Výzkum českých a československých právních dějin po roce 1989 [Research on Czech and Czechoslovak Legal History after 1989]. *Právněhistorické studie* 39/2007, pp. 41–59.

PŘIBYL, S.: *Konfesněprávní studie* [Papers on State Ecclesiastical Law]. Brno: L. Marek, 2007.

PRŮCHA, V. et al.: *Hospodářské a sociální dějiny Československa 1918–1992* [Economic and Social History of Czechoslovakia 1918–1945]. Vol. I, Brno: Doplněk, 2004.

RANDA, A.: *Právo vlastnické dle rakouského práva v pořádku systematickém* [Property Right under Austrian Law in a Systematic Order]. 5th ed., Praha: nákl. knihkupectví Fr. Řivnáče, 1900.

REBRO, K.: *Latinské právnické výrazy a výroky* [Legal Expressions and Sentences in Latin]. Bratislava: Obzor, 1984.

ROSSUM, R. A. – TARR, G. A.: *American Constitutional Law.* New York: St. Martin's Press, 1981.

SCHIAVONE, A. (ed.): *Storia del diritto romano.* 2nd ed., Torino: Giappichelli, 2001.

SCHMIDLIN, B.: *Die römischen Rechtsregeln. Versuch einer typologie.* Köln–Wien: Böhlau, 1970.

ŠINDELKA, J.: *Národnostní politika v ČSSR* [National Minorities Policy in the ČSSR]. Praha: Orbis, 1975.

SKŘEJPKOVÁ, P. – SOUKUP, L.: *Antologie české právní vědy* [Anthology of Czech Jurisprudence]. Praha: Karolinum 1993.

SMITH, L. M.: Cesty k efektivní přímé demokracii: Česká místní referenda v regionálním srovnání [Paths to Effective Direct Democracy: Czech Local Referenda in Regional Comparison]. *Politologický časopis* 4/2006, pp. 399–422.

SMITH, L. M.: *Přímá demokracie v praxi: Politika místních referend v České republice* [Direct Democracy in Practice: The Policy of Local Referenda in the Czech Republic]. Praha: Sociologický ústav AV ČR, 2007.

SOMMER, O.: *Učebnice soukromého práva římského. Obecné nauky* [Textbook of Roman Private Law. General Teachings]. Praha: nákladem vlastním, 1933.

SOMMER, O.: *Učebnice soukromého práva římského. Právo majetkové* [Textbook of Roman Private Law. Property Law]. Praha: nákladem vlastním, 1935.

SOUKUP, L. (ed.): *Příspěvky k vývoji právního řádu v Československu 1945–1990* [Papers on the Development of Legal Order in Czechoslovakia 1945–1990]. Praha: Karolinum, 2002.

SPÁČIL, J.: Neznalost zákona, právní omyl a oprávněná držba [Ignorance of Law, Legal Error and Lawful Possession]. *Právní rozhledy* 5/2000, pp. 189–191.

SPÁČIL, J.: *Ochrana vlastnictví a držby v občanském zákoníku* [Protection of Ownership and Possession in the Civil Code]. Praha: Beck, 2002.

STAŠA, J.: O stavu a perspektivě českého živnostenského práva [On the Situation and Perspectives of Czech Trade Law]. In: Novotný, O. (ed.): *Pocta doc. JUDr. Vladimíru Mikule k 65. narozeninám.* Praha: ASPI, 2002, pp. 343–360.

STEIGERHOF, E. – CRHA, V. (eds.): *Zákony a nařízení týkající se ochrany nájemníků s výkladem* [Acts and Decrees Regulating the Protection of Tenants Annotated]. Praha: Ústřední studentské knihkupectví a nakladatelství, 1933.

STEIN, E.: *Česko-Slovensko. Konflikt, roztržka, rozpad* [Czecho-Slovakia. Conflict, Dispute, Split]. Praha: Academia, 2000.

STEIN, P.: *Regulae iuris. From Juristic Rules to Legal Maxims.* Edinburgh: Edinburgh University Press, 1966.

SUCHÁNEK, R.: Stát jako tvůrce práva [State as the Law Maker]. In: Jirásková, V. (ed.): *Český stát a vzdělanost* [The Czech State and Education]. Papers presented at the conference "Role státu v transformující se české společnosti" held on 6th–7th September 2001 in Lužany. Praha: Karolinum, 2002, pp. 229–243.

SUCHÁNEK, R.: Vývoj svátkového práva od vzniku ČSR po současnost. Státnost česká a československá – tradice a kontinuita [Development of Public Holidays Law since the Establishment of CSR up to Now. Czech and Czechoslovak Statehood – Tradition and Continuity]. Papers presented at the conference held on 4th–5th June 1998 in Zahrádky. *AUC Iuridica* 1–2/1999, pp. 103–114.

ŠULC, Z.: *Stručné dějiny ekonomických reforem v Československu (České republice) 1945–1995* [Brief History of Economic Reforms in Czechoslovakia (Czech Republic) 1945–1995]. Brno: Doplněk, 1998.

ŠVEJNAR, J. et al.: *Česká republika a ekonomická transformace ve střední a východní Evropě* [The Czech Republic and Economic Transformation in Central and Eastern Europe]. Praha: Academia, 1997.

TRETERA, J. R.: *Konfesní právo a církevní právo* [State Ecclesiastical Law and Church Law]. Praha: Krigl, 1997.

TRETERA, J. R.: *Stát a církve v České republice* [State and Churches in the Czech Republic]. Kostelní Vydří: Karmelitánské nakladatelství, 2002.

VALEŠ, L.: Obnova obecní samosprávy v kontextu české tranzice [Restoration of Community Self-Government in the Context of Czech Transition]. In: Jermanová, H. – Masopust, Z. (eds.): *Metamorfózy práva ve střední Evropě: sborník příspěvků z mezinárodní konference "Metamorfózy práva ve střední Evropě" a kolokvia "Metamorfózy veřejné správy", pořádaných Ústavem státu a práva AV ČR a Fakultou právnickou ZČU v Plzni ve dnech 11.–13.června 2008 ve Znojmě* [Proceedings from the international conference "Metamorphosis of Law in Central Europe" and the colloquium "Metamorphosis of Public Administration" organized by the Institute of State and Law of the Academy of Sciences of the CR and the Faculty of Law of West Bohemian University in Pilsen, 11th–13th July 2008 in Znojmo]. Plzeň – Praha: Vydavatelství a nakladatelství Aleš Čeněk – Ústav státu a práva AV ČR, 2008, pp. 372–382.

VIDLÁKOVÁ, O.: Správní reforma v České republice v devadesátých letech (cesta zkoušek a omylů) [Administrative Reform in the Czech Republic in the 1990s (Trials and Errors)]. In: Mikule, V. – Sládeček, V. – Vopálka, V. (eds.): *Veřejná správa a právo. Pocta prof. JUDr. Dušanu Hendrychovi* [Tribute to Professor JUDr. Dušan Hendrych]. Praha: Beck, 1997, pp. 53–69.

VIDMAN, L.: *Psáno do kamene* [Written into Stone]. Praha: Academia, 1975.

VOJÁČEK, L. – SCHELLE, K. – KNOLL, V.: *České právní dějiny* [Czech Legal History]. Plzeň: Aleš Čeněk, 2008.

WESSEL, U.: *Recht, Unrecht und Gerechtigkeit von der Weimarer Republik bis heute*. München: C. H. Beck, 2003.

WILLOWEIT, D. – SEIF, U.: *Europäische Verfassungsgeschichte*. München: C. H. Beck, 2003.

WINTR, J.: *Principy českého ústavního práva* [Principles of Czech Constitutional Law]. Praha: Eurolex Bohemia, 2006.

WINTR, J.: Vliv politických idejí a programů na české zákonodárství v letech 1989–1998 [The Influence of Political Thoughts and Programmes on Czech Legislation in 1989–1998]. In: Gerloch, A. – Maršálek, P. (eds.): *Zákon v kontinentálním právu* [The Act of Parliament in Continental Law]. Praha: Eurolex Bohemia, 2005, pp. 293–341.

WOLODKIEWICZ, W.: *Regulae iuris. Łacińskie inskrypcje na kolumnach Sądu Najwyższego Rzeczypospolitej Polskiej*. Warszawa: C. H. Beck, 2001.

Zákon o zabírání bytů obcemi, ze dne 30. října 1919 č. 592 Sb. z. a n. (úvodem a poznámkami opatřil Jar. Kratoška) [Act on the Appropriation of Flats by Communities, of 30th October 1919 No. 592 Sb. z. a n. (Introduction and notes by J. Kratoška)]. Praha: Ústřední dělnické knihkupectví a nakladatelství (A. Svěcený), 1919.

ZELINKA, J.: *Ochrana nájemníků podle zákona ze dne 27. října 1932 č. 164 Sb. z. a n.* [Protection of Tenants under the Act of 27 October 1932 No. 164 Sb. z. a n.]. Plzeň: nákladem vlastním, 1932.

ZEYER, A.: *Zákon o zabírání bytů ze dne 30. října 1919 čís. 592 Sb. z. a n.* [Act on Appropriation of Flats of 30th October 1919 No. 592/Sb.z. a n.]. Praha: Atlas, 1921.

Archives

The Archives of the Ministry of Foreign Affairs of the Czech Republic
The Archives of the T.G. Masaryk Institute of the Czech Academy of Sciences
The National Archives in Prague, Czech Republic
The National Archives, London, Great Britain

2. THEORETICAL AND CONSTITUTIONAL IMPULSES FOR THE DEVELOPMENT OF LAW

The set of theoretical impulses that affect the development of law at the beginning of the 21ˢᵗ century is much more transparent from the contents point of view than the set of constitutional issues. It includes not just the impulses arising out of the legal system itself and its operation but also the impulses of the fields related to law. We consider business factors, which have a dominant influence on law out of all the external factors, to be very important. The relation between economy and law is a great theoretical topic. It surfaced also as a purely practical topic in our law in the 1990s, not always for the benefit of matters. We are not likely to find a satisfactory answer to the question of whether economy should regulate the law or vice versa. Also the relation between law and language is essential. Language is the most important and the most usual means of communication of legal information and therefore also the means of understanding the law. The linguistic interpretation belongs among the basic methods of the interpretation and the application of law, at the beginning of the 21ˢᵗ century much stronger than before.

Legal theory research focuses on defining the essential elements of a democratic state respecting the rule of law and on the analysis of recent models of courts being bound by statute. Both these issues are of key importance in relation to the tendencies of transforming the application of law in a changing social context. It is pointed out that the scope and content of "the essential elements of the democratic state respecting the rule of law" are not definite. It is not constitutionally defined and it can be deduced from the attributes determined in comparison of the specific forms of democratic states respecting the rule of law. The issue consists not just of the extent of indeterminacy of the conclusions of such analysis, but also in the idea of their invariability, which could hinder social development. The concept of a democratic state respecting the rule of law is dynamic rather than static, and the transformation of social relations in which the concept operates may conflict with the existing ideas of its unchangeable attributes.

The traditional model of law being strictly binding on courts' decisions expanded in the continental legal culture in the 19ᵗʰ century is increasingly confronted with the reality of the plurality of sources of law and their growth and instability. The effort to legitimise the weakening of the law strictly binding on the courts results in critical argumentation with overstretched legal formalism, contrary to desirable judicial pragmatism.

Legalism in law is understood similarly to the free finding of law by courts as an undesirable and extreme approach to contemporary law. The weaknesses of these extremes are shown in detail by theoretical analyses of the decisions of the highest courts, including European courts. It is considered necessary to create sophisticated procedures of legal reasoning *lege artis*, that should represent a substitute for inapplicable simple application models and, at the same time, should restrict the arbitrariness of judicial decision-making.

These conceptual points of departure from legal theory have an immediate impact on constitutional law and international law contexts with consequences for the operation of law in general. The existing model of a legal order based on hierarchy is going through a period of deconstruction and it is being replaced with a network model reflecting the growing entropy in society and diffusion of public authority. This chapter presents the consequences of these processes from the point of view of the definition of the constitutional order of the Czech Republic, relations of constitutional, international and European law and the operation of the constitutional system of the Czech Republic in the current period as well as in the foreseeable future.

2.1 INVARIABILITY AND PURPOSE IN LAW

The idea of invariable and perhaps even eternal law has been present in legal history since the very beginning. The doctrinal opinion considering it inadmissible to change a part of positive law created by people which was taken over by the constitution and the judicial decisions, is one of the new phenomena in law. It has emerged in the second half of the 20th century and it seems to be influential also at the beginning of this century.

Invariability was considered in the past as an obvious feature of natural law as well as positive law. *"In the future, in days to come, at any time, let the king who is in the land, guard the words of righteousness which I have written on my stele."*[185] The wording of the Code of Hammurabi today sounds amusing rather than ceremonial and threatening; however, the words "in the future, in the days to come, at any time" clearly express the intention of perpetual force. The Magna Carta, one of the best known monuments of British constitutional law, speaks about its "complete and firm endurance forever".[186] The conviction of invariability of law appears also in an often unfairly omitted Croatian list of valid law from the times of the Magna Carta, the Vinodol statute, in the following wording: *"...and all the abovesaid elders, [...] have declared and confirmed, establishing and citing the old and tested laws of Vinodol have they confirmed, that their grandfathers and their fathers and all their forbears did ever live according to them."*[187] The issue here was to clarify ambiguities arising out of insufficient knowledge and inaccessibility of common law, rather than enacting new law. Even a random and unrepresentative choice of historical regulations supports the notion that the opinion prevailing for a long time was that law is in principle an unchangeable set of regulations or order in affairs. Hammurabi was aware of the fact that he was creating law; however, he considered himself almost as a god. Otherwise, he would never attempt anything like that.

---

[185]/ retrieved from http://oll.libertyfund.org/index.php?option=comstaticxt&utaicfile=show.pht%Ftitle= 12768layout=htm.
[186]/ retrieved from http://www.constitution.org/eng/magnacar.htm.
[187]/ Margetić, L.: *Vinodolski zakon* [Vinodol Statute]. Rijeka: "Adamić" – vitagraf 1998, pp. 41, 185, 207, the English translation retrieved from http://www.cuvalo.net/?p=50 on 23rd November 2009 at 1.50 pm.

Over time, the idea of unchangeable positive law became contradictory to apparent creation of law by people. Major codifications, such as the Napoleonic Code or the General Civil Code, could not be reasonably perceived as laws valid from time immemorial reduced to writing and systematised. At the point when the law usually contained an abrogation clause and a provision about its effect, the notion of the invariable nature of positive law lost its persuasiveness. It has survived in the form of belief in inborn human rights exempt from the disposition of the law-making and constitution-making bodies. The following sentence from the Declaration of Independence of the USA is among the best known expressions of this belief: *"We hold these truths to be self-evident, that all men are created equal, that they are endowed by their Creator with certain unalienable Rights, that among these are Life, Liberty and the pursuit of Happiness."*[188] Central European legal positivists, however, have been discussing civil rights, rather than human rights, since the 19th century; by doing so legal positivism expressed the belief that they were public rights arising out of positive constitutional law. The idea of unchangeable law was displaced into the tradition of natural law thinking, even though in this area too there were opinions discussing natural law with variable content.

Law usually expresses not just the immediate interests but also the ideals of correct boundaries of interests that prevail and/or are primarily enforced by the authority.[189] It is primarily constitutional law which increasingly confirms certain ideals, values which are to become the basis of the public life. Regulation of such ideals and values becomes one of the purposes of constitutional law. Z. Jičínský in his political polemics repeatedly updated the finding of R. von Jhering that "... the purpose is the source of law in general...",[190] when he stated: *"... there is a purpose in every amendment of a law, and therefore in every change in the constitution. Changes are not made due to legislative aesthetics, they are made because they react to certain social needs."*[191]

The contemporary concept of inadmissibility of change in a small but important part of positive law is luckily based on a unique historical experience of "statutory injustice" (*Gesetzliches Unrecht*) in the Nazi Germany and the concept originates from Gustav Radbruch. His phrase "statutory injustice" and "suprastatutory law"[192] influenced European legal thinking of the second half of the 20th century as well as of the present times. Radbruch probably perceived suprastatutory law as some form of natural law. He invented the term within the framework of his criticism of the alleged historical failure of legal positivism. The idea though has become the starting point of the way towards a core of constitutional order exempt from the disposition of the law-making and constitution-making bodies, i.e. the way towards the idea of a fraction of constitutional law that cannot be changed.

---

[188]/ Jednomyslné prohlášení třinácti Spojených států amerických [Unanimous Declaration of Thirteen United States of America]. In: Tindall, G. B. – Shi, D. E.: *USA (Dějiny států)* [USA (History of States)]. Praha: Nakladatelství Lidové noviny, 1994, pp. 783–785.

[189]/ The definition of the content of legal regulations as a rule defining the boundaries of interests can be found in: Korkunov, N. M.: *Lekcii po obščej teorii prava*. Sankt-Peterburg: Juridičeskij Centr Pres, 2004. Tekst privoditsja po izdaniju 1914 r. pp. 61, 154.

[190]/ Jhering, R. v.: *Der Zweck im Recht*. Vol. I, Leipzig: Druck und Verlag von Breithoff & Härtel, 1893, p. VIII.

[191]/ Jičínsky, Z.: *Ústava České republiky v politické praxi* [The Constitution of the Czech Republic in Practice]. Praha: Linde, 2007, p. 144.

[192]/ Radbruch, G.: Gesetzliches Unrecht und Übergesetzliches Recht. In: *Rechtsphilosophie*. Stuttgart: Koehler, 1950, p. 348.

Shortly after World War II this concept was converted into valid law in the form of Article 79 (3) of the Constitution of the Federal Republic of Germany, which is the Constitution valid until today. The Article states with German precision, but very briefly, that the change of the specified basic components of the content of the Constitution is inadmissible (*unzulässig*). More important than the interpretation of the scope of the provisions that the constitution-maker prohibits from being changed by his followers, is the fact that in this case a specific purpose – the effort to prevent repetition of recent history which was fresh in the minds of the constitution-makers in the year 1949 – prevailed over the contemporary findings of legal sciences. Jhering was probably right in stating that the purpose intended by the legislature is decisive for the content of law. The constitution-maker in this case abandoned invariability which was unsustainable from the scientific point of view and replaced it with a legally acceptable wording of prohibition using the word inadmissibility.

The idea of an unchangeable fraction of positive law would be partially supportable within the framework of the natural law tradition by a claim that this fraction is "merely" a positivisation of natural law. A similar construction is perhaps in the background of the natural law concept of inborn and inalienable human rights, i.e. the natural law interpretation of Article 1, second sentence, of the Charter of Fundamental Rights and Freedoms and Article 12 (1), second sentence, of the Constitution of the Slovak Republic, and it may be found in a majority of the recent constitutions.

A good example of a developed positivist prohibition of changes in the core of a constitution are Articles 9 (2) and (3) of the Constitution of the Czech Republic. A fitting expression of the prohibition can be found in Article 9 (2) of the Constitution of the Czech Republic: *"Amendment of the essential elements of the democratic state respecting the rule of law shall be inadmissible"*. Its interpretation would cause more problems than the similar Article 79 (3) of the Constitution of the Federal Republic of Germany, which additionally refers to Article 1 and Article 20, since the phrase "the essential elements of the democratic state respecting the rule of law" resembles an essay in legal philosophy, rather than the wording of a law. This is why it suits this reflection which focuses on the issue of inadmissibility of change of the core content of the constitution, rather than the exact definition of the extent of this core content. The Czech doctrine of constitutional law repeatedly tackled the cited provision: *"The intent of the constitution-maker was to block the change of democracy and the system of the rule of law. Therefore the provision clearly relies upon standard and modern definition of these concepts."*[193] *Ratio constitutione* is clear in this case; however, this is not enough to overcome the internal contradiction of Article 9 (2) of the Constitution and primarily the contradiction of this article with the findings of legal sciences. A part of the contradictions will recede after reading the explanation of J. Wintr: *"The provision of Article 9 (2) of the Constitution is understood as an element of suprapositive law in the legal order of the Czech Republic. Positive law, law created by people, relying on the will of the legislature, may be as a rule changed any time on the basis of a more recent will of the law-maker. Here the constitution-maker of the year 1992*

---

[193]/ Klíma, K. et al.: *Komentář k Ústavě a Listině* [Commentary on the Constitution and the Charter]. Plzeň: Aleš Čeněk, 2005, p. 77.

declares parts of the constitution-making work invariable – they will form part of our body of law irrespective of the changing will of the people and can be changed only by a revolution that would sweep away the entire current constitutional system."[194] The Czech Republic since becoming independent has not been confronted with the question of a change of the essential elements of the democratic state respecting the rule of law, and therefore neither the Constitutional Court nor other bodies have engaged in the interpretation of Article 9 (2). Perhaps only in the often cited first judgment of the Constitutional Court issued in an abstract review of constitutionality, it is possible to find an indirect statement referring to the notion of the existence of the fundamental indefeasible values of the democratic society (Judgment No. 14/1994 Sb.); the statement is in principle compliant with Article 9 (2) of the Constitution of the Czech Republic.

The constitution-maker of the year 1992 intended to build a legally insurmountable barrier by returning to the period when the state, as he believed, was neither democratic nor respectful of the rule of law. The constitution-maker attempted to prevent democracy from committing suicide in conformity with the Constitution. Is it possible, though, to prohibit the people from freely and democratically deciding also in favour of an arrangement of public affairs that is not a democracy and a state respecting the rule of law? Probably not, but it is possible to refer to such a decision of the sovereign as a revolution even though it may take the form of a peaceful and free vote.

The prohibition of changing the essential elements of the democratic state respecting the rule of law focuses on the future; however, it inheres in the past and wants to prevent its repetition.[195] The ideological basis of such prohibition emerged in contradiction to the development of legal thinking and at the time of the gradual emptying of democratism as well as the legality of public authority.

The concept of law that is created and changed by people, for the content of which various people are responsible to varying extent depending on their possibility to influence the content, has become in the second half of the 20th century, and in the present time still is, the implicit assumption of the majority of otherwise quite heterogeneous legal thought. The aging thesis of N. Luhman, that *"[...] modern industrial society must adapt its law to become positive law amendable by decisions,"*[196] may be seemingly challenged by the argument that it has been historically surpassed. We live in a postmodern time which negates the rationality of modernism. Postmodernism perhaps means loss of control also over creation of law, yet the law and its changes remain in place as partially conscious human work. *"Regulations are created by people in the sense that we can only blame ourselves for the regulations, rather than the nature or God."*[197] This quotation (my favourite) of K. R. Popper reacts to the everyday experience that the regula-

---

[194] Wintr, J.: *Principy českého ústavního práva s dodatkem principů práva evropského a mezinárodního* [Principles of Czech Constitutional Law, plus an Attachment on Principles of European and International Law]. Praha: Eurolex Bohemia, 2006, p. 23–24.

[195] "Legal regulations turn into sediments of the past politics and it becomes more and more difficult for the new political ambitions to remove them." Luhman, N.: *Das Recht der Gesellschaft*. Frankfurt am Main: Suhrkamp, 1995, p. 416.

[196] Luhman, N.: *Rechtssoziologie*. Opladen: Westdeutscher Verlag, 1987, p. 9.

[197] Popper, K. R.: *Otevřená společnost a její nepřátelé* [Open Society and its Enemies]. Praha: ISE, edice Oikoymenh, 1994, p. 63.

tions are created by people, which has become very pronounced since the times when legal customs gave way to other sources of law. H. Jonas subsequently provided a wider basis by saying: *"[...] responsibility is a correlative concept of authority and must be appropriate to the scope of the authority and its enforcement."*[198] It is hard to deny the everyday experience that people create and change law. They are therefore responsible for its contents. Various fields of science proved the limits of validity of "everyday experience" and common understanding. Legal sciences have not joined in and so within the framework of legal sciences it is still possible to argue also with apparentness.

In Czech legal thought it was V. Knapp who repeatedly claimed that law is a work of human beings: *"[...] the sociological concept upon which this work relies considers law as a regulatory system which people create for themselves rather than one being born with people [...]"*.[199]

The provision of the Constitution stipulating that any change of a part of constitutional law is inadmissible relies neither on apparentness nor on everyday experience, which are both contradictory to such provision. Nor does it attempt to rely on scientific legal and philosophical cornerstones. It does not argue against the finding that the law is created by people. The constitution-maker, i.e. a body of people, accepts the responsibility for creating it; however, at the same time it prohibits a part of their creation from being changed. The current constitution-maker cannot prohibit the future constitution-maker from repealing or from changing the original creation. The constitution-maker may only stipulate the manner, the "procedure", how to do it. An attempt to fix the content of law or to make it unchangeable is only a source of future discontinuity when the law must be changed under the pressure of the needs of life and there is no legal possibility to change it.

We agree with V. Knapp, who declared: *"The law cannot make itself unchangeable,"*[200] and continued: *"[...] no legislative body can restrict a future legislative body of the same or higher legislative level [...]"*[201] Creating and changing law is neither merely nor mainly a process of implementation of law; it is rather a process of implementation of political power. In this respect there is no difference and there cannot be any difference between democracy and dictatorship. In a democratic state respecting the rule of law however, the law is created and changed by a procedure stipulated by law. Law is not an entity, it is "merely" a stabilised expression of the past will of the authority and primarily of the state, and so it cannot prevent changes of itself for the future authoritative entity; that is really determined and therefore, to a considerable extent, bound by the material and spiritual conditions of the society. A constitutional prohibition on changing the core of the constitutional order forms part of such spiritual conditions. However another part of spiritual and material conditions supporting change may prevail.

---

[198]/ Jonas, H.: *The Imperatives of Responsibility. In Search for an Ethics for the Technological Age.* Chicago – London: The University of Chicago Press, 1984, p. X.

[199]/ Knapp, V.: *Teorie práva* [Theory of Law]. Praha: C. H. Beck, 1995, p. 28. *"Law is a product of the society, it is not introduced to the society from outside, but it is formed within the society itself."* *"All law [...] is a creation of people [...]"* Knapp, V. et al.: *Teoretické problémy tvorby československého práva* [Theoretical Issues of the Creation of Czechoslovak Law]. Praha: Academia, 1983, p. 7.

[200]/ Knapp, V. *supra* at p. 59.

[201]/ *Ibidem* at p. 60.

If something in law is unchangeable, it must represent some structural invariables, such as binary code in Luhman's interpretation, conditional and teleological standards and the connection with interests and purposes that are variable and create the immediate basis of the development, i.e. the changes of law.

The doctrine and also the constitutional prohibition of changing the essential elements of a democratic state respecting the rule of law represent a legal parallel to F. Fukuyama's "end of history". The sentence *"at the end of history no serious ideological competitors of liberal democracy survived"*[202] expresses the principal idea of Fukuyama's concept. The end of history according to Fukuyama consists in a complete ideological and significant power victory of liberal democracy which is also permanent and irreversible even though the author does not provide the reasons for that. Fukuyama claimed that the final victory of liberal democracy is a historical fact and argued in favour of his claim. The prohibition of changing a part of the constitutional order implicitly admits such change, understands it as evil and wants to prevent it. It stems from bad experience with certain historical alternatives of a democratic state respecting the rule of law. At least in Europe a later wording of Fukuyama applies: *"Even though historically there were many forms of legitimacy around the world, today democracy is the only real source of legitimacy."*[203] This includes also the creating and changing of law by the decision of elected representatives of the people and sometimes also by the people themselves. F. Fukuyama speaks about the alleged final victory of democracy and its transformation into the only source of legitimacy but he does not say anything about democracy as a method of government and decision-making and primarily about democracy as an answer to the question "Who governs?" Ideological victory and an attempt to constitutionally eternalize democracy and the state respecting the rule of law are attended by the emptying of the concepts and their transformation into a dignified part of the constitution.

A major topic of the emptying and formalisation of democracy goes partially beyond the framework of legal philosophy and also beyond the scope of these thoughts. However in the long term, there is a process transferring serious decisions from the elected or politically responsible bodies to extra-constitutional, unofficial bodies or other bodies standing outside of democracies. The most conspicuous examples of such bodies are "coalition councils" and supranational and international institutions. Passing turns of events take place in some revolutionary or other crisis situations.

The transformation of democracy and the state respecting the rule of law into "a dignified part of constitution" is a central issue of legal philosophy and constitutional law. The famous phrase "the dignified part of the constitution" was first used by the classical author of British constitutionalism W. Bagehot: *"In such constitutions there are two parts (not indeed separable with microscopic accuracy, for the genius of great affairs abhors nicety of division) first, those which excite and preserve the reverence of the population — the dignified parts, if I may so call them; and next, the efficient parts — those by which it, in fact, works and rules. [...] every constitution [...] must first win the loyalty*

---

[202]/ Fukuyama, F.: *The End of History and the Last Man*. New York: The Free Press, 1992, p. 211.
[203]/ Fukuyama, F.: *Budování státu podle Fukuyamy* [State-Building According to Fukuyama]. Praha: Alfa Publishing, 2004, p. 37.

and confidence of mankind, and there employ that homage in the work of government."[204] Democracy and the state respecting the rule of law belong to the basis of legitimacy of public authority; however, their importance as an actual order of the content and functioning / operation of public and primarily private authorities is continuously declining. They move to the dignified parts of the constitution, where they get a warm welcome by European monarchies. Constitutional prohibition of changing these parts of the constitution has a chance of succeeding in the long run, for the life of authority and law is increasingly taking place outside of their scope. The life of authority and law has found numerous ways from non governmental arbitration courts, through official torture of prisoners in a leading country of the Western world to creation of law in the EU. Democracy and the state respecting the rule of law are still a reality in Europe, but the prize to be paid for their eternalizing will be their irrelevance for life.

Prohibition of changing the essential elements of the democratic state respecting the rule of law still forms part of the legal order of the state, which is still the most important, yet "merely" one of several legal systems valid and effective on the same territory for the same entities. Legal pluralism has developed at surprising speed from an odd theory describing exotic legal situations into slightly boring analysis of standard disorder of valid law in our country, where on the same territory and for the same natural persons and legal entities at least three legal orders apply at the same time: the legal order of the Slovak Republic, EU law and international law – particularly in terms of human rights and criminal law. It is not important for the issue of attempting to prohibit changes to valid law whether and if so, which other legal orders apply at the same time on the territory of EU Member States; precise definition of the parts of international law which directly bind natural persons and legal entities is not important either.

The provisions on inadmissibility of changes to essential elements of democratic state respecting the rule of law are contained only in the legal order of an individual state. The idea of inalienability and therefore perhaps implied eternality of human rights regularly appears in preambles or introductory provisions of the majority of catalogues of human rights. The expression *"neodňateľných"* [inalienable] is the eighth word in the Slovak translation of the UN Universal Declaration of Human Rights.[205] However, this is not an attempt to prevent future changes in a part of human rights law; the wording of inalienability of human rights at least admits the interpretation as prohibition on taking human rights away from somebody by law or on the basis of law. They can be reasonably interpreted also in ways other than as a prohibition to change a certain part of human rights.

Prohibition on changing essential elements of a democratic state respecting the rule of law therefore remains within the legal order of the state, which is certainly the most visible and perhaps still the most important among the legal orders that apply simultaneously. However, it is not the only legal order and it is giving way to EU law, which on numerous occasions takes the form of a domestic source of law, and thus fogs its actual scope. The opinion of the Federal Constitutional Court concerning the relation of the constitutional law

---

[204]/ Bagehot, W.: *The English Constitution*. London: C. A. Watts and Co. LTD, 1964, p. 61.
[205]/ *Ľudské práva* [Human Rights]. Výber dokumentov OSN. Bratislava: Archa, 1991, p. 12.

of the Federal Republic of Germany and EU law expressed in the Solange I and Solange II decisions and, in particular, in the so called Maastricht decision[206] may also be interpreted as an attempt to maintain the continuity of the human rights basis of all valid law in the context of the growing scope and real dominance of EU law.

Prohibition on changing essential elements of a democratic state respecting the rule of law arises at the time of the gradual emptying of democracy as a method of decision-making as well as decision-making by the people or their representatives by means of transfer of key decisions further away from democratic institutions and is limited to the system of law, the system of law of the state, which in the context of the current European form of legal pluralism is still prevailing even though it is retreating. Therefore there is a danger that it will succeed due to its insignificance, where democracy and the state respecting the rule of law are defined in another way and will be integrated in the dignified part of the constitution (according to Bagehot).

Law is a human creation and so its preservation as well as changing depends on people. The essential elements of the democratic state respecting the rule of law will not change until the people forming the relevant constitution-making body, which can be also the people in a referendum, will respect the constitutional prohibition of change. This is the meaning of Article 9 (2) of the Constitution of the Czech Republic and similar provisions in constitutions of other countries. If they decide not to respect it and will change the essential elements of the democratic state respecting the rule of law through a procedure prescribed by the constitution, such a decision will be valid.

Currently in Central Europe we do not see any attractive alternative to the democratic state respecting the rule of law. In spite of that, we are convinced that it is correct if it is not possible to prevent change of any part of the legal order including the essential elements of the democratic state respecting the rule of law. The basic ideas of central European countries from the period 200 years ago are alien to us and apart from professional historians or specialists in the history of political and legal thinking, nobody understands these ideas. Perhaps our followers will look at democracy and state respecting the rule of law with a similar mixture of surprise and foreignness. We do not know what ideals they will respect, what will be the obvious and indefeasible principles of their public life; however, we do not dare to impose our principles on them. Perhaps they will acknowledge currently a marginal form of communitarism, or the renaissance of republican tradition or something we do not know yet. We do not know.

We are, however, convinced that we are not living in the exceptional moment of history which for the first time identified the permanent basis of organisation of a good society in the form of democracy and the state respecting the rule of law. A new phenomenon in law is the connection of the attempt to make the basis of the current constitutional system eternal and the understanding of variability of all law. The constitution-maker correctly speaks of inadmissibility, rather than invariability of the essential elements of the democratic state respecting the rule of law.

---

[206] *„[...] Federal Constitutional Court guarantees by its jurisdiction for the citizens of Germany that the generally applicable protection of the fundamental rights shall be preserved also against sovereign powers of the communities." Brunner v. The European Union Treaty (1994) 1 CMLR 57.*

At the time when the law faces a maze of challenges as a result of rapid social development, which is difficult to grasp in its complexity for any legislature, the attempt to create a firm point and the ultimate criterion in the basis or the core of the constitutional order is understandable. It represents a certain attitude to the development which, due to concerns about the repetition of history, prohibits entry for the unknown future onto the territory considered as the core of the constitutional system.

The belief of correctness and benefits of maintaining the essential elements of the democratic state respecting the rule of law does not become less firm when it is applied in discussion and confrontation with other opinions, nor when it is not expressed because it is a generally shared view. Currently it is not challenged by attempts to return to the past non-democratic regimes, but it is jeopardized by the emptying of the content in the face of which the constitutional prohibition is powerless.

New phenomena in law react to the new aspects of material and spiritual life of society which form the basis of the interests protected and defined by law as well as the purposes which the law serves. Natural and beneficial conservativism of law prevents the law from converting into a simple normative reflection of social processes. The development of society and maintaining relevance of law as its normative regulator require a reserved openness to changes from the entire legal system, which cannot avoid a priori even the core values of the constitution. Even today there are tendencies towards irrelevance of democracy and a state respecting the rule of law, which result from their initial separation from the authoritative basis of the society. Rational, humanistic and prudent openness to changes, with knowledge that they will occur, forms part of the democratic Enlightenment tradition of the state respecting the rule of law. The constitution-making enthusiasm of the French Revolution is stated in Article 28 of the Constitution of 24th June 1793, which was approved by referendum but has never entered into effect: *"The people shall always have the right to review, amend and change their Constitution. One generation cannot impose its laws on the future generations."*

2.2 THE BINDING EFFECT OF LEGAL TEXTS IN JUDICIAL INTERPRETATION AND APPLICATION OF LAW AND LOGICAL REASONING *LEGE ARTIS*

2.2.1. Introduction

The issue of the extent of the binding effect of the text of legislation or other sources of law on bodies applying the law is certainly not a new one from the formal point of view. The approaches to solving questions raised in the effort to define when it is possible to derogate from the (text of) a law, under what conditions and in what contexts, differ depending on the specific period of social development, on broader political, economic and social contexts, and mainly on the needs and interests of the society or its particular classes.

Considering the variability of individual factors that may be relevant for analysing this issue, it is impossible to resolve it once for all. Despite that, we assume that it is possible to propose acceptable cornerstones for putting the rationality of various approaches to test. As law is a social phenomenon, it is not possible to leave the social context out of consideration. Law is a set of rules that vary depending on many circumstances. It is not a regulatory system created in an abstract manner by some kind of higher authority irrespective of the consequences of such a system.

The development of legal thinking abroad in recent decades, and also in recent years in our legal environment, has been characterised by the development of arguments in favour of the possibility and sometimes even the necessity to depart from the so-called idea of the binding effect of the text of the law or arguments revitalising this concept. These concepts have gained a lot of attention among legal theoreticians as well as a part of the professional public. The main reason for this, in our opinion, is the attraction of these approaches due to their novelty. The traditional concepts of the application of law have been exhausted in two ways. At the theoretical level, they lost the ability to bring something essentially new, something which has not been described, analysed and assessed. At the practical level, a belief emerged at a certain point that these traditional concepts are unable to react to the current social needs brought about by various turning points in the development of a specific society. In our time, which is in principle spared of such turning points causing the need for radical solutions, only the first reason applies, even though certainly it is not the only reason. This development may be caused also by the significant judicialisation of life in general, which is related to the increasing importance of the judicial branch at the expense of other branches of government.

The above mentioned reasons, along with some others, are analysed in the following text with the objective of presenting explicit arguments that are behind the conclusions made by the advocates of the approaches relativising the requirement of the binding effect of the text of laws, and possibly with the aim of relativising some of these arguments.

2.2.2 Statute and law

Submitting specific analysis of the extent of the binding effect of legislation, primarily statutes, when applying law means to answer many fundamental questions which have been dealt with by legal theory from time immemorial because they represent the core of legal research. It is typical that it would be hard to find a generally accepted answer because such an answer will depend on the specific social, cultural, political and economic context and on the needs of the society in a particular period.

One of such core questions is the relation between statute and law. When trying to determine the extent of the binding effect of legal text contained in statutes, it is possible to perceive a certain tension between the concepts of statute and law. Determination of the scope and the content of a statute is quite simple from the technical point of view because the express features of this form of legal rule help us identify the legal rule itself. Law may be considered identical to statute (or legal regulation), but ordinarily law is perceived as a broader term.[207] The first indicated relation between the two concepts is currently con-

---

[207] Here we do not mean only the fact that the legal rules may be expressed also in other sources of law in the formal sense, such as judicial precedents, normative agreements, etc. The issue may be generalised in the sense that the scope and content of law reaches beyond the set of rules of conduct that are expressed in the formalised sources of these rules. For more details on some of these issues see: Gerloch, A. – Maršálek, P. (eds.): *Zákon v kontinentálním právu* [Statute in Continental Law]. Praha: Eurolex Bohemia, 2005. Gerloch, A. – Tryzna, J.:

sidered inappropriate in some cases, and the approach giving priority to law over statute is preferred. Such an approach places emphasis on the conflict between statute and law because we usually resort to the fundaments of this approach (i.e. the assumption of the difference between statute and law) when we perceive the statute as insufficient in a certain respect. In such cases the result usually is to prefer compliance with law rather than statute and such a solution is considered satisfactory. Law in such cases plays the role of the correct and complete measure whereas statute provides criteria that are considered insufficient.

The issue, of course, consists in the fact that it is not always necessarily clear whether such a procedure is admissible, because the relatively determinate content of a statute, which otherwise represents an objective general measure for decision-making, may be replaced with a subjective belief about the content of law. Such subjective beliefs are not always generally shared, and may therefore be contentious.[208]

The need to identify the differences between statute and law while resolving such differentiation arises almost exclusively in the application of legal rules[209] (notwithstanding theoretical research, which has the advantage that it cannot have effect on the legal standing of particular persons if it remains exclusively focused on theoretical terms). If a certain part of the life of an individual or a company is regulated by certain rules, it would be unusual to rely completely on voluntary compliance with such rules; instead mechanisms and institutions are created with the aim of contributing to the reduction of disputes over the rules that apply in specific cases and over the content of such rules.

2.2.3 Law and statute in the context of hard cases[210]

The conflict between law and statute is typically perceived in situations when we assume that the statute is in some respect insufficient, i.e. it results in consequences that are considered unsatisfactory. The frequency of occurrence of such cases depends, of course, primarily on the level of legal regulation of human conduct, i.e. on the extent to which the legislature reflects the prevailing expectations in the society. If the intentional authoritative legislative activity approximates this expectation, there is no significant tension between law and statute and therefore no negative perceptions about it arise. If, however, the legislature deviates to a higher extent or with more intensity from the prevailing belief on the content of legal regulation, i.e. the regulation is deemed to be insufficient (containing loopholes),

Několik úvah nad rolí nejvyšších soudů v podmínkách demokratického právního státu [Some Thoughts on the Role of Supreme Courts in Democratic States Respecting the Rule of Law] In: Šimíček, V. (ed.): *Role nejvyšších soudů v evropských ústavních systémech – čas pro změnu?* [The Role of Supreme Courts in European Constitutional Systems – Time for Change?] Brno: Masarykova univerzita, 2007, pp. 89–102. Gerloch, A. – Tryzna, J.: Nad vázaností soudce zákonem z pohledu některých soudních rozhodnutí [Considering the Binding Effect of Statutes on Judges from the Point of View of Some Judicial Decisions]. *Právní rozhledy* 1/2007, pp. 23–28.

[208]/ We intentionally ignore the evident fact that even statute does not always have to provide in every case a clear answer to the legal question at hand, or a solution that will be identical in all individually solved cases. It may be assumed though that statute has a feature that enables achieving such a solution.

[209]/ We cannot use the phrase "in application of law" here, because for this moment it is necessary to maintain the distinction between law and statute. Otherwise of course normally we would use the phrase "application of law" in the sense of applying individual provisions of legal regulations in specific cases.

[210]/ Sometimes the English term "complex cases" is used for the Czech term "složité případy" is used; both terms are used interchangeably in this subchapter.

the tendency to remove statute in favour of law becomes stronger. Anglo-American cases may be used to illustrate such situation.[211] Based on such cases many assume that the relation between statute and law must be researched on the background of cases called "hard".[212] In contrast with the hard cases there are so-called easy cases, the solution of which does not create a conflict between statute and law. Hard cases usually include various situations the common feature of which is, according to the advocates of such differentiation, the impossibility to solve them according to statute,[213] and it is necessary to solve them on the basis of law. P. Holländer describes such dilemma as a conflict between juspositivism (the solution arises from statute) and jusnaturalism (the solution arises from law).[214] Such a differentiation is, of course, possible, even though currently it is practically impossible to speak about a pronounced conflict, or a conflict that could be referred to as a conflict between legal positivism and natural law.[215]

Some model situations which may be called hard cases are presented below. At this point we will only summarize the general nature of hard cases as the foundation for further thoughts.

All the situations usually referred to as hard cases have one feature in common: a belief of the insufficiency or inappropriateness of the solution arising out of statute (or other formalised sources of law in those legal orders which accept diversity of sources of law). We will refer to the arguments arising out of formalised sources as *institutionalised* arguments and the arguments with weak or no formal support as *non-institutionalised* arguments. Anglo-American theories consider as a hard case usually those legal cases *"representing real reasoning problem of correctness of interpretation of law which cannot be solved by a reference to a clear provision"*.[216] Z. Kühn defines hard cases as *"a large group of various cases that are not merely a logical (or at least quasi-logical) interpretation of legal text or other source of law"*.[217] Classifying a certain case as a hard case is of key importance for the solution of such case because it means that application of

---

[211] It is, of course, questionable whether we could find the same cases in continental law. It seems that the Anglo-American legislatures traditionally rely to a higher extent on the possible creative approach of the courts than the continental legislatures, even though in continental law too we may come across cases when the legislature, being helpless over the content of the adopted legal regulation, leaves it up to the bodies applying the law to find the solution in individual cases. Many of them may be found in the works by Ronald Dworkin (see the following note).

[212] A "hard case" is a term that was probably introduced to modern legal theory by Ronald Dworkin primarily in his book *Když se práva berou vážně* [Taking Rights Seriously]. Praha: Oikoymenh, 2001, p. 112 and subs. Later this concept was taken over in German legal theory, see for example Alexy, R.: *Begriff und Geltung des Rechts*. Freiburg – München: Alber, 1994, p. 18 and subs.; in Czech literature for example P. Holländer: *Filosofie práva* [Philosophy of Law]. Plzeň: Vydavatelství a nakladatelství Aleš Čeněk, 2006, p. 17 and subs.

[213] Or according to any formalised legal rule when it may also be necessary to search for the solution in certain material sources of law.

[214] Holländer, P. *ibidem* at p. 17 and subs.

[215] This conclusion arises indirectly from the frequency of references to natural law in individual judicial decisions, and such references almost do not exist; this applies also to the decisions of the Constitutional Court, even though the judges of this court are to protect natural rights and the specific rights of citizens (see the wording of the promise of a judge of the Constitutional Court in Art. 85 (2) of the Constitution). Even these natural, i.e. inalienable, rights were positivised by constitutional laws, specifically in the Charter of Rights and Freedoms as well as international treaties.

[216] Kühn, Z.: *Aplikace práva ve složitých případech* [Application of Law in Hard Cases]. Praha: Karolinum, 2002, p. 42.

[217] *Ibidem* at p. 45.

various interpretation and reasoning procedures will be accepted in such case, even though they would not or could not be used in other cases.

The differentiation of easy and hard cases is itself quite hard and confusing. There are no objective criteria which would make it possible to differentiate which case is easy and which is hard. Kühn's definition is, however, precise. They are really cases that cannot be solved by interpretation of a legal text. It is necessary to determine why they cannot be solved in this way. In the continental law system, there cannot be a case that would not be resolvable on the basis of legal regulation. The only reason why a case is deemed unresolvable by reference to legislation is the subjective belief of the person making the decision on the case, i.e. the belief that the case cannot be resolved according to statute. A typical example is the decision of the Constitutional Court in the matter of the time limit for exercising presidential veto.[218] The Constitution states that the President may return an adopted statute to the Chamber of Deputies within the time-limit of 15 days of the day when such statute was referred to him. The disputed issue was how to determine the time-limit if the last day is a holiday, which happened in this particular case. The Constitutional Court stated that in such case, the time-limit expires on the closest working day and used various arguments the support of which was beyond the text of the Constitution. But it cannot be stated that the case could not be resolved on the basis of the text of the Constitution. The Constitution stipulates the time-limit for the President and it does not make any provision for any kind of prolongation of the limit due to any reasons. The Constitution also explicitly states in Article 2 (3) that the Government serves all the citizens and governmental powers may be exercised in cases only within the limits and in a manner stipulated by statute. The Constitutional Court nevertheless was under the impression that such a conclusion is unacceptable, thereby classifying the case as hard.[219]

The basic assumption justifying the Court's reasoning is the assertion that the linguistic interpretation is insufficient. Such an assumption is of course disputable; nevertheless, from the point of view of the Court's maintaining the procedure consistent and just, it is necessary. We cannot, however, overlook the consequence arising out of this assumption, which is the possibility to substitute the meaning of the text of a legal regulation with the views of the person deciding the case. The opinion issued is necessarily subjective.[220] It may be shared but it need not be shared. An *a posteriori* agreement or disagreement is irrelevant as the decision on the matter was issued. Some entities, such as the legislature, may react to the expressed conclusions *pro futuro*; it is, however, questionable whether such reaction will be respected.[221]

218/ Judgment No. 30/1998 Sb.

219/ We do not want to assess the correctness or incorrectness of the solution; the aim is only to point out the evident fact that the case could have been solved on the basis of the text of the Constitution.

220/ This evaluation is not meant to be pejorative. Even though such an opinion may be supported by careful reasoning, the choice of submitted arguments is subjective and depends on the person making the decision. Individual arguments and the extent of relevance attributed to them is effectively not subject to any objective control, because such a control is impossible due to the nature of the issue.

221/ We cannot fail to notice the known fact that in an individual case the law is not what is regulated by the law-maker but it is the decision of the court (see also the following note). It is not therefore excluded that an instruction of the legislature will not be respected, even though such an instruction reacts to a particular case by a change of legal regulation in order to remove potential ambiguity in the statute; however, even such a change will not be

The above analysis leads to the following partial conclusion: whether a certain case is considered hard or easy depends on the person deciding the matter. Perhaps every case may be in the first phase considered easy. It is the reasoning of the interpreter, whose motives usually are not communicated explicitly to the addressees of the decision, which makes it a hard case.[222] This reasoning is based on the subjective belief of the interpreter that the solution of the case so far perceived as easy is in a certain respect insufficient (inefficient, ineffective, unjust). In such a case the legitimacy of the solution may certainly be disputed.

When searching for an answer to this question, it is necessary to differentiate the arguments which may be submitted in favour of the solution that is different from the solution that would be based on the text of the legal regulation. The question is whether the solution different from that arising out of the text of the legal regulation is required by institutionalised or non-institutionalised arguments. If the arguments are institutionalised then the deviation from the solution based on the legal regulation may be considered acceptable, because arguments raised are of the same relevance as the conclusions arising from the text of the legal regulation. Only in the case of non-institutionalised arguments the achieved results cannot be considered permissible because the selection of arguments in this case represents purely the subjective choice of the person making the interpretation.

The former acceptable approach may be characterised as a systematic approach. In practice it consists of taking into account arguments that should be taken into account due to the extent of their institutionalisation. Trying to differentiate such situations from the above mentioned "hard cases", these cases may be called "complex" because their solution must be supported by multiple arguments requiring more extensive knowledge of the legal order, the related matters, or other information.

The latter approach is characterised by subjective preference given to various points of view and the common feature is weak or no institutional basis. The decision-maker in these cases typically is not restricted at all in the choice of arguments that are considered relevant. The impulse for such procedure is the subjective unacceptability of the conclusions arising from the case if it were otherwise addressed as easy. Referring to the case as a hard case legitimises, only seemingly though, the application of non-institutionalised arguments because it creates an impression that there are extraordinary circumstances requiring such a procedure. Such a case is then really solved as complex in the meaning described above, but the complexity of the case is declared by the decision-maker.

respected. In relation to the described example the constitution-makers could, for example, react by changing Art. 62 (f) of the Constitution so that it clearly states that an official of the Supreme Court may really be appointed out of the judges of all courts, although the Constitutional Court would remain of the opinion expressed before, despite the fact that such an opinion would completely lose support in the text of the Constitution as a result of the potential amendment.

[222] It is, of course, possible to strive for maximum correctness when drafting the reasoning of individual decisions that would explain all the considerations. However, this is a rare case in our opinion. The real motives of the interpreter remain hidden, and only the arguments justifying the chosen conclusion are presented, or possibly also arguments that cannot be omitted because they were submitted by one of the parties to the case.

2.2.4 Law, statute and justice

In a different context, the issue of the relationship between law and statute takes the form of a potential conflict between statute and justice (or, in yet another context, with morals). The conflict is perceived as a conflict between statute, i.e. positive law, and natural law,[223] usually in the understanding of the traditional Radbruch's formula,[224] or in relation to morals.[225]

P. Holländer mentions in this respect[226] the decision of the Federal Constitutional Court related to decree No. 11 on the Act regulating imperial citizenship of 24th November 1941. In this decision the Federal Constitutional Court concluded that *"Law and justice are not at the disposal of the legislature."* The idea that *"the constitution-makers can arrange everything as they wish would mean a return to the spiritual positions of value-less positivism, which has long been outdated in jurisprudence and legal practice. The period of national socialism in Germany teaches us that the legislature may stipulate erroneous law."*[227]

This concept is clearly relevant for the analysed issue, because it shows how problematic it is to restrict law to statute, because statute, which is also beyond any doubt, can be adapted to the current needs of the limited governing elite and to the detriment of other people. The solution of such potential tension between justice, morals or certain values on the one hand, and the "unjust" statute interfering with these axiomatic principles on the other hand, may be identified according to legal theory (or rather according to an important part of recent legal philosophy) in "judicial decision-making *contra*, or *praeter legem*, as a manner of solution of the tension between morals and law," which relies on the "acceptance of unwritten law."[228]

The described reasoning creates a similarly problematic or disputable assumption of the existence of hard cases. The basic premise is the assumed existence of statutes with extremely unjust content, the legitimacy of which with respect to the content cannot be affirmed by the fact that they are adopted by a body formed (perhaps) legitimately for that purpose. It is based on an unpronounced fact that we are able to differentiate between a good legal regulation and a bad one relying on a certain value system which is immanent for us. In fact, this value system is different in time and space because no recent theory has the ambition to create a universally acceptable value system.

The solution of the conflict between statute and justice (morals, etc.) is sought in the potential of the judge to refuse to obey the literal wording of the statute, *"if it is required due to serious reasons by the purpose of the statute, history of its creation, systematic context or one of the principles embedded in a legal order in conformity with constitution."*[229]

---

[223]/ E.g. in Holländer, P. *supra* at p. 18 and subs.
[224]/ Radbruch, G.: Gesetzliches Unrecht und übergesetzliches Recht. In: Kaufmann, A. (ed.): *Gesamtausgabe Radbruch*. Vol. 3, Heidelberg: Müller, 1990, pp. 83–93; p. 89.: "The conflict between justice and legal certainty probably may be solved only in such a way that positive law ensured by the regulations and the government will have preference also in those cases when it is unjust and inefficient from the content point of view, with the exception of the cases when the conflict between positive statute and justice reaches such an intolerable level that the statute must as undue law give way to justice."
[225]/ Typically R. Alexy, R. Dworkin and others.
[226]/ Holländer, P. *supra* at p. 19 and subs.
[227]/ *Ibidem.*
[228]/ *Ibidem* at p. 41.
[229]/ Judgment of the Constitutional Court file reference Pl. ÚS 21/96.

Such a proposed solution, though, is misleading because it relates to completely different principles than those on which it is built. It is based on the assumption that the legislature creates unjust law, whereas the judge by his judgments provides protection to the addressees of unjust law against potential arbitrariness of the legislature, because he refuses to apply the unjust law. In reality, such a situation is very unlikely. If the legislature starts creating law the content of which is in strong contradiction to the elementary principles of justice, then in such a society an authoritarian or rather totalitarian regime must necessarily exist, which controls more or less the whole society and would therefore probably control the judges as well. We may, of course, imagine that there may be a judge, who would be willing to oppose an unjust statute, but for how long could he resist and how successful could he be? How many judges of the emerging Nazi state successfully opposed it? How many judges in Czechoslovakia successfully opposed the emerging Communist regime and refused to apply the adopted statutes? Realistically, the judge may oppose unjust law only in the environment where he is protected against government interventions, i.e. only in the environment of a democratic state respecting the rule of law, whose institutions heed the very values that the judge relies upon when opposing the unjust statute.[230]

These theories survived also in periods of democratic rule, and therefore they strive to be generally applicable. According to these opinions the judge is authorised to decide even today *contra legem* or *praeter legem*, even though the basic preconditions for such procedure, i.e. the period of rule of extremely unjust statutes, have not been met. Surely we cannot claim that we live currently in a period of rule of extremely unjust statutes, the impact of which must be corrected at any cost. The legislative bodies of individual European states are elected in regular free elections the results of which usually are not disputed. Therefore it is questionable whether in such cases the courts may decide *contra legem*.

Such a judicial procedure of course lacks legitimacy. This is why judges have a tendency to strengthen the legitimacy by a myth of the "unjust" statute, which they must be prepared to oppose. They suppose that general injustice (the statute, as opposed to a judicial decision, applies to entire classes of cases) may be made up for by individual justice. Additionally, judges substitute for objective justice that arises out of statute with subjective justice based on their beliefs and all this is done in a democratic state respecting the rule of law.[231]

We may raise the question whether a state creating rules so extremely unjust that they require corrective intervention of the judge is still a democratic state respecting the rule of

---

[230]/ This issue is explained by O. Weinberger with clearly noticeable irony in the introduction to his paper on the topic of relevance of natural law for legal reasoning. He explains that natural law may be relevant only in those cases when it is able to provide practical arguments for application of law, whereas in general, theoretical respect of the issue of the relation between natural and positive law is completely insignificant. *"Stalin's dictatorship of the party elite (the nomenclature) closely related to the idea of necessary (and therefore natural) development towards dictatorship of the proletariat implemented by Stalin, the party elite and the secret machinery would certainly not capitulate in the face of objections of a professor of legal philosophy that it sharply contradicts the natural law principles in which he believes and that are the real salvation of the humanity."* Weinberger, O.: Přirozené právo a právnická argumentace [Natural Law and Legal Reasoning]. *Právník* 3/1993, p. 194.

[231]/ See Holländer, P. *supra* at p. 45: *"I assume that a possible solution of the tension between morals and law in a democratic state respecting the rule of law consists of conferring the rule-making competence to a judge ..."*

law. The answer is clear: this is not how the conflict between justice and statute arises.[232] It may arise in relation to the general and the unique in those cases when the legal regulation gives space for "discretionary application". However, this conflict usually is not relevant at all in the sense described by the authors of the theses worded on the basis of Nazi law. An apparent legitimacy of the search for resolution of this conflict arises out of a problematic assumption that judges are able to judge what is just and what is unjust better than the legislature. This assumption is not supported by anything. It may be concluded that this ability is not in principle different in case of the representatives of both branches of government; however, from the point of view of conferred legitimacy to make such decisions (as to what is just and what is unjust) it should be the legislature who should be given preference. It may be noted that in the concept of a democratic state respecting the rule of law, one of the fundamental principles often consisted of the significance of the lay element in the judiciary (primarily in the form of a jury system), which was supposed to balance strict legalism.

It is of course necessary to take into account that many cases that are classified as adjudication *contra legem* in fact should not be classified as such because the determined significance of the legal regulation may seemingly contradict the text of the legal regulation; however, this results from application of certain rules contained in the constitutional order. In such a case it is again the systematic interpretation in a broad sense of the word, which is relevant for all formally valid arguments contained in the legal order.[233]

2.2.5 Note on the system of law

Both described situations, i.e. the idea of the existence of hard cases and the alleged necessity to be equipped with a reasoning mechanism in case it is necessary to prevent extreme injustice of a statute, apply to the current arrangement of relations between individual holders of state power.

---

[232]/ After all, Radbruch also pointed out that positive law takes preference also in those cases when it is unjust and incomplete in terms of the content.

[233]/ A possible example of such procedure is the decision of the Constitutional Court file ref. II. ÚS 1856/07, in which the Constitutional Court considered the right to compensation for harm caused by an unlawful decision. In this particular case the claimant sought compensation for harm caused by unlawful prosecution. The general courts partially dismissed the claim for compensation arguing that it was the claimant's fault that the prosecution commenced because, among other things, he intentionally had not told the truth to the prosecuting and adjudicating bodies in relation to the commencement of criminal prosecution, which he later admitted. The Constitutional Court rejected this reasoning, even though Act No. 82/1998 Sb. makes it possible not to award compensation if the aggrieved party "was at fault in terms of the custody, conviction or judgment imposing protective measures" (s. 12 (1) (a) of Act No. 82/1998 Sb.). If this is strictly interpreted it is certainly possible to see the fault relevant for the purposes of the evaluated provision in the fact that the suspect provided untrue information which led to the commencement of criminal prosecution against him. The Constitutional Court however, with respect to Art. 36 (1) and (2) of the Charter stated the following: *"The fault of the claimant causing the commencement of criminal prosecution cannot be seen in the fact that in the position of a suspect, and later of the accused, he used all possible means to defend himself which include primarily the right to remain silent as well as the right not to tell the truth."* The conclusion of the general courts was, strictly speaking, correct. The statute does not define "being at fault" in criminal prosecution, which means that for the purposes of the statute it is any conduct of the suspect that causes him to be accused, i.e. for example his defence consisting of providing untrue information. The Constitutional Court, strictly speaking, interpreted the statute *contra legem*. In fact, of course, this is not an interpretation *contra legem,* because taking into account systematic arguments (i.e. the Charter of Rights and Freedoms) casts doubt on the strict conclusion arrived at by the general courts. Statute cannot be interpreted in contradiction to constitutional law (*lex superior derogat legi generali*).

It is necessary to add that the understanding of law and its content depends of course on the type of legal culture. A broader concept of law, the sources of which are not found exclusively in statutes in the technical sense of the word but in many various sources, is typical of Anglo-American law. Continental law on the other hand is a type of legal culture that is in modern times traditionally based on identification of law with statute. Sometimes such an understanding may currently seem to be outdated even though, in our opinion, it is possible to find formal positively expressed supporting arguments for such an understanding. It is not necessary to rely on the considerations of potential extreme injustice of a statute. It is clear that the contemporary legislature respects the values that may be referred to as generally shared values. These values are at the same time embedded at the constitutional level as well as in treaties regulating human rights and are therefore beyond the sole disposition of the legislature.

2.2.6 Limitation of topic

In relation to the above mentioned and with respect to the below mentioned, it is necessary to express the following limitation which applies to the chosen topic. In the presented study we analyze procedures that may be legitimately used when interpreting statutes. A lot of what has been said so far does not in principle apply to finding the meaning of the statute, but rather to judging its content from the point of view of its acceptability. This blurs the difference between creation of rules and application of law (statute) because the person that applies the law becomes the creator of law whenever he refuses to be bound by law under whatever pretences (of course, with the exception of the above mentioned acceptable "taking into account of systems" arguments).

A necessary condition for the ideas presented here is the acceptance of the fact that the current law-maker is a body which has full democratic legitimacy to make law. Marginal situations which represent the principles of the theses describing a possibility not to respect the text of the statute are not taken into account due to the above explained reasons. It is an effort to find acceptable procedures for interpretation of legal regulations in the relatively stable social environment which is in principle free from excesses that would go beyond the acceptable framework of usual political conflicts in a democratic system.

2.2.7 Why should the judge be bound by statute?

Even though it is currently clear that in some cases application of legal regulations creates a difference between statute and law, there is usually no formal support for such procedures. If we base our considerations on the assumption that the constitutional rules still represent the basis for performance of all activities of state bodies, then it is hard to resist the perception that such a procedure will rarely be contentious.

"The judge, in making decisions, is bound by statute" (Art. 95 (1) of the Constitution of the Czech Republic). *"The exercise of judicial power is governed exclusively by statute"* (Art. 61 of the Danish Constitution). *"Judges are subordinated only to the statute"* (Art. 101 of the Italian Constitution). *"Judges are independent and are subordinated only to statutes"* (Art. 97 (1) of the Constitution of the Federal Republic of Germany). *"The judiciary arises out of the people and is ... on behalf of the King exercised by judges who constitute the judicial branch, are ... bound by statutes and subordinated only to statutes"* (Art. 117

of the Spanish Constitution). *"Judges are independent and subordinated only to statutes"* (Art. 50 (3) of the Hungarian Constitution).

As it becomes clear from the random choice of quotations from the constitutions of various European countries, the principle of judges bound by statute embedded in the constitution is basically shared. It is a concept which in its formal shape has existed for more than two hundred years and is much older if we include various modifications and variants. The requirement for judges to be bound by statute became the basis of modern understanding of law and has had a major influence on the perception of law in many ways.[234]

The continental system of law has been focused on the dominance of legislation, and primarily statutes, since the beginning of the 19th century due to reasons that are in general quite clear and known; in specific legal orders the reasons, however, may be specific and often explained in a simplified manner *ex post*.

The basis of the requirement for the judge to be bound by statute was the idea of a major difference between the rules contained in a statute in a technical sense and other rules which do not have the quality of a statute due to the ways how such rules were created.

General theoretical and philosophical fundamental principles were laid in a new form, among other things, in the works of European philosophers and thinkers such as J. J. Rousseau or Ch. L. Montesquieu, and outside of the European continent the fundamental principles were described for example in the Federalist Papers, and were expressed in the constitutions of many states from those days up to now.[235]

One of general principles for the creation of the binding effect of statute on judges was therefore primarily the effort to divide the power into government branches that are mutually independent and separate and that do not compete with each other in their activities but are rather complementary to each other and maintain balance. The requirement of division of powers and the related requirement of judges being bound by the results of actions of the legislature are, with respect to the previously existing circumstances, logical and of course do not lack rationality even in present times. In addition to this general reason, which had major impact on the relation of judges to statutes, there are also other practical reasons. Statutory law is relatively well arranged, it is easy to systemize, it encourages consistent interpretation and application, and it may be changed quickly if there is a specific need for change, which would take much longer in other manners of creating rules (legal customs, judge-made law). We may assume that the individual reasons depended on the specific conditions more or less relevant in the individual states.

The facts which gave rise to the described problem may be expressed in summary in two or three typical situations. The first situation arises when it seems that the wording of the statute does not offer a solution to a particular legal issue. The necessary condition for such a situation is, of course, the obligation of the judge to decide (prohibition of *denegatio*

---

[234] See in various contexts Gerloch, A. – Maršálek, P. (eds.): *Zákon v kontinentálním právu* [Statute in Continental Law]. Praha: Eurolex Bohemia, 2005.

[235] It is certainly necessary to differentiate between specific circumstances in individual states. For example, it is definitely not possible to compare the situation in the forming United States with the Austrian regime, which was absolutist up to the middle of the 19th century. Of course, even France after the Revolution is not a precise parallel to doctrinal postulates.

justitiae). Another problem consists in the certain rigidity of law which, due to objective reasons, is sometimes unable to react to changes in social circumstances, and therefore the consequences of application of its provisions are perceived as inappropriate and undesirable. And finally the last situation arises when the consequences dictated by the statute are considered as generally undesirable, for example due to evident injustice, unrealistic nature or inefficiency, etc.

In all the above indicated cases, the binding effect of statute (the text) on the judge is perceived as a negative element and a considerable effort is expended to exclude the effect of statute (or in the first situation when the statute is considered insufficient, it is an effort focused on gaining the required legal material that will offer the solution).[236]

The concept of statute in the material sense represents certain solution of the indicated problem, even though it is a solution that rather suggests an effort to avoid the original fundamental postulates and to create the theoretical concept providing reasoning for such procedures. In fact this concept does not offer fundamentally new reasoning that would be different from any other theories pointing out the difference between statute and law and giving preference to law over statute.[237] The statute in the material sense may be understood as the same set of rules that are usually referred to as law. Such an approach may be found only in some branches of law; for example, it is typical of constitutional law,[238] and possibly also in the concept of a material statute in the understanding of the European Court of Human Rights.[239]

2.2.8 What should be the understanding of the binding effect of statute? (Binding effect of statute v. binding effect of the text of the statute)

We may say that the postulate of the binding effect of statute on the judge bears a hidden conflict caused by the substance of this concept. The problem nevertheless can be solved without major difficulties and on a regular basis, which raises a question as to what should be the understanding of the binding effect of statute on the judge. If, for example, adjudication *contra legem* is deemed permissible, then it is certainly necessary to explain the postulate of the binding effect of statute on the judge.

The first possible explanation is the binding effect of statute on the judge in the formal sense, i.e. the judge is bound by the normative legal act that results from the activities of the legislature authorised to take such an activity. This concept rather reflects, as already explained, the traditional division of power. It is to express the subordination of judges to statute, to point out their independence of the executive branch (and possibly of other influences). At the same time, it has a negative connotation. Judges are bound by statute

---

[236]/ Absence of the relevant provision in the statute may be resolved by the so-called negative rule as proposed for example in Normative Theory of Law.

[237]/ A typical example is Dworkin's well-known quotation: "The rule of law is a loftier ideal than the rule of legal texts." See Dworkin, R. *supra* at p. 416.

[238]/ See for example the judgment of the Constitutional Court, file ref. IV. ÚS 2647/07: *"A natural person or legal entity is authorised to file a constitutional complaint if they are of the opinion that a final decision in proceedings which they were a party to, or a measure or other intervention of a public body interfered with their fundamental right or freedom arising out of constitutional law in the material sense of the term."*

[239]/ See for example the judgment of the European Court of Human Rights in *Wieser and Bicos Beteiligungen GmbH v. Austria* (application No. 74336/01).

and only by statute; nothing else than statute is to provide criteria for judicial decision-making.

The binding effect of statutes on judges may also be approached from the material point of view, i.e. from the perspective of the rules that are contained in the statute and how they should be found. This is a fundamental principle similar, to a certain extent, to the material concept of statute described above. The difference consists of the fact that, in the concept analysed here, the source of relevant rules is only the statute, in which the rules are found in a more or less creative manner. As opposed to that, the concept of statute in a material sense, which was described above, represents a concept which also takes into account those rules which cannot be found in statute in the technical sense and the sources of these rules must be found elsewhere, e.g. in judicial decisions representing an original source of such rules.

If we maintain the above indicated differentiation it becomes clear that each of these approaches is as such not problematic; rather, the problem arises out of their interdigitation. So, for example, the formal approach requires that the judge is bound exclusively by statute; the logical consequence of such understanding is, for example, rejection of conclusions expressed by courts in other similar cases.[240] The contents of the statute, i.e. the rules of conduct, are made precise and concrete in individual cases. Why then should a lower court reject interpretive conclusions of a superior court using only this argument? Why should the court reject the interpretation which has been made and can be considered correct in the given case and why should it at any cost insist on autonomous assessment in which it will intentionally disregard the interpretation already made under the pretence of the court's independence of anything apart from statute? By doing so, it may interfere with the consistency of judicial decision-making and the formalised principle of equality requiring that the same cases must be resolved consistently.

We may explain the substance of the indicated conflict in relation to the material understanding of the binding effect of statute on the judge. If we are talking about the binding effect of statute on the judge, we usually mean the binding effect of the text of the statute, which usually cannot be attributed a completely arbitrary meaning.[241] We therefore mean such an approach whereby the decisive legal arguments are inferred by the judge from statute (from its wording) and the judge will suppress all factors that do not arise from the statute (e.g. he will exclude consideration of how just, efficient or effective the statutory solution may be, whether it complies with ethical rules, social belief, etc.).

If the relevance of such rules (factors) is given sufficient space, the binding effect of the text of statute becomes diluted and turns into the binding effect of the statute, which is an approach in which the statute (the text) plays a certain role, but not an exclusive one, and finds itself in competition with other factors. The text of statute cannot be ignored altogether but it may enjoy only a low relevance in a specific case. Examples of

---

[240]/ "Judicial decision is not a source of Czech law", this was the main argument in the "war" between general courts and the Constitutional Court, the substance of which was the dispute over the scope of the binding effect of judgments of the Constitutional Court.
[241]/ If the statute states that a person becomes of legal age by reaching the age of eighteen, it clearly cannot be interpreted as setting forth the becoming of legal age at fifteen.

such an approach include adjudicating *contra legem* or the case of the so-called teleological reduction. The text of statute plays a completely negative role there – it is mentioned only in relation to the explanation why it is not possible to proceed according to the statute.

We may assume that there are many more factors influencing the text of the statute than solely the "mere" need to adapt it to the needs of social life. Various legal principles, values, purposes, interpretation rules and procedures, and methods of reasoning, all have importance and reduce the relevance of the statutory text itself. The cause of the tension which arises has already been indicated. Many of the factors, the practical importance of which may be considered, show a considerably low level of formal validity and, in spite of that, they are able to prevail over statute as the source of normative arguments of strong formal validity.

The issue may nevertheless be considered also from the other point of view, i.e. the text of the statute sets forth a mere principle for identifying the rule itself, the final form of which is influenced by many other factors. This approach reflects the often repeated thesis according to which the linguistic interpretation (i.e. the interpretation focused on the text of the legal regulation) "represents only the first approximation to the meaning of the interpreted legal rule."[242]

The meaning of the term "binding effect" may be perceived in a similar way as the term "statute" in the phrase "binding effect of the statute". Binding effect may mean, for example, the necessity to follow the text of the law in all cases, including those when it seems that its consequences are unacceptable for some reason.[243] Binding effect may also mean the necessity to follow the text of a statute and, when it is not clear, to use one of the above mentioned arguments. Binding effect may mean the necessity to base the considerations on the text of a statute, and only as a last resort to reach a contrary conclusion (as worded by the drafter of the Theresian Code e.g. "to deviate from statute under a trivial pretence of justice").

It is quite clear that the original, or traditional, meaning of the requirement of "binding effect" was closer to the first of the above mentioned alternatives than to the last one. The contemporary status of law primarily in terms of application is such that, at least in some cases, it tends to refer to the last version.

---

[242]/ Critical notes on the substance of linguistic interpretation see Cvrček, F.: Kritické poznámky k výuce interpretace právních textů [Critical Comments on Teaching Interpretation of Legal Text] In: Gerloch, A. – Maršálek, P. (eds.): *Problémy interpretace a argumentace v soudobé právní teorii a právní praxi* [Issues of Interpretation and Argumentation in Contemporary Legal Theory and Practice]. Praha: Eurolex Bohemia, 2003, p. 49 and subs. A critical attitude even though a simplified one with respect to the limited space is, of course, adopted also by the Constitutional Court starting with decision No. 30/1998 Sb., from which the phrase in quotes was stated.

[243]/ It is absolutely necessary to keep in mind in this respect the relativity of such unacceptability – unacceptability from the point of view of the judge who decides the case (i.e. individual unacceptability), unacceptability from the point of view of the society (social unacceptability – the issue again consists of how to find such unacceptability), or unacceptability for a party to the dispute which lost or won the case.

2.2.9 Bound or free application of law?[244]

Considering the scope of acceptance of such rules, we may, in a retrospective view, distinguish various approaches to application of law. These approaches can be classified on an imaginary axis depending on two mutually related criteria. The first criterion is the extent to which the text of the legal regulation is respected, and the second criterion subsists in the extent and scope of acknowledgement of the relevance of the above mentioned less formalised interpretation and reasoning rules. The so-called bound application of law represents one extreme on the scale of various approaches to the application of law. The other extreme is the so-called free application of law, when the judge in principle applies his discretion and is not bound by any rules, or his choice of rules is discretionary, which is effectively the same thing.

It is quite clear that neither of the extreme alternatives is currently strictly applied. It is, however, questionable whether it is possible to speak about a prevailing approach to application of law, as it has only been twenty years since our legal order started to be created anew and the approach to application of law is always related to the participants, i.e. primarily the judges.

The "golden mean" between the ideologies of the bound application of law and the free judicial application of law is considered to be the so-called legal and rational application of law. *"The fundamental values of the ideology of rational and legal application of law are legality on the one hand and rationality on the other."*[245] This concept is deemed to maintain the difference between the creation of rules and the application of law by *"giving rational meaning to the old concept of finding law which is not contradictory to the concept of the so-called formation of law."*

In this approach such a concept could be really an ideal approach to application of law. Unfortunately it is not quite clear what is meant by "rationality" and what is its relation to legality. Z. Kühn, who develops this concept, points out that there are two different aspects. Therefore, it seems that rationality need not be identical with legality. This idea is slightly problematic because it would mean that the legislature creates irrational legal regulation. Therefore, it seems rather that in some cases the legal regulation results in irrational consequences and therefore it is necessary to correct such consequences by interpretation. In such a case there arises a conflict between rationality and legality. The conclusion may be considered rational but will be unlawful; such a conclusion then cannot be considered satisfactory.

The results of partial analysis of the current manner of judicial decision-making show that in an attempt to approximate the description of the realistic manner of application of law it is necessary to somehow change the traditional characteristics of the so-called bound and free application of law. The change may be related to the changing view of the content of law, which is not constituted exclusively by legal regulations *stricto sensu* (rules contained in legislative texts and those inferred from those texts), but rather by many other already mentioned elements such as legal principles. The bound approach to application of law is

---

[244]/ See for example Kühn, Z.: *Aplikace práva soudcem v éře středoevropského komunismu a transformace. Analýza příčin postkomunistické právní krize* [Application of Law by Judges in the Era of Central European Communism and Transformation. Analysis of Postcommunist Legal Crisis]. Praha: C. H. Beck, 2005, p. 4 and subs.

[245]/ Kühn, Z. *supra* at p. 13 and subs.

in the contemporary context understood as an approach which concentrates on the usual set of legal rules contained in texts of legal regulations (including their interpretive consequences), whereas the free approach may be seen as an approach acknowledging other sources of legally relevant rules.

It is, however, necessary to distinguish between two aspects of the issue. It is one thing to acknowledge the existence of material standards of decision-making (rules, principles, purposes, morals, equity), and it is another thing to find ways of dealing with these elements. Although it may be disputed, basically on formal reasons challenging their validity, whether material standards have relevance or support in the given system of law, or it may be disputed whether their existence is justified, even though the formal support is weak or absent at all, in case of the rules of using such material standards it is true that their formal support is very weak or missing and their validity may be based only on their acknowledgement which, of course, depends on the person applying the law to the specific case. Such procedural rules are usually much more important for the final result than individual material standards, because these procedural rules are able to completely exclude application of material rules including those that have strong formal validity.

The most questionable issue, from the point of view of the methodology of the application of law, is primarily the manner of dealing with the two types (i.e. material and formal) of the acknowledged legally relevant factors. We may say without any major doubts that the current status of law is affected by the relative freedom of methodological directives of the interpretation and application of law, which, of course, in many cases leads to disputable results of the application of law in the form of individual judicial decisions. In its complexity, this methodological freedom also contributes to the weakening of what was considered as the binding effect of statute on the judge in the traditional sense. Probably the biggest issue of this methodological freedom subsists in the fundamental difference of individual approaches or even their contradictory nature which results in the contradictory nature of conclusions as well as the absence of authority that would choose one of the models as valid[246] (this is related to the inexistence of formal criteria of determined relevance or validity). This may threaten to cause divergence of adopted conclusions, and inequality of the status of addressees of results of the processes of application of law.

Probably the most problematic are the approaches which seem to reverse the traditional sequence of importance of individual legally relevant rules, or those that clearly do not respect the traditional methodological directives of interpretation of law.

Jurisprudence or recent theories of legal interpretation and reasoning systematically introduce concepts which interfere with the traditional view of the binding effect of statute on the judge and, at the same time, interfere with the traditional methodology of the interpreta-

---

[246]/ This is similar to, for example, the Austrian rule-maker who worded in the General Civil Code the basic interpretation principles. A certain solution, even though perhaps disputable or reflecting methodological freedom, is offered in the manner of the General Civil Code through the draft of the new Civil Code which contains the following provision in s. 3 (2): *"A provision of a statute cannot be attributed other meaning than the meaning arising from the sense of the words in their mutual relation and from the clear intention of the legislature. Nobody, though, may invoke the words of a legal regulation against its meaning."*

tion and application of law. The most important and the most pronounced concepts may be identified and it is possible to analyse the extent of their admissibility. These concepts are quite similar in many respects. Their common feature is the belief that the solution of a legal problem does not arise from the text of legal regulations, but that the legal regulations must be interpreted, which may sometimes lead to unclear results. In some cases the results are clear but they are not in line with the desired direction of the person making the interpretation. It is not necessary to add that this is an idea which has been formed even before the solution of the problem starts to be sought, and usually the idea is based on purely individual personal preferences of the decision-maker. These preferences are so subjective that it is completely impossible to verify and objectivise them.

2.2.10 Jurisprudential alternatives to the weakening of normative relevance of legal texts

Adjudicating contra legem

Probably the most pronounced and the most frequent phenomenon is adjudication *contra legem*. These are cases when the meaning of a legal rule found in the text of a legal regulation is completely denied or is not respected at all. It is questionable which cases are actually adjudication *contra legem* in the true sense of the term. It is beyond any doubt that this phenomenon will not apply to cases when the meaning of one provision of a statute is not respected because this provision is inapplicable due to reasons arising out of systematic interpretation, when there is an exception of one legal rule from another legal rule, or when there is a conflict of legal rules with different legal force. We may, at the most, refer to such adjudication as *contra legem largo sensu*.

Adjudication *contra legem* in a more usual understanding may be caused, for example, by including a legal principle in the reasoning, or by taking another similar factor into account. However, it is questionable whether even in such cases it is really a procedure *contra legem*, because if we understand legal order as a system arranged by the content, which includes various normatively relevant elements, rather than just legal rules *stricto sensu*, it will be again a broad systematic approach taking into account various valid arguments.

We may conclude that something is adjudication *contra legem* in the real sense of the term when factors leading to a conclusion contradictory to the legal rule in the form in which it is expressed in the legal regulation (statute) show a minimum level or no validity at all within the given legal system.[247] The decision of whether a certain argument in the context of a certain legal order is or is not normatively valid, however, is up to the decision-maker. Such decision may be criticised, but the criticism will not realistically influence the result in a certain phase of the process of application of law (e.g. if it is the ultimate decision in the given matter). An example of the theoretical concept justifying similar approaches to the application of law is the classification of sources of law offered by A. Peczenik in *On Law and Reason* (1989), who classifies the legally relevant sources of rules into those that must be used, those that should be used and those which could be used.

---

[247] For example, an action for the payment of the amount in arrears will be dismissed because the defendant is a member of a minority ethnic group, which is certainly an argument which has no support whatsoever in law (it is not excluded that it could find support in the future in the form of some kind of positive discrimination, etc.).

The majority of current theories defending approaches characterised by a methodological freedom which effectively result in the weakening of the importance of law, are based on principles acceptable from the value point of view, which can be agreed upon without major objections. Their potential criticism is therefore, from the very beginning, weakened by the fact that it cannot, if it does not want to lose credibility, question these principles because of their assumed general acceptance.[248] This is not to say that these principles are incorrect or are not to be respected; they undoubtedly cannot be omitted. The problem is the fact that these principles are not invariable, and they are not of an absolute nature. The change of these principles related to, for example, a change of social regime may result in generally unacceptable consequences even if the statutes do not change. In such a case the only possible protection is the unchanged text of the statute interpreted irrespective of its axiological background. It is obvious that the final decision is again up to those who apply the law and the key issue consists of finding a way to set certain limits for their activity.

The so-called loopholes in law

Another situation when the relevance of statute may be weakened is the so-called loophole in law. The concept is interpreted in various ways and, on the one hand, there are opinions denying the existence of such a phenomenon,[249] and, on the other hand, there are attempts to create a more detailed classification of the problem.[250]

The assertion of the existence of loopholes in law is usually linked with the idea of completeness of the legal order, which provides solution for every single case, and on the other hand with the requirement representing the cornerstone of all modern legal orders, which is the duty of the judge to decide the case before him (if possible) according to law. The judge therefore must decide even if the legal regulation is unclear or does not exist at all (or at least seems not to exist). This creates a tension because if the judge is to act according to rules which in a certain specific case do not exist, he either cannot decide according to rules at all (absolute discretion), or he must somehow fill the loophole, i.e. must find the rules for his decision outside of their usual source.

However, considering the existence of loopholes in law, the above mentioned context would be extremely limiting in two ways. First, cases when the legal regulation provides criteria for a decision but the criteria are considered inappropriate or insufficient are considered loopholes in law. Second, the cases when there is no need for an authoritative decision but it is necessary to reach the solution of a question may also be considered as loopholes.

The first group, classified depending on an approach to the existence of loopholes in law, is based on the opinion that it is possible to identify loopholes in law only *de lege ferenda*, and not *de lege lata*.[251] The necessary accessory to this idea is differentiation of individual legal

---

[248]/ For example, it is claimed that specific decisions are to be in accordance with prevailing morals, generally accepted justice, should protect the freedom of an individual, equal status of people, good faith, etc.

[249]/ This refers to typically pure legal science resolving the possible absence of legal regulation by a negative statement.

[250]/ Rüthers, B.: Dotváření práva soudci [Judicial Formation of Law]. *Soudce* 8/2003, p. 3: *"Every legal order, usually even every statute contains loopholes."*

[251]/ Boguszak, J. – Čapek, J. – Gerloch, A.: *Teorie práva* [Theory of Law]. Praha: Eurolex Bohemia, 2001, p. 100.

branches depending on the methods of legal regulation which play an important role in assessing the alleged loopholes. In private law the inexistent legal regulation may be created autonomously by the parties to a legal relation. Should they fail to do so and no explicit regulation exist, the case is decided by analogy the admissibility of which is confirmed by the legal order itself[252] (refusing to decide is inadmissible *denegatio iustitiae*). In public law it applies that state power may be exercised in cases within the limits and in a manner specified by statute, so that if a certain duty is not imposed by statute, it cannot be enforced. Therefore, loopholes in law according to this concept do not exist. A typical advocate of this concept was Hans Kelsen.

The advocates of the opposite approach admitting the existence of loopholes in law, distinguish between two types of loopholes:[253] technical loopholes (also referred to as genuine) and teleological (axiological, recognition) loopholes. The former describe situations when the legal rule does not provide a solution at all to a certain case which itself is legally relevant, so they include situations when the occurrence of a legal case is regulated but the solution of such case is not regulated. These loopholes can be solved only by a factual procedure (the solution usually cannot be found even by a very broad analogy); possibly with respect to the reclusiveness of the legal branch it does not have to be solved at all.[254]

A procedure which relativises the validity of a legal regulation is adopted when addressing the loopholes of the latter type. The common feature of these loopholes is the belief that a particular legal regulation is insufficient when a certain real-life case is regulated and another is not regulated and it seems that it should be regulated. To these cases Kelsen's definition applies according to which these "loopholes are merely another expression for differentiation between positive law and order considered to be better, more just and more correct."[255] B. Rüthers expresses his opinion on the problematic nature of the concept of such loopholes from a different point of view: *"The argument of a loophole is particularly appropriate to loosen the constitutional requirement of the binding effect of statutes on judges or for the judges to get rid of this requirement altogether. Not infrequently it entices the courts, when they are not satisfied with the legal regulation of a particular matter, not to apply the statute that is unsatisfactory for them and to start 'searching for a loophole'."*[256] Irrespective of which understanding of loopholes in law we may choose, Kelsen's definition and Rüthers's additional criticism are fitting.

---

[252]/ The order to proceed according to analogy may be on the one hand considered as an admission of potential loopholes in legal regulation, and on the other hand it may be a remedy for these anticipated loopholes.

[253]/ The terminology of course differs. See e.g. Boguszak, J. – Čapek, J. – Gerloch, A. *supra* at p. 100. Holländer, P.: Mezera v zákoně, § 7 o. z. o. a ryzí nauka právní (Poznámky k úvaze Franze Bydlinského) [A Loophole in Statute, s. 7 of the General Civil Code and the Pure Theory of Law. Comments on the Contemplation by Franz Bydlinsky]. In: Machalová, T. (ed.): *Místo normativní teorie v soudobém právním myšlení (K odkazu Františka Weyra a Hanse Kelsena)* [The Position of Normative Theory in the Contemporary Legal Thinking. Legacy of František Weyr and Hans Kelsen]. Brno: Masarykova univerzita, 2003, p. 130 and subs. Canaris, C. W.: *Die Feststellung von Lücken im Gesetz*. Berlin: Duncker & Humblot, 1964, p. 132 and subs. Kühn, Z. *supra* at p. 200 and subs.

[254]/ For example, we could mention a provision of a criminal act that would define the body of the crime and not the punishment for such a crime. The punishment then could not be imposed due to the relevant provisions of the Charter.

[255]/ Kelsen, H.: *Ryzí nauka právní. Metoda a základní pojmy* [Pure Theory of Law. Method and Basic Concepts]. Praha – Brno: Orbis, 1933, p. 45.

[256]/ Rüthers, B. *supra* at p. 6.

The so-called teleological reduction

While the above mentioned types of situations which may represent a conflict between the text of the statute and its purpose can be relatively well explained and understood, the concept of the so-called teleological reduction belongs rather to the extreme cases of freeing oneself from statute – in this case not from the text of the statute, but from everything which may be presented in the statute including its purpose.

The so-called teleological reduction causes a legal rule contained in statute to be excluded due to certain values or principles. It is therefore an opposite case to teleological loopholes, i.e. the case when a legal regulation offers a certain solution (in case of loopholes such a solution does not exist), but this solution seems to be not only incorrect (then it would rather be a loophole) but rather redundant. The wording of the legal regulation is therefore broader than required by legal principles, values and purposes on which this legal regulation is based and the regulation does not contain the rule which would in accordance with the teleology of the relevant legal regulation stipulate an exception of overly broad legal regulation. The consequence of teleological reduction is the exclusion of such a dictated solution. Similar to the case of teleological loopholes, it is necessary to differentiate the reasons why we resort to teleological reduction and when it is justifiable. If a legal regulation seems to be overly broad for a certain type of cases, it may be because it does not regulate other similar cases sufficiently. Then there are two possible solutions: either to reduce this extension or, on the contrary, to choose an extensive approach to the other curtailed group of cases (which in this respect represents a group subject to a loophole). There may also be cases when an impression of extension as such is created, i.e. the extension is not based on comparison with similar cases but is based on the legal regulation itself.

2.2.11 Instead of conclusion: application and interpretation of law *lege artis*

The above described approaches are not utilitarian concepts adopted on an ad hoc basis. On the contrary, they are relatively thoroughly detailed in theory, and their practical applications are often based on an effort to justify their permissibility (probably because of the awareness of problems related to these approaches).

What is in this context a procedure *lege artis*? Considering the fact that various approaches have their similarly ardent advocates and critics, is it currently possible to identify any of the approaches, the contradictory nature of which is clear, as procedure *lege artis* with the consequence that other procedures are *non lege artis*? If procedure *lege artis* is to mean a procedure that is in accordance with usual generally acceptable methods in a certain branch of science, then it is necessary to first raise the question of whether law actually has any rules like that. The answer to this question leads to rather pessimistic conclusions.

We may therefore assume that rules constituting *lex artis* are formulated differently by the approach of the so-called bound application of law on the one hand, and by the methodology of free application of law on the other hand. This takes us back to the issues of appropriateness of various approaches to law, which reflects considerations of the extent of freedom of the judge in his decision-making, the importance of legal principles and also values.

An important argument in favour of a certain methodological procedure would be its formal embeddedness (to varying degrees) in the legal order. In such an environment it is possible to search for procedures *lege artis*. Basically every legal system when creating legal regulation relies on certain manners of interpretation and application. In the system of statutory law certain principles of interpretation and application are anticipated by the legislature, which, when creating a new legal regulation, implicitly relies on certain procedures of its interpretation. The core of the procedure *lege artis* is therefore the one that is relied upon when the law is created. If a set of such rules is embedded in positive law, then only such procedures are the procedures *lege artis*. Even in case of lack of embeddedness in positive law, such rules can be inferred from the logic of the legal regulation. For example, it is possible to consider the so-called linguistic interpretation as the starting point because the legislature communicated the rules of legal regulation in a natural language. If the legislature assumed that the key means of interpretation was the search of the purpose intended by the legislature, it would probably proceed otherwise.[257]

It has been indicated in many above presented examples that legal theory disposes of various often contradictory procedures from the point of view of procedure and result, which can be used in the interpretation of legal texts. It is clear that with an appropriate combination of these it is possible to reach any desired result. On the one hand, it is possible to exclude applicability of a certain provision referring to its "extreme injustice", which is understood axiomatically, or it is possible to carry out the slightly more acceptable at first sight teleological reduction. On the other hand, it is possible to apply the same legal regulation extensively to cases to which, according to its linguistic expression, it does not apply; this can be justified by an alleged teleological loophole.

Therefore, it is possible to consider as the core of interpretation procedures *lege artis* only those procedures the relevance of which relies on formal validity, which may be either express or implied. The basic rule of interpretation carried out *lege artis* is the acceptance of the requirement to refrain from tendencies to carry out a corrective interpretation of the normative text. It may be assumed that in the conditions of a legal order created by a legitimate democratic legislature (or constitution-makers), it is not necessary to be concerned that law interpreted with respect to this requirement would become "the tool of estrangement and absurdity".

2.3 ANTINOMY IN IMPLEMENTING JUSTICE AND LEGAL CERTAINTY IN CONTEMPORARY LAW

The practical implementation of the values of justice and legal certainty, forming the basis of contemporary law, presents numerous problems in creating as well as applying law. This is caused by the fact that the requirements of these two ideals often collide or exclude each other.[258] The purpose of the following lines will be to contemplate the confrontation of these values in legislative and judicial practice at the beginning of the 21st century, the impact of the confrontation upon the form of legal regulation (tendency towards legislation or

---

[257] The question is how. For example, it would help to find the purpose of a statute by clearly declaring the purpose in its introduction (of course, even the purpose expressed in this way would be interpreted), or possibly the legislature could pay careful attention to the thoroughness of explanatory reports.

[258] Let us mention, for example, a legal regulation using an exhaustive or demonstrative hypothesis of regulations.

judge-made law) and the style of judicial decision-making (the extent to which judges are bound by the law), as well as the theoretical aspects of the confrontation.

2.3.1 Statutory or living justice or a compromise between the two?

Legal thinking on the continent has traditionally preferred statutory justice over living justice, i.e. regulating the life of the society by means of general rules contained in laws over finding justice on a case by case basis.[259] However in practice, statutory justice providing a higher level of legal certainty replaced living justice only in modern times. In the Middle Ages custom and judge-made law dominated over statutes.[260]

The conflict between statutory justice, representing legal certainty, and living justice, formed in the dynamics of social relations, seemed to have been resolved by positivist identification of law and statutes, but it is currently again becoming an issue.

1. Contemporary modern society is extremely dynamic and therefore difficult to regulate. By the time the legislature intervenes, the social reality is another step ahead. This brings up questions whether the legislation is actually able to solve current problems in an appropriate manner and whether law is functional. At the same time the complexity of social relations is growing. It is becoming more and more difficult for the legislature to react to the growing complexity and the related contingencies. Even casuistic legal regulations usually do not cover all the essential aspects and the law lacks continuity. In such a situation there is no choice but to support the lagging statutory justice with the living justice represented by judge-made law. As a result, judges have to play the role of the legislature in many respects by filling the loopholes in law and correcting insufficiencies of statutes. The courts are often forced to substitute for the work of the legislature; however, at the same time they anticipate such work and act in advance of it in those cases when the legislature becomes later inspired by the judge-made law or incorporates it in statutes.[261]

2. However, living justice is not always progressing. Many countries witness legislative optimism – a belief that every problem can be resolved by legislation: it is enough to adopt a legal regulation and everything is in order. In practice such a trend results in severe growth in the number of laws. This is related to the undesirable effect of growing instability and inconsistency of legislation. Legislative expansion, primarily expansion of casuistic regulations, results in the exclusion of the role of courts of justice and administrative bodies as the bodies forming the law in the course of the application process.[262] In recent years these tendencies take the form of officially planned "legislative flurry".

[259]/ More in Tomsa, B.: *Kapitoly z dějin filosofie práva a státu* [Chapters from the History of Philosophy of Law and State]. Praha: Karolinum, 2005, p. 31 and subs.

[260]/ Stieber, M.: *Dějiny soukromého práva v střední Evropě* [History of Private Law in Central Europe]. Praha: proprietary publication, 1930, p. 126 and subs.

[261]/ This phenomenon is researched by legislative sociology. More on the topic e.g. Rehbinder, M.: *Rechtssoziologie*. Berlin – New York: Walter de Gruyter, 1993.

[262]/ Kysela, J.: Zákonodárný proces v České republice jako forma racionálního právního diskursu? [Legislative Process in the Czech Republic as a Form of Rational Legal Discourse?] In: Vostrá, L. – Čermáková, J. (eds.): *Otázky tvorby práva v České republice, Polské republice a Slovenské republice* [Issues of Creating Law in the Czech Republic, Polish Republic and Slovak Republic]. Plzeň: Aleš Čeněk, 2005, p. 69 and subs.

3. From a cross-cultural perspective it seems that there is some kind of "reconciliation" of statutory and living justice. The traditional contrast between statutory law dominating on our continent and judge-made or case law prevailing in Anglo-American law has recently become more balanced. The role of judge-made law (sometimes incorrectly referred to as precedents) is growing in continental law, and statutes are gaining on importance in Anglo-American law (e.g. codes in U.S. law). This phenomenon is a consequence of extensive acculturation of both systems of law. In both legal cultures, in spite of the traditionally different manner of finding justice and legal certainty in practice, legislation and judge-made law cooperate. On our continent, statutes are formed by established practice of the courts that is not binding in terms of form. Although the practice of courts is not binding, it is nevertheless taken into account due to its persuasiveness and the pressure of decision-making in several instances. In the Anglo-American system of law legislation is formed by the system of mostly binding precedents. Such precedents are then considered to be the actual source of law.[263]

All three processes have one thing in common: they change the established relationship between the legislative and the judicial power on the continent. While the judicial power is strengthened in the first and the third situations described above, in the second case the legislative power gains in strength. In general the judicial power is becoming stronger. We may welcome the strengthening of the judicial power particularly in those situations where it helps the society cope with deficiencies of the legislative activity. Yet the process should not lead to the prevalence of the judicial power over the legislative power. It should continue to be true that the legislative power creates law and the judicial power applies law and perhaps forms it to some extent. In doing so the judicial power is bound by statutes. The following thoughts will focus on the reasoning of this opinion.

2.3.2 Neither bound nor free application of law?

Modern theory of law often claims that in theory and practice there are two opposing paradigms of judicial application of law: the ideologies of bound and free application of law. The former is based on the principle that the judge is strictly bound by law, the latter advocates free judicial decision-making.[264] This idea is, however, misleading in many respects. In its pure form such a contradiction has never existed and it does not exist today, neither in the field of theory, nor in practice. The concept of the ideology of application of law is also questionable. This concept has been inappropriately borrowed from the sphere of political sciences and treats judges as beings completely lacking independence – as victims of their education, political interests and public expectations. What is the real status of judicial application of law?[265]

It is clear that the 19th and the 20th centuries saw a gradual loosening of the originally strict tie between the judge and the law. Judges gained the opportunity to construe law

---

263/ Knapp, V. *supra* at p. 95.
264/ Kühn, Z. *supra* at p. 232 and subs.
265/ For more details see Maršálek, P.: *Právo a společnost* [The Law and the Society]. Praha: Auditorium, 2008, p. 158 and subs.

and, eventually, also to form law. This partially modified the previously respected requirement arising out of the division of powers that judges should not decide in a general and normative manner. Some schools of legal theory went even further and required free judicial decision-making. However, they did not become a majority opinion. Theory and practice continued to respect that the judge should be bound by law. Since the 1930s there has been a thesis put forward that over some time laws become wrapped in judicial decisions, principles and conclusions of the doctrine that judges should respect and apply in reasoning their judgments.

The principle of a judge being bound by statute has retained its axiomatic nature till the present times. The reasons are clear. Laws are a practical expression of sovereignty of the people. They are adopted by a legislative body which expresses the general will by means of laws. The laws carry democratic legitimacy which is passed on to the judges' decisions. It is just as important that the laws identify the boundaries of freedom and guarantee legal certainty. In a modern democratic society everybody may do what is not prohibited by law and public bodies may proceed only under, and within the limits set by, the law. Laws define the rights and duties of the addressees of legal regulations.[266]

The principle of judges being bound by statute retains its importance even in the course of structural changes in law currently taking place. The domestic law is increasingly penetrated with treaties and sources of European law which are awarded a privileged position over statutes; nevertheless the vast majority of law is governed by statutes. This is why in most cases international law is not applied due to an overwhelming prevalence of statutory regulation even though the present Constitution explicitly states that the courts are subordinated to statutes and the preferred treaties.

The above lines may make us believe that the position of the principle that judges are bound by law is unswerving. The opposite is true. In spite of its importance and clear correctness, this principle is often questioned or completely rejected. A role in this is played by the sometimes excessively emancipating efforts of justice, or enchantment with Anglo-American law and doctrines of legal realism (which claim that it is the judge who decides what the law is on the issue). It is a paradox that even a part of legal theory places judges beyond the law.[267]

Calls for removing or loosening the principle of judges being bound by statute is often paradoxically combined with an effort to introduce the system of precedents and attempts to refine legal reasoning. The fact that judges are bound by laws enjoying democratic legitimacy is perceived as excessively restrictive on courts. The rigidity and lack of flexibility of the system of precedents, which cannot be compared to our system of established practice of the courts which offers the possibility of derogation, is being overlooked. In the effort of making legal reasoning more "precise" the laws become easy victims of standards of the legal order that are much less certain than the laws themselves (legal principles and values).

---

[266] Gerloch, A.: *Teorie práva* [Theory of Law]. Plzeň: Vydavatelství a nakladatelství Aleš Čeněk, 2004, p. 220.
[267] See Kysela, J.: Kdopak by se „soudcovského státu" bál? [Who is Afraid of "Judicial State"?] In: Šimíček, V. (ed.): *Role nejvyšších soudů v evropských ústavních systémech – čas pro změnu?* [The Role of Supreme Courts in European Constitutional Systems – Time for Change?] Brno: Masarykova univerzita, 2007.

All these tendencies – with the exception of calls for improved legal reasoning – must be rejected. Their protagonists want bad things for bad reasons. They deviate from domestic traditions proven by practice, primarily from the principle of *judex jus dicit inter partes*, and would not result in a decisive comparative advantage. At the end they would result in abandoning the law as a means of enforcement of justice and legal certainty and forming a judicial state (or judgeocracy?) replacing parliamentary democracy. The way to improve the operation of our law subsists in improving the work of legislative bodies and the judiciary rather than in strengthening the independence of judges and blindly following Anglo-American examples.

2.3.3 Wording of the law v. *ratio legis*

The meaning of the concept of the judge being bound by statute may be perceived in a varying scope. In a narrow meaning the concept refers to the binding character of the wording of the law, yet in a wider meaning it refers to the binding nature of the intent or purpose of the law (*ratio legis*). In the widest possible understanding the binding character of laws or statutes becomes a binding character of law. All these interpretations of the principle of judges being bound by statute have their pros and cons. Legal theoreticians and practitioners include advocates as well as critics of each of the interpretations.

To construe the principle as judges being bound strictly by the wording of the law means to adhere to the letter of the law and to construe the regulation primarily using linguistic interpretation. Such an approach guarantees a high level of legal certainty; however, it may prove to be limiting or insufficient. A decision rendered on the basis of such interpretation may be purely formal – unjust or ineffective, or completely absurd due to insufficiency of the language or poor expression of the legislature. It is impossible to use this approach in complex cases of application of law. In such cases the matter cannot be decided only by relying on the wording of the regulation, simply because the wording does not support the decision at all (e.g. in cases of legal loopholes), or the wording may be unclear, conflicting, etc.[268]

The second approach provides a lower level of legal certainty, although on the other hand it enables achieving a more just and effective decision. It does not rely solely on the letter of the law but also on the so called *ratio legis*. Such an approach involves not just standard methods of interpretation (linguistic, logical and systematic interpretation) but also the above-standard methods (historical, teleological and comparative interpretation), which enable the judges to take into account primarily teleological, axiomatic and functional aspects of the law or its provisions.

The third approach in which the binding character of the statutes is substituted by the binding character of law is far too extensive and in fact it is fictitious. We can hardly consider a strictly binding character of legal principles, for example, that are often conflicting as a matter of fact. This is not to say that the judge should not argue using legal principles and values. The opposite is true. However, we can hardly construe that anybody can be strictly bound by these standards.

---

[268]/ Kramer, E. A.: *Juristische Methodenlehre*. Bern – München – Wien: Stämpfli, 2005, p. 173 and subs.

Legal practice spontaneously discovered the benefits and deficits of various approaches to bindingness of the statute on a judge and, in accordance with rationality, took the route of taking into account the wording of the law while at the same time respecting the purpose of the law. This means that the practice chose a less restrictive interpretation of the concept of judge being bound by statute. It is a model of legal and rational application of law.

2.3.4 Justice and legal certainty v. current value and epistemological scepticism in legal thinking and sciences

A difficult search for the balance between justice and legal certainty is not just an issue of legal practice. Legal thinking and legal sciences are also involved to a certain extent. The representatives of these disciplines generally took the view that law helps to at least partially fulfil both the values in the society. By doing so the law itself becomes a social value.[269]

Recently jurisprudence and legal thinking have started to be increasingly subject to value and epistemological scepticism as a result of which the doctrine loses its ability to be a "guiding principle" of legal practice. It is the case primarily because the value basis of law as well as law itself as a means of enforcing justice and legal certainty are being questioned. It is also reflected in the fact that judicial decision-making is often referred to as arbitrariness depending on the person of a judge and on the context of application.

Questioning and rejecting the value basis of modern law, resulting in the requirement for the reconstruction of law and the society as a whole, have been the main features of the Critical Legal Studies (CLS) movement for many years. This school presents a social critique of the legal system. According to this school of thought, law serves the rich and the powerful and is radically unfair.[270]

The postmodernists have introduced criticisms of law and its value basis from a cultural and social point of view. They partially relate to the CLS movement but take a much more sceptical position to law. Their programme is the deconstruction of law. They condemn modern law as a relict of obsolete modern period, as expression of logonomocentrism (dictatorship of law and reason) and European cultural ethnocentrism.[271]

Under a purely economic analysis of law, law is merely a function of economy. Neoliberal supporters of this school of thought consider legal regulation as a more or less inevitable evil that hinders free development of market powers (confines markets and represents considerable costs). Law, they say, also ignores principles of economic efficiency.[272]

We can hear from various sources that law lacks system, flexibility, is uncertain and that it is alienated from real life and therefore it is not functional. Some authors speak about the crisis of law as a social phenomenon. Others predict the end of the state respecting the rule

---

[269]/ See Boháčková, R.: *Dějiny právního myšlení* [History of Legal Thinking]. Brno: Masarykova univerzita, 1994.

[270]/ Kubů, L. et al.: *Dějiny právní filozofie* [History of Legal Philosophy]. Olomouc: Univerzita Palackého, 2002, p. 166 and subs.

[271]/ For more on the topic see Přibáň, J.: *Suverenita, právo a legitimita* [Sovereignty, Law and Legitimacy]. Praha: Karolinum, 1997, p. 187 and subs.

[272]/ See Šíma, J.: *Ekonomie a právo* [Economics and Law]. Praha: Oeconomica, 2004. See Holländer, P.: Bajka o motorkáři (a o Donu Juanovi a Velkém Sběrateli) [A Fable of a Biker]. In: Mikule, V. – Suchánek, R. (eds.): *Pocta Zdeňku Jičínskému k 80. narozeninám* [Tribute to Zdeněk Jičínský on his 80th Birthday]. Praha: ASPI, 2009, p. 161 and subs.

of law, because, they say, the idea of such a state is burdened by insurmountable contradictions. The grimmest vision says that this is a period of the twilight of law.[273]

All these criticisms of modern law and its value basis are extreme and unfounded. They often rely on a clearly speculative basis. They are an expression of legal nihilism and they move legal science away from its main purpose, which is to assist legal practice.

Similarly negative is the impact of some schools of thought dealing with judicial decision-making. It is possible to accept the opinion of legal hermeneutics pointing out the influence of so called pre-understanding in the interpretation and application of law by judges.[274] On the other hand, we cannot accept the teaching of American legal realism, which questions the importance of written law as well as precedents for judicial decision-making and, on the contrary, overemphasizes the influence of extraordinary factors on the result of the procedure. Some representatives of this school do not even believe in the possibility of finding the facts of the case. The judicial decision according to them cannot be anticipated at all. Behavioural jurisprudence is trying to question the independence and objectiveness of judges by empirical research.[275]

What can be added to these theories? Mainly it may be concluded that they are subjective and misleading. Their authors have converted the application of law into dictatorship. They completely forgot about the fact that a judge is bound by statute, they forgot about the institution of judicial independence and *lex artis* that governs the conduct of judges. Justice and legal certainty mean nothing to them.

The outlined picture could lead us to lose the belief in modern legal sciences and legal thinking. However, the situation is not as bad as it may seem at first sight. The opinions of sceptics do not have so many followers and their opponents are able to present a meaningful alternative.[276]

2.3.5 Conclusions
Formation of modern law is influenced by conflicting demands of justice and legal certainty. The development has reached a point of balance between the systems of statutory and living justice. Practice implemented the middle route between bound and free application of law. This balance between the requirements of justice and those of legal certainty shows considerable rationality and therefore viability. This is why the balance will probably survive all the attempts to disturb it – including those inspired by Anglo-American law and value or epistemological scepticism.

---

[273]/ Hurdík, J.: *Institucionální pilíře soukromého práva v dynamice vývoje společnosti* [Institutional Pillars of Private Law in the Dynamics of the Social Development]. Praha: C. H. Beck, 2007, p. 7 and subs.

[274]/ See Gizbert-Studnicki, T.: Der Vorverständnisbegriff in der juristischen Hermeneutik. *ARSP* 4/1987.

[275]/ For more details see Kubů, L. et al. *supra* at p. 153 and subs.

[276]/ In addition to Kramer's work *supra*, see also Larenz, K.: *Methodenlehre der Rechtswissenschaft*. Berlin – Heidelberg – New York: Springer, 1979. Bydlinski, F.: *Juristische Methodenlehre und Rechtsbegriff*. Wien: Springer, 1991. Zippelius, R.: *Juristische Methodenlehre*. München: Beck, 2005. In the Czech Republic we should mention Melzer, F.: *Metodologie nalézání práva* [Methods of Finding Law]. Brno: Tribun EU, 2008.

2.4 POLYCENTRISM AND PLURALISM IN LAW

2.4.1 Polycentrism in current law versus pyramidal structure of the legal order in the conception of traditional sovereignty

The following text does not have the ambition of providing guidelines for solving substantial issues of the development of law at the beginning of the 21st century; it rather aims at summarizing various problems and reflections and at opening them for further research and thought. It represents an introduction into the subject, and it is divided into three parts. The first part establishes the premises and reminds one of the traditional (or, maybe, conservative) approach to the significance of law for state sovereignty and the traditional hierarchical, or pyramidal, structure of law. The second part is based on the motto *"tempora mutantur – times change"* and it demonstrates the gradual transformation of the traditional conception of the hierarchical legal order of a sovereign state – in other words, it explains the issue of "polycentrism" and endeavours to decipher the somewhat complicated title of this subchapter. The third part outlines some problems which have arisen in current Czech law as a result of the transformation of traditional pyramidal structure of the legal order within the conception of traditional sovereignty into polycentrism.

This introduction is then followed by reflections which provide a more detailed analysis of some phenomena and processes which lead to the changes in perception of the legal order on the cusp of the third millennium.

Traditionally, law was understood as a complex system of generally binding legal rules issued by public bodies and enforceable by them. This traditional conception of law was based on the idea of a sovereign state beyond which there is no other power. The state, as a sovereign, determined the rules of the game within the state "in its own image".

However, law was never static; it always reflected changing human ideas of what is beneficial, good and just, of the scope of natural freedom and of the degree of state interference with the life of an individual and society, and of the requisite legal grounding for the exercise of public authority as well as the forms of such legal grounding. The ever quicker development of the society, science and technology in the 20th century must have left its clear traces in the development of law. The same applies to the impacts of various forms of public authority and its tasks in varied types of state (liberal democratic, authoritarian, totalitarian, social or post-colonial) as well as in the groupings, such as the European Communities and the European Union.

The Constitution of the Czech Republic of 16th December 1992 confirmed the traditional conception of law by determining the conditions for the creation of the traditional complex system of generally binding legal rules – constitutional laws, (ordinary) laws, statutory measures of the Senate, decrees of the Government, decisions of the President of the Republic, administrative regulations and generally binding regulations of regions and communities – as well as their mutual relations. These generally binding legal rules can be hierarchically (pyramidally) arranged according to their legal force: the Constitution is on the top of the pyramid and by-laws are at the bottom. This conception of law can be labelled as traditional and it evolved and was applied in the long term mainly within the

European continental legal culture, including Czechoslovakia. But even the long-term application did not remove all problems and arguable issues connected with the mentioned pyramidal structure. We can point, for instance, to the relationship between Constitutional and "ordinary" laws, the solution of non-existence of laws envisaged in the Constitution, the relationship between laws and secondary legislation, implementing regulations, etc. Their listing or analyses are not the subject matter of this paper, or rather, they are not directly connected with our topic.

The Constitution of the Czech Republic includes, or confirms, two "foreign elements" in this principally closed legal order with pyramidal (hierarchical) structure – according to the original Article 10, international treaties on human rights and fundamental freedoms were directly binding and took precedence over statutes[277] and according to Article 89 (2), enforceable decisions of the Constitutional Court are binding on all bodies and persons, i.e. they apply *erga omnes*. The Constitution itself "half-opens" the door to polycentrism in the form of several (three) foci of law – generally binding legal rules, international treaties and the judgments of the Constitutional Court.

The Constitution claims in Article 1 that the CR is an independent (thus sovereign) state, but what does this concept denote? Does sovereignty really mean the situation when there is no other power above the given entity? Who is to be the possessor of sovereignty – the state, the people, the nation, the citizen, law, the Parliament, and what does it actually mean? Is there a set of state competences required so that we can call such a state sovereign? Or can there be sovereignty without competences? Or can we be content with "just" the formal elements (international recognition, state symbols, etc.) for a state to be a state? Has the sovereignty of the Czech Republic been changing in the context of ongoing globalization, universal conception of human rights standards or its accession to the EU?

A sovereign state has the right, or the duty, to regulate social relationships by its legal order. But can they be regulated in whatever way it sees proper? Since the CR has a "tandem" of the two most fundamental Constitutional instruments – the Constitution of the CR and the Charter of Fundamental Rights and Freedoms, the Constitution (Constitutional Act of the Czech National Council No. 1/1993 Sb.) can be perceived as the instrument which represents sovereignty. No state would probably object if the Czech Constitution provided for, for instance, a one-chamber Parliament, direct presidential election, a different number of Constitutional Court Justices and its narrower jurisdiction, a three-tier system of general courts, different names and a different number of higher regional self-governing units, etc. The situation of the Charter of Fundamental Rights and Freedoms is a bit more complicated. The Charter represents the acknowledgement of certain democratic standards of human and civil rights protection and the CR would not "get away with it" in the European or world community if it did not respect these standards. The Parliament thus enjoys much less sovereignty with respect to the Charter than with respect to the Constitution. There is

---

[277]/ Article 10 of the Constitution of the CR, in effect from 1st January 1993 to 31st May 2002: *"Ratified and promulgated treaties on human rights and fundamental freedoms, by which the Czech Republic is bound, shall be directly binding and take preference over statutes."* For comments on this Article see, for instance, Pavlíček, V. – Hřebejk, J.: *Ústava a ústavní řád České republiky* [The Constitution and the Constitutional Order of the Czech Republic]. Vol. 1, 2nd ed., Praha: Linde, 1998, p. 78 and subs.

but one proverbial step from this statement to the question: who is, in reality, the creator of human rights regulation?

In the seventeen years of effect of the Constitution of the CR, there have been other shifts in the conception of the one time exclusively pyramidal structure of generally binding legal regulation, which came in two main "waves". They both have strengthened the position of international treaties, or international law, or the law of the EU.

The first wave was the so-called "Euro-amendment" – Constitutional Act No. 395/2001 Sb. – namely the formulation of the principle in Article 1 (2) of the Constitution of the CR, according to which "*the Czech Republic shall observe its obligations resulting from international law*", and the amendment of Article 10 of the Constitution which, in comparison to the original Article 10, brought substantial extension of the scope of international treaties which are an immediate part of the legal order of the CR and take precedence over laws in application.

The second wave was the accession of the CR to the EU on 1st May 2004 and the requirement to observe obligations resulting from the membership for the CR.

The Euro-amendment, or Article 1 (2), has opened the legal order of the Czech Republic even more and, besides international treaties, other sources of international law, as they are defined by international law itself,[278] have become involved. By the accession of the CR to the EU, "autonomous" EU law has become another focus without the Constitution making the slightest suggestion of their relationship, or the primacy of "general" international law over EU law or the other way round. The guidelines to the solution of this conflict are not provided by the fundamental instrument of the CR but they will probably result from EU law, or from court decisions made outside the CR.

A reduction of the importance of traditional pyramidal structure of the Czech legal order, or the abatement of the role of its main creator, the Parliament, was caused by further flexibility of judicial interpretation (or rather creation) of law. In this context we should not omit the "famous" judgments of the Constitutional Court of CR: judgment No. 403/2002 Sb., which extended the concept of the "Constitutional Order of the CR" to include all ratified and promulgated international treaties on human rights and fundamental freedoms; judgment No. 154/2006 Sb., known as "sugar quotas" judgment; and judgment No. 446/2008 Sb. on the petition to assess the compatibility of Lisbon Treaty and the Constitutional order of the CR.

Thus we can talk of four foci of law:

1. traditional, generally binding legal regulation passed by public bodies of the CR,
2. judge-made law, produced mainly by the Constitutional Court of the CR,
3. international treaties and other sources of international law, including decisions of international courts, and
4. EU law, including decisions of EU courts.

The basic framework of traditional pyramidal structure of national law is laid down by the Constitution of the CR. Even the Constitution, however, is no match for the hectic legisla-

---

[278]/ International customs are also an indisputable source of international law.

tive activity of lawmakers and the executive. The scope of regulation, the number of legal rules and their instability caused by frequent amendments could surely become a topic for an independent scholarly research. Just to illustrate the situation – in 2005, 554 regulations, notifications and decisions were published in the Collection of Laws (Sb.). 101 of them had the force of law, of which only 25 were complete (new) enactments; the rest were direct amendments (*the Act to alter Act on* …, or *the Act to alter some Acts in consequence of the passage of Act on* …). In 2006, 626 items were published in the Collection of Laws, 139 were laws and only 38 of them were complete (new) enactments. In 2007, "only" 393 items were published, 65 having the force of law, out of which only 9 were complete (new) enactments.[279]

Such excessive activity must necessarily establish conflicts in the legal order, diminish the possibility that laws would be accepted by their addressees, and paradoxically it also undermines legal certainty. The consistency of the legal order is an especially sensitive issue in case of overlaps of national, international and European law.

Not even the term "Constitutional Order of the CR", whose content should be the basis of the legal system, is flawless. Does the principle *lex posterior derogat priori* apply within the order, to its individual regulations? It probably does. Does the relationship *lex generalis* and *lex specialis* apply within the order, to its individual regulations? It probably does. Then the Constitutional order itself represents a specific "legal order" (a specific legal order within the legal order of the Czech Republic). The Constitutional order was "weeded" in the course of its more than fifteen-year development by two one-shot Constitutional Acts,[280] which can only have the weight of precedents at present, but they cannot be applied in practice since they were "consummated". Can we be absolutely sure today which legislation the Constitutional order of the CR is composed of? And the situation was made even more complicated by the judgment of the Constitutional Court No. 403/2002 Sb. where, in the reasoning, the Court included also international treaties on human rights and fundamental freedoms in the Constitutional order. If the legal rules of the Constitutional order represent the Constitution of the CR in a wider sense, and if international treaties on human rights and fundamental freedoms do create a part of the Constitutional order, then the Czech Republic will most probably have the most extensive Constitution in the world and the lead over the rest of the world is such that no other state stands a chance to come close. And, unfortunately, we are probably the only state in the world where not even the experts can be sure without any reservation what exactly is covered by the Constitution. And it is supposed to be the

---

[279] They were the following Acts: No. 1/2007 Sb., to regulate enjoyment of some property of the Czech Republic; No. 105/2007 Sb., to regulate a government bonds program to fund principals of government bonds redeemed on the market in 2007; No. 110/2007 Sb., to regulate some measures in the system of central bodies of state administration, connected with the abolition of the Ministry of Informatics, and to alter some Acts; No. 175/2007 Sb., to regulate a government bonds program to partially cover the deficit of the state budget of the Czech Republic for 2007; No. 181/2007 Sb., on the Institute for the Study of Totalitarian Regimes and on the Archives of Security Forces, and to alter some Acts; No. 261/2007 Sb., on stabilization of public budgets; No. 297/2007 Sb., to provide government guarantee of the CR to secure the loan granted to EUROFIMA for the purpose of funding the purchase of rail vehicles; No. 360/2007 Sb., on the state budget of the Czech Republic; No. 378/2007 Sb., on medicines and to alter some related Acts (the Medicines Act).

[280] Constitutional Act No. 69/1998 Sb., to shorten the term of the Chamber of Deputies, and Constitutional Act No. 515/2002 Sb., on a referendum on the accession of the Czech Republic to the European Union and to alter Constitutional Act No. 1/1993 Sb., the Constitution of the Czech Republic as amended.

top of the legal order! And there can be no doubt that the famous *ignorantia juris non excusat –
ignorance of the law is no defence* should apply, too.

It appears that the emergence of polycentrism in current law is a general phenomenon
and the CR can hardly resist it, or even refuse it completely. It results from the above said
that the Constitution of the CR itself has eroded the traditional hierarchical (pyramidal)
structure of the legal order when it leaned to the monistic model of the relationship between national and international law in the CR and when it provided for the generally
binding effect of all Constitutional Court decisions. But if it was provided by the Constitution of the CR, it is possible to proceed on the presumption of correctness. In spite of
this presumption, however, one cannot avoid a feeling of "eagerness" in relinquishing, or
weakening the traditional pyramidal structure of generally binding legal rules in the Czech
Republic.

Is the current situation, when the decisions of the Constitutional Court of the CR are
binding *erga omnes*, really better than was the previous regulation (of the Constitutional Court
of the Czech and Slovak Federal Republic), when the Constitutional Court found an act
to be unconstitutional, but left it to the competent, lawmaking body to tackle the unconstitutionality? Even the Constitutional Court of the CR manifested a degree of "eagerness"
in relinquishing the traditional pyramidal structure of the legal order in the conception of
traditional sovereignty, when it stated in the so-called "sugar quotas finding" that it "*cannot
disregard the fact that several high courts of older Member States ...have never entirely acquiesced in the doctrine
of the absolute precedence of Community law over the entirety of constitutional law ...the Constitutional Court
(of the CR)...interprets constitutional law (of the CR) taking into account principles arising from Community
law...*".

In the case of the CR requirement to observe obligations resulting from international
law, a question arises of whether this regulation is not overly burdensome. Would it not be
more prudent to state the principle that the CR shall observe obligations resulting from
international treaties on the basis of reciprocity? Even that would not mean little. In 2005,
there were 129 notifications of the Ministry of Foreign Affairs published in the Collection
of International Treaties, there were 119 notifications published in 2006 and 89 notifications in 2007.

Both in the case of the Czech Constitutional Court decisions and international obligations and treaties, the Constitution of the CR has laid down a framework, at least some
rules, regardless of whether we approve of them or not. However, we are afraid that the
Constitution of the CR has not provided, or indeed implied, any rules for solving possible
conflicts between "general" international law and EU law with respect to the CR, and thus
these issues have got out of its control completely.

We can conclude by saying that the traditional set of sources of continental law has been
eroded since judicial interpretation (or even creation) of law is being made more flexible.
Changes in the conception of the relationship between international and national law have
taken place, too, which has impacted the structure and content of the legal order. The European Union and its law represent an independent (autonomous) legal system. Thus we
can talk of the plurality of centres of legal orders, or of the plurality of contenders aspiring
to be the centres of legal orders.

2.4.2 Changing structure of the legal order and its attributes

The topic covers a wide range of questions on the border between constitutional law and the general theory of law. From the point of view of organic constitutional law it is the substitution of a different paradigm for the paradigm of a principally closed legal order with pyramidal (hierarchical) structure, deriving from the constitution as a single centre (the expression of a sovereign's will). Legal orders are open to international and European law, each of which claims its primacy. In the perspective of national law, the traditional set of continental sources of law has been eroded because judicial interpretation (creation) of law has been made more flexible and we can encounter so-called *soft law*, etc. We can perhaps talk of the plurality of centres of legal orders, or of the plurality of contenders aspiring to be centres of legal orders. A. Gerloch has written about the multicentric model of law[281] in this context, and polycentrism has been derived from the prefix introduced in Dahl's polyarchy as a realistic image of an ideal democracy; the specific label, however, depends on the author's licence and it is quite possible that the term polycentrism will vanish. An alternative approach has been offered in the thesis of "acentrism" (N. Luhmann), i.e. the absence of any centre; this thesis, however, relates to the world as such, not to law.[282]

In this text we focus on the change in the structure of the legal order from the image of a pyramid to the model of a network and on the conversion of certain traditional characteristics of law. The latter issue is connected with the question of the degree of openness or closeness of the legal system depending on how quick and revolutionary the development of the society may be.

Polycentrism subsists in an attempt at grasping the shift in perception of the structure of legal order, which either loses a single focus (basic rule), or the conception of this focus changes. It is not the top of a pyramid any more (though it was always just a simplified metaphor of the reality), from which lower levels of the legal order evolve, since important parts of the legal order do not originate in the territory of the state, so their existence (applicability) is not derived from this focus. On the other hand, we could talk about the preservation of one focus of the legal order in the case where we do not combine it with origination but with the effects of legal rules created outside the territory of the state (incorporation of international treaties, integration authorization for accession to the European Union, or provisions dealing with effects of European law). Thus the law could still be the "sovereign's order", regardless of whether the "sovereign" creates only some part of it, but the "sovereign" determines what the law is, regardless of its origin.[283]

What is new about the described system is not the mere existence of legal systems outside the territory of individual states, but the intensity of their operation, or their reflections in

---

[281]/ For example, Gerloch, A. – Kysela, J. – Kühn, Z. – Wintr, J. – Tryzna, J. – Maršálek, P. – Beran, K.: *Teorie a praxe tvorby práva* [Theory and Practice of Lawmaking]. Praha: ASPI, 2008, p. 364. Similarly, T. Machalová has acknowledged "multicentric system of law" – see colloquium "Právo a právní kultury v 21. století – různorodost a jednota" [Law and Legal Cultures in the 21st century – diversity and unity]. PF UK, 1st June 2007.

[282]/ Luhmann, N.: *Sociální systémy: nárys obecné teorie* [Social Systems: An Outline of General Theory]. Brno: CDK, 2006, pp. 10 and 496. Put more precisely, Luhmann has written about polycentric theory in an acentric world, and in his conception polycentric means the same as polycontextual.

[283]/ This concept is frequently mentioned in Přibáň, J. *supra.*

constitution-making and the case-law of constitutional courts. As a result, the hierarchical model is at least amended, or maybe even suppressed by networks or network relations.[284] Instead of a clear predominance of higher law over lower (*lex superior derogat legi inferiori*) it is necessary to "translate" from network to network because, among other things, it is not possible to determine what is higher and what is lower since the perspectives differ; this idea is covered by the above-mentioned Luhmann's polycontextualism (cf. also constitutional pluralism later on).

Along the same lines, the European Court of Justice claims primacy of European law over legal orders of Member States, including their Constitutions. On the other hand, Constitutional Courts of the Member States declare their Constitutions to be the supreme law (such as the Polish Constitutional Tribunal in decision No. K 15/04 on the constitutionality of Elections to the European Parliament Act, as well as the Czech Constitutional Court reviewing the Lisbon Treaty – judgment No. 446/2008 Sb.), having the possibility to review European acts as *ultra vires* acts in relation to the delegation of powers. Rigorous international law considers other legal systems to be in principle mere *questiones facti*.[285] In the local course books, the relationship between European and national law is pointed out by J. Wintr who designates the most probably unavoidable differences between the perspectives of the European Court of Justice and national constitutional courts on what is higher law as dualism. The principal collision of perspectives can, according to him, only be solved at the political level.[286] What is important is not whether we label the relationship between the European Court of Justice and constitutional courts as the relationship of cooperation, or rather complementariness as was suggested by S. Bross, Justice of the German Federal Constitutional Court, but what matters is the fact that the relationship is not generally recognized as hierarchical, hence that of subordination.[287]

A practical impact on the development of law is that primacy in abrogation is replaced by primacy in application, when a source of law, or rather a legal rule contained in it, yields in a particular case to another source of law (rule) without removing it finally from the legal order.

How is the concept of "polycentrism" connected with pluralism? First of all, they are not clear cut concepts, i.e. they are not used quite unequivocally. Thus, legal pluralism can

---

[284]/ Similarly Gerloch, A. – Kysela, J. – Kühn, Z. – Wintr, J. – Tryzna, J. – Maršálek, P. – Beran, K., *supra* at p. 363. More generally on the "flattening" of the world where "flat" networks are substituted for hierarchy of authorities, values, organizations, etc., see Friedman, T. L.: *Svět je plochý. Stručné dějiny jednadvacátého století* [The World is Flat. A Brief History of the Twenty-First Century]. Praha: Academia, 2007.

[285]/ "Rigorous" international law should be distinguished from international law which is restrained in its claims and ambitions. Description of both approaches is offered in Malenovský, J.: *Mezinárodní právo veřejné, jeho obecná část a poměr k jiným právním systémům, zvláště k právu českému* [Public International Law, Its General Part and Relationship to Other Legal Systems, Namely Czech Law]. 5th ed., Brno: Masarykova univerzita and Doplněk, 2008, p. 407 and subs.

[286]/ Wintr, J.: *Principy českého ústavního práva s dodatkem principů práva evropského a mezinárodního* [Principles of Czech Constitutional Law, plus an Attachment on Principles of European and International Law]. Praha: Eurolex Bohemia, 2006, p. 153 et subs. Similarly, R. Barents built his book on an insurmountable collision of the perspectives of European and national constitutional law in relation to the autonomy of European law – see Barents, R.: *The Autonomy of Community Law*. The Hague – London – New York: Kluwer Law International, 2004.

[287]/ Bross, S.: *Úvahy o státotvorném procesu v Evropě* [Reflections on the Integration Process in Europe]. Občanský institut Bulletin No. 204, August 2008, p. 7.

both denote a parallel existence and operation of several legal orders (typically national, international and European, possibly with further subdivision of national law into federal and state law), and refer to the socio-legal perception of a variety of laws issuing from the society, among which the law of the state is just one possibility, as the state is no more than one of several social bonds.[288]

Polycentrism in law is certainly connected with the first mentioned sense, and it differs in perspective: primary emphasis is not on the parallel operation of legal orders, but rather on their derivation, origination or focus – i.e. on the change in the image of the legal order structure. So it is a closely related concept, differing mainly in shades of sense and justified by a relatively limited fixation of the compared concept.

Attention paid to the problem of centre, focus, and source of the legal order in incompatible perspectives combines polycentrism with constitutional pluralism, i.e. the model explaining European integration on a basis which differs from the more or less established conception of federal states (classical constitutionalism). Constitutional pluralism also relinquishes the determination of "higher" law, and it rather tries to operationalize competing claims of individual legal systems (and constitutional jurisdictions), so that no stalemates occur. It prefers the dialogue of interested parties to the "powerhouse" last word of authority, which is not necessarily required for maintaining order in law according to "pluralists". However, it does not exist in just one variation, nor does it refer solely to the European Union[289], which can be evidenced, for instance, by the European Court for Human Rights case *Bosphorus Airways v. Ireland* (application No. 45036/98). It shows how international law responds to the co-existence of national and (mainly) European law, the Strasbourg Court claiming the last word this time.

In his meticulous analysis M. Poiares Maduro combines constitutional pluralism with (1) plurality of constitutional sources (sources of constitutional law), (2) pluralism of jurisdictions, (3) pluralism of interpretation, which is based on competences of several institutions that are not organized hierarchically,[290] (4) pluralism of powers, which means the modification of the classical structure of public power with the rise of new forms of public power and private power, and finally (5) pluralism of political communities, which

---

[288]/ See also Maršálek, P. *supra* at p. 189 et subs., or Bárány, E.: *Pojmy dobrého práva* [The Concepts of Good Law]. Bratislava: Poradca podnikateľa, 2007. Incidentally, both the authors are rather critical of legal pluralism, even dismissive, since they connect it with disintegration of the term "law" or "deconstruction of the system of good law". Having that in mind, the advantage of the term "polycentrism" could be its descriptive nature: it does not require that something be organized in some way, nor evaluated, but rather it just endeavours to emphasize a change in a paradigm and to describe it.

[289]/ A remarkably interesting and concentrated introduction to this topic has been provided in the edited record of the European University Institute seminar „Four Visions of Constitutional Pluralism". Eds: Avbelj, M. – Komárek, J., EUI Working Papers, Law 2008/21. My thanks for granting the text are due to J. Komárek.

[290]/ R. Procházka describes varied pretensions of Central European Constitutional Courts to be monopolist interpreters of Constitutions (namely Hungary) or, on the contrary, to participate in interpretation with other constitutional bodies. See Procházka, R.: *Mission Accomplished. On Founding Constitutional Adjudication in Central Europe.* Budapest – New York: CEU, 2002. D. Halberstam has framed the same conflict by the words "departmental" or "coordinated" conception of authority to interpret the Constitution versus judicial supremacy or monopoly – Halberstam, D.: *Constitutional Heterarchy: The Centrality of Conflict in the European Union and the United States.* University of Michigan Law School, Public Law and Legal Theory Working Paper Series, Working Paper No. 111, June 2008, p.7.

assert their claims to self-determination, differ in ways of organization and enable mobility, i.e. transitions from one to the other.[291]

It has appeared, however, that similar to the case of legal pluralism, it is also questionable whether constitutional pluralism is a descriptive, or rather a normative term. Being in a critical mood, J. Baquero Cruz defines pluralism in the quoted proceedings as the word which adds postmodern flavour to constitutionalism with postmodernism featuring a fluid and fragmentary nature. In his opinion, pluralism may realistically reflect the changed reality, but he considers it to be risky.[292]

To a certain degree, D. Halberstam has proceeded similarly to us, when he developed the more or less established concept of constitutional pluralism (the idea of competing claims to constitutional authority within a single system of government) by his own conception of constitutional heterarchy, i.e. non-hierarchical order.[293] According to Halberstam, the European Union and the USA are close in the lack of hierarchy of legal systems and rules of law on the one hand (EU) and the lack of hierarchy of institutions interpreting the Constitution on the other (interpretive pluralism in the USA): in both the systems the ultimate legal authority is missing, and yet there is an explicit order therein. But it does not result from one-sided enforcement of the superior, but from mutual adjustment (accommodation) with the aim of enforcing three fundamental values of constitutionalism, which are the "vote", i.e. the right to be heard, expertise and rights, or protection thereof. These values cannot be unequivocally attributed to individual branches of power, or to the bodies which symbolize them (the President, the Congress, the Supreme Court) - each of the powers invokes the mentioned values in various situational contexts, they all want to be the final arbiter, and each of them succeeds from time to time. So the supreme authority oscillates; it cannot be foreclosed whose opinion will win, yet in "common" matters judicial interpretation prevails.[294]

Polycentrism can also be related to legal pluralism in the second mentioned sense, i.e. to the multiplicity of laws issuing from the society. In this sense it does not work primarily with objective legal orders, but with something like objectivised orders of subjective rights. The relevant context here is multiculturalism based on the premise of the recognition of various cultures which do not claim superiority, but independence.[295] An individual's identity is perceived as an identity shaped in a specific cultural environment, hence created collectively, in the process of socialization. That, indeed, means that restriction of what is declared to be

[291]/ Avbelj, M. – Komárek, J. (eds.) *supra* at p. 6.

[292]/ *Ibidem* at p. 7.

[293]/ Halberstam, D. *supra.*

[294]/ A similar description can be found in *"political jurisprudence"* by M. Shapiro, by means of which he tried in the 1960s to transfer the reality of political pluralism based on the multiplicity of centres of power in the USA, none of which permanently dominates, to the system of legal institutions. Political jurisprudence results from judicial review of actions of public power, namely legislation. See Shapiro, M. – Stone Sweet, A.: Law, Courts, and Social Sciences. In: Shapiro, M. – Stone Sweet, A.: *On Law, Politics and Judicialization.* Oxford: Oxford University Press, 2002, pp. 4–9. Law is an integral part of politics, which is why the judge is a (co-)author of policy, which results in the necessity to make moral (value) choices – Shapiro, M.: *Political Jurisprudence, supra* at pp. 52–53.

[295]/ See, for instance, Barša, P.: *Politická teorie multikulturalismu* [Political Theory of Multiculturalism]. Brno: CDK, 1999. This topic in the legal context is reflected by Scheu, H. Ch.: Současná právní koncepce kulturního konfliktu v Evropě [Current Legal Conception of Cultural Conflicts in Europe]. Colloquium "Právo a právní kultury v 21. století – různorodost a jednota" [Law and Legal Cultures in the 21st century – diversity and unity]. PF UK, 1st June 2007.

a natural, traditional, inherent, etc. part of the culture of a community (typically ethnic or religious) can be considered an attack against the identity of an individual endowed with inalienable natural rights. Making an extreme simplification, we can say there is a contraposition of the requirement of legal status linked primarily to belonging to (sub)cultural groups instead of the state (citizenship).

Derogation from the universality of good law, based on territory, is not a uniform model. It is certainly possible to consider (compare) the reason for, and seriousness of, deviation. And we do not "export" our law out of the Western world, which could lead to us being criticised for cultural imperialism and having to consider what some authors describe as the difference between accommodating universalism and unacceptable cosmopolitanism.[296] On the contrary, we apply law to those who have come here voluntarily but often without any intention of becoming Europeans.[297]

A. Gerloch has rendered the traditional national conception of continental law based on primacy of legislation rather neatly, listing four fundamental postulates: (1) legislation is passed by an elected lawmaking body, which grants it legitimacy; (2) legal order based on legislation is clearer and agrees with legal certainty more than legal orders based on multiplicity of sources of law; (3) legislation can become a means of change of social situations; and (4) it is possible to create an ideal normative world in legislation, and to determine what is right and what is wrong in advance.[298] The problem is that the reality of the beginning of the 21st century is somewhat different from the presented scheme. Disregarding the alienation of citizens from parliamentary political parties, which leads to calls for referenda as well as value divergence (which challenges or even weakens the possibility of *a priori* determination of good and bad), we are left with points (2) and (3); this, however, brings about an incompatibility in understanding legislation.

On the one hand, it is a general, long-term, clear and predictable rule of conduct – a potential programme; on the other hand, it is a tool of government policy, a measure, a plan. C. Schmitt pertinently underlined the distinction made at the end of the 18th century between "classical" legislation and revolutionary measures of Jacobins;[299] indeed, this was reflected in the classification into (regular, general, permanent) laws and (extraordinary, territorially specific, temporary) decrees in the Constitution of 1793, or the period reflections by Hegel. As a result of later fuzziness of the distinction, legislation became both a tool and a restriction of public power. The increased number of tasks of the state raised the pressure

296/ Císař, O.: Teorie demokracie na úsvitu globálního věku [The Theory of Democracy at the Dawn of the Global Era]. In: Hloušek, V. – Kopeček, L. (eds.): *Demokracie. Teorie, modely, osobnosti, podmínky, nepřátelé a perspektivy demokracie* [Democracy. Theory, Models, Persons, Conditions, Enemies and Prospects of Democracy]. Brno: MPÚ, 2003, p. 362.

297/ According to G. Sartori, that is the main difference between most current immigrants from Islamic countries to Europe and immigrants to the USA namely in the 19th and at the beginning of the 20th century. While the latter wanted to become Americans and adopt the values of the new country, which was, of course, easier, since they were mostly Christians, the former intend to live the lives of Muslims, not changing the habits they had brought with them. See Sartori, G.: *Pluralismus, multikulturalismus a přistěhovalci. Esej o multietnické společnosti.* [Pluralism, Multiculturalism and Immigrants. An Essay on Multiethnic Society]. Praha: Dokořán, 2005.

298/ Gerloch, A.: Má zákon budoucnost? Zákony a zákoníky v 21. století [Is There a Future for Legislation? Laws and Codes in the 21st Century]. In: Gerloch, A. – Maršálek, P. (eds.): *Zákon v kontinentálním právu* [Statute in Continental Law]. Praha: Eurolex Bohemia, 2005, p. 18.

299/ Schmitt, C.: *Teorie partyzána* [Theory of the Partisan]. Praha: Oikoymenh, 2008, pp. 82–83.

on passing new laws, which frequently did not create space for individual action but were rather aimed at a predetermined purpose. Stability, a long-term effect, was not their definitive feature any more; we can often see laws deprived of general applicability (not only German "*Einzelfallgesetze*").[300] H. Schneider provides a persuasive summary in three points: (1) from the stabilizing factor in life, legislation evolved into an engine of change; (2) from a tool for separating state domain from the sphere of individual and corporate freedom, it changed into a tool for social support; and (3) regulation, aspiring to be permanent and fair was transformed into a temporary proclamation that special purpose rules be binding (which is connected with item (2).[301]

Then a question of consistency of the legal order has arisen, proportionately to the number of external or domestic sources of law having effect in the territory of the state and their overlapping areas. Thus, polycentrism on the one hand contributes to greater changes in the legal order (transformation of international obligations, transposition of European directives) and, on the other hand, the dynamics created by such changes potentiate the starting situation of polycentrism – i.e. unclearness, conflicts, lower certainty. Since legal certainty is a basic social necessity which cannot be ignored, the role of its "seekers" and guarantors is assumed by courts. Indeed, the above mentioned debate on constitutional pluralism in the European Union is concentrated mainly on courts. Judge-made law, national and European, thus supplements law created through the legislative process, again both at the national (the Parliament, the government and administrative authorities, communities and regions) and European level.

How does the instability of legal order affect the nature of the legal system and its relationship to the environment? Does it tend to be over/under-restrictive or is it a neutral process? Not having any ambition of providing a thorough answer we just note that hectic lawmaking increases the danger of inconsistencies and gaps, the bridging of which is in the competence of judges. They usually base their decisions on standards inherent in the legal order or derived from it (legal principles, analogies, etc.), or they use general clauses, if the legislature included them in the legal order as delegation rules of its kind. By means of legal principles, analogies and general clauses, extra-legal values influence law; however, this is done in a way determined and envisaged by the law. In this respect, law behaves as a self-reflecting and self-reproducing (autopoietic) system.

On the other hand, legitimization of at least statutory law requires contact with the environment, as it is not based on duration but on the consent of the representation of the people, which is presumed at any moment. This reservation applies, unless we include the mentioned legitimization mechanisms in the legal system.

Considering quality, the relationship of law and the environment has not changed and everything is regulated by given procedures. However, we cannot overlook quantitative shifts when recourses to formerly extra-legal values and standards have become more frequent or even common (see also academic emphasis on "*law in context*"). In this respect,

---

[300]/ Compare, for instance, Leisner, W.: *Krise des Gesetzes. Die Auflösung des Normenstaates*. Berlin: Duncker & Humblot, 2001.
[301]/ Schneider, H.: *Gesetzgebung*. 3rd ed., Heidelberg: C. F. Müller, 2002, p. 1. F. A. Hayek and recently also B. Tamanaha have written along the same lines about the changes in legislation.

law has been extending at the expense of other normative systems, which takes us back to the discussion on the diverse conceptions of legal pluralism. And yet the recent development does not appear to have enlightened classical questions, such as whether justice is an immanent element of law or a criterion of its external designation. On the other hand, an opinion has apparently taken hold that a conflict with morals does not constitute invalidity of a legal rule, but "only" its very immorality; it is being potentiated by the cultural diversification of Western societies.

2.5 CHANGES IN CONSTITUTIONAL LAW ON THE THRESHOLD OF THE 21ST CENTURY

2.5.1 Reservation of statute in a democratic state respecting the rule of law

Reservation of statute (a written law) may be subsumed under legal institutions to define a democratic state respecting the rule of law. Reservation of a law has undergone substantial changes in the course of the development of a democratic state respecting the rule of law and, therefore, when analysing the concept it is necessary to take into account the development of the doctrine and judicial decisions of constitutional courts which emphasized the importance of reservation of a law in relation to human rights and fundamental freedoms. The reservation of a law strengthens the democratic principles on the one hand in the structure of relations among constitutional or government bodies and, on the other hand, the relationship between the state and an individual. The principle of the state respecting the rule of law and the principle of democracy bind the legislature to adopt laws for the benefit of the society as a whole.[302] The reservation of a law is a tool used by the constitution-makers to point out the importance of some substantive law relations, the material legal regulation of which is necessary in order to secure legal and social certainty.[303] The reservation of a law does not result in a constitutional duty of the legislature to adopt a legal regulation presumed to exist in the form of statute (a law) by the constitutional order.

The reservation of a law is a tool of formal law used by the constitution-makers to ensure implementation of material, institutional, procedural and other conditions and facts in the form of statute.[304] The purpose of the reservation of a law is the order of the constitution-makers to the legislature that a certain material field shall be *pro futuro* regulated by a law.[305]

[302]/ Von Mangoldt, H. – Klein, F. – Starck, Ch.: *Das Bonner Grundgesetz. Kommentar.* Vol. 2, 4th ed., München: Verlag Franz Vahlen, 2000, p. 687.
[303]/ The rule of law which is dominant primarily in the 2nd half of the 20th century therefore resulted, for example, in extending the rules for publication of legal regulations so that every individual had the possibility to become acquainted with the rules that he/she must follow. See Winkler, G.: *Rechtswissenschaft und Politik.* Wien – New York: Springer Verlag, 1998, pp. 78–79.
[304]/ Klíma, K.: Pyramidální a praktické důsledky vstupu do Evropské unie pro ústavní pojetí pramenů práva v České republice [Pyramidal and Practical Consequences of EU Accession for Constitutional Concept of Sources of Law in the Czech Republic]. In: Gerloch, A. – Maršálek, P. (eds.): *Zákon v kontinentálním právu* [Statute in Continental Law]. Praha: Eurolex Bohemia, 2005, pp. 357–362; Havránek, D.: K hierarchické výstavbě právního řádu a vymezení pojmu právní síly v ústavním prostředí České republiky [Hierarchy of Legal Order and Definition of the Concept of the Force of Law in the Constitutional Environment of the Czech Republic]. *Právník* 5/2007.
[305]/ The reservation of a law is a common feature to the entire constitutional order of the Czech Republic: e.g. Art. 12 (1), Art. 79, Art. 100, Art. 101 (4) and Art. 104 (1) of the Constitution of the CR; Art. 11 (4), Art. 14, Art. 17 (3) and (4), Art. 19 (2) of the Charter of Rights and Freedoms.

The legislature cannot regulate, in the material sense of the word, the field of such legal relations in contradiction to this constitutional order, and this also applies to the situation when similar fields of legal relations are governed by legal regulations not having the force of a law. Reservation of a law must be distinguished from the concept of legislative delegation, the purpose of which, as opposed to the reservation of a law as a stabilising element, is authorisation of other than the parliamentary legislature to issue generally binding legal regulations. Such an authorisation is usually in modern states vested in the Executive which is, from the point of view of availability of expert knowledge, best prepared to fulfil this goal. General authorisation of the Executive to issue legal regulations is a manifestation of dominance of legislative power where the normative activity can be transferred to other public bodies in the country exclusively with the consent of the legislative power.[306]

Reservation of a law is a decision of the constitution-makers who must stipulate which substantive regulation is conditioned by the reservation of a law. Czech constitution-makers have decided to subsume under the reservation of a law the establishment of ministries and other administrative bodies; nevertheless, the manner of action taken by the Government as a constitutional body and the number of its members, as well as the portfolios of individual members, remained to be regulated by an internal normative act of the Government.[307]

Reservation of a law can be classified according to various criteria.[308] In jurisprudence, the reservation of a law is usually classified as a *formal reservation,* whereby the constitution-makers decided that the regulation of certain legal facts shall be in the form of a statute without stipulating the basic material conditions of the legal regulation. A usual formal reservation of a law is the reservation that state power may be exercised only in cases and within the limits stipulated by the law.[309] Government action therefore may never be exercised outside of the legal framework. In this case the constitution-makers did not specify the definition of the limits stipulated by the law; rather, they codified only a general order to the legislature in relation to the exercise and organization of the public power strictly related to the legal regulation. The principle of enumerative claims for the exercise of public authority is a guarantee protecting an individual against unwarranted intervention of the state in the individual's personal sphere. The constitution-makers restricted in a similar

---

[306]/ Kysela, J.: Úvod k teorii zákonodárné delegace: pojem a typy [Introduction to the Theory of Legislative Delegation: the Concept and the Types]. In: Gerloch, A. – Maršálek, P. (eds.): *Zákon v kontinentálním právu* [Statute in Continental Law]. Praha: Eurolex Bohemia, 2005, p. 161. For details on this topic see an excellent monograph Kysela, J.: *Zákonodárství bez parlamentů. Delegace a substituce zákonodárné pravomoci* [Legislation without Parliaments. Delegation and Substitution of Legislative Power]. Praha: Univerzita Karlova v Praze, Právnická fakulta, 2006.

[307]/ We may give examples of the history of governments of the Czech Republic when the ministers were explicitly ministers without portfolio or they became such ministers later if the ministry they were in charge of was cancelled. All such authorisations were granted by a government resolution and a change to the Rules of Order of the Government of the Czech Republic. E.g. Igor Němec – state control minister (the ministry ceased to exist on 30. 6. 1993), after 30. 6. 1993 minister of the government; Pavel Bratinka – minister without portfolio; Vladimír Mlynář – minister without portfolio, spokesman of the government; Jaroslav Bašta – minister without portfolio (22. 7. 1998–23. 3. 2000); Karel Březina – minister (since 23. 3. 2000) and head of the Office of the Government of the Czech Republic.

[308]/ Basic classification In: Walter, R. – Mayer, H. – Kucsko-Stadlmayer, G.: *Bundesverfassungsrecht.* 10th ed., Wien: Manzsche Verlags- und Universitätsbuchhandlung, 2007, pp. 629–631.

[309]/ See Art. 2 (2) of the Charter of Rights and Freedoms.

way the formal as well as material legislature by stipulating that the restrictions upon the fundamental rights and freedoms may be changed exclusively by a law under the conditions set by the Charter of Fundamental Rights and Freedoms.[310] The constitution-makers therefore without a detailed material specification created a constitutional barrier, in the formal sense of the word, and without the fulfilment of this condition it is not possible to restrict fundamental rights and freedoms.[311] Generally speaking, fundamental rights and freedoms can be restricted only if such restriction is carried out in the form of a statute. This usually happens in the public interest or for qualified reasons.[312]

Reservation of a law may also be classified as *material reservation,* i.e. the constitution-makers stipulate for a material regulation, which must have the form of a law, further substantive conditions that must be fulfilled. These are mostly conditions related to the possibility of restricting fundamental rights and freedoms where the goal of the material reservation of a law is to protect the individual against unlawful interventions of public authority and to strengthen the protection of the individual's human rights sphere.[313]

The classification into formal and material reservations stems from the 19th century, when the first catalogues of human rights and fundamental freedoms were created and when human rights and fundamental freedoms were understood as protection against arbitrariness of the executive branch of government and against unlawfulness.[314] The purpose of the reservation of a law therefore was to protect the freedoms as such against a possibility of the legislature to interfere with them or to reduce their material content, rather than the procedural strengthening of the enforceability of human rights of an individual. The understanding of the material reservation of a law changed with the development of international codification of human rights and fundamental freedoms after World War II, when the universal catalogues of human rights and fundamental freedoms started to create a material limit for the constitution-makers on their attempts to reduce or change national catalogues of human rights. Reservation of a law nowadays makes sense primarily in the

---

[310]/ See article 4 (2) of the Charter of Rights and Freedoms.

[311]/ The constitution-makers stipulated without a detailed specification the formal reservation in the Charter of Rights and Freedoms e.g. in Art. 11 (4), where expropriation and forced limitation of ownership was reserved to law. Currently these issues are governed by Act No. 184/2006 Sb., regulating ejection from ownership and limitation of ownership of land or a building (Expropriation Act) which stipulates the basic procedural conditions of expropriation or creation of an easement. Nevertheless the purpose itself that is to be fulfilled by the expropriation or limitation of ownership is regulated by special laws. Sector laws regulate the circumstances under which this law may be applied; these include primarily the Energy Act, Electronic Communications Act, Forest Law, Water Act, Roads Act, etc. However, public interest is not defined in any of these special laws and it must be proved in accordance with the Expropriation Act in administrative proceedings. The constitution-makers therefore followed the axiom that expropriation or limitation of ownership may be imposed only in the public interest under conditions set by law.

[312]/ These are mostly limitations of fundamental rights and freedoms in the public interest for the purpose of the protection of public health, public peace, public security, morals, etc. e.g. qualified reasons for possible interventions in the inviolability of habitation are stipulated in Art. 12 (3) of the Charter of Rights and Freedoms. In this case the constitution-makers stipulated material conditions for intervention in the inviolability of habitation in the form of qualified reasons, the detailed specification of which remains up to legal regulation or application practice.

[313]/ Maurer, H.: *Staatsrecht I. Grundlagen, Verfassungsorgane, Staatsfunktionen.* 5th ed., München: C.H. Beck, 2007, pp. 208–209.

[314]/ See legal regulations from the Austro-Hungarian times: the basic law of the state of 21st December 1867 No. 142 of the imperial collection of laws regulating general rights of the citizens in the kingdoms and countries represented in the Imperial Council; law of 27th October 1862 No. 88 of the imperial collection of laws protecting the habitation.

protection of those human rights and freedoms that are not internationally codified. Treaties regulating human rights and fundamental freedoms have, in the Czech constitutional order, application primacy over national legal regulations irrespective of their legal force.

Reservation of a law may also be classified on the basis of other criteria such as the force of a legal regulation that is reserved, i.e. the reservation of a constitutional law or reservation of an ordinary law. Reservation of a law may be classified by its material content such as reservations entitling interference with human rights of an individual where the intervention subsists in a restriction of the exercise of human rights or a fundamental freedom stipulated by a law, without restricting the human right and fundamental freedom as a whole. We may also speak about a unique reservation of a law where a constitutional law itself stipulates the material content of a human right and when such right may be interfered with only within the framework of a condition set by a constitutional law or by a change of the constitutional law itself.[315] The unique reservation of a law must be distinguished from a general reservation with specific content, which may stipulate that some human rights and fundamental freedoms may be sought only within the statutes specifying such rights and freedoms. The constitution-makers therefore codify certain rights and freedoms, primarily the economic, social and cultural rights that are not directly enforceable and a statute sets the statutory limits for the exercise of these rights.[316] The goal of a general reservation with specific content is to define the jurisdiction of the legislature in regulating the material content of rights that are not directly enforceable in the form of ordinary legislation.[317]

The reservations of a law may be classified also depending on their content into the *institutional reservations of a law* whereby the constitution-makers stipulate how the public authority should be organised, and sets the basic means of the exercise of public authority. The purpose of the institutional reservation of a law is the division and organisation of exercising power into the Executive and Legislative branches, where more detailed regulation of the organisation and constitution of public authority either by the Legislative branch or by the Executive is reserved to a law.[318] The institutional reservation of a law, however, immanently generates a stronger position of the Legislative branch, which determines the scope of competencies and confers the implementation of the competencies on public bodies.[319]

---

[315]/ It is possible to mention as an example the right to personal liberty guaranteed by Art. 8 of the Charter of Rights and Freedoms; the Charter of Rights and Freedoms stipulates strict exemptions of the absolute right without the fulfilment of which personal liberty may never be restricted (detention and arrest related to time limits, custody only on the basis of reasons stipulated by law, etc.).

[316]/ More on enforceability of social rights in Suchánek, R.: K ústavnímu právu na ochranu zdraví a na bezplatnou zdravotní péči [Constitutional Right to Protection of Health and Free Healthcare]. In: Klíma, K. – Jirásek, J. (eds.): *Pocta Jánu Gronskému* [Tribute to Ján Gronský]. Plzeň: Aleš Čeněk, 2008, pp. 249–271.

[317]/ This is Art. 41 (1) of the Charter of Rights and Freedoms which stipulates that the right to free choice of occupation and preparation for the occupation as well as the right to undertake business and to engage in other business activities, the right to raise funds for one's life necessities by work, the right to strike, the right to adequate pay for work, the rights of women, juvenile persons, and disabled persons to a higher level of safety at work or more protection in employment, the right to adequate old-age pension, the right to health protection, etc. may only be enforced within the limits of the laws which execute these provisions of the Charter of Rights and Freedoms.

[318]/ The institutional reservation of a law is very important in federations because the federation may govern only those institutional issues that are not reserved by the constitution to individual states of the federation. See Maurer, H.: *Staatsrecht I. Grundlagen, Verfassungsorgane, Staatsfunktionen.* 5th ed., Münich: C.H. Beck, 2007, p. 210.

[319]/ Ohler, Ch.: Der institutionelle Vorbehalt des Gesetzes. *Archiv des öffentlichen Rechts* 3/2006, pp. 337–377.

Generally, a question arises in relation to the institutional reservation of a law as to whether the Executive branch disposes in some aspects of constitutionally unlimited authority and of absolute freedom to regulate and to create the system of state bodies without intervention of the legislature, i.e. whether the Executive may adapt the system of state bodies to the needs of governance and whether the organisation of state bodies is an autonomous sphere of the Executive branch.[320] In the current concept, the Government as a constitutional body is a top body of the Executive, i.e. the body of the executive branch as well as a body having governance powers within the exercise of its jurisdiction. A strict differentiation between the governance power and the executive power which was typical of the First Republic,[321] was not taken over by the Constitution of the Czech Republic. The general constitutional law axiom of establishing central administrative bodies only in the form of a constitutional act does not exist in the Czech Republic; nevertheless, the institutional reservation of a constitutional law may be applied if the Executive tries to establish by an ordinary law a constitutional body and to expand the system of constitutional bodies over and above the framework of the constitutional order. Establishing state bodies in accordance with Article 79 (1) of the Constitution of the Czech Republic collides on the one hand with the constitutional axiom of the reservation of a law, whereby the intervention of the legislature cannot be excluded even in case of establishing "common" offices, and, on the other hand, with the reservation of a constitutional law, whereby it is not possible to extend the system of constitutional bodies by an ordinary law without changing the Constitution of the Czech Republic. In relation to the institutional reservation of a law, it is necessary to differentiate between the application of the institutional reservation of a law, the purpose of which is a legal form prescribed for establishing a new state body, and between the application of general constitutional reservation whereby the state authority may be applied only in certain cases, within the limits and in the manners specified by law.[322]

The institutional reservation of a law is a measure relating to the state bodies; it has only a certain importance in relation to an individual in terms of the legitimacy and legality of the exercise of authority (power). It cannot be ruled out that the institutional reservation of a law may have an impact on human rights and fundamental freedoms and that it may affect the material exercise of such rights. A democratic state respecting the rule of law must ensure that the human rights of an individual may be interfered with only on the basis of a statute and in a manner stipulated by the statute. Through such a constitutional axiom we may look for the bounds between *re publica* and *re privata*, as the differences in the traditional dualistic structure of law into public and private are blurred in the postmodern democratic state respecting the rule of law.[323] In such circumstances it is very difficult to define an inter-

---

[320]/ Here I am omitting the situation when the legislative branch controls the executive branch through the state budget and the allocation of public resources for the purposes stipulated in advance.

[321]/ For more on the acts of government in the government power and executive power, see Weyr, F.: *Soustava československého práva státního* [The System of Czechoslovak State Law]. Brno: Barvič & Novotný, 1921, pp. 176–183; Neubauer, Z.: Nařízení vládní a ministerská [Government and Ministerial Decrees]. *Právník* 1925; Hoetzel, J.: Literární zprávy – Jaroslav Krejčí: Moc nařizovací a její meze [New Publications – Jaroslav Krejčí: Authority to Order and Its Limits]. *Právník* 1923, pp. 339–345, 390–392.

[322]/ Art. 2 (3) of the Constitution of CR.

[323]/ Winkler, G.: *Rechtswissenschaft und Politik*. Wien – New York: Springer Verlag, 1998, p. 75.

ference with the fundamental rights and freedoms. Often the Executive may interfere with the personal sphere of an individual without being explicitly authorised to do so by the law and in spite of that, such an intervention may be authorised. These cases may involve warnings of state bodies against various dangers when the state authority simultaneously adopts measures preventing or mitigating the damage.[324]

Interventions in the personal sphere of individuals should be justified and adequate.[325] In accordance with the reservation of a law the Legislative branch should be entrusted with the decisions on those facts that are important from the point of view of human rights and fundamental freedoms, but not with obligatory decisions on those issues that are socially burning but do not affect human rights and fundamental freedoms from the point of view of substantive law (e.g. establishment of consultative bodies in state administration). The reservation of a law therefore is not an absolute constitutional law principle. The important point is the regulation of public law relations where an individual in relation to the state[326] is always in a subordinate position and it is substantial for the individual to know who is authorised to exercise public authority against him/her. Authorisation to exercise public authority definitely is not a marginal issue and there should be a procedure for the transfer of information on the legitimacy of an entity authorised to carry out interventions against individuals or citizens.[327] From the point of view of the institutional reservation of a law it is important to define the public law relation, including competences of public bodies; i.e. to define who may act for the state against the individual or, in other words, to define by the law the relation between the individual and the public body.[328]

Stipulating a constitutional requirement to reserve a certain substantive legal regulation to the form of a constitutional law is relatively rare in contemporary constitutional documents. The Constitution of the Czech Republic contains reservation of a constitutional law in Article 2 (2), which provides that a constitutional act may stipulate when the people shall exercise public authority directly.[329] In this respect it is necessary to note that the reservation of a constitutional law is not standard considering possible different legal

---

[324] Hendrych, D. et al.: *Správní právo. Obecná část* [Administrative Law. General Part]. 3rd ed., Praha: C. H. Beck, 1998, pp. 110–111, 118–120.

[325] On this issue, see the judgments of Federal Constitutional Court which created the so called Wesentlichkeitstheorie, BVerfGE 40, 237, 249.

[326] Here we use the concept of state in a broader meaning as a concept referring to all entities that may be authorised to exercise public authority – state bodies, public corporations, public institutes, public enterprises, private law persons authorised to exercise state power, etc.

[327] Schmitt, C.: *Legalität und Legitimität.* 7th ed., Berlín: Duncker & Humblot, 2005, pp. 19–28. More details on legitimacy of law in Přibáň, J. *supra* at pp. 161–185.

[328] We may use as a guiding principle the definition of the jurisdiction of administrative courts in s. 2 of the Act No. 150/2002 Sb., rules of administrative procedure, as amended, which stipulates that: "In the administrative judiciary the courts provide protection to public rights of natural persons and legal entities in a manner stipulated by this law and under the conditions stipulated by this law or by a special law and decide in other matters as stipulated by this law."

[329] On direct democracy and constitutional parameters of referendum in the CR see Mlsna, P.: Úvaha nad přímou demokracií v ČR [Exploration of Direct Democracy in the Czech Republic]. *Právní zpravodaj* 10/2008, pp. 11–14; Mlsna, P.: Přímá demokracie a její ústavní parametry v českém ústavním pořádku [Direct Democracy and Its Constitutional Parameters in Czech Constitutional Order]. In: *Dny veřejného práva, Sborník příspěvků z mezinárodní konference* [Days of Public Law. International Conference Proceedings]. Brno: Masarykova univerzita, 2007, pp. 109–129.

regulations in various parts of the constitutional order. Generally it is impossible to rule out a case where material regulation in one constitutional act would be indirectly amended by another constitutional act or a case of conflict of two constitutional laws. The reservation of a constitutional law is a safety catch of the constitution-makers for the adoption of basic regulations of elementary importance for the state that are given and constant and these qualities should be supported by the form of a constitutional law which requires a qualified majority in both chambers of the Parliament of the Czech Republic in order to enter into force. Article 2 (2) of the Constitution of the Czech Republic contains an optional reservation of a constitutional law, rather than an order of the constitution-makers to adopt a general constitutional act regulating referendum.[330] Article 100 (3) of the Constitution of the Czech Republic is a completely different case, as it assumes that creation or cancellation of a higher self-governing administrative unit may be carried out only by a constitutional act.[331]

Creating a new structure of the territory of the Czech Republic has been reserved to a constitutional act since the beginning of the validity of the Constitution of the Czech Republic. A similar case of the reservation of a constitutional law is Article 11 of the Constitution, which assumes that a change of the state borders of the Czech Republic is possible only in the form of a constitutional act. The constitution-makers therefore assumed that the change of a state border and the territorial structure of the state are such important facts for the existence of the state that the legal regulation of these issues is related to the reservation of a constitutional law. The state territory defined by state borders has a major importance for the perpetual existence of the state and the territorial structure of the state is in turn important for the unitary structure of the Czech Republic.[332]

The constitutional order assumes in certain cases the reservation of an ordinary law as a condition for future legal regulations. The makers of the Constitution of the Czech Republic decided to include an explicit reservation of a law in many provisions of the Constitution as a form of regulation of material relations, primarily of such relations that the constitution-makers considered important for the system of constitutional bodies and the functioning of the state and that may be in many cases subsumed under the Constitution as a body of legal rules dealing with the fundamental conditions for the functioning of the state.

The most frequent case of the reservation of a law is the institutional reservation, the purpose of which is to reserve a law in those legal regulations that aim at creating an

---

[330] Direct democracy and its evaluation in the system of representative democracy is an issue in many European countries. On Slovak case see Nikodým, D.: Ústavnoprávne problémy výkonu štátnej moci občanmi [Constitutional Issues of Exercise of Government by Citizens]. In: Jirásková, V. – Suchánek, R. (eds.): *Pocta prof. JUDr. Václavu Pavlíčkovi, CSc. k 70. narozeninám* [Tribute to Professor Václav Pavlíček on his 70th Birthday]. Praha: Linde, 2004, pp. 359–369.

[331] See Zářecký, P.: K vývoji územní veřejné správy před přijetím Ústavy České republiky [Development of Territorial Public Administration before Adoption of the Constitution of the Czech Republic]. In: Kysela, J. (ed.): *Deset let Ústavy České republiky* [Ten Years of the Constitution of the Czech Republic]. Praha: Eurolex Bohemia, 2003, p. 402 and subs.

[332] Unity of the Czech Republic was not a matter of course in the years of change of 1990–1992; this is confirmed by the government bill regulating the self-government of countries, which assumed that the Czech Republic would be composed of three countries, Bohemia, Moravia and Silesia. See Czech National Council (ČNR) 1992, 6th term of office, print No. 674.

administrative body or a state body to be entrusted with public law competences or the creation of which is assumed by the constitutional order. Another frequent case in the Czech constitutional order is a situation where primarily the Constitution of the Czech Republic assumes the establishment of a certain state body or it may even be said that such state body is established directly on the basis of the Constitution of the Czech Republic; nevertheless, the jurisdiction, functioning and competences remain to be governed by an ordinary law.[333] The constitution-makers however do so only in such cases when the competences of such a state body are crucial for the functioning of the state and when it may be expected that they will be subject to changes, which is a requirement better met by the form of an ordinary law than by the form of a constitutional act. If a key state or constitutional body is established by the Constitution of the Czech Republic and if the existence of this body in the constitutional system of the Czech Republic is indispensable, then the constitution-makers decided to define the jurisdiction of such body directly in the Constitution of the Czech Republic. This is the case of the Constitutional Court of the Czech Republic, the jurisdiction of which is precisely and fully defined in Article 87 of the Constitution of the Czech Republic; the competences of the Court may not be defined in any other way than by the Constitution of the Czech Republic. Considering the legislative technique, defining some competences of the Constitutional Court of the Czech Republic outside of the Constitution of the Czech Republic would not be a problem; the jurisdiction of the Constitutional Court could be defined outside the Constitution in the Constitutional Court Act.[334] The constitution-makers, however, in the case of competences of the Constitutional Court of the Czech Republic, strictly stick to the reservation of a constitutional law and therefore decided, for example, in relation to the Czech Republic's admission to the European Union to define the issues of review of the decision-making process by a referendum on the Czech Republic's accession to the European Union directly in the Constitution.[335] By doing so, the constitution-makers pointed out the importance of the Constitutional Court of the Czech Republic as a constitutional body and at the same time they showed a significant extent of political culture in the Czech Republic, because the constitution-makers did not resolve to govern the Constitutional Court's competences in the form of an ordinary law. Another constitutional body whose competences are only partially defined in the form of a constitutional act is the President. The competences of the President that are not countersigned are precisely and fully defined in Article 62 of the Constitution and the only way to amend them is by a constitutional act. Nevertheless the countersigned competences of the President may be stipulated also by an ordinary law.[336]

A typical institutional reservation of a law is the case when the constitution-makers decided to leave more detailed material regulation of the functioning of a constitutional

---

[333]/ For example, Czech National Bank Act No. 6/1993 Sb.; Supreme Audit Office Act No. 166/1993 Sb.
[334]/ Constitutional Court Act No. 182/1993 Sb.
[335]/ Constitutional Act No. 515/2002 Sb., to regulate the referendum on accession of the Czech Republic to European Union and to change Constitutional Act No. 1/1993 Sb., the Constitution of the Czech Republic, as amended.
[336]/ E.g. s. 10 of the Universities Act No. 110/1998 Sb. on the basis of which the rectors are appointed by the president; s. 10 of Act No. 283/1992 Sb., to regulate the Academy of Sciences of the Czech Republic under which the chairperson of the Academy of Sciences is appointed and removed by the president.

or state body to an ordinary law. This is the case of, for example, Article 79 (2) of the Constitution of the Czech Republic. This provision can be characterised as a reservation of a law under which the legal position of civil servants must be regulated by a law. The constitution-makers therefore stipulated that the legal position of civil servants cannot be regulated in any other way than the law. The intention of the constitution-makers was to differentiate the legal position of civil servants from usual employment contracts concluded under the Labour Code. In relation to this constitutional requirement, the Civil Service Act was adopted in 2002, which treats the legal position of civil servants as a relationship that is different from employment. The legislature wanted to point out the importance of civil servants for the operation of state administration and to set up mechanisms to "protect" civil servants against political pressure in case of changes of government. The Civil Service Act has not so far become effective and it has only been in force for the last 6 years.[337]

Another reservation of a law is contained in Article 80 of the Constitution, which requires a legal regulation of the position and jurisdiction of the Prosecuting Attorney's Office.[338] Further, Articles 97 and 98 of the Constitution leave it up to an ordinary law to define the position, jurisdiction, organisational structure and other details of the Supreme Audit Office and the Czech National Bank. Embedding such institutional reservations of a law in the constitutional order is not an end in itself, because the structure of state bodies reflects the political reality and sets the parameters for subject-matter decisions so that the political power could maintain adequate control over the functioning of the state and so that the structure of the state bodies reflects in a flexible manner the requirements and the development of various social and legal branches.[339]

The main purpose of the institutional reservation of a law incorporated in the Constitution is to guarantee the sharing of political power between the Government and the legislative body, which is an issue closely related to the division of power in the state. Generally speaking, there is no requirement in the Constitution that the constitutional and state bodies with national jurisdiction must be established only by a constitutional act. However it gives a rather unsystematic impression if some bodies are established by a constitutional act, e.g. National Security Council,[340] and their jurisdiction, structure and decision-making rules are regulated by an internal normative act of the government[341] rather than an

---

[337] Act No. 218/2002 Sb. to regulate the service of civil servants in administrative bodies and the remuneration of these servants and other employees of administrative bodies (Civil Service Act).

[338] Prosecuting Attorney's Office Act No. 283/1993 Sb.

[339] German doctrine has been dealing with the relation of politics, law and constitutionality for a long time. The following is a selection of papers: Laufer, H.: *Verfassungsgerichtsbarkeit und politischer Prozeß. Studien zum Bundesverfassungsgericht der Bundesrepublik Deutschland.* Tübingen, 1968; Laufer, H.: *Das Kriterium politischen Handelns.* Würzburg: Dissertation 1961; Novak, M.: Ústavní soud mezi právem a politikou [Constitutional Court between the Law and the Politics]. *Právník* 5/2001, p. 421 and subs.

[340] Article 9 of Constitutional Act No. 110/1998 Sb., on security of the Czech Republic.

[341] Government resolution of 10th June 1998 No. 391 on the National Security Council and on the planning of measures to ensure the security of the Czech Republic, as amended by the government resolution of 22nd August 2001 No. 813, the government resolution of 24th July 2002 No. 741, the government resolution of 12th February 2003 No. 164, the government resolution of 1st October 2003 No. 980, the government resolution of 1st September 2004 No. 828, the government resolution of 10th November 2004 No. 1109, the government resolution of 11th October 2006 No. 1174 and the government resolution of 17th January 2007 No. 54 on the National Security Council and on the planning of measures to ensure the security of the Czech Republic.

ordinary law. Considering the institutional structure of the branches in the state it should apply that the organisational structure of the branches in the state should be governed by the subject-matter principle, the principle of cost-efficiency and if possible the principle of effective of governance.

The reservation of a law is one of the basic legislative institutions of constitutional law. Originally the reservation of a law was perceived as the differentiation between the originators of the acts of power, i.e. a clear definition of those bodies the activity of which may be attributed to the state and that are *stricto sensu* authorised to the sovereign exercise of power.[342] Later the understanding of the reservation of a law changed and it is considered as one of the principles of a democratic state, because in a modern democratic state there is no space for exempting any state body from the principle of parliamentary or judicial control. Primarily in the German doctrine and judicial decisions, the so called *Wesentlichkeitstheorie* is being developed, the purpose of which is to clearly define the state intervention and the scope of such intervention in the fundamental rights and freedoms of a human being and a citizen. Constitutional systems assume that the human-rights sphere of an individual may be interfered with only on the basis of the law. The purpose of the reservation of a law is to legitimise such interventions of the state authority and to create transparent conditions for the cases when the Legislative branch makes general abstract decisions that affect all addressees of such rules.[343] The law hence is to legitimise the Executive branch in its subject-matter interventions in the human-rights sphere of an individual and, at the same time, to protect an individual against unlawful interference with his/her rights by the state.[344] The reservation of a law therefore represents a tool of predictability of the conduct of the state which limits in a subject-matter manner the exercise of state power. If the individual adjusts his/her conduct, then he/she has legal certainty under the transparent legal regulation that the state will not make any arbitrary interventions in the human-rights sphere.[345]

2.5.2 The impact of the Constitutional Court upon the legislative procedure

The abstract review of the compatibility of ordinary laws with constitutional laws belongs among the most significant competences of constitutional courts as specialised judicial bodies protecting constitutionality[346] in a majority of modern democratic states governed by the rule of law in the Continental Europe, based primarily upon written law. This traditional[347]

---

[342] Dagtoglou, P.: *Ersatzpflicht des Staates bei legislativem Unrecht?* Tübingen: J.C.B. Mohr, 1963, pp. 12–18.

[343] Ohler, Ch.: Der institutionelle Vorbehalt des Gesetzes. *Archiv des öffentlichen Rechts* 3/2006, pp. 343–344.

[344] Přibáň, J. *supra* at pp. 175–181.

[345] The issue of legal certainty is made slightly more complex due to the number of legal regulations that the addressee of the legal order should know. The principle *ignorantia legis non excusat* is therefore currently a fiction rather than reality. See Winkler, G.: *Rechtswissenschaft und Politik*. Wien – New York: Springer Verlag, 1998, pp. 153–156.

[346] See the express definition of such role of the Constitutional Court in Art. 83 of the Constitution of the Czech Republic, Art. 124 of the Constitution of the Slovak Republic or Art. 221 of the Constitution of Portugal *("The Constitutional Court shall be the court competent primarily to find the law in the constitutional area.")*

[347] The first European countries introducing the review of constitutionality by a special judicial body – a constitutional court – were Austria (1919) and Czechoslovakia; the latter established the Constitutional Court in 1920 and conferred upon it the power to decide whether ordinary laws were compatible with the Constitutional Charter, its parts, and laws amending and altering it (Art. I – III Act No. 121/1920 Sb. z. a n., which served as a preamble to the Constitutional Charter of the Czechoslovak Republic).

as well as the newly developed role of the constitutional judiciary is part of the catalogue of competences of constitutional courts in many European countries.[348] The constitutional subject-matter, formally distinguished from other laws by its designation and the manner of its passage and alteration (constitution-making process), practically acquires a higher legal force primarily through the judicial competence to repeal laws or other types of legislation which are in violation of the Constitution.

The core of the review of the constitutionality of laws is the review of their substance: the check on compatibility of their contents, i.e. the contents of the rules contained therein, with the contents of constitutional laws forming the constitutional order of the state.[349] However along with its review of the substantive compatibility of ordinary laws and constitutional laws, both being relatively independent bodies of legal rules in the objective sense, recent constitutional judiciary subjects to its review the so-called formal (external) constitutionality, i.e. whether a law, or any other regulation, has been passed by a competent body and whether the competent body or bodies have acted in accordance with constitutional rules regulating the process of their formation.[350] The legislative procedure itself, the rules of which with respect to their formation and application used to be understood as a typical domain of the rule-maker (legislature), has therefore been "constitutionalized" and "judicialised", primarily where a minority in either parliamentary chamber may apply to the Constitutional Court for the repeal of a law.[351]

The Constitutional Court Act [352] (ACC) in its s. 68 (2) stipulates: "In making its decision, the Court shall assess the contents of a statute or some other enactment from the perspective of its conformity with constitutional acts, or, if the matter concerns some other type of enactment, also with statutes, and ascertain whether they were adopted and issued within the confines of the powers set down in the Constitution and in the constitutionally prescribed manner." This provision includes all the three above-mentioned criteria for the review of a law. Reviewing the constitutionality of a law (or delegated legislation) the Constitutional Court regularly observes the following order: (1) to ascertain whether the respective enact-

---

[348]/ See the Constitutions of France (Art. 61), Italy (Art. 134 and 136), Germany (Art. 93 (1)), Portugal (Art. 223 (1), Art. 281 (1), Art. 282 (1) and (2)), Austria (Art. 140), Spain (Art. 161 (1), Art. 162 (1), Art. 163), Bulgaria (Art. 149 (1), Art. 151 (2) and (3)), Romania (Art. 144 a/), Croatia (Art. 125, Art. 126 (1)), Estonia (s. 152 (2)), Lithuania (Art. 105 (1), Art. 106 (1), Art. 107 (1)), Hungary (Art. 32A (1) and (2)), Poland (Art. 188, Art. 190 (3), (4)), Slovakia (Art. 125), Slovenia (Art. 156, Art. 160 (1), Art. 161 (1)), Russia (Art. 125 (2), (6)). See also Suchánek, R.: Ústavní soudnictví ve státech střední a východní Evropy [Constitutional Judiciary in Central and East European Countries]. In: Pavlíček, V. a kol.: *Transformace ústavních systémů zemí střední a východní Evropy* [Transformation of Constitutional Systems in Central and Eastern Europe]. Part I, Praha: PF UK, Vodnář, 1999.

[349]/ The Constitution of the Czech Republic 1992 has introduced the term "constitutional order" for this type of legislation and their body defined in its Art. 112 and Art. 3.

[350]/ Blahož, J.: *Soudní kontrola ústavnosti* [Judicial Control over Constitutionality]. Praha: ASPI Publishing, 2001, p. 267.

[351]/ Section 64 (1) (b) Act No. 182/1993 Sb., on the Constitutional Court, as amended (ACC); formerly Art. 8 (2) Constitutional Act No. 91/1991 Sb., on the Constitutional Court of the Czech and Slovak Federal Republic. The French Constitutional Council began reviewing the constitutionality of all stages of the legislative procedure in the second half of the 1970s, when the change of the Constitution resulted in the power conferred on a minority in both chambers to propose the repeal of a law as part of the abstract control of constitutionality. See Blahož, J. *supra* at p. 329 and subs.

[352]/ Act No. 182/1993 Sb., regulating the rules of procedure before the Constitutional Court under Art. 88 (1) of the Constitution of the Czech Republic.

ment has been passed and issued by a competent body within its constitutionally defined competence; (2) to ascertain whether the respective enactment has been passed and issued in the constitutionally prescribed manner; and (3) to consider whether the content of the respective enactment has been in compliance with legislation having higher legal force. Only after an affirmative answer is given at the first stage the enactment proceeds into the second stage, and if the answer is again positive the enactment is subject to the review of its substantive conformity.[353]

The influence of the Constitutional Court upon the legal system has been generally predetermined by constitutional and ordinary legislation setting rules for the staffing of the Court and for proceedings before it. The abstract checking on the constitutionality of legislation is always subject to the following determinants in the activities of the Constitutional Court:

a) The composition of the Court derived from the consenting wills of the President of the Czech Republic and the Senate; former members of Parliament, both deputies and senators, create not an insignificant number of Justices of the Constitutional Court;[354]
b) Adjudication made only upon an application, i.e. the Constitutional Court may not intervene in the pending suit of its own initiative; however, decision-making of the Court may be affected by the various facts, such as who applies for the decision as well as what his conduct during proceedings is like.
c) The Court being bound by the application, or its prayer for relief (s. 34 (1) ACC); the scope of the reviewing competence of the Court set in s. 68 (2) ACC has its consequences for the application of the principle *judex ne eat ultra petita partium*; the powers of the Constitutional Court to repeal law or other enactments (their individual provisions) in individual cases do not go beyond provisions which the petitioner expressly designated as unconstitutional and therefore applied for their repeal. Since the defects subsisting in the lack of competence to issue an enactment, or in the violation of technical rules of the legislative procedure when the enactment was adopted, do not always apply to the law as a whole, the Constitutional Court has stated several times that "*where the petitioner in the rule control proceedings alleges that the constitutional safeguards of competences and the legislative procedure have been violated (s. 68 (2) ACC), the relief is determined by all provisions forming the enactment allegedly suffering from the deficit of constitutionality.*"[355]
d) The control of constitutionality is subsequent, i.e. the review of constitutionality applies only to enactments, not draft laws or bills not yet promulgated (s. 66 (1) ACC). The Constitutional Court has confirmed that it is competent to determine the constitutionality of individual stages of the legislative procedure including resolutions adopted in its course but the Court may do so only within the competences conferred upon it by the Constitution, i.e. the Court should not be required to intervene in the course of the

---

[353]/ Judgment of the Constitutional Court file reference Pl. ÚS 24/07 (published as No. 88/2008 Sb.).

[354]/ Section 36 (3) of the Constitutional Court Act expressly provides that activities related to the preparation, consideration, or adoption of a statute or some other enactment are not considered a reason for the exclusion of a respective Constitutional Court Justice from the determination and adjudication of an issue.

[355]/ Judgment of the Constitutional Court file ref. Pl. ÚS 24/07 (published as No. 88/2008 Sb.); see also Judgment file ref. Pl. ÚS 7/03 (Judgment No. 113, Vol 34 Sb. n. u., published as No. 512/2004 Sb.).

legislative procedure and to annul one of the resolutions adopted before the termination of the procedure and before the official publication (force) of the law.[356] The facts that the Constitutional Court may not interfere with the legislative procedure but it may assess its course and outcomes may be considered as a loophole in the law;[357] the recognition of such power would permit a preventive control of the constitutionality of (draft) laws.

e) Deciding in a certain time; this is significant particularly today when the legal order is subject to the permanent procedure of changes (s. 67 ACC).

f) Sudden transformation of the relevance of criteria forming the basis for the deciding on the annulment of laws or other enactments; the change was brought in primarily by the amendment of the Constitution (Constitutional Act No. 395/2001 Sb.). Initially it was general incorporation of all treaties ratified by Parliament and published in the Collection of international treaties into the legal order of the Czech Republic. Such treaties have constitutional primacy in their application over ordinary laws (Art. 10 of the Constitution, as amended on 1st June 2002). The second step was incorporation or transposition of EC or EU law into the Czech legal order (as from 1st May 2004). The latter change in particular reduces the space for the Constitutional Court to review the constitutionality of laws and other enactments transposing the EC/EU obligations to mere consideration of relevant procedural and competence elements of the law-making.

The consistency of the contents of a draft law

The issue of monothematic laws is as old as the law-making itself. Even in ancient Rome *"...there was a practice emerging to include into one draft provisions of a variable nature, such as combining an unpopular measure with a welcomed one in order to increase a chance that the draft could be passed as a whole. Therefore in 98 B.C. Lex Caecilia Didia stipulated that a law should be monothematic and should not combine different provisions into one whole..."* [358] The same arguments apply by analogy in a modern democratic state. However, the principle of a monothematic law is not expressly formulated in any piece of legislation although it is considered as an inherent feature of the concept of a state governed by the rule of law (Art. 1(1) of the Constitution). It can be found only in the Government Rules of Legislative Drafting: "One law, including a law providing for an amendment to a different act, may not regulate diverse matters which are not interrelated." (Art. 39 (4)).[359]

---

[356]/ Resolution of the Constitutional Court file ref. II. ÚS 21/02 (No. 3, Vol. 25 Sb. n. u.) on the application that the Constitutional Court should impose a duty on the Chamber of Deputies to refer to the Senate a bill which was agreed by resolution of the Chamber. See also Filip, J.: Ústavní soud a řešení sporů v zákonodárném procesu [The Constitutional Court and the Solution of Disputes in the Legislative Procedure]. *Právní zpravodaj* 1/2002, pp. 9–10.

[357]/ This issue is tackled by Filip, J.: Legislativní technika a judikatura Ústavního soudu [Legislative Technique and Case Law of the Constitutional Court]. *Časopis pro právní vědu a praxi* 3/2005, who compares this situation with the existing powers of competent courts to intervene in the registration stage of elections.

[358]/ Kincl, J. – Urfus, V. – Skřejpek, M.: *Římské právo* [Roman Law]. Praha: C. H. Beck, 1995, p. 17.

[359]/ The Government Rules of Legislative Drafting were passed by the Government Resolution of 19th March 1998, No. 188; they have been amended by nine Government Resolutions. This principle was expressed as early as in 1923 in the Directive for the Uniform Legislative Technique; the Directive provided for various general principles of legislative drafting including the maxim that one draft law should not mix up diverse subjects. See also Šín, Z.: Historie legislativních pravidel v našich zemích [The History of Legislative Drafting Rules in Our Country]. *Právník* 12/2002, p. 1312 and subs.

However, due to the so-called Competence Act, this Resolution applies only to the Government and bodies bound by its resolutions.[360]

Thus a frequently used practice developed in both chambers of the Parliament on the turn of millennia, where a bill (draft law) contains independent amendments of laws not relating (at all or remotely) in their substance to the subject-matter of the introduced bill. One of the first examples is Act No. 170/2001 Sb.[361] but its subject-matter heterogeneity has not been subject to the review of the Constitutional Court yet.

Since this unfortunate practice of "opening" laws through amendments (often introduced surprisingly during the second reading in the plenary session of the Chamber of Deputies or even after the referral of the bill to the Senate) has become more and more frequent such "covert" laws have attracted the attention not only of legal specialists but also citizens have noticed that approach. It should be noted that even the Constitutional Court tolerated such practice for many years.

In its judgment from 2002 on the application of the group of Senators to annul Act No. 217/2000 Sb. containing the amendment of Act No. 10/1993 Sb. on the state budget of the CR for 1993, the Constitutional Court decided not to yet repeal the Act due to its inconsistency.[362] Senators claimed that the Act, or its part, was not adopted in a formally proper manner prescribed by the Constitution. The unconstitutionality of the procedure of adoption of the Act was seen in the following factors: as soon as an amendment of a State Budget Act is included in any other bill, such bill may not be referred to the Senate for consideration and passing a resolution on the bill in accordance with the Constitution because Art. 42 (2) of the Constitution expressly provides that the draft of a State Budget Act may be considered, and the resolution on it passed, solely by the Chamber of Deputies. The Constitutional Court, in accord with the opinions of both parliamentary chambers, fully dismissed as unsubstantiated the application of the group of Senators because "*when considering whether in this particular case the bill may be understood as a "State Budget Act" under Art. 42 (2) of the Constitution it does not suffice to look just at the formal designation of that act (bill). Such approach could consequently lead to potential exclusion of the Senate from the legislative procedure with respect to some important laws just because a particular bill would be called a "State Budget Act" although it would actually regulate the substance not directly applying to the state budget. On the other hand, the Constitutional Court wishes to emphasize that the material understanding of the term "State Budget Act" must not lead to its broad interpretation*

---

[360]/ Section 21 of Act No. 2/1969 Sb. of the Czech National Council, establishing ministries and other central state administration bodies of the Czech Republic.

[361]/ As a result of the unrelated amendment included in the draft an Act was passed whose title speaks for itself: "Act providing for the state bond programme to discharge obligations resulting from the Treaty between the Government of the Czech Republic, the Government of the Slovak Republic and the Government of the Federal Republic of Germany to terminate foreign exchange transactions in convertible roubles and to settle mutual obligations and claims constituting the balance in convertible roubles in favour of the Federal Republic of Germany, and amending Act No. 407/2000 Sb., regulating the state bond programme to partially cover damage incurred by persons engaged in agriculture as a result of drought in 2000, and amending Act No. 424/1991 Sb., providing for assembling in political parties and political movements, as amended". In reaction to the judgment of the Constitutional Court published as No. 98/2001 Sb. and abolishing the financial contribution to a political party for the mandate of a Deputy or a Senator representing that political party, there was a new part incorporated in the Bill, which amended Act No. 424/1991 Sb. in order to quickly re-introduce such financial contribution.

[362]/ Judgment Pl. ÚS 21/01 of the 12th February 2002 (No. 14, Vol. 25 Sb. n. u., published as No. 95/2002 Sb.).

since it is obvious that essentially any bill is, directly or indirectly, relating to the state budget simply because its implementation would usually have an impact on the state budget (either it revenues or expenditures)."

At the same time the Constitutional Court stated: "*It should be added that this practice where one act amends several different laws at a time has been relatively frequent in the legislative procedure. The Constitutional Court generally states that such practice is essentially in conformity with the Constitution only where the amended laws are meritoriously interlinked. On the contrary, the phenomenon, where one bill is to amend acts the subject-matters of which are not directly or immediately interconnected, is undesirable and inconsistent with the sense and principles of the legislative procedure; this happens, for example, in order to speed up the legislative procedure by introducing amendments. (...) Such an approach does not correspond with the basic principles of the state governed by the rule of law, as these principles encompass predictability of a law, its comprehensibility and internal consistency. Where one law (in the formal sense) intervenes in the subject-matter regulated by several other laws and these laws are not interwoven systematically and in their substance, it often gives rise to an obscure legal situation not respecting the principles of predictability, comprehensibility and internal consistency.*"

The Constitutional Court in its judgment of June 2005 on the constitutionality of the legislative procedure applicable to the passage of an ordinary law which, along with its main subject-matter, contains an amendment of a law, the passage of which requires the qualified (constitutional) majority of three-fifths of members in either parliamentary chamber (the "Election Act" under Art. 40 of the Constitution) provides: "It is not possible that different parts of one bill should be subject to different constitutional procedures required for their adoption. In other words: the bill must be subject to the uniform regime of its consideration which cannot be legally good and, at the same time, unconstitutional; where the bill contains parts subject to different procedures for their adoption, the constitutionally conforming adoption of such a bill requires that a stricter procedure be applied to the whole of the bill."[363]

The Constitutional Court made its strictest decision as yet on the subject-matter consistency of a law in its judgment from 2007.[364] A group of Senators objected to Act No. 443/2006 Sb. due to its retroactive applicability[365] as well as the procedure resulting in the alteration of one of earlier amendments of the Banking Act. They found the violation of the principles of regularity and transparency of legislation and the prohibition of arbitrariness in the legislative procedure (Art. 1 and Art. 2 (3) of the Constitution, and Art. 2 (2) of the Charter, Art. 37 (2), Art. 41 and Art. 44 of the Constitution) during the adoption of an amendment in the Chamber of Deputies (introduced as late as during the circumscribed debate in the second reading) altering a law not meritoriously relating to the debated bill. These principles belong to the material maxims of the state governed by the rule of law (Art. 1 and 2 of the Constitution and Art. 1 and 4 of the Charter). Under Art. 48 of the Constitution the

---

[363]/ Judgment Pl. ÚS 13/05 of 22nd June 2005 (No. 127, Vol. 37 Sb. n. u., published as No. 283/2005 Sb.). It should be noted that there was no unanimous opinion of theoreticians and practitioners whether the elections to regional and community councils should be designated as "Elections Act" and why the Constitutional Court subsumed this legislation under Art. 40 of the Constitution as late as in that judgment.

[364]/ Judgment Pl. ÚS 77/06 of 15th February 2007 (published as No. 37/2007 Sb.).

[365]/ The Senators claimed that the Act amended transitional provisions of one of the amendments of the Banking Act (passed as Act No. 319/2001 Sb.), which should have been consumed by that amendment. The Senators challenged the fact that, since the adoption of the amended Act, the legislature had passed several other amendments of the Banking Act containing its own transitional provisions, and then the law-maker intervened backwards in the transitional provisions of one of the former amendments passed much earlier.

Senate expressed its will not to deal with the bill and the President of the Czech Republic left the constitutional period of 15 days run to no effect without the bill being signed or returned thereby.[366] The Constitutional Court, referring to its earlier case law, disposed of the application in the affirmative; the Court inferred from the constitutional principles of a democratic state governed by the rule of law (Art. 1 (1) of the Constitution) and from Art. 2 (3) of the Constitution defining the scope of state authority that the Parliament may not act arbitrarily but is bound by the law: when executing the legislative business the Parliament must comply with the Constitution and with the Standing Rules Acts interpreted in conformity with the Constitution. The Parliament must also follow *"the settled practice of the parliamentary chamber and its bodies which may, due to its repeating for a long time, be considered an unwritten part of the legislative procedure where such part can be deemed compatible with the higher values of law-making, democratic political system, etc."* The background principle for the Constitutional Court is that *"no law or any other enactment may be passed in an unlawful manner"*, one of the examples of unlawfulness in that particular case being the violation of the peremptory regulations governing law-making.[367] As its referential background for considering the constitutionality of the legislative procedure, the Constitutional Court sets the principle of the state governed by the rule of law and the democratic legislative procedure, the principle of constitutional conformity of the interpretation of the sources of law regulating the legislative procedure as well as the existence of safeguards of the constitutionally conforming execution of the legislative procedure. The stated criteria led the Constitutional Court to reject the adoption not only of amendments inconsistent with the subject-matter of the bill in question but, generally, of any laws diverse in their contents whether the inconsistency has been caused by alterations in the draft made by Parliament or the inconsistent law has been introduced to Parliament for consideration.

Since its very beginning the Constitutional Court has emphasized that a law should be predictable in both its form and its contents and it should be a consistent source of law. In 1994 the Court stressed that *"an Act in the state governed by the rule of law is not only an internal circular for the state bureaucracy"*, but that *"it is a generally published tool to suggest primarily to citizens what they may and may not do, and what they may still do and what they must not do."* In the constitutional state *"it is important not only in what way the courts are able to interpret laws but also in what way the laws will be interpreted by citizens. Legal uncertainty in citizens means the loss of their trust in the state and, at the same time, it creates a bar to civic activities."*[368]

The Constitutional Court keeps emphasizing that (a) the principle of clarity and determinacy of a law represents part of the principle of legal certainty and, as a result, of the principle of the state governed by the rule of law;[369] (b) the concept of the state governed

---

[366] Such inactivity of the President cannot be understood as meaning that the performance of his authority is subject to his discretion, but, on the contrary, it should be considered as violation of his duty to act, i.e. to perform his office, unless barred by serious reasons (Art. 66 of the Constitution). The President must either return the passed Act to the Parliament (Art. 62 (h) of the Constitution) or sign it (Art. 62 (i) of the Constitution), *tertium non datur*. The first law when the President acted in this way was Act No. 292/2004 Sb., on the merit of Edvard Beneš.

[367] Knapp, V.: *Teorie práva* [Theory of Law]. Praha: C. H. Beck, 1995, p. 107.

[368] Judgment of the Constitutional Court of 12th April 1994, file ref. Pl. ÚS 43/93, No. 16, Vol. 1 Sb. n. u. (published as No. 91/1994 Sb.).

[369] Judgment of the Constitutional Court of 24th May 1994 file ref. Pl. ÚS 16/93, No. 25, Vol. 1 Sb. n. u. (published as No. 131/1994 Sb.).

by the rule of law implies the principle that neither the legislature nor the executive may dispose of the forms of law, i.e. the source of law, in an arbitrary way, but they must follow the rules of the constitution-maker as well as other principles, particularly transparency, accessibility and clarity;[370] (c) it is necessary, in order to ensure the existence of the internal consistency of the legal order, to make individual laws and other enactments comprehensible and consequences predictable;[371] (d) the predictability, comprehensibility and absence of internal antagonisms of a law belongs among the basic principles of the rule of law;[372] (c) the principle of legal certainty and the protection of trust of citizens in the law implies that any legal person must have a chance to precisely and without any doubts ascertain what properly published rules they must observe in their activities;[373] and (f) an Act in a democratic state governed by the rule of law must be determinate, clear, transparent, comprehensible, unambiguous, without any internal conflict, linguistically and stylistically good.[374] The Constitutional Court in the above-mentioned judgment from 2007 also declared the observance of parliamentary procedures to be a fundamental condition for the ensuring of the formal values of law, such as the order, predictability, absence of arbitrariness, legal equality and legal certainty. The introduction and adoption of a heterogeneous in its subject-matter bill, on the other hand, suggest that there is a conflict with the principles of consistent, transparent and predictable law.

Only several months after this judgment the Government, in the politically important case of Act No. 261/2007 Sb. providing for the stabilization of public budgets,[375] showed how seriously it took the judgment of the Constitutional Court into consideration. The Government bill intended, without any significant unifying idea, to alter a wide and diverse range of other laws, and even incorporated into it three separate laws.[376] Moreover, the Prime Minister, during the circumscribed debate in the second reading and in his capacity as member of the Chamber of Deputies, introduced extensive amendments to this "reform package" bill, and the Chair of the group of the senior coalition party introduced amendments to those amendments.[377] These amendments brought in massive alteration of the bill substantially exceeding the original legislative intention.[378] In addition, the body of

---

[370]/ Judgment of the Constitutional Court of 23rd May 2000 file ref. Pl. ÚS 24/99, No. 73, Vol. 18 Sb. n. u. (published as No. 167/2000 Sb.).

[371]/ Judgment of the Constitutional Court of 4th July 2000 file ref. Pl. ÚS 7/2000, No. 106, Vol. 19 Sb. n. u. (published as No. 261/2000 Sb.).

[372]/ Judgment of the Constitutional Court of 12th February 2002 file ref. Pl. ÚS 21/01, No. 14, Vol. 25 Sb. n. u. (published as No. 95/2002 Sb.).

[373]/ Judgment of the Constitutional Court of 28th May 2003 file ref. I. ÚS 472/01, No. 70, Vol. 30 Sb. n. u.

[374]/ Judgment of the Constitutional Court of 14th July 2005 file ref. Pl. ÚS 23/04, No. 137, Vol. 38 Sb. n. u. (published as No. 331/2005 Sb.).

[375]/ V. PS, 2007, Print No. 222.

[376]/ Particularly, parts 45–47 originally prepared as autonomous laws on environmental taxes became "laws in the law". The absurd outcome of this flagrant violation of the Government Rules of Legislative Drafting has been that Act No. 261/2007 Sb. contains section 1 three times, section 2 three times, etc.

[377]/ V. PS, 2007, Print No. 222/3.

[378]/ The changes expanding the original bill included the amendment of the Public Health Insurance Act (designated as Part 40, Art. LXIV) as a fully new subject-matter. "The Regulation of prices of, and payments for medicinal preparations and food for special medical purposes", which as a separate part encompassing 14 sections and 69 subsections introduced a new system of regulation of prices of medicinal products, i.e. de facto a new law without any formal application of the legislative initiative.

amendments brought in other subject-matters not originally included by the Government in the list of basic topics of the bill and the bill failed to fulfil its purpose.

The Senate raised by the Constitutional Court to the position of a safeguard of the constitutional conformity of the legislative procedure (see below) decided not to deal with the bill thus knowingly[379] contributing to the deterioration of the legal order, which the Senate itself had criticized shortly before.[380] This criticism was referred to by the Constitutional Court in a similar situation in its judgment from 2007 issued with respect to the application of a group of Senators and annulling parts of a bill which the Senate had decided by its resolution not to deal with.[381]

However, the Constitutional Court conceded in many of its requirements when in its judgment from 2009 it did not find Act No. 261/2007 Sb. inconsistent but only "*commingled from the legislative and technical perspective, (...) which becomes partly a 'sweeping-up' amendment and partly a new autonomous (non-amending) regulation*".[382] Although a year ago it insisted on the availability of the text of an Act without the use of electronic information systems,[383] now – a year later – the Court stated that "*in the case of a sweeping-up amendment the amending provisions become part of the consolidated texts of individual amended laws and are available to their recipients through the automated legal information systems; new provisions – non-amending – are available to their recipients in the same way as any other statute.*" Should the maxim of subject-matter consistency of a law, expressed by the Constitutional Court in its judgment from 2007 as "*a law in the formal sense, and in the state governed by the rule of law, may not be considered as a mere carrier of various changes made across the legal order*", be understood as the reason for the annulment of inconsistent parts, then the same maxim in the judgment from 2008 can apply only "*in extreme situations, such as the case mentioned by the petitioner, where the Government would concentrate in one bill all its legislative intentions once a year entitled the regulation of the legal situation in the Czech Republic or even as the Act to improve the destiny of the citizens of the Czech Republic.*" Despite all doctrinal doubts with respect to the applicability and suitability

---

[379]/ All Senators received the detailed opinion of the Legislative Department of the Senate Office of 5th September 2007 on the Bill for the stabilization of public budgets; the opinion expressly notified of, and analysed many legislative mistakes and the conflict between the Bill and judgments of the Constitutional Court.

[380]/ See the Resolution of the Senate of 25th January 2006 No. 303, where the Senate expressed its position with respect to the legislation procedure in the Czech Republic. It said that the legislative procedure in the CR had been, for a long time, deviating from classical ideals of making consistent, transparent and predictable law; the Senate requested the transparency of the law-making procedure and refused the adding of riders to bills having no relevance to their subject-matter.

[381]/ See items 18, 34 and 71 of Judgment of the Constitutional Court published as No. 37/2007 Sb.

[382]/ Judgment file ref. Pl. ÚS 24/07 of 31st January 2008 published as No. 88/2008 Sb.

[383]/ See the reasoning of Judgment from 2007 (published as No. 37/2007 Sb.: "*The requirement of predictability of a law as part of the principle of the state governed by the rule of law fails to be complied with at the moment when an amendment of that law is part of another law in the formal sense and is not relating to it in its subject-matter. The orientation of a recipient within the legal order without using information technology becomes impossible. Needless to say, s. 13 of Act No. 309/1999 Sb., regulating the Collection of Laws and the Collection of International Treaties provides that local government bodies owe a duty to provide access to the Collection of Laws to everyone. The duty to provide access to the information system containing the consolidated versions of legislation in an electronic format is not stipulated by the law. It is more than obvious that without the use of such electronic systems one becomes unable to get knowledge of the legal order of the Czech Republic; thus the application of a general principle that ignorance of law is no defence is more than problematic. Therefore, the law becomes fully unpredictable for its recipients. This principle is conditio sine qua non for the efficiency of any system of positive law; however, it cannot be interpreted only against the recipients but also as an obligation of the state to make the law recognizable because only such law may be observed.*"

of an extensive combination of the sweeping-up amendment and original regulations the Constitutional Court concluded that the considered case was not of that sort. The only signal of criticism by the Court was the censure that the consideration of the Act showed "*the deficit of democratic political culture on the part of the Government majority.*" What is more persuasive than the reasoning of the judgment is the criticism contained in dissenting opinions of four Justices who challenged the judgment. Justice Wagnerová called the judgment as a failed chance "*where the Constitutional Court resigns from the control of the procedure and manner of making the law subject to the review, and shifts the answers to questions linked with the control to a normative area other than where the law is.*" She called the approach of the Constitutional Court very formalistic since a majority of Justices "*were satisfied with the interpretation of procedural constitutional institutions as if the procedure applied to the adoption of ordinary monothematic laws, i.e. they did not react to the unusual extent of formally compiled laws and other circumstances accompanying the passage of the law under review.*"[384]

Constitutionally conforming interpretation of the sources of law regulating
legislative procedure

An inconsistent law may be formed not only due to the original structure of the legislative draft but it may become such within the legislative procedure. The theoretical constitutional background is constituted by the authority of legislative bodies and their members to exceed the intention of a draft law created by an individual or entity having legislative initiative. The intention always predetermines the subject-matter of a new regulation by defining a certain scope of social relations subject to the regulation. Where the activities of the legislature are not confined just to the approval or dismissal of a bill, as is the case of all democratically functioning parliaments, it is important to distinguish between the term "bill" (draft law) and "amendment".

While the institution of a bill (legislative initiative) has been regulated in various contexts usually at the constitutional level[385] the institution of an amendment is often mentioned at the level of parliamentary law contained in special acts, particularly the Act regulating Standing Rules of individual chambers. The Constitution of the Czech Republic recognizes the term "amendment" in the context of relations between institutions involved in the legislative procedure, i.e. the relationship between parliamentary chambers and the relationship between the Chamber of Deputies and the President (Art. 46 (2), Art. 47 (2), (3) and (4), Art. 50 (2)). The institution of "amendment" is one of the main reasons for the existence of the Senate because it enables the Senate to efficiently fulfil its role of the corrective of the legislative work of the other house.

The positive as well as material definition of the concept of "amendment" can be found in the Standing Rules Act of the respective chambers. The first sentence of s. 63 (1) of the Standing Rules Act of the Chamber of Deputies provides that a Deputy may submit in the debate only amendments "*to the issue under consideration*", that they "*should relate to a concrete issue of the item under consideration.*" S. 63 (1) item 5) a) enables a Deputy to submit an amendment which is intended "*to omit, expand or alter some parts of the original draft.*" The right to submit

---

[384]/ Dissenting opinion of Justice Eliška Wágnerová in Judgment of 31ˢᵗ January 2008 file ref. Pl. ÚS 24/07, items 1 and 2.
[385]/ See Articles 41, 42, 44–48 of the Constitution of the CR.

amendments during the parliamentary debate is derived from the right of legislative initiative but it is not identical as it is confined to the exercise of the right of legislative initiative: *"It may be inferred from the need to distinguish between legislative initiative and amendment, the former being subject to stricter constitutional requirements, that an amendment should only modify the introduced regulation, i.e. it should not substantially alter it, nor significantly expand it, and should not at all go beyond the subject-matter of the legislative initiative, or the draft law."*[386]

The Constitutional Court acknowledges that there are several safeguards of constitutionally conforming legislative procedure in order to cease the process of submission of unrelated amendment:

1. Primarily, the person presiding over the session of a chamber (Speaker or Deputy Speakers in the Chamber of Deputies and Presidents or Vice-Presidents of the Senate) should guarantee the observance of the rules of parliamentary procedure. The Court states that it is an authority of, or even a duty imposed upon, the Chair to consider whether a proposal designated as amendment is such in the material sense. This approach can be derived from *"proper interpretation"* of s. 59 (4) and s. 63 (1) of the Standing Rules Act of the Chamber of Deputies.[387] The Constitutional Court shares a quite dangerous maximalist opinion: *"Where an amendment is to change the contents or external format of the proposed law, the Chair should never permit a vote to be taken on an amendment unrelated in its subject-matter, i.e. on a putative amendment."*[388] However, not much is more remote from the role of a Chair as defined in the respective Standing Rules Acts of parliamentary chambers[389] than an idea that the Chair him/herself may decide on the destiny of proposed amendments by authoritatively designating them as either permissible or as unrelated riders. On the contrary, such an approach by a Chair would be directly violating the right of every Deputy to perform in person and without any disturbance his or her own mandate[390] subsisting primarily in that he/she has a real chance, unless barred by any statutory obstacle, to co-decide by voting on every submitted proposal, i.e. to participate in the plenary session and adoption of resolutions of the chamber of which he/she is a member (Art. 39 (2) of the

---

[386]/ Judgment Pl. ÚS 77/06 of 15th February 2007 (published as No. 37/2007 Sb.). Schorm, V.: Bezstarostná jízda [Light-hearted Ride]. *Správní právo* 2/2000, p. 65 and subs.

[387]/ S. 59 (4) of the Standing Rules Act of the Chamber of Deputies reads: "The Deputy should express his opinion on the issue under consideration. Should he derogate from it and exceed the time limit for his speech the chairing person may notify him of that fact and call him to order. Should the Deputy fail to observe in his speech decency rules the Chair may call him to order. Should a double notice fail the Chair may remove the right to the floor from such Deputy. Objections of the Deputy to his removal from the floor are considered by the Chamber without debate."

[388]/ Kysela, J.: Tvorba práva v ČR: truchlohra se šťastným koncem? [Law-making in the Czech Republic: Tragedy with a Happy Ending?]. *Právní zpravodaj* 7/2006, p. 11.

[389]/ See, in particular, s. 54 (1), (2), s. 58, s. 59 (3), s. 59 (4), s. 66, s. 73, s. 76 (1), (6) of the Standing Rules Act of the Chamber of Deputies. The Chair has never the authority to consider amendments under s. 59 (4) of the Standing Rules Act of the Chamber of Deputies, as was suggested by the Constitutional Court; this provision undoubtedly (in the whole context of s. 59) regulates only the rules of oral presentations of a Deputy in the debate and the authority of the Chair to react to such speech. The Chair may do so only by a) notifying and calling to focus on the issue, b) calling to order, and c) removing the right to the floor. The provision does not create the authority to actually exclude an amendment unless the case under s. 72 (3) of the Standing Rules Act of the Chamber of Deputies is at issue.

[390]/ Art. 26 of the Constitution, Art. 21 (1) and (4) of the Charter.

Constitution).[391] The Chair is not, and cannot be, individually responsible for the quality of an emerging law: the Chair is not a judge and is not subject to the presumption of the knowledge of law (*jura novit curia*). The Chair may designate a concrete amendment as "non-votable" only in agreement with the Reporter of a particular bill (typically, the Standing Rules Acts do not mention such authority of the Chair or Reporter) and only if the amendment has been excluded with respect to an amendment passed earlier.[392] The Chair may not assume the authority to decide on a conflict over the substance of a submitted amendment in relation to the original draft because this is not permitted by the law. The Chair should, in accordance with his/her role, use all possibilities to clarify the contentious issue as well as to maintain the democratic manner of decision making, e.g. to move the interruption of the session.[393]

2. The second safeguard should be the consideration of a draft law by the second chamber of Parliament – the Senate. Its role is "*to reveal mistakes in the legislative procedure and adequately react within the scope of powers conferred upon the Senate although it is obvious that its possibilities are limited.*"[394] It should be added to this laconic statement that if the rule of so-called close relationship applies to amendments introduced in the Chamber of Deputies it applies even more to amendments introduced in the Senate. Unlike the legislative initiative itself, a bill passed by the Chamber of Deputies relies on the will of the first parliamentary chamber, which cannot be disregarded in the following stages of the legislative procedure. Since the Senate in its essence does not have powers equal to those of the Chamber of Deputies (at least in passing ordinary laws) but, as follows from Articles 46 and 48 of the Constitution, it acts as a corrector of the Chamber's work, it may neither circumvent the legislative procedure (which it can apply only as the whole house in the manner prescribed by the law[395]) and replace the referred bill by a different text, nor it may add to the referred bill inconsistent and unrelated amendments. Should the Senate do so the Chamber of Deputies serves as a safeguard against such an approach; the latter puts to a vote the bill committed to the Chamber by the Senate as a whole (not its individual Senate amendments) and the Senate text of the bill may not be changed or modified thereby.[396] The above-mentioned idea that where the bill is referred back with amendments by the Senate to the Chamber of Deputies and the limits have been exceeded either intensively or extensively, and the Chair during the debate in the Chamber of Deputies would designate the Senate version of the bill as non-votable, would be in violation not only of the Standing Rules Act but also of the constitutional conception of the role of both chambers.

---

[391] See also the Standing Rules Act of the Chamber of Deputies, particularly s. 69 (5), under which "*The Chamber decides on every amendment by taking the vote. The vote is conducted by the Chair. The Chair is obliged to notify the Chamber that the vote is to be taken.*" Under subsection (6) "*The Chair takes the vote first in favour of the motion and then against the motion.*"

[392] S. 72 (3) of the Standing Rules Act of the Chamber of Deputies.

[393] S. 54 (9) of the Standing Rules Act of the Chamber of Deputies, s. 57 (5) of the Standing Rules Act of the Senate.

[394] Judgment Pl. ÚS 77/06 of 15th February 2007 (published as No. 37/2007 Sb.).

[395] See Part Fourteen (ss. 127–131) of Act No. 107/1999 Sb., on the Standing Rules of the Senate.

[396] Art. 47 (3) and (4) of the Constitution.

3. The Constitutional Court considers as the third safeguard of the due legislative procedure the right of the President of the Czech Republic to return the passed bill back to the Chamber of Deputies (Art. 62 h/, Art. 50 (1) of the Constitution): *"The function of the President within the legislative procedure is certainly not a political one because the function of the President of the Republic does not subsist in the making of a competitive policy in relation to the Government. The President of the Republic is defined by the Constitution a an extra-partisan constitutional body. Considering the conception of the Constitution of the Czech Republic and irrespective of the reality, this characteristics predetermines the President to control the observance of the constitutionality of the legislative procedure through means conferred upon the President by the Constitution, i.e. through the presidential veto."*[397] Although generally one may agree that the suspensive veto of the President may be a tool applied to compel the Chamber of Deputies to think again about its work, one can hardly agree with the above reasons for the President to do so. The thesis that the presidential function is not political since it is conceived as an extra-partisan constitutional institution can rely neither on the constitutional practice nor on the text of the Constitution itself.[398] Although the Constitution did not confer upon the President the right of legislative initiative thus allowing the President to make competitive policy against the Government (unlike the former constitutional situation) it did not define the presidential office as insignificant to such extent that the President cannot enforce his autonomous political will against the Government. Just on the contrary: the power to sign and return bills was incorporated in such an area where the President – not dependent on the countersignature of the Prime Minister – may act freely. It seems to be doubtful whether the President is predestined for the control of the constitutionality of the legislative procedure through his vetoes due to his alleged "extra-partisanship". Should the thesis of the Constitutional Court that the presidential function is not political in the legislative area and non-competitive (non-polemic) with respect to the Government apply, the presidential veto would have to be bound to the countersignature of the Prime Minister, as was the case between 1918 and 1960.[399]

4. Only where the above safeguards fail the Constitutional Court may act if it is called to do so by a regular petition filed by a petitioner having the right to do so.

2.5.3 New phenomena in electoral law

As indicated by a number of comparative studies, a declining turnout in elections is a worldwide trend. According to A. Blais, who researched the development in nineteen countries with a long-lasting democratic tradition, over the last thirty years the average turnout in elections has fallen by 7 percentage points.[400] In addition to that, the trend is growing

---

[397] Judgment Pl. ÚS 77/06 of 15th February 2007 (published as No. 37/2007 Sb.).

[398] President V. Klaus may serve as an example: he was elected President as a member and former Chair of the ODS party and acted as its "honorary chair" during his first presidential term and part of the second term; he actively participated in the party's pre-election campaign in support of its candidates. His political orientation may be traced through his vetoes of bills.

[399] S. 10 and 11 (1) of the interim constitution; s. 47 and 68 of the Constitutional Charter 1920; s. 58 and 77 of the Constitution 1948.

[400] Blais, A.: *To Vote or Not to Vote. The Merits and Limits of Rational Choice Theory.* Pittsburg: University of Pittsburg Press, 2000, pp. 32–36.

stronger, so in the 1990s the election turnout fell on average by one percentage point in every election. Such a development has also applied to the Czech Republic.

The turnout differs depending on the type of election. The highest number of electors can be seen in elections to the Chamber of Deputies, on average more than 68 %, while the turnout is much lower in other types of elections.

The turnout is gradually falling primarily in the Chamber of Deputies elections. In the year 2006 there was a slight improvement which was probably caused by a more intense election campaign that resulted in higher polarization of the society. As is clear from the chart, though, the overall trend has been clearly falling since the 1990s.

It is not only political scientists and researchers who are concerned about low election turnout; surprisingly enough, the voters themselves see it as an issue. According to the public opinion poll carried out by Centrum pro výzkum veřejného mínění (CVVM, Center for Public Opinion Polls) in 2005, more than two thirds of citizens consider low election

Table No. 1: Turnout in elections in the Czech Republic in the years 1994–2008 (percents; Czech Statistics Office).

	1994	1996	1998	2000	2002	2004	2006	2008
Chamber of Deputies of the Parliament of CR		76.41	74.03		58.00		64.47	
Senate PCR – 1st ballot		35.03	42.37	33.72	24.10	28.97	42.09	39.52
Senate PCR – 2nd ballot		30.63	20.36	21.56	32.55	18.41	20.73	29.85
Regional councils				33.64		29.62		40.30
Community councils	60.68		45.02		43.39		46.38	
European Parliament						28.32		

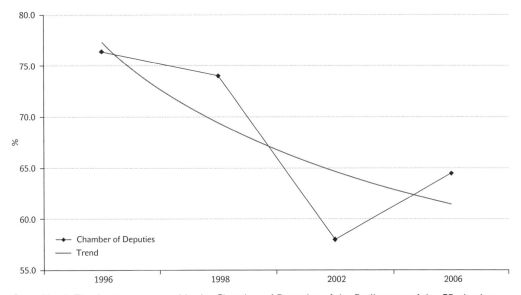

Chart No. 1: Election turnout trend in the Chamber of Deputies of the Parliament of the CR election.

turnout as a social problem.[401] More than a half of the respondents are of the opinion that the government should take steps to increase it.[402]

Electoral law reforms carried out so far have focused primarily on other areas. In addition to purely technical amendments, the basic variables of the electoral system for the Chamber of Deputies were changed several times,[403] which is a key issue for the political parties; however it is not so important for electors and their participation in elections. Gradually the discussion is being launched about such changes that could have a positive influence on the achieved turnout in elections. These include, for example, the expansion of possibilities of remote voting and postal voting or voting via the internet. The universality of suffrage is growing slowly: e.g. voters abroad and foreigners with residence in the Czech Republic have received the opportunity to vote and in the future perhaps even voters younger than 18 may be included.

The defining feature of all forms of remote voting is the fact that the act of voting takes a different form than personally casting a vote in the proper polling station. Some of these forms are already used in the Czech Republic; however, the choice differs in individual types of elections.[404] The universally available option consists of voting using a portable ballot box, which may be requested by an elector who has strong reasons, primarily health-related, in all types of elections. The Code of Good Practice in Electoral Matters[405] does not recommend this manner of voting primarily due to a higher risk of fraud. In our country, though, it is a traditional possibility which has not caused any serious issues.[406] It is also possible to vote in the Chamber of Deputies election, Senate election and European Parliament election using an elector's certificate. Voters who will not be present in their electoral ward on the election day may apply for their elector's certificate which enables them to cast the vote in another polling station.

All forms used so far in the Czech Republic may be included in the group referred to as remote voting in the supervised environment by the Venice Commission.[407] The significant

---

[401] CVVM: *Volební (ne)účast* [(Lack of) Election Turnout]. Press release, 7th March 2005. Praha: SÚ AV ČR.

[402] CVVM: *Možnosti zvýšení volební účasti* [Options for Improving Election Turnout]. Press release, 9th March 2005. Praha: SÚ AV ČR.

[403] Gradual transition towards greater disproportions in the electoral system is in line with the general development trend in the post-communist countries, which was identified in the mid-nineties by M. Kasapovič and D. Nohlen and in 2007 again confirmed by J. Šedo in his very thorough work *Volební systémy postkomunistických zemí* [Electoral Systems of Post-communist Countries]. Brno: Centrum pro studium demokracie a kultury (CDK), 2007, see primarily pp. 86–87.

[404] For more detailed overview see Antoš, M.: *Principy voleb v České republice* [Principles of Elections in the Czech Republic]. Praha: Linde Praha, 2008, pp. 140–146.

[405] European Commission for Democracy through Law (Venice Commission): *Code of Good Practice in Electoral Matters. Guidelines and Explanatory Report.* CDL-AD(2002)023rev. Strasbourg, 23rd May 2003, http://www.venice.coe.int/docs/2002/CDL-AD(2002)023rev-e.pdf. From the point of view of international law, it is a non-binding document worked out by the Venice Commission and approved by the Parliamentary Assembly of the Council of Europe. It is, however, quoted in many recent decisions of the European Court of Human Rights relating to election issues, which gives the document legal importance. This is why I consider it a soft-law.

[406] This does not apply in all cases. In 2004 the Supreme Administrative Court in an action for nullity of a Senate election addressed a problematic course of voting in an elderly care facility in Ústí nad Labem. The court concluded that the members of the district election committee who came to the home with a portable ballot box did not ensure ballot secrecy and therefore the law was breached.

[407] European Commission for Democracy through Law (Venice Commission): *Report on the Compatibility of*

advantage of such forms of voting is their relatively high safety in terms of no interference with the freedom to vote. However, these forms have their limitations with respect to the reducing of time demands for casting votes. If the state is interested in stopping the trend of the falling turnout in elections by providing the electors a simpler access to voting, it will be necessary to use one of the methods of voting in a non-supervised environment.

Postal voting

In the last term of office two bills amending the Electoral Act aiming at introducing postal voting were presented in the Chamber of Deputies with no success. If the bills were adopted all voters could have received a possibility to vote by post in the Chamber of Deputies election.[408] It would be necessary to request ballots no later than 35 days before the date of the election. The modified ballot would be inserted by the voter in an official envelope. At the same time the voter would complete an identification form with his/her name, surname, date of birth and permanent residence address in the Czech Republic or residence outside the Czech Republic. The identification form was also supposed to contain a declaration that the voter was voting personally and was a citizen of the Czech Republic on the day of the election. The completed and signed identification sheet and the official envelope would then be inserted by the voter into the postal envelope and sent to the relevant local authority or embassy.

Due to reasons not related with the core of the amendment, the Chamber of Deputies did not adopt the bill in the third reading.[409] However, there was political consensus on the main principles of the bill, which leads to the assumption that a similar proposal will be discussed again.[410] The dismissed bill contained a number of contentious matters not just of technical nature but mainly in terms of the guarantee of a democratic and free course of elections forming part of the principles of the right to vote. Postal voting in general causes certain conflicts primarily with the principle of secret ballot and with the principle of direct suffrage.[411] Another issue in the Czech Republic subsists in the danger of buying votes. We have some experience in the Czech Republic of some persons standing for election trying to gain votes by, for example, election lotteries or promises to award valuable prizes in case of success in an election. Another form offers various discounts if the customers submit

Remote Voting and Electronic Voting with the Standards of the Council of Europe. CDL-AD(2004)012. Strasbourg, 18th March 2004, http://www.venice.coe.int/docs/2004/CDL-AD(2004)012-e.asp, p. 6 and subs.

[408]/ See print No. 945, Chamber of Deputies, IV term of office, as amended.

[409]/ The comprehensive amendment drafted in the constitutional law committee included a reduction of the share of preference votes required for moving the candidate upwards on the list of candidates from seven to five percent. ODS deputies, who otherwise supported postal voting, did not agree with this change. This is why they did not support the bill in the final vote. The total of 73 deputies voted in favour of the bill and at least 86 votes were needed to pass the bill.

[410]/ This is confirmed by the recurring proposed amendment of the electoral act drafted by the Permanent Commission of the Senate for Compatriots Living Abroad, which was adopted as a Senators' Bill and currently (January 2009) the Government is to issue its opinion (see print No. 332, Senate, 6th term of office 2006–2008 and print No. 706, Chamber of Deputies, V. term of office). According to the bill, postal voting is to be enabled only abroad; the previous bill was similar but the impact was considerably expanded in the course of debate in the Chamber of Deputies.

[411]/ See Birch, S. – Watt, B.: Remote Electronic Voting: Free, Fair and Secret. *The Political Quarterly* 1/2004, p. 63.

the voting papers of particular parties and by doing so they prove that they did not vote for these parties.[412]

This is why remote voting in a non-supervised environment always presents a certain risk that the freedom of choice will be interfered with. It is possible to adopt a regulation to minimise such risk. The simplest way is to enable the voters to vote, in addition to a remote vote, also in a standard manner in the polling station which renders the remote vote void. It is also possible to grant the remote voting option only to those electors who can prove that they cannot attend in the regular polling station, for example because they are abroad.

Vote via the Internet

In addition to postal voting, the alternative of e-enabled voting by means of the internet is becoming internationally quite popular.[413] In Europe the countries that made the biggest progress include the United Kingdom with a number of pilot projects,[414] and primarily Estonia, which became the first country in 2007 that organised a national parliamentary election allowing the internet voting. A total of 30275 votes were cast using this method out of the total 555463 votes, i.e. approximately 5,5 %.[415] This represented almost a triple growth compared to community elections in 2005 and it is assumed that this trend will continue in the future. This may have a positive influence on the overall election turnout primarily in the group of younger voters. According to the results of research carried out for the Council of Europe by a group of experts headed by Professor A. Trechsel from z EUI, approximately one tenth of these voters would not have voted otherwise and thanks to the internet they did cast their vote.[416]

In April 2008 the Chairman of the Czech Statistics Office and the Minister of the Interior signed a memorandum on cooperation in preparing the concept, solution, testing and

---

412/ This is, of course, very disputable "evidence" because every voter has according to current legal regulation the possibility to request in the polling station a new set of all voting papers. This is why it is possible to use one voting paper and the other may be submitted in order to gain the discount. Therefore this is not a way proving that the voter did or did not vote for a particular party.

413/ Covering all the aspects of electronic voting is well beyond the scope of this paper. This is why I refer to the articles covering these issues recently published in the Czech Republic: Filip, J.: Alternativní způsoby hlasování a jejich vliv na aktivitu voličů [Alternative Forms of Voting and Their Impact on Voters' Activity]. *Časopis pro právní vědu a praxi* 1/2007, pp. 5–12; Gottinger, V. – Nováčková, P.: Může být elektronické hlasování alternativou pro místní referendum? [Can Electronic Voting be an Alternative to Local Referendum?]. *Časopis pro právní vědu a praxi* 1/2007, pp. 61–69; Antoš, M.: Hlasování po Internetu: Estonsko [Internet Vote: Estonia]. In: Knoll, V. – Bednář, V. (ed.): *Naděje právní vědy. Býkov 2007* [Hopes of Legal Science. Býkov 2007]. Plzeň: Vydavatelství a nakladatelství Aleš Čeněk, 2009; Šindelář, P.: Elektronické volby jako možný nástroj posílení demokracie [Electronic Election as a Possible Tool for Strengthening Democracy]. *Systems integration* 2006, p. 238 and subs.; Zálešák, M. – Matejka, J.: Nové možnosti (e)demokracie: Vybrané právní a technologické aspekty [New Options of (e)democracy: Selected Legal and Technological Issues]. *ITprávo.cz*. http://itpravo.cz/index.shtml?x=113369.

414/ The Electoral Commission: *Electoral Pilot schemes*. http://www.electoralcommission.org.uk/elections/modernising.cfm.

415/ Estonian National Electoral Committee: *Statistical overview and comparison of the results of I-voting in 2007 parliamentary elections and 2005 local gov council elections*. http://www.vvk.ee/english/Ivoting%20comparison%202005_2007.pdf

416/ Trechsel, A. H. et al.: *Internet voting in the March 2007 Parliamentary Elections in Estonia*. Council of Europe report, 31st July 2007, retrieved from http://www.vvk.ee/public/dok/CoE_and_NEC_Report_E-Voting_2007.pdf, p. 4 and subs.

implementation of systems of electronic voting in the Czech Republic.[417] First of all there is expected to be a pilot project to verify the possibility to vote using electronic identification. Such a project should have only a limited scope and will not be used in regular elections. Both institutions should have submitted a comprehensive report by the end of the year 2009 which would reflect the results and propose necessary legislative changes. Unfortunately, no report was drafted by the end of 2009.

The wording of the memorandum shows that the authors are aware of the issues of electronic voting that must be addressed. Among other things there are the same dangers as described above for postal voting: possibility of duress, buying of votes, etc. In addition to these, there is another group of issues that are specific to electronic voting. It is necessary to make sure that only qualified electors may vote, that their votes cannot be forged and that it is not possible to read or alter the cast vote on the way between the voter's computer and the election server. No voter may be allowed to cast more than one valid vote that would be included in the election result; and, at the same time, it is necessary to make sure that nobody can find out who voted for whom. All ballots must be duly included in the overall election results which must be ensured by sufficient control mechanisms at all stages while not putting in danger the secrecy of the ballot.

Other alternatives

There are also other forms of remote voting that may help achieve the objective of easier access to elections and therefore higher turnout. Introducing the possibility of earlier voting on frequently visited locations may be quite efficient. The United States offers some interesting efficiency data. It turns out that introducing earlier elections has a much bigger impact than postal voting. In North Carolina and Georgia, which gave the opportunity to voters to vote before the day of election for example in shopping centres, last year the number of voters who used one of these forms of voting before the day of election grew two-fold in North Carolina and as much as three-fold in Georgia compared to the election four years ago. The states that provide only the postal voting option did not see such a high growth.[418] Overall 30 % of all votes were cast in the United States before the election day, whereas in 2004 it was only 20 %, which represents an average growth by one half. For comparison: in 1992 it was 7 % and in 1972 it was only 4 %.[419]

Another useful change would be a single national voters' register with remote access instead of the current electoral registers that are maintained by local authorities. The voters then could vote in any polling station even outside of their electoral ward. Currently in order to be able to cast the vote elsewhere it is necessary to apply for an elector's certificate no later than two days in advance,[420] which may deter many voters.

---

[417] Memorandum o spolupráci mezi Českým statistickým úřadem a Ministerstvem vnitra ČR při přípravě koncepce, řešení, testování a realizaci systému elektronických voleb v České republice [Memorandum of Cooperation between the Czech Statistics Office and the Ministry of the Interior of the Czech Republic on Preparing the Concept, Solution, Testing and Implementation of Systems of Electronic Voting in the Czech Republic]. Hradec Králové, 7th April 2008.

[418] McDonald, M. P.: The Return of the Voter: Voter Turnout in the 2008 Presidential Election. *The Forum* 4/2008, Art. 4, p. 5. http://www.bepress.com/forum/vol6/iss4/art4.

[419] *Ibidem* at p. 4.

[420] For more details see Antoš, M. *supra* at pp. 142–143.

Postal or electronic voting could be introduced only as a supplement for a small group of voters who do not have any other practical possibility to participate in an election, which primarily means the voters who are abroad. The risk of fraud would be very low in such a case with respect to considerable geographic dispersion. Postal voting has been introduced in a similar scope in Slovakia in 2004[421] and the limitation applied until recently in Austria.[422] A corresponding recommendation is also given in the Code of Good Practice in Electoral Matters.[423]

Expanding the universality of suffrage

The principle of universal suffrage in its ideal form requires that every person has the right to vote. However certain electoral qualifications are generally accepted. The most permanent position is maintained by the qualification of age and the qualification of citizenship; however, even in these cases some significant shifts are noticeable.

Voting from abroad

The voters who are abroad on the day of election may, since the year 2000, vote in the Czech embassies.[424] This, however, applies only to the Chamber of Deputies election. These votes are then included in the respective region which is drawn in advance by the National Election Committee.

When introducing this option it was assumed that it will be used primarily by the compatriots who have Czech citizenship but live permanently abroad. According to some sources approximately 250,000 Czech citizens are generally staying abroad at the time of elections.[425] These expectations were not confirmed in practice, because of a relatively complex procedure which the applicant for this form of voting must undergo and mainly due to the necessity to appear in person at the embassy. In 2002 less than 4000 electors voted in this way abroad; almost half of this number were persons with an elector's certificate who were abroad only on a short-time basis. In none of these cases the votes from abroad

---

[421]/ See s. 27 (2) and (3) of the Act No. 333/2004 Zb., to regulate elections to the National Council of the Slovak Republic.

[422]/ Prosser, A. – Kofler, R. – Krimmer, R.: Current state of public elections over the Internet in Austria. In: e-Voting.at: Entwicklung eines Internet-basierten Wahlsystems für öffentliche Wahlen. Vienna: Institute für Informationsverarbeitung und Informationswirtschaft, 2002, p. 50.

[423]/ European Commission for Democracy through Law (Venice Commission): Code of Good Practice in Electoral Matters. Guidelines and Explanatory Report. CDL-AD(2002)023rev. Strasbourg, 23rd May 2003, http://www.venice.coe.int/docs/2002/CDL-AD(2002)023rev-e.pdf, p. 34.

[424]/ For a long time in most countries it was possible to vote only in the territory of the state. Mainly the English speaking countries gradually enabled also the voters who were abroad in civil service and in particular in military service. Currently the possibility to vote abroad forms part of the normal standard, yet the conditions differ. According to a comparative study from 2004 this option exists in 40 states out of the 63 that were covered by the study, and it is more frequent in advanced countries than in emerging democracies. Ten of the countries provide the option only for a certain time after an elector moves out of the state: this period ranges from three to twenty years. E.g. in Germany it is generally ten years, but it does not apply to citizens living in another Member State of the Council of Europe (Massicotte, L. – Blais, A. – Yoshinaka, A.: Establishing the Rules of the Game. Election Laws in Democracies. Toronto: University of Toronto Press, 2004, pp. 30–32.). For more information on the Czechoslovak history of voting abroad see Filip, J.: Volební čas v zahraničí jako ústavní problém [Election Time Abroad as a Constitutional Problem]. Časopis pro právní vědu a praxi 1/2002, p. 8–12 (in particular note 6 and 11).

[425]/ See explanatory report in print. No. 945, Chamber of Deputies, IV term of office.

had an impact on the distribution of mandates in the Chamber of Deputies among political parties.[426]

An important growth in the number of votes cast abroad cannot be expected under the current regulation. The embassies are with some exceptions located only in the capital cities and many compatriots would have to travel over considerable distances to cast their votes. A major change could be brought about by the introduction of postal voting which was discussed in the previous section.

Foreigners' right to vote

The qualification of citizenship belongs among the traditional conditions of the right to vote. The extent to which it is applied differs in various countries. For example in the United Kingdom all citizens of the EU and the Commonwealth who have permanent residence in the UK may vote in local, regional and European elections. This option does not apply to the election to the House of Commons, but Irish citizens may take part in these elections.[427] In Hungary persons with permanent residence in its territory may participate in local elections irrespective of their citizenship (Art. 70 (2) of the Constitution). Scandinavian countries also display traditionally open attitudes to this question.

In the EU, since adoption of the Maastricht Treaty, the citizens of the EU have the right to vote in the place of their residence in local and European elections. This is also reflected in the Czech regulation. Their access to elections to local councils is made more difficult by a relatively complex legal regulation which stipulates stricter conditions for this group than for other groups of voters, so they have to request in advance to be added to the annex of the electoral register.[428]

In 1992 the Council of Europe adopted the Convention on the Participation of Foreigners in Public Life at Local Level.[429] This document regulates their suffrage in local elections that they should receive after five years of permanent residence. However, only a small number of states have adhered to the Convention. The Czech Republic signed the Convention in June 2000 but it has not been ratified yet and probably it will not be ratified in the foreseeable future.

The process of expanding the suffrage for foreigners will proceed from the long-term perspective both in horizontal terms (not just EU citizens, but also other foreigners), and in vertical terms (in regional and later also parliamentary elections). One of the reasons speaking in favour of this process is the overall globalisation and integration tendencies as

---

[426] For more details on these issues and on the impact of votes from abroad on the result of the elections see Antoš, M.: Rozhodly letošní volby do Poslanecké sněmovny hlasy ze zahraničí? [Were the Votes from Abroad Decisive in this Year's Chamber of Deputies Election?]. *Právní rozhledy* 17/2006, pp. 642–646.

[427] The Electoral Commission: *Which Non-UK Nationals can vote?* http://www.electoralcommission.org.uk/templates/search/document.cfm/8834.

[428] For more detailed coverage see Antoš, M.: Volební právo cizinců žijících v České republice [The Right to Vote of Foreigners Living in the Czech Republic]. In: Jirásková, V. (ed.): *Interpretace Ústavy České republiky a Ústavy Slovenské republiky. Evropeizace ústavních systémů* [Interpretation of the Constitution of the Czech Republic and the Constitution of the Slovak Republic. Europeisation of Constitutional Systems]. Praha: Univerzita Karlova, Právnická fakulta, 2007, pp. 132–139.

[429] Convention on the Participation of Foreigners in Public Life at Local Level. http://conventions.coe.int/Treaty/Commun/QueVoulezVous.asp?NT=144&CM=8&DF=5/19/2006&CL=ENG.

a result of which permanent as well as temporary migration of people is growing and the other relates to the old principle "no taxation without representation".[430]

Prisoners' right to vote
In the Czech Republic, a traditional impediment to the exercise of suffrage is the restriction of personal liberty due to serving a term of imprisonment. Currently this applies to local and regional elections whereas the convicts may participate in the Chamber of Deputies elections and in European elections. This differentiation may result from practical reasons because in regional and local elections the voter may vote only at the place of permanent residence and the law does not allow for any form of remote voting. Another important factor may relate to the nature of local councils: primarily in case of communities a closer relation between the voters and their representation is assumed. In the case of a voter serving his term of imprisonment it is not possible to assume the same level of awareness of local issues as in the case of other people.

An international comparison shows that even though similar general limitations were applied in the past in many European countries,[431] the current trend is opposite. This was supported by the decision of the European Court of Human Rights in *Hirst v. UK.*[432] Our current legal regulation, however, remains general to a certain extent: the limitation does not apply to all elections but it does apply to all people serving a term of imprisonment irrespective of the length of imprisonment and of the criminal offence committed. Therefore it applies also to voters who may be deemed to remain part of the community with respect to the length of their imprisonment. It would be more reasonable to afford the opportunity to vote to those convicts whose length of imprisonment does not exceed a period over which they may be expected to retain their relation to the community and the region, such as a maximum of four years of imprisonment. At the same time it would be necessary to enable remote voting for these electors.

Breach of equality of the right to vote
A breach of equality of franchise may among other things take place as a result of intentional abuse of electoral boundaries. Almost two hundred years have passed since 1812, when the governor of Massachusetts, Elbridge Gerry,[433] became famous for intentionally manipulating the border of the election district; despite the length of time that has passed since then, it remains an issue to a certain extent in the Czech Republic in relation to the Senate elections. Borders of the election districts are set in a schedule to the Electoral Act and in case the population of an election district grows or falls by 15 % compared to the national

---

[430]/ See Dahl, R. A.: *On Democracy*. New Haven: Yale University Press, 1998, pp. 20–22.
[431]/ Lazarova Trajkovska, M.: *Report on the Abolition of Restrictions on the Right to Vote in General Elections*. European Commission for Democracy through Law (Venice Commission), CDL-AD(2005)011, 4th April 2005, retrieved from http://www.venice.coe.int/docs/2005/CDL-AD(2005)011-e.asp, p. 7 and subs.; Cremona, J. J.: The Right to Free Elections in the European Convention on Human Rights. In: Mahoney, P. – Matscher, F. – Petzold, H. – Wildhaber, L. (eds.): *Protecting Human Rights: the European Perspective*. Köln: Carl Heymanns Verlag, 2000, p. 317.
[432]/ Hirst v. United Kingdom, App. No. 74025/01.
[433]/ Mackie, T.: Gerrymandering. In: Rose, R. (ed.): *International Encyclopaedia of Elections*. London: Macmillian Reference, 2000, p. 144 and subs.

average, the borders must change. The purpose of this measure is to maintain even distribution of mandates as required by the principle of equality of the voting right. The election districts have been changed so far five times.[434] The reason of such frequency is not just a continuous fluctuation of the citizens but mainly inappropriate legal regulation as well as the legislative practice due to which only the most important changes are made at the last moment shortly before the elections. The number of citizens will often narrowly fall within the allowed range and in the following years the issue then reoccurs. The election district No. 27 located in Prague 1, whose territory has been changed three times (in 2002, 2006 and 2008) over the last six years, is an example of a situation that should be avoided.

If this practice was criticised in the past, it was mainly pointed out that it was inappropriate and potentially dangerous, but without a specific suspected abuse. The approach changed in 2008 when ČSSD [Czech Social Democratic Party] deputies objected, during the debate on the amendment of the Electoral Act, to the manner of changes in election districts in the Central Bohemia region. They expressed their concerns that two districts in which elections were taking place that year,[435] were expanded by territories where ODS [Civic Democratic Party] had a dominant position. They argued that the process of preparation of these changes was not transparent and the regional authority did not respect the comments sent by some of the communities concerned.[436]

Due to a significant dominance of ČSSD in the Senate elections in the autumn of 2008, the changes that were carried out did not have any impact and ČSSD's candidates won in all the affected districts. However, this does not suggest that the authors of the changes did not really intend to manipulate the border in a way more advantageous for them in case of a narrow result.[437] A seriously defective legal regulation and the manner of submitting and discussing changes in election districts obviously invite such an abuse.

It is therefore necessary to adopt a completely new philosophy. Following the census once every ten years, a major review should be carried out by a special committee composed mainly of independent experts. At the same time every political party who had more than 10 members in both chambers of the Parliament elected would be represented on the committee by one member. This would ensure transparency of the negotiation for all relevant political entities. As a result of this review, the border of all 81 districts would be newly set so that the differences in the number of inhabitants were kept to a minimum. This should ensure that in the course of the following ten years the maximum allowed deviation would not be exceeded in any of the election districts in spite of the assumed fluctuation of inhabitants.[438]

434/ See the Acts No. 212/1996 Sb., 171/2002 Sb., 418/2004 Sb., 323/2006 Sb. and 261/2008 Sb.

435/ The Senate is re-elected in parts, and this is why the election takes place every two years in one third of the districts.

436/ See the transcript of the 32nd session of the Chamber of Deputies, 4th June 2008, retrieved from http://www.psp.cz/eknih/2006ps/stenprot/032schuz/s032029.htm

437/ For detailed reasoning see Antoš, M.: Mohou se senátní volební obvody měnit účelově ve prospěch vládních stran? [Can the Senate Election Districts be Changed on Purpose in Favour of the Government Parties?]. In: Mikule, V. – Suchánek, R. (eds.): Pocta Zdeňku Jičínskému k 80. narozeninám [Tribute to Zdeněk Jičínský on his 80th Birthday]. Praha: ASPI Wolters Kluwer, 2009, p. 211 and subs.

438/ The current regulation has other defects too, including s. 59 (2) ZVP, according to which the changes in the borders of election districts are carried out only in the years when a Senate election is announced. This creates a significant pressure on the legislative process in order to make the changes before the election is actually

If changes to the electoral legislation are ever discussed in society, in most cases the discussion focuses on the issues of conversion of votes cast to the numbers of mandates for individual political parties made according to the electoral system. In spite of this it turns out that there are also other areas of electoral law which require attention. Numerous phenomena that may be considered new in the Czech Republic have already surfaced in other countries. In addition to gerrymandering, such phenomena include also the issue of compatriots, postal voting or the introduction of electronic voting. We should use the great advantage of having the opportunity to learn from the experience of other countries.

2.6 INFORMATION SOCIETY AND COPYRIGHT

2.6.1 Exploitation and protection of a work of authorship in information society

Copyright law on the threshold of the third millennium is influenced primarily by the phenomenon of information society, a society which extensively and easily uses digitalisation for processing, storing as well as transferring information. If easy availability of works and other intellectual property is not to form, as its consequences, a barrier to creative and artistic activity, it is necessary to strive for such a manner and forms of protection that may appropriately react to new ways of exploitation of individual works and will provide to the authors protection of their independence and dignity, adequate author's fees and control over the work. Efficient protection cannot be provided only by the traditional means of verbal regulation of what is possible and what is prohibited. It is necessary to consistently apply the new technologies of actual protection of works of authorship in order to prevent or to restrict the use of a work in breach of copyright. The role of the law is to prevent bypassing such technical and technological means of protection. The traditional manner of protection and approach to interference with copyright must react to the fact that in the digital environment the services of mediators may be used for activities violating the law. Information society presents new tasks for the bodies charged with the collective management of copyrighted works.

The Copyright Act of the Czech Republic (Act No. 121/2000 Sb., to regulate copyright, rights related to copyright and to change certain laws, as amended) is in line with international treaties regulating copyright as well as with EU law.

The principal international document concerning information society and copyright law is Berne Convention for the Protection of Literary and Artistic Works of 9th September 1886 as amended by the last review of Paris from 1971 (hereinafter the "Berne Convention"). The Czech Republic has been party to the Berne Convention since 1921;[439] it has been bound by the Paris wording of the Convention since 11th April 1980.[440] Other important international treaties include the following:

---

announced. The measure used to judge the district size also cannot be considered ideal: instead of the number of inhabitants it would be better to take into account the number of qualified voters. For more detailed analysis of this issue see Antoš, M. *supra* at pp. 36–42.

[439]/ Regulation No. 401/1921 Sb.

[440]/ Regulation of the Ministry of Foreign Affairs No. 133/1980 Sb. as amended by the Regulation of the Ministry of Foreign Affairs No. 19/1985 Sb.

a) Universal Copyright Convention made in Geneva on 6th September 1952 and reviewed in Paris on 24th July 1971 ("Universal Convention"). Our country has been party to this Convention since 6th January 1960;[441] and it has been bound by the Paris wording since 17th April 1980;[442]
b) The International Convention for the Protection of Performers, Producers of Phonograms and Broadcasting Organizations concluded in Rome on 26th October 1961 (the "Rome Convention"). Our country has been party to the Convention since 14th August 1964;[443]
c) The Agreement on Trade-Related Aspects of Intellectual Property Rights (the "TRIPS Agreement") was concluded within the framework of the Agreement Establishing the World Trade Organisation of 15th April 1994 ("WTO"); the Czech Republic has applied TRIPS as of 1st January 1996.[444]

The latest treaties of major importance for information society include the so called Internet Treaties of 1996 including WIPO Copyright Treaty ("WCT")[445] and WIPO Performances and Phonograms Treaty ("WPPT").[446]

The Convention on the Law applicable to Contractual Obligations opened for signature in Rome on 19th June 1980 ("Rome Convention on Applicable Law")[447] plays an indispensable role in information society.

As for EU law the following directives are relevant for the area of law governed by the Copyright Act:

a) Council Directive 91/250/EEC of 14th May 1991 on the legal protection of computer programs;
b) Directive 2006/115/EC of the European Parliament and of the Council of 12th December 2006 on rental rights and lending rights and on certain rights related to copyright in the field of intellectual property (codified version);
c) Council Directive 93/83/EEC of 27th September 1993 on the coordination of certain rules concerning copyright and rights related to copyright applicable to satellite broadcasting and cable retransmissions;
d) Directive 2006/116/EC of the European Parliament and of the Council of 12th December 2006 on the term of protection of copyright and certain related rights (codified version);
e) Directive 96/9/EC of the European Parliament and of the Council of 11th March 1996 on the legal protection of databases;

---

[441]/ Regulation No. 2/1960 Sb. as amended by the official notice No. 16/1960 Sb.
[442]/ Regulation No. 134/1980 Sb.
[443]/ Regulation No. 192/1964 Sb. as amended by rectification No. 157/1965 Sb.
[444]/ Information of the Ministry of Foreign Affairs No. 191/1995 Sb.
[445]/ Information of the Ministry of Foreign Affairs No. 33/2002 Sb. m. s.
[446]/ Information of the Ministry of Foreign Affairs No. 48/2002 Sb. m. s.
[447]/ Information of the Ministry of Foreign Affairs No. 64/2006 Sb. m. s. as amended by Information of the Ministry of Foreign Affairs No. 21/2007 Sb. m. s.

f) Directive 2001/29/EC of the European Parliament and of the Council of 22nd May 2001 on the harmonisation of certain aspects of copyright and related rights in the information society ("Information Society Directive"). The Information Society Directive is closely related to Directive 2000/31/EC of the European Parliament and of the Council of 8th June 2000 on certain legal aspects of information society services, in particular electronic commerce, in the Internal Market ("Directive on electronic commerce"), Directive 98/84/EC of the European Parliament and of the Council of 20th November 1998 on the legal protection of services based on, or consisting of, conditional access and Directive 1999/93/EC of the European Parliament and of the Council of 13th December 1999 on a Community framework for electronic signatures. Other related directives include Directive 98/48/EC of the European Parliament and of the Council of 20th July 1998 amending Directive 98/34/EC laying down a procedure for the provision of information in the field of technical standards and regulations which defines the concept of information society service;

g) Directive 2001/84/EC of the European Parliament and of the Council of 27th September 2001 on the resale right for the benefit of the author of an original work of art;

h) Directive 2004/48/EC of the European Parliament and of the Council of 29th April 2004 on the enforcement of intellectual property rights ("Rights Enforcement Directive"). The above directive is related to the Proposal for a European Parliament and Council Directive on criminal measures aimed at ensuring the enforcement of intellectual property rights.[448]

European administration is currently interested in some legal aspects of collective management covered primarily by the Commission Recommendation of 18th May 2005 on collective cross-border management of copyright and related rights for legitimate online music services.[449]

Contractual and non-contractual obligations are covered by the following regulations: Regulation (EC) No 593/2008 of the European Parliament and of the Council of 17th June 2008 on the law applicable to contractual obligations (Rome I) and Regulation (EC) No 864/2007 of the European Parliament and of the Council of 11th July 2007 on the law applicable to non-contractual obligations (Rome II).

The objective of the concentrated harmonisation effort at the turn of the century as a consequence of the influence of the Single Market or information society in the field of copyright is to ensure an appropriate balance of rights and interests among various groups and categories of right-holders and users of works protected by copyright. Principal documents related to the topic of the Single Market include the Communication from the Commission to the European Parliament, the Council, the European Economic and Social Committee and the Committee of the Regions of 20th November 2007 – A single market for 21st century Europe;[450] draft Commission Green Paper: Copyright in the Knowledge Economy, the Commission Recommendation of 24th August 2006 on the digitisation and

[448] COM 2006–168, {SEC(2005)848} / COM/2005/0276 final – COD 2005/0127.
[449] 2005/737/EC.
[450] COM (2007) 724 of 20th November 2007, final.

online accessibility of cultural material and digital preservation[451]; and also EP Resolution of 27th September 2007 on "i2010: towards a European digital library" – EUROPEANA[452] which forms part of the current strategy EU i2010.

2.6.2 Prospects of collective management of copyright in information society

Extensive intangible modes of online use resulted in a review of the approach to collective management in particular in terms of compliance of online collective management with competition law. New modes of use in relation to the Treaty Establishing the European Community ("EEC Treaty") and to collective management have recently been clarified primarily by the Commission within the framework of its decision-making powers granted to the Commission in Articles 81 and 82 of the EEC Treaty. The Commission wishes to prevent territorial parcelling of the market by collective managers of online use. Judging by the decisions made so far the Commission supports liberalisation, hence dissolution of territorial monopolies of collective managers. In spite of the fact that this effort of the Commission does not enjoy general support,[453] the Commission's opinion will be decisive for the future development due to the practical role played by the Commission in the application of competition rules. The development in the field of online use will see a trend towards new forms of management including an enhanced role of individual management and supranational cooperation of collective managers. The development of cross-border or even supranational collective management and restriction of the principles of territoriality of collective management are marked trends.

The development of technology gave rise to the phenomenon called DRM (digital rights management). DRM is an application of information technology to facilitate exploitation of rights.[454] Information society and new technologies such as DRM also influence collective management systems. Some DRM systems for example enable the right-holders to monitor and control the process of licensing, use and collection of licence fees (mainly for online use), which enables primarily the strong right-holders to manage their rights directly on an individual basis. Individual management by means of DRM represents an alternative to collective management that may be attractive for some right-holders; however, there is clearly a practical need of specialised entities to manage various rights including rights implemented in the digital environment. The development of a European regulation of collective management shows that the primary issue subsists in an adaptation of collective management to the digital environment, rather than in the replacement of collective management by individual management. The main issue lies in a consistent application of competition rules in the online field.

The opinion that collective management will become even more important in the future may seem paradoxical in the contexts of the development of information technologies and cross-border collective management as well as the growing possibilities of individual

---

[451] 2006/585/EC.

[452] 2006/2040(INI).

[453] See for example Report on the Commission Recommendation of 18th October 2005 on collective cross-border management of copyright and related rights for legitimate online music services (2005/737/EC) (2006/2008(INI) FINAL A6-0053/2007, 5.3.2007.

[454] Intellectual Property on the Internet: a Survey of Issues of December 2002, document WIPO/INT/02, p. 60–62.

management. We must take into account that the current practical development makes rights management more complex and less transparent. As a result of various hybrid forms of rights management and the growth of individual rights management, it is becoming increasingly difficult for the users to find the right-holder and to obtain a licence. In the future we are likely to see the development of new modes of use and pressure on adaptation of collective management coupled with a renaissance of collective management (in a modern form adapted to information society needs) as the reason for its being (i.e. more effective enforcement of rights in the cases where individual management fails) lasts and may grow in importance.

Collective management may also play an important role in addressing various topical issues. For example, massive illegal downloading of music via the Internet (P2P) indicates almost a loss of legitimacy of copyright as all means of combating illegal P2P have failed so far. In this respect we should not turn down the idea of granting "blanket" licences to a collective manager to operate P2P combined with implementation of a special fee for the internet users, which would, similarly to the institution of a blank media levy and a levy on the recording equipment, compensate to a certain extent the expected losses of the right holders. Such ideas are discussed internationally, for example in the proceedings of the international conference on Copyright Policies and the Role of Stakeholders in Athens in June 2008.

Collective management is, on the one hand, facing the need to adapt to the digital needs of information society as a result of which the role of collective management may be reduced in some aspects and this form of management will be restructured, and, on the other hand, collective management will see new opportunities.

2.6.3 Collective management of copyright and related rights in the Czech Republic

The existing Copyright Act regulates collective management in a complex manner compliant with EC regulations.

It is not the objective of this subchapter to deal with its compliance with EU regulations or with the prospects of the development of this institution in the context of European legislation. We will focus briefly on the new phenomena of Czech legal regulation of collective management within the framework of the Copyright Act.

Unlike preceding copyright legislation, the Copyright Act clearly defines the persons holding copyright whose rights are, or may be, subject to collective management. This clears the doubts caused by previous legal regulations, because the list of potential right-holders is exhaustive and clearly defined including the definition of the status of right-holders created by licence. Further, it provides a comprehensive definition of the subject-matter of collective management which clears the doubts about the type of rights that may be managed collectively. It should be admitted that such a comprehensive list may give rise to theoretical discussions on whether the exclusion from collective management of certain subject-matters protected by copyright is justified. Current efforts to amend the Copyright Act strive to resolve these deficiencies.

The Copyright Act defines areas where collective management may be applied. The definition focuses only on collective management of property rights, the management of which is otherwise inefficient or not allowed, and heads towards common interest of right-holders.

The definition of areas where collective management of copyright may be applied represents a new phenomenon. While the previous legal regulations allowed for collective management applicable to rights in published works, the new Copyright Act enables the application of collective management to rights in works offered for publishing, i.e. the works registered by the author with the relevant collective manager.

Another new institution created by the Act subsists in the rights subject to collective management on a mandatory basis. This institution was absent in the previous legal regulation. The exhaustive list of such rights is included in the Act and individual enforcement of such rights is prohibited. The legislature certainly focused on the principal feature of collective management, which is efficiency. Another aspect that was taken into account was the impossibility of individual enforcement of such rights with respect to the growing range of technical means enabling transmission of works protected by copyright to the public, including the possibilities of creating a copy for one's own use. The reasons for creating such an institution are understandable and common in European legislation. However, the Copyright Act, despite its high quality, becomes contradictory to the continuously expanding principle of freedom of contract and to exclusive disposition of intellectual property, because authors who did not make a contract with a collective manager and therefore are not represented by the manager under the contract of representation, should get registered with a competent collective manager to be paid fees for the exercise of rights in copyrighted works subject to the collective management on a mandatory basis, and possibly to exercise their right to remuneration for the use of such works, without having a chance to avoid such representation.

Last but not least, it is necessary to mention the new phenomenon of collective contracts which enables the collective manager and users of copyrighted works to make a contract with a legal entity associating users of the same type of rights and works, and the persons associated in such a legal entity become liable to the collective manager under such a contract. The term *collective contract* is slightly misleading in this case as it does not express the substance of collective management as such, but it identifies the entity associating the users. On the other hand, a typical type of contract for collective management is a bulk contract that is used by the collective manager to grant in its name a bulk licence for exercise of property rights under management of the represented authors in works published or offered for publishing. In this case there is extensive performance of collective management compared to the previous legal regulation, which provided for collective management of rights only in published works. Registration of an unpublished work in the register of collectively managed works perfects the exclusive personal right of the author to publish the work or to decide on the publishing of the work.

Considering the fact that collective management licences are granted by the Ministry of Culture of the Czech Republic in accordance with the Copyright Act and the licensing conditions are exhaustively stipulated, the question arises as to whether collective management regulation really should form part of the Act of a strictly private law nature.

It is beyond doubt that the current collective management system cannot cope with the environment of a growing range of technical means enabling access to works protected by copyright.

2.6.4 Current trends of interpretation of the concept of a three-step test

The term three-step test is sometimes used for the legal construction that defines interpretation rules for the application of legal limitations and exceptions of copyright and other related rights. The concept originated in international law and was used for the first time in the Stockholm Amendment (1967) of Berne Convention where it applied only to the right of reproduction of the work (Article 9 (2)). Later this provision was taken over by TRIPS (Article 13) where it applied to all exceptions and limitations of copyright. The provision was also taken over by WCT (Article 10) in 1996 and by the European Information Society Directive (Article 5.5).

In the course of application of the above test, there were clear tendencies to interpret it extensively. One of the examples of extensive interpretation of the three-step test is the decision of a French court dealing with an appellate review of the Mulholland Drive case of 22nd April 2005.[455]

The decision of a WTO panel in the dispute between EU and USA WT/DS160/R of 15th June 2000[456] is very important for the interpretation of the three-step test. This proceeding scrutinized a provision of the US Copyright Act permitting the playing of radio and television music and other works in some restaurants and retail shops without the payment of a royalty fee within the framework of exceptions stipulated in this Act. The Report of the Panel found this exception to be inconsistent with the three-step test (specifically it is contradictory to normal exploitation of the work) and therefore found it to be in breach of the provision of Article 13 of TRIPS Agreement.[457]

Currently the issue of clarification of the meaning and correct application of the three-step test is being addressed in the *Declaration on a Balanced Interpretation of the "Three-step Test" in Copyright Law* ("Declaration"), which is a result of the work of reputable European experts in copyright law who met at an annual conference of International Association for the Advancement of Teaching and Research in Intellectual Property ("ATRIP") which was hosted by Max Planck Institute (21st–23rd July 2008, Munich).

The Declaration on the one hand states that the three-step test efficiently prevents an overuse of exceptions and limitations of copyright and, on the other hand, points out that there are no complementary mechanisms that would prevent inadequate restrictive interpretation. Further the Declaration indicates that restrictive interpretation of the three-step test by courts and national legislatures was incorrect. In the opinion of the group of experts the three-step test should lead to a proportional interpretation of exceptions and limitations of copyright with respect to their purpose and objective, rather than to the restrictive interpretation as such.

---

[455] http://juriscom.net/documents/caparis20050422.pdf.
[456] http://www.wto.org/English/tratop_e/dispu_e/cases_e/ds160_e.htm.
[457] Telec, I. – Tůma, P.: *Autorský zákon. Komentář* [Copyright Act. Commentary]. Praha: C. H. Beck, 2007.

In its reasoning part, the Declaration deals in detail with an analysis of the balance between the interest of the public and the interest of right-holders. In this context it also mentions the introductory part of TRIPS Agreement which points out the need to maintain balance between the interest of copyright owners and the interest of the general public and, in particular, the general interest in education, research and access to information. Exceptions and limitations of copyright represent the most important legal instrument maintaining this balance between private and public interests in exploitation of the works protected by copyright. When determining the scope of exceptions and limitations, the three-step test should not take into account only the interests of copyright owners.

The text of the Declaration is relatively brief and its full version is available at the Max Planck Institute website.

The importance of the Declaration subsists in a surprising and, to a considerable extent, innovative approach to the three-step test which is supported by well-founded arguments. The Declaration for the first time expresses the idea that the three-step test should not serve only to protect the interests of the copyright holders but, perhaps more importantly, it should help find a balance between the interest of the society as a whole and the interest of the author. As mentioned above in the opinion of the group of experts who drafted the Declaration the exceptions and limitations are not to be interpreted restrictively under the three-step test and they should always be interpreted with respect to their nature and purpose. The Declaration recommends application of the test criteria as a whole rather than individually. These opinions are rather revolutionary and it will be interesting to see what will be the reflection of such ideas in the decisions of judges and legislatures and to what extent the opinions will become common in the thinking of experts in the field.

2.6.5 Possible changes of European legislation relating to exceptions and limitations

The discussion on possible changes in exceptions and limitations of copyright in EU legislation has recently been initiated by the European Commission. Charlie McCreevy, the Commissioner responsible for the internal market and services started consultations on these issues in July 2008 by presenting a Green Paper entitled "Copyright in the Knowledge Economy" (the Commission adopted this Green Paper on 16th July 2008). The purpose of this document is to support dissemination of knowledge in the field of research, science and education in the online environment.

The above presented facts indicate that copyright as such and, in particular, the field of exceptions and limitations are currently a sensitive and frequently discussed topic. Experts are trying in their discussions to find a balance between the interest of the author and that of the society in exploiting works in the rapid development of information society. Current discussion is a logical reaction to the technical development, mainly to the Internet phenomenon and the related digitalisation of works. It will be interesting to see to what extent the rights of an individual, i.e. the author, will keep their position and to what extent compromising solutions in the interest of the general public will be adopted, which could bring the exceptions and limitations concept closer to the institution of "fair use" typical of the American system of copyright where the system of an exhaustive list of exceptions is unified in the general construction of "fair use". If this happens it would be another step in the process of approximation of European and US copyright law which started by accession of the US to the Berne Convention.

2.6.6 Copyright agreements with an international element in digital environment

None of the adopted international conventions which are binding on the Czech Republic contains direct (substantive) rules of copyright contract law in spite of the fact that these conventions assume the possibility of contractual transfer of copyright.[458] The conventions also do not contain any special conflict-of-law rules. Similarly none of the sources of European law harmonizes copyright contract law.[459] The efforts towards unification at the European level resulted in the adoption of the Rome Convention on Applicable Law and culminated by the adoption of Rome I Regulation of 17th June 2008 on the law applicable to contractual obligations which will replace the Rome Convention on Applicable Law as of 17th December 2009. Neither the Rome Convention on Applicable Law nor Rome I Regulation contain special conflict-of-law rules for intellectual property. If the choice of law (*lex electa*) is not carried out, the principle of the centre of a legal relationship applies. At the same time the precedence of imperative provisions applies (in the field of copyright law such provisions may include rules protecting social and cultural values in public interest, or legal guarantees to protect the author if perceived as a weaker party to the contract requiring special protection, or regulations enforcing minimum moral rights in contracts if such rights exist in the system of law in question). Another binding principle is the traditional public policy exception (*ordre public*). One of the application problems may consist of determining (characteristic) subject-matter of performance while determining the centre of a legal relationship, i.e. whether to consider such performance to be in case of licence agreements (or agreements to transfer copyright), the provision of the right by the transferor or, on the other hand, the performance of the obligation (or exercise of the right) when exploiting such a licence acquired, especially in case of exclusive licences (e.g. for the implementation of exploitation of a work by the licensee). The country with the closest relation to the contractual relationship is often the country where the right is exploited, i.e. the same country is determined as in case of application of the general international rule of the country in which protection is claimed (*lex loci protectionis*). In case of a licence agreement assuming exploitation of works protected by copyright by their communication to the public by means of the Internet, the decision on applicable law may give rise to even more questions (the thoughts on subordination to the law of the country where the server is located in the memory of which the shared work is stored, which try to use the parallel to satellite broadcasting, did not become generally accepted[460]).

---

[458]/ For example Article 6 (1) of the amended Berne Convention.

[459]/ Similarly in the field of general civil law of contract a harmonized regulation has not been adopted on the level of the Communities, these activities are under the umbrella of the Commission on European Contract Law which published among other things. *The Principles of European Contract Law*. Hague: Kluwer, 1999 (Parts I, II) and 2003 (Part III).

[460]/ Green Paper COM (95) 382 final, 19. 7. 1995, Communication (follow-up) COM (96) 568 final, 20th November 1996.

The subject-matter applicability of the law of the contract is limited (limitation of the status of obligations). This is primarily related to the status and ownership aspects of the transfer of copyright. There is no common opinion on the choice of applicable law to determine the primary holder (owner) of the copyright. If we use the principle of the country in which protection is claimed (*lex loci protectionis*),[461] it may result in demanding the application of the law of several countries in which the work is supposed to be exploited under the contract, which in some cases may result in controversial conclusions including a potential refusal to recognize the contract in some countries of exploitation. Opinions on the application of the law of the country of origin of the work (*lex originis*) may seem to be more appropriate due to a higher level of legal certainty.[462] Sometimes it is recommended to complement the criterion of the origin of the work with other criteria for the case when the work was first published in a different country than is the country of origin of the work or the country of residence of the author. In cases of employees' works, it is possible to apply the same legal order that applies to the employment contract despite potential criticism of such an opinion on the grounds of potential discrimination against the author.[463] This is why in this case the country of origin principle may be applied. Determining the applicable law may be similarly complicated in cases of admissibility of the translative transfer of rights or of waiver of (moral) rights for the benefit of another, if such act is permissible under the governing law of the contract; however, it is impermissible under the law of the country of origin, and possibly impermissible under the law of the country in which protection is claimed where the work is supposed to be exploited under the contract.[464] The above differences may give rise to serious issues primarily in contracts affecting continental law jurisdictions and the copyright law system,[465] even though within Europe, too, there is not a unified approach to these key issues of copyright law.

2.7 WILL LAW PLAY A MORE IMPORTANT ROLE IN THE MANAGEMENT OF NATIONAL ECONOMIES?

Considering new phenomena in law on the threshold of the third millennium, we should not forget the role of legal tools in the management of national economies. It would be unreasonable to assume that there would be no business interests of individuals, groups and countries that would be contrary to the interests of the society as a whole. Law will therefore remain an important tool for enforcement of the interests of the society.

461/ Knap, K. – Kunz, O.: *Mezinárodní právo autorské* [International Copyright Law]. Praha: Academia, 1981, p. 294.

462/ Čermák, J.: *Internet a autorské právo* [Internet and Copyright Law]. 2nd ed., Praha: Linde, 2003, p. 229; Schack, H.: *Urheber- und Urhebervertragsrecht*. Tübingen: Mohr Siebeck, 2005; Guibault, L. – Hugenholtz, P. B. et al.: *Study on the Conditions Applicable to Contracts Relating to Intellectual Property in the European Union, Final Report*. Amsterdam: Institute for Information Law, 2002.

463/ Knap, K. – Kunz, O. *supra* at p. 294.

464/ Schack, H.: *Urheber- und Urhebervertragsrecht*. Tübingen: Mohr Siebeck, 2005, § 888.

465/ E.g. Dreyfuss, R. – Ginsburg, J. C: Principles Governing Jurisdiction, Choice of Law, and Judgments in Transnational Disputes. *Computer law review international* 2/2003; Kur, A.: Principles Governing Jurisdiction, Choice of Law, and Judgments in Transnational Disputes: A European Perspective. *Computer law review international* 3/2003, pp. 71–72; Weiche, J.: *US-amerikanisches Urhebervertragsrecht*. Baden-Baden: Nomos, 2002, pp. 144–145.

2.7.1 National economy and its operation

A national economy is defined as a set of natural persons and legal entities engaged in business activities within a defined territory of a state. This is rather a historical definition since the modern international environment extends beyond the "national" framework; nevertheless, modern practitioners, including statisticians, still use the term. The businesses including natural persons and legal entities are mutually related by division of labour within the society and the transactions using market mechanisms arising out of the division of labour.

When describing the benefits of the market we must not forget the work of Scottish economist Adam Smith, *An inquiry into the Nature and Causes of the Wealth of Nations* (1776), which deals with the development of division of labour in the society, land and the lease of land, capital and profit, labour and wages and the invisible hand of the market which connects the participants of the division of labour and their interests. These ideas are still very modern and they have not been surmounted yet. Naturally there has been a substantial development of the liberal market theories since the times of A. Smith. However, it turned out that in practice these theoretical postulates are not omnipotent.

Many years of practice show that relying solely on the market self-regulation does not yield reliable results in modern societies and that there are various interventions in supply and demand which may speed up or slow down the development of the society. The society may have available such regulatory tools that may mitigate negative trends and strengthen positive trends.

2.7.2 Economic policy

Economic policy sets out short-term or longer-term goals as well as the means to achieve the goals. The most important means include the instruments of budgetary, tax, monetary,[466] banking and pricing policy. Such means are implemented by legal tools.

The experience of Czechoslovakia proves that economic policy is not identical with the direct system of directive management excluding the freedom of decision on the part of manufacturers as well as consumers, which resulted in overall lagging behind in terms of technical progress, international division of labour and economic growth in general.

It is therefore not surprising that the revolutionary wave after 1989 strongly opposed directive interventions of the state in the economy and excessive interventions of the government by legal regulations, and thus preference was given clearly to the market mechanism. European Union documents lead to critical discussions concerning potential excessive concentration of European interests over national interests as well as the necessity to transpose numerous EU documents into Czech legislation in a relatively short period of time.[467]

Negative phenomena in the course of privatisation, losses in international transactions, a financial crisis and similar issues resulted in a conclusion that there was a "lack" of legislation and change in attitude to the economic policy and the role of the government and

---

[466] For more details see Němeček, E.: *Mezinárodní měnový systém, Otázka konvertibility, stability a likvidity* [International Monetary System. The Issue of Convertibility, Stability and Liquidity]. Praha: Karolinum, 2000.
[467] Tomášek, M.: *Evropské měnové právo* [European Monetary Law]. Praha: C. H. Beck, 2007.

legal regulation at the national as well as international levels. The issue of energy, which cannot be solved only on a national scale, can be mentioned as an example.

2.7.3 Horizontal legal regulation in the market environment

In the market environment, horizontal legal regulation, i.e. regulation of relations between buyers and sellers, suppliers and customers, is very important. A contract or a similar legal document provides a level of certainty concerning time of delivery, quality, place of delivery and the relevant payment conditions. On the one hand it may seem as a redundant administrative intervention, yet on the other hand it cultivates the market relations and brings advantages to both parties.

Many defects in contractual relations, such as late performance and delayed payments, are relatively easy to identify. It is much more difficult to reveal defects in quality, security, etc. which require application of administrative law, such as supervisors, inspectors, occupancy permit procedures as well as criminal prosecution. A certain lack of balance between sellers and purchasers, mainly natural persons, resulted in the adoption of EU consumer protection directives which became an integral part of the Czech legal order.

Horizontal relations in the market environment are distorted by monopoly tendencies that influence the principles of free competition. Such tendencies result in numerous advantages for monopolies primarily in terms of profits on the one hand, and many disadvantages for consumers in terms of pricing on the other hand. One of the biggest issues is a network monopoly in the field of infrastructure supplying energy, gas, water, heat, roads, etc. Measures separating production from network operation, production and sales units in territorial groups have low efficiency. Law enforcement by way of antimonopoly authorities imposing pecuniary fines failed to stop monopolistic tendencies.

Application of legal tools to enforce all components of contractual relations requires high costs for drafting contracts, legal fees including fees paid to attorneys, notaries, executors, etc. This is why it may be necessary to carry out a more detailed analysis of economic aspects of law so that law supports rather than hinders the principles of the market, e.g. in case of real estate transfer.[468] It is often proven that business ethics in the market economy, achieved through education and cultivation of the business environment, reduces transaction costs.[469]

2.7.4 Financial crisis

The most important question is of whether market mechanisms automatically provide for harmonious balanced economic growth or not. The principles of Europeanization, globalisation of world economy coupled with technical development and the extensive wave of demand resulted in a vision of harmonious growth. The global financial crisis of recent years confirmed the cyclical nature of economic development. A period of growth is followed by stagnation, recession with declining economic potential and the resulting social impacts. These phenomena are remarkable at a national as well as an international

---

[468]/ Posner, R. A.: *Economic Analysis of Law*. Boston: 1972, New York: 2007.
[469]/ Putnová, A. – Seknička, P.: *Etické řízení ve firmě, Nástroje a metody, Etický a sociální audit* [Ethical Company Management. Tools and Methods. Ethical and Social Audit]. Praha: Grada Publishing, 2007.

level. As a result of globalisation the phenomena relatively quickly cross the borders of neighbouring economics.

There are various explanations of the reasons for economic cycles and the crises. One of the theories works with the growth of investment as a result of the growing volume of credit transactions. The relations between manufacturing and consumption, and between supply and demand are disturbed in terms of place and time. The growth of investments supported by extensive bank loans is limited in time. The loans are not endless particularly if they are not duly repaid, and if banks fail to maintain adequacy of assets and liabilities.

Anti-crisis plans are put in place by the government authorities in the form of financial intervention in the banking sector, in some preferred industries, in social welfare, etc. Nobody is waiting for the omnipotent market mechanism. Government subsidies will be combined with a number of legal regulations in the banking sector. The concepts of capital adequacy in banks, maintenance of a certain level of regulatory capital, and a stricter regulation of financial markets are being revived. This will remain a topic for future discussions on economic policy at a global as well as national level and on relevant legal frameworks of such policy.

2.7.5 Land use planning

Many European countries including the Czech Republic went through industrial development in the 19th and 20th centuries, including all infrastructural consequences such as transport systems, settlements, culture monuments, etc. The technical development at the beginning of the 21st century and its consequences cannot fit within the historical bounds.

Modern projects require appropriate transport and technical infrastructure. This creates a serious discrepancy between the potential use of the existing production basis and the building of a new basis. New investors do not prefer conducting their activities in old buildings and facilities due to high adaptation or demolition costs as well as the frequent need to clean up the brown field. They prefer green field projects irrespective of the quality of soil at the particular location. It is easier to place technologies in new buildings, as well as to build warehouses and access roads, etc.

The relations are complex also in the historical centres of towns. Private investors require modern functionalist buildings often built on former green space, extension of roads and parking space. The situation in cities is complicated by the fact that the local government has only limited resources for modernisation of infrastructure in order to meet the needs of private developers for the building of commercial buildings or new settlements. The market interests must be therefore regulated by public law tools which evaluate the investment plans and permit their implementation while maintaining certain rules and imposing limitations. The relevant planning authorities, usually local government authorities, may use regulatory tools such as land use planning, application for building permit procedures, conservation of monuments, environmental protection, etc.[470]

---

[470]/ Act to regulate land use planning and building guidelines No. 183/2006 Sb. (Building Act).

2.7.6 Concluding remarks

The above lines, even though rather brief, attempted to show the importance of law in the management of national economies. In spite of the fact that a liberal approach to the development of the market mechanism will continue to prevail, we cannot do without rational economic policy at both the macroeconomic and microeconomic levels. Economic policy must intervene in all cases where market mechanisms have a negative impact, external or internal in nature. Economic policy will use a wide range of tools including appeals, recommendations, material incentives and orders.

Legal tools will remain important means of economic policy. The tools of private law will play the role of providing compensation in cases where market relations fail to ensure the timely and due discharge of obligations in the required manner. Public law tools will always ensure health and safety as well as provide general environmental background.

Efficiency of legal tools cannot be attained by increasing the number of statutes and other regulations. The focus should be on simplification and a more general impact and primarily relatively speedy enforcement of the statutes. The decisive legal regulations, the laws in particular, should not be burdened by details thinking that it improves the health of the economy. Regulations influencing the behaviour of entities in the economy should, to a growing extent, take the form of cross-border, European or global rules.

Comparative research therefore plays an indispensable role. Let us not be afraid of studying in detail the experience of our European neighbours as well as the experience of other countries. Let us not be afraid of opening ourselves to the world, and let us teach it to our students who will take the helm of developing legal sciences over an important part of the third millennium.

2.8 CORPORATE GOVERNANCE IN THE PUBLIC SECTOR: INSTITUTIONAL ECONOMICS VIEW

2.8.1 Introduction

Corporate governance, which refers to tools and mechanisms of supervision over company management and of enforcement of owners' and other stakeholders' interests in corporation management[471], represents an important part of economic institutions. The efficiency of such institutions is one of the key factors for the trust of investors, the efficiency of corporations[472] as well as the well-being of national economies.[473]

471/ The term *corporation* is internationally used to refer to a company independent of members who founded it. Other features include the separation of ownership and management and a large number of scattered owners, most frequently shareholders. The managing bodies of corporations in advanced countries have, in addition to the representatives of owners, the representatives of other groups, primarily employees. In the Czech Republic the term corporate governance refers primarily to stock companies [a.s.] and limited liability companies [s.r.o.] [which are similar to public limited companies and private limited companies in the UK respectively].

472/ This is confirmed by surveys showing that public limited companies that are publicly tradable and comply with best practice corporate governance show on average a higher return on equity. See for example Blažek, L. – Kučera, R.: *Vztahy podniku k vlastníkům* [Relations of a Company to the Owners]. Centrum výzkumu konkurenční schopnosti české ekonomiky [Research Center for Competitiveness of the Czech Economy], Working Paper, 2005, No. 12, is.muni.cz/do/1456/soubory/oddeleni/centrum/papers/wp2005-12.pdf.

473/ See for example Gordon, J.: *The macroeconomic benefits of good corporate governance.* New Delhi: IMF, 2002.

The importance of corporate governance institutions grew substantially after the wave of accounting fraud and the subsequent bankruptcies of several important global corporations. Recently the importance was also proved by the financial crisis in advanced economies with a stunning impact on global economic development. Many problems of these corporations and institutions are closely related to the performance of corporate governance.

New requirements for development of corporate governance have also arisen from other factors in recent years. These include the growing size of corporations and the associated difficulties in achieving balanced respect for interests of individual owners and types of owners (as well as the further weakening of the control function of owners arising from dispersed shareholding), the emergence of new financial tools and processes, the emergence of new institutional owners (hedge funds, private equity funds, sovereign wealth funds, etc.) and the progressing globalisation of corporations, which weakens the influence of traditional national and regional public control or regulatory mechanisms.

Corporate governance in public sector enterprises remains a relatively separate problem because the role of this sector is not diminishing as expected, and in some fields it is actually growing. Development and improvement of corporate governance institutions is important in emerging market economies where many of such institutions are not efficiently functioning.

2.8.2 Corporate governance in the context of institutional economics

As opposed to standard economics relying primarily on the deductive approach, institutional economics places emphasis on the empirical study of economic processes and their historical development and it attempts to show how the economy really operates in practice. It does not question the validity of the basic principles of economics, but it shows that many statements in standard economics rely on assumptions which are fictitious in practice. As opposed to traditional economics, it points out that the behaviour of economic entities is not determined only by individual or profit-focused motives but also by institutional rules, regulations, customs or tradition in the context of which such entities operate. Corporate governance[474] is one of the basic institutions creating conditions for such behaviour.

Corporate governance institutions govern mutual relations among the stakeholders participating in the operation of the corporations. Here too institutional economics shows that some rules of standard economics are very disputable by nature. If standard economics is based on the premise that the corporations operate in the interest of their owners, institutional economics points out the empirical fact that their operation often brings a benefit for the administrators or managers of the corporations rather than the owners. The issue of "information asymmetry"[475] arising between corporation owners and managers represents an opportunity and the danger that the managers will act in their own interests and will not take into sufficient account the interests of the owners.

---

[474]/ See also Urban, J.: Ekonomie s právem a bez něj [Economics with Law and without It]. In: Bažantová, I. (ed.): *K institucionálním základům tržní ekonomiky a k jejich vývoji* [On Institutional Grounds of the Market Economy and Their Development]. Praha: Prospektrum, 2005; and Mlčoch, L.: *Institucionální ekonomie* [Institutional Economics]. Praha: Karolinum, 2005.

[475]/ Stigler, G. J.: The Economics of Information. *Journal of Political Economy* 3/1961, pp. 213–225.

The institutions of corporate governance enforcing primarily the owners' interests in corporate management against the agents hired by the owners represent one of the most important market institutions considering the impact on performance and the efficiency of economy. The absence of efficient tools of corporate governance results in "opportunistic" management behaviour unfavourable not just to the owners of the corporations but also to the economy as a whole.

The firms and organisations of the public sector face specific corporate governance issues. These problems are usually even more visible in post-communist countries.

2.8.3 Problems and reasons of public production

The public sector plays an important role not just in the funding of public and private goods but also in their production by state owned or community owned enterprises within public administration. Public production of goods – production carried out in enterprises in full or majority public ownership – usually focuses primarily on the production of public goods, i.e. goods that the private sector cannot fully supply due to insufficient market motivation, and on the production of publicly provided private goods, i.e. goods and services supplied to users free of charge (these are goods which can be supplied by the private sector; however, the reason for providing them free of charge is the social and political requirement not to restrict the availability of such goods by the income of the people).

Public production does not completely avoid private goods sold to the consumers for market prices. Examples of such goods include electricity, railways, telecommunications and post office services, airways, etc. as well as production of common goods of mass consumption produced by state or community enterprises such as community breweries. Public production of these goods is often carried out simultaneously with their production by private sector enterprises. Therefore it does not take place only in the environment of a natural monopoly (see below), but also on fully competitive markets (e.g. airways).

In spite of the fact that privatisation in the majority of economically advanced countries has been taking place in recent decades also of those areas which were traditionally considered as the domain of state enterprise (such as privatisation of post services), the scope of public ownership of enterprises producing goods and services often remains considerable. The volume of state-owned business in financial services significantly increased as a result of the financial crisis in 2008. These facts lead to a growing interest in the efficiency of public enterprises, which is related to the performance of corporate governance in such enterprises.

Reasons for public production

The most frequently given reason for public production of goods is the argument that the motive of private business entities is to maximize profit, rather than to expand social welfare. This argument does not apply to (perfectly) competitive markets where the effort to maximize profit becomes identical with maximizing the benefit for the entire society. The interest of private producers and the public as a whole are in this case in accordance.

Natural monopoly

A different situation arises in case of the failure of market connected with the termination of its competitive nature when the markets cease to function well. The efficiency of the distribution of resources decreases primarily in the natural monopoly, when the economies of scale are so substantial that only one company can exist efficiently on the market (i.e. when the concentration of all production in a single company becomes the most efficient solution). A private monopoly producer who does not have to worry about competition (as no other company is able to enter the industry) will achieve maximum profit with lower production and higher prices than would be socially efficient.

Solving the issue of a market failure resulting in the natural monopoly requires usually a certain form of public policy interventions; one of such interventions may be public ownership of naturally monopolistic enterprises (another form of intervention may subsist in price regulation). Comparison of the efficiency of regulated public and private natural monopolies often depends on their possibilities of influencing the decision-making of the regulator. The problem of the so called regulatory capture may be, in the conditions of the public natural monopoly, more serious than in the situation of the regulated private natural monopoly.

The reasons for public ownership of a monopoly enterprise may subsist in the interest of the government to provide certain services to the consumers for a uniform price in spite of the fact that the costs of providing the services to various consumers may differ (examples include delivery of letters for a uniform price or electricity supply irrespective of the distance) or an interest in subsidizing the price either from public resources or from the revenues of services rendered by the monopoly. An example of such cross-subsidizing, which is the term sometimes used for this arrangement, is subsidising personal railroad transport from the revenues of cargo transport. The problem of cross-subsidizing lies in the fact that it prefers in treatment one group of consumers at the expense of another group. In both cases, however, the same social objective may be achieved in another, usually more efficient, way (for example by direct subsidizing of selected consumers).

Other reasons of public production

Other reasons for running publicly owned enterprises may also include other market failures, primarily negative externalities (when the costs of the corporation do not include environmental damage or deterioration of traffic circumstances caused by the corporation's activities), but also positive externalities (when corporations do not have the possibility to benefit from a favourable influence their activities may have on the society, such as the social value of jobs created, and they may have tendency to replace manpower with machines) or asymmetric information (when the companies trying to maximize their profit do not provide to customers all the information they need in order to make a decision).

Such market failures certainly exist at least potentially in many areas and therefore it makes sense to deal with them. However, in most cases it is not clear and is difficult to prove on a quantitative basis whether public production in the affected areas solves the issue in a better way than regulatory and other interventions (taxes, subsidies, etc.). Regulatory interventions in private corporations may seem to be more beneficial with respect to the below described issues of public production of goods.

Another reason for public production of goods may be the enforcement of certain political (non-economic) interests and priorities of the government, such as reducing the unemployment rate, keeping certain companies in business, etc. This is often caused by the successful functioning of interest groups (consumers, managers, employees) which have an interest in the production and are successful in transferring the costs of this production to other consumers (the issue of cross-subsidising) or to taxpayers. Keeping companies in public ownership may also be due to purely political reasons, such as the possibility to improve the community budget or to be able to provide sinecures to party men or to political allies.

Summarizing the arguments in favour of the public production of goods, it is clear that none of them will pass the test as a cause for the long-term business engagement of the public sector. In terms of economic or socio-economic reasons, the same objectives may be achieved by appropriate regulation of private corporations; political reasons usually reflect successful lobbying by certain groups resulting in the enforcement of particular interests or an effort to enforce the clientelistic role of the state.

These reasons would not stand the test of a typical problem analysis of public production of goods.

Problems of public production

The main problem of public production of goods usually is low efficiency. Considering enterprises in public ownership fulfilling non-economic or social roles, the issue of low efficiency is often coupled with insufficient transparency of costs of achieving the social objectives. Even if the behaviour of enterprises in public ownership becomes close to society-wide interests, the issues related to inefficiency of public ownership usually prevail over the benefits. The behaviour of natural monopolies publicly owned may serve as an example of the conflicting consequences of public enterprises. Governance of these enterprises usually cannot ignore the interests of citizens and consumers, but the consumers are the people who are most negatively affected by the monopoly position of the enterprise.

The low efficiency of publicly governed companies has been empirically confirmed by numerous international research surveys and comparisons. These surveys showed that the products and services produced by the public sector are substantially more expensive than the same goods produced by the private sector and the goods produced by the public sector were also less competitive due to their higher price.[476]

The economic reasons of lower efficiency include the fact that the public sector usually purchases from third parties for higher than the market prices and that the employment and production costs per one production unit are usually substantially higher in public enterprises compared to similar private companies. Partial economic findings characteris-

[476]/ OECD: *Corporate Governance, State-Owned Enterprises and Privatisation*. Paris: OECD Publishing, 1998. Boardman, A. – Vining, A. R.: Ownership and Performance in Competitive Environments: A Comparison of the Performance of Private, Mixed and State-Owned Enterprises. *Journal of Law and Economics* 1/1989, pp. 1–33. Shleifer, A.: State versus Private Ownership. *Journal of Economic Perspectives* 4/2008, pp. 133–150.

ing decision-making in public companies include lower quality of investment decisions, less efficient organisation of labour, tendency towards bureacratism and buck-passing, as well as the fact that the employees of public enterprises (as a result of a more careless approach to the provision of sick pay) are more often sick compared to the staff of private corporations.

2.8.4 Corporate governance in enterprises with public administration

A comparison of the manner of functioning of private and public enterprises shows that the performance of, as well as the conditions for, corporate governance are materially different in public enterprises.[477]

This is caused by several interlinked factors. Some of them are specific to these enterprises, others are just intensified typical problems of corporate governance of large private corporations with extensive numbers of scattered owners, i.e. the problems of insufficient transparency of their financial management and lack of possibility and interests of individual owners to influence the management. The factors resulting in different performance of corporate governance in private and public enterprises may be briefly summarised in five main points as follows:

(1) The owners of public enterprises, at least in economics, are citizens and these enterprises therefore should be managed from the corporate governance perspective in their interest, i.e. in the public interest.

The idea that public enterprises owned by the state, region or community have more respect for the public interest than private corporations is often oversimplified and incorrect.

This is because defining the public interest is often difficult: if the policy of such enterprises focuses on certain socio-economic objectives (e.g. general availability of certain services, maintaining employment and/or low production prices, etc.), the measures usually bring varying levels of benefit to various groups of citizens. This is because their behaviour and financial management reflects the personal and group interests of those who manage these enterprises, which may be the interests of politicians, government officials or hired managers (public enterprises serving as an instrument for the 'recycling' of politicians may be mentioned as one example of this).

The relative ease of enforcing various priorities through the management of public enterprises is multiplied by the fact that the possibility of citizens as the 'owners' of public enterprises to monitor their functioning and to control their performance is, compared to the owners of large private corporations, much more limited and distant. And this is not just because of the complexity of the collective decision-making process and the intricacy and inefficiency of control mechanisms, but also (paradoxically) as a result of lower transparency of public financial management in comparison to the private sector.

[477] See for example OECD: *Corporate Governance of State-Owned Assets in OECD countries*. Paris: OECD Publishing, 2005. Dewan, S. M. (ed.): *Corporate Governance in Public Sector Enterprises*. Delhi: Pearson Longman, 2006. Dixit, A.: Power of Incentives in Private versus Public Organizations. *The American Economic Review* 2/1997, pp. 378–82. Stiglitz, J. E.: *Ekonomie veřejného sektoru* [Economics of the Public Sector]. Praha: Grada, 1997. Nigro, L. G.: *Decision Making in the Public Sector*. New York: Marcel Dekker Inc., 1984. Carnevale, D. G.: *Organizational Development in the Public Sector*. Boulder: Westview Press, 2002.

(2) The performance of corporate governance in public enterprises is more difficult because it is often complicated to evaluate the overall effect of the public enterprise within the national economy.

The added value of production of any enterprise, state-owned or private, from the national economy perspective, subsists in the difference between the value of its inputs (the value of purchased raw materials) and the value of its outputs (the value of production). The goods or services produced by public enterprises are often not sold for market prices and sometimes are provided to the public for free. This fact prevents not just objective assessment of the added value of public enterprises for the national economy, but also makes it impossible to manage them on the basis of clear business objectives. The volume of their production may be evaluated by the value of their inputs.

In other words, the added value of production of any corporation is an aggregate of the value of wages, paid out interest and profit. For example, if a private corporation increases the wages of its employees by 10% at the expense of its profit, it will not generate any added value from the national economy perspective. In the case of a public enterprise providing its products free of charge, the same increase in wages may be perceived as an increase in its added value, or the value of generated production. Absence of profit does not necessarily mean that the company is managed in the public interest.

(3) Public enterprises tend to be more frequent in specific industries – they are usually large companies operating in industries with cross-section importance.

The reason for state enterprises in these areas may include concerns regarding consequences of private business in these areas (low or unstable supply of goods, possibility of misusing a dominant or monopoly position on the market, capitalising on limited knowledge of consumers or limited possibilities to defend their interests, etc.). These interests or concerns, however, may be solved by regulating private businesses.

The real reason for public production of goods in certain branches of the national economy is often the success of interest groups (connected with the relevant branches) in convincing the public and the politicians that the particular branch requires state enterprise or protection, and also the interest of the politicians in using these large and generally less transparent enterprises (under the excuse of protecting the 'public interest') as a means for ensuring their personal as well as party interests. Public enterprises often act as tools for less transparent redistribution in favour of certain groups or hidden subsidizing of the political sphere.

(4) Public enterprises are often important players with dominant positions on the market. Similarly to private companies that are not exposed to competition, they generally require a certain level of state regulation (in the public interest).

The regulation of public enterprises is not often very effective because the state is usually unable to separate its roles of the owner and the regulator. Regulatory supervision of public enterprises by the state is therefore usually rather weak.

In addition, the state in such a situation often prefers the profitable or fiscal income to the interests of the consumers. This priority ordinarily results in the reduction of general well-being, and the potentially positive impact of public ownership on the consumers and the public as a whole is lost.

A preferential (less competitive) position on capital markets may restrict the performance of public enterprises in a similar manner.[478]

(5) Corporate governance of public enterprises is often restricted by non-transparent nominations of members of governing boards relying on their political rather than professional background. This fact may have a negative impact upon their motivation, priorities as well as independence in performing corporate governance.[479]

As opposed to the managers of private corporations selected directly or indirectly by the owners, management of public enterprises is selected either directly by an elected body or by persons appointed by the elected body. Maintaining good relations with political representatives may be more important for the executive management and the board members in these enterprises than the results to achieve. On the other hand, objectively bad results or provable mistakes in financial management need not become an issue for the managers or governors, providing that they accommodate the representatives of the political power.

As mentioned in the World Bank report, *"SOE [state-owned enterprises] boards rarely play a true corporate governance role. Boards tend to act as a 'parliament' representing various stakeholders. SOE boards in many countries include elected officials, civil servants, and employee representatives, all of whom may have agendas that conflict with the interest of the company as a whole. Unsurprisingly, SOE boards are weak, and decision-making is heavily influenced by the government."*[480]

The link between the enterprise management and the election results shortens the horizon of the management planning and increases the likelihood of political interference in the day-to-day management of public enterprises. It restricts the independence of their boards and audit bodies including their independence of the operative management of the enterprises. Their legitimacy may also rely primarily on the election result or the relationship to the winner of the election.

The majority of the above mentioned factors indicate that if public enterprises are to fulfil their functions in a better way, and if they are to be more efficient and better managed, much better public transparency of their objectives, management and finance will be required.

Corporate governance tools generally used in private corporations do not usually work in public enterprises as indicated above: internal corporate governance (separation and mutual independence of executive management and the board, or audit powers, internal audit, the founder's supervision, etc.) are often formal and do not guarantee efficient performance of corporate governance; external corporate governance tools (supervision of competitive markets of goods, capital and managers) do not usually work in public enterprises.

Carrying out truly independent external audits relying on international benchmarks and standards, publishing external financial flows and relations as well as the criteria and results

[478]/ Boardman, A. – Vining, A. R.: Ownership and Performance in Competitive Environments: A Comparison of the Performance of Private, Mixed and State-Owned Enterprises. *Journal of Law and Economics* 1/1989, pp. 1–33.
[479]/ Shirley, M.: *Why Performance Contracts for State-Owned Enterprises Haven't Worked*. World Bank, 1998. Retrieved from http://rru.worldbank.org/PublicPolicyJournal/Summary.aspx?id=150. Shleifer, A.: State versus Private Ownership. *Journal of Economic Perspectives* 12/2008.
[480]/ *Improving the Corporate Governance of State-Owned Enterprises: The Approach of the World Bank*. World Bank, 2005, p. 23. Retrieved from http://www.ifc.org/ifcext/corporategovernance.nsf/Content/StateOwned_Enterprises.

of personnel decisions, assessment of compliance with international principles of corporate governance in state-owned enterprises (e.g. *Guidelines on Corporate Governance of State-Owned Enterprises* published by OECD[481]) – all of the above factors have a much more important role in performing corporate governance in public enterprises. Apart from government bodies the audit function in public enterprises will always have to be played by non-governmental organisations and private and public media.

2.8.5 Corporate governance in public enterprises: institutional point of view

Why do public enterprises behave differently than private corporations? The main reason usually consists of several mutually related factors. These include primarily the following:

1. The purpose and responsibilities of the enterprise officials often are neither clearly defined, nor consistently enforced and are subject to frequent changes;
2. Their financial management is not very transparent and its control by owners or internal or external audit bodies is often weak and formal;
3. Control powers are concentrated in persons who share the interests with the management of the public enterprises;
4. Compared to private corporations, management and finance of public enterprises is governed by different interests and motivations conditioned by their market position.[482]

These differences may be summarized as differences in the performance of corporate governance conditioned by different degrees of efficiency of internal and external institutions ensuring corporate governance.[483]

The problem of public enterprises subsists in that the maintenance of inefficient corporate governance tools is often supported by strong economic and political interests, which applies primarily in emerging market economies.[484]

Goals of public enterprises

Public enterprises are not often managed on a purely business basis. As opposed to private corporations striving to maximise their profit, public enterprises usually have several objectives the priorities of which are not always clearly set. Unclear objectives of public enterprises (for example lack of clarity in the question of whether it is the objective of the company management to maximise its value for shareholders or to implement certain economic and social policy in the interest of citizens or consumers) make assessment of

---

[481] OECD: *Guidelines on Corporate Governance of State-Owned Enterprises*. OECD, 2005, http://www.ifc.org/ifcext/corporategovernance.nsf/Content/StateOwned_Enterprises.
[482] Dixit, A. *supra* at pp. 378–82. Nigro, L. G. *supra*.
[483] Bati, A.: *Limitations on Effective Corporate Governance in State-Owned Enterprises and How to Deal with Them*. Retrieved from http://www.salans.com/FileServer.
[484] OECD: *Corporate Governance, State-Owned Enterprises and Privatisation*. Paris: OECD Publishing, 1998. World Bank: *Bureaucrats in Business: The Economics and Politics of Government Ownership*. New York: Oxford University Press, 1995. World Bank: *Held by the Visible Hand: The Challenge of SOE Corporate Governance for Emerging Markets*. World Bank, 2006. Retrieved from http://www.ifc.org/ifcext/economics.nsf/Content/CGG_SOE_Governance.

their performance or success more difficult and result in dispersed responsibility of their top representatives.[485]

As a result, management cannot be held responsible, for example, for the failure to achieve specific business objectives, if achieving such objectives is in conflict with simultaneous political objectives enforced by the state as the main shareholder. Another problem of public enterprises often is that because their owners or founders failed to set clear objectives, the objectives of their activity are then set by their management usually in a way that suits the company itself.

Similar issues may sometimes arise also in private corporations, but they are usually of a short-term nature. In the long-term perspective their profit objective is clear and deviation from this goal jeopardizes the existence of the corporation. Assessing the performance of public enterprises focusing on multiple objectives is much more complex.

In addition to the simultaneous focus on multiple objectives, the governance of public enterprises is more difficult because their *objectives may change depending on political cycle*. A change in election results often leads to membership changes in managing and supervisory boards of these enterprises, which may in turn result in different priorities. This may mean for the executive management of a public enterprise, such as a community-owned firm, that in practice the role of the owner of the enterprise that they manage is played by different people with different focuses in different terms of office. Short-term involvement of such "owners" tends to give preference to short-term or personal goals.

Weakening of control functions and responsibilities of corporate management

Public enterprises are usually large organisations and as such they suffer from the same issues as large (stock) companies with many small shareholders. These problems include no or insufficient owner supervision or weak control of management decisions as a result of lack of transparency of their activities.[486]

Similarly to managers of other large corporations, the managers of large public enterprises have considerable ability to enforce their own interests or the interests of other employees of such enterprises, rather than the social interests or the interests of the state (as the only or majority shareholder). As opposed to private corporations, this issue is usually much more significant in public enterprises. In the case of public enterprises, mainly those where the state is the only owner, the problems are further amplified by the absence of pressure on transparency and efficiency of financial management by actual owners motivated by their long-term interest to maintain or increase the value of their property. Such absence often results in weak and formal audit. Collusion between management and those of the administrative or supervisory bodies of the company is not unusual (see below).

Responsibility of managers or managing bodies of public enterprises may be further weakened by splitting the responsibility among various bodies, such as the supervisory board, the ministry and its officials, the cabinet and its members, a political party, etc. Members of such bodies replacing the inexistent real owner may more frequently than in

485/ Stiglitz, J. E. *supra* at p. 157 and subs.
486/ OECD: *Guidelines on Corporate Governance of State-Owned Enterprises*. OECD, 2005. Retrieved from http://www.ifc.org/ifcext/corporategovernance.nsf/Content/StateOwned_Enterprises.

private corporations enforce regulations in administration and control their own interests. The tendency to scatter responsibility of public enterprise officers reflects an inclination to avoiding personal responsibility by the collective manner of decision-making or extended bureaucratic approaches.

Collusion between management and supervisory bodies

Weakened control of public enterprises does not have to arise from their unclear priorities and absence of ownership interest. The cause of insufficient performance of corporate governance may be the fact that personal interests of their managers overlap with personal interests of members of the managing or supervisory boards who are (often formally) authorised to supervise the managers' activities. Motivation and remuneration of control bodies may be presented as an example.

We can use as an example of this problem in the Czech Republic the practice which was applied before privatisation in the state-owned enterprise Český Telecom, a.s.; this practice, however, is or was common in many other companies with majority public ownership.

Český Telecom, a.s. as a state-owned company became a pioneer in a motivation programme under which members of the board of directors were entitled to relatively high bonuses depending on the development of a share price. (This programme was, after the company privatisation, cancelled by the owner similarly to other formerly state-owned companies using a similar arrangement, such as Komerční banka. It is interesting and peculiar that similar systems of top management motivation were introduced in the Czech Republic primarily by state-owned enterprises. It shows a relatively strong position of the management of these companies in relation to the weaker owner – the state.)

The manner of remuneration in which members of the board of directors get bonuses depending on the company performance measured by the price of shares is relatively common around the world. In the case of Telecom as well as other companies applying this programme there may be doubts as to whether the total potential sum of bonuses is appropriate and whether the growth of the share price should not be "reduced" by the impact of the overall trend on the market, i.e. the overall growth of share prices. These objections, however, do not essentially degrade the positive evaluation of this model of motivation and remuneration of top management. The problem is that the same motivation programme in Czech Telecom applied not just to the members of the board of directors but also to the members of the supervisory board.

In the Czech system of corporate governance, the supervisory board plays a key role in the control and supervision of management (in fact consisting of members of the board of directors). Members of the supervisory board are to be independent "non-executive directors" who are able and willing to oppose decisions of management if it is in the interest of shareholders. Members of the supervisory board ideally should be independent of the decisions of top management, and under no circumstances should their income depend on the same indicator as the income of the members of the board of directors. On the contrary, members of the supervisory board must themselves judge whether it is really appropriate to pay out to top managers, for example, up to 200 million CZK in bonuses and whether the same job could be done by somebody else for less money.

It is clear that if members of the board of directors and supervisory board are "all in the same boat" in terms of remuneration (or as it happens to be in some cases, the remuneration of the supervisory board members is approved by the board of directors, which is to be supervised by the supervisory board), their independence is just hypothetical and the supervisory board becomes superfluous. How could a member of the supervisory board control whether the management resorts to steps that will in the short term increase the share price but will damage the company in the long run, if his remuneration also depends on the share price in the short term? This is why the supervisory boards are extremely weak in such a system of "corporate governance".

The idea that the members of the supervisory boards can "emancipate" themselves from executive management and will consistently monitor and defend the interests of shareholders is unrealistic in this situation.

The peculiar feature of corporate governance in public enterprises is primarily the fact that neither the members of the supervisory boards nor the state officials who appointed them have objected to the above described arrangement. This shows that the understanding and acceptance of basic principles of corporate governance is very limited in such enterprises.

2.8.6 Opportunities for improvement of corporate governance in public enterprises

Although numerous factors causing less efficient corporate governance in public enterprises have an objective nature, it is possible to improve corporate governance in these companies.[487] Opportunities for the improvement lie in the key issues of the current practice of corporate governance in these enterprises outlined above.

The main possibilities of improving corporate governance in these enterprises include the following:

1. To create generally accepted and binding rules and procedures of corporate governance in public enterprises;
2. To impose a statutory duty on independent external auditors of public enterprises to express their opinion in compliance with corporate governance principles in public enterprises; to restrict the possibility of public enterprises to make contracts with auditors who are not trustworthy;
3. To state clear and transparent objectives for individual public enterprises including objectives of public and social policy fulfilled by these enterprises; to set forth the duty to publish costs related to the fulfilment of such objectives; to set forth the duty of the company management to explain any material deviations from the defined objectives;
4. To strengthen the role of independent members (non-executive directors) of managing and supervisory bodies of public enterprises (not government officials) including persons

---

[487]/ OECD: *Guidelines on Corporate Governance of State-Owned Enterprises*. OECD, 2005, retrieved from http://www.ifc.org/ifcext/corporategovernance.nsf/Content/StateOwned_Enterprises.

from abroad, and to prevent any conflict of interest of members of managing bodies of the companies;

5. To strengthen the transparency of the financial management of public enterprises and their subsidiaries by introducing a duty to publish the content of contracts made with other companies, and by introducing the duty to get an independent assessment of procurement (public tenders) exceeding a certain financial threshold;

6. To create remuneration committees that generally exist in private corporations; to introduce a duty to publish information about remuneration of individual members of top management or managing bodies;

7. To deregulate markets where public enterprises operate and, by doing so, to subject them to competition; to restrict hidden forms of subsidies for public enterprises;

8. To introduce transparent criteria for the selection of top representatives of public enterprises and their subsidiaries, and a duty to have a public selection process for these positions; and

9. To create ethical standards for the management of public enterprises and to make the representatives personally liable for their compliance with such standards.

Selected bibliography to Chapter 2

Act to regulate land use planning and building guidelines No. 183/2006 Sb. (Building Act).

ALEXY, R.: *Begriff und Geltung des Rechts*. Freiburg – München: Alber, 1994.

ANTOŠ, M.: Hlasování po Internetu: Estonsko [Internet Vote: Estonia]. In: Knoll, V. – Bednář, V. (eds.): *Naděje právní vědy. Býkov 2007* [Hopes of Legal Science. Býkov 2007]. Plzeň: Aleš Čeněk, 2009, pp. 431–439.

ANTOŠ, M.: Mohou se senátní volební obvody měnit účelově ve prospěch vládních stran? [Can the Senate Election Districts be Changed on Purpose in Favour of the Government Parties?]. In: Mikule, V. – Suchánek, R. (eds.): *Pocta Zdeňku Jičínskému k 80. narozeninám* [Tribute to Zdeněk Jičínský on his 80th Birthday]. Praha: ASPI, 2009, pp. 211–220.

ANTOŠ, M.: *Principy voleb v České republice* [Principles of Elections in the Czech Republic]. Praha: Linde, 2008.

ANTOŠ, M.: Rozhodly letošní volby do Poslanecké sněmovny hlasy ze zahraničí? [Were the Votes from Abroad Decisive in this Year's Chamber of Deputies Election?]. *Právní rozhledy* 17/2006, pp. 642–646.

ANTOŠ, M.: Volební právo cizinců žijících v České republice [The Right to Vote of Foreigners Living in the Czech Republic]. In: Jirásková, V. (ed.): *Interpretace Ústavy České republiky a Ústavy Slovenské republiky. Evropeizace ústavních systémů* [Interpretation of the Constitution of the Czech Republic and the Constitution of the Slovak Republic. Europeisation of Constitutional Systems]. Praha: Univerzita Karlova, Právnická fakulta, 2007, pp. 132–139.

AVBELJ, M. – KOMÁREK, J. (eds.): *Four Visions of Constitutional Pluralism*. EUI Working Papers, Law 2008/21.

BAGEHOT, W.: *The English Constitution*. London: C. A. Watts and Co. LTD, 1964.

BÁRÁNY, E.: *Pojmy dobrého práva* [The Concepts of Good Law]. Bratislava: Poradca podnikateľa, 2007.

BARENTS, R.: *The Autonomy of Community Law*. The Hague – London – New York: Kluwer Law International, 2004.

BARŠA, P.: *Politická teorie multikulturalismu* [Political Theory of Multiculturalism]. Brno: CDK, 1999.

BIRCH, S. – WATT, B.: Remote Electronic Voting: Free, Fair and Secret. *The Political Quarterly* 1/2004, pp. 60–72.

BLAHOŽ, J.: *Soudní kontrola ústavnosti* [Judicial Control over Constitutionality]. Praha: ASPI, 2001.

BLAIS, A.: *To Vote or Not to Vote. The Merits and Limits of Rational Choice Theory*. Pittsburg: University of Pittsburgh Press, 2000.

BOARDMAN, A. – VINING, A. R.: Ownership and Performance in Competitive Environments: A Comparison of the Performance of Private, Mixed and State-Owned Enterprises. *Journal of Law and Economics* 1/1989, pp. 1–33.

BOGUSZAK, J. – ČAPEK, J. – GERLOCH, A.: *Teorie práva* [Theory of Law]. Praha: Eurolex Bohemia, 2001.

BOHÁČKOVÁ, R.: *Dějiny právního myšlení* [History of Legal Thinking]. Brno: Masarykova univerzita, 1994.

BRANCATO, C. K. – PLATH, C. A.: *Corporate Governance Best Practices. A Blueprint for the Post-Enron Era*. New York: Conference Board, 2003.

BROSS, S.: Úvahy o státotvorném procesu v Evropě [Reflections on the Integration Process in Europe]. *Občanský institut Bulletin*, http://obcinst.cz/cs/UVAHY-O-STATOTVORNEM-PROCESU-V-EVROPE-c1334/.

BYDLINSKI, F.: *Juristische Methodenlehre und Rechtsbegriff*. Wien: Springer, 1991.

CANARIS, C. W.: *Die Feststellung von Lücken im Gesetz*. Berlin: Duncker & Humblot, 1964.

CARNEVALE, D. G.: *Organizational Development in the Public Sector*. Boulder: Westview Press, 2002.

ČERMÁK, J.: *Internet a autorské právo* [Internet and Copyright Law]. 2nd ed., Praha: Linde, 2003.

CÍSAŘ, O.: Teorie demokracie na úsvitu globálního věku [The Theory of Democracy at the Dawn of the Global Era]. In: Hloušek, V. – Kopeček, L. (eds.): *Demokracie. Teorie, modely, osobnosti, podmínky, nepřátelé a perspektivy demokracie* [Democracy. Theory, Models, Persons, Conditions, Enemies and Prospects of Democracy]. Brno: MPÚ, 2003, pp. 349–376.

COMMISSION ON EUROPEAN CONTRACT LAW: *The Principles of European Contract Law*. Hague: Kluwer, 1999 (Parts I, II) and 2003 (Part III).

CREMONA, J. J.: The right to free elections in the European Convention on Human Rights. In: Mahoney, P. – Matscher, F. – Petzold, H. – Wildhaber, L. (eds.): *Protecting human rights: the European perspective*. Köln: Carl Heymanns Verlag, 2000, pp. 309–324.

CVRČEK, F.: Kritické poznámky k výuce interpretace právních textů [Critical Comments on Teaching Interpretation of Legal Text]. In: Gerloch, A. – Maršálek, P. (eds.): *Problémy interpretace a argumentace v soudobé právní teorii a právní praxi* [Issues of Interpretation and Argumentation in Contemporary Legal Theory and Practice]. Praha: Eurolex Bohemia, 2003, pp. 49–61.

DAGTOGLOU, P.: *Ersatzpflicht des Staates bei legislativem Unrecht?* Tübingen: J.C.B. Mohr, 1963.

DAHL, R. A.: *On Democracy*. New Haven: Yale University Press, 1998.

DEWAN, S. M. (ed.): *Corporate Governance in Public Sector Enterprises*. Delhi: Pearson Longman, 2006.

DIXIT, A.: Power of Incentives in Private versus Public Organizations. *The American Economic Review* 2/1997, pp. 378–82.

DREYFUSS, R. – GINSBURG, J. C: Principles Governing Jurisdiction, Choice of Law, and Judgments in Transnational Disputes. *Computer law review international* 2/2003, pp. 33–39.

DWORKIN, R.: *Když se práva berou vážně* [Taking Rights Seriously]. Praha: Oikoymenh, 2001.

European Commission for Democracy through Law (Venice Commission): *Code of Good Practice in Electoral Matters. Guidelines and Explanatory Report*. CDL-AD(2002)023rev. Strasbourg, 23rd May 2003, http://www.venice.coe.int/docs/2002/CDL-AD(2002)023rev-e.pdf

European Commission for Democracy through Law (Venice Commission): *Report on the Compatibility of Remote Voting and Electronic Voting with the Standards of the Council of Europe*. CDL-AD(2004)012. Strasbourg, 18th March 2004, http://www.venice.coe.int/docs/2004/CDL-AD(2004)012-e.asp

FILIP, J.: Alternativní způsoby hlasování a jejich vliv na aktivitu voličů [Alternative Forms of Voting and Their Impact on Voters' Activity]. *Časopis pro právní vědu a praxi* 1/2007, pp. 5–12.

FILIP, J.: Legislativní technika a judikatura Ústavního soudu [Legislative Technique and Case Law of the Constitutional Court]. *Časopis pro právní vědu a praxi* 3/2005, pp. 236–246.

FILIP, J.: *Ústavní právo České republiky* [Constitutional Law of the Czech Republic]. Vol. 1, 4th ed., Brno: Masarykova univerzita, 2003.

FILIP, J.: Ústavní soud a řešení sporů v zákonodárném procesu [The Constitutional Court and the Solution of Disputes in the Legislative Procedure]. *Právní zpravodaj* 1/2002, pp. 9–10.

FILIP, J.: Volební čas v zahraničí jako ústavní problém [Election Time Abroad as a Constitutional Problem]. *Časopis pro právní vědu a praxi* 1/2002, pp. 8–12.

FILIP, J.: *Vybrané kapitoly ke studiu ústavního práva* [Selected Chapters for the Study of Constitutional Law]. 2nd ed., Brno: Masarykova univerzita, 2001.

FRIEDMAN, T. L.: *Svět je plochý. Stručné dějiny jednadvacátého století* [The World is Flat. A Brief History of the Twenty-First Century]. Praha: Academia, 2007.

FUKUYAMA, F.: *Budování státu podle Fukuyamy* [State-Building According to Fukuyama]. Praha: Alfa Publishing, 2004.

FUKUYAMA, F.: *The End of History and the Last Man*. New York: The Free Press, 1992.

GERLOCH, A. – HŘEBEJK, J. – ZOUBEK, V.: *Ústavní systém České republiky: základy českého ústavního práva* [The Constitutional System of the Czech Republic: the Basics of Czech Constitutional Law]. 4th ed., Praha: Prospektrum, 2002.

GERLOCH, A. – KYSELA, J. – KÜHN, Z. – WINTR, J. – TRYZNA, J. – MARŠÁLEK, P. – BERAN, K.: *Teorie a praxe tvorby práva* [Theory and Practice of Lawmaking]. Praha: ASPI, 2008.

GERLOCH, A. – MARŠÁLEK, P. (eds.): *Problémy interpretace a argumentace v soudobé právní teorii a právní praxi* [Issues of Interpretation and Logical Reasoning in Contemporary Legal Theory and Practice]. Praha: Eurolex Bohemia, 2003.

GERLOCH, A. – MARŠÁLEK, P. (eds.): *Zákon v kontinentálním právu* [Statute in Continental Law]. Praha: Eurolex Bohemia, 2005.

GERLOCH, A. - TRYZNA, J.: Nad vázaností soudce zákonem z pohledu některých soudních rozhodnutí [Considering the Binding Effect of Statute on Judges from the Point of View of Some Judicial Decisions]. *Právní rozhledy* 1/2007, pp. 23–28.

GERLOCH, A. - TRYZNA, J.: Několik úvah nad rolí nejvyšších soudů v podmínkách demokratického právního státu [Some Thoughts on the Role of Supreme Courts in Democratic States Respecting the Rule of Law]. In: Šimíček, V. (ed.): *Role nejvyšších soudů v evropských ústavních systémech - čas pro změnu?* [The Role of Supreme Courts in European Constitutional Systems - Time for Change?] Brno: Masarykova univerzita, 2007, pp. 89–102.

GERLOCH, A.: Má zákon budoucnost? Zákony a zákoníky v 21. století [Is There a Future for a Law? Laws and Codes in the Twenty-First Century]. In: Gerloch, A. - Maršálek, P. (eds.): *Zákon v kontinentálním právu* [Statute in Continental Law]. Praha: Eurolex Bohemia, 2005, pp. 17–21.

GERLOCH, A.: *Teorie práva* [Theory of Law]. Plzeň: Vydavatelství a nakladatelství Aleš Čeněk, 2004.

GIZBERT-STUDNICKI, T.: Der Vorverständnisbegriff in der juristischen Hermeneutik. *ARSP* 4/1987, pp. 476–493.

GORDON, J.: *The macroeconomic benefits of good corporate governance.* New Delhi: IMF, 2002.

GUIBAULT, L. - HUGENHOLTZ, P. B. et al.: *Study on the Conditions Applicable to Contracts Relating to Intellectual Property in the European Union, Final Report.* Amsterdam: Institute for Information Law, 2002. http://www.ivir.nl/publications/other/final-report2002.pdf.

HALBERSTAM, D.: *Constitutional Heterarchy: The Centrality of Conflict in the European Union and the United States.* University of Michigan Law School, Public Law and Legal Theory Working Paper Series, Working Paper No. 111, June 2008.

HAVRÁNEK, D.: K hierarchické výstavbě právního řádu a vymezení pojmu právní síly v ústavním prostředí České republiky [Hierarchy of Legal Order and Definition of the Concept of the Force of Law in the Constitutional Environment of the Czech Republic]. *Právník* 5/2007, pp. 457–478.

HENDRYCH, D. et al.: *Správní právo. Obecná část* [Administrative Law. General Part]. Praha: C. H. Beck, 1998.

HOETZEL, J.: Literární zprávy - Jaroslav Krejčí: Moc nařizovací a její meze [New Publications - Jaroslav Krejčí: Authority to Order and Its Limits]. *Právník* 1923, pp. 339–345.

HOLLÄNDER, P.: *Filosofie práva* [Philosophy of Law]. Plzeň: Aleš Čeněk, 2006.

HOLLÄNDER, P.: Mezera v zákoně, § 7 o. z. o. a ryzí nauka právní (Poznámky k úvaze Franze Bydlinského) [A Loophole in Statute, s. 7 of the General Civil Code and the Pure Theory of Law. Comments on the Contemplation by Franz Bydlinsky]. In: Machalová, T. (ed.): *Místo normativní teorie v soudobém právním myšlení (K odkazu Františka Weyra a Hanse Kelsena)* [The Position of Normative Theory in the Contemporary Legal Thinking. Legacy of František Weyr and Hans Kelsen]. Brno: Masarykova univerzita, 2003, pp. 130–139.

HOLMSTROM, B. - KAPLAN, S. N.: *The State of U.S. Corporate Governance: What's Right and What's Wrong.* research.chicagogsb.edu/economy/research/articles/185.pdf.

HURDÍK, J.: *Institucionální pilíře soukromého práva v dynamice vývoje společnosti* [Institutional Pillars of Private Law in the Dynamics of the Social Development]. Praha: C. H. Beck, 2007.

Improving the Corporate Governance of State-Owned Enterprises: The Approach of the World Bank. WorldBank, 2005. http://www.ifc.org/ifcext/corporategovernance.nsf/Content/StateOwned_Enterprises.

Intellectual Property on the Internet: a Survey of Issues. Geneva: WIPO, 2002.

JHERING, R. v.: *Der Zweck im Recht.* Vol. I, Leipzig: Druck und Verlag von Breithoff & Härtel, 1893.

JIČÍNSKÝ, Z.: *Ústava České republiky v politické praxi* [The Constitution of the Czech Republic in Practice]. Praha: Linde, 2007.

JONAS, H.: *The Imperatives of Responsibility. In Search for an Ethics for the Technological Age.* Chicago - London: The University of Chicago Press, 1984.

KELSEN, H.: *Ryzí nauka právní. Metoda a základní pojmy* [Pure Theory of Law. Method and Basic Concepts]. Praha - Brno: Orbis, 1933.

KINDLOVÁ, M.: Koncept vlády práva v kontextu parlamentní suverenity ve Spojeném království [The Concept of Rule of Law in the Context of Parliamentary Sovereignty in the United Kingdom]. In: Jirásková, V. - Suchánek, R. (eds.): *Pocta prof. JUDr. Václavu Pavlíčkovi, CSc. k 70. Narozeninám* [Tribute to Professor Václav Pavlíček on his 70th Birthday]. Praha: Linde, 2004, pp. 385–405.

KINDLOVÁ, M.: Ústavní zvyklosti jako součást ústavy (komparace commonwealthského přístupu a judikatury Ústavního soudu ČR) [Constitutional Conventions as Part of Constitution (The Comparison of Commonwealth Approach and Case-law of the Constitutional Court of the CR]. In: Klíma, K. - Jirásek, J. (eds.): *Pocta Jánu Gronskému.* Plzeň: Aleš Čeněk, 2008, pp. 300–317.

KLÍMA, K. et al.: *Komentář k Ústavě a Listině* [Commentary on the Constitution and the Charter]. Plzeň: Aleš Čeněk, 2005.

KLÍMA, K.: Pyramidální a praktické důsledky vstupu do Evropské unie pro ústavní pojetí pramenů práva v České republice [Pyramidal and Practical Consequences of EU Accession for Constitutional Concept of Sources of Law in the Czech Republic]. In: Gerloch, A. – Maršálek, P. (eds.): *Zákon v kontinentálním právu* [Statute in Continental Law]. Praha: Eurolex Bohemia, 2005, pp. 357–362.

KLÍMA, K.: *Ústavní právo* [Constitutional Law]. 3rd ed., Plzeň: Aleš Čeněk, 2006.

KNAP, K. – KUNZ, O.: *Mezinárodní právo autorské* [International Copyright Law]. Praha: Academia, 1981.

KNAPP, V. et al.: *Teoretické problémy tvorby československého práva* [Theoretical Issues of the Creation of Czechoslovak Law]. Praha: Academia, 1983.

KNAPP, V.: *Teorie práva* [Theory of Law]. Praha: C. H. Beck, 1995.

KORKUNOV, N. M.: *Lekcii po obščej teorii prava.* Sankt-Peterburg: Juridičeskij Centr Pres, 2004.

KRAMER, E. A.: *Juristische Methodenlehre.* Bern – München – Wien: Stämpfli, 2005.

KUBŮ, L. et al.: *Dějiny právní filozofie* [History of Legal Philosophy]. Olomouc: Vydavatelství Univerzity Palackého, 2002.

KÜHN, Z.: *Aplikace práva soudcem v éře středoevropského komunismu a transformace. Analýza příčin postkomunistické právní krize* [Application of Law by Judges in the Era of Central European Communism and Transformation. Analysis of Postcommunist Legal Crisis]. Praha: C. H. Beck, 2005.

KÜHN, Z.: *Aplikace práva ve složitých případech* [Application of Law in Hard Cases]. Praha: Karolinum, 2002.

KUR, A.: Principles Governing Jurisdiction, Choice of Law, and Judgments in Transnational Disputes: A European Perspective. *Computer law review international* 3/2003, pp. 65–72.

KYSELA, J.: *Ústavní principy, ústavní konvence a ústavní inženýrství* [Constitutional Principles, Constitutional Conventions and Constitutional Engineering]. In: Klíma, K., Jirásek, J. (eds.): *Pocta Jánu Gronskému* [Tribute to Ján Gronský]. Plzeň: Aleš Čeněk, 2008, pp. 121–136.

KYSELA, J.: Úvod k teorii zákonodárné delegace: pojem a typy [Introduction to the Theory of Legislative Delegation: the Concept and the Types]. In: Gerloch, A. – Maršálek, P. (eds.): *Zákon v kontinentálním právu* [Statute in Continental Law]. Praha: Eurolex Bohemia, 2005, pp. 153–170.

KYSELA, J.: *Zákonodárství bez parlamentů. Delegace a substituce zákonodárné pravomoci* [Legislation without Parliaments. Delegation and Substitution of Legislative Power]. Praha: Univerzita Karlova v Praze. Právnická fakulta, 2006.

LARENZ, K.: *Methodenlehre der Rechtswissenschaft.* Berlin – Heidelberg – New York: Springer, 1979.

LAUFER, H.: *Das Kriterium politischen Handelns.* Würzburg: Dissertation 1961.

LAUFER, H.: *Verfassungsgerichtsbarkeit und politischer Prozeß. Studien zum Bundesverfassungsgericht der Bundesrepublik Deutschland.* Tübingen, 1968.

LAZAROVA TRAJKOVSKA, M.: *Report on the Abolition of Restrictions on the Right to Vote in General Elections.* European Commission for Democracy through Law (Venice Commission), CDL-AD (2005)011, 4th April 2005, http://www.venice.coe.int/docs/2005/CDL-AD(2005)011-e.asp.

LEISNER, W.: *Krise des Gesetzes. Die Auflösung des Normenstaates.* Berlin: Duncker & Humblot, 2001.

Ľudské práva [Human Rights]. Výber dokumentov OSN. Bratislava: Archa, 1991.

LUHMANN, N.: *Das Recht der Gesellschaft.* Frankfurt am Main: Suhrkamp, 1995.

LUHMANN, N.: *Rechtssoziologie.* Opladen: Westdeutscher Verlag, 1987.

LUHMANN, N.: *Sociální systémy: nárys obecné teorie* [Social Systems: An Outline of General Theory]. Brno: CDK, 2006.

MACKIE, T.: Gerrymandering. In: Rose, R. (ed.): *International Encyclopaedia of Elections.* London: Macmillian Reference, 2000.

MALENOVSKÝ, J.: Mezinárodní právo veřejné, jeho obecná část a poměr k jiným právním systémům, zvláště k právu českému [Public International Law, Its General Part and Relationship to Other Legal Systems, Namely Czech Law]. 5th ed., Brno: Masarykova univerzita a Doplněk, 2008.

MANGOLDT, H. – KLEIN, F. – STARCK, CH.: *Das Bonner Grundgesetz. Kommentar.* Vol. 2, 4th ed., München: Verlag Franz Vahlen, 2000.

MARGETIĆ, L.: *Vinodolski zakon* [Vinodol Statute]. Rijeka: „Adamić" – vitagraf, 1998.

MARŠÁLEK, P.: *Právo a společnost* [The Law and the Society]. Praha: Auditorium, 2008.

MARŠÁLEK, P.: Zákon v nacionálně socialistickém státě [Statute in a National Socialist State]. In: Gerloch, A. – Maršálek, P. (eds.): *Zákon v kontinentálním právu* [Statute in Continental Law]. Praha: Eurolex Bohemia, 2005, pp. 83–95.

MASSICOTTE, L. – BLAIS, A. – YOSHINAKA, A.: *Establishing the Rules of the Game. Election Laws in Democracies.* Toronto: University of Toronto Press, 2004.

MAURER, H.: *Staatsrecht I. Grundlagen, Verfassungsorgane, Staatsfunktionen.* München: C. H. Beck, 2007.

MCDONALD, M. P.: The Return of the Voter: Voter Turnout in the 2008 Presidential Election. *The Forum 4/2008,* http://www.bepress.com/forum/vol6/iss4/art4.

MELZER, F.: *Metodologie nalézání práva* [Methods of Finding Law]. Brno: Tribun EU, 2008.

MIKULE, V. – SUCHÁNEK, R. (eds.): *Pocta Zdeňku Jičínskému k 80. narozeninám* [Tribute to Zdeněk Jičínský on his 80th Birthday]. Praha: ASPI Wolters Kluwer, 2009.

MLČOCH, L.: *Institucionální ekonomie* [Institutional Economics]. Praha: Karolinum, 2005.

MLSNA, P.: Přímá demokracie a její ústavní parametry v českém ústavním pořádku [Direct Democracy and Its Constitutional Parameters in Czech Constitutional Order]. In: *Dny veřejného práva* [Days of Public Law], Sborník příspěvků z mezinárodní konference [International Conference Proceedings]. Brno: Masarykova univerzita, 2007, p. 36.

MLSNA, P.: Úvaha nad přímou demokracií v ČR [Exploration of Direct Democracy in the Czech Republic]. *Právní zpravodaj* 10/2008, pp. 11–14.

NĚMEČEK, E.: *Mezinárodní měnový systém, Otázka konvertibility, stability a likvidity* [International Monetary System. The Issue of Convertibility, Stability and Liquidity]. Praha: Karolinum, 2000.

NEUBAUER, Z.: Nařízení vládní a ministerská [Government and Ministerial Decrees]. *Právník* 1925, pp. 621–629.

NIGRO, L. G.: *Decision Making in the Public Sector.* New York: Marcel Dekker Inc., 1984.

NIKODÝM, D.: Ústavnoprávne problémy výkonu štátnej moci občanmi [Constitutional Issues of the Exercise of Government by Citizens] In: Jirásková, V. – Suchánek, R. (eds.): *Pocta prof. JUDr. Václavu Pavlíčkovi, CSc. k 70. narozeninám* [Tribute to Professor Václav Pavlíček on his 70th Birthday]. Praha: Linde, 2004, pp. 359–369.

NOVAK, M.: Ústavní soud mezi právem a politikou [Constitutional Court between the Law and the Politics]. *Právník* 5/2001, pp. 421–439.

OECD: *Corporate Governance of State-Owned Assets in OECD countries.* Paris: OECD Publishing, 2005.

OECD: *Guidelines on Corporate Governance of State-Owned Enterprises.* OECD, 2005. http://www.ifc.org/ifcext/corporategovernance.nsf/Content/StateOwned_Enterprises.

OHLER, Ch.: Der institutionelle Vorbehalt des Gesetzes. *Archiv des öffentlichen Rechts* 3/2006, pp. 336–377.

PAVLÍČEK, V. – HŘEBEJK, J.: *Ústava a ústavní řád České republiky* [The Constitution and the Constitutional Order of the Czech Republic]. Vol. 1, 2nd ed., Praha: Linde, 1998.

PAVLÍČEK, V. et al..: *Ústavní právo a státověda* [Constitutional Law and the Theory of State]. Vol. II, Part 1, 2nd ed., Praha: Linde, 2008.

POPPER, K. R.: *Otevřená společnost a její nepřátelé* [Open Society and its Enemies]. Praha: ISE, edice Oikoymenh, 1994.

POSNER, R. A.: *Economic Analysis of Law.* Boston: 1972, New York: 2007.

PŘIBÁŇ, J.: *Suverenita, právo a legitimita* [Sovereignty, Law and Legitimacy]. Praha: Karolinum, 1997.

PROCHÁZKA, R.: *Mission Accomplished. On Founding Constitutional Adjudication in Central Europe.* Budapest – New York: CEU, 2002.

PROSSER, A. – KOFLER, R. – KRIMMER, R.: Current state of public elections over the Internet in Austria. In: *e-Voting.at: Entwicklung eines Internet-basierten Wahlsystems für öffentliche Wahlen.* Vienna: Institute für Informationsverarbeitung und Informationswirtschaft, 2002, pp. 47–56.

PUTNOVÁ, A. – SEKNIČKA, P.: *Etické řízení ve firmě, Nástroje a metody, Etický a sociální audit* [Ethical Company Management. Tools and Methods. Ethical and Social Audit]. Praha: Grada Publishing, 2007.

RADBRUCH, G.: Gesetzliches Unrecht und übergesetzliches Recht. In: Kaufmann, A. (ed.): *Gesamtausgabe Radbruch.* Vol. 3, Heidelberg: Müller, 1990, pp. 83–93.

RADBRUCH, G.: *Rechtsphilosophie.* Stuttgart: Koehler, 1950.

REHBINDER, M.: *Rechtssoziologie.* Berlin – New York: Walter de Gruyter, 1993.

Report on the Commission Recommendation of 18 October 2005 on collective cross-border management of copyright and related rights for legitimate online music services (2005/737/EC) (2006/2008(INI) FINAL A6-0053/2007, 5 March 2007. http://www.europarl.europa.eu/sides/getDoc.do?type=REPORT&reference=A6-2007-0053&language=EN.

RESCHOVÁ, J.: *Evropský konstitutionalismus: zdroje, formy a tendence* [European Constitutionalism: Sources, Forms and Trends]. Praha: VŠE, 2003.

RÜTHERS, B.: Dotváření práva soudci [Judicial Formation of Law]. *Soudce* 8/2003 (pp. 2–6) and 9/2003 (pp. 11–14).

SARTORI, G.: *Pluralismus, multikulturalismus a přistěhovalci. Esej o multietnické společnosti* [Pluralism, Multiculturalism and Immigrants. An Essay on Multiethnic Society]. Praha: Dokořán, 2005.

SCHACK, H.: *Urheber- und Urhebervertragsrecht.* Tübingen: Mohr Siebeck, 2005.

SCHMITT, C.: *Legalität und Legitimität.* Berlín: Duncker & Humblot, 2005.

SCHMITT, C.: *Teorie partyzána* [Theory of the Partisan]. Praha: Oikoymenh, 2008.

SCHNEIDER, H.: *Gesetzgebung.* 3rd ed., Heidelberg: C. F. Müller, 2002.

ŠEDO, J.: *Volební systémy postkomunistických zemí* [Electoral Systems in Post-Communist Countries]. Brno: Centrum pro studium demokracie a kultury (CDK), 2007.

SHAPIRO, M. – STONE SWEET, A.: *On Law, Politics and Judicialization.* Oxford: Oxford University Press, 2002.

SHIRLEY, M.: *Why Performance Contracts for State-Owned Enterprises Haven't Worked.* World Bank, 1998. http://rru.worldbank.org/PublicPolicyJournal/Summary.aspx?id=150.

SHLEIFER, A.: State versus Private Ownership. *Journal of Economic Perspectives* 4/2008, pp. 133–150.

ŠÍMA, J.: *Ekonomie a právo* [Economics and Law]. Praha: Oeconomica, 2004.

ŠIMÍČEK, V. (ed.): *Role nejvyšších soudů v evropských ústavních systémech – čas pro změnu?* [Role of the Supreme Courts in European Constitutional Systems – Time for a Change?] Brno: Masarykova univerzita, 2007.

ŠINDELÁŘ, P.: Elektronické volby jako možný nástroj posílení demokracie [Electronic Election as a Possible Tool for Strengthening Democracy]. *Systems integration* 2006, pp. 238–249.

SLÁDEČEK, V. – MIKULE, V. – SYLLOVÁ, J.: *Ústava České republiky.* Komentář [The Constitution of the Czech Republic. Commentary]. 1st ed., Praha: C. H. Beck, 2007.

STIEBER, M.: *Dějiny soukromého práva v střední Evropě* [History of Private Law in Central Europe]. Praha: vlastním nákladem, 1930.

STIGLER, G. J.: The Economics of Information. *Journal of Political Economy* 3/1961, pp. 213–225.

STIGLITZ, J. E.: *Ekonomie veřejného sektoru* [Economics of the Public Sector]. Praha: Grada Publishing, 1998.

SUCHÁNEK, R.: K ústavnímu právu na ochranu zdraví a na bezplatnou zdravotní péči [Constitutional Right to Protection of Health and Free Healthcare] In: Klíma, K. – Jirásek, J. (eds.): *Pocta Jánu Gronskému* [Tribute to Ján Gronský]. Plzeň: Aleš Čeněk, 2008, pp. 249–271.

TELEC, I. – TŮMA, P.: *Autorský zákon. Komentář* [Copyright Act. Commentary]. Praha: C.H. Beck, 2007.

TINDALL, G. B. – SHI, D. E.: *USA (Dějiny států)* [USA (History of States)]. Praha: Nakladatelství Lidové noviny, 1994.

TOMÁŠEK, M.: *Evropské měnové právo* [European Monetary Law]. Praha: C.H. Beck, 2007.

TOMSA, B.: *Kapitoly z dějin filosofie práva a státu* [Chapters from the History of Philosophy of Law and State]. Praha: Karolinum, 2005.

TRECHSEL, A. H. et al.: *Internet voting in the March 2007 Parliamentary Elections in Estonia.* Council of Europe Report, 31st July 2007. Retrieved from http://www.vvk.ee/public/dok/CoE_and_NEC_Report_E-Voting_2007.pdf.

URBAN, J.: Ekonomie s právem a bez něj [Economics with Law and without It]. In: Bažantová, I. (ed.): *K institucionálním základům tržní ekonomiky a k jejich vývoji* [On Institutional Grounds of the Market Economy and Their Development]. Praha: Prospektrum, 2005, pp. 7–22.

URBAN, J.: *Teorie národního hospodářství* [Theory of National Economy]. Praha: ASPI, 2006.

VOSTRÁ, L. – ČERMÁKOVÁ, J. (eds.): *Otázky tvorby práva v České republice, Polské republice a Slovenské republice* [Issues of Creating Law in the Czech Republic, Polish Republic and Slovak Republic]. Plzeň: Aleš Čeněk, 2005.

WALTER, R. – MAYER, H. – KUCSKO-STADLMAYER, G.: *Bundesverfassungsrecht.* Wien: Manzsche Verlags- und Universitätsbuchhandlung, 2007.

WEICHE, J.: *US-amerikanisches Urhebervertragsrecht.* Baden-Baden: Nomos, 2002.

WEINBERGER, O.: Přirozené právo a právnická argumentace [Natural Law and Legal Reasoning]. *Právník* 3/1993, pp. 193–202.

WEYR, F.: *Soustava československého práva státního* [The System of Czechoslovak State Law]. Brno: Barvič & Novotný, 1921.

WINKLER, G.: *Rechtswissenschaft und Politik.* Wien – New York: Springer Verlag, 1998.

WINTR, J.: *Principy českého ústavního práva s dodatkem principů práva evropského a mezinárodního* [Principles of Czech Constitutional Law, plus an Attachment on Principles of European and International Law]. Praha: Eurolex Bohemia, 2006.

ZÁLEŠÁK, M. – MATEJKA, J.: Nové možnosti (e)demokracie: Vybrané právní a technologické aspekty [New Options of (e)democracy: Selected Legal and Technological Issues]. *ITprávo.cz.* http://itpravo.cz/index.shtml?x=113369.

ZÁŘECKÝ, P.: K vývoji územní veřejné správy před přijetím Ústavy České republiky [Development of Territorial Public Administration before Adoption of the Constitution of the Czech Republic]. In: Kysela, J. (ed.): *Deset let Ústavy České republiky* [Ten Years of the Constitution of the Czech Republic]. Praha: Eurolex Bohemia, 2003, pp. 399–411.

ZIPPELIUS, R.: *Juristische Methodenlehre.* München: Beck, 2005.

Public law within the legal system of the Czech Republic as an EU Member State contains many elements connecting it not only to other branches of national law but also with the legal systems of other EU Member States. Europeanization is considered the most important feature. The current process of Europeanization of Czech law after the Czech Republic's accession to the EU in 2004 has not been solely a process of approximation of Czech law with that of the EC/EU; it has represented an integration of European legal thinking into the development of the legal system of the CR as an EU Member State. The phenomenon of Europeanization has an impact on Czech public law as a whole, but its individual parts are affected in various magnitudes and in varying degrees of complexity. There are differences between branches where a considerable portion of powers have been delegated to the EC bodies, such as finance or environmental law, and branches where the Czech Republic still holds its sovereignty, such as criminal law. The research in the latter branch focuses on the tools of Europeanization in areas such as common criminalization and decriminalization of certain types of conduct, or the principles of criminal liability of legal entities within the EU. On the other hand, the research in branches of Czech law, functioning more or less within the powers delegated to the EU bodies, concentrates on, and analyses, the reflection of European rules in the Czech legal system and also the feedback provided by Czech law with respect to European law-making in the relevant fields.

Globalization is another factor having significant influence upon Czech public law. It is necessary to define the limits for the process of internationalization of public law within the functioning of Czech law under globalization. An increasing amount of legal regulation resulting in the differentiation or fragmentation of international law into more subject-areas also deserves attention since it presents risks of mutual competition between those areas and endangers the unity of the international legal order. Some other issues arise such as the accord or conflict between the regulation of human rights and the procedural mechanisms for their protection within the Council of Europe and the European Union, or the position of the EU in international relations and international law, or, at the most general level, the balance between universalism and regionalism in international law. It has been shown that the risk of fragmentation should not be exaggerated since individual subsystems cannot exist in isolation from general rules. Thus, general international law remains the referential framework for the defining of individual subsystems. Internationalization brings forth in Czech public law the concepts of human rights, international security or international criminal justice.

Czech public law stems from the continental legal tradition. It presumes the division of powers and the primacy of written law not resulting from judicial interpretation or customs; it has been derived from legislation passed by elected representatives. Laws have been enforced by the executive branch of government and by courts. Judicial interpretation should ideally be limited in such a way that it does not derogate from the intent of the legislature. Basic rights and freedoms require their legislative anchoring in order to ensure their applicability to individuals and, in particular, to protect them against state power. Nevertheless, it should be added that Montesquieu's original conception that a judge should only be the "*bouche de la loi*" ("mouth pronouncing the words of the law") has been essentially disregarded in continental law. The substantial disadvantage of written law has been its static nature and its lack of flexibility, resulting in its inability to react to changing circumstances. The judge may not in his interpretation derogate from the initial legislative intent; therefore, many situations remain uncovered by law. This problem has been obvious in Czech law, where judges feel strongly bound by a narrow interpretation of the law. One of the important elements of the development of public law in the beginning of the 21st century is the enhancement and expansion of the catalogue of human rights and freedoms, which often stands beyond the state. Such a catalogue is derived from the international obligations of the state and enables individuals to directly and immediately invoke their rights against their own state. This fact contributes to the approximation of public law systems within the EU; for example, the human rights dimension in criminal law appears to be a much more efficient mechanism of approximation than EU legislative acts may have been.

3.1 UNIVERSALITY OF INTERNATIONAL LAW: WHAT IS THE ROLE OF GENERAL INTERNATIONAL LAW IN THE PERIOD OF ITS FRAGMENTATION?

3.1.1 Research premise: the concept of fragmentation of international law

Fragmentation of international law is a complex process of content expansion and specialization of this area of law (both substantive and procedural), which features a number of aspects. The subject matter of international law has been split into separate subsystems, such as "human rights law", "international criminal law", "international environmental law", "the law of the sea", "international trade law", "international investment law" or "international refugee law". The ever more specialized process of the creation of international law rules, their interpretation and application has continued within their framework. The process has been accompanied by the establishment of specialized international bodies and organizations operating in individual subsystems. Simultaneously, there has been an increasing interconnection and overlap among jurisdictions of decision-making bodies, active at international or mixed international-domestic levels, which apply international law. The overlap has resulted in a possible danger of competition or even direct conflict of case-law of individual bodies.

This situation has attracted the attention of both the theory and practice of international law, which was evidenced, for example, by the fact that in 2002–2006 the fragmentation of international law became a point on the agenda of the International Law Commission (ILC), the main body of the United Nations for the codification and promotion of the progressive development of international law.[488] Hence, a question has arisen: does this phenomenon really endanger the unity of international law and is this law still capable of playing the integrating role of a legal order common to the whole international community?

The researched issue can be structured into several areas. The study of the International Law Commission was focused on the fragmentation of substantive law only. An equally important feature of international law fragmentation is the process of splitting in the area of institutions and procedure, connected with a speedy growth of the number of international decision-making mechanisms. The Commission did not deal intentionally with the second topic, since it feared that its activities in this sphere could be perceived as an undesirable interference with the activities of other UN bodies (The International Court of Justice, *ad hoc* criminal tribunals, etc.).[489]

The starting point of research into the substantive fragmentation of international law, which cannot be avoided, must logically be the outcomes of the work of the International Law Commission on this topic; not just relatively short reports of the Commission should be examined, but mainly a much more detailed report of the Study Group of the Commission, edited (and to a large extent written) by a special rapporteur Koskenniemi.[490] We, of course, consider a wider doctrinal debate[491] and the relevant case-law of international courts.

3.1.2 The relationship between general and special rules of international law
A. Varied conception of normative conflicts related to lex specialis

The relationship between the special and general rules of international law (*lex specialis* and *lex generalis*) is an example of the typical manifestation of the substantive fragmentation of international law. It is a classic case of conflict of rules which can take on several shapes.[492]

(a) A conflict between a general rule and a special interpretation of a general rule
Firstly, it is the case of questions which were resolved in the decisions of some international courts (namely ICJ, ICTY and ECHR) that achieved diametrically different results. Here belongs the standard of control required for attributing actions of persons, who are not its

---

[488] *Report of the International Law Commission*, GAOR, Sixty-first session, Suppl. No. 10 (A/61/10), pp. 400–423.

[489] This problem was studied in detail by the same group of authors in the grant project of the Ministry of Foreign Affairs of the Czech Republic, MZV ČR No. 1/2007. Having been amended, the final treatise was published as an independent monograph: Šturma, P. et al.: *Konkurující jurisdikce mezinárodních rozhodovacích orgánů* [Competing Jurisdictions of International Decision-Making Bodies]. Praha: Ed. středisko PF UK, 2009.

[490] Koskenniemi, M.: *Fragmentation of International Law: Difficulties arising from the Diversification and Expansion of International Law*. Report of the Study Group of the International Law Commission, UN doc. A/CN.4/L.682 (2006).

[491] See, for instance, Dupuy, P. M.: *L'unité de l'ordre juridique international: cours général de droit international public*, RCADI. Leiden: Martinus Nijhoff, 2003; Simma, B. – Pulkowski, D.: Of Planets and the Universe: Self-contained Regimes in International Law, *EJIL* 3/2006, pp. 483–529.

[492] Koskenniemi *supra* at p. 25.

bodies, to a state. The decisive test is whether, in the period when the considered actions occurred, the persons were subject to real control of the state to which their actions are attributed.

This question was for the first time resolved by the ICJ in the Nicaragua case in 1986.[493] In this case, based on interpretation, the USA was not held liable for actions of Nicaraguan contras merely on account of organizing, financing, training and equipping them. This level of involvement failed to meet the test of "effective control" of the state over the activities of non-state actors.

On the other hand, the International Criminal Tribunal for Former Yugoslavia (ICTY) examined in 1999 whether the actions of the Bosnian Serb militia during conflicts in the territory of former Yugoslavia were to be attributed to the former Federal Republic of Yugoslavia (Serbia and Montenegro). The Tribunal concluded that the standard of effective control was set too high for attributing actions of that militia to a foreign state and used the conception of "overall control" instead. According to the ICTY it is sufficient that the foreign power has a "role in organizing, coordinating, or planning the military actions of the military group" for the conflict to be qualified as an international armed conflict.[494]

The contrast between the judgments in Nicaragua and Tadić is an example of a normative conflict between an earlier and a later interpretation of the rule of general international law. There is also a different interpretation of contrasts between judgments in Nicaragua and Tadić which aims at reconciling them. According to this interpretation, both the issues of law and of fact were different in the two cases. In the Nicaragua case, the ICJ resolved the question of responsibility of a state, while in the Tadić case, the Tribunal concentrated on the questions of criminal liability of an individual and the control test did not concern liability, but the applicable rules of international humanitarian law. This position, explained in the dissenting opinion of judge Shahabuddeen,[495] was later accepted by the International Law Commission in the commentary to Article 8 of the Draft Articles on the responsibility of states, as well as by the ICJ in the case Bosnia Herzegovina v. Serbia (2007).

The ICJ returned to the question of standard (degree) of control in its recent judgment in the Case Concerning Application of the Convention on the Prevention and Punishment of the Crime of Genocide (2007).[496] The Court examined the issue of responsibility of the respondent State, i.e. Serbia, as the successor of the FRY. According to the test formulated in this judgment it must be shown that "effective control" had been exercised, or that instruc-

---

[493]/ *Military and Paramilitary Activities in and against Nicaragua* (Nicaragua v. United States), Merits, ICJ Reports 1986, pp. 64-65, para. 115.

[494]/ ICTY, Prosecutor v. Duško Tadić, Judgment of 15 July 1999 (Appeals Chamber), Case No. IT-94-1-A, paras. 115, 116–145.

[495]/ ICTY, Prosecutor v. Duško Tadić, Judgment of 15 July 1999 (Appeals Chamber), Case No. IT-94-1-A, Separate Opinion by Judge Shahabuddeen, paras. 17–18.

[496]/ *Application of the Convention on the Prevention and Punishment of the Crime of Genocide (Bosnia and Herzegovina v. Serbia and Montenegro)*, Judgment of 26 February 2007, ICJ Reports 2007. Concerning this judgment see Šturma, P.: MSD k aplikaci Úmluvy o zabránění a trestání zločinu genocidia [The ICJ on the Application of the Convention on the Prevention and Punishment of the Crime of Genocide]. *Právní zpravodaj* 10/2007, pp. 11–15.

tions had been issued for every operation in which alleged violations occurred, not only for the overall actions of persons or groups who committed these violations.[497]

In light of the new critique of both ICJ judgments and the commentary of the International Law Commission by Professor A. Cassese, former judge (and President) of the ICTY, it is clear that the conflict between the two standards of control cannot be reconciled on the basis of the different contexts of decisions in the ICJ and ICTY.[498] In spite of enormous efforts, neither the judgment in Tadić nor its subsequent doctrinal defense is problem-free.

It was indirectly confirmed also by the recent decisions of the ECHR on inadmissibility in the cases of Behrami and Saramati (2007).[499] In fact, the ECHR did not explicitly apply any of the competing standards of control. Instead, it used the phrase that the UN Security Council retained "ultimate authority and control".[500] However, it definitely does not follow from the judgment that the Court had applied the test of "overall control". The ECHR concentrated on the analysis of the chain of command. Having performed this test, the ECHR reached the conclusion that the UN Security Council retained ultimate authority and control and that effective command of the relevant operational matters was retained by NATO. Therefore, the Court determined that KFOR had exercised lawfully delegated powers of the Security Council under Chapter VII and, consequently, their actions had been essentially attributable to the UN.[501]

(b) A conflict between a general rule and a special rule that claims to exist as an exception to general law

This area is not merely a conflict of diverse interpretations of the same general rule, but the creation (or just a postulate) of a special rule which takes the position of lex specialis in competition with a general rule. This may be illustrated by the treatment of reservations by international human rights bodies. According to the Vienna Convention on the Law of Treaties (1969), the rule on reservations is very liberal and leaves every state with the right to decide the compatibility of the relevant reservation "with the object and purpose of the Convention", and it is implemented only in cases where the specific treaty does not provide for reservations otherwise.[502]

Regional instruments, such as the European Convention on Human Rights (1950) and the American Convention on Human Rights (1969), which established human rights courts, represent exceptions. So it is not by chance that the European Court of Human Rights made a landmark decision regarding reservations in the 1988 *Belilos* case. It viewed an interpreting declaration made by Switzerland in its instrument of ratification as in fact a reservation (according to the actual content) and struck it down as incompatible with

---

[497] *Application of the Convention on the Prevention and Punishment of the Crime of Genocide (Bosnia and Herzegovina v. Serbia and Montenegro)*, Judgment of 26 February 2007, ICJ Reports 2007, para. 406.
[498] Cassese, A.: The Nicaragua and Tadić Tests revisited in Light of the ICJ Judgment on Genocide in Bosnia. *European Journal of International Law* 4/2007, p. 649.
[499] *Behrami and Behrami v. France, Saramati v. France, Germany & Norway*, ECHR (GC), Decision as to the Admissibility, 2 May 2007.
[500] *Ibidem* at p. 39, para. 134.
[501] *Ibidem* at p. 41, paras. 140–141.
[502] Article 20 (Acceptance of and objection to reservations).

the object and purpose of the Convention. The ECHR held Switzerland bound by the Convention "irrespective of the validity of the declaration."[503]

In subsequent cases, the European Court has pointed out that the normal rules on reservations to treaties do not as such apply to human rights law. Thus in the *Loizidou* case, the Court, having analyzed the object and purpose of the European Convention, concluded that the states could not make their acceptance of an opt-out conditional on an effective exclusion of an area of law and practice within their jurisdiction from the control of the bodies of Convention. Any restriction of their competence *ratione loci* and *ratione materiae* is incompatible with the nature of the Convention.[504] In the mentioned case the Court declared invalidity of the restriction *ratione loci* under Articles 25 and 46 of the Convention (according to the applicable numbering) in the declaration made by Turkey. At the same time it confirmed the validity of the declaration itself (i.e. its remainder), which makes it possible for the Court to deal with individual complaints against this state. In the ECHR's view " a fundamental difference in the role and purpose of the respective tribunals (i.e. of the ICJ and the ECHR), coupled with the existence of a practice of unconditional acceptance ... provides a compelling basis for distinguishing the Convention practice from that of the International Court."[505]

ECHR case-law, indicating the creation of an exception from general rules on treaty reservations, has inspired other human rights bodies. The Human Rights Committee, authorized to control the observance of the International Covenant on Civil and Political Rights, took an essential position on the question of reservations in its General Comment No. 24 (of 1994). The Committee endeavours to justify the opinion that human rights treaties are specific.[506]

(c) A conflict between two types of special law

The third case of conflict of laws is a disagreement between special rules of different areas of international law. It may be illustrated by rules regulating international trade and the rules of environmental protection. In the famous 1998 *Beef Hormones* case the Appellate Body of the World Trade Organization (WTO) considered the status of the so-called precautionary principle under the WTO covered treaties, especially the Agreement on Sanitary and Phytosanitary Measures (1994). It concluded that whatever the status of that principle under international environmental law, it had not become binding on the WTO.[507] Should it not be just an issue of competence of the respective WTO body to consider only WTO covered treaties, but a problem of substantive law, it would be rather a serious example of fragmentation. The mentioned approach in fact suggests that international environmental law and trade law might be governed by different principles. As there are no clear bounda-

---

[503]/ *Belilos v. Switzerland*, judgment of 29th April 1988, ECHR Series A (1988) No. 132, p. 28, para. 60.

[504]/ *Loizidou v. Turkey*, judgment of 23rd March 1995, ECHR, Series A, No. 310, paras. 77–89.

[505]/ *Ibidem* at p. 29, para. 85.

[506]/ CCPR/C/21/Rev.1/Add.6 (11 November 1994). See also Šturma, P.: Výhrady k mezinárodním smlouvám [Reservations to International Treaties]. In: Vanduchová, M. – Gřivna, T. (eds.): *Pocta Otovi Novotnému k 80. narozeninám* [Tribute to Oto Novotný on his 80th birthday]. Praha: ASPI Publishing, 2008, pp. 384–398.

[507]/ Measures Concerning Meat and Meat Products (Hormones), 13 February 1998, WT/DS26/AB/R, WT/DS48/AB/R, paras. 123–125.

ries between the two branches of international law, the response to a specific problem is bound to vary depending on which specific branch one chooses as the relevant frame of legal interpretation.[508]

Another example is the conflict between rules regulating the protection of foreign investment and European law. The relationship between the EC/EU law and the international law on foreign investment has been attracting increased attention recently. It is mainly due to the ongoing procedure before the European Court of Justice (ECJ) to decide compatibility of bilateral investment agreements of EU Member States with the EC law.[509] Several arbitration proceedings initiated by investors against EU Member States were concerned with substantive provisions related to a certain degree to the EC/EU law. Probably the most famous, and from the Czech Republic's perspective the most interesting, case is *Eastern Sugar*.[510] Also these disputes have stimulated discussions on new competences of the EC in relation to direct foreign investment under the Lisbon Treaty.

B. Examples of reference to special rules in international law

The Report of the International Law Commission Study Group provides a number of examples of special rules. In some cases they are but very general, or even blanket provisions. This is obvious namely in the text and commentary to Article 55 of the Draft Articles on Responsibility of States for Internationally Wrongful Acts (2001). This Article, called *lex specialis*, provides that "these Articles do not apply where and to the extent that the conditions for the existence of an internationally wrongful act or the content or implementation of the international responsibility of a State are governed by special rules of international law."

Without referring to specific rules, this provision establishes a normative priority for any special rules in its field of application. According to the Commentary of the Commission this means that these Articles, codifying rules for responsibility, operate as subsidiary or residual rules.[511] For other rules to be applicable as real *lex specialis*, there must be actual incompatibility between them. Otherwise a general rule would apply alongside a special rule. For special rules to derogate from general rules, it is required that the special (derogating) rules have at least the same legal rank as the general (derogated from) rule. Consequently, in the sphere of responsibility, it is not possible to derogate from those general laws on the responsibility of states that provide for "serious breaches of obligations under peremptory norms of general international law".[512]

Other examples can be found in abundant case law of the European Court of Human Rights. That is why it is necessarily a question of choice, which can occasionally be quite misleading as regards the efforts to show the clear distinction between the application or elaboration of a general standard and derogation from it on the basis of *lex specialis*. The

---

[508]/ Koskenniemi *supra* at p. 28.
[509]/ Opinion AG Poiares Maduro, Case C-205/06, *Commission v. Austria*, and Case C-249/06, *Commission v. Sweden* of 10 July 2008.
[510]/ Eastern Sugar B.V. (Netherlands) v. The Czech Republic, ad hoc UNCITRAL Arbitration, Partial Award of 27 March 2007.
[511]/ Draft Articles on State Responsibility. In: *Report of the International Law Commission*, GAOR, Fifty-third session, Suppl. No. 10 (A/56/10), p. 356.
[512]/ Fragmentation of International Law *supra* at pp. 31–32.

first situation can be illustrated by a frequently cited ECHR judgment in the *Neumeister* case (1974), where the Court correctly observed that the provision on compensation in case of unlawful arrest in Article 5 (5) of the Convention was not *lex specialis* in relation to the general rule on compensation (so called just satisfaction) in Article 50. In this case, one rule does not exclude the other, they work concurrently. When applying one provision, the ECHR considers the other.[513] A rather obvious solution follows from the wording of both the provisions and their purpose, which is in the case of Article 5 (5) of the Convention a substantive obligation that contracting parties provide intra-state compensation to a victim of unlawful arrest, while compensation under Article 50 (presently Art. 41 of the Convention as amended by Protocol No. 11) is a form of international contractual liability (or rather obligation) in case the Court finds there has been a violation and the national law of the contracting party allows for only partial reparation to be made. A more complicated question, not asked by the International Law Commission in this context, arises whether this rule on compensation (just satisfaction) according to the Convention is in itself a *lex specialis* – as primary liability constituted *ex contractu* – in relation to the general rules of responsibility of states.[514]

In other cases, though, the ECHR clearly supported the application of the *lex specialis* principle when solving the relationship between, for instance, Articles 5 (4) and 13 of the Convention regarding an effective remedy.[515] Article 13 provides for less stringent requirements and thus it has to yield to Article 5 (4) as well as to Article 6 of the Convention, because the right to independent and impartial court proceedings is understood as *lex specialis* in relation to the more general requirement of effective remedy.[516] However, the conception of a special rule as such that excludes the concurrent application of a general rule appears to be relative in the light of the decision in *Kudla*.[517] In some cases the Court permitted concurrent application and found a violation of some aspects of Articles 6 (1) and 13 of the Convention.

Explicit determination of the relationship to the European Convention can be found in the Charter of Fundamental Rights of the EU. In the relationship between substantive rules of the European Convention and the EU Charter the *lex posterior* principle will not apply. Its application is excluded by special provisions in Chapter 7 of the Charter. On the contrary, the principle of priority of ECHR interpretation of human rights contained both in the

---

[513]/ Neumeister v. Austria, Judgment of 7 May 1974 (Article 50), ECHR Series A, No. 17, p. 13, para. 29.
[514]/ But a discussion has been going on in the Czech international law theory where some authors underline the different nature of this contractual obligation. See Šturma, P.: *Úvod do evropského práva ochrany lidských práv* [Introduction to European Human Rights Law]. Praha: Karolinum, 1994, pp. 98–100; Čepelka, Č. – Šturma, P.: *Mezinárodní právo veřejné* [Public International Law]. Praha: C. H. Beck, 2008, pp. 426–428. A different position presents Malenovský, J.: Smluvní ochrana občanských a politických práv v teorii a praxi mezinárodního práva [Contractual Protection of Civic and Political Rights in the Theory and Practice of International Law]. In: Šturma, P. (ed.): *Právní následky mezinárodně protiprávního chování. Pocta Čestmíru Čepelkovi k 80. narozeninám* [Legal Consequences of Internationally Wrongful Acts. Tribute to Čestmír Čepelka on his 80th Birthday]. Praha: PF UK, 2007, pp. 132–144. It appears that the solution of this theoretical dispute may consist in the conception of interpretation maxim *lex specialis*.
[515]/ See, for instance, Brannigan & McBride v. UK, Judgment of 28 May 1993, ECHR Series A, No. 258, p. 57, para. 76; Nikolova v. Bulgaria, Judgment of 25 March 1999, ECHR 1999-II, p. 25, para. 69.
[516]/ See, for instance, Yankov v. Bulgaria, Judgment of 11 December 2003, ECHR 2003-XII, para. 150.
[517]/ Kudla v. Poland, Judgment of 26 October 2000, ECHR 2000-XI, p. 234–236, paras. 164–168.

Convention and the Charter (Art. 52 (3)) is introduced, as well as the principle of the right to more extensive protection, or prohibition of restriction of a recognized higher protection (Art. 53 of the Charter).[518] Generally, these are examples of a contractually established application (or interpretation) hierarchy and the *lex specialis* principle.

A slightly different situation occurs in cases when, in relations between parties, a bilateral contract is to replace *lex generalis*, namely customary international law. This was the case in *Amoco International Finance Corporation*, where the Iran–US Claims Tribunal stated that this did not mean, however, that customary rules were irrelevant in the case. On the contrary, they "may be useful in order to fill in possible *lacunae* of the Treaty, to ascertain the meaning of undefined terms or, more generally, to aid interpretation and implementation of its provision."[519] A similar situation exists with respect to applicable law in the case of more modern bilateral investment promotion and protection agreements which are also interpreted and applied on the basis of general rules of international law.

On the contrary, other cases confirmed the stronger position of *lex specialis* as an exemption from general rules. It may be illustrated by the advisory opinion of the ICJ in the case *Legality of Nuclear Weapons* (1996). The ICJ considered the issue of the relationship between the International Covenant on Civil and Political Rights (1966) and the law applicable to armed conflicts. Specifically, it dealt with the human right not to be arbitrarily deprived of life. The ICJ stressed that this right was applicable even in armed conflicts. At the same time it observed that "the test of what is an arbitrary deprivation of life, however, then falls to be determined by the applicable *lex specialis,* namely, the law applicable in armed conflict which is designed to regulate the conduct of hostilities."[520]

Put more generally, the ICJ in this statement expressed the relationship between human rights law and international humanitarian law. The Court pointed out that human rights continued to apply even in armed conflicts. Humanitarian law (as *lex specialis*) does not supersede completely the human rights law; rather, it just constitutes an exception in certain aspects. Thus the ICJ asserted a pragmatic justification of the existence of two sets of rules and the determination whether the real situation is "normal" or "exceptional" then leads to the application of general or special law.[521] A similar solution was repeated by the ICJ in a more recent advisory opinion concerning the legal consequences of the construction of a wall in the occupied Palestinian territory.[522]

---

[518]/ Svák, J. – Šikuta, J.: Dvojsystémová ochrana ľudských práv v Európe [Dual System of Human Rights Protection in Europe]. In: *Zborník z medzinárodnej konferencie Zmluva o Ústave pre Európu a ústavy členských štátov EÚ.* Bratislava: BVŠP, 2005, pp. 116–117; Šturma, P.: Charta základních práv Evropské unie, její povaha a účinky [The Charter of Fundamental Rights of the European Union, its Nature and Effects]. *Ibidem* at pp. 132–134.

[519]/ *Amoco International Finance Corporation v. Iran*, Iran-US C.T.R., vol. 15, 1987-II, p. 222.

[520]/ *Legality of the Threat or Use of Nuclear Weapons, Advisory opinion, ICJ Reports 1996*, p. 240, para. 25.

[521]/ Fragmentation of International Law *supra* at pp. 47–48. A different perspective on the relationship between human rights and humanitarian law is presented in Bílková, V.: Ochrana lidských práv za ozbrojeného konfliktu – přístup Evropského soudu pro lidská práva [The Protection of Human Rights in Armed Conflicts – ECHR Approach]. *Právník* 1/2008, pp. 38–45.

[522]/ Šturma, P.: Posudek MSD o právních následcích stavby zdi na obsazeném palestinském území [ICJ Advisory Opinion Concerning the Legal Consequences of the Construction of a Wall in the Occupied Palestinian Territory]. *Právní zpravodaj* 9/2004, pp. 13–17.

3.1.3 Self-contained regimes

A. Definition of the term self-contained regime

An extreme form of application of the *lex specialis* principle, and at the same time one of the most controversial topics connected with fragmentation of international law is so called *self-contained regime*. This term was used for the first time by the Permanent Court of International Justice in its judgment in the case *S. S. Wimbledon* (1923).[523] The Court was deciding whether the provisions of the Treaty of Peace of Versailles, which regulated waterways in Germany, was applicable also to the Kiel Canal which was governed by a special section of the Treaty differing in many aspects from the general regulation. The court answered the question in the negative and stated in its reasoning that *"the provisions relating to the Kiel Canal in the Treaty of Versailles are therefore self-contained; if they had to be supplemented and interpreted by the aid of those referring to the inland navigable waterways of Germany ... they would lose their "raison d'être". ...The idea which underlies them is not to be sought by drawing an analogy from [general] provisions but rather by arguing a contrario".*[524] So the self-contained regime was originally perceived as a connected set of primary contractual provisions relating to a specific question.

The successor of the Permanent Court, the International Court of Justice, transferred the concept into the sphere of secondary norms by its famous and frequently quoted judgment in the *Case concerning the United States Diplomatic and Consular Staff in Tehran* (1980).[525] It used it to denote a subsystem of international law which contains an independent, connected regulation of secondary consequences of unlawful acts, while at the same time excluding the application of sanctions provided for in general international law, such as reprisals. In the given case it was diplomatic law, which according to the Court *"constitutes a self-contained régime which, on the one hand, lays down the receiving State's obligations regarding the ... privileges and immunities to be accorded to diplomatic missions and, on the other, foresees their possible abuse ... and specifies the means at the disposal of the receiving State to counter any such abuse. These means are, by their nature, entirely efficacious".*[526]

Finally, the term has been used recently to denote those functional or territorial subsystems of international law, which allegedly extricated themselves completely from the influence of the general rules of this law, and not only sanctioning rules, and were transformed into independent legal regimes. As typical examples, the following are usually mentioned: human rights law, environmental law or the WTO regime in the area of functional specialization and European law in the area of territorial specialization. Thus, in this sense, a self-contained regime denotes a complex set of primary and secondary rules, which had initially originated in general international law, but gradually became quite independent.

It is obvious at first sight that there is a significant disparity among the three meanings attributed to the concept of *self-contained regime*. They refer to different types of international law (primary, secondary or both) and require a different degree of specialization (subsidiary

---

[523] PCIJ, *Case of the SS "Wimbledon"*, P.C.I.J. Ser. A, No. 1, 1923, pp. 23–24.

[524] *Ibidem* at p. 24.

[525] ICJ, *Case concerning the United States Diplomatic and Consular Staff in Tehran* (*United States v. Iran*), Judgment, 24 May 1980, ICJ. Reports 1980, para. 86.

[526] *Ibidem.*

applicability of international law, its complete exclusion). Many authors quite reasonably argue that using the term in the first and the last sense causes problems. There is no point in a discussion on self-contained regimes within primary legislation, as there is no general system of primary (unlike secondary) laws in international law: all primary legislation is more or less specialized, and the relations between legislation having a differing degree of specialisation are solved by the *lex specialis* principle.

To understand the self-contained regime as a functionally or territorially specialized set of primary and secondary rules, completely distinct from general international law, is not correct either. If a normative set actually achieved such a degree of complexity and consistency that it was self-sustaining and did not need the institutes of general international law, it would be more appropriate to consider it a new legal order, not just a subsystem of international law. Subsystems are gradually becoming more complex and, if the states wish so, there is no reason why one of them could not cover all the relevant aspects of life in a certain functional or territorial area some day.

While the described development represents a theoretical option, it should be added that none of the subsystems of international law has undergone such a development yet. Not even so highly integrated regimes, such as European law or WTO law, regulate all legal institutions in an exhaustive manner; they have to utilize the general regulation of international law (e.g. in the fields of sources of law and interpretation of contracts). The fact that these regimes "*are not to be read in the clinical isolation from public international law*",[527] was recognized even by their decision making bodies. The doctrine also maintains that "*no treaty, however special its subject-matter or limited the number of its parties, applies in a normative vacuum but refers back to a number of general, often unwritten principles of customary law*".[528] With regard to this situation, as well as to the fact that – as was mentioned above – a really self-contained regime would cease to be a regime of international law, the use of this term in its third possible sense is not appropriate.

Since the use of the term in its first sense is amiss and in its third impractical, we tend to accept the second proposed explanation and perceive the self-contained regimes as "*a particular category of subsystems, namely those that embrace a full, exhaustive and definitive, set of secondary rules*"[529] and thus "*exclude the application of general international law in relation to legal consequences of breaches of ... obligations*".[530] In this conception *self-contained* only refers to secondary (sanctioning) rules, including the possibility to apply reprisals. It does not cover the area of general, non-sanctioning rules, such as those which determine the sources of law, regulate personality or provide for the regime of concluding and interpreting international treaties.

The key issue relating to self-contained regimes which needs clarification is their relationship to the secondary rules of general international law. Is the application of these rules in

[527] WTO, *US – Standards for Reformulated and Conventional Gasoline*, Report of the Appellate Body, 29 Apr. 1996, WT/DS2/AB/R, s. 17.
[528] Koskenniemi, M.: *Study on the Function and Scope of the lex specialis Rule and the Question of "Self-Contained Regimes"*, Preliminary Report by the Chairman of the Study Group submitted for consideration during the 2004 session of the ILC, Doc. ILC(LVI)SG/FIL/CRD.1 and Add. 1, quoted in B. Simma *supra* at p. 492.
[529] Simma *supra* at p. 493.
[530] Homsi, C. S.: „Self-Contained Regimes" – No Cop-Out for North Korea. *Suffolk Transnational Law Review* 1/2000, s. 89.

self-contained regimes really absolutely excluded, or do they remain a realistic option which can be used where the rules of the regime are insufficient or fail completely?

B. Approach of international law theory

In theory, there are two main approaches to self-contained regimes. According to the first one, so called *universalism* or a system-oriented model, international law is a compact unit[531] whose individual subsystems may be specialized to a degree, yet they remain a part of a homogeneous corpus. This corpus represents a basic standard which is always applicable unless explicitly provided otherwise. This applies also to secondary rules where something like *"presumption against the creation of a wholly self-contained regime"*[532] operates. The presumption can only be refuted by proving a clear and undisputable intention on the part of states to derogate from the general regulation and replace it with special rules. Even then, however, general international law serves as a supporting tool for those cases which the specialized regime governs either insufficiently or not at all. This approach is adopted by all special rapporteurs of the ILC and it was also recognized by the ICJ in its decision in *ELSI* (1989). The Court declared it unacceptable that "an important principle of customary international law should be held to have been tacitly dispensed with, in the absence of any words making clear an intention to do so".[533] In the given conception, general international law is a norm and self-contained regimes represent an exception to it, while their existence must be clearly and persuasively proved.

The second approach, so called *particularism* or a concept-oriented model, perceives the matter from the opposite perspective. According to this approach, international law is primarily a set of specialized subsystems. They are interconnected by a number of structural relations, but they also retain a high degree of autonomy. This applies also to the sanctioning rules where there is a *"presumption in favour of complete and exhaustive regulation in the respective regime"*.[534] Again, the presumption can only be refuted by proving a clear and undisputable intention on the part of states, but this time it is the intention to open a subsystem of the rules of general international law. If such intention cannot be proved, the self-contained regime remains wholly closed to general rules and they are not applicable even to fall back on in cases of loopholes in regulations or failures of the system. This approach is, rather logically, adopted by experts and decision making bodies of individual subsystems (e.g. the European Court of Justice).

The German lawyer Simma draws an analogy between both the approaches and two possible perspectives in astronomy. From the first perspective, the universe and constellations are considered the basic unit; its laws (= international law) are generally applicable and they uniformly control the operation of all the planets, which, in spite of their dissimilar appearance and composition, are very much alike in the end. The second perspective, on the other hand, focuses on individual planets, emphasizes the differences among them and

531/ Dupuy, P.-M.: *L'unité de l'ordre juridique international: cours général de droit international public.* Leiden: Martinus Nijhoff, 2003.
532/ UN Doc. A/CN.4/507, J. Crawford, *Third Report,* 2000, para. 147.
533/ ICJ, *Elettronica Sicula S.P.A. (ELSI) (United States of America* v. *Italy),* Judgment, 20 July 1989, ICJ Reports 1989, p. 42, para. 50.
534/ Simma *supra* at p. 505.

maintains that because of these differences each planet must be subjected to specific laws (= self-contained regime law) and no common rules are possible.[535] Simma correctly points out that the disagreement between the two perspectives, based in different axiological (hence unverifiable) systems, is substantially implacable, and he suggests avoiding it.

He elaborates on the concept of *"the rights or facultés of unilateral reaction"*[536] which the states as sovereignties enjoy in imaginary international "natural condition". This *faculté* became embodied in secondary sanctioning normativity of a horizontal, decentralized system of international law, which is primarily based on self-help. States are willing to give up their *faculté* and replace it by another, more centralized and vertical set of sanctions only if the given procedure ensures the same or higher efficacy of sanctioning unlawful acts. The waiver is non-automatic; moreover, it is conditioned on the functionality of the special regulation.

Where a self-contained regime fails because of any reason, or proves insufficient, the original *faculté* is restored and the states regain the possibility to return to unilateral sanctioning means of international law. In other words, "we have posited that states only intend to relinquish their *facultés* under general international law in favour of a special regime's procedures to the extent that and as long as a subsystem's procedures prove efficacious".[537] Simma believes that this scenario could be carried out in three situations, namely in the case of a continuous violation of an obligation under a special system, despite a decision to the contrary by the system's competent body; in the case of an injured state's failure to obtain reparation, despite such a decision; and if a unilateral action is necessary as a defensive measure.[538] The proposed compromise appears to be reasonable; however, no relevant actor in international relations, neither a state nor a judicial body, has rallied to it (or even commented on it), and it has not actually aroused much interest in the doctrine.

C. Situation of individual self-contained regimes

The main candidates for inclusion among self-contained regimes are usually considered to be diplomatic law, human rights law, the law of WTO and European law.

Diplomatic law was the first one to appear on the list of self-contained regimes; however, its inclusion has given rise to much uncertainty until now. It is undisputable that this subsystem contains some specific sanctioning elements which do not exist in general international law (the institution of declaring someone *persona non grata*) or even deviate from it (the prohibition of reprisals against specific groups of persons, i.e. diplomats), yet it is hardly possible to talk about a really complex set of sanctioning rules which would, at least in common

---

[535] *"Depending on whether we choose a universalistic or a particularistic perspective, whether we first see the universe or the planets, the analysis tends to yield different results. If we focus on the universe, the law of the universe (general international law) governs the planets. If we focus on the planets, planetary rules (the rules of the subsystem) leave little room for universal law." Ibidem at p. 506.*

[536] *Ibidem* at p. 508. The concept was originally coined by the special rapporteur of the ILC, G. Arangio-Ruiz, see Arangio-Ruiz, G.: *Summary Records of the Meetings of the Forty-fourth Session.* ILC Yearbook, Vol. I, 1992, retrieved from http://untreaty.un.org/ilc/publications/yearbooks/1992.htm, p. 77.

[537] Simma *supra* at p. 516. See also *"if instead of enhancing the effectiveness of the relevant obligations the regime serves to dilute existing standards [...] then the need for a residual application, or a 'fall-back' onto the general law of State responsibility may seem called for".* Koskenniemi, M. *supra* at Add. 1, para. 119.

[538] Simma *supra* at p. 509. This idea is not brand new, a very similar conception appeared in Czech theory, see Šturma, P. *supra* 1994 at pp. 102–103.

situations, be self-sustaining. Simma correctly states that diplomatic law, for example, does not deal with the issue of compensation. Since it cannot be expected that states would like to exclude this institution from the subsystem, it is obvious that the regulation of general international law must apply here. Thus, diplomatic law is not so much a self-contained regime, but rather a subsystem with certain specific features, whose relation to general international law can be solved by the *lex specialis* principle.

The situation is more complicated in the three other regimes. In the recent decades, *human rights law* has developed into a complex subsystem operating at universal and regional levels and containing primary rules as well as complicated institutional mechanisms (courts, quasi judicial bodies) aimed at ensuring their observance. The subsystem as such is fragmented, i.e. sanctioning rules and institutions connected to them do not have general character and they are always bound to a specific treaty. Human rights' specificity and independence, based on their integral (not strictly bilateral and reciprocal) nature, was reiterated by judicial bodies operating within the system and outside of it.[539] But few bodies contemplated what implications this feature had for secondary rules. The ICJ probably got farthest in this respect when it declared in its 1986 decision in *Military and Paramilitary Activities in and against Nicaragua* that *"where human rights are protected by international conventions, that protection takes the form of such arrangements for monitoring or ensuring respect for human rights as are provided for in the conventions themselves".*[540] However, not even the ICJ states whether the given regulation has the character of exclusivity or just priority and whether it enables supportive application of general sanctioning rules of international law.[541]

A part of the doctrine accepts this option. Its arguments rely mainly on the fact that sanctioning mechanisms within the human rights regime are either not binding (submitting reports regularly) or aimed at individuals (individual complaints), so they can hardly replace the classical institution of binding interstate responsibility. Moreover, specific procedures may fail or prove inefficient, in which case the only way to provide further operation of the regime is to utilize traditional tools. It should be added that traditional tools could be also implemented in relations among states, which are not parties to the same human rights conventional system and are bound only by obligations issuing from customary rules. In general it appears that human rights law, with regard to its fragmentation, has not created a genuine self-containted regime. There has been a development in this direction (conventional systems at regional levels), which, however, has touched only some parts of the subsystem, where a relatively large space for implementation of the sanctioning provisions of general international law has remained.[542]

---

[539]/ *"Unlike international treaties of the classical kind, the Convention comprises more than mere reciprocal engagements between contracting States. It creates, over and above a network of mutual, bilateral undertakings, objective obligations which, in the words of the Preamble, benefit from a 'collective enforcement'."* ECHR, *Ireland v. UK*, Application No. 5310/71, 1978, Ser. A Vol. 25 para. 239.

[540]/ ICJ, *Military and Paramilitary Activities in and against Nicaragua (Nicaragua v. United States of America)*, Merits, Judgement, 27 June 1986, ICJ Reports 1986, par. 134.

[541]/ The question is even more complicated, because states usually do not damage other states by human rights violations, and interstate responsibility is thus based only on the fact that those rights apply *erga omnes*, i.e. among all. This fact requires some sort of modification of the classical rules of state responsibility, as is shown in Articles 48 and 54 of the *Draft Articles on State Responsibility for Internationally Wrongful Acts*.

[542]/ It is indicated, for instance, by imposing economic and other sanctions (i.e. countermeasures) on states, which,

WTO law offers a different picture. When compared with the GATT system, which *"was a self-contained regime [...] only in aspiration, but not in reality"*,[543] the WTO system achieves a higher degree of integration and self-sustainment in the regulation of imposing sanctions. Article 23 of the *Dispute Settlement Understanding* directly orders that states drawing consequences from wrongul acts *"shall have recourse to, and abide by, the rules and procedures of this Understanding."* Some take this provision as an example of a clause which guarantees the exclusivity of the self-contained regime regulation and excludes simultaneous application of the rules of general international law.[544] There is some uncertainty as regards completeness of the system of reprisals and compensation for damage. The *Understanding* does not explicitly provide for these institutions, but the opinion that compensation and the suspension of concessions under Article 22 are in fact their functional equivalents modified to fit the specific needs of the WTO system, has been more widely recognized. While sanctioning rules of general international law remain "in reserve" for cases of extreme failure of the system, a complex set of autonomous secondary rules is currently available to the WTO law and it can aspire to be included in the list of self-contained regimes with more chances than the previous candidates.

The last candidate, *European law* (or *Community law*), holds an even better position. The European Court of Justice has reiterated that by concluding the Treaty of EC (TEC) the states "have created their own legal system"[545] which "constitutes a new legal order of international law".[546] There is a centralized, collective system of imposing responsibility and coercion and the Member States have waived the possibility to enforce the observance of a law by unilateral actions.[547] The role of international law is minimal even in gap-filling, when the European decision making bodies rather follow the analogy with institutions inside the system or implement the general principles of Community law. The possibility to apply secondary sanctioning norms of international law has remained limited to cases of non-operation, or principal failure of the system, which confirms that European law is probably "the most self-contained" regime of the present day.

3.1.4 Principle of systematic integration of rules from various areas of international law

Unlike the previous subchapters which endeavour to diagnose the phenomenon of fragmentation of international law generally and some of its manifestations, this subchapter

---

according to other states, violate human rights enormously. Very active in this field has been the USA as well as the European Union.

[543]/ Kuyper, P.: The Law of GATT as a Special Field of International Law. *Netherlands Yearbook of International Law* 1994, p. 252, quoted in Simma *supra* at p. 519.

[544]/ *"In some cases it will be clear from the language of a treaty or other text that only the consequences specified are to flow /.../ An example /.../ is the World Trade Organization Dispute Settlement Understanding as it relates to certain remedies."* Arangio-Ruiz *supra* at p. 357, quoted in Simma *supra* at p. 520.

[545]/ ECJ, *Costa v. ENEL,* Case No. 6/64, EC Reports 1964, p. 593.

[546]/ ECJ, *Van Gend en Loos,* Case No. 26/62, EC Reports 1963, p. 12.

[547]/ ECJ, *Commission v. Luxemburg and Belgium,* Joint Cases No. 90/63 and 91/63, EC Reports 1964, p. 625. See *"A member State cannot under any circumstances unilaterally adopt, on its own authority, corrective measures or measures to protect trade designed to prevent any failure on the part of another member State to comply with the rules laid down by the Treaty."* ECJ, *Mutton and Lamb,* Case No. 232/78, EC Reports 1979, p. 2729.

attempts to search for a possible therapy. The point is whether along with separative forces, resulting in specialization and particularization of international law, there are counter forces which lead to integration of international law rules into a system.

As was shown when we explored the *lex specialis* principle, it is not quite possible to separate legal interpretation from solving the conflict of rules. The purpose of interpretation of an international treaty is to find out the real meaning of its text. There are many interpretation principles and maxims; those referring to treaties are collected in the Vienna Convention on the Law of Treaties (1969) which laid down the fundamental interpretation maxim. Under this general interpretation rule, a treaty shall be interpreted in *good faith* in accordance with the *ordinary meaning* to be given to the terms of the treaty in their *context* and in the light of its *object and purpose* (Art. 31). For the purposes of interpretation, the context shall comprise, in addition to the text, including its preamble and annexes, any agreement relating to the treaty which was made between all the parties in connection with the conclusion of the treaty. The context shall also comprise any instrument which was made by one or more parties in connection with the conclusion of the treaty and accepted by the other parties as an instrument related to the treaty (it can be, for instance, an interpretive declaration).

Under Article 31 (3) there shall be taken into account, together with the context, any subsequent agreement between the parties regarding the interpretation of the treaty or the application of its provisions; any subsequent practice in the application of the treaty which establishes the agreement of the parties regarding its interpretation; any relevant rules of international law applicable in the relations between the parties. It is the last reference to any relevant rules of international law (Art. 31 (3) (c)) that is potentially a very strong means which, through interpretation, ensures a systematic integration of treaties from various areas, hence unifying international law. This provision is crucial, since it reminds us that all treaty rules draw their force and validity from general law, and constitute rights and obligations which exist alongside rights and obligations constituted by other treaties and rules of customary international law.[548]

Both older and more recent international law specialists agree that any international treaty must be interpreted in the context of all applicable principles and rules of international law. Lord McNair stated in his classical work on the law of treaties that treaties must be performed and interpreted on the background of general principles of international law.[549] French professors Daillier and Pellet expressly declare that "a treaty cannot be assessed separately. It is not only entrenched in the social reality, but its provisions must be confronted with other legal rules with which they can compete".[550]

It is worth mentioning that the European Court of Human Rights, which has formulated its own approach to the European Convention interpretation (based on dynamic interpretation and the application of the *effet utile* principle), referred to Article 31 (3) (c) of the Vienna Convention in several landmark cases. In one of its classical judgments in *Golder* the Court made use of this interpretation rule when it was to decide whether Article 6 of

---

[548]/ *Ibidem* at p. 175.
[549]/ McNair, A. D.: *The Law of Treaties*. Oxford: Clarendon Press, 1961, p. 466.
[550]/ Daillier, P. – Pellet, P.: *Droit international public*. 7ᵗʰ ed., Paris: LGDJ, 2002, p. 266.

the Convention (the right to a fair trial) guarantees the right of access to the courts for any person wishing to file a claim to achieve a decision on his civil rights and obligations.[551] The ECHR, having referred to other rules of international law, interpreted the meaning of Article 6 of the Convention to guarantee the right of direct access to the courts, because this right follows also from a general legal principle as one source of international law under Article 38 of the Statute of the ICJ.

Later, the ECHR resorted to the interpretation applying Article 31 (3) (c) of the Vienna Convention in some complicated cases related to the application of other rules of international law in addition to the European Convention. The first well known case is the decision in *Loizidou*, where the Court, on the basis of this interpretation, referred to the UN Security Council resolutions and the states' practice, which confirmed the position that the so called Turkish Republic of Northern Cyprus is not considered to be a state under international law.[552]

On the other hand, construction applying other rules of international law served to form a more restrictive interpretation of the Convention in other cases. According to the opinion expressed in *Al-Adsani* decision, where most judges gave preference to the rules on state immunity, the Court was to consider the relevant rules of international law. "The Convention should so far as possible be interpreted in harmony with other rules of international law of which it forms part, including those relating to the grant of state immunity."[553]

Another, and probably even more controversial, case was the decision on inadmissibility made by the Grand Chamber of the ECHR in the *Banković* case against Belgium and other European NATO member States, where the Court, on the basis of other rules of international law, refused the claim that injured parties fell within the jurisdiction of the respondent states through the bombing of the building of Radio Televizije Srbije (Radio-Television Serbia, RTS) in Belgrade. In this case it refused to apply the theory of extraterritorial jurisdiction implied from having control over the circumstances under Article 1 of the Convention.[554]

Examples of the use of a relevant interpretation rule to systematically integrate the rules from various areas of international law can be found in the decisions of the Appellate Body of the WTO. The first case of this kind was the decision in the *Shrimp* case, where the Body, having referred to Art. 31 (3) (c) of the Vienna Convention, enabled the application of general principles of international law to interpret the provisions of WTO agreements (in this case exceptions provided for in Article XX (g) GATT)[555]. By this interpretation the Appellate Body established the application of multilateral treaties in the field of environment; however, it has never decided that these rules prevail over the obligations under WTO agreements.[556]

---

[551]/ *Golder v. UK*, Judgment of 21 February 1975, ECHR Series A, No. 18, pp. 13–14, paras. 27–31.

[552]/ *Loizidou v. Turkey* (Merits), Judgment of 18 December 1996, ECHR 1996-VI, p. 2231, para. 44.

[553]/ *Al-Adsani v. UK*, Judgment of 21 November 2001, ECHR 2001-XI, p. 100, paras. 55–56. See Caban, P.: *Jurisdikční imunity státu* [Jurisdictional Immunity of States]. Praha: PF UK, 2007, pp. 140–142.

[554]/ *Banković v. Belgium and others*, Decision of 12 December 2001, Admissibility, ECHR 2001-XII, p. 351, para. 57. See criticism regarding this decision in Bílková *supra* at pp. 25–29; Orakhelashvili, A.: Restrictive Interpretation of Human Rights Treaties in the Recent Jurisprudence of the European Court of Human Rights. *EJIL* 3/2003, p. 529.

[555]/ *United States – Import Prohibition of Certain Shrimp and Shrimp Products*, 12 October 1998, WT/DS58/AB/R, DSR 1998: VII, pp. 2793–2798, paras. 126–134.

[556]/ Koskenniemi, M. *supra* 2006 at p. 188.

In some cases, the decision making in disputes within WTO suggested a rather narrow interpretation of what are "any relevant rules of international law applicable in the relations between the parties" under Art. 31 (3) (c) of the Convention. In the case concerning products made of genetically modified organisms, the European Community defended the prohibition of their imports in the EU states by some rules outside the scope of WTO law, such as the Convention on Biological Diversity (1992) and the subsequent Cartagena Protocol on Biosafety (2000). However, the WTO panel interpreted "the rule applicable in the relations between the parties" in such a way that it applied not only to the parties to the dispute, but that all parties to the interpreted treaty must be the parties to the other treaty as well.[557] Due to the fact that the USA was a party neither to the Convention nor to the Cartagena Protocol, these agreements could not be taken into account.

Finally, probably the strongest application of Art. 31 (3) (c) of the Vienna Convention was made by the International Court of Justice in the *Oil Platforms* case (2003). Although the jurisdiction of the ICJ was limited to disputes arising from the interpretation or implementation of the Treaty of Amity, Economic Relations and Consular Rights between the United States and Iran (1955), the Court inferred from general interpretation rules (including the quoted rule) that the provision of Article XX (1) (d) of the bilateral treaty, concerning the exception permitting the application of security measures, was not "intended to operate wholly independenty of the relevant rules of international law on the use of force... The application of the relevant rules of international law relating to this question thus forms an integral part of the task of interpretation entrusted to the Court by the 1955 Treaty."[558]

Therefore, the ICJ applied the general rules of international law to the actions of the USA whose navy had destroyed three oil platforms in the Persian Gulf. It arrived at a conclusion that these measures could not be justified under the 1955 Treaty, as these actions represented the use of armed force not qualifying, under international law, as acts of self-defence, and thus did not fall within the category of measures contemplated in the measures of the Treaty.[559]

We can concur with the opinion that the ICJ judgment in the *Oil Platforms* case represents a major example of application of Art. 31 (c) of the Vienna Convention. By the use of integrating interpretation, the Court managed to work around the technical aspects of the bilateral treaty and got to the gist of the dispute, which was the application of force.[560] Because of jurisdictional restrictions it could not apply the UN Charter directly, but it involved a substantial part of general international law in the interpretation of a partial provision. Thus it recognized for the first time the great potential which Article 31 (3) (c) has for the systematic integration of international law rules.

557/ *EC – Measures Affecting the Approval and Marketing of Biotech Products*, 7 February 2006, WT/DS291-293/INTERIM, pp. 299 – 300.
558/ *Oil Platforms case (Iran v. US), Merits, ICJ Reports 2003*, p. 161, para. 41.
559/ *Ibidem* at para. 78.
560/ Koskenniemi, M. *supra* 2006 at p. 194.

3.1.5 Conclusions: the role of general international law

The analysis has shown that the continuing branch specialization is an objective procedure and a necessary toll paid for the development of current international law. Function oriented legal regimes identify and express the need to regulate a specific area of international relations and, of course, endeavour to regulate these relations most effectively. The fact that it is possible to adjust international legal regulation to definite conditions and requirements is based on the prevailingly directory nature of international law; it reflects the increasing necessity to specifically regulate a given area. Such branch specialization occurred originally mainly at the primary rules level, but now it happens more and more at the secondary rules level, which regulates responsibility and coercion. Thus a fear is aroused of fragmenting international law into individual branches and of weakening of the role of general international law.

It is in the areas where there are specialized sets of primary and secondary rules, which are usually connected with the existence of specialized judicial dispute-resoluting bodies (or controlling bodies), that the theoretical conception of so-called *self-contained regimes* is most justified. At a closer look, however, we will discover that it is not an entirely exclusive phenomenon. First of all, we can perceive these regimes as a stronger version of special regulation (*lex specialis*). Special rules, of course, exist in the whole context of international law (as well as in any legal system) without endangering its coherence. There are interpretation principles and methods in international law which make it possible to solve the relationship between general and special regulation.

In addition, even strong self-contained regimes (such as WTO law) cannot and do not exist in a legal vacuum; rather, they utilize their footing in general international law. This is manifested namely in the relationship to the general rules of conventional law (namely the interpretation of treaties). The self-contained character of such regimes is limited also in the sphere of secondary rules. Both in the area of human rights mechanisms and in the field of international economic law, etc., it has become apparent that special legal consequences prevail, and in principle exclude the applicability of general rules of responsibility, as long as these special institutional mechanisms based on treaties operate effectively. In case of their failure, however, the persons can resort to the measures of general international law.

Similarly, there are rules for the solution of relationships between older and more current rules concerning the same matter (*lex posterior*), and in the area of conventional law they are even codified in the Vienna Convention on the Law of Treaties (1969).

Remembering the extraordinary role (or "responsibility") of international treaties as regards specialization or fragmentation of international law, it is rather logical that we can find another remedy in the Vienna Convention on the Law of Treaties, i.e. the means to maintain the unity of general international law. In spite of diverse methods in its application in the case-law of various international judicial bodies, we can deem the interpretation based on Art. 31 (3) (c) of the Vienna Convention to be an important means of achieving systematic integration, and thus *formal unity* of international law.

In spite of ongoing specialization of international law, we need not overvalue the danger of its fragmentation, since there are also means of systematic integration. Individual subsystems cannot forever exist independently of general rules (perhaps with the exception of

EC law which was separated from international law). For the future, general international law remains not just a natural environment, but it also creates an indispensable reference framework, in relation to which individual subsystems (regimes) can qualify.

3.2 ROLE OF COURTS IN THE PROTECTION OF THE ENVIRONMENT

3.2.1 Introductory notes and background

Protection of the environment clearly seems to be one of the major tasks of humankind in the 21st century[561] – in its own and innermost interest. From among the most substantial issues of the environment that was dramatically destroyed and damaged because of the influence of the human population particularly during the last century, let us stress, above all, the changes of climate, diminishing the ozone layer of the Earth, acid rains, loss of biological diversity and/or enlargement of the deserts.

Courts all over the world have been performing an important and still expanding role in the protection of the environment during the last couple decades. This public interest (interest of the community as a whole) is gradually becoming separate from the interests in the preservation of life, health and property and gains its own and unique dimension and value as well as its own subject matter.

Issues relating to the legal protection of the environment by courts are being dealt with by numerous international conventions of which the most significant seems to be the Aarhus Convention. The Convention granting the public rights regarding access to information, public participation in decision-making procedures and access to justice on matters concerning the environment (Aarhus, Denmark, 1998) is based on three pillars the third of which is the role of judiciary in the protection of the environment.

There are several established judicial institutions which, within their jurisdictions, more or less deal with the issues of the environment and its protection at the international level, primarily the United Nations International Court of Justice (ICJ) in the Hague, International Court of Maritime Law (ITLOS) in Hamburg, or specialized "Green Courts" which are effective at regional levels and whose nature is that of an arbitrative body rather than that of a court. There are also other judicial institutions which play an important role within the scope of environmental issues in Europe, whether within the European Union or within the Council of Europe, including the following: the Court of Justice of the EU, the General Court (formerly the Court of First Instance), or the European Court of Human Rights (ECHR). The frequency and the importance of environmental cases decided by the above mentioned judicial authorities have been significantly increasing from year to year.

3.2.2 Decision-making in environmental issues in the Czech Republic

Adjudication of individual courts is one of the two fundamental principles of the institutionalized decision-making process in legal matters concerning the environment in Continental Europe (besides administrative decision-making carried out by executive bodies). In the

---

[561] Damohorský, M. et al.: *Právo životního prostředí* [The Law of the Environment]. 2nd ed., Praha: C. H. Beck, 2007, p. 3 and subs.

field of the protection of the environment and nature not only the creation but mainly the functioning of all of the three pillars of branches (legislative, executive and judicial) is crucial. This includes especially their interactive balancing as well as effective operations.

Administrative bodies are those which decide to the greatest degree in issues of environmental protection but, to a certain extent, also in matters of "creating" the environment in the Czech Republic. Their decisions are still, within the frame of the so called administrative judiciary, subject to judicial review. Substantial majority of decision-making processes concerning the environment are carried out in the form of administrative decisions, i.e. individual administrative acts according to the Code of Administrative Procedure (Act No. 500/2004 Sb.). Public administrative bodies are also entitled to pass the so-called measures of a general nature that are of mass effect and even generally binding decrees, i.e. government decrees, executive regulations of ministries and other central state authorities.

The agenda of courts in the scope of environmental protection can be divided, in accordance with various spheres of issues decided, into the branches of criminal law (criminal acts against the environment), civil law (rights of ownership, damages, neighbours's rights), administrative law (judicial review of decisions of administrative bodies in matters of environmental protection within the scope of administrative judiciary) and constitutional law (scrutiny and protection of the constitutionality and legality of delegated legislation). The points at issue are addressed to varying degrees in the four above mentioned legal spheres. Regarding the protection of the environment, the major role is evidently played by the judiciary of criminal and administrative law; the public law branches stay nearest to the protection of the environment.

Procedural rules applicable to the environmental protection in the Czech Republic may be subdivided as follows: criminal proceedings, civil proceedings, administrative proceedings and other specific proceedings and procedures (e.g. land-use planning, environmental impact assessment [SEA or EIA]). The role of procedure, undoubtedly, gradually plays a more important and more significant role in the protection of the environment, however, this is linked mainly to mistakes and defects in the functioning of central state authorities and has nothing to do with the increasing necessity of the protection of the environment.

3.2.3 International Court of Justice and International Tribunal for the Law of the Sea

The beginning of the international judicial decision-making in the sphere of the protection of the environment cannot be seen without the context of the origins and development of environmental law as an autonomous legal branch, i.e. roughly the beginning of the 1970s. Although the judgments of the International Court of Justice and the International Tribunal for the Law of the Sea possess a strong influence on forming the rules of international law, their influence has been marginal in the sphere of environmental law up to this date. The reason might be not only quite a small number of cases disputed in connection with the protection of the environment, but also the attempts to seek compromises that are not only legally justified but also politically acceptable.

The International Court of Justice (ICJ), established in 1945, with its seat in the Hague, dealt with its first case concerning the protection of the environment, *Corfu Channel,* as early as in 1947. From that time this judicial institution adjudicated a couple more disputes relating to environmental issues (still the proportional percentage of these disputes is very small). In the *Corfu Channel* case the International Court of Justice recognized *"every State's obligation not to allow knowingly its territory to be used for acts contrary to the rights of other States"*.[562] Other most frequently cited cases are *Fisheries Jurisdiction* (1972), *Nuclear Tests* (1973) and above all *Gabčíkovo-Nagymaros Project* (1993). Recently commenced and still pending proceedings are worth mentioning, namely the cases *Pulp Mills on the River Uruguay* and *Aerial Herbicide Spraying*.

The International Tribunal for the Law of the Sea (ITLOS) was established as a determined judicial institution by the United Nations Convention on the Law of the Sea (UNCLOS) in 1982. Its headquarters is in Hamburg, Germany. The tribunal has a considerable potential from the point of view of development of international environmental law: its subject-matter jurisdiction covers, among other fields, the spheres of protection of maritime climate against the pollution and sustainable usage of biological maritime sources – considering the fact that it came into force in 1994 it hasn't had enough opportunities for its implementation yet. The cases of *Southern Bluefin Tuna* (1999) and *MOX Plant* (2001) dealing with the protection of the environment were the major ones. It could be stated, though, that likewise the ICJ the ITLOS is in its "environmental contemplations" relatively restrained.

International environmental law at the present time still finds a relatively limited reflection among judgements of major international judicial authorities. This is so probably because this legal branch is quite new and only a few of its rules can be considered properly stabilized and generally recognized at the international level. Both current major institutions involved in the international adjudication on matters concerning the protection of the environment still rather repeatedly confirm the established principles of this legal branch and only gradually and carefully acknowledge new environmental rules – fundamental conclusions can hardly be expected. Because of the ever growing importance of international environmental law the development in this direction is nevertheless essential; the question arises not whether but when and how it will take place.

3.2.4 Role of the European Court of Human Rights in environmental protection

The role of the European Court of Human Rights, established as an international inspection body supervising the compliance with the Convention for the Protection of Human Rights and Fundamental Freedoms[563], in the protection of the environment is quite remarkable. This is because, contrary to the absence of any reference concerning the protection of the environment in the European Convention, it gave rise to relatively prolific environmental jurisprudence thanks to its creative and progressive interpretation of its own provisions. Its origin should be viewed within the framework of acknowledging specific environmental damage as a source of the breach of the European Convention and, therefore, forming *indirect* environmental protection embodied through the European Convention.

The right to life (Art. 2 of the Convention), the right to respect private and family life (Art. 8 of the Convention), and the right to the peaceful enjoyment of possession (Art. 1

---

[562]/ Sands, P: *Principles of International Environmental Law.* 2nd ed., Cambridge: Cambridge University Press, 2003, p. 217.
[563]/ 213 U.N.T.S. 222 (1950). CSFR signed the Convention in 1991; it was published as No. 209/1992 Sb.

of the Protocol No. 1 to the Convention) belong to the traditional protected rights, where the Court inferred the possibility of their breach as a consequence of major impact on the environment.

The following cases can be considered corner-stones of substantive environmental jurisprudence of the European Court of Human Right: *Powell and Rayner*[564], *López Ostra*[565] (the first case in which the Court stated the breach of the Convention as a consequence of damage to the environment and acknowledged environmental content of rights embodied in Art. 8 of the Convention), *Hatton*[566], *Taskin*[567], *Fadeyeva*[568], *Öneryildiz*[569] and, from the very recent past, *Budayeva*.[570] In all of these cases the European Court applied certain explanatory principles and criteria which are typical of any of its environmental decisions: what we have in mind is the so called horizontal effect of the Convention, inference of the existence of the so called positive duties of the states, the issue of considering intrastate legality as well as the criterion of a fair balance between the rights of an individual and the interest of the society as a whole.

Particularly the derived positive duties of states to regulate and to control the sources damaging the environment, if they cause collision with the rights protected by the Convention, possess indisputable significance in the protection of the environment; on the other hand we have to consider their elementary limitations resulting from the very essence underlying the protection of human rights – namely that these duties are not targeted primarily at the protection of the environment but at the protection of individuals against particularly serious environmental risks, as the Court expressed, for example, in the case of *Kyrtatos*[571].

Considering the procedural aspects of the protection of the environment, environmental case law of the European Court of Human Rights has inferred mainly the rights of individuals to obtain full information on the environment, to participate in decision-making procedures and to judicial protection in cases of the breach of rights in environmental matters (especially the cases of *Guerra*[572] and *Öneryildiz* and *Taskin* already mentioned).

Environmental case law of the European Court of Human Rights shows what the extent of the environmental protection might be when it is based on the existing human rights protection without explicit anchoring of specific environmental rights. Thanks to the Court's will to see the breach of human rights in cases of significant damage to the environment the Convention guarantees both the basic substantive aspects of the protection of the individual against excessive interference with the environment connected with their life, health and privacy, as well as the major procedural requirements. Despite its evolutionary nature the Convention still lacks the guarantee of the right to favourable living environment in

---

[564]/ *Powell and Rayner v. The United Kingdom*, 12 ECHR 355 (ser. A) (1990).
[565]/ *López Ostra v. Spain*, 20 ECHR 277 (1994).
[566]/ *Hatton v. The United Kingdom*, 37 ECHR 28 (2003).
[567]/ *Taskin v. Turkey*, 42 ECHR 50.
[568]/ *Fadeyeva v. Russia*, 2005 IV 45 ECHR 10.
[569]/ *Öneryildiz v. Turkey*, 2004 XII 41 ECHR 20.
[570]/ *Budayeva v. Russia,* ECHR, judgement of 20th March 2008.
[571]/ *Kyrtatos v. Greece* 40 ECHR, 16, 399 (2003).
[572]/ *Guerra v. Italy*, 26 ECHR 357 (1998), p. 53.

its qualitative sense as independent of the impact on the individuals. Conclusions of the Court point at the very core of the issue in the *Kyrtatos* case: the protection of the environment through the human rights protection complaints shall be limited by the breach of concrete protected rights against individuals. If the life, health, privacy, possession or other protected rights of the complainant were not sufficiently affected by the environmental damage, the environment cannot be successfully defended by the protective mechanisms of the Convention.

3.2.5 Role of the Court of Justice of the European Union in environmental protection

One of the most important institutions of the European Union in connection with the protection of the environment at the Community level is the Court of Justice of the European Union which quite frequently decides on environmental issues. Environmental protection is primarily considered by the Court of Justice based in Luxembourg and, to a lesser extent, by the General Court (former Court of First Instance).

Decisions of the Court of Justice of the European Union within the protection of the environment are based, besides quite exceptional cases before the General Court, on just two legal bases: the action of the Commission in proceedings for the breach of the Treaty on the Functioning of the European Union (Articles 258 and 260 TFEU) and decision-making upon the reference for preliminary ruling (Art. 267 TFEU). On the contrary, another available type of proceeding, the control of fulfilling or infringement of the obligations under the Treaty on the Functioning of the European Union by Member States between each other, according to Art. 259 TFEU, is not utilized at all by Member States, within the scope of environmental protection. A principal role in supervising the conformity with EU law within the scope of environmental law is attributed to the European Commission, which closely observes how EU law is implemented into practice by individual Member States.

Since 1987, when the European Court of Justice decided to systematically focus on the issues relating to the legal protection of the environment, it has issued more than 450 decisions concerning the protection of the environment, especially in connection with waste management, protection of nature, water protection, environmental impact assessment and protection against the detrimental impact of chemical substances.

Regarding the proceedings in cases of a violation of the Treaty on the Functioning of the European Union, the Commission, according to Art. 258 TFEU, generally initiates the so-called infringement procedure on the basis of *non-transposition*, or *non-communication*, *non-conformity* or *bad application*. The first step of the Commission is usually the request of the Commission for the explanation delivered to the Member State concerned, wherein the request usually specifies the subject matter of proceeding for all potential stages to follow. If the Member State does not fulfil the obligation under the Treaties in connection with the request for the explanation, the Commission will deliver to it a *reasoned opinion* on the matter, including the time limit for removal of deficiencies. Unless the Member State fulfils the obligation, the Commission may bring the matter before the Court of Justice of the European Union. The judgement of the Court, if issued, is usually with respect to non-fulfilment of an obligation of the Member State arising out of the specific directive.

If any Member State has not complied with the decision of the Court of Justice, the Commission may initiate new proceedings against the Member State under Art. 260 TFEU due to that Member State's breach of EU law. The procedure is identical to the proceedings according to Art. 258, the difference being the right of the Commission when bringing the case before the Court of Justice to concurrently specify the amount of the lump sum and penalty payment to be paid by the Member State concerned which the Commission considers appropriate in the circumstances. Although the European Commission fairly frequently uses the possibility of the lump sum and recurring penalty payment, the Court, during the time of its existence, imposed a financial sanction only in four cases, while in three of these four cases environmental protection was the issue.

Environmental protection, waste and packaging management, nature and landscape protection, and environmental impact assessment can be recognised, within the scope of EU law in the field of environmental protection, currently as well as from the long-term perspective, as the most frequent types of judicial review by the Court in preliminary ruling proceeding.

Of the most significant recent cases we can especially refer to the cases of C-121/03 *Commission v. Spain*[573], C-176/05 *KVZ Retec*[574], C-252/05 *Thames Water Utilities*[575], C-216/05 *Commission v. Ireland*, C-290/03 *Barker*[576], C-209/04 *Commission v. Austria*[577], C-244/05 *Bund Naturschutz in Bayern*[578] and C-117/03 *Società Italiana Dragaggi SpA*[579].

The Czech Republic has never had to defend any ruling against itself either for breach of the Treaties according to Art. 258 or for non-fulfilment of a judgement pursuant to Art. 260 TFEU. In only one case an action was brought, in the case of C-140/06 Commission of the European Communities v. Czech Republic for non-transposition Directive 2002/49/EC relating to the assessment and management of environmental noise; however, before issuing the decision, it was withdrawn by the Commission. It is possible, though, that in the future some decisions of the Court of Justice will concern the Czech Republic directly, whether as a suing party or a party sued, respectively, in the case of a preliminary ruling.

3.2.6 Constitutional judiciary and the protection of the environment

Approximately since the 1970s the Constitutions of European states are loaded with such principles as the state liability to ensure the protection of the environment, the right of citizens to a healthy (favourable, sustainable, etc.) living environment, the duty of all persons in the state, both natural and artificial, to protect the environment or at least not to damage it beyond a certain limit, and also principles of the protection of natural sources, of nature and landscape protection as well as of the protection of animals and plants as cultural and natural heritage. Some institutions also deal with the ownership of natural resources and

---

[573]/ ECR [2005] I-7569.
[574]/ ECR [2007] I-1721.
[575]/ ECR [2007] I-3883.
[576]/ ECR [2006] I-3949.
[577]/ ECR [2006] I-2755.
[578]/ ECR [2006] I-8445.
[579]/ ECR [2005] I-167.

of the compartments of the environment. The protection of the environment is laid down in the Constitution, the provisions of which are followed by quite a number of statutes and other legislation which these rights and duties, also under the influence of international and European law, further regulate, expand and guarantee.

Enforcement of these rights, duties and principles thoroughly depends on the decision-making of constitutional courts as the supreme judicial authorities in European countries. The constitutional order of the Czech Republic also provides for a number of rights and duties mentioned above. The following articles deserve special mention: Article 7 of the Constitution (the principle of state liability), Article 11 (relation of the right of ownership and environmental protection), Article 14 (relation of free movement rights and environmental protection), and mainly Article 35 (the right to a favourable environment and the duty to protect it, as well as the right to access environmental information) of the Charter of Fundamental Rights and Freedoms.

The Constitutional Court of the Czech Republic has been frequently – directly or indirectly – engaged in the issues concerning the environment and its compartments in recent years (particularly from 1993 to 2006). The interpretation of the environment as public property, questions concerning the existence of the right to a favourable environment and issues connected with the right of all authorized persons (both natural and juridical) to a favourable living environment were debated (all in connection with Art. 35 (1) of the Charter). The Constitutional Court also dealt with the issues connected with the relation of the right to a favourable environment to other fundamental rights or with defining the term "right to a favourable environment". The following decisions of the Constitutional Court as examples of the most important cases should be mentioned as well as compared: Judgment file No. Pl. ÚS 15/96 (published in the Collection of Laws of the Czech Republic under No. 280/1996 Sb.), Judgment file No. III ÚS 70/97 (published in the Collection of Judgments and Resolutions of the Constitutional Court, Sb.n.u. Volume No. 8, Judgement No. 96), Resolution file No. I.ÚS 282/97, Resolution file No. Pl.ÚS 24/2000, Judgment file No. Pl.ÚS 17/95. These judicial decisions, no matter how remarkable and significant, do not possess, considering their consequences and importance, a breakthrough quality. Together with the growing extension of environmental, economic and social problems and with the growing number of cases we may expect increasing activity in this very peculiar segment of Czech judiciary.

3.2.7 Role of judiciary in the protection of the environment through criminal law

The concept of criminal liability in environmental protection started to penetrate into Czech law as late as during the first half of the 1990s in connection with the development of environmental law legislation. The basic modification was brought by two amendments to the Criminal Code at the turn of the 1980s and the 1990s which introduced into the Czech Criminal Code (although broadly and vaguely formulated) the elements of the crime of endangering or impairing the environment (ss. 181a, 181b).[580] The objective of criminal acts against the environment is the interest of the society in ensuring the protection of the

---

[580]/ Damohorský, M. et. al. *supra.*

environment and its individual compartments. Thus this concept follows and develops the content of Article 7 of the Constitution and Article 35 of the Charter.

One of the major reasons why the area of environmental protection has recently been included in the scope of criminal law is the constant growth and mainly gravity of criminal acts committed against the environment. These cannot be punished at the level of administrative law mainly because of their gravity.[581] In Czech law as well as in international law this tendency towards a more profound implementation of the instruments of criminal law in the protection of the environment by introducing specific provisions (new elements of crimes) into the national criminal codes can be observed roughly from the beginning of the 1990s. Within the scope of re-codification of Czech criminal law (the new Criminal Code, Act No. 40/2009 Sb.) criminal acts against the environment are becoming part of a separate chapter, as it is common in other countries of the EU.

The growing impact of criminal liability within environmental law can be recognized at a Community level at which the European Court of Justice recently played an important role. In 2001, on the basis of the 6th Environment Action Programme of the European Community, the draft of the Directive on the protection of the environment through criminal law was adopted. The purpose of the Directive was to ensure more effective implementation of environmental protection legislation at the EC level through adopting the basic code of criminal offences within the EC. Articles 174 and 175 TEC created the legal basis of this Directive. During the hearing of the proposal in the European Parliament questions arose whether the Directive was not contrary to the EC Treaty (intrusion into national competencies of Member States) and so the Council of the European Union instead adopted, in 2003, Council Framework Decision 2003/80/JHA on the protection of the environment through criminal law, having regard to the Treaty on the European Union, in particular Art. 34 (2). This was based on the so-called Third Pillar of the EU Treaty – police and judicial cooperation. This established the first internal legislation of the EU in the area of combating crime against the environment, the inspiration of which was Strasbourg Convention of the Council of Europe on the protection of the environment through criminal law passed in 1998. The European Court of Justice, on the grounds of the petition by the Commission against the Council concerning the legal basis of the Framework Decision passed, cancelled this decision (Case C-176/03 Commission of the European Communities v. Council of the European Union) with the argument that the Framework Decision should have been properly adopted under Article 175 EC.

At the present time a new proposal of the Directive concerning the protection of the environment through criminal law is being drafted[582] in compliance with Art. 175 (2) TEC. Both the Council Framework Decision from 2003 and the draft Directive EC from 2007 introduce harmonization in the area of (1) criminal acts, and (2) liability of natural persons and legal entities. The draft Directive requires that effective, proportionate and dissuasive criminal penalties be implemented but the type and the level of punishment remain within the jurisdiction of individual Member States. All elements of criminal acts are based on illegality.

---

[581]/ *Government Decree No. 1044, 23rd October 2000:* Updated Concept of Protection against Organized Crime.
[582]/ Commentary 2007/51 *in fine.*

Criminal law is, by its oppressive nature, an important instrument for the protection of the environment. No matter how the role of the protection of the environment through criminal law grows, it is not utilized effectively enough, especially in comparison with administrative punishment. Major impact of the case law of the Supreme Court of the Czech Republic in the field of the protection of the environment through criminal law on theory as well as on the practice still subsists in the harmonization of judicial decisions of lower courts and in the interpretation of elements of individual crimes against the environment.

3.2.8 Administrative judiciary and environmental protection

Legislation on environmental protection is mainly provided and ensured by public law. The public right to a favourable environment provided for by Article 35 of the Charter of Fundamental Rights and Freedoms imposes on the state the responsibility to create the legal basis on which this right may be secured.[583] The state, using its executive power, has created the system of administrative procedures to control the activities that may bear potential hazard to the environment. By limiting its negative impact on the environment[584] the state provides for the guarantee of the environment relating to standards set up by the Charter.[585] Activities of state authorities, and in some cases also of bodies of local self-government, may significantly encroach on the legal sphere of holders of public duties and, at the same time, on the legal standing of holders of public rights, mainly the right to a favourable living environment. The role and the importance of administrative courts in protecting persons (both natural and juridical) arise from the scope of legal regulation of the environmental protection on one hand and from their status as independent and impartial bodies on the other.

Legal regulation of administrative judiciary,[586] as provided for by the Code of Administrative Justice (Act No. 150/2002 Sb., CAJ), represents the basic legislation concerning the protection of environmental rights by courts. Besides, the courts adjudicate on other issues, the hearing of which is imposed upon them by CAJ. Considering environmental protection, the following sections stipulate the pivotal powers of the courts: actions against the decision of an administrative body (sec. 5 and subsequent sections CAJ), actions for the protection against the failure to act (sec. 79 and subsequent sections CAJ), actions for the protection against illegal interference of an administrative body (sec. 82 and subsequent sections CAJ), actions for the cancellation of the so-called measure of a general nature, or its part, for its conflict with the law (sec. 101 and subsequent sections CAJ), and finally actions for the protection of public interest (sec. 66 and subsequent sections CAJ).

---

[583]/ Pavlíček, V. et al.: *Ústava a ústavní řád České republiky, 2. díl Práva a svobody* [The Constitution and Constitutional Order of the Czech Republic, Part 2 Rights and Freedoms]. 2nd revised and expanded ed., Praha: Linde, 1999, p. 282.

[584]/ Limits of a negative impact on the environment are expressed especially in Art. 35 (3) of the Charter.

[585]/ The Charter of Fundamental Rights and Freedoms does not limit endangering or damaging environment absolutely but with the reference to acceptable limits as specified by implementing statutes. Similarly the extent of favourability of the environment used in Art. 35 (1) is defined by implementing statutes (comp. Art. 41 (1) of the Charter).

[586]/ Concerning the regulation of administrative judiciary in general see e.g. Hendrych D. et. al.: *Správní právo: obecná část* [Administrative Law: General Part]. 6th ed., Praha: C. H. Beck, 2006, p. 540 and subsequent sections, Vopálka, V. (ed.): *Nová úprava správního soudnictví* [New Regulation of Administrative Justice]. Praha: ASPI Publishing, 2003.

The key document in the field of judicial control of the executive power in the area of environmental protection is the Convention on Access to Information, Public Participation in Decision-making and Access to Justice in Environmental Matters (Aarhus Convention) of 25th June 1998. This Convention[587] regulates the access of the public to basic tools enabling the protection of the fundamental right – the right for life in a favourable living environment[588]. In this connection the so-called three pillars of the Aarhus Convention are being mentioned which regulate, as indicated by the name of the Convention, the following: (1) access to information, (2) participation in decision-making, and (3) access to justice in regard of the environment. While the duties of the parties to the Convention related to the first two pillars are usually carried out at the level required, the third pillar, covering the judicial review, constitutes the major issue.

The European Union, which is also a party to the Convention,[589] regulates within Union law some of the key decision-making procedures, the parameters of which must comply with the Aarhus Convention requirements. It concerns mainly environmental impact assessment (EIA/SEA) and integrated prevention and pollution control (IPPC). Besides decision-making procedures the access to information in environmental matters[590] is also an objective of the European Union legislation.

Access to justice is provided for in Article 9 of the Aarhus Convention. The Convention deals separately with the protection of rights regarding the access to information embodied in Article 4 and the rights to take part in decision-making procedures ensured by Article 6. In both cases the Convention presupposes the existence of an independent and impartial authority constituted under the law, in particular the court to which anyone from the public has access in cases of an alleged breach of his or her rights. It is presumed, and in cases concerning access to information it is even required, that the possibility of review by an authority other than court exists. The purpose of this procedure is not to exclude the possibility of judicial review but to ensure a prompt review by another, mainly administrative authority, the decision of which may constitute the prerequisite for the access to justice.

Beyond the scope of protection of rights laid down by its first and second pillars, the Convention also requires the existence of the possibility to seek administrative as well as judicial review to challenge acts and omissions of private persons and public authorities by members of the public, if they meet the criteria, if any, laid down in national law, when these acts or omissions contravene provisions of national law relating to the environment (Art. 9 (3)).

The way of transposition of requirements resulting from European Union law and consequently the obligations set up by the Aarhus Convention are considered, at the level of national legislation in the Czech Republic, to be sufficient with the exception of the access to justice. Possible deficiencies of domestic legislation arise mainly from insufficient determination of entities that may seek legal protection of their rights. The illustrative example of

---

[587] Published as No. 124/2004 Sb.m.s.; binding on the Czech Republic as of October 4th, 2004.
[588] the Preamble to the Convention, recital 7.
[589] EC ratified the Aarhus Convention on 17th. February 2005; Council Decision 2005/370/EC.
[590] Directive 2003/4/EC.

insufficient legislation of this kind is the insufficient transposition of Article 10a of Directive 85/337/EEC[591] as alleged by the European Commission.[592] The subject matter of the issue in question is the possibility, or lack thereof, of the affected public in the sense of the quoted Article[593] to resort to the judicial review of acts or omissions of an administrative body in the procedure of environmental impact assessment according to Act No. 100/2001 Sb., on environmental impact assessment, in which the affected public participates. Access to judicial review is reserved to a limited section of the public (environmental NGOs) which have access to the relating decision-making procedures in the position of participants in proceedings. Unfortunately, the legislative draft[594] which was submitted for consideration of the Parliament of the Czech Republic does not eliminate this defficiency since it focuses only on one section of the affected public, i.e. the organized public. Without a relevant change in legislation the right to judicial protection in the sense of the quoted Article of the Directive, and consequently the Aarhus Convention, is still denied to a certain section of the affected public.

3.2.9 Conclusions

Should we draw certain fundamental conclusions on the grounds of the above-mentioned descriptions and analyses of the position and activities of individual courts, it is quite obvious, and in connection with the increasing frequency and gravity of environmental issues also understandable, that the role and the importance of courts of all categories and at all levels will substantially grow in the future, together with the growth of its overall agenda. What we have in mind is the increase of both a "direct" (environmental), and an "indirect" (through the protection of life, health and property) agenda for all categories of courts, including international, European and national (domestic) in individual countries

In our opinion, mainly criminal and administrative (public) law will possess constantly growing importance in this development but an increasing influence of private law (especially civil law) can also be expected, particularly in relation to "compartments of the environment that may be subject to ownership", i.e. primarily to natural resources. Constitutional judiciary will surely not remain silent.

Substantive law will undoubtedly perform an important function in the area of the protection of the environment. The key role will obviously be played by continuing European integration and harmonization of law but also by broader international cooperation in this field in the intercontinental (global) scope.

An important and key role is being, and will be, played by the established practice of courts, their judicial decisions and their unifying role in environmental protection. Although in the continental legal system judicial decisions do not play such an important role as in the Anglo-American legal system based on precedents, they will certainly possess an increasingly important inspirational and unifying function. European continental law (including

---

[591] Directive 85/337/EC as amended by Directive 97/11/EC and Directive 2003/35/EC.
[592] Letter from 29th June, in which the Czech Republic delivered to the European Commission the reasoned opinion on the matter.
[593] Article 10a Directive 85/337/EC is the transposition of Article 9 (2) the Aarhus Convention.
[594] Parliamentary Print No. 599/1.

Czech law) should be more inspired by the British and American legal systems (not only by precedents but especially by more general wording of legal rules). Nevertheless, the role of administrative and criminal law and its tools and methods will most likely prevail in the environmental protection in Central European countries.

The growing importance of courts in environmental protection will certainly require the increase of professional legal qualification and also of general awareness of judges concerning environmental issues and the need for environmental protection. This important function may be implemented by Law Faculties of Czech public universities and also by other institutions, e.g. the Judicial Academy of the Ministry of Justice in Kroměříž, Moravia. Courts will not be able to fulfil their role without their cooperation with prosecutors, policemen, administrative officers and experts from other branches of similar function.

3.3 EUROPEANIZATION OF CRIMINAL LAW

3.3.1 The background of the Europeanization of criminal law

European cooperation in criminal matters has always maintained specific features within international cooperation. The first signs of European cooperation in criminal matters emerged at the beginning of the 19th century. The first document was the French-Belgian Convention of 12th August 1843 providing for cooperation in tax issues, and the second document was the so-called Mannheim Convention of 17th October 1868 regulating the international regime of navigation on the Rhine; this latter Convention regulated illegal activities relating to navigation along this river.[595] The idea to enhance criminal cooperation among European countries was developed after World War I. In Paris in 1924 the International Association of Penal Law was established; its main objective was to promote the conception of universal criminal law within the League of Nations.[596] Many promoters of the unification of criminal law tried to achieve this aim by approximating not only the physical elements of a crime referring to the fact that criminal conduct was committed, or caused consequences, in several states, but also the mental elements of crimes according to the perpetrators' affiliation to more than one country.[597] The idea of cooperation among European countries and within the international community was also welcomed by its supporters in pre-war Czechoslovakia. For example, Czech internationalist A. Hobza argued that *"the situation when all delicts are considered by every state independently of other states does not comply with the present needs of our world"*.[598]

The Czechoslovak doctrine of international and criminal law was very positive about harmonization of criminal law. This was clear at the 10th Congress of the International Penal and Penitentiary Commission held in Prague in 1930. The Czechoslovak Minister of Foreign

---

595/ Legros, R.: *La pénétration du droit européen dans la justice répressive belge.* Bruxelles: Bruylant, 1970.
596/ Pella, V. V.: *Vers l'unification du droit pénal par la création d'un institut international auprès de la Société des Nations.* Paris: Sirey, 1928.
597/ Donadieu de Vabres, H.: *La justice criminelle d'aujourd'hui.* Paris: Armand Collin, 1929.
598/ Hobza, A.: Mezinárodní delikt [International Delict]. In: *Pocta k 70. narozeninám univ. Prof. dra Augusta Miřičky* [Tribute to Professor August Miřička on his 70th Birthday]. Praha: Československá společnost pro právo trestní, 1933, pp. 129–138.

Affairs Edvard Beneš, in his address to this Congress, stated that *"individual national cultures are approximating each other; modern science compels the legislatures in individual states to balance differences and to unify legislation, to modify their social, economic, legal and cultural institutions as a result of their mutual influence"*.[599] These eternal ideas of the famous Czechoslovak politician were reflected in practice. Czechoslovakia was one of the first countries ratifying in 1931 the International Convention for the Suppression of Counterfeiting Currency of 1929.[600] On the other hand, the practical implementation of international law into national legislation was somehow complicated in Czechoslovakia. The Czechoslovak legal order was strictly based on the principle of sovereignty and enforced primacy of Czechoslovak law over international law.[601] The law-making conception of the Czechoslovak legislative assembly was considered to be unlimited in its essence; the National Assembly, respecting the constitutional rules in force, could provide for anything and in any manner irrespective of international obligations. The Czechoslovak conception of the relationship between national and international law was dualistic although jurisprudence acknowledged that the monistic concept should have rather been enforced, for example, within the League of Nations. This approach caused international law to be perceived by the Czechoslovak system of law, as well as by many other legal systems in Europe, as a set of contractual rules the validity of which was derived from the validity of national constitutional law. Even the theory of Czechoslovak international law of that time claimed that no system of law expressed the requirement that a special simultaneous transformation of each rule of international law into national legislation should have been pursued.[602] Nothing to this end was contained in the Constitutional Charter. For example, Bohuš Tomsa, great Czech legal philosopher and internationalist, wrote that there was no regulation within the Czechoslovak legal order which would have required such transformation.[603] František Weyr,[604] another outstanding constitutionalist in pre-war Czechoslovakia, stated that, as a result of the dualistic theory maintained in Czechoslovak practice, the custom was developed to assign international treaties just "interim national force". Since it was clear that an international treaty without having the binding effect in national law was in fact insignificant and since it was sometimes impossible to wait for Parliamentary consent to a treaty, the Government was from time to time authorized to publish treaties with interim force in the Collection of Laws and Decrees. However, Weyr argued that such practice just showed the weak aspects of the dualistic conception of the relationship between international and national law in Czechoslovakia.[605]

---

[599] The speech of Minister Dr. E. Beneš at the 10th International Congress on Penal Law and Penitentiary 1930, In: Věstník Československé společnosti pro právo trestní, 1930.

[600] Multilateral Convention for the Suppression of Counterfeiting Currency (No. 15/1932 Sb.) was signed in Geneva on 20th April 1929. At the same time, all participating countries signed the explanatory Protocol; some states (such as Austria, Colombia, Cuba, Greece, Portugal, Romania, Yugoslavia and Czechoslovakia) also signed the optional Protocol to this Convention.

[601] Weyr, F.: Pojem, změny a doplnění normy [The Concept, Changes of, and Amendments to the Rule]. *Vědecká ročenka Právnické fakulty Masarykovy university* 1932, pp. 26–40.

[602] Hobza, A.: Publikace a platnost mírových smluv v Čsl. republice [The Publication and Validity of Peace Treaties in the Czechoslovak Republic]. *Právník* 1923, pp. 11–22.

[603] Tomsa, B.: *Právo mezinárodní* [International Law]. Bratislava: Právnická fakulta University Komenského, 1930.

[604] Weyr, F.: *Československé právo ústavní* [Czechoslovak Constitutional Law]. Praha: Melantrich 1937.

[605] See also Budník, J.: Několik poznámek k vnitrostátní platnosti mezinárodních smluv [Several Notes on National Validity of International Treaties]. *Časopis pro právní a státní vědu* 1937, Vošta, L.: Několik poznámek k otázce

Essential progress on the way to harmonization of criminal law in the European continent was made after World War II. This was seen at the European Convention on Extradition 1957 and the European Convention on Mutual Assistance in Criminal Matters 1959. The Council of Europe initiated the conclusion of other similar agreements which furthered, through recommendations of the Council of Europe, the harmonization of some features in national systems of criminal law. The collection of agreements on criminal cooperation concluded within the Council of Europe was complemented by the Maastricht Treaty in 1992, which explicitly provided for cooperation in criminal matters within the newly established third pillar of the European Union. A more significant contribution by the European Union to this area can be seen after the adoption of the Amsterdam Treaty in 1997. The whole context of mutual applicability of mechanisms of criminal cooperation within the Council of Europe on the one hand, and the European Union on the other, has been substantially complemented by Schengen agreements forming particular mechanisms of police and judicial cooperation. Both cooperation in criminal matters within the Council of Europe and cooperation in criminal matters established by the European Union are significant elements of the Europeanization and internationalization of criminal law. However, both processes undoubtedly have led to the weakening of two traditional principles of criminal law, namely the principles of territoriality and sovereignty of national legislatures.

3.3.2 The relationship between European law and national criminal law

Criminal law plays a secondary role in the legal systems of Member States as it protects social values and relations regularly governed by other branches of law. Thus, criminal law often is, to a greater or lesser extent, dependent upon other legal branches (such as the issue of unlawfulness of a crime which is considered from the perspective of the whole legal system).[606] Where such branches of law have already been harmonized within the European Community, criminal law is dependent on EU law through the harmonized branches although it is not, and cannot be, directly influenced thereby. European law has tackled a serious issue recently in this respect, namely whether it is possible to affect criminal law through competences conferred upon the Community by Member States although criminal law is not subject to such competences. European law has been created synthetically by transferring powers from individual Member States to the European Union in sectors falling within the ambit of the establishing treaties, the nature of which is that of international treaties. In this context European law can be defined as a set of legal rules in those areas where the regulation of legal relations was transferred from Member States' bodies to the bodies of the European Union upon common will shared by the Member States. The common will of Member States expressed in the establishing treaties, as international

vnitrostátní platnosti mezinárodních smluv [Several Notes on the Issue of National Validity of International Treaties]. In: *Pocta k šedesátým narozeninám Dr. Emila Háchy* [Tribute to Dr. Emil Hácha on his 70th Birthday]. Praha: Frant. Řivnáč, 1932, pp. 319–323, or Peška, Z.: Příspěvek k otázce transformace mezinárodních smluv v právo vnitrostátní [Contribution to the Issue of Transformation of International Treaties into National Law]. In: *Pocta k šedesiatym narodeninám Dr. Karla Laštovku* [Tribute to Dr. Karel Laštovka on the Occasion of his 60th Birthday]. Praha: Frant. Řivnáč, 1936, pp. 296–306.

[606] Novotný, O. – Vanduchová, M. et al.: *Trestní právo hmotné – I. Obecná část* [Criminal Substantive Law I. General Part]. 6th updated and expanded ed., Praha: ASPI, 2010.

treaties, determines not only the contents of the legal rules creating European law but also the scope of areas covered by European law.

The need to affect criminal law by European rules was originally meant as the expression of the common will that some types of conduct should be criminalized in the legal systems of all EU Member States. At the beginning of the 1990s EU Member States came to the conclusion that if the international community was able to agree on the common criminalization of some types of conduct (such as drug trafficking) it would have been rather sad if the common criminalization of some types of conduct had not been agreed by such an integrated community as the European Union undoubtedly is. The impact of European law upon criminal law of the Member States also emerged from another side. For more than fifty years, European law has been built upon the principle of non-discrimination on the grounds of nationality with respect to competences conferred upon the Community by individual Member States. However, this development has shown that where certain legal relations of sovereign states are integrated and subject to the control of common bodies, specific processes may commence to expand the common and coordinated activity into other branches of law and other sectors of the life of society. This expansive logic of European integration, this "fuse effect", can be best explained by intensive expansion of economic and political needs of integration of the Member States. Particularly here a phenomenon arises which has been called "Europeanization" and which, along with "globalization", has become a regular part of our vocabulary. This is a process where European law influences those national legal relations which originally and apparently should not have been subject to European law. More concretely, where criminal law touches, or even gets in conflict, with "Europeanized" legal relations, the problem of the general supremacy of European law over national law must emerge. In other words, European law clearly affects non-criminal law, which subsequently induces an impact on criminal law as a result of the subsidiary nature of criminal law.

The accord of Member States with respect to the common criminalization of certain types of conduct and the restriction of the criminal sovereignty of Member States for the sake of free movement of four basic freedoms, i.e. competences transferred to the Community, has not been meant, by its nature, as a shift of the subsidiarity of criminal law from national law towards supranational law, i.e. European law. European law harmonizes national non-criminal law; the resulting outcome of this process serves, under the principle of criminal law subsidiarity, to derive a national criminal rule. The category of criminal law subsidiarity directly within European law can be acknowledged only when EU primary law starts to create certain protected interests, the protection of which is required of the Member States to provide for in their criminal law, such as measures against euro counterfeiting.

The decision of the European Court of Justice in the case *Commission v. Council*[607] has been considered a clear transfer of criminal law subsidiarity from national law to European law. The European Court of Justice has acknowledged that criminal law plays a subsidiary role in the legal system of Member States as it protects social values and relations regularly governed by other legal branches. Where such legal branches have been harmonized within

---

[607]/ ECJ decision in case C-176/2003, *Commission v. Council* of 13th September 2005, ECR 2005, I-7879.

the EU, criminal law is, through the harmonized branches, also dependent on EU law; however, it is not, and cannot be, affected directly. The European Court of Justice has thus supported the functional understanding of European law[608] under which the European legislature has an 'implicit' sectoral power in criminal law as an exception to the general exemption of criminal substantive law and criminal procedure from the EU. The existence of EU pillars raised a fundamental theoretical question of whether the designation of conduct as criminal by an EU rule did not deny the principle under which criminal law could not be a transferred competence. The new construction of shared competences as contained in the Lisbon Treaty has removed this ambiguity.

3.3.3 The relationship with the protection of basic rights and freedoms

Fundamental rights and freedoms create an important background of Europeanization of criminal law. Primarily and in connection with criminal law, these are rights and freedoms enabling individuals to defend their liberty and dignity within relevant institutional guarantees. In the Czech Republic it was the Czech Constitutional Court which dealt in its case called the sugar quotas[609] for the first time with the relationship between national and European law with respect to a potential conflict between the two systems, as well as the relationship between the competences of the European Court of Justice on the one hand and national courts, i.e. the Constitutional Court, on the other. The Constitutional Court in its judgment accepted, in compliance with the European doctrinal approach, the supremacy of application of Community law and the absence of its own competence to review its constitutionality. The Court expressed the basic legal principle of the relationship between Czech and Community law as follows: *"At the moment of accession of the Czech Republic to the European Community certain competences of bodies of the Czech Republic were conferred upon the EC and its bodies. The scope of competences exercised by EC bodies subsequently reduced the competences of all respective national bodies regardless of whether the competences are of a normative or individual decision making nature. The Constitutional Court considers the referral of part of competences to be conditional since the Czech Republic remains the original holder of sovereignty and powers resulting therefrom, as is stipulated by Art. 1 (1) of the Constitution. Under this provision the Czech Republic is a sovereign, uniform and democratic state based on the rule of law and the respect for rights and freedoms of people and citizens. Delegation of a part of competences of national bodies may persist as long as EC bodies exercise these competences in a manner compatible with the preservation of the fundaments of state sovereignty of the Czech Republic and in a manner not endangering the material substance of the state based on the rule of law."* The Constitutional Court has concluded that the application of Community law within national law should be approached in such a way so as not to conserve the effects of Community law in the national system of law. Such approach would correspond to the fact that the rigidness of effects caused by Community acts to national law has been subject to a dynamic development. Such understanding would also best serve that what was mentioned above, namely the conditional nature of the referral of part of competences. However, it should be emphasized that the

---

[608]/ Tomášek, M. et al.: *Europeizace trestního práva* [Europeanization of Criminal Law]. Praha: Linde, 2009.
[609]/ Judgment of the Constitutional Court Pl. ÚS 50/04 to annul sections 3 and 16 of Government Regulation No. 548/2005 Sb., stipulating certain conditions for the implementation of measures of the common organization of the markets in the sugar sector of 8th March 2006, published as No. 154/2006 Sb.

Constitutional Court consistently refers to Community law in its judgment; the ratification of the Lisbon Treaty changes the situation. Moreover, the judgment did not deal with the referral of competences, or their part, in criminal law. Later the Constitutional Court in its decision on the implementation of the European arrest warrant[610] (EAW) did not consider "classical" implementation of Community law, i.e. its first pillar, but rather the implementation of the Framework Decision of the Council of the EU, which belongs to the third pillar of EU law. In its judgment of dismissal the Constitutional Court resorted to constitutionally conforming interpretation; the Court tied the national applicability of the Framework Decision to Art. 1 (2) of the Constitution stipulating the duty of the Czech Republic to observe its international obligations. The wording of Art. 1 (2) of the Constitution along with the principle of loyal cooperation stipulated in Art. 10 of the European Community Treaty give rise, in the Court's opinion, to the constitutional principle under which national laws, including the Constitution, should be interpreted in conformity with the principles of European integration and cooperation between Community bodies and national bodies of the respective Member State. Thus, the Constitutional Court identified itself with the opinion of the European Court of Justice in the *Pupino* case[611] under which the conforming interpretation of national law in the light of European law must take into consideration not only EC rules, i.e. the first pillar, but also the legal rules of the European Union.

Considering the exercise of some basic rights and freedoms in the area of cooperation in criminal matters the Member States may go beyond the framework of the European dimension of the protection of rights of persons in criminal proceedings. The judgment of the Supreme Court of the Czech Republic of 22nd July 2004[612] illustrates this situation: the principle of *ne bis in idem* is violated where the accused person is prosecuted and convicted for the same fact which was, as conduct of a criminal nature, earlier considered by the competent administrative authority and resulted in a legally effective and final decision; the decision determined the fact as an administrative infraction unless the decision of the administrative body was reversed.[613] This legal opinion may be understood as the application of the *ne bis in idem* principle within one Member State. Considering the relationship with other Member States this opinion goes beyond the horizon of Article 50 of the Charter of Fundamental Rights of the EU since the Charter requires the applicability of the *ne bis in idem* principle to judgments of conviction in criminal proceedings and not with respect to administrative proceedings.[614] However, the acknowledgement of the *ne bis in idem* principle in such a context may raise some doubts with respect to the legal practice in the concrete

---

[610]/ Judgment of the Constitutional Court Pl ÚS 66/04 in the case to repeal s. 21 (2) of Act No. 140/1961 Sb., the Criminal Code, as amended, and to repeal s. 403 (2), s. 411 (6) e), s. 411 (7) and s. 412 (2) of Act No 141/1961 Sb., the Criminal Procedure Code, as amended, of 3rd May 2006, published as No. 434/2006 Sb.

[611]/ Judgment of the Court of Justice, Case C-105/03 Tribunale di Firenze v. Maria Pupino of 16th June 2005, ECR 2005, p. I-5285.

[612]/ Judgment of the Supreme Court of the Czech Republic of 22nd July 2004, No. 11 Tdo 738/2003.

[613]/ See, for example, Grivna, T. – Sekvard, O.: Nový pohled Nejvyššího soudu na zásadu ne bis in idem? [A New View of the Supreme Court upon the Ne Bis in Idem Principle?]. *Právní fórum* 3/2005, pp. 98–103.

[614]/ Tomášek, M.: Soudcovská tvorba ochrany základních práv a svobod v procesu europeizace trestního práva [Judge-made Protection of Basic Rights and Freedoms in the Process of Europeanization of Criminal Law]. *Acta Universitatis Carolinae Iuridica* 1/2006, p. 31 and subs.

areas of Europeanized criminal law, in particular in the protection of financial interests of the EC. In the sense of Council Regulation No. 2988/95 on the protection of the European Communities' financial interests,[615] the checks and inspections of economic natural or artificial persons on the spot in order to reveal frauds or fraudulent practices against the financial interests of the Community do not exclude simultaneous judicial proceedings against such persons in a Member State as such cases are not subject to the principle of *ne bis in idem*.[616] This is not a simultaneous concurrence of different criminal proceedings, but rather the administrative proceedings – controlling competence of the Commission – and potential criminal proceedings in the respective Member State.[617]

3.3.4 The issues of implementation

The implementation into the national system of law of a Member State is an important dimension of the Europeanization of criminal law. The Czech approach to this issue was indicated in the implementation of the Framework Decision on the European Arrest Warrant and the Surrender Procedures between Member States of 13th June 2002. The Czech Republic, upon its accession to the European Union, was obliged to implement the European arrest warrant, as part of EU *acquis*, as of the date of accession, i.e. 1st May 2004. The amendments of both the Criminal Code and the Criminal Procedure Code containing the provision implementing the Framework Decision nationwide, had been duly prepared but the issue resulted in tough political debate and the amendments were passed as late as on 1st November 2004.

Originally, the Government of the Czech Republic along with the above mentioned amendments also introduced an amendment of Art. 14 of the Charter by inserting the fifth paragraph reading: "*A citizen may be surrendered to a Member State of the European Union for criminal proceedings or serving the term of imprisonment if such surrender results from the obligations of the Czech Republic as a Member State of the European Union, which may be neither restricted nor excluded.*" The proposed amendment of the Charter was dismissed by the Chamber of Deputies on 2nd April 2004. Then the amendments of the Criminal Code and the Criminal Procedure Code respectively were passed by the Chamber of Deputies overruling the veto of the President arguing for its unconstitutionality.[618]

The amendments of the Criminal Code and the Criminal Procedure Code were a subject-matter of the complaint submitted to the Constitutional Court of the Czech Republic.[619] A group of Czech members of the Chamber of Deputies of Parliament of the Czech Republic and a group of members of the Senate of Parliament of the Czech Republic filed an ap-

---

[615]/ Council Regulation No. 2988/95 of 18th December 1995 on the protection of the European Communities' financial interests. OJ EC L 312 of 23rd December 1995.

[616]/ Tomášek *ibidem*.

[617]/ Tomášek, M.: Odhalování podvodů proti finančním zájmům Evropských společenství prostřednictvím kontrol na místě [Discovering Frauds against Financial Interests of the European Communities through On-spot Checks]. *Trestněprávní revue* 6/2005, pp. 149–152.

[618]/ Vantuch, P.: Evropský zatýkací rozkaz [European Arrest Warrant]. *Právní rádce* 4/2004, p. 61.

[619]/ Similarly in Germany, the law implementing the Framework Decision was subject to a constitutional complaint. The Federal Constitutional Court repealed the Act on the European arrest warrant on 18th July 2005 which led to many problems. A new implementing law (Act on international legal assistance in criminal matters – IRG) became effective as late as on 2nd August 2006.

plication with the Constitutional Court to repeal s. 21 (2) of the Criminal Code and s. 403 (2), s. 411 (6) e), s. 411 (7) and s. 412 (2) of the Criminal Procedure Code.

The complaint was considered by the plenary session of the Constitutional Court.[620] The Court in the reasoning of the judgment stated that Art. 1 (2) of the Constitution of the Czech Republic along with the principle of cooperation stipulated in Art. 10 of the EC Treaty establish a constitutional principle under which national legislation, including the Constitution, should be interpreted in compliance with the principles of European integration and cooperation between Community bodies and the bodies of a Member State. Should there be more ways of interpretation of the Constitution, having the Charter of Fundamental Rights and Freedoms as one of its parts and only some of the rights and freedoms would lead to the fulfilment of obligations owed by the Czech Republic due to its membership in the EU, such mode of interpretation should be selected which would support the fulfilment of those obligations and not the mode of interpretation which would render their fulfilment impossible. The Constitutional Court found unsubstantiated the allegations of complainants that the national adoption of the EAW would disturb the permanent relationship between the citizen and the state. A citizen rendered to another EU Member State for criminal proceedings still enjoys the protection of the Czech Republic including during the time of the criminal proceedings. The European arrest warrant only allows for the surrender, limited in time, of a Czech citizen for prosecution in another EU Member State for a clearly defined crime; the citizen would face no obstacles to return to the Czech Republic after the proceedings terminate. The citizen has the right to apply for any remedial measure against the acts of investigative, prosecuting and adjudicating bodies during his surrender under the EAW; these remedial measures include a constitutional complaint.

The Constitutional Court referred to the historical motives for the formulation of the second sentence in Art. 14 (4) of the Charter of Fundamental Rights and Freedoms. This provision was originally included in Art. 15 (2) of the draft Charter as described in the report of the Constitutional Committees of the Chamber of the People and the Chamber of Nations respectively adopted on 7th January 1991. Experience with the crimes of the former Communist regime played an important role in the shaping of the Charter. Other experience, quite fresh at that time, was extremely relevant in drafting the existing Art. 14 (4) of the Charter at the turn of 1990 and 1991; the experience was drawn from the action called "Asanace" in Czech which was meant as "cleansing" or "decontamination" of the society since the Communist regime compelled inconvenient persons to leave the Republic. The historical interpretation shows that Art. 14 (4) of the Charter of Fundamental Rights and Freedoms has never applied to extradition.

Czech citizens enjoy advantages resulting from their status as EU citizens; it is then natural in this context that a certain extent of responsibility should be accepted along with these advantages. Investigation and abatement of crime committed in the European area cannot be successfully pursued within only one Member State but it requires wide international cooperation. One of the results of such cooperation is the replacement of former

---

[620]/ Judgment of the Constitutional Court Pl. ÚS 66/04 in the complaint to repeal s. 21 (2) of Act No. 140/1961 Sb. the Criminal Code, as amended, and to repeal s. 403 (2), s. 411 (6) e), s. 411 (7) and s. 412 (2) of Act No. 141/1961 Sb., the Criminal Procedure Code, as amended, of 3rd May 2006, published as No. 434/2006 Sb.

procedures of surrendering suspects with new and more efficient mechanisms reflecting the reality of the 21ˢᵗ century. The Constitutional Court states that the existing standard of the protection of fundamental rights within the European Union provides no reason to believe that this standard, through the application of principles resulting therefrom, is of a quality lower than that of the protection provided in the Czech Republic.

The Constitutional Court argues that the right of a citizen to be protected by the state can also be traced in the fact that Art. 14 (4) and Art. 36 (1) of the Charter of Fundamental Rights and Freedoms as well as Art. 6 (1) of the Convention for the Protection of Human Rights would be violated if a citizen was surrendered for criminal proceedings to a state that fails to comply with the standards of criminal proceedings stipulated by the constitutional order of the Czech Republic, for example, if the right of a citizen to a fair trial was endangered (Art. 36 (1) of the Charter), or the citizen was exposed to torturing or to any other inhumane and degrading treatment or punishment (Art. 3 of the Convention, Art. 7 (2) of the Charter). However, this is not the case of the European arrest warrant.

The Constitutional Court explicitly points out that all EU Member States are signatories of the Convention for the Protection of Human Rights and Freedoms. Therefore, the rights of citizens could not be prejudiced if their criminal case was considered in another EU Member State since every EU Member State is bound by the standard of human rights protection equivalent to that in the Czech Republic; the legal systems of all EU Member States are built upon the values the Czech Republic commenced to share after 1989. The Czech Charter is also based on the European Convention for the Protection of Human Rights and Freedoms.

A person to be surrendered to another EU Member State is secured the right to file a complaint against the measures taken by investigative, prosecuting or adjudicating bodies and the complaint has a suspensory effect (s. 411 (5) of the Criminal Procedure Code); he can also file a constitutional complaint and time-limits for surrender are suspended during the time when the Constitutional Court considers the complaint (s. 415 (3) of the Criminal Procedure Code). These provisions ensure the protection of a citizen, or of any other person, to be surrendered for criminal proceedings; simultaneously, the condition is preserved that the surrender of a citizen may not, in any individual case, violate the constitutional order of the Czech Republic.

The allegation that the relationship between a citizen and the state would be disturbed by the national regulation of the European arrest warrant is not substantiated according to the Constitutional Court. A citizen surrendered for criminal proceedings in another EU Member State remains under the protection of the Czech Republic in the course of the proceedings. The European arrest warrant only enables a citizen to be, for a limited period of time, surrendered for his prosecution of a specifically defined crime in another EU Member State and nothing may hinder him from returning back to the Czech Republic as soon as the criminal proceedings terminate (or from serving his term of imprisonment in the Czech Republic). The Criminal Procedure Code specifies the reasons for which a person may not be surrendered to another Member State (s. 411 in particular). The citizen has the right to apply for any remedial measure against the acts of investigative, prosecuting and adjudicating bodies during his surrender under the EAW; these remedial measures have a suspensory effect (s. 411 (5)) of the Criminal Procedure Code) and include a constitutional complaint. Where the surrender may violate the constitutional order of the Czech Republic, it will not be pursued.

Persons suspected of a crime and surrendered under the EAW are not prosecuted for the commission of a crime under s. 412 (2) of the Criminal Procedure Code (CPC) but the criminal proceedings will be conducted with respect to crimes defined in criminal substantive law of the requesting EU Member State. The statutory enumeration of offences in s. 412 (2) of the CPC (Art. 2 (2) of the Framework Decision) serves only for procedural purposes for a court. Where, in the European arrest warrant, the competent body of a requesting state designates the conduct of the surrendered person as one of the crimes listed in s. 412 (2) of the CPC or Art. 2 (2) of the Framework Decision, the Czech court does not examine whether the conduct at issue is a crime under Czech law. The adoption of s. 412 of the CPC does not result in the applicability of criminal law of all EU Member States in the Czech Republic. It only means that the Czech Republic assists the other EU Member States in enforcing their criminal law. Therefore persons in the Czech Republic (citizens, individuals with long-term residency and other persons habitually staying in the CR) are not required by s. 412 of the CPC to know the criminal law of all EU countries.

Removing the principle of dual criminality with respect to EU Member States the Czech Republic has not violated the principle of legality. Generally speaking, the requirement of dual criminality may be, as a safeguard, abandoned in the relations among EU Member States which have a sufficient level of mutual approximation of values and mutual confidence; these are democratic states observing the rule of law and bound by their duty to respect this principle. This is the situation where the approximation of 27 EU Member States has reached such a level of mutual trust that they do not feel the need to insist on the principle of dual criminality.

The surrender of a citizen or any person legally staying in the Czech Republic for criminal prosecution in another EU Member State will be applicable only when the criminal conduct was committed in another EU Member State and not in the Czech Republic. Where the crime is committed partly in the Czech Republic and partly abroad, criminal prosecution will be pursued in the Czech Republic. This gives rise to the obstacle to surrender of the person abroad (s. 411 (6) (d) of the CPC) unless, due to the nature of the conduct, prosecution in another EU Member State appears to be more effective because, for example, the relevant evidence is in that state or the essential part of the crime was committed there.

The character of the Framework Decision also results in some problematic issues brought in by the European arrest warrant. What is meant are individual problems in application aimed at the principle of dual criminality. A significant change, if compared with extradition proceedings, is the formulation of dual criminality in the European arrest warrant as a list of types of criminal conduct where the dual criminality test is not required. Other types of criminal conduct are, if the surrender under the EAW is at issue, subject to the condition that the conduct designated in the EAW is considered a crime in the requested state. Experience suggests that some crimes are defined too widely (e.g. computer crime) and that national laws of individual EU Member States, when implementing the Framework Decision, provide quite different definitions of conduct where dual criminality is not required.

3.3.5 The specificity of the Europeanization of criminal law in the field of health

The specificity of doing business in the medical area and the performance of medical professions as a regulated occupation have been, in particular since the accession of the Czech Republic to the EU, subject to intense professional debate and observed by the lay public. Professional ethics self-regulation plays a significant role in the further development of legal regulation. Medical law as an interdisciplinary branch in its practical application as well as a branch of science is becoming more and more important due to the speedy development of biomedicine and biotechnology in general, and in connection with possible cross-border exchange of scientific knowledge and personal data in particular.

The Convention for the Protection of Human Rights and Dignity of the Human Being with regard to the Application of Biology and Medicine (the Convention on Biomedicine) is of great significance for the development of medical law in the Czech Republic; the Convention became part of Czech legal order on 1st November 2001.[621] The Convention on Biomedicine is an international treaty under Art. 10 of the Constitution of the CR which means that it has supremacy in application over Czech primary and secondary legislation.[622] Considering any case in this area should start with interpretation of the Convention; the procedure provided under the law is relevant only where the Convention remains silent or where it explicitly refers to the law. If the law in any manner restricts the rights stipulated in the Convention such law may not essentially be applied. The only exception is the procedure under Art. 26 of the Convention permitting, under certain circumstances, the restriction of rights stipulated by the Convention. Should a concrete case be considered it is not sufficient just to examine whether the restriction of a patient's rights was permitted by the law but whether in that particular case it was necessary to restrict his rights due to any reason stipulated in the Convention. Many problems can be expected in its practical application. The use of the institution of necessity under the Czech Criminal Code may cause difficulties. The Convention in Articles 8 and 9 contains its own rules for necessity and they differ from the regime stipulated in the Czech code. The possibility to apply the provisions of the Czech Criminal Code appears to be tied in concrete cases to the fulfilment of the condition of the public interest in the sense of the Convention.

The relationship between the Convention and the Charter of Fundamental Rights and Freedoms seems to be a bigger problem. The Convention, based upon the primacy of the freedom of a patient to decide even over his own health and life,[623] may conflict with the provision of the Charter stipulating the imprescriptible right to life.[624] Such problems may occur in relation to abortions or when the patient refuses a life-saving intervention.[625] Article 9 of the Convention may also be considered quite disputable as it stipulates the right to make binding wishes in advance, thus enabling the patient to waive in advance the right to

---

[621]/ The Convention was published under No. 96/2001 Sb.m.s. in the Collection of International Treaties.
[622]/ Art. 10 of Constitutional Act No. 1/1993 Sb.
[623]/ Resulting from Art. 5 of the Convention.
[624]/ Art. 1 in connection with Art. 6 of the Charter.
[625]/ A traditional example is the refusal by Jehova's Witnesses of blood transfusion to save one's life; such situation may occur regarding fatal diseases when the patient refuses to undergo further drastic treatment and prefers palliative care instead.

have his life saved or even to prohibit any attempt to rescue his life. Emphasizing the will of the patient, the Convention indirectly comes closer to the legalization of passive euthanasia as is suggested by some opinions. In this context it should be noted that, unlike criminal law, this area is not part of the third pillar; what is important is the fact that the Czech Republic is bound by European legislation in the field of medicine and health care although it has not transposed this legislation into its legal system. The Convention on Biomedicine was ratified before the accession of the CR to the European Union but other legal documents are binding on the Czech Republic per se. It is obvious that there should be a body responsible not only for acquiring information about what legislation is binding on the Czech Republic but also for the distribution of the relevant information among competent institutions. There is no body in charge of cooperation with international organizations and other institutions so that we can deal with the solution of topical issues in the medical field. The issues deserving attention are cloning, euthanasia, transplantation, using modern technology (robotics) and drugs in a way compatible with processes and their theoretical and practical solutions in Europe and worldwide. Terminology should also be clarified, namely whether the terms "patient" and "client" should be distinguished and when either one may be conveniently used following the pattern of Anglo-American law.

3.4 CRIMINAL LIABILITY OF LEGAL ENTITIES
DE LEGE FERENDA IN THE CZECH REPUBLIC

3.4.1 Introduction

Debates on whether to introduce criminal liability of legal entities began in the Czech Republic at the end of the 1990s; the first scholarly articles and treatises were published, particularly within the context of discussions on the future development of criminal law in the Czech Republic. There were many scholarly essays written[626], articles published dealing with individual aspects of the criminal liability of legal entities and its sentencing,[627]

---

[626]/ Solnař, V. – Fenyk, J. – Císařová, D.: *Základy trestní odpovědnosti* [The Basics of Criminal Liability]. Praha: Orac, 2003, pp. 258–261. Musil, J.: Trestní odpovědnost právnických osob: Historický vývoj a mezinárodní srovnání [Criminal Liability of Legal Entities. Historical Development and International Comparison]. In: Musil, J. – Vanduchová, M. (eds.): *Pocta Otovi Novotnému* [Tribute to Oto Novotný]. Praha: Codex, 1998, pp. 76–98. Kratochvíl, V.: Jednání za jiného – možná cesta k trestní odpovědnosti právnických osob? [Acting for Another – a Potential Way to Criminal Liability of Legal Entities?]. In: Kratochvíl, V. (ed.): *Sborník z mezinárodního semináře o hospodářské kriminalitě* [Proceedings from the International Seminar on Economic Crime]. Brno: Masarykova univerzita, 1999, pp. 88–99. Musil J.: Trestní odpovědnost právnických osob – ano či ne? [Criminal Liability of Legal Entities – Yes or No?]. *Trestní právo* 7–8/2000, pp. 2–10. Musil, J. – Prášková, H. – Faldyna, F.: Úvahy o trestní odpovědnosti právnických osob de lege ferenda [Considerations of Criminal Liability of Legal Entities de Lege Ferenda]. *Trestní právo* 3/2001, pp. 6–17. Kratochvil, V. – Löff, M.: *Hospodářské trestní právo a odpovědnost právnických osob* [Economic Criminal Law and Criminal Liability of Legal Entities]. Brno: Masarykova univerzita, 2003. Janda, P.: Trestní odpovědnost právnických osob [Criminal Liability of Legal Entities]. *Právní fórum* 5/2006, pp. 168–178.

[627]/ Hurdík, J.: Trestní odpovědnost právnických osob? [Criminal Liability of Legal Entities?]. *Časopis pro právní vědu a praxi* 1/1996, pp. 28–33. Teryngel, J.: K trestní odpovědnosti právnických osob a osob za ně jednajících [On Criminal Liability of Legal Entities and Persons Acting on Their Behalf]. *Trestní právo* 1/1996, pp. 15–18. Teryngel, J.: Ještě k rozlišení odpovědnosti právnických a fyzických osob [Distinguishing between Criminal Liability of Natural Persons and Legal Entities Revisited]. *Trestní právo* 12/1996, pp. 9–12. Novotný, O.: O otázkách hospodářského trestního práva [Some Issues of Economic Criminal Law]. *Právní praxe* 6/1997, pp. 375–401. Pipek, J. –

unsuccessful legislative projects described,[628] and information provided on relevant foreign legislation within the continental system of law.[629] Jiří Jelínek, co-author of this subchapter published a monograph in 2007 summarizing the scholarly debate on the introduction of criminal liability of legal entities to the Czech Republic and comparing it with foreign legal systems (primarily those based on continental law).[630]

The duty to introduce criminal, or adequate non-criminal liability, for legal entities is imposed on the Czech Republic by its own Constitution, Art. 1(2)[631] stipulating that the Czech Republic is obliged to fulfil its obligations resulting from international law. The Czech Republic, in the situation when most Member States of the European Union have already incorporated the criminal liability of legal entities into their legal systems, has been exposed to even more intense pressure, primarily by international organizations (OECD, the Council of Europe, the UN, GRECO)[632] compelling the Czech Republic to comply with its international obligation in this respect. In addition to various framework decisions adopted by the Council within the so-called third pillar of the EU, this requirement has begun to be voiced in directives of the European Community (Directive 2008/99/EC of

Bartošíková, M.: Vztah obchodněprávní a trestněprávní odpovědnosti statutárních orgánů a členů statutárních orgánů [The Relationship between Business and Criminal Liability of Governing Bodies and Their Members]. *Právní praxe v podnikání* 1/1999, pp. 1–17. Šámal, P. – Púry, F. – Sotolář, A. – Štenglová, I.: *Podnikání a ekonomická kriminalita v České republice* [Undertaking Business and Economic Crime in the Czech Republic]. 1st ed., Praha: C. H. Beck, 2001, pp. 7–11. Král, V.: K trestní odpovědnosti právnických osob – východiska, obsah a systematika zákonné úpravy [On Criminal Liability of Legal Entities – Background, Contents, and the System of Legislation]. *Trestněprávní revue* 8/2002, pp. 221–223. Pipek, J.: Princip ne bis in idem v konkurenci jurisdikcí [The Principle of Ne Bis in Idem in the Conflict of Jurisdictions]. *Trestněprávní revue* 4/2004, pp. 97–107. Jalč, A.: Korupcia – trestnoprávny vývoj, rekodifikácia a trestná zodpovednosť právnických osôb [Bribery – Criminal Law Development, Recodification and Criminal Liability of Legal Entities]. *Justičná revue* 1/2005, pp. 1–8. Vaníček, D.: Trestní sankce ukládané právnickým osobám [Criminal Sanctions Imposed on Legal Entities]. *Trestní právo* 7–8/2006, pp. 12–19.
[628] Čečot, V. – Segeš, I: Trestná zodpovednosť právnických osôb? [Criminal Liability of Legal Entities?]. *Justičná revue* 1/2001, pp. 19–26. Šámal, P.: K úvodním ustanovením připravované rektifikace trestního zákona [The Introductory Provisions of the Draft of Rectification of the Criminal Code]. *Trestněprávní revue* 12/2002, pp. 349–357. Vantuch, P.: K návrhu zákona o trestní odpovědnosti právnických osob [The Draft Law on Criminal Liability of Legal Entities]. *Trestní právo* 3/2003, pp. 2–9.
[629] Kratochvíl, V: Trestní odpovědnost právnických osob a jednání za jiného (Stav de lege lata, de lege ferenda v České a Slovenské republice) [Criminal Liability of Legal Entities and Acting for Another (The Situation de Lege Lata, de Lege Ferenda in the Czech and Slovak Republics]. *Právny obzor* 4/2002, pp. 365–372. Doelder de, H.: Kriminalizace korporativního chování, možnosti trestního postihu korporace [Criminalization of Corporate Conduct, Possibilities of Punishing Corporations]. In: Kratochvíl, V. (ed.): *Trestněprávní reforma v České republice* [The Reform of Criminal Law in the Czech Republic]. Brno: Masarykova univerzita, 1994, pp. 60–68. Musil, J.: Trestní odpovědnost právnických osob v novém francouzském trestním zákoníku [Criminal Liability of Legal Entities in the New French Criminal Code]. *Kriminalistika* 4/1995, pp. 305–315. Huber, B.: Trestní odpovědnost korporací [Corporate Criminal Liability]. *Trestní právo* 9/2000, pp. 2–9. Čentéš, J. – Palkovič, J. – Štoffová, Z.: Trestná zodpovednosť právnických osôb [Criminal Liability of Legal Entities]. *Justičná revue* 4/2001, pp. 416–423. Čentéš, J. – Štoffová, Z.: Trestná zodpovednosť právnických osôb v Belgicku [Criminal Liability of Legal Entities in Belgium]. *Justičná revue* 10/2001, pp. 990–999. Čentéš, J. – Palkovič, J. – Štoffová, Z.: Trestná zodpovednosť právnických osôb v slovinskom právnom poriadku [Criminal Liability of Legal Entities in the Slovenian Legal Order]. *Trestní právo* 5/2002, pp. 8–12. Madliak, J. – Porada, V. – Bruna, E.: Niekoľko úvah o trestnej zodpovednosti právnických osôb v podmienkach SR [Several Remarks on Criminal Liability of Legal Entities in the Slovak Republic]. *Karlovarská právní revue* 3/2006, pp. 26–29. Príbelský, P.: Trestná zodpovednosť právnických osôb v Rakúsku [Criminal Liability of Legal Entities in Austria]. *Trestněprávní revue* 1/2007, pp. 12–18.
[630] Jelínek, J.: *Trestní odpovědnost právnických osob* [Criminal Liability of Legal Entities]. Praha: Linde, 2007.
[631] Constitutional Act No. 1/1993 Sb., the Constitution of the Czech Republic.
[632] Group of States against Corruption.

the European Parliament and of the Council of 19 November 2008 on the protection of the environment through criminal law).

The aim of this subchapter is not to deal with individual theoretical aspects supporting or rebutting the regulation of the criminal liability of legal entities. Its purpose is to describe various legislative initiatives introduced in the Czech Republic in the past so that the criminal liability of legal entities could be incorporated in the legal system, to explain reasons why these initiatives have not been successful, and to propose ways of possible legislative solution of this issue. This subchapter deals with the description of an unsuccessful legislative project of a separate law on the criminal liability of legal entities and proceedings against them.[633] The explanation of the basic conception of the Bill and its basic institutions is followed by reasons why this Bill was refused by the Parliament of the Czech Republic. The next parts then contain considerations of further legislative procedure where the possibility of administrative liability or a combination of administrative and criminal liability of legal entities is debated.

3.4.2 Bill on the criminal liability of legal entities
The Bill on the criminal liability of legal entities considered by the Chamber of Deputies of the Parliament of the Czech Republic in the first reading on 2nd November 2004 was intended to be the response to international and European requirements for introducing the liability of legal entities for criminal wrongs; it was brought in at the time when not many states in the region had adopted such regulation. The Bill was part of extensive recodification of Czech criminal substantive law (and partly criminal procedure) formed by the draft of the new Criminal Code, the Bill amending legislation relating to the adoption of the Criminal Code and the Bill on the criminal liability of legal entities. Although the first two drafts were immediately referred for consideration in committees of the Chamber of Deputies and then submitted for the approval in the second reading, the Bill on the criminal liability of legal entities faced a different approach. As early as in the first reading the Bill was subject to devastating criticism not only by the opposition but also by the coalition; it was outvoted by a count of 69 to 43 of 125 deputies present. It is also quite alarming that only 125 out of 200 deputies took part in consideration of such an important draft law; the vote was cast by only 112 deputies.

3.4.3 Substantive law aspects of the Bill
The draft law on the criminal liability of legal entities was built upon their actual criminal liability. This means that legal entities were supposed to be subject to criminal punishments (except for imprisonment) as are individuals.[634] Typologically such an approach to the liability of legal entities can be designated as the model of so-called "vicarious liability"; however, this model was modified, or complemented with certain elements of the original

---

[633] The Parliament of the Czech Republic. The Chamber of Deputies. 2004. 4th term. Parliamentary print No. 745 – the Government Bill on criminal liability of legal entities and proceedings against them ("Bill on criminal liability of legal entities", BCLLE).
[634] Kratochvíl, V. *supra* 2002 at p. 366.

liability of legal entities.[635] Under s. 5 (1) BCLLE, unlawful conduct committed on an entity's behalf, in its interests or against its interests or in the interests of another, could be imputed to the legal entity. Such conduct would include not only that of its governing bodies and top management members but also its representatives (agents). Next, the legal entity could have been assigned a crime committed by individuals performing their controlling and managing functions provided that their conduct had established causal nexus between the conduct and the consequences of the crime. However, the liability of a legal entity was constructed in such an extensive way that a legal entity could have been criminally liable for the conducts of its employees; this was partly rectified by subsection (2) stipulating that criminal liability could have arisen for the legal entity only if its bodies or above-mentioned persons had decided to commit a crime, had approved or ordered it (paragraph a). Subsection (1) is an apparent manifestation of the vicarious liability model where a legal entity is ascribed conduct of natural persons acting not only as its "governing mind" but also as individual employees. Subsection (2) in its paragraph b) introduced the element of original liability where liability arises as a result of cumulative conduct of an individual employee and negligent conduct of the legal entity (its bodies or representatives) subsisting in insufficient control or supervision. Therefore it cannot be argued that the criminal liability of a legal entity was constructed in BCLLE upon so-called no fault liability; it is not true that the legal entity would be criminally liable for its acts arising irrespective of "conduct imputable to the legal entity".[636]

Under the refused BCLLE there was no requirement for establishing the criminal liability of a legal entity to ascertain a concrete natural person whose conduct could have been imputed to the legal entity; thus, there was no requirement for conducting simultaneous or cumulative criminal proceedings against the natural person. The criminal liability of a legal entity was not hindered by the fact that an acting individual himself was not criminally

---

[635]/ Section 5 (1) and (2) BCLLE:

(1) A crime committed by a legal entity is the crime committed in its name, in its interests, against or in the interests of another, where such a crime accomplishes the elements of any offence listed in s. 4, and may be imputed to the legal entity, should the act have been committed by

a) the governing body or a member thereof;

b) a person authorized to act on behalf of the legal entity or as its representative;

c) a person performing, within the legal entity, managing or controlling functions should his conduct have been at least one of requirements giving rise to criminal liability of the legal entity; or

d) an employee in the course of fulfilling his employment duties.

(2) The commission of a crime listed in s. 4 of this Act may be imputed to a legal entity if

a) the crime has been committed as a result of the decision, approval or instruction of its bodies under (1) a), b) or c), or

b) the crime has been committed because the bodies under (1) a), b) or c), have failed to take measures that they should have taken under the law or that may have been reasonably required, particularly, the bodies have failed to pursue obligatory or necessary control over activities of their employees or other inferior persons, or the bodies have failed to take necessary precautions to avoid or prevent the consequences of the crime committed.

[636]/ See the Explanatory Report on BCLLE which reads: "Such liability based upon the imputability of a crime to a legal entity should be understood as special liability based on fault of a legal entity, which differs from the guilt (fault) of a natural person, but it should not be maintained that such liability is strict (no-fault) (in its essence this type of liability – liability for quasi-wrong – is similar to that constructed in s. 337 of the draft criminal code regarding the crime of drunkenness, or in s. 201 of the existing Criminal Code regarding the same offence). Such construction of a crime requires both the connection with the commission of a crime and taking into account the nature of a legal entity whose interests may differ from those of an individual."

liable. Criminal liability was not conditional upon any profit attained by the legal entity as a result of wrongful conduct.

BCLLE failed to define the perpetrator – a legal entity; thus, it was necessary to use the definition provided by civil and business law.[637] The draft even presumed the criminal liability of a non-existing entity as provisions for imputation of conduct of natural persons was intended to be used in the case when the crime had been committed before the legal existence of a company. Similarly, the provisions applied to the invalidity of a company[638] and to cases when the legal act intended to constitute authority to act on behalf of the legal entity was invalid or ineffective. The draft also stipulated the criminal liability of a successor of the legal entity should it have known of the crime or could have known due to the circumstances of the case.

On the other hand, the Czech Republic,[639] its territorial self-governing units – regions and communities, as well as the Czech National Bank were immune from criminal liability under the draft. Such construction seems to be quite understandable as one can hardly imagine that the state would prosecute itself, or that the state would prosecute its political subdivisions established thereby.[640] However, the immunity did not cover legal entities in the activities of which the above-mentioned criminally immune public corporations participated, or those legal entities which managed or administered the property of the public corporations.

BCLLE provided an exhaustive list of crimes to determine the scope of the criminal liability of legal entities. The range of crimes was quite wide since it included more than 130 offences belonging to all titles of the special part of the Criminal Code except for crimes against conscription duties and military crimes. Thus, a legal entity could commit various offences ranging from rape and sexual abuse, through environmental offences to economic crime. It was a very wide and definite set of crimes far exceeding in its volume the set of crimes whose prosecution was binding on the Czech Republic by international treaties. The selection of this extensive alternative to be considered by Parliament appears to have been a mistake.[641]

The principle of personality applicable to natural persons was replaced by the principle of incorporation which was modified in that it was sufficient when the legal entity had its registered office or organizational unit (branch) in the Czech Republic, or it performed

---

[637] For more details see s. 18 and subs. of Act No. 40/1964 Sb., the Civil Code, as amended, and s. 56 of Act No. 513/1991 Sb., the Commercial Code, as amended.

[638] S. 68a of the Commercial Code.

[639] Beran, K.: Proč není stát právnickou osobou? [Why Is the State Not a Legal Entity?]. *Právní rozhledy* 7/2006, pp. 255–261.

[640] Beran, K.: *Právnické osoby veřejného práva* [Legal Entities in Public Law]. Praha: Linde, 2006.

[641] The second alternative contained a narrower set of offences, approx. 70, as it encompassed only types of criminal conduct whose prosecution was necessary under a duty imposed on the Czech Republic in international treaties. The third alternative, designated as not fully relevant by the sponsor himself in the Explanatory Report, subsisted in the reference to the Criminal Code which stipulates that a legal entity is criminally responsible for conduct "unless the nature of the crime itself excludes it." Such an approach would be quite advantageous due to potential amendments of the Criminal Code and expansion of the catalogues of respective crimes. Thus it would not be necessary to simultaneously amend BCLLE and the Criminal Code in order to extend the list of crimes attributable to legal entities. This advantage, on the other hand, would probably fail to balance the disadvantage of legal uncertainty in determining what conduct may be, due to its nature, considered as a crime of a legal entity.

its business or had its property located in the Czech Republic. Legal entities not fulfilling the above-mentioned requirements (i.e. foreign entities without property and not doing business in the Czech Republic) were excluded from the applicability of BCLEE even where they committed a crime in the Czech territory. Thus, the usual scope of territorial applicability of the Criminal Code was reduced in BCLLE. This rule, however, should not have applied to crimes committed for the benefit of an entrepreneur – a natural person or a legal entity having its registered office, branch, shop or place of business in the Czech Republic, although the crime had been committed outside the territory of the CR; the rule should not have applied to crimes stipulated by a binding international treaty.

BCLLE also included criminal cooperation in preparing and committing a crime in the form of counselling, aiding and organizing. These modes of criminal cooperation were subject to the provisions of the Criminal Code as subsidiary legislation.

3.4.4 Sanctions and protective measures

The third title of BCLLE governed punishments and protective measures. The draft stipulated general principles of sentencing which were intended to serve as a guide for courts when determining the type and scope of punishment; courts should have considered "*internal and external relations of the legal entity including its recent activities and property situation ...*". This rule clearly shows that sentencing was also based upon issues which may not be considered in sentencing individuals. External relations of a legal entity encompass, for example, its significance regarding employment in the respective region or its involvement in some activities beneficial for the public. Courts were expected to obligatorily consider these aspects when deciding on the punishment to be imposed upon the legal entity; but decision making with respect to the commission of a particular crime by the legal entity, i.e. the issue of its guilt in the procedural sense of the word, was not prejudiced thereby.

BCLLE introduced both monetary and non-monetary sanctions. The monetary sanction allowed for an amount ranging between CZK 1,000 to 1,000,000 per day; forfeiture of property was another type of punishment applicable to cases where the legal entity had obtained (or intended to have obtained) any property benefit as a result of the crime committed. Unlike the original proposal, BCLLE did not contain a provision distinguishing between property acquired due to the crime and other property, the former to be subject to the forfeiture, the latter to be used, for example, in bankruptcy or insolvency proceedings to reimburse creditors. Another type of punishment primarily applicable to natural persons was included in BCLLE, namely forfeiture of a particular item of property; the respective provision stipulated that where a legal entity was subject to bankruptcy proceedings "*only addictive and psychotropic substances or any other items may be forfeited which endanger the safety of persons or property*". Where the activities of a legal entity subsisted primarily or only in the commission of a crime or crimes the court might impose upon the entity the punishment of dissolving the legal entity. This punishment was not applicable to entities established by a law. Other non-monetary penalties included the prohibition of activities; this sentence, if to be imposed upon banking institutions, insurance companies, reinsurance companies and other entities in the capital market, required an official opinion of the state body in charge of issuing relevant licences or any other types of authorization for those legal entities. The opinion was not binding on the court but the court should have considered and dealt with it in the reasoning of its judgment. The last types of punishment were the ban on a legal entity's participation in the government contract bidding and public tenders, the ban on a legal entity's acceptance of grants and subsidies, and the reputational punishment of publishing the respective judgment in mass media.

3.4.5 Procedural aspects of BCLLE

As suggested by the title of the draft, BCLLE included special provisions for criminal proceedings with the Criminal Procedure Act being the general law. In the course of preparation of BCLLE, a proposal based on the principle of opportunity (i.e. the principle of expediency) of criminal proceedings was refused; thus, the principle of officiality (duty to prosecute by virtue of office) was maintained. Similarly, most principles of criminal procedure applicable to the prosecution of crimes of individuals applied to legal entities as well, such as the principles of legality, economy and speedy trial, publicity, etc.

A legal entity was supposed to possess the same rights in proceedings as an individual did unless the nature of legal entities excluded them (e.g. the institutions of custody and detention and rights relating thereto were inapplicable); the exception was the institution of mandatory defence which was not stipulated with respect to legal entities. A legal entity had a duty to be represented in proceedings by a representative determined upon, or even without, the application of the legal entity. The representative was only a natural person authorized to perform all acts envisaged for the accused person by the Criminal Procedure Act. Thus, the representative acted on behalf of the legal entity within the scope of all rights and duties of the accused. Simultaneously, a legal entity could hire its own defence counsel. The generally applicable principle of criminal procedure "*nemo tenetur se ipsum accusare*"[642] was functioning only partly with respect to the legal entity since its full scope could be enjoyed just by its representative. Other natural persons through which the legal entity acted (members of governing bodies, agents under powers of attorney, etc.) did not enjoy the rights and duties of an accused person (unless these persons were prosecuted as co-offenders), thus having the position of witnesses in proceedings. The following reasons could justify such an approach: should the opposite be chosen, investigative, prosecuting and adjudicating bodies would face a lack of evidence, especially when there is no formal burden of proving introduced in Czech criminal procedure which might partly result in the shifting of the burden of proving to the legal entity; the Czech procedural rules prefer the investigative principle and the principle "*in dubio pro reo*".[643] [644]

BCLLE also contained provisions relating to the enforcement of newly introduced types of punishments.

---

[642]/ No one is bound to incriminate himself.
[643]/ When in doubt, in favour of the accused.
[644]/ Kuchta, J.: Trestní řízení proti právnickým osobám z pohledu některých zásad trestního práva procesního. [Criminal Proceedings against Legal Entities from the Viewpoint of Some Principles of Criminal Procedure.] In: Neckář, J. – Radvan, M. – Sehnálek, D. – Valdhans, J. (eds.): *Acta Universitatis Brunensis Iuridica No. 337*. Brno: Masarykova univerzita, 2008, p. 1745.

3.4.6 Reasons for refusal

As suggested earlier, BCLLE was subject to extensive criticism as early as in the first reading in the Chamber of Deputies.[645] The criticism was directed against the actual foundations of the draft as well as against particular provisions. Some deputies claimed that the regulation of the criminal liability of legal entities was redundant, alien to Czech law, introducing a diversion from the criminal liability of natural persons, which Czech criminal law had been built upon for hundreds of years. The draft was mostly criticized for its "hypertrophy" of criminalization of legal entities, particularly with respect to a wide range of wrongful conduct of natural persons attributable to the legal entity. All those presenting their negative opinions in the parliamentary debate argued that a legal entity could not be criminally liable for many crimes enumerated in the draft, particularly for those whose criminal nature was not stipulated by international or European obligations. Examples of such crimes were given: sexual coercion, detriment caused to the right of another, sexual abuse, spreading of an infectious disease, inciting an aggressive war, poachery or spreading of false news (hoaxing), in particular where it was possible to prosecute a concrete natural person who had committed the crime at issue. The wide scope of imputability of crimes to a legal entity expecting that the legal entity would be held criminally liable for conduct of its employees would make it possible to attribute to the legal entity practically any crime irrespective of its remoteness, and it in fact created no-fault liability of a legal entity without any chance for this entity to exonerate or liberate. The combination of these two factors could lead to the criminalization of business. The criminal liability of a legal entity could also become a tool for an unfair competition fight.[646]

Another aspect of BCLLE also subject to criticism was the issue of collective guilt. Some deputies argued that the regulation of the criminal liability of legal entities would include individuals who had not participated in the actual commission of a crime and therefore could not have been held liable, such as ordinary employees or small shareholders.[647]

The criticism was also directed against provisions for types of punishment and procedural fines. For example, it was noted that the rate of monetary penalty was fixed as an amount per day but the duration of penalty (or its maximum number) was not stipulated in the draft; thus a question was raised whether it was virtually possible to impose a monetary penalty for an indefinite time. The provision for punishing a legal entity by publishing a judgment against it in mass media was subject to criticism, particularly because it stipulated the maximum fine (of up to CZK 500,000) for the legal entity's failure to publish the judgment, although the act of publishing itself (not the application therefor) would be independent of the will of the convicted entity.[648]

The sentence of the ban on activities (primarily long-term ban) was opposed with arguments that such sentence would practically mean a concealed liquidation of the convicted

---

[645]/ Parliament of the Czech Republic. The Chamber of Deputies. 4th term. Transcripts 37, session on 2nd November 2004. Digital library, http://www.psp.cz/eknih/2002ps/stenprot/037schuz/s037044.htm, retrieved on 12th May 2009.
[646]/ *Ibidem.*
[647]/ *Ibidem.*
[648]/ *Ibidem.*

legal entity; a company making business in a narrow field would hardly be able to return to business after, for example, fifteen years of such a ban.[649]

The draft, according to its opponents, attempted to introduce unequal positions (a) among entities of public law (some bodies exempt from the applicability of BCLLE); (b) among legal entities themselves (entities on the capital market, requiring a banking or other licence for their business under the special law, would enjoy increased protection since in order to sentence them the opinion of the relevant state body deciding on such licences was considered); and (c) between natural persons and legal entities (the latter would be liable without individual fault, would be given higher procedural fines and monetary penalties, etc.).[650]

Some opposing arguments can be accepted, and some not. It should be taken into account, however, that debate over BCLLE was carried out at a time when only one third of the EU Member States had the criminal liability of legal entities introduced into their legal systems. Central Europe was, in this respect, represented by Poland and Slovenia; the Polish regulation of imputability of a crime committed by a natural person to a legal entity is not as wide as it was proposed in BCLLE. In addition, the Polish law set forth that the criminal liability of a particular legal entity is conditional upon the ruling of guilt of the acting natural person (except for conditional discontinuance of criminal prosecution or discontinuance of prosecution due to reasons excluding the sentencing of a perpetrator).[651]

International requirements of that time to introduce the criminal liability of legal entities were not so extensive and did not deal with so many types of criminal conduct as they do today. It is quite likely that should the Czech draft have been introduced in Parliament after the passage of the Austrian law in 2005[652] extending the liability of legal entities even to all crimes and attributing to a legal entity conduct of the scope of natural persons similar to that defined in BCLLE, the Czech draft would not have faced such a strong and one-sided opposition.

The dismissal of BCLLE by the Chamber of Deputies has resulted in continuing applicability of the existing law where legal entities can be held responsible under (a) civil law rules (liability for damage, defects, etc.) and (b) the rules of imposing administrative sanctions, which are scattered over (and hidden in) an enormous number of special laws. The Commercial Code[653] provides for separate public liability *sui generis* with respect to business companies and cooperatives, subsisting in the dissolution of a company or cooperative due to serious breaches of the law circumscribed by the Code. However, such regulation of liability for wrongs (delictual liability) does not fulfil the requirements of international documents and European legislation. The general regulation of proceedings of administrative wrongs (delicts) of legal entities is also missing.

---

[649]/ *Ibidem.*
[650]/ See the course of the whole debate in the source quoted.
[651]/ Art. 3 and 4 of Act No. 197/2002 Dz. U., regulating the liability of mass entities for prohibited acts subject to punishment.
[652]/ Ss. 1 and 2 of the Federal Act No. 151/2005, Federal Law Gazette Austria, on the responsibility of associations.
[653]/ S. 68 (3) d) and subsection (6), s. 254 (2) c), s. 257 (1) of Act No. 513/1991 Sb., the Commercial Code.

3.4.7 The outline of the law on the liability of legal entities for administrative delicts

The years following the dismissal did not pay much attention to legislative attempts to deal with delictual liability of legal entities. Unlike the original concepts of real criminal liability of legal entities, the German alternative of non-criminal (administrative) liability of legal entities was preferred. As late as in January 2008, the Government in its resolution entitled "On the conception of the fight against organized crime" of 23rd January 2008, No. 64, imposed on the Minister of the Interior a duty to submit, by 31st December 2008, an outline of the subject-matter of a law introducing into the legal system of the Czech Republic administrative liability of legal entities for wrongful conduct, prosecution of which is required by international treaties on the fight against organized crime.

On 16th December 2008, the Ministry submitted to interdepartmental comment procedure "The outline of the law on the liability of legal entities for administrative delicts caused by conduct punished as a crime if perpetrated by natural persons, and the punishment of which is required by international treaties or the legislation of the European Communities" (the Outline). The Outline (after introducing the reasons for the regulation of the delictual liability of legal entities) analyses certain alternatives of solution, including a "zero" alternative; all of them are subsequently compared. The alternatives are as follows:

a) Introducing criminal liability;
b) Regulating the issue within administrative law;
c) Finding solution in both administrative and criminal law.

The "zero" alternative suggesting that no new regulation would be made was refused at the very beginning.

3.4.8 The alternative of criminal liability of legal entities

The Outline considers this alternative to be the most suitable solution, i.e. the regulation of the delictual liability of legal entities within criminal law. Such solution would best respond to the international and European requirements and facilitate effective cooperation in criminal matters. Due to the earlier dismissal of BCLLE by the Chamber of Deputies the Outline has focussed on the other two alternatives in the area of administrative law and the combination of administrative and criminal law.

3.4.9 The alternative of administrative liability of legal entities

Regulation of liability solely in the area of administrative law is found in the Outline to be problematic in many respects. Primarily, the limited possibilities of international cooperation are a disadvantage. There are no relevant international treaties concluded in the field of administrative sentencing which would facilitate international legal assistance; should any treaties be concluded the Czech Republic is not their contracting party, or such treaties require that the respective delicts be tried by (criminal) courts. Administrative bodies would not be allowed to use request and other institutions of international legal assistance, which would be inconsistent with obligations under international treaties requiring the effective prosecution of unlawful behaviour of legal entities committed abroad, because the absence of these efficient tools of legal assistance would render the criminal prosecution hardly practicable.

Another problematic issue in this type of regulation within administrative law subsists in a certain inefficiency of the whole conception where the same conduct would be subject to the decision-making of investigative, prosecuting and adjudicating bodies in criminal proceedings against a natural person and, simultaneously, subject to the consideration of administrative bodies in proceedings to determine the liability of a legal entity. Many steps taken in these two types of proceedings would be repeated. There is a related question to be solved, namely what bodies would be competent to decide on delicts of legal entities since no administrative body having general jurisdiction over such cases exists in the Czech Republic. Customs authorities may be taken into consideration as they are endowed with law enforcement powers and have lost a substantial portion of their duties as a result of the membership of the Czech Republic in the European Community and its joining the Schengen area. However, the Minister of Finance maintains that the extension of respon-sibilities of customs authorities to include deciding on delicts, which are considered crimes if committed by natural persons, would not be possible since these authorities lack the required professional, personnel and material background. The establishing of brand new administrative authorities specialized in this area appears to be rather uneconomical.

For all these reasons the solution to confine the issue just to administrative law has been found improper; thus the Ministry of the Interior has been inclined to favour alternative C, which is also widely analysed in the Outline.

3.4.10 Alternative of combined administrative and criminal liability of legal entities

The C alternative subsists in the regulation of substantive law aspects (individual elements of delicts and other conditions for the liability of legal entities) in administrative law as well as procedural issues in criminal law. Administrative delicts (wrongs) would be dealt with by investigative, prosecuting and adjudicating bodies and sanctions would be imposed by criminal courts. This alternative is preferred in the Outline because it eliminates the above-mentioned disadvantages of liability under administrative law, i.e. it allows for international cooperation in the area of wrongs committed by legal entities, it facilitates the use of inves-tigative institutions of criminal law (searches and seizures) in relation to the constitutional right to defence;[654] it seems to be the most effective of the three alternatives.

The liability of legal entities is drafted in the Outline as liability for "culpable" conduct of the legal entity itself. The fault of a legal entity is determined in cases identical with those stipulated in BCLLE where the conduct of a natural person could be imputed to a legal entity but this conduct must always be in the interests of the legal entity.

The scope of criminalization (the number of sets of elements) contained in the Outline is narrower than that in BCLLE. Only subject to punishment are those types of conduct which are contained in international documents and European legislation; the final draft of

---

[654]/ Art. 40 of the Charter of Fundamental Rights and Freedoms.

the law should directly contain typological elements of conduct as regulated by international treaties (legislation of the European Community or European Union, EC/EU) along with reference to relevant articles in those legal documents.

Cessation of the liability of a legal entity should be tied to the lapse of a subjective time-limit of one year from the date when an administrative body becomes aware of the commission of an administrative delict, or to the lapse of an objective time-limit of 10 or 15 years from the date when the administrative delict was committed. Most other aspects (territorial and personal applicability of the law, transition of liability to a legal successor or separation of proceedings against a legal entity from those against a natural person) follow the regulation contained in BCLLE. The selection of sanctions is also identical with that contained in the original Bill on criminal liability of legal entities; what differs is the determination of individual rates of monetary penalty (fine), which is not fixed as a daily rate but scaled according to the term of imprisonment applicable to corresponding crimes with respect to natural persons. The Outline also uses quite a special construction when individual elements of delicts are mentioned in reference to the wording of relevant international treaties and European legislation: the definitions of corresponding crimes are not included but the rates of penalties are derived from the rates of punishments available for the commission of those crimes. The decision-making body will be allowed to impose a penalty lower than the statutory rate, but lower only to a certain extent, scaled according to the rates of punishment for corresponding crimes. The punishment of the ban on activities will not be imposed for a time period longer than five years and the activities required from a legal entity by the law will not be subject to any ban.

Since the Outline proposes that administrative delicts of legal entities will be dealt with by investigative, prosecuting and adjudicating bodies, it will be necessary to amend the relevant provisions of procedural legislation. Primarily, amendments or alterations should be made with respect to the Criminal Procedure Act in order to establish the jurisdiction of investigative, prosecuting and adjudicating bodies for administrative delicts of legal entities. The provisions for jurisdiction should be complemented, as well as provisions for joint proceedings regarding a crime committed by a natural person and the administrative delict of a legal entity, provisions for searches and seizures or a court's duty to inform. Finally, in the regulation of enforcement procedure, it will be necessary to take into account the modes and concrete conditions for the enforcement of administrative punishments imposed. The concrete regulation would probably follow the dismissed BCLLE.[655]

3.4.11 Issues in the Outline subject to criticism

Similar to BCLLE several years ago, the Outline was subject to devastating criticism, this time as early as during the comment procedure. Essential comments were made by the Minister chairing the Legislative Council of the Government and the Minister of Justice. In addition to some legislative and technical comments the opponents argue that the C alternative actually appears to be the conception of criminal liability of legal entities regulated in a special law and formally designated as liability for administrative delicts. They argue that

---

[655]/ See above.

no administrative liability arises where the case is not decided by administrative authorities. The Outline in the C alternative created an artificial construction fully alien to the Czech legal order and intended just to cover the criminal substance of the liability of legal entities, apparently in order to avoid dismissal in Parliament, as was the case of BCLLE.

The Minister of Justice argues that the Outline fails to contain an alternative in the field of administrative law, which would be fully compatible with international treaties and European legislation; such solution appears to be practicable if, for example, a first instance case was tried by administrative bodies and the appeal was heard by criminal courts. Administrative authorities would have efficient tools available (in special cases with the approval of court) to conduct effective procedure while using evidence obtained and collected by investigative bodies. In addition to many other material defects, the Minister of Justice considers inappropriate the formulation of physical elements (actus reus) of delicts through typological elements contained in international treaties or EC/EU legislation, particularly because the terminology used in international documents differs from that used in Czech law; references to individual articles of international treaties could cause many problems in application not only in state bodies but also for the recipients of legal rules; this could be incompatible with the requirement of transparency and determinacy of a legal rule. There is no reason why the elements of individual delicts cannot be defined in reference to corresponding crimes.

3.4.12 Proposals for the direction of future legislative attempts

The Minister chairing the Legislative Council of the Government (similarly to many other proponents of comments) finds as the best solution to leave the existing proposals for regulation within administrative law and to redraft a bill introducing the criminal liability of legal entities; only such regulation would be fully in compliance with international obligations and seems to be more efficient if compared to administrative law. The criminal liability of legal entities has been incorporated in the legal systems of many EU Member States and has been sufficiently elaborated in scholarly publications. When preparing the new proposal it would be highly desirable to take the opinions and comments on BCLLE into account and to adjust to them, for example, by reducing the scope of criminalization of legal entities or altering the imputability of conduct.

Having discussed the comments and after a common meeting with the Ministry of Justice and the Office of the Government, the Ministry of the Interior concluded that the proposed C alternative should not be recommended to the Government for approval. The future legal regulation of delictual liability of legal entities should be based on criminal law (alternative A), or administrative law, which would have to comply with the obligations imposed by international treaties and EC/EU legislation (modified alternative B). Even if alternative B has been modified in the required way (e.g. according to the comments by the Minister of Justice), its other drawbacks will survive, particularly its higher complexity, lower efficiency and higher costs. This is the reason why the work on the Outline has been suspended. A new decision of the Government will be necessary whether to continue the proposal of administrative liability of legal entities, or to return to the originally proposed concept within criminal law. Due to the recent political situation in the Czech Republic, where a caretaker government was appointed, it is hard to predict when the required decision may be adopted. Under these circumstances, enactment of delictual liability of legal entities appears to be unattainable.

3.4.13 Conclusion

The issue of criminal or any other corresponding type of liability of legal entities has been topical also in the Czech Republic. The absence of the liability of legal entities is more and more perceived as a debt owed by the Czech legislature to international recommendations and obligations. For example, the Criminal Law Convention on Corruption (No. 70/2002 Sb.m.s.) relies in its Art. 18 on the duty of contracting states to pass a legislative measure introducing the liability of legal entities for crimes of corruption. A similar provision (Art. 2) is contained in the Convention on Combating Bribery of Foreign Public Officials in International Business Transactions (No. 25/2000 Sb.m.s.). Criminal liability of legal entities is envisaged in many Framework Decisions of the Council of the EU and, recently, in the Directive on the protection of the environment through criminal law.[656]

The preparatory work to introduce liability for legal entities into Czech law originally focussed on pure criminal liability. This was the approach of the first Bill on the criminal liability of legal entities presented in Parliament for approval in 2004. Criminal liability was drafted in this proposal in a scope much wider than was usual at that time. The Bill was subject to strong criticism and subsequently dismissed in the first reading.

The legislative work was then directed to the concept of administrative liability. However, with problems occurring quite soon it was clear that the creation of a model of administrative liability similar to that used in Germany would be very difficult, primarily due to its high costs, lower efficiency and difficult applicability of instruments of international cooperation. A "hybrid" concept was also unsuccessful; its main aim was to mend the problems connected with the administrative alternative. The Government of the Czech Republic should issue a new and essential decision on the new direction of the legislative work in the area of liability of legal entities. However, it is obvious that the Government should not stop trying to adopt the relevant legislation either in criminal or administrative law. The attitude to the contrary would further increase the international pressure to introduce delictual liability of legal entities; it could also lead to proceedings for the breach of the TEC under Art. 226 and subsequent provisions of TEC.

Considering individual alternatives of regulation we are inclined to support pure criminal liability of legal entities as the solution apparently least complicated, ensuring the fulfilment of international obligations even for the future, and quite usual in other EU Member States. Due to the preceding failure of BCLLE in the Chamber of Deputies we suggest that the proposal should be drafted in a way making legal entities liable only for those types of conduct whose punishment results from international treaties and EC/EU legislation. In addition, the possibility to impute the conduct of an employee to the legal entity should be at least partially restricted. What appears to be appropriate is to determine the

---

[656]/ Directive 2008/99/EC of the European Parliament and of the Council of 19 November 2008 on the protection of the environment through criminal law.

scope of criminal sanctions as widely as possible, the individual rates and scales being set sufficiently wide in order to facilitate just and reasonable sentencing of a liable legal entity.

3.5 TAX LAW IN THE CZECH REPUBLIC IN THE CONTEXT OF THE LAW OF THE EUROPEAN UNION

3.5.1 Tax law in the Czech Republic

Tax law is fundamentally relating to the term "tax". When defining tax law we should proceed from the definition of the term "tax". Everyone is aware of the existence of taxes. This is so because taxes concern every single person and everybody is supposed to pay them. In this connection, we can mention Benjamin Franklin's well-known quotation: "Nothing is certain but death and taxes." What are the means by which taxes can be classified and defined?

Taxes are usually described as obligatory charges that the state imposes by the law to gain revenues for the coverage of the needs of society, i.e. for public budgets, without providing any equivalent consideration to the taxed person. A conceptual characteristic of taxes is its irretrievability.[657]

At present the main features of taxes are the following:

a) irretrievability,
b) non-purposefulness (absence of any special purpose),
c) non-voluntariness (obligation to pay taxes),
d) legality (taxes can be imposed only in accordance with the law),
e) taxes are imposed by the state or other public corporations,
f) determination of tax yield as revenues going to the public budget, and
g) the absence of immediate consideration provided by public authorities.

From the above mentioned the following definition of taxes may be inferred: Taxes are non-purposeful and irretrievable obligatory payments imposed, under the law, by the state or other public bodies, the revenue of which goes into the public budget whilst for the payment of taxes no immediate consideration is provided.

The set of legal rules by which taxes are regulated may be designated as tax law. Tax law is most frequently defined as a subsection of financial law.[658]

In this connection, we should point out that the authorial team led by Professor Babčák from the Faculty of Law in Košice (Slovakia), takes the legal opinion that tax law has already separated from financial law and established itself as an autonomous legal branch of the Slovak legal order.[659] Tax law is thus comprehended as an autonomous legal branch. Even in foreign countries there are no identical opinions on the issue of whether tax law is a part

---

[657]/ Bakeš, M. – Karfíková, M. – Kotáb, P. – Marková, H.: *Finanční právo* [Financial Law]. 5th ed., Praha: C. H. Beck, 2009, p. 154.

[658]/ See, for example, Bakeš, M. – Karfíková, M. – Kotáb, P. – Marková, H. *ibidem*, or Mrkývka, P. et al.: *Finanční právo a finanční správa* [Financial Law and Financial Administration]. Vol. I, Brno: Masarykova univerzita, 2004.

[659]/ Babčák et al.: *Daňové právo* [The Law of the Taxation]. Košice: Univerzita Pavla Josefa Šáfarika, 2005.

of financial law or if it has established an autonomous legal branch.[660] Opinions favoring the idea that tax law is an integral part of financial law still prevail.[661]

Viewing tax law as an autonomous legal discipline can undoubtedly be marked as a "new phenomenon in law on the threshold of the 21st century". Financial law jurisprudence should definitely tackle this issue in the near future.

The essential concept of Czech tax law is the term "tax system". Tax system is defined as an aggregate of all taxes in any particular state.[662] The specification of taxes which will become part of the tax system is within the competence of a legislative body; however, the above mentioned constitutional rules for imposing taxes, fees and other obligatory payments should be observed.

After the accession of the Czech Republic to the European Union in 2004 the Czech constitutional rules are not the only rules which the legislature should comply with. Under Art. 10a (1) of the Constitution of the Czech Republic certain powers of the authorities of the Czech Republic may be transferred to international organizations or institutions, as specified by an international treaty. According to the explanatory note substantiating the draft amendment to the Constitution of the Czech Republic, by which the provision of Art. 10a (1) was included into the Constitution of the Czech Republic, this constitutional provision was to prepare the Czech Republic for its EU or EC membership, especially from the point of view of the accession of the state to this supranational organization. This is a standard integration article containing the mandate to transfer certain powers from the constitutional authorities to the international institution.[663] It is obvious that the legislature, while imposing taxes, is bound to respect obligations of the Czech Republic arising from its membership in the European Union or in the European Communities.

The so-called energy taxes[664] can be mentioned as an example: the introduction of these taxes into the Czech legal order was part of the duty of the Czech Republic to transpose relevant directives, since Art. 1, Council Directive 2003/96/EC, restructuring the Community framework for the taxation of energy products and electricity, as amended, explicitly reads: "*Member States shall impose taxation on energy products and electricity in accordance with this Directive*".

The tax system in the Czech Republic has until recently been regulated by Act No. 212/1992 Sb., on the system of taxes, as amended by Act No. 302/1993 Sb., which was, effective as of January 12, 2004, repealed by Act No. 353/2003 Sb., on excise taxes. In consequence, the current legal order of the Czech Republic does not contain a law explicitly providing for taxes that can be imposed in the Czech Republic. This situation is not surprising, though, since Act No. 212/1992 Sb. was not a Constitutional Act but just an "ordinary" one, it could have been amended at any time reflecting the existing needs.

---

[660]/ Blumenstein, L.: *System des schweizerischen Steuerrechts*. Zürich: Schultness, 2002, p. 16.

[661]/ For example, Tipke, L.: *Steuerrecht*. Köln: Verlag Dr. Otto Schmidt, 2005, p. 4, Amann, R.: *German Tax Guide*. The Hague: Kluwer Law International, 1997, p. 3, or Kosikowski, C.: *Prawo finansowe. Ogólna Częśc*. Warszawa: Dum wydawniczy ABC, 2003, pp. 39–40.

[662]/ Bakeš, M. – Karfíková, M. – Kotáb, P. – Marková, H. *supra* at p. 155.

[663]/ Constitutional Act No. 395/2001 Sb., amending the Constitutional Act of the Czech National Council No. 1/1993 Sb., the Constitution of the Czech Republic, as amended.

[664]/ Energy taxes are sometimes called ecological or environmental taxes.

The tax system is composed of direct and indirect taxes. Direct taxes affect the taxable income at its source and there is no possibility to pass the tax duty on to another individual or entity. Direct taxes can be subdivided into direct income taxes, the object of which is the revenue (income), and direct property taxes, the object of which is the estate, in abeyance or in transfer. On the contrary, indirect taxes affect the income at the stage of its consumption and the taxpayer is a different person than that which actually bears the tax duty, the one who is economically affected by the tax. Indirect taxes can be subdivided into general taxes, those affecting all products and services, and special taxes, those affecting just some products and services.

Taxes which form the Czech system of taxation can be divided between direct and indirect in the following way:

i. direct taxes
   a. income taxes
      i. personal income tax
      ii. corporate income tax
   b. property taxes
      i. affecting estate in abeyance
         1. real estate tax
         2. road tax
      ii. transfer taxes
         1. inheritance tax
         2. gift tax
         3. real estate transfer tax
ii. indirect taxes
   a. general
      i. value added tax
   a. special
      i. excise taxes
         1. mineral oil tax
         2. alcohol tax
         3. beer tax
         4. wine and intermediate product tax
         5. tobacco and tobacco product tax
         6. energy taxes
            a. natural gas and other types of gas tax
            b. solid fuel tax
            c. electricity tax

The tax system of each State should fulfill certain basic requirements, which are termed as the principles of the tax system or simply tax principles. To define these is the task of legal theory which should deduce, on the basis of application in practice, certain general knowledge. Amongst the major principles on which the tax system should be based are:

i.   legal certainty,
ii.   foreseeability,
iii. fairness,
iv.   solidarity,
v.   lucidity,
vi.   comprehensibility,
vii. clarity,
viii. unambiguity,
ix.   transparency,
x.   the "ability to pay" principle, or acceptability.

At present, especially the following two sections of principles are being discussed:

1. legal certainty, lucidity, comprehensibility, clarity, unambiguity and transparency on the one hand, and
2. fairness, solidarity and acceptability on the other hand.

In relation to the first group of principles, the legal regulation of taxes, specifically direct income taxes and value added taxes, is changing from year to year. The frequency of tax law amendments is enormous. The Act on Income Taxes,[665] as an example, had been amended more than 100 times by the end of 2009. Besides, the extent of legal regulation has been increasing. When the Income Tax Act was passed it contained about 12,000 words; at present it comprises nearly 70,000.

The frequency of amendments and the scope of legal regulation is not the only issue – there is also the method of legal regulation, which deserves attention. In this connection, we have to point out certain basic rules of the law-making procedure which are included in the Legislative Rules of the Government.[666] According to these rules, a section of a statute should contain only provisions relating to the very same matter, while preference should be given to shorter sections. There should not be more than six subsections in one section; otherwise, following the principle of lucidity, the division of the matter into more sections is preferred.[667] Concerning paragraphs, in accordance with the Legislative Rules of the Government, if all letters are used up no double letters should be used. On the contrary, further paragraphs should be incorporated into a new subsection at the beginning of which the relevant introductory part of the provision should be stated.[668]

The provision of sec. 24 of the Income Tax Act contains 14 subsections and the provision of subsection 2 contains 43 paragraphs which are marked from (a) to (zt). This legal provision contains more than 6,000 words. It is beyond any dispute that such a legal regulation is not only in contradiction to the above mentioned general rules of the law-making

---

[665] Act No. 586/1992 Sb., on icome taxes, as amended.
[666] The Legislative Rules of the Government passed by the Government Resolution, 19th March 1998, No. 188, as amended (LRG).
[667] Art. 39 (2) LRG.
[668] Art. 26 (4) LRG.

procedure comprised in Legislative Rules but it also violates the principles of lucidity, comprehensibility, clarity, unambiguity and transparency of tax law. Unfortunately, provisions similar to the provision of sec. 24 of the Income Tax Act are not unique in Czech tax laws; conclusions relating to sec. 24 of the Income Tax Act may apply to other provisions of the Act and to other tax laws.

Another aspect which contradicts the tax principles mentioned above is the erroneous systematics of some tax laws. The Income Tax Act may serve as an example. This law regulates personal income tax in Part One, corporate income tax in Part Two and common provisions for personal income tax and corporate income tax in Part Three. However, provisions (35ba) and (35c) regulating tax credits exclusively concerning the personal income tax are components of Part Three.

The first group of principles mentioned above seems to be violated only in connection with the legal regulation concerning income taxes, as governed by the Act of 1992. However, even the legislation having become effective relatively recently, e.g. the Act on Excise Taxes, as amended,[669] and the Act on VAT,[670] violates a couple of principles mentioned above within the first group. Section 13 of the Act on Excise Taxes contains 25 subsections and sec. 80 of the Value Added Tax Act contains 19 subsections.

As can be seen, the contemporary tax system of the Czech Republic does not comply with the requirements of legal certainty, lucidity, comprehensibility, clarity and transparency.

The principles of fairness, solidarity and acceptability are discussed mainly in connection with the adjusted tax base of the income from employment and benefits thereof and the rate on personal income tax.

Effective as of January 1, 2008, a linear (flat) income tax instead of the then-existing progressive tax rate was introduced, for the first time since 1993. At present, the linear income tax is imposed at the level of 15 %, whilst before 2008 a progressive sliding-scale rate of 12 %–32 % applied. These adjustments intensified theoretical discussions in relation to which of these rates is of more fairness and solidarity.

In jurisprudence as well as in economic theories, the progressive tax rate is understood as bringing in the elements of solidarity since the entities with higher income are subject to a higher rate of tax. Consequently, this reality suggests a higher solidarity of higher-income (natural or artificial) persons with lower-income persons. On the contrary, there are objections that the progressive tax rate has an anti-motivational effect, and that persons are tempted to evade their tax duties. Mainly the persons with higher revenues consider this rate as unfair.

At first the linear tax rate seems more just than the progressive sliding-scale tax rate since the whole income is taxed by the same rate, a concept which can be seen as "fair". On the contrary, opponents of the linear tax argue that it lacks the element of solidarity.

This is about an "eternal" quarrel of especially economic and political thoughts and we cannot a priori condemn or favour either approach to taxation. Nevertheless, current legal regulation of personal income tax comprises a significant deviation from standard

---

[669] Act No. 353/2003 Sb., on excise taxes, as amended.
[670] Act No. 235/2004 Sb., on value added tax, as amended.

methods when applying the linear tax rate. The linear tax rate just appears to be flat at the amount of 15 %. The reason is a new definition of the partial tax base of the income from employment and benefits thereof. Effective as of January 1, 2008, the partial tax base of the income from employment and benefits thereof means the income from employment and benefits thereof increased by the amount equal to the social security insurance levies, contribution to the national employment policy and to the general health insurance levies. According to specific legal regulations the employer is bound to pay these charges based on its income by itself. In practice this partial tax base is called "the super gross wage". This statutory rule consequently means that the rate of personal income tax from employment and benefits thereof is not 15 % but 23.1 %. Different types of income are taxed by different rates which can be considered unfair.

The current personal income tax regulation can be viewed as a non-systematic solution which, as a result, can be unfair although at first sight it appears that the tax rate is linear and thus fair.

3.5.2 Tax Law Of The European Union

Tax issues at the level of the European Union fall under both the tax law of the EU and the tax law of individual Member States. The objective of the EU tax law is the legal regulation at the EU level. Once we are concerned with the tax law of individual Member States, this should be the subject matter of comparative law, which infers general legal conclusions by comparing tax systems of individual Member States of the EU.

Tax law of individual Member States the European Union, taken as a whole, is character-ized as a high-tax area.[671] In 2005 the overall tax ratio in the Member States of the European Union amounted to 39.9 % of GDP; this value is about 12 percentage points above those recorded in the United States and Japan. The high overall tax burden by no means implies that it is the same in every EU Member State. On the contrary, ten Member States display ratios below 35 %. The differences in taxation levels across the Union are quite significant (e.g. from 49.1 % in Denmark to mere 28.6 % in Romania). It should be added that these overall tax ratios include social security contributions, which are in this context considered taxable income.

Characteristic features of the tax law of individual Member States of the European Union include the shift from direct taxes (especially corporate income tax) to indirect taxes (especially value added tax and excise taxes).

Corporate income tax is subject to tendency to lower its rates. Individual Member States certainly compete amongst each other, and so the reduction of a tax rate in one Member State initiates the other Member States to decrease corporate income tax as well. The reasons and targets are strictly economic: a state imposing a lower rate of corporate income tax is more attractive for foreign and domestic investors than any other state where the business corporations and other legal entities face higher corporate income taxes.

The following graph displays the decline of the average corporate income tax rates in EU Member States between 1995 and 2008. The graph shows not only the continuous reduction

---

[671] See *Taxation trends in the European Union – Main results*. Luxembourg: European Communities, 2008.

Graph 1

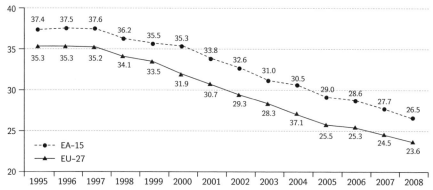

Source: *Taxation trends in the European Union – Main results.*
European Communities, 2008.

Graph 1

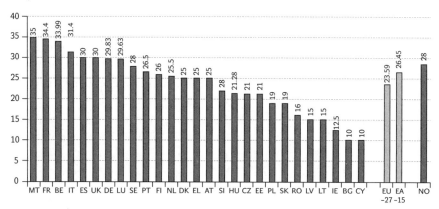

Source: *Taxation trends in the European Union – Main results.*
European Communities, 2008.

Graph 1

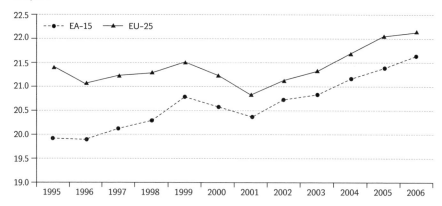

Source: *Taxation trends in the European Union – Main results.*
European Communities, 2008.

of the corporate income tax rate but also the corporate income tax rate in the states of the Eurozone[672] higher than in other EU Member States.

The actual corporate income tax rates are shown in the graph below; it is apparent that although the continuous downward trend of corporate income tax rates is quite general, these rates still substantially vary among the Member States. The tax rate on corporate income varies between a maximum of 35 % in Malta and a minimum of 10 % in Cyprus and Bulgaria.

The decline of the corporate income tax rates is, however, counterbalanced by the increased indirect taxes, especially VAT, imposed on products and services. The implicit tax rate of indirect taxes on consumption in individual Member States of the EU has been increasing since 2001.

The above-mentioned data suggest two principal trends in tax law of individual Member States of the European Union to be clearly recognized:

1. decrease of corporate income tax rates, and
2. increase of rates of indirect taxes.

Tax charge is being shifted from direct taxes to indirect taxes.

The autonomous tax law of the European Union is based on primary legislation, mainly on the Treaty on the Functioning of the European Union (TFEU).[673] The free movement of goods, the free movement and establishment of persons, the free movement of services, and the free movement of capital belong to the basic rights and freedoms, which are regulated by the Treaty. The economic goal of the TFEU is the creation of the Common Market and of the European Monetary Union. These basic rights and economic goals within the protection of economic competition, taxes and approximation of legal rules are reflected in Title VII, Part 3 of the Treaty on the Functioning of the European Union.

It can be stated that the essentials of EU tax law are incorporated in Chapter 2 and 3, Title VII, Part 3 of the TFEU which deals with tax provisions and approximation of laws in Articles 110-118 of the Treaty.

The rules prohibiting any limitation of the free movement of goods with respect to taxation are contained especially in Article 110 TFEU. According to this provision, no Member State may impose, directly or indirectly, on the products of other Member States any internal taxation of any kind in excess of that imposed directly or indirectly on similar domestic products. Furthermore, no Member State may impose on the products of other Member States any internal taxation of such a nature as to afford indirect protection to other products. This provision prevents Member States from the blocking of the free movement of goods using tax law regulations.

Approximation of laws and regulations of individual EU Member States results primarily from the fundamental provision of Article 113 TFEU, according to which the Council, acting unanimously in accordance with the special legislative procedure and after consulting the

---

[672] The Eurozone consists of the EU Member States having adopted the Euro currency as their sole legal tender.
[673] Treaty establishing the European Economic Communities signed in Rome on March 25, 1957 (The Treaty of Rome), as amended.

European Parliament and the Economic and Social Committee, shall adopt provisions for the harmonization of legislation concerning turnover taxes, excise duties and other forms of indirect taxation to the extent that such harmonization is necessary to ensure the establishment and the functioning of the internal market and to avoid distortion of competition.

From what has been stated two basic facts arise:

1. tax harmonization according to Art. 113 of the TFEU can only concern indirect taxes, and
2. the Council must adopt the rules of harmonization unanimously.

The following legislation harmonizing legal regulation of value added tax and excise duties, including taxes on energy, was issued:

1. Council Directive 2006/112/EC, of 28th November 2006, on the common system of value added tax, as amended,
2. Council Directive 92/12/EEC, of 25th February 1992, on the general arrangements for products subject to excise duty and on the holding, movement and monitoring of such products, and
3. Council Directive 2003/96/EEC, of 27th October 2003, restructuring the Community framework for the taxation of energy products and electricity, as amended.

Especially within the area of value added tax, relatively frequent legislative activities of relevant institutions of the European Union can be recognized. For example, at the beginning of 2008 two new directives concerning VAT were adopted, and they are:

1. Council Directive 2008/8/EC, of 12th February, 2008, amending Directive 2006/112/EC, as regards the place of supply of services, and
2. Council Directive 2008/9/EC, of 12th February, 2008, laying down detailed rules for the refund of value added tax, provided for in Directive 2006/112/EC, to taxable persons not established in the same Member State of refund but established in another Member State.

The objective of Directive 2008/8/EC is to ensure that the value added tax on supply of services will return to the country where these services were rendered and, by this, to prevent the obstruction of economic competition among the Member States imposing different VAT rates. In the case of the supplies of services to taxable persons, the general rule with respect to the place of supply is that the place of supply should be based on the place where the recipient is established, rather than where the supplier is established.

On the contrary, direct taxes cannot be harmonized under Art. 113 TFEU since individual Member States are not willing to relinquish sovereignty and to confer to the European Union their legislative powers in the area of direct taxes. Nevertheless, certain harmonization efforts have succeeded. This is not because of the above-mentioned Art. 113 TFEU, but rather because of the provision of Art. 115 TFEU.

Art. 115 TFEU concerns the provision of approximation of laws within the common market. According to this provision the Council, acting unanimously in accordance with the special legislative procedure and after consulting the European Parliament and the Economic and Social Committee, may issue directives for the approximation of laws, regulations or administrative provisions of Member States, which directly affect the establishment or functioning of the internal market. In accordance with this provision of the Treaty, directives harmonizing certain particular areas of income tax related to the EU common market are issued.

Unlike indirect taxes, the harmonization of direct taxes in the European Union is carried out much more slowly and much less consistently. One of the reasons is the different legal classification of harmonization of direct taxes and connected powers of EU institutions. By comparison with straight and "strong" authority concerning harmonization of indirect taxes which is contained in Art. 113 TFEU, the basis for harmonization of direct taxes in primary Community legislation is formed just by the general provision of Art. 115 TFEU (falling not within Chapter 2 dealing with tax provisions but within Chapter 3 relating to the approximation of laws). Mandate conferred by this provision to the Council in connection with the issuing of directives concerning approximation of laws, regulations and administrative provisions of Member States can be utilized for harmonization of taxes other than indirect taxes only when the requirement stated therein is fulfilled, namely that such harmonization has a direct impact on the establishment or functioning of the common market.

De lege ferenda proposals at the EU level in the area of corporate income tax include a common consolidated corporate tax base[674] and common taxation for small and medium sized enterprises in accordance with the tax base rules effective in the home state of the registered office of the parent company.[675]

The introduction of a single common consolidated corporate income tax base has been considered by the EU since 2001. The fundamental objectives of CCCTB working group[676] are:

i. to examine the definition of a common consolidated tax base for companies operating in the EU,
ii. to discuss the basic tax principles,
iii. to discuss the fundamental structural elements of a uniform tax base, and
iv. to discuss other necessary technical details such as a mechanism for "sharing" a uniform tax base for companies between individual Member States.[677]

The communication entitled "Implementing the Community programme for improved growth and employment and the enhanced competitiveness of EU business" of May 2, 2007, suggests that the Commission believes that a comprehensive approach involving the

[674] CCCTB – Common Consolidated Corporate Tax Base.
[675] Home State Taxation for Small and Medium Sized Enterprises.
[676] Common Consolidated Corporate Tax Base Working Group (CCCTB WG).
[677] http://ec.europa.eu/taxation_customs/taxation/company_tax/common_tax_base/index_en.htm, retrieved on 29th May 2009.

introduction of a common corporate tax base could provide the largest overall benefits as regards the taxation of profits of companies operating in the internal market.[678] However, we cannot anticipate the future success of this project, especially in regard of the above-mentioned unwillingness of Member States to harmonize legal regulations of direct taxes.

The mentioned analysis clearly shows that the Czech tax system will be continuously adjusted to the EU legislation, which itself is subject to frequent alterations.

3.5.3 Conclusions

Tax law undoubtedly occupies a significant role in the tax system of any state mainly because of the importance, which taxes bear as the revenue to the public budget. However, the doctrine of financial law in the Czech Republic will have to cope with a "new feature in law on the threshold of the 21st century", which introduces the conception of tax law as an autonomous legal branch. In this context, serious scholarly discussions should be held in order to unify opinions of experts focusing on financial law in the Czech Republic regarding the position of tax law as a subsection of financial law or as an autonomous legal discipline.

The fact that the current tax system of the Czech Republic does not comply with the requirements for legal certainty, lucidity, comprehensibility, clarity and transparency can be considered as a serious problem of Czech tax law. This is a big challenge addressing jurisprudence as well as legal practice in implementing the above-mentioned principles in the 21st century.

What should be taken into account when regulating the current tax system is the legal regulation of EU tax law relating to both indirect taxes, which is harmonized, as well as to the regulation of direct taxes, the approximation of which is possible only under the rules of the common market. Further, we can be inspired by the tax law legislation of individual Member States. Two principal trends are more than obvious: the decline of corporate income tax rates and the increase in indirect tax rates. Thus, tax burden is being shifted from direct taxes to indirect taxes.

It is obvious that the Czech tax system will be continuously adjusted to the European Union legislation, which itself is subject to frequent alterations.

This fact can be easily marked as "a new phenomenon in law on the threshold of the 21st century", since before the accession of the Czech Republic to the EU and completion of the Association Agreement the obligation to harmonize legal rules of taxation had not existed in the Czech Republic.

The final conclusion in this subchapter concerning tax law and the tax system in the Czech Republic may be found in the reasoning of the judgment of the Supreme Administrative Court of the Czech Republic, file No. 2 Afs 62/2004, which reads:

"The tax system represents not only an indispensible means for the existence of the state but above all the test of its legitimacy. The tax system must be, from the point of view of its concept and actual application, transparent, predictable and acceptable. Otherwise, the above mentioned legitimacy function cannot be fulfilled and, as a

---

[678] General Report on the Activities of the European Union in 2007 /Summary Report of Activity of the European Union, 2007, ISBN 978-92-79-07098-3. Luxemburg: European Communities, 2008.

final consequence, the significance and the functioning the State is challenged." Let us hope that in connection with the legal regulations of individual taxes in the upcoming years the tax system of the Czech Republic will more consistently comply with the above-mentioned general principles.

Selected bibliography to Chapter 3

ACEVEDO, M. T.: The Intersection of Human Rights and Environmental Protection in the European Court of Human Rights. *New York Environmental Law Journal* 8/2000, pp. 437–496.

AMANN, R.: *German Tax Guide*. The Hague: Kluwer Law International, 1997.

BABČÁK, V. et al.: *Daňové právo* [Tax Law]. Košice: Univerzita Pavla Jozefa Šafárika, 2005.

BABČÁK, V.: Daňové právo a príprava daňovej reformy v Slovenskej republike [Tax Law and the Preparation of Tax Reform in the Slovak Repblic]. *Acta Universitatis Carolinae* 3–4/2003, pp. 9–26.

BABČÁK, V.: Úvahy o mieste daňového práva v systéme slovenského práva [Reflections on the Role of the Tax Law in the Slovak Legal System]. In: *Finančnoprávne epištoly – Medzinárodný finančnoprávny zborník k nedožitým 80. narodeninám Prof. JUDr. Jordána Giráška, DrSc* [Financial Law Epistles – International Proceedings of Financial Law on the Occassion of 80th Birthday of Professor Jordán Girášek in Memoriam]. Bratislava: EPOS, 2005, pp. 21–28.

BAKEŠ, M. – KARFÍKOVÁ, M. – KOTÁB, P. – MARKOVÁ, H.: *Finanční právo* [Financial Law]. 5th ed., Praha: C. H. Beck, 2009.

BALAŠ, V. – ŠTURMA, P.: *Kurs mezinárodního ekonomického práva* [The Course of International Economic Law]. Praha: C. H. Beck, 1997.

BÁNDÍ, G. et. al.: *The Environmental Jurisprudence of the European Court of Justice*. Budapest: Monnet Program of the EC Commission, 2008.

BERAN, K.: *Právnické osoby veřejného práva* [Legal Entities in Public Law]. Praha: Linde 2006.

BERAN, K.: Proč není stát právnickou osobou? [Why Is the State Not a Legal Entity?]. *Právní rozhledy* 7/2006, pp. 255–261.

BÍLKOVÁ, V.: Ochrana lidských práv za ozbrojeného konfliktu – přístup Evropského soudu pro lidská práva [The Protection of Human Rights in Armed Conflicts – ECHR Approach]. *Právník* 1/2008, pp. 19–47.

BIRNIE, P. – BOYLE, A.: *International Law and the Environment.* 2nd ed., Oxford: Oxford University Press, 2002.

BLAHOŽ, J.: Základní lidské a občanské právo na zdravé životní prostředí: srovnávací pohled [Basic Human Rights for a Healthy Living Environment: a Comparative Approach]. *Právník* 12/2002, pp. 1253–1265.

BLUMENSTEIN, L.: *System des schweizerischen Steuerrechts*. Zürich: Schultness, 2002.

BONĚK, V. – BĚHOUNEK, P. – BENDA, V. – HOMES, A.: *Lexikon – Daňové pojmy* [Lexicon – Tax Terms]. Ostrava: Jiří Motloch – Sagit, 2001.

BOYLE, A.: Human Rights or Environmental Rights? A Re-assessment. *Fordham Environmental Law Review* 2006–2007, pp. 471–511.

BUDNÍK, J.: Několik poznámek k vnitrostátní platnosti mezinárodních smluv [Several Notes on National Validity of International Treaties]. *Časopis pro právní a státní vědu*, 1937.

BUJŇÁKOVÁ, M.: Opodstatnenosť daňového práva ako samostatného odvetvia práva v právnom poriadku Slovenskej republiky [Legitimacy of Tax Law as an Autonomous Legal Branch in Legal Order of the Slovak Republic]. *Mezinárodní a srovnávací právní revue* 14/2005, pp. 4–12.

CABAN, P.: *Jurisdikční imunity státu* [Jurisdictional Immunity of States]. Praha: PF UK, 2007.

ČEČOT, V. – SEGEŠ, I: Trestná zodpovednosť právnických osôb? [Criminal Liability of Legal Entities?]. *Justičná revue* 1/2001, pp. 19–26.

ČENTÉŠ, J. – PALKOVIČ, J. – ŠTOFFOVÁ, Z.: Trestná zodpovednosť právnických osôb [Criminal Liability of Legal Entities]. *Justičná revue* 4/2001, pp. 416–423.

ČENTÉŠ, J. – PALKOVIČ, J. – ŠTOFFOVÁ, Z.: Trestná zodpovednosť právnických osôb v slovinskom právnom poriadku [Criminal Liability of Legal Entities in the Slovenian Legal Order]. *Trestní právo* 5/2002, pp. 8–12.

ČENTÉŠ, J. – ŠTOFFOVÁ, Z.: Trestná zodpovednosť právnických osôb v Belgicku [Criminal Liability of Legal Entities in Belgium]. *Justičná revue* 10/2001, pp. 990–999.

ČEPELKA, Č. – ŠTURMA, P.: *Mezinárodní právo veřejné* [Public International Law]. Praha: C. H. Beck, 2008.

CÍSAŘOVÁ, D. – FENYK, J. – GŘIVNA, T. et al.: *Trestní právo procesní* [Criminal Procedure]. 5th ed., Praha: ASPI, 2008.

CÍSAŘOVÁ, D. – SOVOVÁ, O. et al.: *Trestní právo a zdravotnictví* [Criminal Law and Medicine]. Praha: LexisNexis, Orac, 2004.

DALLIER, P. – PELLET, A.: *Droit international public.* 6th ed., Paris: Librairie Générale de Droit et de Jurisprudence, 1999.

273

DAMOHORSKÝ, M. – MÜLLEROVÁ, H.: Ochrana životního prostředí v ústavách zemí Evropské unie [Environmental Protection within the Frame of the Constitutions of the EU Countries]. In: Klíma, K. – Jirásek, J. (eds.): *Pocta Jánu Gronskému* [Tribute to Ján Gronský]. Plzeň: Aleš Čeněk, 2008, pp. 375–381.

DAMOHORSKÝ, M. et al.: *Právo životního prostředí* [Environmental Law]. 2nd ed., Praha: C. H. Beck, 2007.

DAMOHORSKÝ, M.: *České právo životního prostředí* [Czech Environmental Law]. Praha: Právnická fakulta Univerzity Karlovy, 2006.

DAMOHORSKÝ, M.: Role soudů při ochraně životního prostředí [The Role of Judiciary in Environmental Protection]. In: *Jaké jsou limity soudní ochrany v Čechách?* [What Are the Limits of the Judicial Protection in the Czech Republic?] Praha: Zelený kruh, 2008, pp. 31–34.

DAVID, L.: Zásada komplementarity neoslabuje státní suverenitu [The Principle of Complementarity Does Not Weaken State Sovereignty]. *Trestněprávní revue* 6/2005, pp. 141–144.

DEJEANT-PONS, M.: Les droits de l'homme à l'environnement dans le cadre du Conseil de l'Europe. In: Masclet, J. C. (ed.): *Environnement et renouveau des droits de l'homme*. Paris: La Documentation Française, 2006, pp. 75–89.

DELMAS-MARTHY, M.: Vers un droit pénal européen commun. *Archives de politique criminelle* 19/1997, pp. 7–23.

DOELDER DE, H.: Kriminalizace korporativního chování, možnosti trestního postihu korporace [Criminalization of Corporate Conduct, Possibilities of Punishing Corporations]. In: Kratochvíl, V. (ed.): *Trestněprávní reforma v České republice* [The Reform of Criminal Law in the Czech Republic]. Brno: Masarykova univerzita, 1994, pp. 60–68.

DOUMA, TH. W. (ed.): *European Environmental Case Law*. The Hague: T.M.C. Asser Press, 2002.

DRACHOVSKÝ, J.: Dávky veřejné [Public Benefits]. In: Hácha, E. et al. (eds.): *Slovník veřejného práva* [Public Law Dictionary]. Brno: Polygrafia, 1929, pp. 314–317.

DRGONEC, J. – HOLLÄNDER, P.: *Moderná medicína a právo* [Modern Medicine and the Law]. Bratislava: Obzor, 1988.

DUPUY, P. M.: *L'unité de l'ordre juridique international: cours général de droit international public*. Leiden: Martinus Nijhoff, 2003.

ENGLIŠ, K.: *Soustava národního hospodářství, sv. 2* [The System of National Economy, Vol. 2]. Praha: Melantrich, 1938.

FENYK, J. – KLOUČKOVÁ, S.: *Mezinárodní justiční spolupráce v trestních věcech* [International Judicial Cooperation in Criminal Matters]. Praha: Linde, 2005.

FILIP, J.: Evropský a ústavní kontext sporu o transpozici eurozatykače [The European and Constitutional Context of the Dispute over the Transposition of the European Arrest Warrant]. In: Hurdík, J. – Fiala, J. (eds.): *Východiska a trendy vývoje českého práva po vstupu České republiky do Evropské unie* [Starting Points and Trends of the Evolution of Czech Law after the Accession of the Czech Republic to the European Union]. Brno: Masarykova univerzita, 2005, pp. 26–58.

GŘIVNA, T. – SEKVARD, O.: Nový pohled Nejvyššího soudu na zásadu ne bis in idem? [A New View of the Supreme Court upon the Ne Bis in Idem Principle?]. *Právní fórum* 3/2005, pp. 98–103.

HOBZA, A.: Mezinárodní delikt [International Delict]. In: *Pocta k 70. narozeninám univ. Prof. dra Augusta Miřičky* [Tribute to Professor August Miřička on the Occasion of his 70th Birthday]. Praha: Československá společnost pro právo trestní, 1933, pp. 129–138.

HOBZA, A.: Publikace a platnost mírových smluv v Čsl. republice [The Publication and Validity of Peace Treaties in the Czechoslovak Republic]. *Právník* 1923, pp. 11–22.

HUBER, B.: Trestní odpovědnost korporací [Corporate Criminal Liability]. *Trestní právo* 9/2000, pp. 2–9.

HUGHES, D.: *Environmental Law*. 4th ed., Butterworths, LexisNexis, 2002.

HURDÍK, J.: Trestní odpovědnost právnických osob? [Criminal Liability of Legal Entities?]. *Časopis pro právní vědu a praxi* 1/1996, pp. 28–33.

JALČ, A.: Korupcia – trestnoprávny vývoj, rekodifikácia a trestná zodpovednosť právnických osôb [Bribery – Criminal Development, Recodification and Criminal Liability of Legal Entities]. *Justičná revue* 1/2005, pp. 1–8.

JANDA, P.: Trestní odpovědnost právnických osob [Criminal Liability of Legal Entities]. *Právní fórum* 5/2006, pp. 168–178.

JELÍNEK, J.: *Trestní odpovědnost právnických osob* [Criminal Liability of Legal Entities]. Praha: Linde, 2007.

KARFÍKOVÁ, M.: Úloha daňového systému při zajišťování funkcí státu [The Role of the Tax System in Ensuring the Functions of the States]. In: Klener, P. (ed.): *Český stát a vzdělanost* [The Czech State and Education]. Praha: Karolinum, 2002.

KMEC, J.: *Evropské trestní právo* [European Criminal Law]. Praha: C. H. Beck, 2006.

KMEC, J.: K některým aspektům zásady „ne bis in idem" ve světle judikatury Evropského soudu pro lidská práva [On Some Aspects of the Ne Bis in Idem Principle in the Case-law of the European Court of Human Rights]. *Trestní právo* 1/2004, pp. 21–24, 2/2004, pp. 20–23, 3/2004, pp. 16–18.

KOSIKOWSKI, C.: *Prawo finansowe. Ogólna Część* [Financial Law, General Part]. Warszawa: Dum wydawniczy ABC, 2003.

KOSKENNIEMI, M.: *Fragmentation of International Law: Difficulties arising from the Diversification and Expansion of International Law. Report of the Study Group of the International Law Commission.* UN doc. A/CN.4/L.682, 2006.

KRÁL, V.: K trestní odpovědnosti právnických osob – východiska, obsah a systematika zákonné úpravy [On Criminal Liability of Legal Entities – Background, Contents, and the System of Legislation]. *Trestněprávní revue* 8/2002, pp. 221–223.

KRÁLIK, J. – JAKUBOVIČ, D.: *Finančné právo* [Financial Law]. Bratislava: VEDA, 2004.

KRATOCHVÍL, V. – LÖFF, M.: *Hospodářské trestní právo a odpovědnost právnických osob* [Economic Criminal Law and Criminal Liability of Legal Entities]. Brno: Masarykova univerzita, 2003.

KRATOCHVÍL, V.: Jednání za jiného – možná cesta k trestní odpovědnosti právnických osob? [Acting for Another – Potential Way to Criminal Liability of Legal Entities?]. In: Kratochvíl, V. (ed.): *Sborník z mezinárodního semináře o hospodářské kriminalitě* [Proceedings from the International Seminar on Economic Crime]. Brno: Masarykova univerzita, 1999, pp. 88–99.

KRATOCHVÍL, V: Trestní odpovědnost právnických osob a jednání za jiného (Stav de lege lata, de lege ferenda v České a Slovenské republice) [Criminal Liability of Legal Entities and Acting for Another (The Situation de Lege Lata, de Lege Ferenda in the Czech and Slovak Republics)]. *Právny obzor* 4/2002, pp. 365–372.

KRUŽÍKOVÁ, E. – ADAMOVÁ, E. – KOMÁREK, J.: *Právo životního prostředí Evropských společenství: praktický průvodce* [Environmental Law of the European Community: Practical Guide]. Praha: Linde, 2003.

KUCHTA, J.: Trestní řízení proti právnickým osobám z pohledu některých zásad trestního práva procesního [Criminal Proceedings against Legal Entities from the Viewpoint of Some Principles of Criminal Procedure]. In: Neckář, J. – Radvan, M. – Sehnálek, D. – Valdhans, J. (eds.): *Acta Universitatis Brunensis Iuridica No. 337.* Brno: Masarykova univerzita, 2008, pp. 1741–1748.

LÁCHOVÁ, L.: Perspektivy majetkových daní [Prospects of Property Taxes]. In: Kubátová, K. – Vybíhal, V. et al.: *Optimalizace daňového systému ČR* [Optimization of the Tax System of the Czech Republic]. Praha: Eurolex Bohemia, 2004, pp. 141–161.

LANGROVÁ, V.: *Soudní judikatura ve věcech životního prostředí* [Case law in Environmental Matters]. Praha: ASPI, 2007.

LEGROS, R.: *La pénétration du droit européen dans la justice répressive belge.* Bruxelles: Bruylant, 1970.

MACH, J. et al.: *Zdravotnictví a právo, komentované předpisy* [Medicine and the Law, Commented Statutes]. Praha: Orac, Digesta, 2003.

MADLIAK, J. – PORADA, V. – BRUNA, E.: Niekoľko úvah o trestnej zodpovednosti právnických osôb v podmienkach SR [Several Remarks on Criminal Liability of Legal Entities in the Slovak Republic]. *Karlovarská právní revue* 3/2006, pp. 26–29.

MALENOVSKÝ, J.: *Mezinárodní právo veřejné. Jeho obecná část a poměr k vnitrostátnímu právu, zvláště právu českému* [Public International Law. General Part and Relationship to Domestic Law, Namely Czech Law]. 4th ed., Brno: MU – Doplněk, 2004.

MALENOVSKÝ, J.: Smluvní ochrana občanských a politických práv v teorii a praxi mezinárodního práva [Contractual Protection of Civic and Political Rights in the Theory and Practice of International Law]. In: Šturma, P. (ed.): *Právní následky mezinárodně protiprávního chování. Pocta Čestmíru Čepelkovi k 80. narozeninám* [Legal Consequences of Conduct Contrary to International Law. Tribute to Čestmír Čepelka on the Occasion of his 80th Birthday]. Praha: PF UK, 2007, pp. 121–144.

MARGUENAUD, J.-P.: Environnement et renouveau des droits de l'homme – La jurisprudence de la Cour EDH. In: Champeil-Desplats, V. (ed.): *Environnement et renouveau des droits de l'homme – actes du colloque de Boulogne-sur-Mer 20–21 novembre 2003.* Paris: Documentation Française, 2006, pp. 101–107.

MARKOVÁ, H. – BOHÁČ, R.: *Rozpočtové právo* [Budgetary Law]. 1st ed., Praha: C. H. Beck, 2007.

MARKOVÁ, H.: Vlastní nebo sdílené daně obcím? [Own or Shared Taxes for Communities?]. In: *Dny veřejného práva* [Days of Public Law]. Brno: Masarykova universita, 2007, pp. 503–511.

MRKÝVKA, P. et al.: *Finanční právo a finanční správa, 2. díl* [Financial Law and Financial Administration, Part 2]. Brno: Masarykova univerzita, 2004.

MUSIL J.: Trestní odpovědnost právnických osob – ano či ne? [Criminal Liability of Legal Entities – Yes or No?]. *Trestní právo* 7–8/2000, pp. 2–10.

MUSIL, J. – PRÁŠKOVÁ, H. – FALDYNA, F.: Úvahy o trestní odpovědnosti právnických osob de lege ferenda [Considerations of Criminal Liability of Legal Entities]. *Trestní právo* 3/2001, pp. 6–17.

MUSIL, J.: Trestní odpovědnost právnických osob v novém francouzském trestním zákoníku [Criminal Liability of Legal Entities in the New French Criminal Code]. *Kriminalistika* 4/1995, pp. 305–315.

MUSIL, J.: Trestní odpovědnost právnických osob: Historický vývoj a mezinárodní srovnání [Criminal Liability of Legal Entities. Historical Development and International Comparison]. In: Musil, J. – Vanduchová, M. (eds.): *Pocta Otovi Novotnému* [Tribute to Oto Novotný]. Praha: Codex, 1998, pp. 76–98.

Nalogovoje pravo. Učebnik. Moskva: Rgist, 2004.

NOUZHA, CH.: Réflexions sur la contribution de la Cour internationale de justice à la protection des ressources naturelles. *Revue juridique de l'environnement* 3/2000, pp. 391–419.

NOVOTNÝ, O. – VANDUCHOVÁ, M. et al.: *Trestní právo hmotné – I. Obecná část* [Criminal Substantive Law I. General Part]. 6th updated and expanded ed., Praha: ASPI, 2010.

NOVOTNÝ, O.: O otázkách hospodářského trestního práva [Some Issues of Economic Criminal Law]. *Právní praxe* 6/1997, pp. 375–401.

ONDŘEJ, J.: Mezinárodněprávní ochrana životního prostředí na konci 20. století [International Legal Protection of the Environment at the End of 20th Century]. *AUC-Iuridica* 3–4/1998, pp. 73–88.

Parliament of the Czech Republic. The Chamber of Deputies. 4th term. Transcripts 37, session on 2nd November 2004. Digital library.

PAVLÍČEK, V. et al.: *Ústava a ústavní řád České republiky, 2. díl Práva a svobody* [The Constitution and Constitutional Order of the Czech Republic, Part 2 Right and Freedoms]. 2nd revised and expanded ed., Praha: Linde, 1999.

PEKOVÁ, J.: Majetkové daně zdaňující převod vlastnických práv k majetku [Property Taxes on the Transfer of Rights in Rem]. In: Mácha, P.: *Dědění, darování, převádění nemovitostí* [Inheritance, Gift and Real-Estate Transfer]. Praha: Newsletter, 1995, pp. 13–15.

PELLA, V. V.: *Vers l'unification du droit pénal par la création d'un institut international auprès de la Société des Nations.* Paris: Sirey, 1928.

PEŠKA, Z.: Příspěvek k otázce transformace mezinárodních smluv v právo vnitrostátní [Contribution to the Issue of Transformation of International Treaties into National Law]. In: *Pocta k šedesiatym narodeninám Dr. Karla Laštovku* [Tribute to Dr. Karel Laštovka on the Occasion of his 60th Birthday]. Praha: Frant. Řivnáč, 1936, pp. 296–306.

PETROVA, G. V.: *Financovoje pravo* [Financial Law]. Moskva: Velbi, 2006.

PIKNA, B.: *Mezinárodní terorismus a bezpečnost Evropské unie* [International Terrorism and the Security of the European Union]. Praha: Linde, 2006.

PIPEK, J. – BARTOŠÍKOVÁ, M.: Vztah obchodněprávní a trestněprávní odpovědnosti statutárních orgánů a členů statutárních orgánů [The Relationship between Commercial and Criminal Liability of Governing Bodies and Their Members]. *Právní praxe v podnikání* 1/1999, pp. 1–17.

PIPEK, J.: Princip ne bis in idem v konkurenci jurisdikcí [The Principle of Ne Bis in Idem in the Conflict of Jurisdictions]. *Trestněprávní revue* 4/2004, pp. 97–107.

PLAGRET, B.: *Droit public, droit financier, droit fiscal.* Vol. 2, Paris: édition Sirey, 1989.

POLÁK, P. – FENYK, J.: Etiologie projevů trestního práva v Evropské Unii [Etiology of the Expression of Criminal Law in the European Union]. *Acta Universitatis Carolinae Iuridica* 2/2005, pp. 7–44.

PRÍBELSKÝ, P.: Trestná zodpovědnosť právnických osôb v Rakúsku [Criminal Liability of Legal Entities in Austria]. *Trestněprávní revue* 1/2007, pp. 12–18.

RADVAN, M.: *Zdanění majetku v Evropě* [Property Taxation in Europe]. 1st ed., Praha: C.H. Beck, 2007.

RASHBROOKE, G.: The International Tribunal for the Law of the Sea: A Forum for the Development of Principles of International Environmental Law. *The International Journal of Marine and Coastal Law* 4/2004, pp. 515–535.

REPÍK, B.: Chrání Evropská úmluva o lidských právech právo na životní prostředí? [Does the European Convention on Human Rights Protect the Right to the Environment?]. *Bulletin advokacie* 7–8/2005, pp. 20–24 (part I), 9/2005, pp. 65–68 (part II).

ROTHWELL, D. R.: The Contribution of ITLOS to Ocean Governance through Marine Environmental Dispute Resolution. In: Ndiaye, T. M. – Wolfrum, R.: *Law of the Sea, Environmental Law and Settlement of Disputes.* Leiden, Boston: Martinus Nijhoff Publishers, 2007.

RŮŽIČKA, M. – POLÁK, P.: Nad jedním rozhodnutím Nejvyššího soudu týkajícím se problematiky *ne bis in idem* z hlediska jeho aspektů mezinárodních a vnitrostátních [On One Decision of the Supreme Court Dealing with *Ne Bis in Idem* and Considering Its National and International Aspects]. *Státní zastupitelství* 6/2005, pp. 2–16.

ŠÁMAL, P. – PÚRY, F. – SOTOLÁŘ, A. – ŠTENGLOVÁ, I.: *Podnikání a ekonomická kriminalita v České republice* [Undertaking Business and Economic Crime in the Czech Republic]. 1st ed., Praha: C. H. Beck, 2001.

ŠÁMAL, P.: K úvodním ustanovením připravované rektifikace trestního zákona [The Introductory Provisions of the Draft of Rectification of the Criminal Code]. *Trestněprávní revue* 12/2002, pp. 349–357.

SANDS, P.: *Principles of International Environmental Law.* 2nd ed., Cambridge: Cambridge University Press, 2003.

SHELTON, D.: Human Rights, Environmental Rights, and the Right to Environment. *Stanford Journal of International Law* 28/1991, pp. 103–138.

SIMMA, B. – PULKOWSKI, D.: Of Planets and the Universe: Self-contained Regimes in International Law. *EJIL* 3/2006, pp. 483–529.

ŠIROKÝ, J.: *Daně v Evropské unii* [Taxes in the European Union]. Praha: Linde, 2006.

ŠIROKÝ, J.: *Daňové teorie s praktickou aplikací* [Tax Theories with a Practical Application]. Praha: C. H. Beck, 2003.

ŠIŠKOVÁ, N.: *Dimenze ochrany lidských práv v Evropské Unii* [Dimensions of Human Rights Protection in European Union]. 2nd ed., Praha: Linde, 2008.

SMOLEK M. – STEJSKAL, V.: *Právo životního prostředí a jeho prosazování* [Environmental Law and Its Enforcement]. Praha: Karolinum, 2006.

SMOLEK, M.: Implementace a prosazování norem mezinárodního práva a práva Evropských společenství v oblasti ochrany životního prostředí [Implementation and Enforcement of the Rules of International Law and European Union Law in the Protection of the Environment]. *AUC Iuridica* 1/2005, pp. 9–144.

SMOLEK, M.: Judikatura Evropského soudního dvora [Case law of the European Court of Justice]. *Ekologie a právo* 2005–2007.

SOLNAŘ, V. – FENYK, J. CÍSAŘOVÁ, D.: *Základy trestní odpovědnosti* [The Basics of Criminal Liability]. Praha: Orac, 2003.

Souhrnná zpráva o činnosti Evropské unie 2007 [General Report on the European Union's Activities in 2007]. Luxembourg: Evropská společenství, 2008.

SPÁČIL, B.: *Teorie finančního práva ČSSR* [Theory of Financial Law in the Czechoslovak Socialist Republic]. Praha: Orbis, 1970.

STEJSKAL, V. – SOBOTKA, M.: Právo životního prostředí v judikatuře českých soudů [Environmental Law in the Case law of Czech Courts]. *Jurisprudence* 2/2006, pp. 77–85.

STEJSKAL, V.: *Prosazování právní odpovědnosti v ochraně biodiversity* [Enforcement of Liability in the Protection of Biodiversity]. Praha: Eva Rozkotová-IFEC, 2006.

STEJSKAL, V.: *Trestněprávní odpovědnost na úseku ochrany životního prostředí* [Criminal Liability in the Environmental Protection]. Praha: Univerzita Karlova, Právnická fakulta, 2002.

STEJSKAL, V.: *Úvod do právní úpravy ochrany přírody a péče o biologickou rozmanitost* [An Introduction to the Legal Regulation of Environmental Protection and Biological Diversity Care]. Praha: Linde, 2006.

ŠTĚPÁN, J.: *Právo a moderní lékařství* [Law and Modern Medicine]. Praha: Panorama, 1989.

ŠTURMA, P. et al.: *Konkurující jurisdikce mezinárodních rozhodovacích orgánů* [Competing Jurisdictions of International Decision-Making Bodies]. Praha: Ed. středisko PF UK, 2009.

ŠTURMA, P. et al.: *Mezinárodní právo životního prostředí. I. část (obecná)* [International Law of the Environment. Part I (General)]. Beroun: IFEC, 2004.

ŠTURMA, P.: Charta základních práv Evropské unie, její povaha a účinky [The Charter of Fundamental Rights of the European Union, Its Nature and Effects]. In: *Zborník z medzinárodnej konferencie Zmluva o Ústave pre Európu a ústavy členských štátov EÚ*. Bratislava: BVŠP, 2005.

ŠTURMA, P.: Evropská unie a členské státy před Evropským soudem pro lidská práva (ve světle případu Bosphorus) [European Union and the Member States before the European Court of Human Rights (in the light of Bosphorus case)]. *Právník* 1/2008, pp. 1–18.

ŠTURMA, P.: MSD k aplikaci Úmluvy o zabránění a trestání zločinu genocidia [The ICJ on the Application of the Convention on the Prevention and Punishment of the Crime of Genocide]. *Právní zpravodaj* 10/2007, pp. 11–15.

ŠTURMA, P.: Posudek MSD o právních následcích stavby zdi na obsazeném palestinském území [ICJ Advisory Opinion Concerning Legal Consequences of the Construction of a Wall in the Occupied Palestinian Territory]. *Právní zpravodaj* 9/2004, pp. 13–17.

Taxation trends in the European Union – Main results. 2008 ed., Luxembourg: European Communities, 2008.

TERYNGEL, J.: Ještě k rozlišení odpovědnosti právnických a fyzických osob [Distinguishing between Criminal Liability of Natural Persons and Legal Entities Revisited]. *Trestní právo* 12/1996, pp. 9–12.

TERYNGEL, J.: K trestní odpovědnosti právnických osob a osob za ně jednajících [On Criminal Liability of Legal Entities and Persons Acting on Their Behalf]. *Trestní právo* 1/1996, pp. 15–18.

TICHÁ, T.: Trestněprávní ochrana životního prostředí – zásadní vývoj v evropském právním prostředí [Criminal Protection of the Environment – Fundamental Development in European Legal Environment]. *České právo životního prostředí* 2/2005, pp. 9–17.

TIPKE, K.: *Die Steuerrechtsordnung*. Köln: Verlag Dr. Otto Schmidt, 2000.

TIPKE, L.: *Steuerrecht*. Köln: Verlag Dr. Otto Schmidt, 2005.

TOMÁŠEK, M. et al.: *Europeizace trestního práva* [Europeanisation of Criminal Law]. Praha: Linde, 2009.

TOMÁŠEK, M.: Mechanismy resistence národního ústavního práva vůči právu evropskému [Resistance Mechanisms of Domestic Constitutional Law to European Law]. *Právník* 11/2003, pp. 1057–1075.

TOMÁŠEK, M.: Soudcovská tvorba ochrany základních práv a svobod v procesu europeizace trestního práva [Judge-made Protection of Basic Rights and Freedoms in the Process of Europeanisation of Criminal Law]. *Acta Universitatis Carolinae Iuridica* 2/2006, pp. 7–33.

TOMSA, B.: *Právo mezinárodní* [International Law]. Bratislava: Právnická fakulta University Komenského, 1930.

VANÍČEK, D.: Trestní sankce ukládané právnickým osobám [Criminal Sanctions Imposed on Legal Entities]. *Trestní právo* 7-8/2006, pp. 12–19.

VANTUCH, P.: K návrhu zákona o trestní odpovědnosti právnických osob [The Draft Law on Criminal Liability of Legal Entities]. *Trestní právo,* 3/2003, pp. 2–9.

VOŠTA, L.: Několik poznámek k otázce vnitrostátní platnosti mezinárodních smluv [Several Notes on the Issue of National Validity of International Treaties]. In: *Pocta k šedesátým narozeninám Dr. Emila Háchy* [Tribute to Dr. Emil Hácha on the Occasion of his 70th Birthday]. Praha: Frant. Řivnáč, 1932, pp. 319–323.

WEYR, F.: *Československé právo ústavní* [Czechoslovak Constitutional Law]. Praha: Melantrich, 1937.

WEYR, F.: Pojem, změny a doplnění normy [The Concept, Changes of, and Amendment to the Rule]. *Vědecká ročenka Právnické fakulty Masarykovy university* 1932, pp. 26–40.

WINISDOERFFER, Y. – DUNN, G.: Le Manuel sur les droits de l'homme et l'environnement: ce que les états membres du Conseil de l'Europe retiennent de la jurisprudence „environnementaliste" de la Cour européenne des droits de l'homme. *Revue juridique de l'environnement* 4/2007, pp. 469–478.

4. TRANSFORMATION OF PRIVATE LAW

A new impulse for Czech private law at the beginning of the 21st century is brought in by the intended recodification of private law in the Czech Republic; its purpose will be primarily to reconstruct the understanding of a Civil Code as the general code of private law. The draft of a Civil Code is introduced along with the draft of a new Commercial Code and the draft of a new Private International Law Act. The background of private law has been significantly affected by the phenomenon called publicisation of private law which has brought elements of public law in the originally pure private law domain. This tendency may lead to a certain relativization of the concept of "private law", typically in company law to provide one example. Needless to say, procedural law as a whole, including civil procedure, is public law by its nature. Public law has been significantly projected in, for example, labour law, the trends of which seem to be quite autonomous when compared to the development of private law at the general level.

Private law has been undergoing a specific development within the process of European integration. Although the European Union has been originally linked primarily with public law serving as an integrating tool in many fields of approximation of the law of individual EU Member States in order to achieve the single market and other components of the single European area, private law has recently, however slowly, occupied a certain position within the European Union. What helps to promote the standing of private law in the EU is the process of harmonization of laws of individual EU Member States; directly unifying legislative acts are not exceptional, particularly those regulating private international law and procedure. On the other hand, a strong pressure to unify the rules of civil substantive law has been exercised primarily by academic jurists and the authors of individual subchapters are highly interested in the developments in this area. European private law and European private international law are phenomena that may not be disregarded and underestimated.

Private law should not be considered only from the European perspective of the unification within the European Union or the Council of Europe. Some authors pay attention to wider and global contexts and trends producing significant impacts upon private law as well, particularly the process of globalization affecting, for example, company law and labour law. Naturally, what should also be taken into consideration is the fact that we live in a postmodern society with more and more emphasis on the individual and his liberties, various cultures, various life styles and the need of coexistence and mutual respect. Post-modernism has an impact on private law although we do not always realize this effect.

Interesting aspects from common law have been applied not only in Czech law but generally in the continental system of law; typically this can be seen in European law where a certain kind of approximation and blending of both legal systems occurs. The process of penetration of common law into continental law cannot be stopped and it is necessary to get more information on the system as such and to take into account the positive features common law brings in. Comparison of various solutions of concrete issues in Czech law and common law has been paid some attention in Czech law although common law would deserve a more systematic treatment.

4.1 IS IT POSSIBLE TO BREAK THE BARRIER SEPARATING THE PROPERTY OF A BUSINESS COMPANY FROM THE PROPERTY OF ITS OWNERS?

4.1.1 The concept of penetration

The question forming the title of this subchapter has been raised by Czech case law only exceptionally. Czech jurisprudence deals with this topic primarily in comparative texts focussing on foreign legal doctrines, in references to interesting decisions of courts in some European countries and to decision-making of the European Court of Justice.[679] However, the whole topic denoted illustratively as the *piercing* or *lifting of the corporate veil* by the common law terminology or as *Durchgriff* by German legal terminology has been attracting attention in Western countries for decades.

The biggest interest is shown in the penetration through the veil of "capital" companies (limited), particularly one-member private limited liability companies because their legal construction seems to be the most appropriate vehicle for the enforcement of individual interests of their members. The penetration in the legal personality of a legal entity, or a business company, is – in its proper and narrower sense – mostly understood as disregarding one of its attributes, namely the property separate from that of its members. Jurisprudence speaks about the principle of separation of property of the legal entity and its members which is broken through penetration.[680] The capital company and its members are seen as if no line existed between them. Figuratively speaking, the veil covering the holder of rights and protecting its members is being pierced. The practical question is whether, and under what circumstances creditors may satisfy their claims against the company from the property

---

[679] Kühn, Z.: Fikce samostatnosti právnických osob a její prolomení [The Fiction of the Separate Nature of Legal Entities and Its Breakthrough]. *Právní rozhledy* 11/2003, pp. 542–552; Pauknerová, M.: *Společnosti v mezinárodním právu soukromém* [Companies in Private International Law]. Karolinum, Praha 1998; Glückselig, R.: Průlom do právní autonomie obchodních společností [Penetration into the Legal Autonomy of Business Companies]. *Právní rozhledy* 5/2002, p. 219 and subs.; MacGregor, R.: Americká koncepce akciové společnosti a vztahů v ní [The American Concept of a Stock Corporation and Relations Therein]. *Právní rozhledy* 23/2004, p. 868 and subs.; Černá, S.: Evropský a tuzemský přístup ke skupinám společností [European and National Attitude to the Group of Company]. In: Eliáš, K. (ed.): *Soukromé právo v pohybu* [Private Law in Motion]. Plzeň: Aleš Čeněk, 2005, pp. 16–24; Černá, S.: K rozdílům mezi německou a francouzskou koncepcí skupin společností [On the Differences Between German and French Conceptions of the Groups of Companies]. *Právní rozhledy* 8/2004, pp. 288–292.
[680] Schmidt, K.: *Gesellschaftsrecht*. 4th ed., Köln: Carl Heymanns Verlag, 2002, pp. 217, 218.

of members disregarding the generally acceptable and legally governed construction of a capital company as an autonomous entity with respect to its property.

The main function of penetration is the protection of creditors in the widest sense of the term, i.e. not only creditors holding the position of a party in private relations, but also the protection of public interests incorporated in legislation regulating taxation, banking law, environmental protection, etc.

The core of the issue is to define the theoretical background and concrete solutions built upon allowing third persons to reach a company member who is otherwise protected by the wall of separate property liability of a business company, and to treat him as a holder, or co-holder, of duties arising out of acts or omissions of a company.[681] At the same time the question arises of what other solutions are available in addition to penetration.

The theory as well as case law in countries mentioned below is based on the principle that the limits of a legal entity should not be easily surpassed, i.e. it may happen only exceptionally. The concept of penetration conflicts with the principle of legal certainty establishing one of the cornerstones of private relations. Nevertheless, such solution is acceptable when breaking the barrier separating the property of a business company from the property of its owners is justified by extraordinary circumstances. Penetration then serves as a corrective measure of the principle of property separation where its absolute preservation would lead to apparently unjust conclusions.

4.1.2 Case law and the doctrine in Anglo-American law

Anglo-American case law, and subsequently jurisprudence, dealt with the issues of penetration much earlier than European law on the Continent. The common law doctrine of piercing or lifting the veil of a company appears to be a product of the extensive law of precedents created by English and American courts.[682] The attention of jurisprudence was attracted by an enormous number of cases where plaintiffs challenged particularly the separation of company property from that of its members in situations where, due to the circumstances of individual cases, they considered such separation to be openly unjust. Although they did not cast doubt on the dogmatic and legally stable doctrine that the capital company itself, not its members, would be fully liable for its debts, the courts in individual cases did not respect this doctrine and determined that the members were liable for the debts of the company. Such relativization of the borders of a legal entity was a reaction to the abuse and even harmfulness of the separation of a company's property from that of its members.

Anglo-American case law has been quite multifarious, not uniform in its arguments and different in the classification of relevant criteria that it appears to be rather impossible to categorize the grounds for penetration. English courts have considered penetration (lifting the veil) quite exceptional but possible where there are circumstances requiring that justice

---

[681]/ The concept of penetration is much wider and encompasses (1) unlimited ("personal") companies as suggested primarily by German case law and practice, (2) penetration against the company, and (3) penetration in favour of the company and its members. Penetration is not confined just to business companies. Keeping the wider context in mind I will focus on capital companies, particularly private limited liability companies.

[682]/ The doctrine of lifting the veil is a combined outcome of both common law and the law of equity.

disregards the separation of a company's property. A typical situation based on qualified grounds has been the abuse of formation and activities of a group of companies for fraudulent purposes, particularly in the case of evading duties which would have essentially been enforceable by the original company.[683] The abuse of a holding group of companies may subsist in "the breach of trust" among their members to such an extent that risky activities are "delegated" to subsidiaries so that these subsidiaries will bear all risk whilst the holding company will collect the profit.[684] The variance of case law solutions has been reflected on by the doctrine which lacks an agreement with respect to the arrangement of the whole issue and to drawing up general conclusions.

A uniform doctrine of penetration has not been established even in the USA although the issue has been one of the most debated areas within corporate law. The basis has been formed, and is developed by case law, particularly in connection with solving the consequences of the creation of groups of companies.[685] In both the UK and the US, separate property of a legal entity has been a general principle and any breach of this principle may be pursued with ultimate care. Nevertheless, the breach is practicable primarily where there is such confusion with respect to the property and interests of the holding company and its subsidiary that the border between the two erodes and the subsidiary loses its autonomy acting as an agent of its holding; the elements essential for the subsidiary as a legal entity become erased in that relationship.

In the absence of a uniform doctrine, case law (see Judge McHugh in Laya v. Erin Homes, Inc.)[686] has attempted to create a list of reasons (far from being exhaustive) which should be take into account when deciding on penetration. These are cases where a company's property is commingled with property of its members, or where a company's property is used for private purposes of members, or where a member causes third persons to believe that he is personally liable for the debts of the company. Other situations may occur, namely where identical persons act on behalf of two or more companies; or a company has been operated exclusively in order to accomplish a particular trade transaction of an individual or a legal entity; or where all shares in a company are in the hands of one person or family, or the assets and liabilities have been distributed among "enterprises" in such a way that assets concentrate on one part and the liabilities on the other; or a company has been used to undertake unlawful business and/or to reduce the risk resulting from default; or a company has been formed to assume the debts of another person; or a company has insufficient initial capital considering the business risk involved which should have been envisaged by its founding members at the time of formation;[687] or the formation and subsequent operation of a company does not comply with relevant substantive and procedural legislation

[683]/ See, for example, Creasy v. Breachwood Motors, Ltd. [1993] BCLC 480, [1992] BCC 638 (Q.B.).
[684]/ Wallersteiner v. Moir [2A All E.R. (All England Reports) 217 (Court of Appeal 1974)]. *Ibidem.*
[685]/ Only Texas has passed legislation regulating the piercing of corporate veil.
[686]/ Merkt., H. – Göthel, S. R.: *US-amerikanisches Gesellschaftsrecht.* 2nd ed., Frankfurt am Main: Verlag Recht und Wirtschaft GmbH, 2006, p. 239.
[687]/ Usually, the insufficient initial capital itself does not suffice for the purpose of piercing and other conditions must be fulfilled. However, if a company has insufficient capital subsequently as a result of unexpected circumstances this does not establish the reason for permission to pierce the corporate veil (see Truckweld Equipment Co., Inc. V. Olson, 618 P.2d 1017, 1022 (Wash. Ct.App.1981); Fletcher, Cyc. Corp. § 41.72). *Ibidem* at p. 243.

(no constituting general meeting is held, investments have not been paid up, etc.) The last example given proves the courts' position that the members of a company may not acquire and use advantages of corporate law if they have failed to comply with requirements establishing those advantages (e.g. paying up their investments). The above-listed reasons, although there are many more to consider, are not self-sufficient. A US judge, in order to consider the piercing, must give an affirmative answer to the question whether the rigid preservation of the principle of a company's separate property may protect fraudulent conduct or support injustice, i.e. that persons behind the company intended to use it to twist the third parties in fraudulent and mischievous ways. The described connection must therefore be abused in a qualified way.

It seems to be logical that piercing has not applied to stock corporations (joint-stock companies) but exclusively to one-member private limited companies, or multi-member family companies as the pre-requisite of the piercing is personal and active participation of a member in the company governance. More often the courts tend to penetrate the separate liability of a company with respect to contractual obligations rather than tortious duties, although they may argue that in contracts the creditor can direct the choice of his debtor and therefore the creditor should bear a greater risk of failure.

The doctrine, in order to draft at least a rough classification of concrete reasons for penetration, states that the main and most frequent reason is control[688] as a product of common law, having an instrumentality test as its basis.[689] The second group of grounds for penetration encompasses a large number of cases where penetration is justified by claiming public interests (public policy), or that the company itself should assist its member to evade the statutory ban protecting public policy. These cases are subject to the so-called *alter ego test*.[690] The final group of grounds (belonging to the law of equity) is immediately connected neither with dominance nor evasion of the statutory ban and subsists in the failure to comply with formalities in operation of the company, and in insufficient capitalisation.

The piercing of the corporate veil as the legal institution of corporate law is not the only or standard solution of creditors' and public policy protection, but it is part of a wider system of protective measures. It applies as an extraordinary means of the protection of creditors, in addition to the protection based on the doctrine of equitable subordination[691] and upon the institutions of tort law based primarily on statutes of fraud and general liability for damage.

---

[688]/ Cohen, H.: Grounds for Disregarding the Corporate Entity and Piercing the Corporate Veil. *American Jurisprudence* 1/1998.

[689]/ The instrumentality test is to ascertain the dominance or neglect of the barrier between a company and its members. A judge will not consider the company to be the autonomous holder of rights if the company is subject to such circumstances that it lacks its own will and becomes a mere instrument of its members; dominance has been used to commit fraud or any other wrong, i.e. for unlawful purposes, and such a manner of governance and use of the company gives rise to damage or unjust injury.

[690]/ This test subsist in that the company is not considered as an autonomous holder of rights where the interests and property are interwoven to such an extent that there is almost no chance to separate them; their separation would permanently preserve fraud or support injustice.

[691]/ The doctrine of equitable subordination can be used by creditors for their protection against the company becoming insolvent. Its origin lies in the law of precedents; it became a basis for the Bankruptcy Act 1978, as amended.

4.1.3 German approach

Scholarly debate in Continental Europe focused on penetration is much younger. In Germany, it developed after the 2nd World War and was inspired by the Anglo-American theories. Legal practitioners in Germany discuss the borders of separate property of a company particularly in relation with "destructing" intrusions of a company member in the company's property, or removing the company's property to the detriment of its creditors, and in relation to the protection of creditors of such a company finding itself in a critical position due to such removals. The principle of legal personality and the related principle of separate corporate property has been firmly rooted in German law. However, German case law raised the question whether penetration, or external sanction of a company member by its creditors, would be possible. Such sanction applies almost exclusively to members of a private limited company. The background for decision-making of German courts subsists in their attempt to clear the loophole in the statutory protection of basic capital, or in the protection of creditors through sufficient basic capital of the company.

Judgments of German courts have undergone an interesting development in the last thirty years. The Federal Court of Justice of Germany in its judgments from the 1980s and 1990s was hesitant to create any independent conception of penetration but it formed, by statutory analogy,[692] the so-called external sanctioning of a governing member abusing his position in the company. The Court permitted that, under specific circumstances, the member who is the person managing the actual holding, will not compensate every individual injury caused to the company regulated thereby but he will be obliged to pay directly for the debts to the creditors of the company regulated. Such approach is built upon *the doctrine of a qualified holding company as a matter of fact* which denotes a business entity in Germany based on the actual control where the regulating company applies its influence in such a compact manner that individual interventions cannot be separated and, as a result, potential negative consequences cannot be repaired through compensation of every single injury. Should such a company be subject to *bankruptcy*, which means the termination of the holding entity, the court may decide, upon the petition of creditors, that the case will be adjudicated by analogy according to s. 303 of the Shares Act (Aktiengesetz) imposing on the regulated company a duty to ascertain claims of creditors when the holding terminates. It would be irrational to require the holding company just to provide security for its debts; therefore the Court came to the conclusion through extensive interpretation that, instead of providing security for debts, the regulating company would be directly obliged to pay the creditors' claims against the company regulated. Where no contract to control the company has been made but the regulating company executes upon the other member of the holding its influence intensively and in a compact way *disregarding its interest*, it is not acceptable that the regulating entity be in a more advantageous position than that with the existence of a controlling contract stipulating a stricter regime for the contractual holding (as a matter of law).

---

[692]/Judgment Autokran of 16th September 1985, II ZR 275/84, GmbHR 1986, 78; judgment Video of 23rd September 1991 II ZR 135/90, GmbHR 1991, 520. A certain shift in decision-making of the Federal Court of Justice indicating further conceptual changes was judgment TBB of 29th March 1992 BGHZ, 122, 123.

In its judgment in Bremer Vulkan of 17th September 2001,[693] the Federal Court left its references to securities law and formed an independent concept of liability of the controlling member for the destruction of the company. The member, regardless of holding law, is liable for damages to the company if he is at fault and liable for the destruction of the company through his determinative influence. This judgment has brought light in ordinary cases but lacked the conception of penetration to be used in extreme cases.

In its judgment in KBV of 24th June 2002[694] the Federal Court of Justice formulated penetration (Durchgriff) *stricto sensu*; the principle of penetration was made the basis for separate company's property and the conclusion the Court arrived at provided protection to creditors built upon company law. The general premise in this judgment has subsisted in the denial of the right of members having abused the legal form of a limited liability company to seek the privilege of no liability for debts of such company stipulated in s. 1 (2) GmbHG.[695] The abuse subsisted in such intrusion by members in the property of the company that its capability of fulfilling its obligations against creditors was minimized. The deprivation of the privilege was conditional on the fact that the members themselves failed to respect the company's property separate from their own property and that the company concerned failed to take any measure to remove such situation under ss. 30 and 31 GmbH. Simplifying the context of the case we may say that the Court accepted an approach similar to the Anglo-American piercing/lifting the corporate veil. German case law has recognized the possibility of creditors to have recourse against the member having abused his managing position in the company resulting in the bankruptcy, even through the application of general liability for damage.

In 2007 however, the Federal Court of Justice in its Trihotel judgment on 16th July 2007[696] diverted not only from the conception of penetration being the institution of company law (having been criticized by some legal theoreticians), but also from external recourse of the creditor against the member within tort law. The existing concept was replaced by the concept of internal tort liability under s. 826 BGB, i.e. liability to the company of the member for his intentionally causing damage in a way contrary to good morals (Innenhaftung). The creditor would be protected indirectly since the claim for damages may be raised only by the company itself against its member under the general provision for liability for civil wrongs.

One of the motives for the German shift to internal liability has been the original French regulation of the action for complementing receivables (replaced by Art. 625-1 CC) and similar Italian and Spanish provisions missing in Germany, and the English and Scottish regulation of wrongful and fraudulent trading permitting expansion of the recourse from only governing persons to include real directors.[697] Such foreign insolvency solutions are

---

693/ II ZR 178/99, GmbHR 2001, 1036.
694/ II ZR 300/00, GmbHR 2002, 902.
695/ "GmbH" – The Act on Private Limited Companies of 20th April 1892, as amended.
696/ II ZR 3/04, GmbHR 2007, 927.
697/ The English regulation and case law has reached the protection of creditors of an insolvent company through the combination of liability of the bodies of a company for defective governance and expansion of the liability to shadow persons (the conception of so-called wrongful trading). English law creates special facts of unlawful conduct subsisting in delaying the critical situation in the company. The objective presumption of liability of the governing

understood as the institutions of company law since they are built upon the breach of duty by a member against the company. External or direct liability of a member for damage caused to the creditors of the company should be complemented with the fact that even in France and the United Kingdom, which have special provisions for the protection of creditors of an insolvent company and for the purposes of solving extraordinary cases of abuse of a member's position in the company, courts accept the concept of penetration behind the veil of separate company's property in its narrow sense as well as the principles of the general law of obligations.

However, the Trihotel judgment has not been accepted only positively in Germany.[698] Primarily, the objection is that the application of the general rule of civil law (s. 826 BGB) may not be restricted by the decision of a court with reference to a better applicability of its own decision. The elements of conduct stipulated in s. 826 are to protect any injured party including a company as well as its individual creditors, if the party establishes that he has been intentionally injured by a company member, in a way incompatible with good manners, through abuse of the legal form of the company. Other objections are raised in the field of conflicts of laws. In this context it should be noted that the second chamber of the federal Court of Justice has only indicated the direction to be followed in similar cases. Future development in this area is expected.

4.1.4 French doctrine and case law

France also recognizes the rule of maintaining the separate property of a capital company from that of its members. However, the application of this rule has also been limited. French courts are in a better position than those in Germany when punishing a member controlling the company since the French Commercial Code provides creditors with special means to involve the holding company in the solution of crisis in its subsidiary.

Under Art. 625-1 Code de commerce[699] where a legal entity (including a business company) becomes insolvent and the situation is solved by bankruptcy procedure (liquidation judiciare) the court may, during the proceedings, decide that the person having been a member of its body (dirigent de droit) or a director as a matter of fact, or actual director (dirigent de fait) should bear partial or full liability for the debts of the company (l'obligation des

---

body for damage caused to creditors is not to permit any further reduction of chances of creditors to have their claims satisfied (s. 14 (3) Insolvency Act), where the situation of the company dramatically worsens. Members of the "endangered" company must do their best to prevent damage to property of creditors (to apply for liquidation, to restore the company, etc.) The cumulative requirement for liability for damage to arise (being of a subjective nature) is that company members foresaw and could have foreseen that insolvency was inevitable (real success need not be achieved). Liability for defective governance acquires a wider dimension and is also held by a member managing the company informally (shadow director).

[698]/ Dauner-Lieb, B.: Die Existenzvernichtungshaftung als deliktische Innenhaftung gemäss § 826 BGB. *ZGR* 1/2008, p. 34 and subs., Schanze, E.: Gesellschafterhaftung für unlautere Einflussnahme nach § 826 BGB: Die Trihotel-Doktrin des BGH. *NZG* 18/2007, pp. 681–686. Theiselmann, R.: Die Existenzvernichtungshaftung im Wandel. Das „Trihotel"-Urteil des BGH vom 16. 7. 2007 – II ZR 3/04 und seine Praxisfolgen. *GmbHR* 17/2007, pp. 904–907, Krolop, K.: Die deliktische Haftung der Gesellschafter wegen Gläubigerschädigung bei der GmbH und der in Deutschland aktiven Limited im Licht des MoMiG und der Aufgabe des bisherigen Konzepts der Existenzvernichtungshaftung. *NotBZ* 8/2007, p. 265 and subs.

[699]/ This provision was incorporated in the Commercial Code by Act No. 2005-845 of 26th July 2005, which became effective on 1st January 2006 (except Art. 190).

dettes sociales). This will happen in the situation where he committed any of the enumerated defects contributing to the company's failure to pay its debts. The Act provides for five reasons when collective proceedings against the legal entity may be expanded to its legal or actual director. These are cases when the person governing the company "legally" or "as a matter of fact" disposed of its property as if it was his own property; covered his operations with the veil of the legal entity and made the company's transaction in his own interest; used the company's property and loans contrary to the interests of the company for personal purpose of for the benefit of another entity in which he was directly or indirectly involved; abusing the property caused the deficit of the legal entity, rendering it unable to pay its debts as they fell due; embezzled or concealed all assets of the legal entity, or their part, or fraudulently increased its liabilities. The list shows that the approach is similar to the grounds enumerated above in relation to the decision-making of Anglo-American courts in piercing or lifting the corporate veil.

In addition to special provisions of insolvency law the French legal environment has formed concepts enabling creditors, in order to satisfy their claims against a company, to reach the liable member without the solution being connected with insolvency. This possibility is provided by the concept of a fictitious company (société fictive), which reacts to the situation when a company is just a dummy company. The background idea is that a company may not be a tool for the enforcement of the interests of (typically) one member but that it is based on *affectio societatis* and that it has its own interests separate from those of its individual members, which is expressed in its organizational and property autonomy. The French doctrine and case law have not been so strict to always apply this principle when the company has one member with 100% share and the member is also the only director; but along with other circumstantial evidence such as operating his own trade under the name of the company, absence of the organizational autonomy of the company, etc., such conclusion can be reached.[700]

Another background solution for the sanctioning of an abusing member has been the concept of joining the property (*confusion de patrimoine*). This partly overlaps with the concept of a fictitious company but, in addition to a high property share in the company and involvement in its governance, there should also be disappearing borders between the property of the member and that of the company. This approach is quite close to the German "penetrating liability of members" for the debts of the company (*Durchgriffgshaftung*) in the German understanding explained above. The number of French judgments based on this concept significantly exceeds the number of German judicial decisions.

French courts sometimes affirm the application of a creditor requiring satisfaction of his claim against the company by its controlling member under the doctrine of apparentness (théorie d'apparence). This happens when the member, being the holding company, causes the impression of identity with its subsidiary particularly because their names are interchangeable, or the companies have the same registered offices, or they use the identical head-letter paper, or negotiations to make a contract are held once under the name of

---

[700]/ Meyer, J.: *Haftungs-beschränkung im Recht der Handelsgesellschaften*. Berlin, Heidelberg, New York: Springer, 2000, pp. 452, 453.

the holding and once under the name of the subsidiary, the holding company intentionally causes the creditor to think that he is to be a real debtor, etc.[701]

In addition to the approaches resulting from the legal principles and doctrines built-upon, the creditor, in order to protect himself against the member, may apply general tort law, namely Art. 1382 of the French Civil Code; this provision creates the liability to damages. The provision includes damage caused to the property of the creditor by intentional conduct of the member contrary to good morals pursued using the legal form of a private limited company.

4.1.5 Possibilities of recourse against a company member by creditors of the company under Czech law

The Czech business environment is also typical of attempts by creditors to reach the property of a company's member in situations when members, through their destructive intervention in the company property, caused the company to become insolvent, or its insolvency deeper and more extensive. Czech law also permits arguments resulting from the understanding of a business company (typically a private limited company) as a set of interlinked and mutually conditional constructing elements. The privilege of limited liability is subject to the condition that property brought into the company should be multiplied, tied to the fulfilment of the purposes of the company and used to discharge debts incurred by the company in reaching its objectives; at the same time, members should respect the separation of their property from that of the company and give regard to the interest of the company as a separate legal entity. The privilege of no liability should restrict business risks. However, it protects members who act fairly. On the contrary, the breach of the prohibition to abuse the law or the legal form of a business company (if proven) should make ineffective the mandatory provision of a law stipulating no liability of company members. This solution of the abusive intrusion of a member into the company's property, and the protection of creditors built thereupon is the legal institution of company law. However, such an attitude allows for an intervention into legal certainty, or more concretely, into the separate property status of a business company as a deeply rooted institution of company law. Thus, two legal principles conflict, namely abrogative consequences of a breach of law and legal certainty.

Since penetration into the separate nature of a company's property must be considered as an *ultima ratio*, the question should be primarily posed whether the protection of creditors is to be built upon standard legal measures, and whether such protection can be sufficiently effective. In other words, what chances are offered to the creditors by the special and general parts of tort law.

Abusive intrusion into the company's property is more likely to be pursued by a member with dominant or at least significant influence; therefore a question arises to what extent the legal regulation of an actual holding company (i.e. a holding company as a matter of fact) punishing such dominance provides the creditors with any measure to "reach" the controlling member. The answer is negative since the basic function of the legal regime of

---

[701] *Ibidem* at pp. 453, 454.

the actual holding company under Czech law is to protect the controlled company and its members. Provisions for the holding company generally prohibit the controlling person to apply its dominance to the detriment of the controlled company, but they stipulate conditions which, if respected, legalize the "negative" influence.[702] The controlling company is obliged to compensate its subsidiary for harm caused due to its exercising of the dominance by the end of the accounting period within which the harm was caused, or to enter into a contract on compensation (s. 66a (8) Commercial Code, ComC).[703] Should the harm fail to be compensated, the controlling company owes the duty to reimburse the damage caused thereby (s. 66a (14) ComC). At the same time the controlling company has a duty to cover the loss sustained by members of the subsidiary due to the failure to compensate the harm (s. 66a (14) ComC). Another tool for the protection of the controlled company, although not very efficient, is the secondary liability of persons (standing as sureties as of law) establishing the governing body of the controlling company for the fulfilment of duties of the controlling company to reimburse the damage to the subsidiary (s. 66a (15) first sentence, ComC). Members of the governing body of the subsidiary are also liable if they have drafted an incomplete report on the relations between the interlinked persons (s. 66a (15) second sentence, ComC).

We can summarize that the Czech regulation of the actual holding company does not stipulate any special duty of the controlling persons against creditors of the controlled person or against third persons.[704] The regulation is directed "into" the holding company, it protects the controlled person (subsidiary) and creditors are protected indirectly through the law providing for the removal of negative consequences of the controlling influence and for the fostering of the ability of the subsidiary to fulfil its obligations.

The legal regime of the actual holding is primarily aimed at protecting the controlled person. The Czech legislature in subsection 190 (5) ComC copied German provisions of s. 302 AktG under which, briefly speaking, the controlling person must compensate to the controlled person for uncovered annual loss; however, the Czech legislature failed to incorporate in the Czech legislation s. 303 AktG creating the duty of the controlling person, after the contractual holding has terminated, to ascertain all claims of creditors against the controlled company occurred before the registration in the Commercial Register of the termination of the controlling contract, or the contract for the transfer of profits, if the creditors so require within the prescribed time-limit. Subsection 190 (5) ComC enables the creditors of the controlled company to raise against the controlling company, and under specified circumstances, the claim resulting from the secondary liability for the discharge of obligation to compensate the damage sustained as a result of the breach of duties by persons giving orders and instructions on behalf of the controlling person to the governing body of the controlled company. This provision applies to a member of the controlled company only if it is a controlling person at the same time. Another consequence is that there is no duty

---

[702] Černá, S. – Čech, P.: Ke způsobům prosazování rozhodujícího vlivu v ovládané akciové společnosti, jeho podmínkám a důsledkům [On the Modes of Enforcing the Dominant Position in the Controlled Joint-stock Company, Its Conditions and Consequences]. *Obchodněprávní revue* 1/2009, p. 14 and subs.

[703] Act No. 513/1991 Sb., the Commercial Code, as amended ("ComC").

[704] The only exception is the above-mentioned duty of the controlling persons to cover the loss sustained by members of the controlled person (s. 66a (14) ComC).

to pay for the claims of creditors against the controlled company, but statutory (secondary) liability for the obligation to compensate damage caused to the creditor.

Section 66c ComC is the provision stipulating the sanctions against the company member whose actions have a negative impact upon the company. The section reads: "*Everyone who uses his dominant position in the company and intentionally compels persons acting as the governing body, or a member thereof, members of the supervisory board, the proctor or any other authorized representative of the company, to act to the detriment of the company or its members, shall be liable for the fulfilment of duty to compensate damage caused due to such conduct.*" As can be inferred from this provision, the establishing of an intention to cause damage is the essential element of such conduct. The provision describes unlawful conduct, i.e. a wrong, giving rise to secondary liability. Unlike subsection 66a (6) ComC this provision does not require continuing influence but only one intervention suffices. The mode of influence is determined by the group of persons subject to the influence (see above). The provision governs the sanctioning secondary liability held by the person exercising its dominance for the fulfilment of obligation to compensate damage caused to the company or its members by persons subject to such dominance. The prerequisite of such secondary liability is that any of the above-listed persons becomes liable for damage to the company or its members. Should no such liability arise no secondary liability may follow. If we consider the quoted provision from the point of view of external sanctions against members for their abusive intervention in the company's property and as a potential tool for the protection of creditors, it becomes quite clear that the provision can fulfil such a function only indirectly and does not allow for direct sanctions against the member by creditors. Secondary liability ensures that the obligation to compensate the damage sustained by the company and its members be discharged; the obligation is owed by the above-listed persons having breached their duties against the company. The provision is not formulated in a way to primarily protect third persons unless members of the company concerned are included.

The bridge across which the creditor could reach the member is constructed in subsection 66 (6) ComC. This provision allows for the extension of both primary liability and statutory (secondary) liability stipulated in the Commercial Code or special legislation applicable to persons acting as governing bodies, or members thereof, of the company, i.e. including the member who, as a so-called actual director, has a significant impact upon the company's activities. This provision covers cases deviating from the framework defined by the law of holding companies. Its wording may also apply to abusive intrusion in the company's property if exercised by a member through persons who, in their capacity as governing bodies, or members thereof, of the company subject to the impact, determine the activities of the company concerned.

The requirement for the expansion of applicability of the provision for primary liability and secondary (i.e. statutory at the same time) liability of a member is that the member's impact upon the activities of the company is substantial (see the wording of s. 66 (6) ComC – "*person who … substantially affects …*"), i.e. restricting the autonomous decision-making of the company in a substantial manner. Usually it will take a longer time (see the wording of s. 66 (6) ComC above), but it may be repeated, if not continuous, and exceptionally one occurrence is permissible. Substantial impact apparently does not cover such conduct of the actual director that has a single effect where the influence is not significant.

Secondary liability to creditors for the debts of the company may, in a limited scope, be extended to a member in his capacity as actual director. The scope of his potential secondary liability will be confined to the damage which has not been compensated by persons having caused harm to the company (i.e. including the member in his capacity as actual director (ss. 66 (6), 135 (2) and 194 (6) ComC). The requirement for the secondary liability of so-called legal as well as actual directors to arise is the failure to reimburse the damage caused and, at the same time the insolvency of the company or the fact that the company suspended its payments. However, sanctioning the member due to his statutory (secondary) liability is usually very problematic. Practical experience suggests that the procedure described is used quite exceptionally.

The external sanctioning of a member by creditors, in a wider sense of the term, may include the duty of the member to pay damages to the creditors. Under s. 66 (6) ComC, the company as well as third persons may, under the circumstances defined, claim damages against the member acting in his capacity as actual director. This liability may be therefore divided into its internal part (to the company) and external liability to third persons, i.e. including creditors. Outside the scope of the Commercial Code, there are some special, usually narrowly defined, provisions governing direct liability for damage applicable to persons – bodies, or members thereof, along with members (applying s. 66 (6) ComC) who exercised their impact upon them "from the shadow". However, such provisions are quite rare. They can be found in the regulation of transformation of business companies and cooperatives, namely s. 50 of Act No. 125/2008 Sb., providing for no-fault liability for damage caused to creditors[705] by a breach of duties of a member of the governing body of the participating company or cooperative.

The special regulation of civil liability of governing bodies along with dominant company members for damage caused to creditors is governed by insolvency law, namely the breach of a duty to file an insolvency petition (ss. 98a and 99 of Act No. 182/2006 Sb. on insolvency and the modes of its solution, the Insolvency Act). If it is established that the governing persons have breached their duty to file the petition due to the qualified impact of a member, creditors may "reach" him. This is the damage caused to the creditors due to the failure to file the petition and not the secondary liability for debts of the company.[706] Therefore, the creditor shall not satisfy his claim against the company from the property of the member but he claims the compensation for damage sustained due to the breach of non-contractual duty of the members of the governing body adversely affected by the member. These provisions do not respond to the intervention of the member in the company property causing or deepening its insolvency, but they relate to specific and factually different cases.

---

[705] In addition to creditors some other persons are also protected by damages, namely persons participating in the transformation and their members.

[706] See the judgment of the Supreme Court of the Czech Republic 29 Odo 1220/2005 of 27th September 2007, which applies to the duty under Act No. 328/1991 Sb., on bankruptcy and composition, namely s. 3 (l) and (2).

Considering the potential of s. 66 (6) ComC in the light of the protection of creditors it provides for only a limited possibility to impose direct sanctions upon the member either under statutory liability for the debts of the company (typically as a result of the breach of duties of so-called governing persons in their governance of the company under the significant influence of the member) or under direct liability for damage caused to creditors in special cases. Special regulation of tort law is applicable to the latter cases.

Concrete circumstances of a particular case need not, however, allow for the sanctioning of the member under the regulation of primary or secondary liability of bodies or their members. In situations where the impact of the member upon the company is exercised outside the structure of company bodies, or only partly through them, and the interventions of the member in the company's property are performed by various means and through various persons, the application of general law of obligations may be considered, i.e. general civil regulation of tort liability (due to its subsidiarity). Section 424 of Act No. 40/1964 Sb., the Civil Code, provides for the duty to compensate damage caused by intentional conduct against good morals. The intrusion of the member into the company's property removing the property from its original purpose and causing or deepening its insolvency may be, depending on the circumstances, considered as a subgroup of the category of intentionally causing damage by conduct against good morals. This general clause of tort law allows for reaching not only company members themselves and members of the governing bodies but also other persons who remove property from the company in any other way thus assisting in the intentional detrimental conduct against good morals.

4.1.6 Conclusion

The protection of creditors should not be understood in a paternalistic way since the creditors themselves should, using the instruments of contract law, take all necessary steps in order to satisfy their claims. Both contractual and non-contractual means for the protection are the issues to be solved by individual Member States. The European Court of Justice has expressed its opinion that it is up to Member States within their freedom of establishment to ensure the protection of creditors against fraudulent activities.[707] The efficiency of means for the protection of creditors is one of the factors to strengthen competitiveness of the legal environment of every Member State. The protection of creditors using the penetration through the veil of separate property of the company as the institution of company law represents an extreme solution. However, such mode of the protection of creditors should not be refused *a priori*. Such a solution will be marginal if there are other means for the protection, namely special regulation of the law of obligation or, as subsidiary regulation, general tort law. Only where these tools fail or are ineffective it is possible, in justified cases, to consider the abrogative use of the prohibition to abuse the legal form of a business company.

---

[707] Judgment of the European Court of Justice in *Centros* of 9th March 1999, case C-212/97.

4.2 CONTRACTUAL OBLIGATIONS AND OBLIGATIONS RESULTING FROM TORTS: EUROPEAN TRADITION AND CZECH PERSPECTIVE

The law of obligations belongs to the branches most influenced by Roman law. The survival of the Roman tradition has been typical of the whole West European continent (France, Belgium, Switzerland, Germany, Italy, etc.), but Roman law has also its significance in the Far East (the Japanese Code) and South America (the Civil Codes of Argentina, Brazil, Colombia or Chile). Thus it is not surprising that there is the highest number of similarities – both systemic and material – in the law of obligations compared to other branches of law in the European legal systems. A more concrete example of the converging tendencies was an attempt to draft a common code of obligations for France and Italy between the world wars.[708] Although the draft was not enacted it served as evidence of the common basis of obligations in these two countries. The original system of obligations was created for a totally different economic system, namely the economic system of Ancient Rome, but during more than two thousand years of its development the law of obligations gradually adapted to the needs of modern societies, and it managed to enhance and strengthen contractual activities. Obligations of today belong to the most dynamic parts of civil law, whether it be contract law or the law of civil wrongs (also termed delicts or torts).

In the beginning of the 21st century no one dared underestimate the significance of either contract law or tort law. The basic function of the law of obligations has remained identical despite the bustling developments in the society. The purpose is that the legal framework makes the fulfilment of any human needs practicable through mutual cooperation in a modern highly technological and information society functioning through the Internet and oriented at education. The attention drawn to the law of obligations at the European and international level proves its significance. The European intercommunity trade, and attempts to improve it and increase its quality, was one of initializing moments for the supranational harmonizing tendencies to pursue. National legal systems of EU Member States have witnessed Europeanization of the whole private law, particularly the contours of the main principles of European contract law can be seen more clearly (*Lando's Commission on European Contract Law, Gandolfi Academy of European Private Lawyers*). The tendency is visible in the law of torts. Inspired by "The Principles of European Contract Law", the European Centre for Tort Law (ECTIL) has recently published "The Principles of European Tort Law" which have or may become a stimulating basis for legislatures in individual EU Member States. Today the inspiring and synthesizing value of "The Principles" should not be disregarded by drafters of national legislation.

4.2.1 Classification of the law of obligations

Various criteria may be chosen to classify obligations. What has a practical impact is the categorization of obligations according to the legal grounds for their creation. The whole law of obligations is then subdivided into two large groups: the law of contractual obligations and the law of obligations resulting from torts (delicts). Where a contract is the legal title for the creation of an obligation, the law of contractual obligations is considered; if

---

[708]/ The Obligation Code Draft was passed in Paris in October 1927.

the title arises from unlawful conduct (usually based on fault) or from a wrong defined by statute then tort law is at issue.

The contract becomes a decisive element in considering whether the nature of a particular legal relation is private or public. Where a contract creates the basis of a legal relation and the parties may derive their respective rights and duties from this contract the legal relation falls within private law; where a legal relation is based upon an administrative decision the relation belongs to public law.[709] It should be noted that substantial differences between contracts in private law and public law are obvious and are well-known in the legal systems abroad. For example, the same fact having occurred during the effect of the contract may be solved in a totally different way in public law and in private law (such as the impact of changing relations upon the duration of obligations in France).[710] The fostering of contractual elements is a result of penetration of common law legal principles, which are traditionally hostile with respect to legislation and provide wide space for parties to regulate their relations in the form of a contract. Contractual elements are enhanced also as a result of economic liberalism, globalization, new technologies supporting a massive development of electronic trade, the evolution of social relations and due to the existence of Community law.[711] Contracts are expanding not only their economic and legal background but also their social dimensions. The legal regulation of Brazil, which belongs to the Roman-Germanic legal culture despite its geographical distance from Europe, may be mentioned in this context. Its law has significantly emphasized the social role of a contract due to Brazilian political and social development. Under sec. 421 of the new Brazilian Civil Code the freedom to contract may be pursued with respect to the social function of the contract. There is a similar provision in the Quebec Civil Code. Under its sec. 1994 the lessor, at the request of a lessee who has suffered a reduction of income or a change in the composition of his household, is bound to reduce his rent during the term of the lease; if the lessor refuses to do so the lessee may seek protection in court. If the income of the lessee returns to or becomes greater than what it was, the former rent is re-established. The social function of civil law in a society is supported also by Swiss civilists.[712]

4.2.2 Prospects of codification

The law of obligations along with the law of property create the core of private law (civil) and it should be regulated in a basic code, i.e. the Civil Code. Great codifications in the 19th and 20th centuries respected this requirement and included the legal regulation of obligations; this applies to French private law codification (Code civil 1804), as well as to the Austrian General Civil Code (ABGB 1811). Both magnificent pieces of legislation are based primarily on the theory of natural law although its reflection is stronger in the Austrian Code; they both pay primary attention to two fundamental principles of private law, namely family and property. Obligations including contracts are "hidden" in the French

---

[709] Knappová, M. – Dvořák, J. In: Eliáš, K. a kol.: *Občanský zákoník. Velký akademický komentář* [The Civil Code. Comprehensive Academic Commentary]. Vol. 1, Praha: Linde, 2008, p. 30.
[710] Dvořák, J.: Pacta sunt servanda? In: Dvořák, J. – Kindl, M. (eds.): *Pocta Martě Knappové k 80. narozeninám* [Tribute to Marta Knappova on the Occasion of Her 80th Birthday]. Praha: ASPI, 2005, p. 45 and subs.
[711] Spinosi, C. J.: Le contrat. In: *Le contrat: Journées Brésiliennes*. Paris: Société de législation comparée, 2005, p. 3.
[712] See *Le centenaire du Code civil suisse*. Paris: Société de législation comparée, 2008.

Code civil in Book III entitled "Of the different modes of acquiring property" (section 711 and subsequent). The Austrian Civil Code provided for obligations and civil wrongs in Part II "Of the rights of persons to property", section 859 and subs., and in Part III "Provisions common to personal and property rights" section 1342 and subs. The enactment of the German Civil Code (BGB 1896) represented a certain change compared to the French and Austrian civil codes: its system was based upon the Pandect law approach and, for the first time, included a general part in the code. The general part also deals with general provisions applicable to contracts. The law of obligations was contained in Book II of the Code. The Swiss Civil Code 1907 was quite remarkable at its times as it fully omitted obligations; the Law of Obligations Act adopted in 1912 made the whole area of civil law complete. The Swiss Civil Code contributed to the civilist legislation with one more element, namely the regulation of business relations in the Civil Code. Such inclusion of business relations into a civil code signifies a phenomenon denoted as the *commercialization of civil law*. In other sources this approach is designated as a monistic conception of the law of obligations later applied in Italian, Dutch or Russian legislation. The type of regulation of obligations designated as dualistic, where autonomous laws are enacted for civil law and business law respectively, was chosen as the legislative approach in the Czech Republic, Slovakia, Austria and France.

Lex ferenda in the Czech Republic will remove the dual system of obligations in the Civil and Commercial Codes by means of the adoption of a civil code which is supposed to become the basic (general) regulation of private law including the law of obligations. The same intention has been expressed in Slovakia where the outline of the legislative draft of the Civil Code has been introduced.[713]

4.2.3 The development of the law of contractual obligations

Contractual obligations have been a fast-growing area. A significant impulse for its further development was the change in the structure of the offer and supply having occurred primarily in the second half of the 20th century. *"The twentieth century witnessed an overproduction of means: the means were produced more and more quickly, they overtook all means already known, not mentioning urgent means. The abundance of means had to begin finding aims to serve. What happened was that available solutions were desperately looking for potential problems to solve."*[714]

The end of the twentieth century became the era of consumption and consumers.[715] As a result of the fact that consumers contracts are not in their essence negotiated and are formed upon acceptance of a fixed price and general terms the law of obligations have been used to assist the consumers. The first provisions in this respect were incorporated in national

---

[713]/ Lazar, J. (ed.): *Návrh legislatívneho zámeru kodifikácie súkromného práva. Ministerstvo spravodlivosti SR* [The Outline of the Legislative Intent of the Codification of Private Law. Ministry of Justice of the Slovak Republic]. Bratislava: Ministerstvo spravodlivosti Slovenskej republiky, 2008.

[714]/ Bauman, Z.: *Individualizovaná společnost* [An Individualized Society]. Praha: Mladá Fronta, 2004, p. 174.

[715]/ See, for example, Schulte-Nölke, H.: Spotřebitelské právo v občanskoprávní kodifikaci? [Consumer Law in the Codification of Civil Law?]. In: Švestka, J. – Dvořák, J. – Tichý, L. (eds.): *Sborník statí z diskusních fór o rekodifikaci občanského práva* [Proceedings from the Discussion Fora on the Recodification of Civil Law]. Praha: ASPI, 2008, p. 106 and subs.; Fiala, J. – Hurdík, J. – Selucká, M.: *Současné aktuální otázky spotřebitelského práva* [Recent Topical Issues of Consumer Law]. Brno: Masarykova univerzita, 2008.

legislation of some EU Member States (Germany and France); this was followed by a systemic and purposeful structure of EU directives whose transposition into national legal systems has been pursued under the supervision of the EU. A consumers' or consumerist plethora has led to considerations whether there is time to *"provide in legislation for the protection of a consumer against consumption itself"*.[716] Such ideas seem to be unsuccessful in the Czech society from the very beginning; socialist legal principles such as that forbidding excessive accumulation of things are forgotten not only by lawyers.[717] Any intervention in the freedom of acquiring property would be perceived with high sensitivity and negation.

The theory of law admits without any doubt that the protection of a weaker contracting party may apply to categories of contracting parties other than the consumer and his supplier.[718] Similar "balancing" provisions should apply to other paired categories of "lessor-lessee", "employer-employee", "insurer-the insured", and so on. A weaker party is usually less informed, not as professional, having unequal chance to use legal aid, sometimes even lacking social intellect or being insufficiently, but blamelessly, reasonable, etc.[719]

Another new phenomenon in the law of obligations is the idea of *legitimate expectations of the performance of a contract*. Legitimate expectations of a *consumer* is regulated in Czech law with respect to, for example, the sale of goods in a shop, namely s. 616 (2) of the Civil Code. The thing subject to the sale in a shop is in conformity with a contract if it shows the quality and fitness properties corresponding to the content of the contract, description by the seller, producer (his sales representative or importer) or with what can be *reasonably expected* considering the advertisements publicized, or if they correspond to what is usual for things of the same kind.

Substantive protection of a consumer is enhanced in civil procedure through the powers of consumers, or their associations aimed at consumer protection, to file class actions. The practical value of such actions is that the solution of litigation between two or more parties to court proceedings becomes legally effective for other parties in identical situations and with no duty to seek their protection in court (see ss. 83 and 159a of the Civil Procedure Act).[720] Section 54 (2) of the Commercial Code provides for a special regulation of the burden of proof in cases where the plaintiff is a consumer who, in the cases mentioned above (i.e. in the cases where a legal entity protecting the interests of consumers may bring an action), seeks the refraining from unfair conduct or the removal of a defective status. The special

---

[716]/ Hulmák, M. in Švestka, J. – Spáčil, J. – Škárová, M. – Hulmák, M. et al.: *Občanský zákoník I. Komentář* [The Civil Code I. Commentary]. 1st ed., Praha: C. H. Beck, 2008, p. 416.

[717]/ S. 129 of Act No. 64/1964 Sb., the Civil Code, in its original wording stipulated that only one family house may be owned by one person. Under s. 130(2) things accumulated contrary to the interests of the society in excess of the scope of personal needs of the owner, his family and household do not enjoy the protection of individual ownership.

[718]/ Section 52 of the Civil Code identifies as a supplier any person who, in the course of making or performing a contract, acts within his commercial or any other business activity. A consumer is a person who, in the course of making or performing a contract, does not act within his commercial or any other business activity.

[719]/ Zoulík, F.: Soukromoprávní ochrana slabší smluvní strany [Protection of a Weaker Party under Private Law]. *Právní rozhledy* 3/2002, p. 109. Spáčil, J.: Prodej nemovitosti za nepřiměřeně nízkou cenu a lichevní smlouvy v českém občanském právu [The Sale of Immovables for Unreasonably Low Prices and Usurious Contracts in Czech Civil Law]. *Právní rozhledy* 7/2003, pp. 331–333.

[720]/ For more details see Winterová, A.: Procesní důsledky skupinové žaloby v českém právu [Procedural Consequences of Class Actions in Czech Law]. In: Dvořák, J. – Winterová, A. (eds.): *Pocta Jiřímu Švestkovi k 75. narozeninám* [Tribute to Professor Švestka on the Occasion of His 75th Birthday]. Praha: ASPI, 2008, p. 347.

regulation subsists in that "the wrongdoer must prove that he did not commit unfair competition". Such provision, usually called the transfer of the burden of proof, is in fact the provision for a rebuttable legal presumption that unfair competition was committed and the defendant should prove the opposite in the proceedings, i.e. rebut the presumption. The grounds for such provision resulting from EU legislation are clear: a consumer is assumed to be a weaker party in litigation, who usually lacks funds and chances to collect the evidence. Procedural consequences of the quoted provision are that the plaintiff-consumer has an advantage, supposing all the above-mentioned requirements are fulfilled, that no other plaintiff might have, such as a legal entity protecting consumer interests. The legal entity in its capacity as plaintiff will have to prove that the defendant did commit unfair competition. This statutory solution is subject to doubts due to the creation of apparent inequality of parties.[721]

The legal protection of consumers brings other questions of a more general nature: how to determine the extent of legal protection of a weaker party when experience shows that incorrectly determined scope of legal protection of one party may lead to an effect contrary to what was initially intended. Practical cases have confirmed the fact that unreasonable protection of tenants results in the reduction of the owner's investment in the house; similarly, legal advantage given to one category of employees results in the lack of interest on the part of employers to hire such employees for an indefinite time, etc. On the other hand, a seemingly weaker party may abuse its position against the interests of others (against a majority). The Commercial Code in its section 56a stipulates that the abuse of a majority, as well as a minority, of votes in a company is forbidden.

4.2.4 The position of parties

The law of contract does not insist on balanced (equivalent) performance by parties. The parties are assumed to be fully responsible for their conduct, they have sufficient knowledge, are prudent, farsighted and aware of legal consequences which their conduct may result in (*vigilantibus jura*). However, the law becomes active as soon as one party has obtained unreasonable advantage against the other party just because that party acted under pressure, without knowledge and experience, lacking any legal aid, etc. Obligations created by such contracts are not supported by the legal order. They are usually subject to invalidity. Despite the absence of explicit legislative provisions in this respect, Czech lawyers consider such contracts to be invalid because they are against good morals (usurious contracts). *Lex ferenda* contains explicit solution even for cases where the party receives consideration not even reaching a half of what that party provided to its counterpart (lesion beyond moiety – *laesio enormis*).

4.2.5 Impact of the European Union

Legislative activities in the law of obligations carried out in Europe at the end of the 20th century can be subdivided into two groups. Primarily, harmonizing streams in the European Union can be seen in the area of contract law; their recurring and motivating idea contained in the documents of the European Parliament and the Commission has been that

---

[721] *Ibidem.*

the single internal market cannot fully operate without civil law legislation being further harmonized.[722] The outcomes achieved in this field are extraordinary and remarkable. The published Principles of European contract law were drafted by the Lando commission and the recently published Draft Common Frame of Reference (*DCFR*) is the common outcome of the work of the Study Group on a European Civil Code and the Research Group on EC Private Law (Acquis Group); both documents are paid extraordinary attention by legal theoreticians and practitioners. Although the Draft is a model and not legally binding (*soft law*) it is considered to be a real framework for the purposes of legal science, academia, judiciary and legislature.[723]

Legislative activities of individual Member States have been pursued independently of the harmonizing processes; states try to improve the quality of their legal orders and focus on the law of obligations and torts. A relatively extensive reform of the law of obligations in the German Civil Code (2002) attracted deserved attention and became an inspiration for many legislative changes in Poland. Immediately after the celebration of the bicentennial anniversary of the Code civil the legislative drafts of the reform of the law of obligations and statutes of limitation were completed in France, which are known under the name of their coordinator as so-called *l'avant-project Catala*.[724]

4.2.6 The legal substance of a contract

The legal substance of the contract itself has been newly subject to critical and open examination. Does a contract really create a legal fact establishing between parties a contradictory or even antagonistic relationship where each party focuses on the satisfaction of its private interests? Or can there be seen, or sometimes prevail, the elements of contractual solidarity in a contract? The position of parties to the content of the contract results in distinguishing two groups of contract: (a) contracts whose basis is created by the exchange of values (typically the sales contract); and (b) contracts whose purpose is identical for all parties thereto, namely contracts of association or organization. Both types of contracts, however, confirm their elementary function: they become a synonym for the assumption of an obligation.[725]

The recent legal regulation has paid special attention to the procedure of the forming of a contract, namely to individual steps preceding the creation of a contract as a perfect legal

---

[722]/ See the Resolutions of the European Parliament of 26th May 1980, 6th May 1994, 15th November 2001, 2nd September 2003, and finally the Resolution of the EP on European contract law and the revision of the acquis: the way forward (2005/2022(INI).

[723]/ Von Bar, Ch.: O celoevropské odpovědnosti národní kodifikační politiky [On the European Responsibility for National Codification Policies]. In: Švestka, J. – Dvořák, J. – Tichý, L. (eds.): *Sborník statí z diskusních fór o rekodifikaci občanského práva* [Proceedings from the Discussion Fora on the Recodification of Civil Law]. Praha: ASPI, 2006, p. 11 and subs.; Von Bar, Ch.: Úvod do akademického komunitárního (společného) referenčního rámce [An Introduction to the Academic Community (Common) Frame of Reference]. In: Švestka, J. – Dvořák, J. – Tichý, L. (eds.): *Sborník statí z diskusních fór o rekodifikaci občanského práva* [Proceedings from the Discussion Fora on the Recodification of Civil Law]. Praha: ASPI, 2008, p. 95 and subs.; Lando, O., Návrh společného referenčního rámce, český návrh občanského zákoníku a dobrá víra [The Draft of the Common Reference Frame, the Draft of the Czech Civil Code, and Good Faith]. In: Švestka, J. – Dvořák, J. – Tichý, L. (eds.) *ibidem* at p. 134 and subs.

[724]/ Hondius, E.: *La reformé du droit des contrats aux Pays-Bas. Le contrat en Europe aujourdhui et demain.* Paris: Société de législation comparée, 2008, p. 41 and subs.

[725]/ Terré, F. – Simler, Ph. – Lequette, Z.: *Les obligations.* Paris: Dalloz, 2005.

fact. The law governs this pre-contract process through particular requirements imposed: generally speaking, it is the principle of *culpa in contrahendo* (fault in the course of creating a contract). Express legal regulation of this doctrine was carried out within the obligations reform in Germany in 2002 (see the newly adopted section 311). The German regulation of this doctrine follows von Savigny's theory formulating a thesis that any fault occurring in the course of creating a contract and subsequent damage caused gives rise to liability on the wrongdoer's part. Von Savigny considers the beginning of negotiating a contract as creating a special (contractual) legal relation imposing on every party a duty to act prudently; the breach of this duty creates *culpa in contrahendo* giving rise to liability. Many national legislatures have incorporated this doctrine into their national laws although, unlike German legislation, they consider this liability to be in tort rather than in contract (e.g. France, Luxemburg).

4.2.7 Culpa in contrahendo

The institution of *culpa in contrahendo* is one type of expression of the principle of fairness and loyalty. National laws in many European countries usually denote this principle in a way which may be quite surprising to a Czech lawyer: *good faith and fair dealing, Treu und Glauben, redelijkheid eb bilijkheid, dobra wiara, buona fede, bonne foi*, etc. In this context, however, legal terminology should be clarified. If the institution of *good faith* in the sense of a *legal maxim* or *principle* is used, its *objective* meaning is considered. It should be noted that *good faith* as an abstract concept may be understood at two referential levels in different circumstances. In addition to the concept of *good faith* as designating an objective maxim, Czech legislation uses the term of *good faith* as denoting the subjective feeling and state of mind of a party; this understanding prevails in Czech laws.

The objective meaning of *good faith* essentially implies a certain general clause (behaviour pattern) referring to particular general moral values, which some authors recognize as generally acknowledged and accepted in a society. Good faith in this sense should be interpreted as the category of moral (ethical) rules of interpersonal interaction, i.e. a certain objective standard to measure the conduct of a particular person in a particular case. The result of such test may be a conclusion that certain conduct is either compatible with the principle of good faith, or it does not comply with the maxim.[726]

On the other hand, the subjective category of *good faith* is usually understood as a certain obligatory element of a particular situation (merits) to be fulfilled in order to form legal consequences intended by the law (e.g. in order for a party to acquire a right or to reach a particular legal position).[727] In this respect good faith represents the subjectively erroneous, but excusable in a particular case, belief of a person that he or she acts lawfully or that no harm may be caused to another as a result of such act. The subjective sense of good faith includes the mental category (psychological part) of an acting individual.

---

[726]/ We can see certain analogy between this understanding of good faith and the category of good morals (*boni mores*) that is typically used in Czech law.

[727]/ The institution of *prescription of an ownership right* may serve as an example. In order to establish prescription along with the acquisition of a property right the essential elements must be fulfilled and the element of good faith must be met as one of them (good faith meaning the ignorance or unawareness of the possessor).

Although there are significant differences in their content and subject-matter between the two meanings of good faith both Czech law[728] and foreign legal systems quite often use just one term *good faith* to denote either of them. The issue is whether such approach of the legislature subsisting in using one common term for two different concepts (two different sets of facts) can be denoted as correct and proper. It should be emphasized that traditional principles of legislative technique allow for identical designation of only such concepts that have the same content, i.e. they are of the same meaning. The use of one term for two different legal institutions may be found dangerous and misleading.

It should be added, however, that the general concept of good faith (if used interchangeably for both meanings) in legislation is essentially quite simple to interpret, at least to determine whether objective or subjective understanding applies in a particular situation. However, theoretically there may be borderline contexts of different situations where the use of good faith may result in some ambiguity in interpretation. Thus, distinguishing between the two meanings of good faith seems to be a better and correct solution. This approach seems to be chosen for the draft of a new Czech Civil Code. The drafters intend to use the term *good faith* just in its subjective meaning. The objective elements are to be expressed by terms such as fairness or fair observance of good morals.[729]

It should be admitted that it would be very difficult to exclude the concept of good faith in its objective meaning from the legal order of the Czech Republic. Harmonization in the field of consumer law has been a concrete reason for introducing the objective good faith in legislation of some EU Member States (Czech law inclusive). Section 53 (3) and section 56 (1) of the Czech Civil Code (regulating consumer contracts) provide for objective good faith. Since the objective good faith seems to survive in future European directives the proper approach to its translation into the Czech language should be considered. As will be seen later, this terminological phrase may be interpreted as having various, and even very different, meanings. Transposing European directives into Czech law, extraordinary attention should be paid to the correct interpretation of the sense of good faith in a particular provision in a particular directive so that the most appropriate Czech equivalent can be chosen for that particular case.[730]

Looking into some foreign legal systems we can find out that very often good faith means more (or even something different) than a synonym for honesty and confidence. The commonly used term *good faith* (or *good faith and fair dealings*) is usually explained specifically in contract law as a duty to take legitimate interests of the other party into account when negotiating a particular contract; it includes the duty not to conceal, distort or wrench the facts (prohibited *misrepresentation*) relevant for an appropriate decision of the other party (so-called duty to inform). This rule applies primarily within the context of so-called pre-contractual liability. The duty to act in compliance with good faith is not confined just to

---

[728]/ See, for example, section 53 (3) and section 56 (1) of the Civil Code (objective good faith) and section 486 or section 161 of the Civil Code (subjective good faith).

[729]/ See the following passage of the subchapter for the criticism of the term proposed.

[730]/ Generally speaking, the expression *good faith* seems to be more than suitable to denote the subjective part of this institution. On the other hand, the Czech phrase *dobrá víra* (literally translated as *good faith*) can hardly semantically suggest in the Czech language any moral or ethical category, or connection with honesty and integrity. Such interpretation would be extremely cumbersome and, as suggested earlier, may lead to interpretive ambiguity.

the stage before the entering into a contract. This imperative is effective in the course of concluding the contract, during the life of the contract, in exercising the rights and fulfilling duties resulting from the contract and even when these are altered or terminated (*post contractum finitum*).

In addition, the application of this principle is also explained in contract law as the duty of mutual loyalty, cooperation, notification, etc. Contracting parties are obliged to act in the performance of their contract (i.e. exercising their rights as well as discharging their obligations) in such a way that the intended purpose and objective of their contract can be achieved and that rights and legitimate interests of the other party can be respected.

Sometimes this principle is explained as the order to exercise rights and duties in a reasonable (appropriate) manner. This belongs to the classical category designated as the abuse of law (*abusus juris*). The borderline between the duty to act in compliance with good faith and the prohibition to abuse law is rather vague and their dimensions are often unclear. Some authors tend to understand them as one whole, others consider the abuse of law as a subcategory of the objective good faith. In particular, recent publications reflect tendencies to understand good faith as reasonableness, or adequacy.[731]

Good faith is not the principle binding just the recipients of legal rules in their exercising private rights and duties, e.g. parties to an obligation. In the same way it may be (and often is) an order for the judge to take this maxim in individual cases into account and to use it to measure the correctness (appropriateness) of his decisions. For example, some legal systems allow for judicial intervention in the content of contractual provisions where a significant change of circumstances occurs in the time between the entering into the contract and the moment of agreed performance, the change being connected with an extreme difficulty (not impossibility) in the performance of an obligation on the part of the debtor. In such a case the debtor may apply to court to alter the contract (its content), to moderate his duty (the court may, for example, decide that the original scope of the debtor's duty is to be reasonably reduced), or even to cancel his obligation in an extraordinary situation. However, before intervening in the contract, the court must decide whether any fixing of the debtor's original obligation (insisting on the original performance), or its consequences, can be inconsistent with the requirement of good faith, i.e. incompatible with the principle of reasonableness, adequacy and justice. Should the conclusion be affirmative, only then may the court decide on the alteration or cancellation of the contract. Where it concludes that the excessive difficulty in discharging the obligation is not crucial enough to allow for the judicial intervention in the contract, the court may not satisfy the debtor.[732] Sec. 6:258 of the Civil Code of the Netherlands, or sec. 357 of the Polish Civil Code may serve as examples of such principle.

Considering the above-mentioned issues just through the traditional legal principle of *pacta sunt servanda*, the right of courts to unilaterally intervene in contractual provisions

---

[731]/ See, for example, Antoniolli, L. – Veneziano, A.: *Principles of European Contract Law and Italian Law.* Hague: Kluwer Law International, 2005, p. 49. The author examines good faith as contained in the Principles.

[732]/ It is our intention not to mention here a common duty imposed upon courts and regulated by many Civil Codes, namely to direct the parties to newly negotiate the conditions of their contract where substantial alteration of circumstances of their contract occurs.

may appear to be doubtful and lacking any conception.[733] Should a view further be taken it seems to be clear that rigid adherence to this principle is not always the best solution. Sometimes it is necessary to admit that the maxim may be avoided (which is suggested in the institution *clausula rebus sic stantibus*). However, this is an example of the conflict of two legal principles, namely the principle that contracts bind on the one hand, and the principle of fairness and confidence on the other. Jurisprudence has already firmly concluded that legal principles may be conflicting (different principles protect different values: for example, one principle protects the freedom of speech, another principle protects the privacy of an individual). Should the conflict occur it must be decided which of the conflicting and competing principles ought to be preferred in a particular case. The Czech Constitutional Court refers to this situation as weighing principles.

4.2.8 The principle of good faith

Neither the Czech Civil Code, nor any other piece of Czech legislation, regulates (defines)[734] the institution of good faith in its general sense and, naturally, it provides no direction with respect to the interpretation of that institution. The explanation of this term has been therefore a task for legal theoreticians and courts. However, considering applicable doctrines or case law we can see quite an unfortunate approach: neither Czech legal theory nor practice have tried seriously to define the scope of the term *good faith*. The problem does not subsist in the total absence of interpretive interest in that term; difficulties result from the fact that when authors attempt to explain good faith they usually fail to distinguish properly between objective and subjective good faith and use the two concepts interchangeably. Some opinions even suggest that legal rules containing the subjective good faith principle are interpreted as the legal principle of good faith (i.e. as fairness and integrity).

The principle of good faith has usually been explained as one aspect of the principle of legal certainty. Under this theory, other aspects creating the legal certainty principle are: (a) the principle of protection of good faith, (b) the principle of protection of third parties rights, (c) the principle that the law may not apply retrospectively and forever, and (d) the principle of protection of acquired rights.[735] Briefly speaking, *legal certainty* as such is traditionally featured as one of three pillars of a democratic state based on the rule of law. The other two pillars are the *rule of law* and *reasonableness of law*. This is, for example, the approach of Hurdík. In his work on the principles of private law he correctly (and as one of a few authors in Czech law) points out that there are two different meanings of the concept at issue. Hurdík understands objective good faith as a moral category which "(...) *tends to become, or actually becomes a general principle having an impact on the creation and pursuance of all private relations*".[736] Hurdík also emphasizes that "(...) *some codes of private law identify good faith, or replace good faith, with the concept of fairness or other concepts with meanings shifted from the mental category*

---

[733]/ This is, for example, an approach of French lawyers. See Dvořák, J. *supra* at p. 54 and subs.
[734]/ Despite that, private law explicitly refers to objective good faith (see above) but it does so only in very specific and exceptional provisions.
[735]/ Hurdík, J.: *Zásady soukromého práva* [The Principles of Private Law]. Brno: Masarykova univerzita, 1998, p. 115 and subs.
[736]/ *Ibidem.*

to the moral category (...)".[737] Hurdík concludes his explanation of objective good faith with the following statement: *"Good faith in its sense of an objective moral category assumes the significance of a general principle applicable to the whole field of civil, or more precisely private law, expressing fairness of the attitude of participants to the creation and performance of civil relations."*[738]

The drafters of a new Czech Civil Code intend to include in the Code a general clause on good faith directly in the introductory provisions of the law. The general rule contained in section 7 should read: *"A person who acted legally in a certain way is assumed to have acted fairly and in good faith."*[739] The explanatory report states that "(...) the proposed provision presumes the existence of good faith in compliance with all legal systems of continental Europe. Anyone denying good faith must successfully bear the onus of proving. The existing Civil Code has been the only European civil code lacking provisions for the general presumption of good faith."[740] Section 8 is drafted as follows: *"Apparent abuse of law shall not enjoy legal protection."* If we have a closer look at both provisions we can see that section 7 intends to merge the presumption of existence of both objective and subjective good faith. Such an approach is very unusual in two points: first, it is quite unique if a law speaks about objective and subjective good faith in one sentence at one place; second, this situation need not have necessarily adversarial consequences. What is more problematic is the fact that the Draft has the aim to presume the existence of objective good faith through a rebuttable presumption without imposing upon all participants in civil (private) relations the general duty to act in compliance with the principle of good faith. We consider this issue a handicap of the Draft Code. Where the Draft is compared with civil codes of most European countries it becomes clear that this approach constitutes derogation from the "general standard". The absence of an explicit duty to act (to exercise one's rights and discharge one's duties) in compliance with the principle of good faith (or fairness) represents a significant inconsistency of the drafters.

Section 6 of the Draft supposed, along with the already discussed sections 7 and 8, to create one interwoven and logical whole, is intentionally mentioned as the second since no consistent body of the three sections has been formed. Subsection 6 (1) reads: *"The right may be duly exercised, and the duty duly discharged only if good morals are observed with regard to the habits of civil life."* Subsection 6 (2) expresses an idea that *"No one may turn to account his own unlawfulness and unfairness."*[741] Although all the three sections are supposed to be interlinked and interwoven (since their main sense seems to be the determination of basic limits and restrictions in the way of exercising rights and discharging duties of parties to civil relations, we argue that their purpose is not met and the reader of the Draft may be puzzled. Subsection 6 (1) provides for the application (uplatnění) of rights. However, it is not clear whether this *ap-*

---

[737]/ *Ibidem* at p. 124.

[738]/ *Ibidem* at p. 125.

[739]/ Objective good faith should be replaced with the term *fairness* (poctivost). We consider this terminological choice to be good because if we want to avoid the use of *good faith* for its objective meaning we can hardly find a more suitable Czech equivalent.

[740]/ The Explanatory Report on the Draft Civil Code, section 7.

[741]/ A similar provision was contained in subsection 8 (2) in the earlier draft of the Code and its wording was as follows: *"No one may benefit from his using the right of another or failing to act in good faith."* It is clear what changes have been introduced to the draft in the process of its compiling, sometimes the changes affecting significant and decisive areas.

plication is confined to judicial proceedings, which would be a rather dangerous restriction, or whether any exercise of rights is implied. The authors of the Draft themselves appear to be inconsistent since in the explanatory report they explicitly use the *exercise* of rights which is a wider terms than *application*. We also argue that the use of the phrase *fair observance of good morals* is not correct. Our concern is that its opposite meaning "unfair observance of good morals" is not possible *per definitionem*. If a person observes good morals it means *eo ipso* that he behaves himself morally (ethically). There is no need for a legal rule to provide for another value criterion of observance of good morals. This is a theoretical approach *non lege artis*.

Subsection 6 (2) reflects the rule of *nemo turpitudinem suam allegare potest*. There is also a certain inaccuracy, at least in formulation. We claim that the term *turn to account* (těžit) used in the provision should be replaced with a more appropriate term *rely on* or *take advantage,* etc. In addition we consider the phrase *turn to account his own unlawfulness* as quite incomprehensible. A clearer formulation should be used such as *to benefit (take advantage) from his unlawful and unfair conduct.*

The essential problem found in section 6 is the conflict between its intended purpose and the reading. The explanatory report quite explicitly explains the aim of the drafters to introduce to Czech private law the rule that conduct should be in compliance with the good faith principle. The explanatory report reads: *"Standard civil codes link the exercise of rights and discharge of legal duties with the criterion of honesty and the absence of bad will or fraudulent intent. (...) European languages express analogical requirement using Treu und Glauben (loyalty and faith), good faith, bonne foi, buona fede (good faith), redelijkheid eb bilijkheid (honesty and fairness), etc. However, the term "good faith" in our legal language has acquired a particular legal meaning as internal (subjective) conviction of the actor of his own legal conduct; thus "good faith" may not be correctly translated into Czech as "dobrá víra". Where it happened due to a mechanical translation of foreign texts, for example in s. 56 (1) of the existing Civil Code, it leads to misunderstanding and scholastic distinguishing between good faith in objective and subjective senses of the word. (...) The category of good morals is inherent in Czech private law despite a long totalitarian interruption of its use. Therefore it is proposed to use this category when providing for the rule well-known in many European and non-European civil codes (...) in the new Czech civil code. The existing Civil Code has suffered from the deficiency absent in traditional civil codes, namely that the Code prohibits breaching good morals but does not compel people to act in compliance with them."*[742]

If one accepts these arguments he must also accept the conclusion that the category of good morals is to substitute for the institution of objective good faith in Czech law in the future. We have already argued that such approach is incorrect since the two concepts are far from being identical and should not be used interchangeably. Besides, the proposed sections 6 and 7 are not sufficiently interlinked with each other as the relationship between the institution of *fair observance of good morals* in section 6 and the term *fairness* in section 7 is not clear. Should the terminological phrase *fair observance of good morals* really denote what is commonly termed *good faith* in foreign legal systems the question arises how *fairness* in section 7 should be understood. Are both concepts considered identical (and if so, why two different terms are used), or are there two different legal situations? Our understanding

---

[742]/ The Explanatory Report on s. 6 of the Draft Civil Code.

of the Draft is that its authors have attempted to regulate the same issue in both sections; however, the language of the Draft does not speak for itself.

The principle of fairness and confidence should play one of the most important roles in the reviving Czech private law. However, the draft of a new Czech civil code in its latest version is quite confusing in its relevant provisions and far from the objectives declared. We can only hope that the Draft will be subject to further changes to form a better position of the principle of fairness in the Czech legal order.

4.3 CODIFICATION OF PRIVATE INTERNATIONAL LAW IN THE EU: DOES IT MAKE SENSE TO RECODIFY CZECH PRIVATE INTERNATIONAL LAW?

4.3.1 Significance of private international law and the basic sources of its regulation

Private international law regulates private relations containing the so-called foreign or cross-border element. Recently, a new concept of "Community foreign element" has been introduced within the EU, which signifies that certain legal instruments of European law confine their regulation only to relations created within the European Union. It should be noted that such restriction of legal regulation just to Community relations is not simple and the existing case-law interpretation of the European Court of Justice has not been fully persuasive.[743] Some newer laws, particularly those within the European Union, directly define this cross-border or foreign element.[744] I would argue that, generally, this need not be a convenient solution: it will rather depend on a concrete situation which might stay outside the scope of the definition.

The most important rules of private international law, i.e. conflict-of-law rules, determine what law should apply to the respective private relationship. The second significant category of rules usually attached to private international law are rules applicable to international civil procedure regulating civil proceedings in private cases containing a foreign element.

A special construction of conflict-of-law rules, their specific aspects, such as the issue of how the governing law is determined, the application of foreign law determined by the relevant conflict-of-law rule, or instruments correcting the effects of conflict-of-law rules are similar in different legal systems. This is obvious particularly when substantive rules in various countries, which are essentially disparate, are compared. A certain parallel may be found in international civil procedure. States very often come to similar solutions despite their dissimilar national regulations of civil procedure, which are quite different even within one legal context, i.e. being of identical or similar legal culture.

This leads to the development of comparative legal studies, to searching and finding common solutions in certain areas. What is quite significant is unification, or harmonization of the conflict of laws as well as international civil procedure. Private international law,

---

[743]/ See, in particular, *Owusu* case C-281/02, [2005] ECR I-1383.
[744]/ For example, Art. 3 of Regulation (EC) No 1896/2006 of the European Parliament and of the Council creating a European order for payment procedure, states that "a cross-border case is one in which at least one of the parties is domiciled or habitually resident in a Member State other than the Member State of the court seised."

however, is national law by its nature; each state has its own private international law and this branch is a special, autonomous branch of national law.[745]

Emphasizing these apparently elementary principles serves a particular purpose. They create an important background for both theoretical research and legislative work. This background is also relevant in assessing with what instruments and to what extent it is possible to unify private international law at the level of the European Union, and what significance can be assigned to the codification of private international law at the level of individual countries, particularly in individual EU Member States.

4.3.2 Joining the conflict-of-law rules and international civil procedure and the position of private international law with the system of private law

Modern types of legislation usually consolidate the conflict of laws rules and the rules of international civil procedure.

The consolidation of conflict-of-law rules and international civil procedure rules has not been new in Czech law. The Czechoslovak Act No. 97/1963 Sb., as amended, on private international law and procedure (PILA) was one of the first laws globally combining conflict-of-law rules and international civil procedure rules into one piece of legislation. Such consolidation has proven to be useful: the rules governing jurisdiction and competence of courts and the recognition and enforcement of foreign judgments are interconnected with, and follow the conflict-of-law rules. Consolidation of conflict-of-law rules and the rules of international civil procedure is contained in the legislation of some other states; however, these were passed later than the Czech PILA. In the European context, laws of the following countries can be listed: Hungary (1979), former Yugoslavia (1982), Switzerland (1987), Italy (1995), Belgium (2004), Bulgaria (2005) and, most recently, Turkey (2007) and Macedonia (2007).

Consolidation of conflict-of-law rules and the rules of international civil procedure has gradually been reflected in the legislation of the European Communities (EC), particularly in the Council Regulation Proposal of 2006 to amend Regulation No. 2201/2003 concerning jurisdiction and the recognition and enforcement of judgments in matrimonial matters and the matters of parental responsibility. The Proposal should be expanded: the existing procedural provisions will be complemented with the relevant conflict-of-law rules governing divorce and separation of marriage (so-called Rome Regulation III).[746] Another example to illustrate the trend is the recent Council Regulation No. 4/2009 on jurisdiction, applicable law, recognition and enforcement of decisions and cooperation in matters relating to maintenance obligations (so-called Maintenance Regulation). The Green Paper entitled "Successions and wills" of 2005[747] and the Green Paper on conflict of laws in matters concerning matrimonial property regimes of 2006[748] expressly foresee the consolidation

---

[745]/ See, in particular, Kučera, Z.: *Mezinárodní právo soukromé* [Private International Law]. 7th ed., Brno – Plzeň: Doplněk and Aleš Čeněk, 2009, p. 30.

[746]/ Proposal for a Council Regulation amending Regulation No. 2201/2003 as regards jurisdiction and introducing rules concerning applicable law in matrimonial matters, COM(2006) 399 final.

[747]/ COM (2005) 65 final.

[748]/ Green Paper on conflict of laws in matters concerning matrimonial property regimes, including the question of jurisdiction and mutual recognition, COM (2006) 400 final.

of conflict-of-law rules and procedural rules in one instrument. The outlined tendency has been quite straightforward within the European Union. Should any doubts ever occur they concern the question whether the European Community is competent to unify conflict-of-law rules in those areas, rather than the issue of consolidating rules itself.

Consolidation of conflict-of-law rules and the rules of international civil procedure has been observed in a wider extent exceeding the frontiers of the European Union, namely in the Hague Conventions adopted within the Hague Conference on Private International Law; examples of such approach are the Hague Convention on Jurisdiction, Applicable Law, Recognition, Enforcement and Co-operation in Respect of Parental Responsibility and Measures for the Protection of Children,[749] or the newest regulation of maintenance in the Hague Convention 2007 and its Protocol of 2007.[750] Conflict-of-law rules along with the rules of international civil procedure can also be seen in many bilateral treaties on legal assistance.[751]

What should be considered as positive is the fact that the Czech legislature has come to the conclusion that the consolidation of conflict-of-law rules and the rules of international civil procedure should be preserved in the draft of a new Private International Law and Procedure Act which has been part of the recodification of Czech civil law. Professor Eliáš as the leading expert in this process in the Czech Republic admits that such approach is "due to practical reasons",[752] "practical reasons" are apparently not meant as a negative feature reduced just to the practical needs of a judge deciding the case. Czech scholarship clearly considers the consolidation of both types of rules as positive.[753] There are primarily theoretical reasons, namely a close relation and interconnection between private international law and international civil procedure. Their practical application is quicker and smoother if there is no need to look for relevant rules in various pieces of legislation, which might lead to the overlooking of important provisions or even to their omission. Another significant aspect is that the application of conflict-of-law rules is preceded by the solution of the international civil procedure issue, particularly the issue of jurisdiction. Considering different national legislation allowing for proceedings on the same matter in various states, the application of the rules of international civil procedure may have an impact on the substantive result of a particular case. This is the reason why the rules governing jurisdiction of courts should precede the relevant conflict-of-law rules, as can be seen in modern codification of private international law, for example, in Switzerland, Italy or Belgium.[754]

---

[749]/ See Communication No. 141/2001 Sb.m.s., published in the Collection of International Treaties of the Czech Republic.

[750]/ See Convention of 23 November 2007 on the International Recovery of Child Support and Other Forms of Family Maintenance, and Protocol of 23 November 2007 on the Law Applicable to Maintenance Obligations.

[751]/ See, for example, the Treaty between the Czech Republic and the Republic of Poland on legal assistance and the regulation of legal relations in civil, family, employment and criminal matters, Regulation No. 42/1989 Sb., which is applicable to the areas not covered by European private international law.

[752]/ See Eliáš, K.: Charakteristika návrhu nového občanského zákoníku [Characteristics of the Draft of a New Civil Code]. In: Švestka, J. – Dvořák, J. – Tichý, L. (eds.): Sborník statí z diskusních fór o rekodifikaci občanského práva [Proceedings from the Discussion Fora on the Recodification of Civil Law]. Praha: ASPI, 2006, p. 33.

[753]/ See Kučera, Z.: Legislativní úvahy k připravované kodifikaci mezinárodního práva soukromého [Legislative Considerations on the New Codification of Private International Law]. In: Štenglová, I. (ed.): Pocta Miloši Tomsovi k 80. narozeninám [Tribute to Miloš Tomsa on the occasion of His 80th birthday]. Plzeň: Aleš Čeněk, 2006, p. 217.

[754]/ See Kučera, Z. – Pauknerová, M.: Nad mezinárodním právem soukromým a procesním [On Private International Law and Procedure]. Právní rozhledy 10/2000, p. 458 with other references.

4.3.3 The significance of codification of private international law in the Czech Republic and EU Member States

Codification of private international law in the Czech Republic has had a long history. So-called Vienna Draft of Private International Law of 1913, ordered by the Austrian Ministry of Justice and written by Austrian professor Gustav Walker, was the basic source of the Act of 1948 regulating private international law and the position of foreigners in international private law; it was in its essence also the basic source of our current Act of 1963, whose tradition will apparently continue with the draft of a new Private International Law Act. The Government proposal of the Civil Code, introduced in Parliament in 1937,[755] followed Professor Walker's Vienna Draft. The passage providing for conflict-of-law rules was removed from the Government bill after World War II; it was introduced with marginal modifications, and passed by Parliament, as separate Act No. 41/1948 Sb.[756] The Private International Law and Procedure Act of 1963, still in effect, was passed within the great codification initiative in the middle of the 1960s. The Act includes conflict-of-law rules, rules governing the legal status of foreigners and the rules of international civil procedure. At that time, the Act was considered a complex regulation reflecting the tendency obvious in private international law for many preceding years, namely the consolidation of conflict and procedural rules.

At the time of their enactment, solutions contained in PILA represented a quite progressive approach to the legal regulation, for example in the conception of unlimited choice of law in obligations, the principle of reasonable arrangements of a legal relationship, etc. Although those solutions may seem too simplistic in our complicated era, and some of them may even be out-of date, until recently they represented quite a solid standard. However, the newest developments and directions in private international law, both in Europe and worldwide, cannot be disregarded.

The draft of a new Czech Private International Law (and Procedure) Act, written by its spiritual father Professor Zdeněk Kučera, is a modern type of regulation; it takes into account progressive types of codification of private international law in Europe, particularly Switzerland, and incorporates the results of unifying laws, primarily the Hague Conventions and some European instruments. At the same time, the Draft follows the traditional approach contained in the existing PILA. The Draft is well-grounded and conceptually compact; particularly the construction of the general part suggests that the Draft is an academic piece of work based upon cultural traditions and the great scholarship of the author.

4.3.4 General trends of the codification of private international law in EU Member States

Codification initiatives in private international law have emerged in many other countries. In post-communist countries new codification was induced by the changing of the whole system of private law (in addition to the above-mentioned states, also in Russia, Lithuania, Estonia); but changes have occurred also in Western countries. Recently, many such states have

---

[755]/ Ledrer, E.: *Mezinárodní právo soukromé, Nové zákony a nařízení* [International Private Law. New Laws and Regulations]. Praha: V. Linhart, 1948, p. 18.
[756]/ *Ibidem* at pp. 18–62 for more details.

passed new laws governing private international law, where certain more general tendencies may be traced. Due to its limited extent this article will focus only on conflict-of-law rules.

The structure of legal regulation

Modern types of codification of private international law usually opt for the following order of topics in the special part:

1. international jurisdiction of courts of the respective country,
2. conflict-of-law regulation, and
3. recognition and enforcement of foreign judgments.

The special part is preceded by the general part.

The general part of private international law

Unlike modern types of codification of substantive law, the codification of private international law basically encompasses rules relating to the general part of private international law; it is not exceptional today that issues such as qualification, overriding mandatory rules, public order reservation, application of foreign law, avoidance of the law, etc. are codified. Although their codification is not sometimes welcomed by the professional public arguing that the theory of private international law is part of academic textbooks and therefore unnecessary to be included in the law, it should be noted that this is a trend tending to expand. The general part is essentially aimed at the conflict of laws, or some procedural issues such as the application of foreign law or basic provisions for cases with a foreign element.

Differentiation of connecting factors

Unlike the former, more general formulation of conflict-of-law rules, the connecting factors of today are more differentiated and sometimes even fragmented; a more casuistic approach can be traced. The main argument in favour of that trend is that such mode of codification will contribute to a higher degree of legal certainty. Although personally I have been very reserved with respect to this argument, my disagreement stemming from the Czech legal tradition, this trend apparently influenced by the Anglo-American legal tradition should be respected.

Nationality and its replacement with the factor of habitual residence

A clear shift can be seen from the criterion of nationality to the criterion of habitual residence in the law of persons, family law and succession law.[757] The law applicable to such cases is

---

[757] See, in particular, Struycken, A. V. M.: *Les conséquences de l'intégration européenne sur le développement du droit international privé, Recueil des Cours, Académie de droit international de la Haye*. The Hague: Martinus Nijhoff Publishers, 1992, pp. 257–384; Lagarde, P.: Développements futurs du droit international privé dans une Europe en voie d'unification: quelques conjectures. *RabelsZ* 2004, p. 225; Borrás, A. – Gonzáles Campos, J. D.: La loi nationale à l'heure de la réforme du droit international privé espagnol. In: *Le droit international privé: esprit et méthode: Mélanges en l'honneur de Paul Lagarde*. Paris: Dalloz, 2005, p. 137; Mansel, H. P.: Das Staatsangehörigkeitsprinzip im deutschen und gemeinschaftsrechtlichen Internationalen Privatrecht: Schutz der kulturellen Identität oder Diskriminierung der Person?" In: Jayme, E. (ed): *Kulturelle Identität und Internationales*

not determined, not primarily at least, according to the nationality of spouses, mother, child, etc., but in accordance with their usual place of residence, which better corresponds to the recent situation of the persons concerned. On the other hand, the criterion of nationality should not be fully removed; it still remains irreplaceable as a complementary criterion.

Expansion of declaratory (directory) regulation

The fact that the choice of governing law is permissible in areas traditionally subject to mandatory conflict-of-law rules is also a new phenomenon. It should be emphasized that new laws offer to their recipients to choose the governing law not only for their obligations but also with respect to their non-contractual relations and compensation for damage *ex delicto*. The choice of governing law is becoming more relevant in marriage law and will affect succession law in the near future.

The protection of a weaker contracting party

A weaker contracting party is protected by national substantive rules as well as by private international law; typical examples of such protection are consumer, employment and insurance contracts. Protection is usually more closely bound to the place of habitual residence or to the residence of a weaker party, to the place of work performance, etc. The choice of governing law is usually restricted in order to reflect these criteria.

The impact of unified regulation

Unified instruments have had a significant impact upon private international law and procedure. Primarily Hague Conventions adopted within the Hague Conference on Private International Law, some conventions adopted within the Council of Europe initiatives as well as individual pieces of European legislation belong to this category of legal regulation. What is clear is the tendency to incorporate solutions, originally intended to be followed just by the state parties to a particular convention, into national legislation which may lead to its more universal effect against third parties – non-contracting states. Conflict-of-law rules contained in the European legislation are understood as universal, i.e. they will apply generally regardless of whether the relation at issue is between Union Member States or with third parties – non-EU countries.

4.3.5 The phenomenon of European private international law as the most dynamically developing branch of European private law

The concept of European private international law has become a component part of European private law and private international law in the EU Member States.

The development of this branch has been quite unique; it is an outcome of the last decade when formal preconditions were adopted within the European Union allowing for the adoption of unified regulation directly binding on individuals in all Member States. The uniform regulation includes a significant portion of international civil procedure and only

Privatrecht. Heidelberg: C. F. Müller Verlag, 2003, p. 119. For more details on the author's opinion see Pauknerová, M.: Private International Law in the Czech Republic: Tradition, New Experience and Prohibition of Discrimination on Grounds of Nationality. *Journal of Private International Law* 1/2008, p. 83.

partly affects conflict-of-law rules. In the near future, we can expect that other legislative instruments will be adopted in order to unify conflict and procedural rules so far regulated by national laws of individual Member States or international conventions or treaties. Some ideas have even emerged to carry out complete codification of private international law and procedure within the European Union. There are the first systems of European private international law proving the significance of this new branch and its position with respect to national legal systems of EU countries.[758]

The Amsterdam Treaty – judicial cooperation in civil matters

The concept of European private international law and procedure stems from the definition of judicial cooperation in civil matters stated in Art. 65 of TEC which created the legislative basis for new European instruments in this area. Measures taken in the area of "judicial cooperation in civil matters" provided for in Art. 65 TEC must fulfil three general criteria according to the TEC (see Art. 65 TEC): (a) civil matters, (b) foreign element, and (c) needed for the proper functioning of the internal market.

These measures are restricted to a certain extent: the limits are represented by the principles of subsidiarity and proportionality. The position of European private international law and procedure has not been changed much with the Lisbon Treaty. Judicial cooperation is newly stipulated in Chapter 3, Art. 81 of the Treaty on the Functioning of the European Union and the reading is very similar to that contained in the Treaty on the European Community. A major difference subsists in the usage of one word: the Lisbon Treaty replaces the former reading of the requirement for the adoption of measures in judicial cooperation in civil matters "when necessary for the proper functioning of the internal market" with a more general wording "particularly when necessary for the proper functioning of the internal market". We can see a shift to a more liberal understanding of areas to which the provision may apply.

External powers of the EU in the regulation of private relations with a foreign element

The European Union possesses the power to conclude international treaties with third parties or international organizations in the area in private international law. The question is whether this external power of the EU is exclusive, or whether there are common or shared powers of the EU and its Member States. This issue is of practical importance in private international law, particularly with respect to concluding international treaties drafted by EU Member States within the Hague Conference on Private International Law. The Czech Republic has been a contracting state to many Hague Conventions, thus an answer to this question is extremely relevant.

[758]/ Bogdan, M.: *Concise Introduction to EU Private International Law*. Groningen: Europa Law Publishing, 2006; Stone, P.: *EU Private International Law: Harmonization of Laws*. London: Elgar European Law Publishing, 2007; in Czech sources see Rozehnalová, N. – Týč, V.: *Evropský justiční prostor* [The European Judicial Area]. Brno: Masarykova univerzita, 2003, and Pauknerová M.: *Evropské mezinárodní právo soukromé* [European Private International Law]. Praha: C. H. Beck, 2008. For general conceptual ideas in Czech sources see Rozehnalová, N.: Evropské soukromé právo v. evropské mezinárodní právo soukromé [European Private Law v. European Private International Law]. In: Hurdík, J. – Fiala, J. – Selucká, M. (eds.): *Tradice a inovace v občanském právu* [Tradition and Innovation in Civil Law]. Brno: Masarykova univerzita, 2007, p. 112 with other references.

The situation has been partly solved by the well-known judgments of the European Court of Justice (No. 22/70 AETR/EART[759] and the opinion No. 1/03 Lugano Convention II[760]). Although the ECJ opinion on the Lugano Convention has been partly criticized[761] it represents the principal position in, and background for further analysis of external powers of the EU in private international law. Another factor played an important role, namely the accession of the EC/EU as the Regional Economic Integration Organization (REIO) to the Hague Conference on Private International Law on 3rd April 2007.

It is clear now that EU Member States are not free in concluding their individual treaties in areas which have been unified within the "judicial cooperation in civil matters". This seems to be quite topical with respect to bilateral treaties on cooperation and legal assistance made between EU Member States and third party countries; such treaties may no longer be concluded or re-negotiated without prior agreement of the European Union.

4.3.6 The current situation and the near future – unified and harmonized regulation of private international law in the EU

The list of the most significant regulations containing conflict-of-law rules and the rules of international civil procedure is rather extensive.[762] The existing Czech Private International Law and Procedure Act encompasses many provisions transposing into Czech law directives relevant for the arrangements of private relations with a foreign element. Most of them belong to so-called sectoral directives governing a particular legal area: for example, the law applicable to insurance, participation in payment systems, participation in settlement systems, insolvency of a financial institution, or financial security in relation with a foreign element. Directives in the area of private international law can be found in the Czech system in other laws, such as the Civil Code with respect to the regulation of consumer contracts (see s. 51a and subsequent provisions), or Act No. 480/2004 Sb. providing for certain services of the information society (for example s. 9 contains a conflict-of-law rule).

Naturally, these cases do not represent unification of legal systems but only harmonization dependent on concrete measures of individual EU Member States. Nevertheless, harmonization plays a significant role in the piecemeal unification of the national legal systems.

---

[759] Case 22/70, Commission of the European Communities v Council of the European Communities, [1971] ECR 263.
[760] Opinion of the European Court of Justice 1/03 of 7 February 2006 Lugano Convention II [2006] ECR I-1145.
[761] Pocar, F. (ed.): *The External Competence of the European Union and Private International Law*. Studie pubblicazioni della Rivista di diritto internazionale privato e processuale. Padova: CEDAM, 2007.
[762] In particular: Regulation No. 44/2001 on jurisdiction and the recognition and enforcement of judgments in civil and commercial matters (Brussels I); Regulation No. 2201/2003 concerning jurisdiction and the recognition and enforcement of judgments in matrimonial matters and the matters of parental responsibility (Brussels IIa); Regulation No. 1206/2001 on cooperation between the courts of the Member States in the taking of evidence in civil or commercial matters; Regulation No. 1346/2000 on insolvency proceedings; Regulation No. 805/2004 creating a European Enforcement Order for uncontested claims; Regulation No. 1896/2006 creating a European order for payment procedure; Regulation No.861/2007 establishing a European Small Claims Procedure; Regulation No. 864/2007 on the law applicable to non-contractual obligations (Rome II); Regulation No. 1393/2007 on the service in the Member States of judicial and extrajudicial documents in civil or commercial matters (service of documents); Regulation No. 593/2008 on the law applicable to contractual obligations (Rome I); Regulation No. 4/2009 on jurisdiction, applicable law, recognition and enforcement of decisions and cooperation in matters relating to maintenance obligations.

It can be stated that the unified and harmonized regulation has already covered a substantial portion of the rule of the conflict of laws and international civil procedure. It is apparent that the regulation has only been fragmentary and, as such, does not claim to be universally applicable.

Regulations governing conflict-of-law rules, such as Regulation No. 864/2007 on the law applicable to non-contractual obligations (Rome II), state that "any law specified by this Regulation shall be applied whether or not it is the law of a Member State" (see Art. 3 entitled "Universal application"). In other words, this Regulation foresees cases where the conflict-of-law rule determines the law of a non-Member State as governing law. For example, in the case when Norway is the country where the damage occurred, the judge is obliged to apply this law.

On the other hand, Regulations in the area of international civil procedure are applicable within the Union. For example, Regulation No. 1896/2006 creating a European order for payment procedure governs the proceedings for the European payment order dealing with non-contentious money claims in cross-border cases; a cross-border case is one in which at least one of the parties is domiciled or habitually resident in a Member State other than the Member State of the court seised (see Art. 1 and Art. 3). It means that this Regulation is not universally applicable; only Regulations dealing with the conflict of laws are universally applicable, not Regulations focusing on international civil procedure.

Many other instruments are being prepared. The Draft Regulation of the Council to amend Regulation (EC) 2201/2203, i.e. Brussels IIa Regulation, with respect to jurisdiction and which is to introduce new rules to determine the law applicable to matrimonial cases (so called Regulation Rome III)[763] is aimed at the unification of the conflict of laws and international civil procedure with respect to divorce and separation. The Rome III Regulation is facing a long journey, particularly because experts in Member States have not uniformly come to a conclusion on whether the Union should govern conflict-of-law rules of family law. "Regulation Rome IV" is the working title of the draft to regulate property rights of spouses; its purpose is to unify conflict-of-law rules and the rules of international civil procedure in this field. So far, the above-mentioned Green Paper on conflict of laws in matters concerning matrimonial property regimes, including the question of jurisdiction and mutual recognition of 2006, was published.[764] Preparatory work has intensified in international succession law, which should have its outcome in an EC Regulation on applicable law, jurisdiction, recognition and enforcement of judgments in inheritance and wills cases, as is foreseen by the Green Paper "Successions and wills".[765] The proposed Regulation tries to arrange just for one inheritance proceeding to be pursued with respect to property of one deceased person in order to exclude duplicity in the

---

[763]/ See Proposal for a Council Regulation amending Regulation (EC) No 2201/2003 as regards jurisdiction and introducing rules concerning applicable law in matrimonial matters z 28.6.2007, JUSTCIV 183, Committee on Civil Law Matters (Rome III).

[764]/ Green Paper on conflict of laws in matters concerning matrimonial property regimes, including the question of jurisdiction and mutual recognition, COM (2006) 400 final.

[765]/ Green Paper "Successions and wills", COM (2005) 65 final; Proposal for a regulation on jurisdiction, applicable law, recognition and enforcement of decisions and authentic instruments in matters of succession and the creation of a European Certificate of Succession, CM (2009) 154.

case where, for example, immovable property located in the Czech Republic is dealt with by a Czech court whilst movables are subject to the proceeding before the court of the state of nationality of the deceased person. In order to follow modern trends the proposal considers the habitual residence of the deceased, not his or her nationality. The proposal was planned to be completed in 2009 but due to sensitive political issues the procedure has been delayed.

4.3.7 Remarks on codification of European private international law

Codification of private international law at a more universal level seems to be a dream of most professors of private international law all over the world; such considerations can be found in all major monographs dealing with private international law, usually in connection with comparative law.

There is possibly a more realistic view within the European Union than in a global context. Considering the ambitious list of legislation and the plan of ongoing or prepared codifying projects we may conclude that the idea of codification of private international law and procedure is not as impracticable as it was a couple of years ago.[766]

The formal background

A closer look at the formal background of the unification of private international law within the European Union suggests that the heading of Title IV, Part Three of the EC Treaty on free movement of persons, must be interpreted in such a way that it does not preclude the conclusion that Title IV TEC encompasses practically the whole of private international law should not be excluded.[767] This should be understood as a basic formal source for further considerations regarding the unification of European private international law.

The current situation

Proprietary rights and personal status issues have remained untouched by unifying initiatives pursued within the conflict of laws branch.[768] As far as company law is concerned, there is a proposal for a uniform conflict regulation prepared, or debated, in Germany.[769] There is an academic opinion published that most building stones are, or will be in the near future available.[770]

The general part of private international law has not essentially been regulated, although many uniform European instruments provide for general institutions being regular elements of the general part of private international law, such as renvoi, public order reservation,

---

[766]/ For the first ideas on communitarization of private international law see the frequently quoted article by Basedow, J.: The communitarization of the conflict of laws under the Treaty of Amsterdam. *CMLR* 3/2000, p. 687.
[767]/ Bogdan, M. *supra* at p. 9. See Title V of the Treaty on the Functioning of the EU.
[768]/ Lagarde, P. *supra* at p. 225.
[769]/ See, in particular, Sonnenberger, H. J.: *Vorschläge und Berichte zur Reform des europäischen und deutschen internationalen Gesellschaftsrechts.* Tübingen: J.C.B. Mohr Siebeck, 2007, and Sonnenberger, H. J. – Bauer, F.: *Vorschlag des Deutschen Rates für Internationales Privatrecht für eine Regelung des Internationalen Gesellschaftsrechts auf europäischer/nationaler Ebene.* Heidelberg: Verl. Recht und Wirtschaft, 2006, pp. 1–24.
[770]/ Kreuzer, K.: Was gehört in den Allgemeinen Teil eines Europäischen Kollisionsrechtes? In: Jud, B. – Rechberger, W. – Reichelt G. (eds.): *Kollisionsrecht in der Europäischen Union.* Wien: Jan Sramek Verlag, 2008, p. 1.

or mandatory rules and their application; attention is also drawn to the applicability of foreign law referred to by the conflict-of-law rule. The defining of general issues of private international law has been enhanced through judgments of the European Court of Justice, particularly with respect to the concept of the "European public order". The first contours of the general part of private international law code have been shaped.[771]

Unlike the conflict-of-law rules area, the branch of international civil procedure contains many unifying instruments – so far with respect to the relations with a foreign element. However, many intensive debates have focussed on finding the answer for the question of whether the regulation of the European payment order or the European small claims procedure should apply to all proceedings or just those with a foreign or cross-border element. All those debates ended up with the restrictive solution confining the applicability of those Regulations only to cross-border relations.

4.3.8 The first proposals of codification of European private international law and their evaluation

The initiative of famous German expert in private international law Professor Kreuzer who introduced a European Code of Private International Law has been a significant contribution to the unification and prospective codification of European private international law.[772] His extensively cited treatise on the European Code has been inspiring for the whole European Union. Kreuzer asks the question of whether the European Code of private international law should have universal or only particular effect. Consequently, Rozehnalová considers the distinction between European v. universal private international law, which is another significant aspect.[773] Should the conflict-of-law branch be unified, it should be treated at the universal level; this corresponds with the nature of private international law, which should not be confined within the borders of the EU.

Kreuzer intends to codify European private international law in the form of a Regulation.[774] A Regulation seems to be the only format in order to ensure the effective enforcement and uniform adoption of the legal instrument in all EU Member States (except for the United Kingdom, Ireland and Denmark); but it should be noted that this approach will not be easy to pursue and Member States will be rather reluctant to accept it.

The first more concrete ideas aimed at the codification of European private international law were uttered during the meetings of the European Group for Private International Law GEDIP (*Groupe européen de droit international privé*). Undoubtedly, this was due to a strong professorial interest of most members of the Group in this issue. However, not only academic ideas were introduced: most members possess deep knowledge of, and extensive experience in, the preparation of legislative instruments within the EU and often in legislative initia-

---

[771] *Ibidem* at p. 1 and subs. For a more general approach see, for example, Grundmann, St.: Binnenmarktkollisionsrecht – vom klassischen IPR zur Integrationsordnung. *RabelsZ* 2000, pp. 457–477.

[772] Kreuzer, K.: Zu Stand und Perspektiven des Europäischen Internationalen Privatrechts – Wie europäisch soll das Europäische Internationale Privatrecht sein? *RabelsZ* 1/2006, p. 1.

[773] Rozehnalová, N.: Evropské kolizní právo – začátek společné cesty? [The European Conflict of Laws?] In: Hurdík, J. – Fiala, J. – Selucká, M. (eds.): *Evropský kontext vývoje českého práva po roce 2004* [The European Context of the Development of Czech Law]. Brno: Masarykova univerzita, 2006, p. 388.

[774] Kreuzer, K. *supra* at p. 88.

tives regarding private international law in their home countries (e.g. drafting the Private International Law Act of 2004 in Belgium).[775]

We may agree with Siehr's opinion that no other way but a uniform and comprehensive codification of European private international law and procedure can be envisaged.[776] On the other hand, the European unification of the whole private international law should not be understood as the issue to be completed in the near future.

4.3.9 Conclusion: The issue of further codification of private international law within the national legal system of EU Member States

Private international law (and procedure) possesses certain specific features which I personally consider significant with respect to the potential unification of these rules in a wider extent. Primarily, it should be emphasized that conflict-of-law rules and some rules of international civil procedure have partly been formulated in a very similar pattern in the legal systems of various states, and even in the legal systems belonging to different legal cultures. This proximity and similarity of regulation may lead to certain autonomy of those rules in the sense of their independence of a particular social, political and economic system. Another substantial feature of conflict-of-law rules and the rules of international civil procedure has been their neutrality. Unlike substantive rules, both these categories of rules are "neutral" by themselves in the sense that they only determine the governing substantive law, or identify the competent court, without defining the relevant substantive law to be applied by the court seised. This is of extreme importance for the potential unification of the systems. Countries may feel themselves to be less affected by any such unification than they would have been had the unification of substantive law been pursued.

These two specific features, non-existent in the case of substantive law, may play a crucial role for the unification within the European Union, as it can be seen in the successful unification of private international law. Unlike conflict-of-law rules unification, substantive unification intervenes in the very traditional roots and solutions adopted in different legal cultures and states are very reluctant and reserved should any change be compelled from outside. A similar situation exists in civil procedure: we can see the difference between the rules of international jurisdiction of courts and the recognition and enforcement of judgments on the one hand, and the remaining issues on the other hand.

European private international law is gradually replacing national autonomous private international law, primarily by means of Regulations[777] as directives seem to be less important. On the other hand, a realistic view should be taken: private international law is part of national law; every state has its own private international law, and its interest is that both the conflict-of-law rules and the rules of international civil procedure correspond to its own

---

[775] See, in particular, Groupe européen de droit international privé, Seizième réunion, Coimbra 2006, Compte rendu des séances du travail, to be retrieved from http://www.gedip-egpil.eu/.

[776] Siehr, K.: Auf dem Weg zu einem Europäischen Internationalen Privatrecht. *Europäische Zeitschrift* 5/2005, p. 90.

[777] For example, Rome III Regulation will replace national legislation of EU Member States on jurisdiction in matrimonial matters (new Art. 6 on residual jurisdiction replacing the existing Art. 7 of Brussels IIa Regulation); see the criticism by Jayme, E./Kohler, Ch., Europäisches Kollisionsrecht 2006: Eurozentrismus ohne Kodifikationsidee?, IPRax 2006, p. 539.

legal culture. New national codifications are adopted even in EU countries (e.g. Belgium, Bulgaria, the Czech Republic in the future). New legislative instruments, such as the Rome I Regulation No. 593/2008 on the law applicable to contractual obligations, sometimes expressly envisage a simultaneous existence of relevant national legislation foreseeing the applicability of the more convenient of the two laws in the particular case.[778]

The following conclusions are considered to be relevant:

1. The issue of a comprehensive codification of European private international law is not of ultimate significance today but it should be discussed and considered since the tendency has been quite obvious.
2. National codifications of private international law in EU Member States retain their significance and should be further worked on. This applies also to the Czech codification of private international law.
3. The two levels influence each other, the impact is not one-way. Uniform European instruments are based on the legislative conceptions of individual EU Member States on the one hand, and European law, i.e. what has already been unified, on the other hand, has an impact on the autonomous legal systems of individual Member States; this leads, in fact, to a certain degree of unification.

Unification has been carried out in both directions. This is a significant conclusion from the point of view of legal certainty of parties to private relations with a foreign element.

4.4 SELECTED ISSUES OF THE RECODIFICATION OF FAMILY LAW IN THE CZECH REPUBLIC

4.4.1 General remarks on family, law and the relationship between them

Family is the basic and the most important social group and institution representing a fundamental part of the social structure as well as a basic economic unit. Family results from marriage or blood relations (parenthood, siblings, etc.)[779] This encyclopaedic definition of family is one of many ways of describing and understanding the concept. Various branches of scientific and scholarly knowledge usually emphasize different aspects typical of family as the basic social institution. Family, whatever definition may be chosen, is primarily an institution where day-to-day coexistence is pursued by persons connected through narrow ties of their relationship, mutual assistance and moral responsibility. In other words, family (understood as the basic social institution) is the environment where most members of the society live their everyday personal lives.

These relations in personal lives, relations between women and men or parents and children, appear to be the least capable of coping with intervention by external powers whatever nature and form such intervention may have including the application of general rules binding on the modes of human conduct. "*Should there be other borders which may be reached*

---

[778]/ Art. 7/3 e) Rome I Regulation (insurance contracts).
[779]/ *Všeobecná encyklopedie v osmi svazcích* [General Encyclopaedia in Eight Volumes]. Vol. 6, Praha: Diderot, 1999, p. 417.

by law these would be much more fateful in this field. Should there be a need to override the law by justice this is the field where such an approach is a life necessity. Where it starts to be necessary that the law should decide a dispute between a husband and wife or between parents and children the situation itself is already a misery if not even a dead failure. If there is something able to show how far we are from moral perfection it would undoubtedly be the fact that the law must deal with the issues of family life."[780]

Legal rules regulate these relationships in such a way that they do not take the family as their recipient or addressee. Family has not been traditionally considered as the holder of rights and duties in our territory.[781] Legal rules have addressed individual persons having several roles in a family. Therefore family law may be defined as *"a set of laws whose subject-matter is rights and duties involved in various roles in the family and similar unions. These are rights and duties of spouses, parents and children or other relatives, as well as of these individuals and other persons fulfilling various roles in relation to children, replacing, or complementing the functions of their parents."*[782]

4.4.2 Family law in the draft of a new Civil Code[783]

It was clear that the recovery of the democratic state based on the rule of law at the end of 1989 and beginning of 1990 could not dispense with essential changes in the legal order. Whilst the most urgent amendments of the Civil Code (CC) were completed as early as in 1991,[784] the Family Act (FA) was subject to its first amendment as late as in 1998.[785] The amendment of FA of 1998[786] originated in Parliament, avoiding the standard and consistent legislative procedure. Due to its conceptual and subject-matter insufficiency the amended FA was still considered by jurisprudence to be provisional.[787] Even amendments passed after 1999 did not heal this unfortunate situation. Moreover, some of them seem to have brought in more opacity and ambiguity.

Partial amendments across the whole legal order having attempted to adapt to the conditions of the democratic state based on the rule of law were by themselves unable to remove the legal order which had been built upon totally different conceptual foundations for 50 years. The idea of recodification of private law emerged for the first time as early as in the beginning of the 1990s. The first draft of a new code was published in the *Právní praxe* journal in 1996. After a short period of silence the work on the new Draft started. In April 2001 the Government approved the outline of its legislative intent, becoming the starting point for the legislative procedure and drafting. Professor Dr. JUDr. Karel Eliáš and As-

---

[780]/ Svoboda, E.: *Rodinné právo československé* [Czechoslovak Family Law]. 1st ed., Praha: Vesmír, 1935, p. 7.

[781]/ The General Civil Code of 1811 (Imperial Patent No. 946/1811 Sb. z. s., GCC) defined a family in its s. 40; however, its purpose was just to set the terminology as was the case of "relationship" and "relationship-in-law".

[782]/ Radvanová, S. in Knappová, M. et al: *Občanské právo hmotné* [Civil Substantive Law]. Vol. III, 3rd ed., Praha: ASPI, 2002, p. 16.

[783]/ Hereinafter referred to as "the Draft".

[784]/ Act No. 509/1991 Sb., to alter, amend and regulate the Civil Code.

[785]/ However, it should be noted that one amendment to FA was made in 1992; the amending law was Act No. 234/1992 Sb., altering and complementing Act No. 94/1963 Sb., the Family Act, as amended by Act No. 132/1982 Sb. This law enabled individuals to enter into marriage also before a church or any other religious society.

[786]/ Act No. 91/1998 Sb., altering and amending Act No 94/1963 Sb., the Family Act, as amended, and changing amending other laws.

[787]/ For example, Radvanová, S. – Zuklínová, M.: *Kurs občanského práva – Instituty rodinného práva* [The Course of Civil Law – Family Law Institutions]. 1st ed., Praha: C. H. Beck, 1999, p. 11.

sociate Professor JUDr. Michaela Zuklínová, CSc. became the main authors of the Draft (the latter drafter in charge of family law). The drafting was coordinated by the Ministry of Justice of the Czech Republic having established the Recodification Committee as the body assembling outstanding experts both from jurisprudence and legal practice.[788] After comprehensive debates and within the standard legislative procedure, the Draft was referred to the Government for consideration in January 2009.

Provisions for family law are contained in Part II of the Draft[789] entitled "Family Law". This reflects on the whole system of the Draft apparently built upon the anthropocentric conception. The focus is on individuals, his or her family and only then does property follow. The emphasis upon an individual and the family surrounding him or her has been a characteristic feature of traditional European codes of private law.[790]

Part I of the Draft deals with marriage. Although it follows a traditional understanding of marriage[791] the Part also reacts to some new social phenomena relating to marriage. Considering the issues connected with the formation of marriage, the drafters originally intended, in compliance with the approved outline of the legislative intent, to introduce some changes. They intended to omit the mandatory provision defining the main purpose of marriage (the existing s. 1 (2) FA), the provision strictly separating secular and religious aspects of wedding and marriage through the removal of legal consequences from ceremonies held before a church or any other religious society, and, finally, the removal of the categorical requirement for a ceremonial form of wedding (relating to the preceding step). These issues became the subject matter of not only wide discussion among lay people and legal experts, but also of tough political debates, particularly at the latest stages of the consideration of the Draft.

As far as the religious wedding is concerned the Draft was amended reflecting on the public opinion and distributed in two alternatives for comments within the regular comment procedure. The first alternative presumed that the declaration resulting in the formation of marriage under "secular" law can be made solely before state bodies. The second alternative preserved the *status quo*.[792] Failure to admit secular legal consequences to declarations made by prospective spouses before church bodies was perceived by the society primarily as the return to the totalitarian regime and the denial of the legitimate right of choice. The public talked about the "prohibition of religious weddings" which was rather schematising. The "prohibition of religious weddings" would have meant the prohibition for churches and

---

[788] The composition of the Committee members was subject to gradual changes.

[789] The authors of this chapter are referring to the text of the Draft submitted to the Government in January 2009.

[790] See, for example, the French Code Napóleon of 1804. Provisions for marriage are contained in Title V of Book One of its original text (for details see, for example, *CodeNapóleon*. Édition seule officielle pour Le Grand-duché de Berg. Düsseldorf: X. Levrault, Imprimeur du Gouvernement, 1810, p. 71 and subs.). Considering more recent codes, Book One of the Dutch Civil Code is entitled "Personal and family law".

[791] Under s. 578 of the Draft, marriage is a "permanent union of husband and wife created in the manner prescribed by this law." For the conceptual features of marriage see, for example, Hrušáková, M. – Králíčková, Z.: *České rodinné právo* [Czech Family Law]. 3rd ed., Brno: MU Brno and Jan Šabata, 2006, p. 51 and subs.

[792] It should be added that the first option was to extend the possibility of making the declaration on the entering into marriage to all churches and religious societies; later the existing regulation was preferred, i.e. the right to solemnize marriage having effects for secular law was confined just to those churches and religious societies having authority to exercise "special rights" under s. 7 of Act No. 3/2002 Sb., regulating churches and religious societies, as amended.

religious societies to hold ceremonies relating to the formation of marriage at both the state law and religious levels. This would have been contrary to the constitutionally guaranteed freedom of worship and freedom to express beliefs[793] and the Draft did not contain any such provision. *"The difference between the totalitarian regulation introduced by Act No. 265/1949 Sb., and subsequently in the original text of the Family Act 1963, on the one hand, and the regulation proposed in the Draft subsists primarily in that religious wedding may be entered into anytime and anywhere independently of the civil wedding. Particularly such situations where the religious wedding was solemnized before the civil wedding, were forbidden and even prosecuted by the totalitarian regime (s. 207 Criminal Act 1950, s. 211 Criminal Act 1961) having been inspired by Bismarck's Kulturkampf. If the religious wedding is solemnized without any status effects for the state the real religious nature of the ceremony may be preserved (for example, the wedding in the Catholic Church represents the grant of sanctity of marriage)."*[794]

Since the legal effects of the formation of marriage under civil law were confined just to declarations made before state bodies the requirement of ceremonial form of such declaration was omitted. There was a presumption that persons practising any religion would consider as decisive – therefore ceremonial – the moment when their marriage assumed the religious effects, i.e. the solemnization of their marriage by church or a religious society. Should the ceremonial form of "secular" marriage have been insisted on the worshippers would have had to undertake two ceremonies. Those entering just into civil marriage would have a choice whether their declaration to the state was ceremonial or not.[795]

These questions were eventually solved at the political level. The result of negotiations was to preserve in the Draft the existing situation. The text of the Draft submitted to the Government presumes that the legal effect of the formation of marriage will be connected with both the declaration before the state and the declaration before a church or religious society being authorized to exercise "special rights". The solemnization of wedding will continue to be ceremonial.[796]

The same destiny has applied to the provision that the main purpose of marriage is to create family and regularly raise children. This provision had been returned to the Draft before the Draft was submitted to the Government.

It is a generally well-known fact that the number of marriages has been falling. Those deciding in favour of marriage perceive this event much more intensively as the essential moment in their lives. Prospective spouses spend a lot of energy and money to make the solemnization of their marriage fulfil their dreams. This is why the organization of large (as well as modest) wedding ceremonies has recently become the subject of business. It is not surprising that "ordinary" wedding halls often fail to correspond with the plans of prospective spouses for their wedding ceremony. Therefore there has been an increasing number

---

[793]/ Articles 15 and 16 of the Resolution of the Czech National Council declaring the Charter of Fundamental Rights and Freedoms as part of the constitutional order of the Czech Republic under No. 2/1993 Sb., as amended (the Charter).

[794]/ The Explanatory Report on the Draft in the wording of May 2008.

[795]/ This is in accordance with the fact that entering into marriage is a private business of the prospective spouses and the state just passively accepts their declaration and takes it into account; thus there is no reason to regulate such event by mandatory provisions more than necessary.

[796]/ Paradoxically, there is a disadvantage on the part of prospective spouses in comparison with those intending to enter into the registered partnership. The latter may choose (at least at some Vital Statistics Registry) whether they want a ceremonial or just "common" declaration to enter into the registered partnership.

of applications of prospective spouses to organize their wedding ceremony at special and extraordinary places.[797] The Draft takes this tendency into consideration expressly providing for the duty of the state body to reflect the will of prospective spouses with respect to the place of their wedding ceremony.[798] However, such a liberal approach is absent should the prospective spouses – Czech citizens – choose to be married outside the Czech Republic. Unlike the existing regulation, the Draft provides that marriage may be entered into in the Czech Embassy or consular department only in cases deserving special attention.[799] As far as the concept of impediments of marriage and the effects of their breach is concerned we can summarize that this issue follows the existing regulation. Situations where marriage is not formed are contained in the provision intended to create an exhaustive list. Unlike the existing s. 17a FA the Draft explicitly provides for the requirement of different sex of prospective spouses.

The expanding property stratification of the society results in the increasing importance of the legal regulation of property relations between spouses. The interest intensifies in arranging for legal regulation of property in the way best corresponding to the concrete situation of the (prospective) spouses. The Draft respects this trend and provides for many ways of contractual modifications of community property and its administration. Following the existing regulation the Draft distinguishes the regime of separate property, the regime stipulating the constitution of community property as late as on the date of termination of marriage, as well as the regime to expand or reduce community property within the statutory limits. The contract of marital property must be made in the form of a public instrument (deed). Unlike today, the Draft does not require the form of a notarial deed. What is new is the possibility to make a contract arranging for property relations between spouses in the case of termination of their marriage. Considering termination by divorce, such possibility seems to be relevant. The rising number of divorces is the fact which must be considered by the legislature as objective although negatively perceived. Attempts to fight this trend with instrument of purely legal and political nature (e.g. making the conditions for divorce much harder) have no chance to be accepted by the society today.[800] Where a contract is made to arrange for the settlement of property relations in the case of termination of marriage by divorce before the actual breakdown between spouses, such contract – made when the atmosphere was not extremely emotional – may prevent any other conflicts and may contribute to peaceful and cultured parting of spouses. The Draft newly provides that the

[797] Even under water or in deep coal mines.

[798] However, this seems to be a declaratory provision rather than a duty since its practical application will depend, in a particular case, upon the abilities and readiness of the registrar and solemnizing officer to serve at the place chosen by prospective spouses.

[799] This requirement was submitted and insisted on by the Czech Ministry of Foreign Affairs within the comment procedure; they claim that some Czech diplomatic missions in attractive tourist destinations had been overwhelmed by applications for a wedding ceremony. However, only the practical application of the new code will show whether the expectations of the Ministry are met. It may be reasonably presumed that the number of applications for a wedding ceremony in attractive tourist destinations will not decline but it will require more time to check whether each individual application is a case deserving special attention, whilst today this can be solved just by making a waiting list and setting dates when the wedding "in the whisper of turquoise green sea and palm trees" will take place.

[800] At best, the increasing number of divorces would transform into the increasing number of marriages formally existing but practically dysfunctional.

property relations may be arranged by a contract for the case of dissolution of marriage generally, i.e. including death. In such case, however, the contract in the relevant part becomes an inheritance contract and must contain the respective elements.[801]

It should be added that the provisions for marital property law in the Draft, unlike the existing Act, attempt to increase the protection of one spouse against harassing conduct of the other, as well as protection of third persons in contacts with spouses relating to property issues. The Draft reacts to the fact that an increasing number of marriages are such that one spouse is fully dependent in property issues on the other.[802] One example is the provision regulating situations when a husband administering all community property under contract may legally act only with the consent of the other spouse.[803] The protection of a weaker spouse is especially treated in the Draft when common residence is considered. Sections 659–666 contain "some provisions for the housing of spouses", followed by "special provisions against domestic violence" (ss. 667–669).

The expression of an increased protection of third persons is the provision for the public list of contracts to alter the statutory property regime between spouses. Under s. 637 of the Draft, a contract may be included in the list should one spouse propose so. This is an approach to the protection of third persons well-known in Germany, Italy and many other states. "*If a contract and all documents altering the statutory regime of property of spouses are put on the public list changes made between spouses will be effective against third persons. However, it is up to the parties to a marriage contract and to their will whether they intend to constitute such effects. Should no spouse propose that the contract of the marital property regime be included in the list third persons may rely on such contract only if they have knowledge of it. It is obvious that spouses may provide in the contract that the content will not be made public.*"[804]

The regulation of divorce also follows, to a certain extent, the existing legal situation. The only reason for divorce has been and remains the breakdown of marriage. In addition to divorce where reasons for breakdown are examined (including so-called harsh divorce) the Draft has taken over the other type, informally called "agreed" or "uncontested" where no grounds are examined. The Draft incorporated a comment made by the Ministry of Culture stating that a court will divorce marriage without examination of grounds when – in addition to all reasons stipulated in the existing legislation – "*spouses have attempted to conciliate with respect to the reasons for their breakdown.*" "*Today divorce is understood as a legitimate solution of the dispute between spouses.*"[805] Divorce without examining the grounds for breakdown may be reached by those spouses who are able to agree on a matter relating to the termination of their marriage.[806]

[801]/ The inheritance contract subsists in that one party – the testator, calls the other party or a third person to inherit or to become a beneficiary, and the other party accepts it. The inheritance contract must be in the form of a public instrument. For details see s. 1408 and subs. of the Draft.

[802]/ Despite all antidiscrimination measures it is more and more difficult for mothers before or after maternity leave or middle-age women to get a job in the labour market.

[803]/ These are situations when community property as a whole would be disposed of, or residential premises as part of community property are at issue which is the family common household, or the residence of one family member or a minor child below the legal age and in custody of spouses as well as establishing permanent encumbrance of immovable property which belongs to community property (s. 645 (2) of the Draft).

[804]/ Explanatory report on the Draft in the wording of January 2009.

[805]/ Hrušáková, M. – Králíčková, Z. *supra* at p. 118.

[806]/ That is the regulation of the situation of a minor child after divorce, property issues and housing.

This can be done only by such spouses who by themselves have somehow settled their new situation. Proving that they "*have attempted to conciliate with respect to the reasons for their breakdown*" will be practically confined to a purely formal declaration that the attempt was to no effect. This provision has no other meaning than to make the formal declaration by spouses, or to "attempt to conciliate" should they intend to reach this type of divorce.

Debates on the regulation of divorce in the Draft included maintenance and support of a spouse after divorce. It was shown that the principle of good morals – as the only and very abstract principle referred to by courts when they do or do not award this type of maintenance – is rather difficult to tackle in its practical application by both professionals and lay people. Some concrete cases were even covered by media. There is a prevailing opinion today that divorce means the cessation of former spousal and family relations so that divorced partners become full strangers to each other. The Draft intends to respect this approach and circumscribes the criteria for awarding maintenance to a former partner as well as provides for much stricter rules than the existing legislation. "*It is proposed, particularly in reference to German regulation (s.1570 and subs. BGB) and Swiss law (Art. 125 ZBG), that the extraordinary nature of this type of maintenance be emphasized; there should be more aspects determined which will be relied on within the existing general good morals criterion hardly tackled in the practice of today. If this is not specifically regulated any of the divorced partners might be subject to unjustified claims for maintenance even a long time after divorce, because the claim for maintenance under the existing law lapses only due to a new marriage entered into by the potential claimant or by death. The essential restriction of time to five years after divorce, still applicable in Poland, was abolished in Czech law in 1982. Imposing a risk upon persons entering into marriage that their potential divorce would entitle the other partner to claim maintenance any time after divorce, may be rather demotivating for the prospective spouses.*"[807] Therefore the Draft proposes that maintenance may be claimed only by the partner who is unable to support him or herself. The duty to maintain, to a reasonable extent, will be owed only by such partner who may be justifiably required to do so (the general criterion), particularly with respect to his/her age, health condition at the time of divorce, or termination of custody of common child(ren), etc. More concrete determination of the conditions for awarding maintenance subsists in that courts will take into account the duration of marriage and time lapsed after divorce as well as whether the divorced partner has failed to get an adequate job although no objective obstacle barred him or her from doing so, whether the divorced partner has been able to support him/herself by better management of his/her property, whether the divorced partner participated in the care of common family household during marriage, whether the divorced partner did or did not commit against the other partner or any other close person conduct of a criminal nature, or whether there is any other serious reason. This criterion provides a court with tools to deal with individual cases upon individual bases considering the concrete circumstances of each of them.

Title Two starts with provisions for kinship (family relationship). The Draft defines kinship as the relation of persons created either upon a natural tie, or by adoption. This is a traditional understanding of the concept. The Draft attaches importance to both the relations instituted by nature as well as those established by law.

---

[807] / Explanatory report on the Draft in the wording of January 2009.

Motherhood is the relationship between mother and her child. The Draft follows the pattern constituted by s. 50a FA stipulating that mother is a woman giving birth to the child. Thus nothing is changed in the fact that motherhood is established by the objective factor of delivery and as such established forever, i.e. it may not be "waived" or "abandoned"[808] nor contractually transferred to another woman.

Determination of paternity in the Draft is constructed upon the traditional system of presumptions. The first one is the statutory presumption of paternity of the husband of the mother. This has been complemented with provisions governing paternity cases where the child is born between the date of commencement of divorce proceedings and the 300th day after divorce. If during that time the husband, or ex-husband, declares that he is not the father of the child whilst another man declares he is the father of the child the latter is assumed to have been the father if the mother confirms both declarations. This regulation is not identical with that contained in the existing Family Act. The legal effect of declaration under s. 58 (1) (second sentence) FA is the denial of paternity, not its determination as is intended by the Draft. Thus the Draft makes the whole situation easier for the persons concerned. The Draft has also taken into consideration the extensive developments in assisted reproduction: it introduces a new presumption covering cases when a child was conceived by artificial insemination and is born to an unmarried woman.[809] In such a case it is presumed that the man having agreed to artificial insemination is the father of the child. Unlike the existing s. 54 (3) FA, the Draft allows for this presumption to be used not only in paternity proceedings before courts (under s. 54 (1) FA) but generally anytime a child is born as a result of artificial insemination. Should paternity fail to be determined by any of the described ways it may be constituted by a consenting declaration of the mother and the man intending to be father. Under the existing law (s. 52(3) FA) the declaration of the mother is not required if she is incapable, due to mental disorder, of assessing the significance of her conduct or where making the declaration is barred by a hardly surmountable obstacle. The Draft in this respect deviates from the existing law since it provides in s. 697 that the determination of paternity is not possible if the mother cannot, due to her mental disorder, assess the significance her declaration or her making the declaration is barred by a hardly surmountable obstacle. The provision in the Draft clarifying the applicability of general clauses stipulating legal conduct is essential. Unless provided otherwise, such special expression of will is subject to general provisions for legal conduct. There is an exception regarding the restriction of time when one may invoke the invalidity of such expression of will. S. 698 of the Draft stipulates that invalidity of paternity declaration may be raised only within the time-limit for the denial of paternity. Where paternity is not established by the consenting declaration, the mother, the child or a man claiming his paternity may apply to court for judicial determination of paternity. The man having had intercourse with the mother during the period between the 160th and 300th day before the birth of the child is presumed to have been the father unless his paternity is excluded due to serious reasons. The Draft maintains the third paternity presumption which may be claimed only in court

---

[808] When we get information from media that a woman "waived" or "abandoned" her motherhood it factually and legally means that the mother has agreed to the adoption of her newly born child.
[809] The birth of a child is normally covered by the statutory presumption of paternity of the husband of the mother.

proceedings. What is new is the reduction of the relevant time of intercourse before the birth of a child from the existing 180 days to the proposed 160 days. The Draft thus reacts to the recent developments in premature birth care.

Recently the DNA analysis has been a standard way of determining contested paternity in court proceedings. Its advantage has been, unlike formerly used methods, that paternity of a particular man may be fully excluded. Should paternity fail to be excluded then the computation of probabilities is pursued to determine how probable the paternity is.[810] Therefore courts do not examine whether the mother, during the relevant period of time, had intercourse with the respective man but they directly move to expert evidence based on the DNA analysis. Even the Constitutional Court, in its judgment I ÚS 987/07 provided its opinion: *"It is apparent that with the development of modern medicine the whole concept of s. 54 (1) and (2) of the Family Act has become obsolete. The so-called basis of the third presumption is the fact that the man had intercourse with the mother during the period between the 180th and 300th day before the birth of the child (...). This construction of the factual basis of the presumption originated in the time when it was not possible for the forensic expert to unambiguously determine whether the defendant was or was not the father; therefore it was necessary to tie the presumption to another fact, namely the sexual intercourse of the mother and the defendant. (...) If it is practicable for the analysis of desoxyribonucleic acid to unambiguously determine whether the defendant is the father of the child or not there is no need to tie the third presumption to the fact of intercourse which is an indirect indication of paternity. This is why the wording of s. 54 (2) FA is lagging behind the development of modern medicine and fails to correspond to the recent social reality. Until the legislature reacts to the changes described the concrete situation should be solved by interpretation (...)."* The Constitutional Court states that paternity proceedings *"are governed by the principle of arbitrary (not legal) order. Therefore it is not possible to consider as the only correct approach one where the court first examines whether there was any sexual intercourse between litigants and only if the result is affirmative the court orders to carry out the DNA analysis to find out whether any serious circumstances may exclude paternity of the defendant. It is not a defect in proceedings if the court directly applies for the DNA analysis as expert evidence: such an approach is in accordance with not only the principle of arbitrary order but also with the principle of procedural economy."* Thus the question arises whether paternity procedure in the Draft should be regulated in a way different from the existing law so that the new methods of proving paternity can be better taken into consideration.[811]

The regulation of the denial of paternity is in the Draft, in its essence, taken over from the existing legislation. The right of denial of the Supreme Prosecuting Attorney has been preserved with small clarification added. The Draft puts a stronger emphasis upon the biological relations of the child, stating in s. 7023 (2) that the Supreme Prosecuting Attorney may file the application for the denial of paternity if all the circumstances prove that the man considered to be the father of the child is not his father and the time-limit set for either

---

[810] For more details on the DNA analysis see, for example, Brdička, R. - Loudová, M. - Sieglová, Z.: Znalec sám proti sobě. Řešení sporného otcovství [The Forensic Expert Against Himself. The Solution of Contested Paternity]. *Právní rádce* 8/2000, p. 14 and subs., Loudová, M. - Sieglová, Z.: Metodiky analýzy DNA jednoznačně řeší otázku sporného otcovství [The Methodology of DNA Analysis Solves Contested Paternity Unambiguously]. *Právo a rodina* 4/2002, p. 13 and subs.

[811] However, it should be noted in this context that the same conception (i.e. paternity tied to the sexual intercourse during the relevant period of time unless serious circumstances exclude paternity) is still maintained, for example, by Swiss or German civil codes.

parent to deny paternity has lapsed, unless the welfare of the child exceptionally requires that the denial should not be claimed. The phrasing *"if all the circumstances prove that the man considered as the father of the child is not his father"* is openly directed to the outcome of the DNA analysis carried out. The biological aspect prevails but even in this case the paternity denial claim may not be raised without any other supporting arguments. The Supreme Prosecuting Attorney must consider whether the particular case is not the exceptional situation where the welfare of the child would exclude the denial to be claimed.[812]

Although the regulation of paternity in the Draft is very similar to the existing legislation it also contains a brand new institution. The Draft in its s. 710 presumes that paternity may be denied by the child after he or she reaches the legal age but not later than within one year of the legal age, or within one year of becoming aware of the fact casting doubt on the paternity of his/her father should the child learn of the fact after reaching the legal age. The Draft respects the strong tendency emphasizing the right of a child to know his/her biological origin. The importance of knowing one's own biological origin is increasing for medical purposes where the knowledge of genetic inheritability may be crucial in certain circumstances.

4.4.3 Conclusions

This subchapter has focused on some aspects of the recodification of family law as contained in the Draft of a new Czech civil code. The authors, using several examples, have pointed out that the final version of the Draft is not the work of just two main drafters or of the relatively narrow Recodification Committee. The Ministry of Justice of the Czech Republic, at the first stage of the comment procedure, received more than three hundred comments.

The general comparison of the existing legislation with the Draft shows that there is no legal discontinuance. The existing regulation was not prejudicially refused but the Draft builds upon it. The debate over the Draft very often criticised its discontinuance with the recent law but the criticism was justified just to a limited extent. The whole part dealing with family law does not bring anything revolutionary,[813] and its relationship to the existing law is merely evolutionary.[814] A different approach to family law is not possible as we

---

[812] Such an exceptional situation may be where the denial of the paternity of a man who considers himself to be the father would be claimed by, for example, the biological father who had known of the birth of his child but did not want to admit his paternity. The mother of the child subsequently met another man who acknowledged his paternity at a very young age of the child (despite the fact that he might have known he had not been the biological father). After four years, the biological father tries to disrupt the functioning family with the "new" father, threatening them he will apply to the Supreme Prosecuting Attorney for filing the paternity claim in his favour. In this case the welfare and interests of the child must be protected to allow the child to be raised by persons known to him/her. It is not in the interest of the child to destroy his or her confidence in the social role of those raising him or her and providing everyday care, particularly in the situation where the child, reaching the legal age, may decide by him/herself whether he or she denies the paternity of the "new" father (see below).

[813] With the exception of the regulation of adoption which deserves special attention but which would go beyond the scope of this chapter.

[814] However, no other solution was practicable in those parts of private law whose objective has been to introduce regulation comparable with that contained in standard codes of private law (e.g. succession law). Discontinuance of certain parts of the Draft should not be understood as the aim of the drafters but rather as the tool to attain another objective, namely to introduce such legal regulation which may be comparable to the traditional codes of private law in Europe.

stated in the introduction: *"Should there be other borders which may be reached by law these would be much more fateful in this field."*[815] The social schemes of family law are strongly rooted and cannot be changed from one day to another. Legal regulation which would be inconsistent would never cross the border protecting the internal life of the family, and it would not become part of the real law – the law which is perceived by people as just and good and thus voluntarily observed.

4.5 THE CHANGE OF CIRCUMSTANCES AND ITS CONSEQUENCES FOR CONTRACTUAL RELATIONS

4.5.1 Defining the subject-matter

The purpose of this subchapter is to deal with the main problems potentially affecting contractual relations, which may result from the change of circumstances, unforeseeable alteration of the situation, acts of god, etc. The research was based on a relatively extensive background analysis (both factual and legal). Essentially, the change of expectations of contracting parties is at issue if these are compared to their position at the time of their entering into the contract.

Four basic questions emerged in the course of the analysis:

1. What are the reasons for, and the nature of, the relevant change of the circumstances?
2. Do the relevant changes have an impact upon the contract, particularly upon the performance of contractual obligations?
3. Is there any chance to perform contractual obligations and to exercise rights under the circumstances changed, and if so, under what conditions?
4. What are the consequences of the situation where neither the performance of contract nor the exercise of rights are practicable?

Legal regulation and doctrines

Although legal systems address the issue, which has existed since the era of Roman law, its understanding seems to be rather different in various systems. It is different despite the fact that the whole issue is reduced basically to one scheme: to what extent, or in what way, it is necessary to make exceptions to the principle of *pacta sunt servanda* in favour of the maxim of *rebus sic stantibus*. Different approaches in different national jurisdictions exist not only due to their evaluation of the key principle. As we will see later, the changes may be identical or very similar, and may lead to different consequences. Individual legal systems may also qualify them differently and may use different legal institutions to tackle them. Approaches may differ when considering legislative techniques. Sometimes we can see rather circumscribed legislation, and other jurisdictions lack any regulation in this sense, although they belong to the legal culture of continental legal systems with a strong tradition of regulation.

---

[815]/ Svoboda, E. *supra* at p. 7.

Neither the Czechoslovak, nor Czech legislature has paid much attention to this issue, and national case-law is far from being voluminous.[816] However, a certain recently significant development should be followed: special regulation of the change of contractual relations has been incorporated in the Draft of a new Czech civil code. More intensive attention paid to this issue has been apparent at supranational and international levels. Particularly, there is a project of so-called spontaneous harmonization or unification in the form of the Principles of European Contract Law,[817] the Principles of International Commercial Contracts UNIDROIT[818] and, finally, DCFR[819] of the Study Group for the European Civil Code.[820]

Basic concepts and evaluating views

Managing a particular issue requires a certain set of concepts and terms to be available. The set serves a better understanding of the issue, as well as prevention, or exclusion, of any misunderstanding. We are aware of the fact that the risk of misunderstanding is higher where the research is more extensive, i.e. more legal systems are subject to comparison. Our analysis is therefore based upon certain generally comprehensible terms.

It should also be noted that, since the very beginning whether we admit it or not, we impute our own individual evaluating criteria to the whole issue. This applies even to the arrangement of the substance as it is described. Such impact is more than apparent in the analysis or comparison themselves. Thus, it is necessary to introduce the criteria chosen for our research first.

Concepts

a) *The change of circumstances (situation)*

The change of circumstances is a wide concept encompassing any external or internal significant intervention in the basic factual and legal circumstances of the legal act concerned (situation). It includes (or is connected to) many phenomena (concepts and categories) such as acts of God, mistake, impossibility of performance, frustration of a contract or incidental (unexpected) circumstances.

b) *The change in time*

Long-term contracts create a specific category of the legal acts concerned; these contracts are typically subject to the change of external or internal situations. The specificity of such situations is that their development usually passes at normal pace, but sometimes it is "jumping".

c) *The change and impossibility of performance*

The change of situation may, but need not, result in the factual, legal, economic impos-

---

[816] Particularly, Škárová, M., in: Švestka, J. – Spáčil, J. – Škárová, M. – Hulmák, M. et al.: *Občanský zákoník I. Komentář* [The Civil Code I. Commentary]. 1st ed., Praha: C. H. Beck, 2008, commentary on s. 575 and subs., p. 1521.

[817] Lando, O. – Beale, H. (eds.): *Principles of European Contract Law*. Dordrecht: Nijhoff, 1995; Lando, O. – Zimmermann, R. – v. Bar, C.: *Principles of European Private Law*. 2nd ed., Dordrecht: Nijhoff, 2002.

[818] The Principles of International Commercial Contracts, translation from French, Praha 1998.

[819] Von Bar, C. – Clive, E. – Schulte-Nölke, H.: *Draft Common Frame of Reference*. Munich, 2008.

[820] The third volume of DCFR with commentary to be published in 2009.

sibility of performance by one or both parties to the contract. Impossibility does not represent a change but rather its consequence.

Evaluating criteria

Evaluating criteria are understood as views of, or grounds for, the arrangement, analysis and evaluation of our issue; there are *a priori* criteria which may be undoubtedly subject to criticism.

Our choice of the criteria results from a particular typology introduced and analysed later. The grounds relate first to the objective factors representing the change (change and its foreseeability); the objective criterion must be fully supplemented with a subjective criterion, i.e. the view of relevant persons or parties. This is why we place the "personal" view (parties and their positions) second. Whilst foreseeability is a purely objective category, causal nexus and causality includes several subjective elements. The next criterion (impossibility and purposes) relates to the evaluation of an impact of the change, i.e. consequences of a change in the contractual relationship. Finally, the last criterion signifies a possibility of intervention by the state or any other "out-of-contract" entity in order to adapt the contractual situation as an alternative to the termination of the contractual relationship. This is a certain concession by contractual autonomy in favour of procedural intervention.

4.5.2 Development and status

The Czech Republic

a) Existing legislation

Czech law recognizes two sets of facts as exceptions to the basic principle of *pacta sunt servanda* in contract law: impossibility to perform and frustration of the purpose of a contract, the latter being stipulated only in the Commercial Code and applying just to commercial obligations.

The basis is contained in the mandatory nature of section 575 of the Civil Code (CC) which is complemented with other clauses (ss. 576 and 577).

This general regulation is expanded for commercial contracts through declaratory provisions of the Commercial Code (ss. 352–354 ComC). Special regulation of international trade is stipulated in s. 731 (3) of the Commercial Code providing for the failure to issue a permission in connection with the discharge of obligations.

The existing legislation (the Civil Code and the Commercial Code) has evolved from the preceding International Trade Act (s. 252 ITA) which governed certain issues of both the impossibility (ss. 254–250) and frustration of the purpose of a contract (s. 275). Section 575 of the valid Civil Code does not essentially differ from s. 93 of the original wording of the Civil Code adopted in 1964, and has been apparently influenced by the ITA. The regulation of frustration has been incorporated, under the influence of the ITA, only to the Commercial Code (s. 275). Both codes are relatively new in Czech law, i.e. they do not follow the previously existing general Austrian civil code, or the so-called "middle" civil code.

The existence of frustration of the purpose of a contract is subject to three requirements to be met: (a) the purpose is expressed in the contract; (b) frustration occurred as a result of a substantial change of circumstances; and (c) the change of circumstances does not include a change in the situation of a party or a change in the economic and market situations.[821]

b) The characteristics of the Czech doctrine of impossibility
The recent approach to impossibility has been relatively tough and restrictive, which corresponds to the previous theoretical and practical treatment of this institution resulting from the International Trade Act.

Several elements are typical of such an approach or conception. Czech law does not provide any special regard to contractual relations of long-term duration when assessing impossibility of performance. The law applies to them but their existence undoubtedly deserves special attention, which is paid neither by theory nor by case law. Czech law, as has already been stated, recognizes another institution in addition to impossibility, namely the frustration of the purpose of a contract. This regulation contained in the Commercial Code should be understood as relating to impossibility although neither the theory nor judicial practice does so.

Czech jurisprudence has shown rather a superficial position in this respect. Since monographs of a more significant nature are absent it would be desirable to at least have textbooks mention the specificity of this legal regulation. The specificity subsists in the absence in legislation of any reasons or grounds for the impossibility of performance. Tackling the issue in textbooks would be desirable also because the rigid approach to impossibility fails to differentiate when evaluating the concrete situation. Differentiation can be reached only if the reasons for impossibility are discerned. Hence jurisprudence just takes over brief comments on the impossibility of performance applicable to the International Trade Act which was incorporated in the Civil Code and Commercial Code respectively in the 1990s.[822] As is well-known,[823] the International Trade Act did not provide for any reasons for impossibility and therefore could not provide for any differentiation thereof.

c) Absence of the doctrine of Wegfall or Störung der Geschäftsgrundlage, frustration and imprévision.
Czech law does not recognize the doctrine of the disappearance of the basis of transaction (such as German and Austrian Wegfall der Geschäftsgrundlage). What should be mentioned is the category of frustration of the purpose of contract stipulated in the Commercial Code, although this category has been somehow disregarded by jurisprudence and case law.

d) Differences in approaches
Czech law differs from traditional conceptions in two basic features.

The understanding of *mistake* has been specific. Primarily, Czech law does not permit "consensual" mistake by both parties. Such situation would require very complex inter-

---

[821]/ Pelikánová, I., et al.: *Obchodní právo* [Business Law]. Vol. II, 2nd ed., Praha: Codex Bohemia, 1998, p. 218.
[822]/ Pelikánová, I. *ibidem*, and Kopáč L., in: Bystrický, R., et al.: *Právo mezinárodního obchodu* [International Trade Law]. Praha: Svoboda, 1967, p. 311 and subs.
[823]/ Kopáč. L., *ibidem* at p. 309 and subs.

pretation of the institution of mistake explicitly designated as "unilateral". However, this type of mistake is not understood as a potential fact which may establish the change of circumstances, nor is it viewed as a possible consequence of such change (also due to the fact that the law so provides).

Czech law (with certain exceptions with respect to the termination of contract) does not consider the differences in the situation changed between short-term or fixed-term contracts on the one hand and long-term contracts, particularly those made for indefinite time, on the other. Neither case law nor legal theory reflects this difference.

e) Absence of the intervention by court
Recent regulation[824] does not permit, and did not in the past, any potential intervention of courts in the contract in the meaning of some adaptation of contractual relations that have become unbearable for either party. No Czech judgment has dealt with such an issue. The intervention is not stipulated in legislation but, theoretically, its solution by court is not excluded. Silence with respect to this issue remains on the part of jurisprudence.

Germany
The development of the doctrine of lapse of the basis of transaction, or its disruption
The doctrine of (subsequent) change in circumstances of contractual relations has been known on the Continent since the Roman Empire and was dealt with by glossarists and post-glossarists.[825] Grotius and Puffendorf played a significant role there.[826] It was Winscheid in the second half of the 19th century who developed the theory of presumption.[827] Under this theory a party enters into a contract presuming that the intended legal effect is real only under certain circumstances ("Gewollte rechtliche Wirkung besteht nur bei einem gewissen Zustand der Verhältnisse."). The contracting party concerned may, should a situation occur that such presumption is missing, require the other party to cancel the existing contract. Certain hesitations on the part of German legal scholars and mainly the problems arising in its practical application resulted in extensive scholarly research culminating in the work of Oertmann on the economic basis of a contract.[828] As did Winscheid, Oertmann also builds upon the conclusion that the discharge of a contract may be considered as a result of the change in circumstances if the expectations, ideas and presumption of parties are frustrated due to various events after the contract has been entered into (lapse of the basis of a contract). Today this theory understands the basis of a contract as having three modes. The first mode means that the principle of equivalence has been substantially disrupted.[829] The second mode subsists in making a significant change in the purpose of the contract by

---

[824] See particularly Kopáč, L. *ibidem*.
[825] However, the *clausula rebus sic stantibus* was not accepted. (see Zweigert, K. – Kötz, H.: *Einführung in die Rechtvergleichung*. 3rd ed., Tübingen: Mohr Siebeck, 1996, p. 518.)
[826] Zweigert, K. – Kötz, H. *supra* at p. 518, Kegel, G.: *Empfiehlt es sich, den Einfluß grundlegender Veränderungen des Wirtschaftslebens auf Verträge gesetzlich zu regeln?* Verhandlungen des 40. Deutschen Juristentages, Vol. I., Tübingen: Mohr, 1953, p. 135.
[827] Winscheid, F.: *Der Grund der Obligationen*. Leipzig: 1847, p. 428 and subs.
[828] Oertmann, R.: *Geschäftsgrundlage*. Berlin: A. Deichert, 1921.
[829] For example, Medicus, D.: *Bürgerliches Rechts*. 21st ed., Köln: C. Heymann, 2007, p. 99.

one party[830] and the third type covers situations where the parties share the consequences of common substantial mistake.[831] The doctrine of lapse of the basis of contract results in the necessity to adapt the contract and only if adaption is not practicable, the contract is terminated. The substantial issue is that the reform of BGB led to incorporation of the doctrine in the Code itself (s. 311 BGB), petrifying the preceding case law.[832]

The doctrine of impossibility applies where a factual or legal obstacle hinders the performance and the debtor is unable to surmount this obstacle in any way (s. 275/1 BGB). The contract specifies conduct or results thereof which are the content of performance. Should circumstances fail to create insurmountable obstacles with respect to one part of performance no impossibility may occur. No reason arises for this.

Where the performance becomes impossible for the debtor he is relieved from concrete performance (s. 275 BGB). The contract remains valid and the debtor is responsible for damage unless he can prove that he bears no responsibility for the obstacle arisen or – in the case of impossibility – for his ignorance of the existence of an obstacle (ss. 273, 280/1, 311a/2 BGB). Generally, the debtor's liability is determined by the standard of negligence applied. The standard of no-fault liability is appropriate where the contract expressly or impliedly provides so (s. 276/1, first sentence BGB).

Austria

The institution of disappearance of the economic basis of contract plays a significant role in Austria, too. It is considered as the main means for the solution of legal consequences of incidental change of circumstances although its legal basis is not explicitly stipulated in ABGB. However, it represents just a supporting mechanism. The institution applies where written law fails to govern the allocation of risk with respect to the changing circumstances in contractual relations.[833] ABGB contains many provisions to apply to special types of contract affected by incidental change of circumstances, such as in labour law, contracts, lease contracts, business agency contracts, pledge/lien contracts, contracts of donation, etc. Besides, there are many general provisions applicable to contract law should circumstances change, such as s. 871 for mistake, ss. 901, 918, 920, 934 and 1435 (subjective mistake, mistake in motivation, impossibility, default, excessive price, *condictio causa data causa non secuta*). There are other conceptions of regular and extraordinary termination of long-term contracts.

Disappearance or absence of the contractual basis provides to the party concerned the right to terminate or invalidate the contract, particularly when the existence of special circumstances is considered as fundamental by both parties, or when the change of these basic circumstances was unforeseeable by one of the parties at the moment of entering into contract. Disappearance or absence of the contractual basis provides to the party concerned the right to request that the contract be modified where both parties would

---

[830]/ Fikentscher, W.: *Geschäftsgrundlage als Frage des Vertragsrisikos*. Munich: Beck, 1971, 29 and subs, passim.

[831]/ Kramer, E.: *Münchener Kommentar*. Vol. II, 13th ed., Munich: Beck, 1998, p. 42, II.

[832]/ Regierungsbegründung BT-Druck, 14/6040, p.175.

[833]/ Rummel, P.: *Kommentar zum ABGB*. Vol. I, 3rd ed., Wien: Manz-Verlag, 2000, § 901, N. 4, 6, Gschnitzer, H., in: Klang, H.: *Kommentar zum ABGB*. Vol. IV, 2nd ed., Wien: Österreichische Staatsdruckerei 1968, p. 335; Rummel, P.: Anmerkungen zum gemeinsamen Irrtum und zur Geschäftsgrundlage. *JBl* 1981, p. 1.

have made a contract with different contents should they have envisaged the change of circumstances (hypothetical test by analogy with the provision for mistake under s. 872 ABGB).

The Netherlands

Articles 6:258 and 6:260 of the Civil Code (NBW) contain provisions for the changing circumstances. Under Art. 6:258 the court may modify the contract or terminate it due to unforeseeable circumstances of such a nature that the contracting parties may not, under equity criteria and reasonableness, expect that the original text of the contract will be observed. This rule was used by the Supreme Court (Hoge Raad)[834] long before 1992 as a logical consequence of the permanently expanding principle of good faith. The Code equipped the judiciary with relatively wide discretion with respect to their intervening in contracts, their modification and termination with retroactive effects. Modification can be applied as a result of court discretion under certain circumstances. The court may intervene in the offer of a party only if the changed circumstances were not foreseeable by either party and were not considered in their evaluation of risks. Third, the parties affected by the changed circumstances cannot be held responsible for their consequences.[835]

Hungary

Hungarian law denotes as frustration any situation where the duty cannot be fulfilled as a result of circumstances arising after the contract has been made. Under the Hungarian Civil Code[836] frustration may occur not only where its reason cannot be imputed to either party but also when one party is responsible for the event causing frustration. Several types of frustration are distinguished: impossibility (physical frustration) occurs when pre-conditions for performance are destroyed or frustrated after the contract has been entered into; subsequent unlawfulness (legal frustration) arises when performance cannot be perfected because a law, passed after the contract has been made, prohibits it.

The Civil Code in such cases permits that the parties may terminate the contract or apply to court for its modification. The court may change the contract if it becomes incompatible with legal interests of either party as a result of circumstances arising after the contract has been made. The court, upon application of the party, modifies the contract *pro futuro*.[837]

Sweden

Swedish case law and jurisprudence distinguish among five types of grounds for adaptation:[838] (a) promise and guarantee. The contract becomes invalid if the defendant fails to fulfil his promise; (b) information. Invalidity occurs when one party acts erroneously or is at fault either intentionally or by negligence; (c) the third assumption is based on facts known

[834] HR of 16th December 1977, NJ 1978, 156, and the judgment HR of 10th July 1989, NJ 1989, p. 786.
[835] Hartkamp, A. S.: *Asser's Handleiding tot de boevefening van het Nederlands Burgerlijk Recht.* Deventer: Kluwer, 2005, p. 341 quoted according to the national report, p. 28.
[836] Sections 399–400 of the Civil Code – Act No IV from 1959, and s. 545 of the Civil Code providing for the contract for work and insurance contract.
[837] See the national report p. 22.
[838] *Ibidem* at p. 39.

to the defendant or facts shared by both parties and defaulted; (d) unexpected profit. This assumption is based on facts known to the other party, or common to both parties, and the other party, at the same time and as a result of erroneous assumption, gained profit; and (e) the defendant acted fraudulently or in bad faith at the moment of entering into contract.

Italy

The settlement of a conflict between two old principles of contract law, namely *pacta sunt servanda* and *clausula rebus sic stantibus* has been found in general provisions for extraordinary difficulties in the Civil Code (CC Art. 1467-1469).[839] Art. 1467 reads: (1) In contracts for continuous or periodic performance or for deferred performance, if extraordinary and unforeseeable events make the performance exceedingly burdensome, the party who owes such performance can demand a dissolution of the contract, with the effect set forth in art. 1458. (2). The dissolution cannot be demanded if the supervening onerosity is part of the normal risk of the contract. (3) The party against which the dissolution is demanded can prevent this by offering to modify equitably the conditions of the contract.

Spain

Spanish law, as a result of the significance of the *pacta sunt servanda* principle (see Art. 1091 Código civil), shows a little interest in exempting a party from a duty due to changing circumstances. However, Spanish courts have developed the doctrine of *clausula rebus sic stantibus* allowing a party in extraordinary difficulties due to the change of circumstances to be released from contractual duties or to apply to court for adaptation of their contract reflecting the circumstances changed. Requirements for such application are very strict:[840]

1. The contract must be a long-term contract, or such where duties have not been fulfilled, or a contract where one party has performed its part and the other has not.
2. The change in the basis of a contract must exist. This is possible where
    a) the contract has become extraordinarily onerous for either party, or
    b) the purpose of the contract has been totally frustrated.
3. The change of circumstances must be extraordinary and unforeseeable. Neither party may have reasonably presumed damage when entering into the contract.
4. Neither party can accept the risk of the change of circumstances as their contractual obligation. The clause of *rebus sic stantibus* shall not apply to aleatory contracts.
5. The person relying on the change of circumstances may not be held responsible for that change under the contract or according to the public opinion.

France

The key concept of *imprévision* is considered where incidental economic circumstances arise after the contract has been entered into; the circumstances make the performance extremely difficult, or significantly more expensive, but still practicable. *Imprévision* includes the im-

---

[839]/ *Ibidem* at p. 41.
[840]/ *Ibidem* at p. 46.

balance between contractual obligations stipulated by the parties at the time of making the contract, or at the time of its performance.[841]

England and Scotland

The modern theory of frustration of contract is common to both English and Scottish law. However, there are certain differences; they are caused due to the fact that English courts use the reform law[842] not applicable in Scotland and Scottish courts follow the principle of *condictio causa data causa non secuta*. Two sources are relevant for Scottish law: (a) the maxim of *rei interitus*, i.e. the term describing the breach of contract, either partial or total, affecting a very particular element which is essential for the performance of contract.[843] Case law has been partly influenced by the doctrine and has applied the principle of *condictio causa data causa non secuta* and another principle of *naturalis aequitas*.[844]

The common core

The working group within the project "Common Core of European Private Law" carried out empirical research where individual members were solving several typical situations of changing circumstances in selected jurisdictions in compliance with prevailing opinions of jurisprudence and case law. The results of the empirical research may be evaluated as follows:

In the case of unexpected intervention by the state due to the significant legislative increase of performance price, two states allowed for an adaptation of the contract, eight countries considered such intervention as the grounds for termination of contract, three states saw the intervention as no reason for the change of the relations and one state permitted an alternative solution either as adaptation or termination of the contractual relation.

In the case of unexpected profit of one party (lessee) generated after a long-term lease contract had been entered into, two states allowed for adaptation of the lease, none of the countries saw any reason for termination, and the majority (10) countries advised to continue the legal relations unchanged because they did not consider the unexpected profit of one contractual party as the material change of contractual relations.

Another extraordinary situation subsisted in the lapse (ban on or restriction) of the physical object of performance as a result of the state's confiscation of petrol supplies due to the beginning of war. Most jurisdictions (6) preferred the performance to be deferred until such serious measure of the state would terminate, four states saw the solution in the termination of contract and one country allowed for adaptation or, should it have failed, for suspension of performance.

The breach of promise, or agreement on the purpose of the house to be sold for a much lower price than market value because of its cultural purposes, was another special situation subject to the research. One state considered the new situation as a reason for adaptation of the contract; none of the countries suggested that the contract be terminated; three

---

[841]/ *Ibidem* at p. 49.
[842]/ *Ibidem* at p. 61, Treitel, G. H.: The Law of *Contract*. 10th ed., London: Sweet & Maxwell, 1999, p. 805 and subs.
[843]/ Law Reform, Frustrated Contracts 1943.
[844]/ Cooper, P. M.: Frustration of Contract in Scots Law. *Journal of Comparative Legislation* 1946, p.1 and subs.

countries saw no grounds for any change in such breach of the agreement on the purpose of the contract; one country considered this as a reason for action to perform in compliance with the original terms in the contract; two states preferred adaptation of the contract or, should it have failed, termination of the contractual relation.

Mutual mistake regarding the price of share to be sold was considered by two states as the reason for adaptation, two other countries preferred termination; all Member States considered the mutual mistake to be of such a material nature that it should have an impact upon the duration of the contractual relation and result in changes. One country saw the mutual mistake as grounds for adaptation or, if failed, for termination of the contractual relation; one state considered that situation as a reason for the return of consideration without the sales contract being terminated.

4.5.3 Analysis and comparison

The aim of this subpart is to introduce certain typologies, i.e. relevant situations – sets of fact or model cases deserving specific attention and "typological" solution, as suggested above. These sets of facts result from a certain compromise regarding the principle of *pacta sunt servanda*, and the application of the maxim of *rebus sic stantibus* that is necessary in order to maintain a just and fair legal transaction based on legal certainty and fairness. An analysis of information relating to factual situations and their legal evaluation is based on the empirical research and study. The method subsists in a certain intersection of information sets and individual categories derived from the criteria contained in 4.5.1. Typological situations are certain "pure" cases of coming to a solution as a result of weighing interests of both principles.

These criteria (pure types) are used to assess legal regulation, case law and theory with respect to our issue in individual selected jurisdictions.

The concept and outline of problems, typology

This part analyses five main aspects of the issue. These aspects were formulated with respect to the defined criteria in 4.5.1 used in the evaluation of the empirical research results. First, we deal with a phenomenon creating the basis for considering potential changes of contractual relation. The reason for the change is considered, i.e. for new facts absent at the time of making a contract and which may be taken into account in regard of the impact upon further actions of parties and its assessment. Second, the impact of the new situation upon the contractual relations is analysed. The third aspect subsists in the legal evaluation of the impact; the fourth aspect relates to some specific questions of the impact upon the contract, or the subject-matter of the contract; the final part introduces solutions. The concept of mistake is tackled separately as, in fact, the sixth aspect of the change of circumstances.

The definition of a (material) change of the situation and unexpected circumstances

This is the basic category representing a particular kind of situation where, after the contract has been entered into and its performance has begun, changes occur; the contracting parties are facing circumstances different from those existing at the moment of making the contract and their expectations. The basic issue in this category is the moment of the change. The parties must solve a problem unexpected by them. The material change of circumstances is irretrievable and unforeseen.

Such situation may be subject to typology under relevant criteria. The typology is significant not only for better understanding of the whole area but it also encompasses a basis of its solution, i.e. primarily of the consequences of the change.

The change of circumstances may be analysed, or considered from various perspectives. In order to attain a certain typological definition of the change ((f) below) it is relevant to analyse the nature of the change ((a) below) first, followed by the significance of the change ((b) below), to characterize it according to its grounds ((c) below), their duration ((d) below) and, finally, to focus on the subjective aspect of the change, i.e. whether it is possible to foresee its occurrence or not ((e) below).

a) Changes according to their nature
i.   The change in the functioning of natural laws and their perception. This is a relatively new aspect dependent upon the development and potential of our knowledge. Examples may be acid rain, global warming, ice melting, water level rise, etc.
ii. Natural disasters. Gradual changes should be distinguished from phenomena such as floods, fire, earthquake. These are immediate quality changes more or less occurring at particular places under certain circumstances. However, some can be hardly predictable, such as earthquake or tsunami waves.
iii. Changes as a result of technological development. These are changes caused by people; no more precise information exists regarding their significance. An example may be using the Internet and other outcomes of industrial revolutions.
iv. Effects of economic phenomena. Although the recurring economic cycle is a stable fact some economic phenomena cannot be predicted in a more accurate way and their significance and expression qualified. An example may be the financial and banking crises in 2008. They have relatively an extraordinary character and are very insidious due to their stealthy nature. Even specialists are neither able to foresee them nor evaluate their significance, expansion and consequences.
v.   Political phenomena. The change of circumstances does not usually include strikes, war, riots, insurrection, etc. However, the issue is whether unexpected beginning of such phenomena can be understood in this way. What is meant here are potential consequences of these phenomena and their solution also with respect to the global interlinking and active approach by states. Another type of political phenomena are certain legislative measures and other steps taken by the state that may substantially change not only the legal, but also the factual situation, and any generally accessible information on them is missing.
vi. Conduct of the state as a contracting party. Although conduct of the state should be foreseeable as a matter of fact, some steps of the state may unexpectedly and significantly change the conditions of the contractual relation.

b) Significance of the change of circumstances
This is primarily an objective criterion and only secondarily a subjective one. The change means "the development" of a situation in time. The change in quality is relevant, i.e. accession of new elements or properties or phenomena essentially altering the existing situation.

An example may be the change of a river channel, several rises in the exchange rate, introducing mobile phones in the market and the decline of surface lines, etc.

c) Changes according to their reasons
Considering the origin of (reasons for) changes in relation to contracting parties two categories can be distinguished, namely changes caused by external (objective, independent of the parties) reasons, and changes due to internal (subjective) reasons subsisting primarily in the position of parties.

i.   Examples of external reasons are natural disasters, economic, political and social changes including legal changes.
ii. Internal reasons for the change are conduct designated as mistake or breach of contract or acting against its purpose.

Both aspects are relevant in examining the reasons. However, it is disputable to what extent the internal reasons can determine the nature of the change as a qualified change in our understanding.

d) Permanent character of changes
Sometimes so called temporary changes are considered. These are cases where the changed situation returns to its original shape after certain time. The question is how long the temporary period can be during which the restoration is completed. This is the first aspect. The second aspect is permanency of the impact of changes upon the contractual relations: to what extent it is practicable to distinguish between the phenomenon itself and its consequences, i.e. to what extent the change, whose reason ceased to exist, can lead to permanent consequences. Examples of this may be extinguishing fire or managing the consequences of floods. It is important to distinguish between the reason and consequences. Should the change be irretrievable or irreparable by a person, a qualified change in our sense may be considered.

e) Unforeseeability of changes
This is a "subjective" category. Regarding the prediction of a change there are foreseeable and unforeseeable changes. The former type means that the change can be expected, and therefore its existence or occurrence is irrelevant for our analysis. What is relevant is the extent of (un)foreseeability. Although this is a subjective category foreseeability can be primarily examined from the objective perspective and only then particular positions of parties should be considered. The aspect of foreseeability is usually missing in individual jurisdictions.

f) Typological definition of the change of situation (pure type)
Considering all relevant aspects of our analysis we can define the qualified change of circumstances as an unexpected substantial change of the situation followed by consequences which cannot be restored to their previous position without specific efforts being made.

The mode and extent of effects (impact upon contractual relations)
This part is devoted to the impact of the qualified change upon the "factual" situation of the contracting parties.

a) Significance and quantity of the impact
There are two issues to be dealt with: first, to what extent the physical object of performance or the position of parties have been affected; the second step is to consider the change of the parties' understanding of the purpose of their contract. What may be debatable is partial impact upon the situation, examples of which are partial destruction of the object of performance, certain shift in price which need not represent a material change but may be perceived as quite sensitive due to the long duration of the contract, etc.

b) The quality and manner of the impact
The subject-matter of the change (impact) is relevant, whether it be material things or money, costs or other intangible property. The impact upon the manner, kind and other issues relating to performance is taken into account.

c) The contract as a whole or its part
When the part of a contract affected is significant, then a more relevant or substantial solution should be found.

d) Parties subject to impact
Changes may affect the parties themselves, particularly one of them, as we can see in most cases of consequences of the qualified change of circumstances.

e) Typological definition
Relevant consequences as part of the material change of situation are taken into account if a loss, substantial disruption of the object or mode of performance, or a change in the quality of the position of at least one party, occurs.

The nature of affected contractual relations as a complementary criterion
We focus on the extent to which our typological definition can be used with respect to the nature of contractual relations. We will consider the effect of consequences of the change in regards to the nature of the contracting parties, types of contracts, or the position of a weaker party to the contract, such as a consumer or employee.

a) Long-term or short-term contract
The longer the contractual relation the more vulnerable the balance between the parties is, and thus impact upon their relations is more significant.

b) The area of contractual relations
What is at issue is determination of a particular economic situation in the relevant area, not the definition of the type of contract (e.g. a lease, or a lease of a petrol station as a special subcategory of a lease contract).

339

c) Balanced contracts or contracts with a weaker party

Contracts (e.g. employment or consumer contracts) where one party is a weaker participant in the contractual relation is not very much relevant for our analysis because we focus on the objective aspects and only secondarily we consider subjective criteria including the position of parties. In this context, the extent of the impact of the change of the relation with the weaker party may be regarded, whether the impact is limited or not. This criterion may be significant in the case of renegotiation or adaptation of the contract.

d) Typological definition

The position of a party as a weaker partner in the relations concerned is a complementary or secondary criterion. This relationship is relevant particularly with respect to adaptation of the contract and its enforcement.

The characteristics of impacts and the doctrinal definition

This is a legal qualification of the situation concerned, or the impact of new circumstances upon the contractual relations, the facts being the distinguishing factor.

The variability of the legal qualification is apparent in the following example. A producer of artificial fertilizers makes a long-term contract, upon which he is obliged to produce in his factory a fertilizer for growing tobacco, and an exporter agrees to export the fertilizer overseas. Impossibility of performance occurs when the factory is nationalized after the contract has been made, or where the production of such a fertilizer is prohibited by the state. The disturbance of equivalence of performance occurs when the raw materials for the production of fertilizers are subject to tax or customs duties; frustration of the purpose of contract occurs when countries to which the fertilizer should be imported prohibit the import. In such case the fertilizer can still be produced and accepted by the exporter.

a) Impossibility of performance

This is a permanent, "consequent" incapacity to fulfil contractual obligations.

b) Lapse (disruption) of the basis of contract

This is a German theory applied not only in Germany but also in Austrian and Swiss case law (Wegfall der Geschäftsgrundlage, Störung der Geschäftsgrundlage).

c) Cessation of a presumption

This is Winscheid's theory on the presumption of contractual relations and its termination which is still relevant in some jurisdictions (e.g. Italy).

d) Frustration

This is an Anglo-American doctrine of frustration of the purpose of contract.

e) Disturbance of equivalence of performance or contractual relations

The change of circumstances results in the imbalance of the relationship between contracting parties.

f) Mutual (common) mistake irrelevant

Although we consider a subjective view in some cases, mistake of parties is not determined as a special category of the change of circumstances, its reasons, or impact upon the contractual relations. Mistake is a "psychological" category and expresses the mental

perception of factual or legal concepts. We have already excluded this subjective understanding of the change of the relations since we do not accept the subjective element as
relevant in our analysis of the whole issue. A different typological issue may be included,
such as the change in perception of the functioning of natural laws, economic situations
and other phenomena, etc.

g) *Typological definition*

Except for mistake, all other consequences may be described as the lapse of the basis of
contract, cessation of the presumption, frustration of contract or disturbance of equivalence of performance or contractual relations.

Assessment

The new situation is the result of the changed situation and its impact upon the contractual relations and it represents an essential problem. Lawyers have been trying to solve
this problem from the very beginning of modern legal thinking, i.e. since Roman jurisprudence. Considering various national jurisdictions, we can see several solutions which
may be applied cumulatively in some cases. However, their alternative application is more
common.

a) *Termination (discharge) of obligation*

The "primary" consequence or solution of the impact of the changed situation is the
termination of the obligation to perform the contract. This is relevant particularly in the
case of impossibility.

b) *Termination (discharge) of contract or contractual relationship*

This occurs in the case of frustration of the purpose of contract. Where performance or
any other right become incapable of being accomplished, the contract loses its sense for
the parties and ceases to exist.

c) *The right to withdraw or similar means of legal protection*

The creation of an option for the party concerned to withdraw from the contract or to
choose a similar means of legal protection is a less radical type of solution (cancellation,
revocation, etc.). This option may commonly arise for application by the obligee, but
the obligor may seek it as well.

d) *Liability for damage*

Liability for damage arises when the obligor fails to fulfil his obligation fully or he performs only partly or with defects. As a result damage may be caused to the obligee who
may claim his right to compensation (damages).

e) *Liability for unjust enrichment*

This is a secondary consequence, the discharge of contract being the primary consequence.

f) *Adaptation of contract*

Many jurisdictions recognize this institution, i.e. the right to adaptation of contract due
to the changed situation. This right is enforceable in some of those jurisdictions.

The problem of mistake

Although many jurisdictions consider mistake to be a significant factor of the change of situation, we do not accept this category as relevant. This results from our "objective" approach to the analysis. Unilateral mistake is a specific problem not belonging to the area of changed relations and is often solved in a specific manner within the scope of the general part of civil law. So-called mutual or common mistake is a specific case of the solution of the change of situation or its impact upon the contractual relations.

Comparison. "Pure types" and their use in the analysis

Basic classification of individual jurisdictions may be made from the point of view of their approach to the solution of the issue. Considering the extent of the relationship between two basic principles, namely the primary principle of *pacta sunt servanda* and the principle for an exception – *rebus sic stantibus*, we can identify the approaches of individual jurisdictions as either conservative or liberal.

However, the qualification is not identical in every model situation since other criteria are also taken into account. We assess, in particular, the following aspects:

a) *The approach to the phenomenon designated as the change of circumstances*
   A relatively liberal approach is taken by Germany, Austria and the Netherlands. They are not influenced by Oertmann's theory of the lapse of the basis of contract, or disruption of contract. These jurisdictions include the "subjective phenomenon" of mistake in the change of relations. Other jurisdictions are much more reserved, including the system of Scandinavian countries, former socialist countries, France and Spain.

b) *The extent and mode or scope of the impact*
   When the perception of the negative consequences is more sensitive, whether in respect of quality or quantity, the approach taken is more liberal and the reliance on the basic principle (*pacta sunt servanda*) is stronger.

   Approaches vary as the category is still very complex. However, a certain generalization can be made. The limit of sensitivity is the lowest in the Netherlands, Scotland and Great Britain. On the other hand, Romanic countries, particularly France, Spain and Italy are conservative in a sense that they do not permit any intrusion in the principle of *pacta sunt servanda* with respect to measuring the extent of the consequences of the changed situation.

c) *Legal qualification, mistake*
   The more differentiating the assessment of the impact of the changed situation, i.e. taking into account both objective and subjective elements and categories (foreseeablity, expectation, surprise, mistake) the larger the space for exceptions to the principle of *pacta sunts servanda*.

   Mistake is the only typological example of the subjective character of the changed situation. Mistake is taken into account by jurisdictions irrespective of their belonging to various legal cultures (families). The category of mistake is almost absent in former socialist countries but is strongly represented in Germany or Spain. English and Scottish law is more reserved in this respect as are Austria and France.

d) Modes of solution

More solutions offered represent the strengthening of the exception to the principle of *pacta sunt servanda*. Where the party concerned may choose exoneration, termination of contract, renegotiation or resort to court, it gets a tool to reduce the meaning of being bound by contract.

Countries permitting the breaking of the principle of *pacta sunt servanda* provide the parties with a possibility of renegotiation or judicial intervention in the contractual relations. This applies primarily to Germany, Austria and the Netherlands.

4.5.4 Our own solution

The analysis may result in a certain solution as a logical conclusion derived from the facts collected; it can be a middle ground, considering solution in various jurisdictions mentioned above. Our own solution is based on a "balanced" ratio between the principle of *pacta sunt servanda* and the exception to this principle represented by *rebus sic stantibus*.

It should be emphasized (and repeated) that our approach is "inductive". It is not an application of a particular doctrine *a priori* (which is the case of deduction) but we analyse "empirical" knowledge and the solution is reached using the transparent method based on the criteria set, thus resulting in flexible and pragmatic conclusions. Our solution results from the facts – typology (pure types) of individual issues presented above, which are elements of a complex area being the subject-matter of our research.

1. The first requirement is the existence of a change which is essential and irretrievable. It occurs after the contract has been made.
2. The change is a consequence of "external" reasons. Its occurrence does not depend upon the conduct of the parties.
3. The change represents an essential obstacle representing either permanent impossibility of performance, cessation of the physical object of performance, frustration of the purpose or lapse of the basis of the contractual relation.
4. The consequence for, or impact upon the essential element of the contractual relation must be permanent and its remedy in the form of its restoration into the original position is not worthwhile in terms of costs.
5. The change or its consequence results in the prevention of performance of obligation or the exercise of right.
6. Legal solution of the relationship subsists in the termination of contract as of the moment of an impact of the change upon the contractual relations without any other legal consequences.
7. Parties may govern their legal relations by contract. In addition, the party concerned may seek adaptation of the contract in order to restore its original "balance".

4.6 REFLECTION OF GLOBALIZATION IN CZECH LABOUR LAW

4.6.1 Introduction

Global competition and the world economy have undoubtedly had an impact not only upon individual legal orders in their entirety but also upon different legal branches including labour law. Labour legislation should respect both globalization and liberalization of the world economy bringing in requirements for a flexible legal regulation.

A higher degree of flexibility is not only the basic requirement when considering the change of the Czech rigid and mandatory labour legislation into a modern European labour regulation, but it is also the key term in the world trends in labour law.[845] Global economic competition generally leads to reducing labour protection of employees. Attempts to create a "friendly framework" and "friendly" business atmosphere for investors result in the following trends:

a) To eliminate the expansion of the binding nature of collective contracts;
b) To restrict national collective contracts and to confine collective bargaining to individual businesses;
c) To allow for individual collective contracts to go below the level reached in collective contracts at a higher level;
d) To allow for bargaining and agreements going below the minimum statutory standards (at least with respect to working hours, work overtime and similar issues);
e) To introduce new restrictions on strikes;
f) To provide for special exceptions for working conditions in small and mid-size businesses;
g) To substantially extend the probationary period;
h) To admit new special individual employment contracts with a lower degree of social protection (so-called precarious employment) – an example may be stronger liberalization of individual fixed-term employment contracts;
i) To create a longer time period for the calculation of overtime work in order to enable the employer to extend the time for no overtime compensation;
j) To reduce payments not directly tied to the employee's performance including vacations, holidays, work incapacity, etc.[846]

Regulation by so-called soft law, i.e. primarily through collective contracts against statutory regulation, has been another aspect of the global trends.

Needless to say, the enforcement of the above-mentioned trends is not always straightforward and unambiguous.

The tendency towards liberalization resulting from world-wide globalization would have, sooner or later, or has already had an impact on the law of individual countries including the Czech Republic.

---

[845] See the presentation of general reporter Lance Compa on the first topic "Liberalization of trade and labour law" during the World Congress of Labour Law and Social Security Law. *General Reports*, Paris 5 – 8 September 2006.
[846] *Ibidem.*

4.6.2 The Green Paper of the EU Commission from the point of view of Czech labour legislation

The world-wide trend aimed at a certain liberalization resulting from the needs and general interests was taken into account by the European Union, as is stated in the Green Paper of 23rd November 2006 entitled "Modernizing labour law to meet the challenges of the 21st century";[847] according to the Green Paper more flexibility should be provided in labour law along with the basic protection of employees' rights being preserved. The Green Paper concentrates on the situation in employment and assumes that European labour markets are facing a task to be more flexible and to maximise the securing of jobs for everyone. The need to modify labour legislation is emphasized in order to support the flexibility and the security of employment. The Green Paper primarily deals with the question of what role should be played by labour law in the process of enforcing *flexicurity*, i.e. the combination of flexibility and security. The Green Paper is another step taken to pursue the trend started and serves as confirmation that the European Union has realised the need to increase its competitiveness against other parts of the world. In the past, the labour law and employment area concentrated on social issues and the security of employees which can be traced in most pieces of legislation passed in this sector within the European Communities.

The concept of *flexicurity* is by itself contradictory in its very core. Naturally, flexibility requires a lower degree of legal regulation, or even deregulation. Flexibility means that contracting parties creating their employment relations may regulate their mutual rights and duties in the most liberal way practicable and, if possible, with minimal restrictions imposed by the legislature, whether at the national or European levels. Social security, on the other hand, means that the labour market, as well as working conditions are protected through the intervention of the legislature, whether national or European. The concepts of flexibility and security are, to a certain extent, contradictory in many respects including the extent or intensiveness of legal regulation.

The Green Paper results from the fact that, due to quicker technological development, strengthened competition resulting from globalization, changing demand on the part of consumers and the significant expansion of services, more flexibility in labour law is required. Contractual conditions heavily protecting employees may discourage potential employers from hiring workers even in times of economic vitality.

The attempts to find the balance between "flexibility" of labour law and its protective function, part of which is a certain degree of security for employees, have not been new. Labour law has been dealing with the issue from the very beginning of its existence as a branch of law. It is a well-known fact that labour law as applied in European countries has undoubtedly been the most "social" in the world-wide context and provides employees with the highest degree of security.

The problem of countries of the former Eastern socialist block, recently acceding to the European Union, the Czech Republic being a typical example, subsists in the fact that the original "socialist" labour codes effective in those countries were, by nature, anti-liberal and

---

[847]/ The Green Paper may be retrieved, for example, from http://ec.europa.eu/employmentsocial/labourlaw/greenpaperen.htm

mandatory. The European Union directives governing labour law that are to be transposed into Czech law also restrict freedom to contract the employment relationship. Moreover, EU directives tend to be rather casuistic. What should be kept in mind is the difference between the "old" EU Member States and, for example, the Czech Republic: the old Member States originally had a liberal regulation of the labour market into which the European Union, step by step, has intervened with its restrictive directives. This means that the generally liberal employment legislation has only been modified due to the transposition of the directives. On the contrary, the anti-liberal character of employment legislation in the Czech Republic has been intensified as a result of the transposition of the directives in Czech law. In other words, the old Czech mandatory, quite casuistic in some issues, and anti-liberal Labour Code was complemented by international obligations binding on the Czech Republic. If we consider the recent extent of the EU directives in the area of labour law, it is obvious that harmonization of Czech employment legislation with that of the European Union has not contributed to the flexibility of Czech labour law but has had a fully opposite effect.

The Green Paper states that since the beginning of the 1990s the reforms of national labour legislation in individual EU Member States have been aimed at easing the existing regulation in order to facilitate a larger scope of diversity of contractual relations. The reforms have tended to increase the flexibility "on the margins", i.e. to introduce more flexible types of employment with a lower degree of protection against dismissals; the aim has been to support the involvement of new workers and disadvantaged job applicants in the labour market, and to provide a wider choice of jobs for those who want to choose. On the other hand, if we follow the development of labour law in the Czech Republic, the situation has been rather different.

Unlike the necessary partial liberalization carried out at the very beginning of the 1990s which was required due to the transition of centrally managed economy to market economy, the subsequent development of labour law in the Czech Republic cannot be described as "the easing of the existing regulation in order to facilitate a larger scope of diversity of contractual relations". The opposite is true. Particularly, the end of the last century and the beginning of the 21st century saw the strong tendency in the Czech Republic towards larger and stricter regulation, primarily as a result of harmonization of Czech legislation with that of the EU.

One of the clear outcomes of the Green Paper has been the discussion commenced within the EU on flexibility and security in the area of employment policy and working conditions. The EU may not close their eyes so as not to see the consequences of globalization. The protectionist (in the sense of labour law, i.e. in favour of employees) and social system of labour law in both EU legislation and the laws of individual Member States do not positively contribute to the competitiveness of the EU in the worldwide context.

On the other hand, it should be noted that the impact of legislation of individual EU Member States has been quite incongruous. EU legislation transposed into national law may have positive effects in one country but give rise to serious problems in another.

I argue that further labour regulation by the EU should not be pursued as far as flexibility or at least flexicurity are concerned. Either concept will not be positively developed by an influx of European directives. Instead, the EU should support debates, comparative analyses and gradual and voluntary approximation of national labour systems. The attempts to draft an academic model of the "European Code of Labour Law" should also be appreciated. I maintain that all initiatives should be confined to, and based on debates and the exchange of opinions rather than on directive regulation. Generally, the EU should stay rather reserved and forethoughtful as far as the further regulation of labour relations is concerned; it should always be pursued after intensive debates and more extensive analyses of labour legislation, as well as the needs of industry, in individual EU Member States.

The essential issue with respect to flexibility is not the issue of further regulation but rather the opposite, i.e. deregulation of the European labour law. It should be noted, however, that even if deregulation is to be pursued the review of the existing directives should be carried out very carefully.

4.6.3 Czech labour legislation

The above-mentioned worldwide globalizing trends which have undoubtedly had an impact on the law of the European Union will, sooner or later, have an impact on Czech labour law. Today the impact seems to apply "later" rather than "sooner".

If we have a closer look at the Czech legislative reality, i.e. the new Labour Code 2006 (effective as of 1st January 2007), we can see that the Code as a whole goes strictly against those trends so the Czech labour legislation seems to be "swimming against the stream".

If we consider the extent of international obligations of the Czech Republic, in particular the extreme extent of the EU Directives, it appears to be quite clear that the drafters of the Labour Code 2006 should not have chosen the way of more or less copying provisions of the old Code to the new one, as was the case, but rather they should have considered and respected the existing international labour obligations of the CR. Other provisions, both mandatory and regulatory, should have been subject to a prudent analysis with regard to their historical, economic and social background in order to find out whether they should have been incorporated in the new Code in addition to the international obligations of the Czech Republic.

Unfortunately such an approach was not chosen: despite all initial proclamations the new Code is neither new nor liberal or flexible. Moreover and quite paradoxically, the new Code has led to diminishing the role of collective bargaining; under normal circumstances, it is collective bargaining that helps reach outcomes above the standard provided by the legislation. The non-liberal and casuistic Labour Code does not provide sufficient space for collective bargaining.

One clear example of this fact may be given, namely the abolition of a parallel part-time employment contract. This is not to say that the institution was ideal and its regulation optimal; but the reality is that the EU tries to introduce more flexible forms of employment with a lower degree of protection against dismissal whilst the Czech Republic in its Labour Code 2006 abolishes one of such forms without any possibility of replacement.

It is quite logical that the worldwide development and trends that can be seen in the legislation of the EU will not halt at the borders of the Czech Republic. It may be assumed that a more flexible regulation of labour law will have to be considered even in the Czech Republic. The issue of how extensive and intensive further legislative steps should be in order to make the legislation more flexible will naturally be subject to future election debates and preferences. Nevertheless, I believe that the liberalizing direction pursued worldwide cannot stay outside the Czech Republic and will have effect upon our labour legislation.

More visible approximation of labour legislation in individual EU Member States is another issue to be considered in the future, although the future seems to be quite far. Nevertheless this is the trend which, as soon as it starts, will be running slowly in some countries and more quickly in others, and may result in the constitution of a uniform European labour code, which is considered just as an "academic unrealistic vision" today. The future will definitely see stronger enforcement of institutions such as "home-working", "tele-working", "job-sharing", "agency employment", etc.

The new Czech Labour Code 2006 is very far from satisfying such needs. The necessity to pass a new law in the area of labour relations was quite urgent and without doubt and was invoked as a result of the changing situation in the society; what was also changed was the nature and intensiveness of general interests. The new law was expected to bring liberalization into those relations as well as to reduce significant imbalance among all parties to labour relations having been established by the old code. The changes in, and needs of the society should result in the liberalization of labour relations and the removal of asymmetry in the labour relations, which originated during the totalitarian regime; the explicit asymmetry established by the law, as well as other residuary aspects of the totalitarian regime still surviving have no place in a democratic state based on the rule of law. The intervention of the state, carried out through legislation, should always respect the principle of proportionate (just) balance between the requirement of the general interest of the society and the requirement of the protection of basic rights of an individual; therefore the Labour Code 2006 was presumed to remove unjustified but significant intervention in the constitutionally guaranteed rights and freedoms.

In consideration of the needs of the society and general interests, the Code was presumed to remove unjustified and still surviving mandatory nature of labour legislation, unjustified regulatory approach to all areas of employment relations as well as objectively unreasonable favouritism regarding employees and trade unions against employers accompanied by significant and inconsistent intervention in the constitutionally guaranteed rights and freedoms. The proportionality principle should be a decisive factor when we evaluate the new Code, i.e. not only the position of the employer and employee, but also the position of trade unions and generally employees' representatives, the position of "different" employers; what should also be considered is the reasonability of the intervention in proprietary rights (not only those of employers), the proportionality of the intervention in the freedom to contract, and its scope, in various types of employment relations, and the mode of the regulation of the freedom to contract itself and its applicability in connection with the general conception of delegation in the Civil Code.

The key words for the new labour legislation ought to have been liberalization and flexibility.[848] The reason for liberalization and flexibility was primarily the fact that the old

[848]/ For more information see Bělina M.: Postavení českého pracovního práva v rámci systému evropského a českého práva [The Position of Czech Labour Law within the Systems of European and Czech law]. *AUC Iuridica* 3–4/2007, p. 7 and subs.

Labour Code 1965 was passed in the middle of the 1960s, i.e. it was drafted and enacted by parliament of the socialist country with directive management of the economy. This mere fact should necessarily lead to the conclusion that the legislation drafted for different social and economic conditions and for a different era (the new Code was intended to apply in the 21st century) must conceptually result from a fully different background and understanding. The more so because necessary amendments to the old Code passed in the 1990s and the beginning of the 21st century did not affect its conceptual basis and introduced just changes required by the new social and economic conditions and obligations of the Czech Republic resulting from our accession to the European Communities.

However, the Labour Code 2006 to which so much hope was attached has become rather controversial in many respects, and it can be seen as symptomatic that the Code has not satisfied expectations with respect to its novel approach.

4.6.4 Constitutional conformity of the Labour Code 2006

Part of the legitimate expectations of all persons concerned with respect to the Labour Code 2006 has been the assumption that the new regulation is in conformity with the constitutional order.[849] However, since the very beginning of its legislative procedure, the Labour Code 2006 has given rise to rather emotional discussions particularly regarding its constitutional conformity.

Due to the preceding debates and doubts it was not surprising that as early as before the effect of the Labour Code 2006 a group of Senators of the Parliament of the Czech Republic brought an action before the Constitutional Court in order to have two provisions of the Code repealed; they were followed by a group of Deputies of the Parliament of the Czech Republic applying to the Constitutional Court for the repeal of dozens of provisions.

Since both applications challenged the provisions of one Act, the plenary session of the Constitutional Court held on 9th January 2007 decided to join the applications to one case under the file number Pl. ÚS 83/06.

The plenary session of the Constitutional Court at its hearing on 12th March 2008 held that 11 provisions of the Labour Code were repealed, and the remaining claims dismissed. It was important that the respective provisions of the Labour Code 2006 were repealed under the Constitutional Court decisions as of the date of publication of the Court's decision in the Collection of Laws of the Czech Republic.

This was the most massive challenge of legislation during the existence of the Constitutional Court and, subsequently, the most extensive repealing judgment of the Constitutional Court with respect to one piece of legislation; moreover, it affected the law of a codex type.[850]

The above mentioned judgment of the Constitutional Court of 12th March (published under No. 116/2008 in the Collection of Laws of the Czech Republic) directly affected the conception itself. The Labour Code 2006 has introduced two new conceptual elements:

849/ See Svitáková V. – Bělina, M.: Splňuje nový zákoník práce legitimní očekávání? [Does the New Labour Code Fulfil Legitimate Expectations?] *Právní rozhledy* 2/2007, p. 43 and subs.

850/ See Bělina M.: Nález ÚS zasáhl koncepci zákoníku práce [The Constitutional Court Judgment Affected the Conception of the Labour Code]. *Právní zpravodaj* 4/2008, p. 1 and subs.

first, it is a new regulation of the relationship between the Civil Code and the Labour Code upon the delegation principle, and, second, the principle governing contract law, namely "what is not prohibited is permitted" is stipulated.

4.6.5 Delegation and subsidiarity

The old Labour Code of 1965 was based on the independence and autonomy of labour law with respect to the Civil Code thus cutting the historical ties between civil law and labour law. The Civil Code was fully inapplicable in labour relations (the only possible application may have been by analogy); the Labour Code 1965 paraphrased general institutions of civil law such as representation, statute of limitations, time computing, etc. The historical tie between civil law and labour law is based on the principle of subsidiarity in their relationship in all continental legal systems. This historical tie was interrupted only temporarily in the legislation of some former socialist countries. The Labour Code 2006 was legitimately expected to amend the unfortunate situation caused by the codifications in the 1960s and return the relationship between civil and labour law to that existing in most countries, namely to the relation between the general and the special. Civil Codes have traditionally been *lex generalis* for labour relations whilst labour legislation has been considered *lex specialis*.[851]

The Labour Code 2006 did not choose the traditional way of subsidiarity but opted for a novel (and never before tried) way of delegation. Section 4 provides that the Civil Code applies to labour relations only when the Labour Code permits that. As a result, the Labour Code contains many delegating provisions at various parts (primarily in sections 18 and 326).

The newly regulated conception of delegation of the Civil Code, as stipulated in the Labour Code, constituted legal uncertainty and instability (incompatibility with Art. 1 (1) of the Constitution) because when the draft of a new Civil Code is enacted it will be necessary to substantially amend the Labour Code if not even to pass a fully new law.

The principle of delegation also brings significant problems in application as a result of obscurity and ambiguity of the legal rules. The conception as contained in the Labour Code is inconsistent with the principle of quality law and denies the confidence in law. Application problems may arise as a result of two simultaneously existing, but not mutually corresponding and consistently interconnected provisions of the Labour Code 2006 and the Civil Code, which must be applied at the same time and not in the subsidiary regime due to the mandatory legacy of the Labour Code. There may even be a case where it will be impossible to identify the situation and to reach a respective legal decision without using other provisions and principles not explicitly referred to in the Labour Code 2006, which as such will cause the provisions and principles to be inapplicable. The new regulation may result in the situation that courts if they want to decide such cases will have to "free" themselves from the applicable provisions of the Labour Code 2006 and disregard them. This is strictly against the principle of legal certainty as one of the basic features and

---

[851]/ On the principle of will autonomy and contractual dimension see judgment No. 73, Vol. 18 SbNU, p. 135 and judgment No. 135, Volume 28 SbNU, p. 151.

requirements of a state governed by the rule of law, which the Czech Republic is declared to be in Art. 1 (1) of the Constitution.[852]

The Constitutional Court accepted the objections of the applicants challenging the principle of delegation, and repealed section 4 of the Labour Code 2006. In its reasoning, the Court did not find the principle of delegation, as stipulated by the Labour Code, as compatible with the rule of law principle. The Constitutional Court has emphasized that what essentially applies is that civil law is general private law (i.e. the Civil Code is a general private law code) with subsidiary application in all other private branches. Legislation regulating those branches is essentially preferred but if a particular issue is not explicitly stipulated the general Civil Code applies. This approach corresponds to the historical development of private law which originally was just internally differentiated; only later individual branches of law became separate, such as business law, labour law, family law, etc. The method of delegation used in section 4 of the Labour Code 2006 significantly restricted the subsidiary application of the Civil Code in employment relations, which led to the interruption of basic ties between the general and the special and, at the same time, brought a certain extent of uncertainty in labour relations. The Constitutional Court has concluded that various references contained in the Labour Code cannot cover all situations appearing in employment. When general subsidiarity of the Civil Code is excluded uncertainty arises what law will govern the relations concerned should the Labour Code have no prepared hypothesis with respect to the relevant rules for their solution. The uncertainty in employment relations does not correspond with the principle of predictability of the effect of the law and, as such, is incompatible with the rule of law principle in the meaning of Art. 1 of the Constitution, which is relevant when the content of each normative act is considered and evaluated.

The repeal of section 4 of the Labour Code has led to the abolition by the Constitutional Court of the delegation principle in the relationship between the Civil Code and the Labour Code, and to its replacement with the principle of subsidiarity. This means that provisions of the Civil Code, as the general part of private law, shall apply where the Labour Code, as the special part of private law, lacks special regulation. This represents the general complementary role of civil law, or its subsidiary applicability. Subsidiary applicability of the Civil Code, unlike the delegation principle, allows for the application of the Civil Code in all its implications without individual provisions being ripped out of context. Provisions of the Civil Code may apply to employment relations only if the Code itself does not regulate the issue in a different way. Moreover, the Civil Code provisions incompatible with the basic principles of the Labour Code (section 13) and of employment relations may not be applied as well. The nature of the whole issue suggests that subsidiary application of the Civil Code to employment relations will be used mostly with respect to Part I - General Part of the Civil Code and Part VIII - Obligations, particularly its Title I - General provisions. Part VI - Unjust Enrichment - may also be considered.

The judgment of the Constitutional Court repealing section 4 of the Labour Code, thus changing the relationship between the Labour Code and the Civil Code based on the principle of delegation to that based on the subsidiarity principle, has been entirely essential

852/ See judgment No. 27, Vol. 32 SbNU, p. 255 and judgment No. 22, Vol. 21 SbNU, p. 195.

and unprecedented. The Constitutional Court has recognized the constitutional dimension in the relations between individual branches of law and codes and acknowledged the Civil Code as general subsidiary legislation for the whole area of private law. The Constitutional Court has agreed with the strong voice of the legal public having challenged the delegation principle from the very beginning of the legislative procedure.

4.6.6 Directive nature

The directive (or declaratory) nature of legislation is undoubtedly linked with its flexibility. The second conceptual change brought in by the Labour Code 2006 is the introduction of the private law principle that "what is not explicitly prohibited is permitted", which is contrary to the leading principle of the old Labour Code of 1965, i.e. "what is not explicitly permitted is prohibited." This conceptual change itself has been welcome. However, the definition contained in section 2 (1) of the Labour Code 2006 of what provisions are mandatory and what declaratory gave rise to many doubts. The application submitted by a group of Deputies challenged the legal regulation of this definition in section 2 (1) as contradictory, which fails to correspond with the freedom to contract and is, as such, incompatible with the rule of law and contractual freedom (i.e. against Art. 1 of the Constitution and Art. 2 (3) of the Charter of Fundamental Rights and Freedoms).

As has already been mentioned, the Labour Code 1965 was, from its very beginning, drafted as a mandatory law and was based on the maxim "what is not explicitly permitted is prohibited". This approach to the regulation of employment relations resulted from the context based on different economic and social conditions of the pre-November 1989 era. The change of the economic and social environment invoked the need to change the very nature of a Labour Code aimed at liberalization of employment relations incorporating the opposite principle of "what is not explicitly prohibited is permitted", as it is phrased in Art. 2 (4) of the Constitution and Art. 2 (3) of the Charter of Fundamental Rights and Freedoms, the latter being promulgated as part of the constitutional order of the Czech Republic by resolution of the Presidium of the Czech National Council No. 2/1993 Sb. The society therefore legitimately expected that the principle of freedom to contract would be introduced to labour relations where the mandatory nature of provisions should be preserved only where the public interest existed and the real protection of employees was justified; all other areas would be subject to agreement of the contracting parties and what types of contracts other than those contained in the Labour Code could also be made. Although the Labour Code 2006 appears on its surface to have incorporated the expectations, the opposite is true: the regulation contained in section 2 (1) of the Labour Code 2006 is contradictory, unclear and indeterminate and as such inapplicable, and definitely fails to create the freedom to contract.

It should be emphasized that the Constitutional Court has recognized the constitutional dimension of the autonomy of will and freedom to contract in many of their judgments. The Constitutional Court maintains that the protection of the freedom of will to contract is a consistent part of the rule of law in a democratic state; the freedom is a derivative of the constitutional protection of property rights under Art. 11 (1) of the Charter having *jus disponendi* as its basic component. The Court has not confined the freedom to contract only to property rights although its constitutional background is the strongest in that context. In its judgment No. I. ÚS 113/04 of 4th May 2004 (published as judgment No. 63, Vol. 33 SbNU, p. 129) the Court stated that respecting the autonomy of an individual is the general requirement for the functioning of the state based on the rule of law in the sense of Art. 1 (1) of the Constitution and Art. 2 (3) of the Charter. The right of an individual to autonomy of his or her will, i.e. to freedom of that individual, corresponds with the requirement imposed on the state so that the state should recognize autonomous manifestation of will of individuals and their relevant conduct. Where such conduct does not interfere with the rights of third persons the state must (even through legislation) respect such conduct or acknowledge it. The freedom of an individual may be intervened by the state only if the public interest justifies such intervention, if the intervention is proportionate (reasonable) with respect to its objective to be achieved. The new Labour Code 2006 regulates the basic maxims and principles, including the freedom to contract, in such a way that it contravenes the very basis of the rule of law; section 2 (1) introduces the approach not only legally and factually imperfect but even unconstitutional.

The Constitutional Court supported the applicants' position with respect to section 2 (1) of the Labour Code 2006: it stated that new possibilities would be open to parties to employment relations not only to regulate their mutual rights and duties in a way different from that contained in the Labour Code 2006, but also to regulate matters not even stipulated therein. Any conception chosen corresponds undoubtedly with the nature of private relations and is generally more liberal than the preceding regulation. However, the Constitutional Court concluded that the legislature, when defining and drafting provisions intended to be mandatory, had not considered the fact that the conception chosen should represent a fully new and principal right for the parties to employment relations, which becomes the right of "interpretation". The Constitutional Court stated that, in the light of the above-mentioned, the challenged provision of section 2 (1) is rather complicated and indeterminate for its recipients. Due to the legislative technique selected it has been quite difficult to identify in many provisions of the Labour Code 2006 what prohibitions were intended to be introduced by the legislature. The principle of legal certainty belongs to the fundamentals of the system based on the rule of law, and the foreseeability of law is one of its component parts. The definition of mandatory provisions in the Labour Code 2006 has been pursued in such a complex and vague way that the comprehensibility, transparency and clarity principle has been contravened, as has repeatedly been declared by the Constitutional Court in its judgments. Therefore the Court repealed section 2 (1) except for the first and fourth sentences since the generally declared liberal regulation allowing for the expansion of contractual freedom of parties to labour relations was, due to the mandatory nature of many provisions, restricted to such an extent that contractual freedom as the basis of the relationship between the employer and the employee was denied, and if a limited space was available it was in favour of just one of the parties.

Thus the judgment of the Constitutional Court has substantially affected even the second conceptual change introduced by the new Labour Code 2006 when it recognized the constitutional dimension in regard of the reflection (or rather insufficient reflection) of the contractual freedom principle in the Labour Code 2006.

4.7 INSOLVENCY LAW WITHIN THE EUROPEAN CONTEXT

The terms *insolvency law* and *insolvency proceedings*, used quite freely today, have been introduced primarily due to the integrating features of European law. The terms denote proceedings whose purpose and objective are to solve insolvency (bankruptcy). In the past, such types of proceedings had no uniform designation. Different countries used different names for such proceedings, such as bankruptcy, composition, insolvency proceedings, and, lately, also "collective hearing". The issue is what is common to all these types.

What can be traced is the common subject-matter, namely the solution of the inability of an individual or entity to pay debts as they fall due, whether termed insolvency or bankruptcy or otherwise. Despite some nuances in definitions applicable in different countries, there are essentially two forms of insolvency: (a) equitable (or equity) insolvency, and (b) balance-sheet (or technical) insolvency.[853] Should a definition of insolvency be missing in some legal systems, none of the above-mentioned types of proceedings would be applicable. However, there are some types of procedure whose regulation and course are similar to those of insolvency proceedings. The so-called universal execution applicable to the whole of the debtor's property is the most frequent example.[854] Despite many similarities this cannot be considered to be insolvency proceedings, which means, for example, that exceptions to the rule of fair trial may not apply.[855] It also means that insolvency and its consequences may be solved only in the course of insolvency proceedings and no other type of procedure may be used even in order to decide on preliminary issues.

The principle of *par conditio creditorum*, i.e. equal conditions for all creditors, has been considered as basis for all types of insolvency procedure. It was the attempt to enforce this principle which led to the constitution of bankruptcy as the oldest type of insolvency procedure so that all creditors may get a relevant share in the remaining debtor's property. The principle was subject to violation in the course of its history since certain ranks of creditors gradually gained a more advantageous and preferred position. On the other hand, the principle was always observed among creditors in the same rank. One of the modern tendencies focuses on the expansion of the principle so that all creditors who have submitted their claims may share the bankrupt's estate although their portions may differ.

Three stages of the development of insolvency procedure can be traced. They differ in their social function, economic background and procedural formats, which all have common features despite modifications in individual legal systems. The insolvency law of today is at the beginning of its third stage.

Bankruptcy proceedings as the initial form of insolvency solution seem to have originated in the statutory law of North Italian cities in the Middle Ages. Bankruptcy law was

---

[853]/ The Czech term *insolvence* was traditionally used only to denote the first form in Czech law, i.e. in the meaning of *equitable insolvency*. The European context shows that the term *insolvency* is almost identical with the meaning of *bankruptcy* as inability to pay debts as they fall due. This tendency has been reflected in the new legal regulation of the Insolvency Act No. 186/2006 Sb.

[854]/ Czech law regulates procedure similar to insolvency proceedings, which subsists in the enforcement of judicial decision (execution) by selling an enterprise under ss. 338f – 338zr of the Civil Procedure Code; this execution does not apply to the whole of the debtor's property but covers a significant portion.

[855]/ For more information see Zoulík, F.: Právo na spravedlivý proces a konkursní řízení [Right to Fair Trial and Bankruptcy Proceedings]. In: Štenglová, I. (ed.): *Pocta Miloši Tomsovi k 80. narozeninám* [Tribute to Miloš Tomsa on His 80th Birthday]. Plzeň: Aleš Čeněk, 2006, p. 436 and subs.

revived at the beginning of the Modern Era. It was due to both the expansion of the market economy having led to the bankruptcy of unsuccessful entrepreneurs, and exhaustive wars (the Thirty-Year War in particular) having caused the insolvency of lower nobility as well as of some large noble estates.

The second stage of insolvency procedure formally started with the French *Code de commerce* of 1807, whose third part was devoted to bankruptcy law. This law reflected preceding developments (Colbert's measures in particular) and what was typical was its close connection with commerce as it applied only to merchants.[856] Another important feature of this law was that it distinguished between no-fault bankruptcy (*faillite*) and culpable bankruptcy (*banqueroute*) subject to criminal prosecution. The French law had an impact on later regulation including laws in Central Europe (Prussia 1855, Austria 1868, Germany 1877); the difference was that the concept of a bankrupt included persons other than merchants and that the defaming consequences of culpable bankruptcy were reduced.

This stage can be called "classical" as the solution of insolvency became part of almost all legal systems; in addition to bankruptcy, regulation of composition was introduced, and the principles upon which individual systems were based, became general.

Insolvency procedure seems to undergo crisis today resulting from the fact that economic factors relevant during the second stage of insolvency law have ceased to apply. Instead, new approaches emerge and are reflected in recent legislation on insolvency law.[857]

1. The most significant social and economic change applies to the structure of typical bankrupts. Middle-size entrepreneurs (those employing several hundreds or even thousands of employees) become bankrupt more often than earlier; even large enterprises, such as joint-stock companies (or public limited companies), may be subject to insolvency procedure, one of the main reasons being the growing concentration of capital. There is an increasing number of non-business persons facing insolvency, namely consumers; this is caused primarily due to the expanding loan business (particularly instalment purchases) and inability of consumers to pay their debts.

2. The changes have caused insolvency cases to lead to serious consequences, although historically no fatal impact occurred even in the times of large economic crises. For example, the insolvency of a mid-size business may have a negative impact on the economic situation in the respective region and the insolvency of a large joint-stock company may adversely affect macroeconomic factors. The insolvency of consumers may become a significant social burden as it is necessary to provide these people with basic support.

3. The manifold and complex system of economic and legal relations in the modern society is the reason why insolvency procedure is not confined to a small number of participants but the number of creditors is gradually rising; they include business partners of the

---

[856] For more information see Pelikánová, I.: *Úvod do srovnávacího práva obchodního* [Introduction to Comparative Commercial Law]. Praha: C. H. Beck, 2000.

[857] Zoulík, F.: K některým problémům zákona o konkursu a vyrovnání [On some issues of the Bankruptcy and Composition Act]. *Právo a podnikání* 2/1993, pp. 2–8; Schelleová, I. et al.: *Konkurz a vyrovnání* [Bankruptcy and Composition]. Praha: Eurolex Bohemia, 2005, p. 59 and subs.

bankrupt as well as his or her employees. The role of banks and other financial institutions is also expanding; they are usually creditors claiming the largest portion of debts of a particular bankrupt, therefore having the biggest impact on the procedure.

4. Economic results of entrepreneurs are subject to various factors; thus the results are variable and fluctuating between stability and crisis, the most serious of which is insolvency. The crises of enterprises become a common element in business and are subject to microeconomic examination. The aim is usually to find such solutions which would lead to the survival of the enterprise even if some restrictions may apply.

5. Composition as a solution of insolvency may hardly be used in the system of developed economic relations. Therefore other methods are being sought which would allow for some kind of restoring settlement of the situation.

These social and economic changes have been projected in the area of law.

First, the change of a typical insolvent entrepreneur is, due to a large volume of the estate, the reason why bankruptcy may not be just realization of property and other values "item by item". To isolate individual items is problematic and substantial is the fact that separate realization of individual items usually bears loss. Thus, running the business of the bankrupt with some kind of revitalizing program is not only in the interest of the bankrupt but also of his/her creditors who may reach a share better than that obtainable should full liquidation of the bankrupt's enterprise be carried out. Legal regulation prefers (or provides more space for) restructuring modes of insolvency solutions to solutions based on the liquidation of a business. Since composition as a traditional restructuring means loses its practical applicability, so-called reorganization (for insolvent entrepreneurs) and discharge for insolvent private individuals has been introduced.

The second substantial change subsists in the fact that insolvency is no longer just a property issue between the debtor and his or her creditors (although this is the essential factor) but there are wider economic and social circumstances. This is why it is extremely important to keep the bankrupt's business running. Social factors can be also traced in other modes of insolvency solution, namely the subsistence welfare of the bankrupt's employees is usually preserved by special legislation. Private individuals subject to bankruptcy give rise to another social problem as they find themselves in permanent indebtedness after the closing of bankruptcy procedure, which prevents them from reasonable social performance. Modern legislation in some countries attempts to reduce the time-period during which debts may be enforced, or the state is involved to pay substitute performance.

Legal regulation must also react to a high number of creditors, particularly in the case of mid-size and large businesses. Generally, the structure of creditors' bodies is being altered. The creditors' committee becomes the decisive body replacing the meeting of creditors; it is not exceptional that the only purpose of the creditors' meeting is to constitute the creditors' committee. Since the importance of creditors' committees is growing, the issue of proportionality is raised so that all groups of creditors can be represented thereby; thus legislation usually regulates the manner in which the committee may be constituted.

Considering procedural aspects of insolvency there has been tendency to solve the problems at their very initial stages as the solution seems to be the most efficient as far as the debtor's and creditors' positions are concerned. Thus the debtor is usually imposed with a duty to apply to court for insolvency proceedings as soon as his or her crisis reaches the insolvency stage; failure to fulfil this duty is usually subject to various types of penalty, the most effective of which being property liability of all members of the governing body of the company. In addition, some countries provide for an opportunity on the part of the debtor to apply for insolvency procedure as early as at the stage of imminent insolvency, which may be connected with certain advantages for the debtor.

The feature common to all other changes in procedure is the attempt to increase the efficiency and speed of proceedings. What generally appears ineffective is setting procedural time-limits; these are usually formalistic and impose unnecessary burden upon all participants applying for their extension. The desired aim may be better reached through a simplification and concentration of proceedings. The hearing of incidental disputes within insolvency proceedings (not separately) may serve as a positive example.

The changed concept of insolvency procedure imposes more duties upon administrators of the insolvency estate. They must understand various types of solving insolvency ranging from liquidation to restructuring. Their procedural role has expanded as it comprises not only realization of property but many other activities. Stricter requirements apply to their selection and qualification.

The so-called negative definition of insolvency represents a specific issue; it means that some institutions may never be subject to insolvency procedure although they formally comply with the conceptual definition of insolvency. These are primarily state institutions – the state and its subdivisions, bodies of local self-government and some other institutions whose position is defined by a particular law. In addition, some financial institutions are exempt from liquidation, especially banks, insurance companies and some others. The reason is not favourable treatment but rather the protection of their clients; these institutions also possess an enormous number of contracting partners (sometimes reaching millions) and their liquidation could produce significant macroeconomic consequences. They are not totally excluded from insolvency but the procedure may start only after their licence has been withdrawn or cancelled, which is preceded by a complex process aimed at diverting adverse consequences.

The growing number of cases of consumer insolvency requires a special legal approach. These persons usually have no property to be realized. On the other hand, they may be receiving regular income, for example from employment. To solve their insolvency, the "instalment (or payment) schedule", or "discharge", has been introduced. Its purpose is that a significant portion of the debtor's income is paid off by monthly instalments, and the rest need not be paid. In some countries there is a special system of social benefits to help solve the indebtedness of the debtors.

New trends of the development of insolvency law representing the third stage were seen firstly in the federal law in the USA called the Bankruptcy Reform Act (or the Bankruptcy Code including all its implementing laws) which was enacted in 1978 and became effective a year later. This Code represents a complex and substantial innovation of insolvency law. Its typical feature is a certain mode of protection of the debtor's property on condition that the property can be kept and used in business. That is why restructuring modes of insolvency solution are preferred and out-of court-settlement also plays a significant role. The classical way of solving insolvency called "liquidation" still applies (Chapter 7 of USBC) and it remained a prevailing manner a long time after the passage of the law. Another way was introduced, namely "reorganization" (Chapter 11) for enterprises, and the so-called "instalment payment schedule" (Chapter 13) for natural persons.[858] The US Bankruptcy Code has influenced the legal systems in almost all developed countries although not to the same extent and depth; it may also be due to the specificity of the US legislative technique which could be only adapted to national systems but not fully adopted by them. The US solution was, from the very beginning, subject to objections that it preferred debtors and introduced rather lengthy judicial procedure. The Code was amended in 1994 in order to remove those deficiencies.

British regulation has been the second modern type of insolvency solution. It is based on the Insolvency Act 1986 complemented and amended by a relatively large volume of secondary legislation called the Insolvency Rules. Similar regulation was introduced in Scotland and Northern Ireland; therefore the whole country is subject to essentially the same system. A strong position of creditors is the core feature of the British regulation; they essentially influence all types of insolvency procedure. In addition to liquidation in the form of court proceedings there is also extrajudicial resolution of insolvency with courts having a limited supervising position: it is voluntary liquidation by creditors and so-called administrative receivership. A relatively high speed and efficiency of procedure was appreciated but the decisive role of creditors frequently led to premature liquidations and unnecessary bankruptcies, which had a negative impact on the business environment. The Enterprise Act as new legislation was passed in 2003; it pays substantial attention to insolvency law and introduced many changes following the US regulation; it applies primarily to the protection of bankrupts directed to the restructuring of their businesses and to the mitigation of some harsh consequences of bankruptcy.

New German regulation is a European alternative and was influenced by the US concept of insolvency. Its basis is created by the Insolvency Procedure Code (Insolvenzordnung), passed in 1994; the period between the force and effect of this law was quite long and the law became effective as late as in 1997.[859] This law replaced all existing pieces of insolvency legislation. It was not just the legislative and technical consolidation, but a uniform procedure was created which may result in alternative solutions of insolvency. The German

---

[858]/ The English terminology corresponds to the English tradition and differs from the Czech understanding: The English term "liquidation" under Chapter 7 is "bankruptcy" (konkurs in Czech) since the word "liquidation" (likvidace) in Czech law denotes a certain type of out-of-court cessation of the existence of a company. The English term "reorganization" under Chapter 11 has been widely spread in international terminology and as such introduced in the Czech Insolvency Act No. 186/2006 Sb.; but still it may be quite misleading in Czech law because the Czech term "reorganizace" denotes mechanical, organizational changes whilst the US law understands reorganization as substantial changes in business, traditionally designated in Czech as "restructuralization" (restrukturalizace) or "revitalization" (revitalizace). See Winterová, A. et al.: *Civilní právo procesní* [Civil Procedure]. 5th ed., Praha: Linde, 2008, p. 663. The US "payment schedule" is termed "discharge" (oddlužení) in Czech.

[859]/ US, British and German legislation has been analyzed in many specialist books and treatises published in many foreign languages. Particular attention should be paid to a very inspiring and comparative article by Franks, J. R. – Nyborg, K. G. – Torous, W. N.: Srovnání amerického, britského a německého zákona o úpadku [A Comparison of US, UK and German Insolvency Codes]. *Financial Management* Fall 1996, pp. 88–101 (available in Czech translation).

regulation respects modern trends in the development of insolvency law and provides a wide area for restructuring approaches. Its social aspects are a positive novelty subsisting primarily in the settlement of the situation of bankrupt individuals; the focus is on the termination (or substantial alteration) of their debts which enables them to keep fulfilling their social and economic roles.[860]

Many European countries have followed the German pattern and passed new legislation on insolvency law reflecting the modern trends and fully replacing the existing laws. The Czech Republic is one of them: Act No. 186/2006 Sb. provides for insolvency and modes of its solution, complemented with relating secondary legislation and its legislative and technical amendment passed before the Act became effective.

Some countries have amended and complemented their existing legislation in order to keep up with the modern tendencies. This applies primarily to Austria and Italy. Austria has preserved its Bankruptcy Procedure Code of 1914 (Konkursordung), but amended it and certain consequences of insolvency are regulated by special laws;[861] this has been the way of incorporating modern features in Austrian law, amortization of residual debt being a specific Austrian trait. The situation is similar in Italy: the basis is created by the Insolvency Act of 1942 complemented by the Act providing for crises of large enterprises and certain concepts of banking law.

France has undergone a different process.[862] It tried to preserve its very specific way of dealing with insolvency, which used to be a pattern followed by foreign countries. Thus the law constituting part of the *Code de commerce* was amended twice, but later it was detached and formed into a separate piece of legislation almost identical as far as the content was concerned, except for minor modifications depending on the legal nature of a bankrupt. In 2004, the new Insolvency Code was passed and it became effective in 2007; this law fully accepts modern trends although it differs in terminology.

Post-communist countries underwent a long interruption in the regular development of insolvency law. These countries had found it necessary to reintroduce insolvency law along with the transformation of their economies into the market system. The task was usually solved at two stages. First, the basic issues were regulated following the domestic tradition as well as foreign patterns, the Hungarian law of 1991 being one example. Czech law No. 328/1991 Sb., providing for bankruptcy and composition, belongs to this stage. It dealt with the most important aspects, but faced many problems in its practical application. It was amended many times, each amendment solving just a partial issue. The process of modernization of Czech insolvency law was completed by passing the new Insolvency Act in 2006 (No. 186/2006 Sb.). Russian and Polish approaches also deserve mentioning. The federal Insolvency Act was passed in Russia in 1998; it subsists in the traditional distinction between bankruptcy and composition, but allows for some novelties, such as arbitration and receivership. The law includes extensive special provisions dealing with

---

[860] See, for example, Hartl, J.: České a německé konkursní právo ve vzájemném srovnání [Czech and German Insolvency Law in Comparison]. *Právní rozhledy* 8/1999.
[861] Sojka, D. – Sojková, P.: *Konkurz na počátku třetího tisíciletí* [Bankruptcy at the Threshold of the Third Millenium]. Praha: Linde, 2002.
[862] Pelikánová, I., *supra*.

individual categories of bankrupts. Polish regulation is based on the Act of 2003 designated as the Bankruptcy and Restructuring Law; most provisions deal with bankruptcy and its circumstances (including compulsory composition); restructuring is admitted only in the case of imminent bankruptcy, the relevant provisions being brief and creating just the framework.

Insolvency law in European countries is subject to certain approximation, but only at the conceptual and general levels. Legislation of Member States provides for many specific features based on, and resulting from different legal traditions and the conflict of interests among certain professional groups. Thus, uniform European insolvency law is just a prospect for the future, which is not very near.

However, insolvency procedure at the EU level[863] should be mentioned although it applies only to certain issues. Even this regulation faced many difficulties. At the beginning, it concentrated on the solution of some partial problems, in particular the protection of employees of an insolvent employer and the special regime of insolvency of financial institutions (banks and insurance companies). Next, cross-border issues were tackled applicable to insolvency of a business run or having its property in more than one EU Member State. In 1995, the European Union Convention on insolvency proceedings was prepared to tackle these issues and the nature of subsidiary agreements between Member States. However, the Convention has not been ratified and has not come into force. The issues were eventually solved by Council Regulation No. 1346/2000 on insolvency proceedings, which became effective on 31st May 2002 in all Member States except Denmark.

Regulation No. 1346/2000 is the basic piece of European legislation on insolvency law. It does not represent harmonization or even unification of insolvency law in individual Member States, but it regulates the consequences of the existence of the single internal market of the EU for insolvency procedure.[864] Rules of the conflict of laws providing for applicable law create just a small portion of the Regulation. International jurisdiction is stipulated depending on the place of the main interest of the debtor. Automatic recognition of the commencement of insolvency proceedings in all Member States is another issue tackled. The Regulation introduces so-called secondary proceedings carried out in other Member States where the debtor's property is located; as it applies just to liquidation it forms so-called partial bankruptcy (already known). The Regulation also provides for the rules for informing creditors and recognizing their claims. It is clear that the substance prevails in the Regulation. However, the impact of the Regulation is wider since it must be directly applied by national courts, their case law creating the uniform conceptual background.

It should be noted that, legislatively, the first steps towards uniform European insolvency law have been represented by the Regulation as well as conceptual approximation of laws in

---

[863]/ Rozehnalová, N. – Týč, V.: *Evropský justiční prostor (v civilních otázkách)* [The European Judicial Area (in Civil Matters)]. Brno: Masarykova univerzita, 2005, particularly p. 372 and subs.

[864]/ Despite the short existence of the Regulation there have been many published treatises and articles analysing the substance. See especially Fritz, D. F. – Bähr, R. M.: Die Europäische Verordnung über Insolvenzverfahren – Herausforderung an Gerichte und Insolvenzverwalter. *Deutsche Zeitschrift für Wirtschafts- und Insolvenzrecht* 6/2001, pp. 221–235. In the Czech sources see Bělohlávek, A. J.: Evropské insolvenční právo [European Insolvency Law]. *Bulletin advokacie* 11/2007, pp. 38–53.

individual Member States. The actual functioning of insolvency procedures within Europe is another issue which significantly differs from that in North America. Reorganization as one of the restructuring solutions of insolvency is meant here. It seems to be an effective and functioning institution in the US and a large number of insolvency cases have been treated through reorganization (although not with ultimate success in all cases). On the contrary, most European countries have shown some hesitation with respect to reorganization, which is used only rarely and its effectiveness appears to be low. On the other hand, it is clear that bankruptcy does not satisfy modern requirements and can be used only partially; its substitution is needed. There is an implicit question, however, whether reorganization is not a product of the specific features of US law and whether it may function in a different environment.

I maintain that such doubts are not justified. Reorganization as any other novelty will need some time to domesticate in national legal systems. Reorganization by itself represents a lengthy process usually taking several years. Its efficiency may be considered after several decades of its existence, which is the case in the US, where it was introduced in 1978. European countries have incorporated reorganization into their system quite recently; the longest history applies to Germany, where it started in 2000.

The Czech Republic may be taken as an example of the system that must be very patient in reaching any decisive conclusions. The new Insolvency Act became effective on 1st July 2007; as is stipulated in its section 432, insolvency proceedings commenced before this date must be considered under then existing legislation. As a result, a dual system of procedure and application of relevant legislation should be managed for several years. In addition, since the accession to the EU, Czech courts have applied Regulation 1346/2000, thus creating a certain triple system. This will definitely lead to growing demands but not necessarily in the negative.

Experience in their practical application and the economic impact of new solutions will be relevant. Certain problematic issues have already occurred.

The most serious of them is the fact that some entrepreneurs cannot opt for any restructuring mode of their insolvency. Reorganization under section 316 (4) of the Insolvency Act is essentially permissible only if some quantifiable parameters have been satisfied (such as turnover of CZK 100 mil. during the last accounting period, or 100 employees in their main employment). Should the requirements fail to be met, reorganization can be permissible only upon the submission of a reorganization plan approved by one half of secured creditors and one half of unsecured creditors. Since the condition to which the exception to the impermissibility is tied will not always be met many small and some mid-size entrepreneurs will be excluded from reorganization and any other restructuring solution will be unattainable.

Other problems may occur. For example, the question is whether the new Insolvency Act can react to specific circumstances of some businesses, such as farming and agriculture.

It is not essential whether other problems occur, what number can be envisaged and how serious they may be. It is crucial that their solution is open because the Czech Republic has new modern regulation of insolvency law corresponding to its prospects.

Selected bibliography to Chapter 4

ANTONIOLLI, L. - VENEZIANO, A.: *Principles of European Contract Law and Italian Law - A Commentary.* Hague: Kluwer Law International, 2005.

BAR, CH. von: O celoevropské odpovědnosti národní kodifikační politiky [On the European Responsibility for National Codification Policies]. In: Švestka, J. - Dvořák, J. - Tichý, L. (eds.): *Sborník statí z diskusních fór o rekodifikaci občanského práva* [Proceedings from the Discussion Fora on the Recodification of Civil Law]. Praha: ASPI, 2006, pp. 11–27.

BAR, CH. von: Úvod do akademického komunitárního (společného) referenčního rámce [An Introduction to the Academic Community (Common) Frame of Reference]. In: Švestka, J. - Dvořák, J. - Tichý, L. (eds.): *Sborník statí z diskusních fór o rekodifikaci občanského práva* [Proceedings from the Discussion Fora on the Recodification of Civil Law]. Praha: ASPI, 2008, pp. 95–105.

BARTOŠEK, M.: *Encyklopedie římského práva* [Encyclopaedia of Roman law]. 2nd ed., Praha: Academia, 1994.

BAUMAN, Z.: *Individualizovaná společnost* [An Individualized Society]. Praha: Mladá Fronta, 2004.

BĚLINA, M.: Nález ÚS zasáhl koncepci zákoníku práce [The Constitutional Court Judgment Affected the Conception of the Labour Code]. *Právní zpravodaj* 4/2008, pp. 3–6.

BĚLINA, M.: Postavení českého pracovního práva v rámci systému evropského a českého práva [The Position of Czech Labour Law within the Systems of European and Czech Law]. *AUC Iuridica* 3–4/2007, pp. 7–21.

BĚLOHLÁVEK, A. J.: *Evropské a mezinárodní insolvenční právo* [European and International Insolvency Law]. Praha: C. H. Beck 2007.

BĚLOHRADSKÝ, S. J.: *Reforma manželského práva* [The Reform of Marriage Law]. Praha: Stáňa J. Bělohradský, 1919.

BRDIČKA, R. - LOUDOVÁ, M. - SIEGLOVÁ, Z.: Znalec sám proti sobě. Řešení sporného otcovství [The Forensic Expert against Himself. The Solution of Contested Paternity]. *Právní rádce* 8/2000, pp. 14–15.

BYSTRICKÝ, R., ET AL.: *Právo mezinárodního obchodu* [International Trade Law]. Praha: Svoboda, 1967.

ČERNÁ, S. - ČECH, P.: Ke způsobům prosazování rozhodujícího vlivu v ovládané akciové společnosti, jeho podmínkám a důsledkům [On the Modes of Enforcing the Dominant Position in the Controlled Joint-stock Company, Its Conditions and Consequences]. *Obchodněprávní revue* 1/2009, pp. 10–17.

ČERNÁ, S.: Evropský a tuzemský přístup ke skupinám společností [European and National Attitude to the Group of Company]. In: Eliáš, K. (ed.): *Soukromé právo v pohybu* [Private Law in Motion]. Plzeň: Aleš Čeněk, 2005, pp. 16–24.

ČERNÁ, S.: K rozdílům mezi německou a francouzskou koncepcí skupin společností [On the Differences between German and French Conceptions of the Groups of Company]. *Právní rozhledy* 8/2004, pp. 288–292.

CodeNapóleon. Édition seule officielle pour Le Grand-duché de Berg. Düsseldorf: X. Levrault, Imprimeur du Gouvernement, 1810.

COMPA, L.: Liberalization of trade and labour law. Presentation delivered at the World Congress of Labour Law and Social Security Law. *General Reports,* Paris, 5th - 8th September 2006.

DĚDIČ, J. - ŠTENGLOVÁ, I. - ČECH, P. - KŘÍŽ, R.: *Akciové společnosti* [Joint-stock Companies]. 6th amended ed., Praha: C. H. Beck, 2007.

DVOŘÁK, J.: Pacta sunt servanda? In: Dvořák, J. - Kindl, M. (eds.): *Pocta Martě Knappové k 80. narozeninám* [Tribute to Marta Knappova on the Occasion of her 80th Birthday]. Praha: ASPI, 2005, pp. 45–57.

ELIÁŠ, K. - ZUKLÍNOVÁ, M.: *Principy a východiska pro nový kodex soukromého práva* [The Principles and Backgrounds of the New Code of Private Law]. 1st ed., Praha: Linde, 2001.

FIALA, J. - HURDÍK, J. - SELUCKÁ, M. (eds.): *Současné aktuální otázky spotřebitelského práva* [Recent Topical Issues of Consumer Law]. Brno: Masarykova univerzita, 2008.

FRITZ, D. F. - BÄHR, R. M.: Die Europäische Verordnung über Insolvenzverfahren–Herausforderung an Gerichte und Insolvenzverwalter. *Deutsche Zeitschrift für Wirtschafts- und Insolvenzrecht* 6/2001, pp. 221–235.

GLOS, J. et al.: *Rodinné právo* [Family Law]. 2nd ed., Bratislava: Obzor, 1971.

GLÜCKSELIG, R.: Průlom do právní autonomie obchodních společností [Penetration into the Legal Autonomy of Business Companies]. *Právní rozhledy* 5/2002, pp. 219–223.

HARTL, J.: České a německé konkursní právo ve vzájemném srovnání [Czech and German insolvency law in comparison]. *Právní rozhledy* 8/1999, pp. 407–409.

HONDIUS, E.: *La reforme du droit des contrats aux Pays-Bas. Le contrat en Europe aujourdhui et demain.* Paris: Société de législation comparée, 2008.

HRUŠÁKOVÁ, M. - KRÁLÍČKOVÁ, Z.: *České rodinné právo* [Czech Family Law]. 3rd ed., Brno: MU Brno and Jan Šabata, 2006.

HURDÍK, J.: *Zásady soukromého práva* [The Principles of Private Law]. Brno: Masarykova univerzita, 1998.

JIREČEK, J. (ed.): *Práva městská Království českého a Markrabství moravského od M. Pavla Krystyana z Koldína* [Municipal Rights of the Czech Kingdom and Moravian Margrave Lands by M. Pavel Krystyan from Koldin]. 5th ed., Praha: Všehrd, 1876.

KNAPP, V.: *Předmět a systém československého socialistického práva občanského* [The Subject-matter and System of Czechoslovak Socialist Civil Law]. Praha: Nakladatelství ČSAV, 1959.

KNAPPOVÁ, M. et al.: *Občanské právo hmotné. Obecná část* [Civil Substantive Law. General Part]. Vol. I, 4th updated and expanded ed., Praha: ASPI, 2005.

KNAPPOVÁ, M. et al: *Občanské právo hmotné* [Civil Substantive Law]. Vol. III, 3rd ed., Praha: ASPI, 2002.

KUČERA, Z.: *Mezinárodní právo soukromé* [Private International Law]. 7th ed., Brno – Plzeň: Doplněk and Aleš Čeněk, 2009.

KÜHN, Z.: Fikce samostatnosti právnických osob a její prolomení [The Fiction of the Separate Nature of Legal Entities and Its Breakthrough]. *Právní rozhledy* 11/2003, pp. 542–552.

LANDO, O.: Návrh společného referenčního rámce, český návrh občanského zákoníku a dobrá víra [The Draft of the Common Reference Frame, the Draft of the Czech Civil Code, and Good Faith]. In: Švestka, J. – Dvořák, J. – Tichý, L. (eds.): *Sborník statí z diskusních fór o rekodifikaci občanského práva* [Proceedings from the Discussion Fora on the Recodification of Civil Law]. Praha: ASPI, 2008, pp. 134–144.

LANDO, O. – BEALE, H. (eds.): *Principles of European Contract Law.* Dordrecht: Nijhoff, 1995.

LANDO, O. – ZIMMERMANN, R. – V. BAR, C.: *Principles of European Private Law.* 2nd ed., Dordrecht: Nijhoff, 2002.

LAZAR, J. (ed.): *Návrh legislatívného zámeru kodifikácie súkromného práva. Ministerstvo spravodlivosti SR* [The Outline of the Legislative Intent of the Codification of Private Law. Ministry of Justice of the Slovak Republic]. Bratislava: Ministerstvo spravodlivosti Slovenskej republiky, 2008.

Le centenaire du Code civil suisse. Paris: Société de législation comparée, 2008.

LOUDOVÁ, M. – SIEGLOVÁ, Z.: Metodiky analýzy DNA jednoznačně řeší otázku sporného otcovství [The Methodology of DNA Analysis Solves Contested Paternity Unambiguously]. *Právo a rodina* 4/2002, p. 13–16.

PAUKNEROVÁ, M.: *Evropské mezinárodní právo soukromé* [European Private International Law]. Praha: C. H. Beck, 2008.

PAUKNEROVÁ, M.: Private International Law in the Czech Republic: Tradition, New Experience and Prohibition of Discrimination on Grounds of Nationality. *Journal of Private International Law* 1/2008, pp. 83–105.

PAUKNEROVÁ, M.: *Společnosti v mezinárodním právu soukromém* [Companies in Private International Law]. Praha: Karolinum, 1998.

PELIKÁNOVÁ I. – ČERNÁ S. et al.: *Obchodní právo. Společnosti obchodního práva a družstva* [Business law. Business Companies and Cooperatives]. Vol. II, Praha: ASPI, 2006.

PELIKÁNOVÁ, I., et al.: *Obchodní právo* [Business Law]. Vol. II, 2nd ed., Praha: Codex Bohemia, 1998.

PELIKÁNOVÁ, I.: *Úvod do srovnávacího práva obchodního* [Introduction to Comparative Business Law]. Praha: C. H. Beck, 2000.

PIĄTOWSKI, J. S. (ed.): *System prawa rodzinnego i opiekuńczego* [The System of Family and Custody Law]. Vol. I, Wrocław: Zakład Narodowy im. Ossolińskich – Wydawnictwo, 1985.

RADVANOVÁ, S. – ZUKLÍNOVÁ, M.: *Kurs občanského práva – Instituty rodinného práva* [The Course of Civil Law – Family Law Institutions]. 1st ed., Praha: C. H. Beck, 1999.

ROZEHNALOVÁ, N. – TÝČ, V.: *Evropský justiční prostor (v civilních otázkách)* [The European Judicial Area (in Civil Matters)]. Brno: Masarykova univerzita, 2005.

ROZEHNALOVÁ, N. – TÝČ, V.: *Evropský justiční prostor* [European Judicial Area]. Brno: Masarykova univerzita, 2003.

SCHULTE-NÖLKE, H.: Spotřebitelské právo v občanskoprávní kodifikaci? [Consumer Law in the Codification of Civil Law?]. In: Švestka, J. – Dvořák, J. – Tichý, L. (eds.): *Sborník statí z diskusních fór o rekodifikaci občanského práva* [Proceedings from the Discussion Fora on the Recodification of Civil Law]. Praha: ASPI, 2008, pp. 106–116.

SKŘEJPEK, M.: Maxima [Maxims]. *Soudce* 6/2003, pp. 14–15.

SOJKA, D. – SOJKOVÁ, P.: Konkurz na počátku třetího tisíciletí [Bankruptcy at the Threshold of the Third Millenium]. Praha: Linde, 2002.

SPÁČIL, J.: Prodej nemovitosti za nepřiměřeně nízkou cenu a lichevní smlouvy v českém občanském právu [The Sale of Immovables for Unreasonably Low Prices and Usurious Contracts in Czech Civil Law]. *Právní rozhledy* 7/2003, pp. 331–333.

SVITÁKOVÁ, V. – BĚLINA, M.: Splňuje nový zákoník práce legitimní očekávání? [Does the New Labour Code Fulfil Legitimate Expectations?] *Právní rozhledy* 2/2007, pp. 43–50.

SVOBODA, E.: *Rodinné právo československé* [Czechoslovak Family Law]. 1st ed., Praha: Vesmír, 1935.

ŠVESTKA, J. – DVOŘÁK, J. – TICHÝ, L. (eds.): *Sborník statí z diskusních fór o rekodifikaci občanského práva* [Proceedings from the Discussion Fora on the Recodification of Civil Law]. Praha: ASPI, 2008

ŠVESTKA, J. – SPÁČIL, J. – ŠKÁROVÁ, M. – HULMÁK, M. et al.: *Občanský zákoník I. Komentář* [The Civil Code I. Commentary]. 1st ed., Praha: C. H. Beck, 2008.

TERRÉ, F. – SIMLER, PH. – LEQUETTE, Z.: *Les obligations*. Paris: Dalloz, 2005.

Všeobecná encyklopedie v osmi svazcích [General Encyclopaedia in Eight Volumes]. Vol. 6, Praha: Diderot, 1999.

WINTEROVÁ, A.: Procesní důsledky skupinové žaloby v českém právu [Procedural Consequences of Class Actions in Czech Law]. In: Dvořák, J. – Winterová, A. (eds.): *Pocta Jiřímu Švestkovi k 75. narozeninám* [Tribute to Professor Švestka on His 75th Birthday]. Praha: ASPI, 2008, pp. 347–356.

ZOULÍK, F.: K některým problémům zákona o konkursu a vyrovnání [On Some Issues of the Banktruptcy and Composition Act]. *Právo a podnikání* 2/1993, pp. 2–8.

ZOULÍK, F.: Právo na spravedlivý proces a konkursní řízení [Right to Fair Trial and Bankruptcy Proceedings]. In: Štenglová, I. (ed.): *Pocta Miloši Tomsovi k 80. narozeninám* [Tribute to Miloš Tomsa on His 80th Birthday]. Plzeň: Aleš Čeněk, 2006, pp. 436–444.

Soukromoprávní ochrana slabší smluvní strany [Protection of a Weaker Party under Private Law]. *Právní rozhledy* 3/2002, pp. 109–116.

ANNEX

EVALUATION DU MANUSCRIT "CZECH LAW BETWEEN EUROPEANIZATION AND GLOBALIZATION"[1]

Cet ouvrage juridique, destiné à marquer l'anniversaire prestigieux de l'Université Charles, se trouve au carrefour de plusieurs disciplines, dans une perspective dynamique donnant toute sa part à l'intégration européenne. Quatre grands chapitres regroupent les études thématiques, permettant d'ordonner la diversité des points de vue.

Le premier chapitre intitulé "*Historical impulses for the development of law*" comporte lui-même des sous-sections qui traduisent bien la richesse de cette approche partant de l'exploration juridique du passé. Un premier thème porte sur la question du droit de propriété, telle qu'elle s'est posée à des périodes de crise politique et sociale entre 1918 et 1948, au regard de la problématique contemporaine des privatisations et des indemnisations. Un autre thème relève du droit constitutionnel, d'abord dans sa dimension comparatiste, en évoquant aussi bien la "légalité" des régimes autoritaires que l'interprétation de la Constitution américaine, puis dans sa dimension proprement nationale, avec des thèmes aussi cruciaux que la question du fédéralisme et de l'ethnicité. Une section est également consacrée aux relations de l'Eglise et de l'Etat, du point de vue de l'histoire du droit, avec là – aussi un parallèle entre le droit tchèque et l'expérience américaine. Enfin une section sur le droit romain permet d'aborder la question des méthodes juridiques ou des aspects techniques, comme l'usucapion.

Le deuxième chapitre reprend des thèmes de droit constitutionnel ou de droit privé pour les projeter vers l'avenir, sous le titre générique "*Theoretical and constitutional impulses for the development of law*". Il s'agit de débats théoriques, portant aussi bien sur "l'invariabilité de la loi" que sur le "polycentrisme et le pluralisme juridique, pour déboucher sur l'examen de la "*changing structure of the legal order*". L'accent est également mis sur les mutations du droit constitutionnel, à l'aube du XXI° siècle, à travers notamment la procédure parlementaire et le droit électoral. Une place est faite à la nouvelle "société de l'information", comme à la gouvernance économique du secteur public.

---

[1] This review of the manuscript was sent to the Karolinum Press by Professor Emmanuel Decaux on 6th January 2010.

Le troisième chapitre regroupe les études internationales, à travers le débat sur la fragmentation du droit international, abordé sous l'angle original du droit général, la question de la protection internationale de l'environnement et des études européennes, en matière pénale ou fiscale.

Enfin, le dernier chapitre porte sur le droit privé, sous le titre "*Transformation of private law*". Les questions abordées sont également très stimulantes, responsabilité des entreprises et responsabilité des actionnaires, obligations contractuelles et responsabilité pour faute, changement des circonstances et relations contractuelles, l'insolvabilité. Plusieurs études portent sur la codification, en général, ou dans certains aspects, comme la recodification du droit de la famille ou la "globalisation" du droit du travail.

Ce survol trop rapide montre assez la richesse et la diversité des questions soulevées par les meilleurs spécialistes du sujet. Loin de donner une vision fragmentée, il se dégage de l'ensemble une conception ouverte et moderne du droit, intégrant pleinement les nouvelles perspectives du droit européen et du droit comparé, mais plus largement les phénomènes transnationaux liés à la globalisation du monde contemporain. Ce faisant, les professeurs de l'Université Charles démontrent l'utilité de la science juridique pour répondre aux nombreux défis nés de l'histoire récente et aux perspectives d'un monde en profonde mutation, sans dogmatisme, mais avec méthode, rigueur et dynamisme. La traduction anglaise de tous les textes devrait contribuer à la diffusion de cet ouvrage d'exception qui atteste la qualité et l'originalité de l'école juridique tchèque.

C'est pourquoi je recommande très vivement la publication de cet ouvrage juridique intitulé "*Czech law between Europeanization and globalization*", dans la maison d'édition Karolinum.

Fait à Paris, le 6 janvier 2010
Professeur Emmanuel Decaux,
Directeur du Centre de recherche sur les droits de l'homme et
le droit humanitaire de l'Université Paris II (Panthéon-Assas)

366

REFERENZ-GUTACHTEN ZUR VERÖFFENTLICHUNG "CZECH LAW BETWEEN EUROPEANIZATION AND GLOBALIZATION"[2]

Es gibt nicht viele Fakultäten in Europa, die anlässlich einer 660-Jahrfeier ihrer Universität das ehrgeizige Projekt unternommen und schließlich bewerkstelligt haben, ein wissenschaftliches Werk herauszugeben, das sich mit den Grundsatzfragen der Rechtsentwicklung zum Beginn des Dritten Jahrtausends in ihrem Land beschäftigt. Das zu begutachtende Werk von sechzig Wissenschaftlern der Juristischen Fakultät der Karls-Universität Prag stellt schon für sich nach Anspruch und Erscheinung ein "Opus Magnus" im besten Sinne des Wortes dar. Es wirkt noch um so eindrucksvoller, wenn in Betracht gezogen wird, dass es sich bei dem Werk um nur einen Band aus einer insgesamt fünf Bände umfassenden Veröffentlichungsreihe von Forschungsarbeiten handelt, die unter dem Leitthema "Quantitative und qualitative Transformation der Rechtsordnung am Beginn des Dritten Jahrtausends" unter Mitwirkung zahlreicher Mitglieder der Fakultät ausgearbeitet wurde. Während die zuletzt genannten Bände in tschechischer Sprache erscheinen, ist der hier zu besprechende Band in englischer Sprache verfasst. Dieser ist erkennbar adressiert an einen internationalen Leser- und Forscherkreis und nach Qualität und Originalität der Beiträge darf mit Fug und Recht erwartet werden, dass das Opus im kontinentaleuropäischen Rechtskreis und darüber hinaus nicht nur wahrgenommen, sondern auch viel beachtete Aufmerksamkeit stiften und nachhaltiges Interesse generieren wird.

Aufbau und Struktur des Werkes sind mit einem einleitenden historischen Teil, einem zweiten Teil, der die konzeptionellen und konstitutionellen Aspekte der Rechtsentwicklung behandelt, sowie den dem Öffentlichen Recht und dem Privatrecht gewidmeten beiden weiteren Teilen umfassend angelegt; zudem werden jeweils sowohl europäische als auch internationale Einflüsse auf das tschechische Recht einbezogen. Dadurch bietet das Werk mehr als nur eine Innensicht auf die Rechtsentwicklung in Tschechien als neuem Mitgliedstaat der Europäischen Union; es bietet zugleich eine glänzende Darstellung und Analyse der Wirkweise und Bedeutung der gleichsam äußeren Einflüsse des europäischen

---

[2]/ This review of the manuscript was sent to the Karolinum Press by Professor Dr. Dr.h.c. Marian Paschke on 29th January 2010.

und internationalen Rechts, der gesellschaftlichen und politischen Entwicklungen und nicht zuletzt der Änderungen von ökonomischen und außerökonomischen (etwa umweltbezogenen) Rahmenbedingungen. Durchweg geht es den Verfasserinnen und Verfassern der Einzelbeiträge erkennbar nicht um enzyklopädische Dokumentation, sondern vor allem um sorgfältige Reflektion und Bewertung des jeweiligen Forschungsgegenstandes. Damit entwickelt das Werk in seinen Teilen und seiner Gesamtheit eine Wirkkraft, die diese rechtswissenschaftliche Arbeit auf einen Spitzenplatz internationaler Aufmerksamkeit katapultieren wird, der bisher wohl nur wenigen rechtswissenschaftlichen Veröffentlichungen in Tschechien zuteil geworden war.

In dem hier begrenzten Rahmen ist es nicht möglich auf einzelne Beiträge und die dabei entwickelten Detailerkenntnisse einzugehen. So bemerkenswert und originell die einzelnen Beiträge auch geschrieben sind, das Werk wäre letztlich wohl falsch verstanden, wollte man es aus der Perspektive der Einzeldisziplin, der Detailentwicklung und der Darstellung von Einzelphänomenen lesen und würdigen. Die Kraft des Textes entfaltet sich vor allem aus seiner vom Herausgeber glänzend arrangierten ganzheitlichen Konzeption und der diesbezüglichen Wahrnehmung des Lesers. Mit dieser Darstellung der Entwicklungen des tschechische Rechts, seiner vielfältigen und zum Teil bodenstürzenden Neuerungen in zahlreichen Bereichen sowie der ordnungs- und gesellschaftspolitischen Bewältigung der mit ihnen verbundenen Herausforderungen wird dem ausländischen Leser (nicht anders als dem inländischen) wie in keiner bekannten Veröffentlichung zuvor vor Augen geführt, welcher Prozess von historischen Ausmaßen, von intellektuellen Herausforderungen und von weit mehr als akademischen Anstrengungen in den letzten Jahren der Rechtsentwicklung in Tschechien zu durchlaufen war und noch immer zu bewältigen ist.

Die Veröffentlichung des Werkes *"Czech law between Europeanization and globalization"* ist ein Zeitzeugnis besonderer Art, ein Zeitzeugnis des tschechischen Rechts und der Rechtsentwicklung in Europa. Dem Herausgeber und den Autoren ist ein Werk von historischem Rang gelungen. Es ist Wert, nicht nur heute gelesen und studiert zu werden; die Beiträge legen Zeugnis ab von einem Anpassungsprozess im Recht, dessen Bedeutung wir Heutigen vielleicht erahnen, aber wohl erst von den künftigen Generationen wahrlich verstanden und gewürdigt werden kann. Der Unterzeichner ist begeistert und beglückt, die Schrift gelesen zu haben; er zollt allen Beteiligten tiefe Anerkennung für die Leistung.

Hamburg, den 29. Januar 2010
Univ. Professor Dr. Dr.h.c. Marian Paschke
Direktor am Institut für Seerecht und Seehandelsrecht
Fakultät für Rechtswissenschaft, Universität Hamburg

NOTES:

NOTES:

NOTES:

NOTES:

NOTES:

NOTES:

NOTES:

NEW PHENOMENA
IN LAW AT THE
BEGINNING OF
THE 21ST CENTURY

CZECH LAW
BETWEEN
EUROPEANIZATION
AND GLOBALIZATION

Professor JUDr. PhDr. mult. Michal Tomášek, DrSc. et al.

Charles University in Prague
Karolinum Press
Ovocný trh 3–5, 116 36 Prague 1, Czech Republic
Prague 2010

Vice-rector-editor Professor PhDr. Mojmír Horyna
Cover and graphic design Zdeněk Ziegler
Typesetting MU typografické studio
Print Tiskárny Havlíčkův Brod, a. s.

First edition
ISBN 978-80-246-1785-5